ROUTLEDGE HANDBOOK OF AFRICA–ASIA RELATIONS

The *Routledge Handbook of Africa–Asia Relations* is the first handbook aimed at studying the interactions between countries across Africa and Asia in a multi-disciplinary and comprehensive way. Providing a balanced discussion of historical and on-going processes which have both shaped and changed intercontinental relations over time, contributors take a thematic approach to examine the ways in which we can conceptualise these two very different, yet inextricably linked areas of the world.

Using comparative examples throughout, the chronological sections cover:

- Early colonialist contacts between Africa and Asia;
- Modern Asia–Africa interactions through diplomacy, political networks and societal connections;
- Africa–Asia contemporary relations, including increasing economic, security and environmental cooperation.

This handbook grapples with major intellectual questions, defines current research, and projects future agendas of investigation in the field. As such, it will be of great interest to students of African and Asian Politics, as well as researchers and policymakers interested in Asian and African Studies.

Pedro Miguel Amakasu Raposo de Medeiros Carvalho is Assistant Professor at Lisbon School of Economics & Management (ISEG), University of Lisbon.

David Arase is Resident Professor at Johns Hopkins-Nanjing Center for Chinese and American Studies, USA.

Scarlett Cornelissen is Professor in the Department of Political Science at Stellenbosch University, South Africa.

ROUTLEDGE HANDBOOK OF AFRICA–ASIA RELATIONS

Edited by Pedro Miguel Amakasu Raposo de Medeiros Carvalho, David Arase and Scarlett Cornelissen

LONDON AND NEW YORK

First published 2018
by Routledge
2 Park Square, Milton Park, Abingdon, Oxon OX14 4RN

and by Routledge
711 Third Avenue, New York, NY 10017

Routledge is an imprint of the Taylor & Francis Group, an informa business

© 2018 selection and editorial matter, Pedro Miguel Amakasu Raposo de
Medeiros Carvalho, David Arase and Scarlett Cornelissen; individual
chapters, the contributors

The right of Pedro Miguel Amakasu Raposo de Medeiros Carvalho, David
Arase and Scarlett Cornelissen to be identified as the authors of the
editorial material, and of the authors for their individual chapters, has been
asserted in accordance with sections 77 and 78 of the Copyright, Designs
and Patents Act 1988.

All rights reserved. No part of this book may be reprinted or reproduced or
utilised in any form or by any electronic, mechanical, or other means, now
known or hereafter invented, including photocopying and recording, or in
any information storage or retrieval system, without permission in writing
from the publishers.

Trademark notice: Product or corporate names may be trademarks or
registered trademarks, and are used only for identification and explanation
without intent to infringe.

British Library Cataloguing-in-Publication Data
A catalogue record for this book is available from the British Library

Library of Congress Cataloging-in-Publication Data
Names: Carvalho, Pedro Miguel Raposo de Medeiros, 1969- editor. | Arase,
David, editor. | Cornelissen, Scarlett, editor.
Title: Routledge handbook of Africa-Asia relations/edited by
Pedro Miguel Amakasu Raposo de Medeiros Carvalho,
David Arase and Scarlett Cornelissen.
Other titles: Handbook of Africa-Asia relations
Description: Abingdon, Oxon; New York, NY: Routledge, 2018. | Includes
bibliographical references and index.
Identifiers: LCCN 2017019482 | ISBN 9781138917330 (hardback) |
ISBN 9781315689067 (ebook)
Subjects: LCSH: Africa–Foreign relations–Asia. | Asia–
Foreign relations–Africa. | Africa–Foreign economic relations–Asia. |
Asia–Foreign economic relations–Africa.
Classification: LCC DT38.9.A78 R68 2018 | DDC 303.48/2605–dc23
LC record available at https://lccn.loc.gov/2017019482

ISBN: 978-1-138-91733-0 (hbk)
ISBN: 978-1-315-68906-7 (ebk)

Typeset in Bembo
by Sunrise Setting Ltd, Brixham, UK

Printed and bound by CPI Group (UK) Ltd, Croydon, CR0 4YY

CONTENTS

List of figures	*ix*
List of tables	*x*
List of contributors	*xi*
List of abbreviations	*xvi*
List of terms	*xxi*

Introduction: is it too early for an Afro-Asian view of the world?
'New' research perceptions between Africa and Asia   1
Pedro Miguel Amakasu Raposo de Medeiros Carvalho

PART I
Africa and Asia early contacts   **19**

Early colonialism

1 Africa and Asia diaspora: reconstructing a neglected history   22
Samuel Ojo Oloruntoba and Sabelo Ndlovu-Gatsheni

2 Iberian trade and slave connections   33
Daniel B. Domingues da Silva

Late colonialism

3 Lost and found: sovereignties and state formations in Africa and Asia   46
Kwame Nimako

4 South Asian Muslims in East Africa   60
Iqbal Akhtar

Contents

Postcolonial interactions

5 Religion and development in Africa and Asia 76
Jörg Haustein and Emma Tomalin

6 Nationalism in Africa and Asia 94
Christopher J. Lee

PART II
Asia–Africa modern interactions 109

Diplomatic and political exchanges

7 The discourse of 'Datsu-A ron': Japan and Africa in the network
of modern history and contemporary politics 112
Kweku Ampiah

8 The role of aid in South Korea's relations with Africa
during the Cold War 126
Hyo-sook Kim

9 Asia–Africa political and diplomatic interactions: 1970–1990 139
Sanjukta Banerji Bhattacharya

10 From Bandung to BRICS: Afro-Asian relations in the
twenty-first century 153
Seifudein Adem and Darryl C. Thomas

Political-economic connections

11 Africa's rising commodity export dependency on China 168
Alicia Garcia-Herrero and Carlos Casanova

12 Bridging Asia with Africa: the case of Malaysia 185
Evelyn S. Devadason and V.G.R. Chandran Govindaraju

13 Navigating the One China policy: South Africa, Taiwan
and China 202
Ross Anthony and Yejoo Kim

Societal-level interactions

14 Africa–Asia relations in academic network formation 216
Takuo Iwata

Contents

15 Dreaming Afrasia: an essay on Afro-Asian relations in
   space–time perspectives   233
   Yoichi Mine

16 The role of Islam in forging linkages between Africa and Asia from
   the 1970s: the case of Islamic relief and development support   249
   Mayke Kaag

17 Civil society and the rise of NGOs in Africa and Asia: parallel trajectories? 259
   David M. Potter

18 Education and gender in the Global South: inadequate policy
   environment at the confluence in sub-Saharan Africa   273
   Emefa Juliet Takyi-Amoako

PART III
Africa–Asia contemporary relations   291

Economic and development cooperation

19 BRICS in Africa and human rights   294
   Ian Taylor

20 Contemporary Sino-Africa relations   307
   Zhang Chun

21 Asia in Lusophone Africa   321
   Carmen Amado Mendes

22 Africa–Asia regional partnerships and South–South development
   cooperation   335
   Annette Skovsted Hansen

23 Asia and Africa and post-2015 development agenda   352
   Shalini Chawla

Security and governance

24 Religions, (in)security and conflict in Africa and Asia   372
   Jeffrey Haynes

25 The land–water–food–energy nexus: green and blue water dynamics
   in contemporary Africa–Asia relations   386
   Larry A. Swatuk

vii

Contents

26 Developments in European Union–Africa relations and their
   implications for Asia   406
   Laura C. Ferreira-Pereira and Alena Vieira

Migration, environment and politics

27 Migration and global politics in Africa and Asia: patterns and
   drivers of change throughout time   424
   Pedro Miguel Amakasu Raposo de Medeiros Carvalho

28 Asian stakes in Africa's natural resources industries and prospects
   for sustainable development   439
   Thomas Feldhoff

29 Refugees and internally displaced persons in Africa and Asia   457
   Pablo Shiladitya Bose

   Conclusion   472
   Pedro Miguel Amakasu Raposo de Medeiros Carvalho

   Index   478

FIGURES

11.1	Bilateral trade links	173
11.2	Exports to China as a percentage of GDP for key African countries	174
11.3a	Exports by commodity	174
11.3b	Imports by product	175
11.4	Commodity price index	175
11.5	Commodity dependence increase: Africa	178
11.6	Chinese import penetration	179
11.7	TiVA has not grown as fast as gross trade	181
11.8	The ratio of TiVA/gross fell significantly	182
12.1	OFDI flows of Malaysia in Africa	193
12.2	Malaysia–Africa trade, 1992–2013	195
15.1	Projection of population growth by region	235
15.2	Projection of fertility change by region	236
18.1	International commitment: treatises and promises	282
20.1	China–Africa trade relations, 1950–2015	309
20.2	African countries with bilateral trade volume over US$ 1 billion, 2014	310
20.3	China's investment in Africa and its growth rate, 2003–2014	311
28.1	Macro-level contributions of mining in low- and middle-income countries	448
28.2	A four-layer approach to the implementation of a natural resource-based economy	449

TABLES

11.1	Trade with China versus trade with the US	172
11.2	Intraregional exports and imports as a percentage of total exports and imports	180
12.1	Progressive developments between Malaysia and South Africa	191
12.2	Selected Malaysian companies in Africa	194
12.3	Malaysia–Africa: market concentration of trade	196
12.4	Malaysia–Africa: product concentration of trade	197
17.1	Colonial era legal foundations of non-profit organisations in South Asia and Tanzania	262
18.1	The confluence defined further	278
18.2	Effect of colonialism on gender in sub-Saharan Africa elaborated	280
20.1	Peacekeeping operations, China participating, August 2016	313
20.2	The six FOCAC ministerial conferences to date	314
20.3	Sub-forums of FOCAC	315
25.1	Selected dam projects in Africa	398
28.1	Announced green-field FDI projects by region/country (2013–2014)	443
28.2	Announced green-field FDI projects by industry (2013–2014)	444
28.3	Africa's merchandise exports by region	445

CONTRIBUTORS

Samuel Ojo Oloruntoba is Senior Lecturer at the Thabo Mbeki African Leadership Institute, University of South Africa. He obtained his PhD in Political Science with specialization in International Political Economy of Trade and Finance from the University of Lagos, Nigeria. His book on *Regionalism and Integration in Africa: EU–ACP Economic Partnership and Euro-Nigeria Relations* was published by Palgrave Macmillan in 2016.

Sabelo Ndlovu-Gatsheni is the founding Head of the Archie Mafeje Research Institute for Allied Social Policy (AMRI) at the University of South Africa (UNISA) and is the current Director: Scholarship in the Change Management Unit (CMU) in the Vice-Chancellor's Office at UNISA. He has published 12 books, over 50 journal articles and over 50 book chapters. His latest publication is *The Decolonial Mandela: Peace, Justice and Politics of Life* (2016).

Daniel B. Domingues da Silva is Assistant Professor of African History at Rice University, USA. His research focuses on the transatlantic slave trade and it has received funding from several institutions, including the National Endowment for the Humanities. He is co-manager of *Voyages: The Trans-Atlantic Slave Trade Database*.

Kwame Nimako is the founder and director of the Summer School on Black Europe in Amsterdam, and has taught at the University of Amsterdam and University of California, Berkeley. He is author or co-author of some 30 books, reports and guide-books on economic development, ethnic relations, social policy, urban renewal and migration.

Iqbal Akhtar is a historian of religion with a dual-appointment assistant professorship in the Department of Politics & International Relations and Religious Studies at Florida International University, USA. He completed his doctoral studies at the University of Edinburgh and his most recent monograph is entitled *The Khōjā of Tanzania*.

Jörg Haustein is Senior Lecturer in Religions in Africa at SOAS University of London, UK. His expertise is centred on newer developments in African Christianity and Islam and their societal impact, including issues of development. He has published widely on Ethiopian Pentecostalism and is currently researching the impact of German colonialism on Islam in East Africa.

Contributors

Emma Tomalin is Professor of Religion and Public Life and the Director of the Centre for Religion and Public Life at the University of Leeds, UK. Her main research interests are focused around 'Religions and Global Development' and 'Religion, Gender and Society'. Her most recent book is titled *The Routledge Handbook of Religions and Global Development* (2015).

Christopher J. Lee is Associate Professor of History at Lafayette College, USA. He has published several books, including *Making a World after Empire: The Bandung Moment and Its Political Afterlives* (2010), *Unreasonable Histories: Nativism, Multiracial Lives, and the Genealogical Imagination in British Africa* (2014), *Frantz Fanon: Toward a Revolutionary Humanism* (2015), and *A Soviet Journey: A Critical Annotated Edition* (2017).

Kweku Ampiah is Associate Professor of Japanese Studies at the University of Leeds, UK.

Hyo-sook Kim is Assistant Professor of International Relations at Kansai Gaidai University in Japan. Her research focuses on international norms and policymaking in donor countries. She is co-editor of *Foreign Aid Competition in Northeast Asia* (2012) and author of 'South Korea's Aid to Africa and Compliance with International Norms' (2017), published in the journal of *African and Asian Studies*.

Sanjukta Banerji Bhattacharya retired as Professor of International Relations, Jadavpur University, Kolkata, India in mid 2016 after a long academic career of over 35 years. She has published four books and over 50 articles and chapters in national and international journals and edited volumes. Her academic interests include US politics, Third World studies, India's history and foreign policy, West Asia, Africa, terrorism, refugees and migration studies, and religion and politics.

Seifudein Adem is a former Research Associate Professor of Political Science and Associate Director of the Institute of Global Cultural Studies at Binghamton University, New York, USA, and he was also President of the New York African Studies Association (2010–2011). His most recent publications include *China's Diplomacy in Eastern and Southern Africa* (2013).

Darryl C. Thomas is Associate Professor in the Department of African American Studies, Pennsylvania State University, Pennsylvania, USA. His most recent publication is 'Cedric J. Robinson's Meditation on Malcolm X's Black Internationalism and the Future of the Black Radical Tradition', In Gayle Theresa Johnson and Alex Lubin (eds), *The Future of Black Radicalism* (2017).

Alicia Garcia Herrero is a Senior Fellow at Bruegel. She is also the Chief Economist for the Asia Pacific at NATIXIS. Currently, she is Adjunct Professor at City University of Hong Kong and Hong Kong University of Science and Technology (HKUST) and visiting faculty at China–Europe International Business School (CEIBS).

Carlos Casanova is the Asia Pacific Economist at Coface in Hong Kong. His areas of expertise include economic developments in the Asia Pacific region and China.

Evelyn S. Devadason is an Associate Professor at the Faculty of Economics and Administration, University of Malaya. She received her PhD (Economics) from the University of Malaya in

2006 and M.Soc.Sci (Economics) from the National University of Singapore in 1992. Her research focuses on international trade and regional integration.

V.G.R. Chandran Govindaraju is an Associate Professor at the Faculty of Economics and Administration, University of Malaya. He received his PhD (Economics) from the University of Malaya in 2010. His research focuses on industrial competitiveness, innovation and technology policy, regional and industrial development and policy evaluation.

Ross Anthony is the Director of the Centre for Chinese Studies at Stellenbosch University, South Africa. His research focuses on Chinese politics and culture, both domestically and in its relationship with Africa. He has written on issues of security, nationalism, infrastructure, migration and environment.

Yejoo Kim is a Research Fellow at the Centre for Chinese Studies at Stellenbosch University, South Africa. Her research agenda centres on Africa's development with reference to East Asia.

Takuo Iwata is Associate Professor at Ritsumeikan University, Kyoto, Japan. His research focuses on comparative politics and African studies, democratization studies, and also decentralization, local governments' international cooperation, border issues, ICT in politics, symbolic power, Africa and Asia relations, and laughter in African politics.

Yoichi Mine is Professor at the Graduate School of Global Studies, Doshisha University, Kyoto, Japan, and Professor Extraordinaire at the Department of Political Science, the University of Stellenbosch, South Africa. His research interests include human security, development economics, comparative history and African area study. His co-edited works include *Preventing Violent Conflict in Africa: Inequalities, Perceptions and Institutions* (2013).

Mayke Kaag is a social anthropologist and a senior researcher at the African Studies Centre, Leiden University, Netherlands. She is the convenor of a collaborative research group on 'Africa in the World'. Recent publications include 'Islamic Charities from the Arab World in Africa: Intercultural Encounters of Humanitarianism and Morality' in Volker Heins, Kai Koddenbrock and Christine Unrau (eds), *Humanitarianism and Challenges of Cooperation* (2016) and (with Annalies Zoomers) *The Global Land Grab – Beyond the Hype* (2014).

David M. Potter is a Professor of International Relations in the Faculty of Policy Studies, Nanzan University, Japan. His research focuses on official development assistance and international non-governmental organizations. He is author and co-author of multiple books, journal articles and book chapters on related topics.

Emefa Juliet Takyi-Amoako is Executive Director of Oxford ATP International Education. She is also Education Consultant and Senior Quality Assurance Expert on higher education in Africa and elsewhere. Her research interests are in the areas of education policy, globalization, partnerships, gender and pre-tertiary and higher education. She has published works on education including her edited book, *Education in West Africa* (2015). She holds a doctorate in Comparative and International Education from Oxford University, UK.

Ian Taylor is Professor in International Relations and African Political Economy at the University of St Andrews, UK and also Chair Professor in the School of International Studies,

Renmin University of China. He is also Professor Extraordinary in Political Science at the University of Stellenbosch, South Africa.

Zhang Chun is a Senior Fellow and Deputy Director of the Center for West Asian and African Studies at the Shanghai Institutes for International Studies, China.

Carmen Amado Mendes is Assistant Professor of International Relations and former head of the International Relations Office at the School of Economics, University of Coimbra, Portugal, and author of *Portugal, China and the Macau Negotiations 1986–1999* (2013) and several articles and book chapters on China's foreign policy and Macau.

Annette Skovsted Hansen is Associate Professor of Japanese and Global History at Aarhus University. Her current research is on cultural histories of global networks linked to Japanese development cooperation. Her 2015 publications include 'Global Alumni Networks: The Inclusion of Fellow Experts from Developing Countries in Epistemic Communities', *Forum for Development Studies*, Volume 42 (2).

Shalini Chawla is a Senior Fellow at the Centre for Air Power Studies, New Delhi, India. The focus of her studies is on South Asia with specialization on China, Pakistan and Afghanistan. She has published widely in national and international journals. Her prominent works include *Pakistan's Military and Its Strategy* (2009) and *Nuclear Pakistan* (2012).

Jeffrey Haynes is Professor of Politics, and the Director of the Centre for the Study of Religion, Conflict and Cooperation at London Metropolitan University, UK. He is the author, co-author, editor or co-editor of more than 40 books. The most recent are *Faith-based Organizations at the United Nations* (2014) and the *Routledge Handbook of Religion and Politics* (2016).

Larry A. Swatuk is Professor of International Development in the School of Environment, Enterprise and Development (SEED) at the University of Waterloo, Canada and Extraordinary Professor, Institute for Water Studies, University of the Western Cape, South Africa. Prior to joining the University of Waterloo he spent 11 years at the University of Botswana where he was Associate Professor of Natural Resources Governance at the Okavango Research Institute and Lecturer in the Department of Political and Administrative Studies. He is author of *Water in Southern Africa* (2017) and co-editor (with Corrine M. Cash) of *Water, Energy, Food and People across the Global South* (2017).

Laura C. Ferreira-Pereira is Professor of Political Science and International Relations at the University of Minho, Portugal. She has recently acted as the leading guest editor of a Special Issue of *Cambridge Review of International Affairs* entitled 'The Strategic Partnerships of the European Union: Conceptual Insights, Cases and Lessons' (2016). She is the author of *Portugal in the European Union: Assessing Twenty-Five Years of Integration Experience* (2014).

Alena Vieira is Integrated Member of Centro de Investigação em Ciência Política (CICP) and Assistant Professor at the University of Minho, Portugal. Together with Laura C. Ferreira-Pereira, she has co-edited a Special Issue of the *Cambridge Review of International Affairs* entitled 'The Strategic Partnerships of the European Union: Conceptual Insights, Cases and Lessons' (2016).

Contributors

Pedro Miguel Amakasu Raposo de Medeiros Carvalho is PhD in economics from Okayama University, Okayama and in policy studies from Nanzan University, Aichi, both in Japan. He is Assistant Professor at ISEG, University of Lisbon, Portugal and researcher of CEsA (Centre for African, Asian and Latin American Studies). His research focus on Asian development studies in Africa, particular China and Japan's development cooperation, and Africa–Asia relations.

Thomas Feldhoff is Professor of Human Geography in the Department of Geography at Bochum University, Germany. His research focuses on Material Political Geographies, Space and Place in Public Policy. His work has been published widely in books, edited volumes and journals, including the *Journal of Transport Geography*, *International Planning Studies* and *Urban Design International*.

Pablo Shiladitya Bose is a migration scholar and urban geographer whose main interests focus on the relationships between people and place. His major current projects are on refugee resettlement in North America and Europe, forced displacements caused by development and environment across the world, and urbanization and transnationalism in cities of the Global South. Among his other research has been work on food and migration, transportation and mobility for underserved populations, and culture, place-making and national identity.

ABBREVIATIONS

AA	Afro-Asian
AADUN	Africa–Asia Development University Network
AALCO	Asian–African Legal Consultative Organization
AAPSO	Afro-Asian Peoples' Solidarity Organization
AARP	Africa–Asia Regional Partnerships
A-ASIA	Asian Studies in Africa
AASROC	Asia–Africa Sub-Regional Organization Conference
ABEDA	Arab Bank for Economic Development in Africa
ACBF	Africa Capacity Building Foundation
ACP	African Caribbean and Pacific
ADB	Asian Development Bank
AEC	ASEAN Economic Community
AEGIS	Africa–Europe Group for Interdisciplinary Studies
AF	Africa Fund
AFC	Asian Financial Crisis
AfDB	African Development Bank
AFRASO	Africa's Asian Options
AM	Artisanal mining
AMA	African Muslims Agency/Association des Musulmans d'Afrique
ANC	African National Congress
APF	African Peace Facility
ARC	Asian Relations Conference
ARF	ASEAN Regional Forum
ASA	African Studies Association
ASAP	Africa and Structural Adjustment Programmes
ASEAN	Association of the Southeast Asian Nations
ASM	Small-scale mining
ATEF	Africa Taiwan Economic Forum
AU	African Union
BC	Bandung Conference
BCE	Before the Common Era

Abbreviations

BR	Berg Report
BRAC	Bangladesh Rural Advancement Committee
BRICS	Brazil, Russia, India, China and South Africa
CAADP	Comprehensive Africa Agriculture Development Programme
CBTI	Cross Border Transport Infrastructure
CE	Common Era
CFSP	Common Foreign and Security Policy
CGIAR	Consultancy Group on International Agricultural Research
CI	Confucius Institute
CMR	Critical Maritime Routes Programme
COSATU	Congress of South African Trade Unions
CPLP	Community of Portuguese-Speaking Countries
CRIMARIO	Critical Maritime Routes in the Indian Ocean
CRS	Corporate Social Responsibility
CSDP	Common Security and Defence Policy
CSO	Civil Society Organization
DAC	Development Assistance Committee of the OECD
DFID	Department for International Development
DID	Development-induced Displacement
DIRCO	Department of International Relations and Cooperation
DRC	Democratic Republic of Congo
DTI	Department of Trade and Industry
EAC	East Africa Community
ECAS	European Conference on African Studies
ECFA	Economic Cooperation Framework Agreement
ECOSOC	UN Economic and Social Council
ECOWAS	Economic Community of West African States
EFA	Education for All
ENE	National Electricity Company (Angola)
EOWAS	Economic Organization of West African States
EPA	Economic Partnership Agreement
ESDP	European Security and Defence Policy
ESS	European Security Strategy
EU	European Union
FAO	Food and Agriculture Organization of United Nations
FBO	Faith-based organizations
FDI	Foreign Direct Investment
FfD	Forum on Financing for Development
FICCI	Federation of Indian Chambers of Commerce and Industry
FNLA	National Front for the Liberation of Angola
FOCAC	Forum on China–Africa Cooperation
FPA	Framework Participation Agreement
G8	Group of Eight Most Industrialized Countries
G22	Group of 20 Countries or Willard Group
G77	Group of 77 Countries
GDP	Gross Domestic Product
GFC	Global Financial Crisis
GMR	Global Monitoring Report

xvii

Abbreviations

HUFS	Hankuk University of Foreign Studies
IAFS	India–Africa Forum Summit
IAFSC	India–Africa Framework for Strategic Cooperation
IAR	India–Africa Relations
IASF	India Africa Summit Forum
ICACPPS	Initiative on China–Africa Cooperative Partnership for Peace and Security
ICC	International Criminal Court
ICNPO	International Classification for Non-profit Organizations
ICT	Information and Communication Technology
IDA/IDP	Indian Diaspora in Africa/India's Diaspora Policy
IDP	Internally Displaced Persons
IFAD	International Fund for Agricultural Development
IFI	International Financial Institutions
IIRO	International Islamic Relief Organization
IMF	International Monetary Fund
INGO	International non-governmental organization
IPKF	India and UN Peacekeeping Missions in Africa
ISIS	Islamic State Movement in Iraq and Syria
ITEC	Indian Technical and Economic Cooperation
IWMI	International Water Management Institute
JAAS	Japan Association for African Studies
JBIC	Japan Bank for International Cooperation
JETRO	Japan External Trade Organization
JICA	Japan International Cooperation Agency
KAF	Korea–Africa Forum
LDC	Least Developed Countries
LIC	League against Imperialism and Colonialism
LNG	Liquefied Natural Gas
LPA	Lagos Plan of Action
LTTE	Liberation Tigers of Tamil Eelam
M&A	mergers and acquisitions
MAP	Millennium Partnership for the African Recovery Programme
MASSA	Malaysian South–South Association
MASE	Programme to Promote Regional Maritime Security
MASSCORP	Malaysian South–South Cooperation
MDGs	Millennium Development Goals
METI	Ministry of Economy, Trade and Industry
MNC	Multinational Corporation
MoFA	Ministry of Foreign Affairs of Japan
MPLA	People's Movement for the Liberation of Angola
MTCP	Malaysian Technical Cooperation Programme
NAASP	New Asian–African Strategic Partnership
NAI	New African Initiative
NAM	Non-Aligned Movement
NCCIM	National Chambers of Commerce and Industry
NDB	New Development Bank
NEP	New Economic Policy
NEPAD	New Partnership for Africa's Development

Abbreviations

NIEO	New International Economic Order
NIF	National Islamic Front
NGO	Non-governmental organizations
NPO	Non-profit organization
NVDP	Narmada Valley Development Programme
OAS	Organization of African States
OAU	Organization of African Unity
ODA	Official Development Assistance
OECD	Organization for Economic Co-operation and Development
OFDI	Outward Foreign Direct Investment
OPEC	Organization of the Petroleum Exporting Countries
OPEP	Organization of the Petroleum Exporting Countries
OSPAAAL	Organización de Solidaridad con los Pueblos de Asia, África y América Latina
PA	People's Assembly
PAC	Pan-African Congress
PPP	Public Private Partnership
PRAI	Principles for Responsible Agricultural Investment
PRC	People's Republic of China
PWYP	Publish What You Pay
ROC	Republic of China
SAARC	South Asian Association for Regional Cooperation
SACP	South African Communist Party
SADC	Southern African Development Community
SADCC	Southern African Development Coordination Conference
SADR	Sahrawi Arab Democratic Republic
SALW	Small Arms and Light Weapons
SAR	Special Administrative Region
SDG	Sustainable Development Goal
SDP	Spatial Development Programme
SEWA	Self Employed Women's Association
SEZ	Special Economic Zone
Sinopec	China Petroleum & Chemical Corporation
SMEs	small and medium-sized enterprises
SOEs	state-owned enterprises
Sonangol	Angolan Oil Company
SP	Strategic Partnership
SPLA	Sudan People's Liberation Army
SSA	Sub-Saharan Africa
SSC	South–South Cooperation
SSDC	South–South Development Cooperation
STAP	Pakistan's Special Technical Assistance Programme
SWAPO	South West African People's Organization
TABA	Taiwan African Business Association
TFR	Total Fertility Rate
TICAD	Tokyo International Conference on African Development
TNC	Transnational Corporations
UMNO	United Malays' National Organization
UN	United Nations

xix

Abbreviations

UNCTAD	United Nations Conference on Trade and Development
UNDP	United Nations Development Programme
UNGA	United Nations General Assembly
UNGEI	United Nations Girls' Education Initiative
UNIDO	United Nations Industrial Development Organization
UNITA	Union for the Total Independence of Angola
UNP	United National Party
UNSC	United Nations Security Council
US	United States
USSR	Union of Soviet Socialist Republics
WB	World Bank
WIL	World Islamic League
WMR	World Migration Report
WNF	World Network of Friends
WTO	World Trade Organization
WWII	World War Two

TERMS

A-a hyeopryeok   Economic cooperation between Asia and Africa that President Chun Doo-hwan suggested when he visited Africa in 1982

Ezulwini Consensus   A common African position on the proposed reform of the United Nations, adopted by the Executive Council of the African Union on March 2005, advocating for a stronger representation of Africa in the Security Council

Gaebal jeonseon   Development front as a new basis for cooperation among developing countries

Hanguk munje   The Korean question

Hyeolmaeng   A blood pledge

Lusophone Africa   Five former Portuguese colonies in Africa

Portuguese-speaking countries   Angola, Brazil, Cape Verde, East Timor, Guinea-Bissau, Mozambique and São Tomé and Principe

Saemaul Undong ODA   New Community Movement, a representative aid model to share South Korea's development experience

Seonkyeonghyeop-husugyo   Aid as a precondition for establishing diplomatic relations

Ujamaa   Family-like solidarity

INTRODUCTION: IS IT TOO EARLY FOR AN AFRO-ASIAN VIEW OF THE WORLD?

'New' research perceptions between Africa and Asia

Pedro Miguel Amakasu Raposo de Medeiros Carvalho

If one considers the current and increasing Afro-Asian economic vitality, development, political and diplomatic interfaces all together it seems Europe no longer is the object of reference, as Africa and Asia want to recover the civilizational advantage they had over Europe in the past. Given the technical, cultural, ethnical and historical contributions of Africa and Asia to the formation of the world, this Handbook aims at providing insights into the nature of interactions between Africa and Asia in historical and contemporary terms. How did Africa and Asia interactions evolve through time? How should we conceptualize Africa and Asia? How does scholarship interpret these interactions? How do Africa and Asia interact in today's globalized world? The discussion in this Handbook includes diplomatic and political exchanges, economic and development connections, societal-level interactions, security and governance dynamics, academic insights and research networks over which African–Asian relations are played out. This introductory chapter questions whether it is too early for a non-Western Afro-Asian perspective of the world as opposed to the Western/Eurocentric–Orientalist view of history. However, to answer properly the above question, first one needs to conceptualize Africa and Asia's interactions and place them within European capitalist ascendency. In this process, the first section of the chapter criticizes the Eurocentric view of history and analyzes why and how Africa and Asia lost their preeminence to Europe. The second section examines Asia and Africa counteractions (though failed) to Eurocentrism through Pan-Afro-Asianism. The third section examines the obstacles for an Afro-Asian view of the world through an analysis of the lack of education, in particular tertiary, which ultimately affects African and Asian studies as a discipline. Here, the focus is on the revitalization of public universities as a means to economic and social development and a necessary step towards building research networks. The fourth section analyzes the linkage of knowledge, agency in Africa and Asia for a desirable worldview, followed by an outline of the structure of the Handbook and summary of the chapters, and then concludes.

An Afro-Asia worldview: how Africa and Asia lost their preeminence

In ancient times Africa, Asia and the Middle East, not Europe, were the civilizational, economic and trade centers of the world. Their traditions, values and knowledge inspired and modeled the world. In this sense, according to Moghalu (2014:13) the Africa and Asia worldview reflected the inner world of the mind of an individual or group because their actions influenced the world. Goody (2004:68), however, notes that Asia was a way ahead of Africa. With the exceptions of Egypt and North Africa, Ethiopia and the coastal Swahili towns of East Africa, the rest of Africa did not match the technological, agricultural and commercial or literature levels of the major states of Eurasia. For millennia, Africa and Asia developed and interacted independently of Europe. Their worldview was based on peaceful trade interactions. Arguably, this began to change in Africa after 1415 when the Portuguese Prince Henrique captured Ceuta and in Asia after 1498 when Vasco da Gama sailed to Calicut in southwestern India, and when Columbus discovered America in 1492. Although Portuguese inroads were limited to coastal areas, gradually the world shifted from an *Afro-asiacentric* view to one along the lines of a *Eurocentric* view in relation to geopolitics, economic and social relations, but also science, culture and academic knowledge, just to name the most important. The problem of Eurocentrism, say Anievas & Nisancioglu (2015:4–5), is that it conceives the origins and sources of capitalist modernity as a product of European development, not Asian, much less African, where Europe is conceived as the permanent 'core' and prime mover of history. As a result, Patel (2015:54) notes that Eurocentrism became a style of thought that ontologically and epistemologically divided the 'Occident' and the 'Orient' to create knowledge on and of the Occident and the Orient as distinct. However, as Keita (2005:2) notes, before the Columbian age the world was more Oriental than Western, though this division was not as straightforward as the later opposition constructed upon the knowledge between the West and the East that lasted from the fourteenth century to the late twentieth century. Prior to 1750 or even 1800, the world was Afro-Asian, with ancient Egypt being at the crossroads between the two continents. Those who later become 'Arab,' 'Asiatic' and 'Oriental' were engaged in social and politico-economic intercourse with those now called African (ibid.: 8). Within this geopolitical space, what we needed to know about Afro-Asia interactions rested in Africa (Egypt, Kush, Nubia, Ethiopia, Mogadishu and Adullis) and the modern states of Aden, Oman and Yemen into Indian Ocean within the purview of the 'Orientalist' notes. Given the technological advance of Asia over Europe, at least until the industrial revolution from 1750–1780 onwards, European advantage remains debatable (Goody, 2004). Other scholars, such as Kang (2012) and Hobson (2012:46), have also called into question the Eurocentric assumption of history, with the last arguing that,

> Europe was not merely a latecomer to the infant global economy, but it was also a late-developing civilization as it assimilated many inventions that had been pioneered in the East, mostly from China but also in North Africa, Middle East, and India.

In fact, as Pomeranz (2000:44–45) notes, in terms of technology until early 1750 in the fields of irrigation, textile weaving and dyeing or as late as 1827 and 1842 for the manufacturing of porcelain, Europe lagged behind China, India, Japan and many parts of Southeast Asia. Africa was also ahead of Europe in the production of iron, which in terms of quality was as good as that available in Europe (ibid.). Therefore, the idea that Europe was the 'civilizational light' in terms of knowledge, technology, economic power and industrial output or that Africa and Asia in particular were civilizationally backwards compared with Europe is misleading. In fact,

Introduction

African and Asian scientific and technological contributions to the world go back to the origins of humankind. A few examples demonstrate this. In 3400 BCE it was Egypt (called Kemet by Africans and much later called Egypt by the Greeks) that was the first major civilization of Africa and in the world (Asante, 2015:22). The first book of mathematics was Kemetic. Its architecture with its great sphinxes was grandiose and its philosophy was also advanced. Imhotep was the first philosopher to deal with the questions of volume, time, the nature of illness, physical and mental disease, and immortality. The dynasties of Kemet lasted until 341 BCE when Persian kings and later Alexander the Macedonian fought for the Kemet empire (Asante, 2015:67). Other powerful kingdoms followed the Kemet, such as Nubia, Axum, Carthage, Ghana, Mali, and the Songhai empire in 1456; these were the most important in African history. By this time the Arab invasions had converted the North African and also the east coast to Islam. Although a great Indian Ocean trading complex involving East Africa antedated Arab conquests, the incorporation of the East African coast into the Islamic system in the thirteenth century gave a new impetus to trade. Slavery always formed a minor item in this trade, institutionalized as it was in African and Arab societies, but it was with the Portuguese discoveries of the fifteenth century that slave trading expanded and constituted a very large part of all international economic transactions in the period 1451–1870, first under Iberian control, then French, English and Dutch dominion. Eventually, the collapse of the last great African empire, the Songhai, coincided with the internationalization of slave trade that served both European and African economic interests. Asia also fell into the hands of Western commercial interests and as in Africa, colonization, slave trade and indentured labor also affected Asia (Jayasuriya & Angenot, 2008:1). However, Western dominion in Asia was not as straightforward as in Africa. According to Hobson (2012:46), Pomeranz (2000:31), Goody (2004:17) and many other scholars, Europe only came to play a dominant role in Asia and the world after 1800. The same applies to Africa, as before the Berlin Conference (1884–1885) Europeans only controlled one-tenth of the African landmass. However, by 1900, nine-tenths of Africa had been colonized (Osborne & Kent, 2015:75). This did not happen in the case of Asia. Given the important role China had in the development of the global economy after 1492, the Chinese empire not only controlled the global silver recycling processes, but also led the world in GDP, manufacturing production and manufactured exports. Hobson (2012) downplays the thesis of a Eurocentric world history in general and the place of Asia and Europe in particular. Not surprisingly, in the seventeenth century, China and India had the world's largest cotton industries and dominated the cotton trade across the Indian Ocean and as far as West Africa against Great Britain which could not possibly compete with them unless it cut its wage bills (Allen, 2011:32). Japan, Egypt, Sudan and Persia were also significant players in a 'polycentric' world. To the Eurocentric mindset the arrival of the Portuguese in Calicut in 1498 meant that India would lose the monopoly of trade to Portugal and other European powers. Again, Hobson (2012:54) notes that the Portuguese only had 6 percent of total shipping tonnage in the sixteenth century. The same applies to the Dutch in their dealings with the Indians and other Asians in general. The question is how and why did Asian and African civilizations lose their scientific, cultural and development edge as well as their status, power and economic dynamism to Europe after the fifteenth century? Without question, a worldview based on slavery and the slave trade, imperialism, and colonialism and the emergence of capitalism as a mode of production based in colonial exploitation played a strong role in the development of Europe at the expense of Africa and Asia. However, it does not justify why ultimately Asia and Africa stayed behind.

The "rise of the West and decline of the East," to use Anievas & Nisancioglu's (2015) expression, in terms of economic growth and development divergence derives from the application of steam power to manufacturing processes, transport communications (steamships and railways) associated with the industrial revolution in England and France, and the gains from globaliza-tion as a result of the fall of transportation costs which made the world economy more inte-grated. Further, the combination of several economic, social, demographic and geopolitical factors worked in favor of Europe's colonial powers, but not Asian and African colonies, which were subordinated to the interests of their colonial masters (Allen, 2011:57). Anievas & Nisancioglu (2015:246–247) argue that the very preconditions for growth in Asia led to economic and social crisis: the growing population and income, economic and social polarization constrained effect-ive demand at the bottom, put pressure on resources and increased the availability of cheap labor in Asia more than elsewhere in the world and led to crisis. In Asia, a particular case is the Dutch who insisted on the exploitation of labor power as the basis for capital accumulation. After they gained control, from the Portuguese and other European powers, of pepper-producing areas, rice and especially textiles, they were able to integrate intra-Asian trade into a network of trade centered on the Asian sub-continent, and thus increased capital through connecting the dispersed mass of labor power (ibid.: 233–234). As for Britain, its colonization of India in the very heart of Asia provided the material inputs for Britain's industrialization, and also took advantage of the above crisis conditions to catch up and overtake Asia in the international system (ibid.: 247).

Bandung and Pan-Afro-Asianism: the return of Asia and Africa?

Returning to our introductory question – whether it's too soon for an Afro-Asian view of the world – one argues that it is not only a question of time in terms of power warfare but of intellectual, political, economic (resources), social and (why not?) academic readiness in terms of knowledge production. Mullen (2003:219) notes that Du Bois in his novel *Dark Princess*, published in 1928, actively supported the rise of Pan-African and Pan-Asian politics. He notes (ibid.: 234) that by enacting Afro-Asian linkages amidst world wars, colonialism, Orientalism (here understood as the Asiatic) and rising Pan-Africanism, *Dark Princess* also anticipated the roots and routes of a number of Afro-intellectuals, such as Aimé Césaire or Léopold Senghor who would support the cause of both Asian independence and Afro-Asian solidarity. Du Bois in *Dark Princess* goes further and predicts the historical event of the 1955 Asian–African confer-ence, when the Princess Kautilya declares near the novel's end, "The colored world goes free in 1952" (cit. in Mullen, 2003:235). After the 1885 scramble for Africa and the formation of the Indian National Congress the same year, at the first Pan-African Congress in London in 1900, Du Bois turned his attention to the linkages between African and Asian liberation movements.

Again, the question is not whether Africa and Asia, as well as the world (Western and non-Western), were or are predisposed to overcome the problems of *Africaness* (and/or *Asianess*), regarded has having no essence (Abrahamsen, 2003:196). In this context, Ndlovu-Gatsheni (2012:76–77) notes that the processes of slave trade, imperialism and colonialism contributed to this identity emptiness within a contextually dependent form of identification in terms of racial identity or lack thereof, geographical or historical constructs and its representation through Eurocentric categories and conceptual systems. However, the dreams of a worldview based on pan-Afro-Asian unity proved to be short-lived. In Asia the Opium War of 1839–1842 between China and Great Britain awoke China to consider the questions of Asian solidarity. Also, the Japanese triumph in the war with Russia in 1904–1905, which was an important turning point supported by many including Du Bois himself (Mullen, 2003:218), accelerated the spread of Pan-Asian ideas throughout the continent. Hence, in 1926–1927 the first Pan-Asian and anti-colonial doctrines were formulated in Bierville, France, which gave rise to the League against Imperialism (Mackie, 2010:10). Gradually, Pan-Asianism served as justification for the policy of expelling

Western influence from, and establishing Japanese hegemony over, East Asia within the slogan 'Asia for the Asians,' where only Asians should be allowed to determine how they lived. The problem was that other Asians did not share the Japanese definition of Pan-Asianism (McNeil & Iriye, 1971:232). After 1945, Pan-Asianism no longer figured in debates on foreign relations in Japan or elsewhere. As a result, Saaler & Szpilman (2011:17) note that researchers, politicians and diplomats disregarded Pan-Asianism as its connections with Japan's geopolitical ambitions led to another problem, which is the ambiguity and contradictions of the concept involved as it could be used to legitimize both the anti-colonial struggle against the West and the domination of one Asian nation by another. Similarly, Zeleza (2006:18) notes that in Africa the construction of Pan-Africanism was not without problems as its six versions (transatlantic, Black Atlantic, continental, sub-Saharan, Pan-Arab and global) reflected conflicting racial and ideological tendencies of Pan-Africanism. Despite the establishment of the Organization of African Unity (OAU) in 1963, Ndlovu-Gatsheni (2014:25) observes that the tensions over the imperatives of Pan-Africanism between African leaders did not end, as while some emphasized economic cooperation with France, a former colonial power, a second group of Ghanaians under Nkrumah's leadership, which was ideologically socialist, continued to stress a stronger political unity as a pre-requisite for economic cooperation (ibid.). However, it was a third group, the so-called Monrovia, who favored the absolute equality and sovereignty of African states, and principle of non-interference in the domestic affairs of African states, as well as supporting the total decolonization of Africa that informed the construction of the OAU (ibid.). Unfortunately, the Cold War's (1945–1989) ideological divide of socialism versus capitalism undermined the ideals of Pan-Afro-Asianism at the Conference of Bandung in 1955, which signaled the spirit of anti-imperialist self-determination among the emergent new nations in Asia and Africa (Chakrabarty, 2010:51–52).

Rebuild Africa–Asia interactions in the twenty-first century beyond politics: the importance of education to economic growth

According to Lumumba-Kasongo (2015:15) the leadership of Pan-Afro-Asianism as an alternative worldview to the Cold War depends on the ability of Afro-Asian states to transform long-term solidarity into an effective ideological foundation of their actions. But what kind of ideology do we need, Lamumba-Kasongo asks? The academic challenge is how to rebuild Afro-Asia interactions within and beyond the 'politico-ideology' spirit of the Bandung Conference, and theoretical dependency approaches that support the theory that underdevelopment is not internally generated but a structural condition of global capitalism itself. Khudori (2006:123) points out that the early spirit of the Bandung Conference of 1955 associated with the struggle against the domination by the powerful over the weak still persists in today's economic globalized world. Despite the political impact of the Bandung Conference in speeding up the process of decolonization or in bringing China as well as Japan more fully into the Asian family of nations through the Non-Alignment Movement (NAM) established in 1961, the four meetings (1964–1989) of the Asian and African countries that followed did not produce the expected economic and development results, at least in Africa. Nevertheless, the conference enacted a new worldview under the idea of the Third World as an alternative to American and Soviet imperialism, committed to human rights, self-determination and world peace (Lee, 2010:15). It also helped to establish the principles for a future worldview based on South–South economic relations and growth strategies that, as this Handbook will examine, are much in vogue (Fosu & Ogunleye, 2015:25). Still, one can question why Africa failed to develop and Asia has not, or why economic growth over the 1960–1998 period was more vigorous in Asia than in Africa (see Khudori, 2006:124).

Henley (2015:49) argues that in the search for the origins of the development divergence between Africa and Asia, the higher ethnic fragmentation, resource endowments, geography obstacles or even the nature of institutions are without doubt important reasons that explain Africa's much lower development performance in relation to Asia. However, as he writes 'history is not destiny' (ibid.), and so the pessimistic burden of history can no longer be an excuse to adapt to changing times. Here, the Northeast and Southeast Asian countries economic miracle was achieved with different economic approaches, for example in the quest for how to achieve rapid economic growth through interventionist industrial policy as in Japan and South Korea, or without it as in Thailand, or even by abandoning it, as in Malaysia and Indonesia demonstrates two things. First, the dependency theory no longer seems to be an acceptable theoretical approach to explain the continued impoverishment of former colonized countries in Asia or in Africa. Second, despite its relative success in challenging the modernization theory—which explains underdevelopment in terms of the lack of certain qualities in 'underdeveloped societies', such as drive, entrepreneurial spirit, creativity, and problem-solving ability—the Asian economic miracle also demonstrates that through investment in human resources endowments is possible to break the cycle of poverty (ibid.).

In this context, a Group of 16 socially engaged intellectuals, academics and activists from Africa, Asia, Latin America, Europe, and USA gathered in Indonesia in 2005 and instituted the so-called Yogyakarta Commemoration Group "to look for alternatives to the present undesirable World Order and Globalisation" (Khudori, 2006:121). The Group criticized, mainly, the domination of the rich countries in the world order, the model of development of OECD countries, which has not changed, and the dominant Western "neo-liberal" paradigm and worldview (ibid.: 126). As a result, they launched a movement related to the fiftieth anniversary of the Bandung Asian–African Conference – Bandung II, which accordingly can play an important role to build a different and more egalitarian world. Given the several weaknesses of Africa when compared to Asia, they are of opinion that strong efforts should be made to change the present state of globalization based on the neo-liberal agenda that has failed to reduce gaps between rich and poor (Khudori, 2006:124). The call for a *Global Civil Society Movement* relates to the fiftieth anniversary of the Bandung Asian–African Conference, with education as one of the most important areas needed to preserve Human Dignity within the six areas besides politics, economics, culture, environment, and communication (ibid.: 132).

Accepting that growth is a necessary condition for development for this to occur it requires a different type of economic growth not "extensive" in terms of more quantities of factor endowments of land, labour, capital and resources, rather more "intensive" and sustainable growth (Moghalu, 2014:213). This latter kind results from technological innovation, which are only possible through an educated workforce, as a means to economic growth. In other words, the modernity theory incorporates two narratives: the superiority of Western civilization through progress and reason and the continuous growth of capitalism through modernization, development, the creation of new markets, and recently the expansion of urbanization and industrialization (Patel, 2015:53; Goody, 2004:6). Hence, to raise the quality of education in Africa is fundamental to the revitalization of African universities as a means to contribute more directly to poverty reduction and sustainable development (Akalu, 2015:221). Despite the promise, numbers of enrollment in higher education in Africa that between 2000 and 2010 more than doubled from 2.3 million to 5.2 million, Africa still lags behind Asia-Pacific that in 2014 reached 109 million enrolled students in tertiary education. Although Africa saw an impressive expansion in primary education in the 1960s and 1970s, in terms of gross enrollment ratio in 1989 sub-Saharan African (SSA) countries reached 69 per cent, however the secondary level remained low, at 18 per cent. In contrast, some Southeast Asian countries have reached 56 per cent in early 1990s (Aryeetey & Nissanke, 2003:44). For this difference, several reasons can be advanced. First, the need to "Africanize" the teaching staff of African diaspora meant fewer funds to support higher education and research in Africa. Second, the almost exclusive focus on primary education from 1980 onwards in the wake of structural adjustment programs explains the disregard for higher education in Africa (Akalu, 2015:220). Third, the failure of Sub-Saharan Africa to "change" the educational system from its colonial nature and globalization means that to a certain extent the past hegemony of Western philosophy is still rooted in African academia (Namuddu, 1991:49). Finally, some point out that as long as those who provide the resources monopolize the ownership of policy, it is unlikely that the educational project in Africa as a whole can provide avenues by which the continent effective integration into the world economy can became a reality (Akalu, 2015:221).

African and Asian studies: from colonial scholarship towards a flourishing Africa–Asia 'new' scholarship

In other words, the question is whether colonial (or western or European neo-imperialism/ neo-colonialism) (i) is responsible for a continued lack of educational achievement in Africa/ Asia and the state of Africa/Asia's scholars' participation in scholarly debates internationally; and (ii) is a constraining factor in network formation and collaboration between African/Asian scholars working on Africa–Asia relations.

In answering these questions, one should note that both continents educational systems were influenced by centuries of western occupation. Before independence, much of the foreign-inspired educational research in Africa and Asia was conducted at the universities and ministries of the colonial powers (Namuddu, 1991:45).

After independence, Huat (2015:67) argues that the neo-colonial appropriation of Asian scholarship by western academics became a reality as scholars were trained (and still are, though less so) in Euro-American universities with the ideological and intellectual "imprint" of Western academia circles. Gradually, the field of Asian studies also known as Oriental studies, with focus on the history, culture, arts and societies of Asia, developed. Unfortunately, it was a biased development because Asia and the non-West (Africa included) have been at best laboratories to validate Western based theories (Ngo, 2015:20). This also explains why Asia has no Western international relations theory (Acharya & Buzan, 2010). Two major reasons are advanced: First, the mainstream international relations theory derives from Western philosophy, political theory and history. Second given that World history is mostly based on a Eurocentric point of view, the analysis of the thinking and approach of Asian scholarship has been mainly undertaken by biographers and area specialists rather than scholars specializing in international relations theories (Acharya & Buzan, 2010:6, 11). Still, they do admit the existence of non-Western IR theories. However, historical, cultural, political, institutional and linguistic barriers on the one hand, and the lack of receptiveness to non-Western contributions arisen from the ethnocentrism of Western scholarship, on the other hand hinders global and local debates linked to less theoretical disciplines, such as history, law and area studies (ibid.: 18, 21). Similarly, the field of African studies, which began in the West (Britain, France and the United States), comprises all the disciplines of the humanities, the arts, and the social sciences, with focus on Africa and the African peoples from early times to present. Prior to the 1950s it was not even considered a discipline, although some historians and anthropologists were going in that direction (Azevedo, 2005:7). The emergence of the nation-states independence during the 1960s revolutionized the field of

African Studies as until then Africa was excluded from the academic community (ibid.: 8). The reason is simple. As in Asia, historiographers of the colonial period treated Africa as an extension of Europe, using European concepts within a Eurocentric rather than an Afro-centric approach to study the continent (ibid.:10). Despite the creation of the African Studies Association in 1957, this new field did not develop until the 1970s. Because of the economic crisis and of structural adjustment programmes during the 1980s, sub-Saharan Africa reduced its per capita expenditure on education from US$42 in 1980 to US$28 in 1992. In contrast, Asian countries devoted an average of US$30 in 1980 to $49 in 1992 (UNESCO, 1995:6). Finally, the end of the Cold War diverted foreign assistance funds from Africa to Eastern Europe. To worsen the status of educational research in Africa, governments and donor's agencies prevented an autonomous African research agenda with most of the sub-Saharan countries having no priority research projects beyond those identified by governments and donor agencies. As far as African Universities and African researchers are concerned the absence of academic freedom, the different systems of education based on different colonial systems across Africa, the insufficient human and material resource, and the lack of instructional quality at all levels affects, negatively, the dissemination of results and the mobility of students across Africa (Namuddu, 1991:50–1; Diarra, 2009:20). Only 0.6 per cent of world researchers and 0.9 per cent of the world share of scientific publications were provided by sub-Saharan African countries in 2001 with half of this output was accounted by South Africa alone (UNESCO, 2009:7). Despite external donors allocations of US$600 million annually to higher education in sub-Saharan Africa between 2002–2006, only US$152 million directly benefited universities and research centers in the region (World Bank, 2010:94–6). According to Diarra (2009:20) all these problems coupled with the lack of funds, limits information exchange and the potential for networking centres of excellent and collaborative research, which are essential to facilitate the transfer of knowledge across Africa and for the creation of the Pan African University. Finally, through research and increased knowledge, higher education can also help to address the challenges arising from population growth, limited arable land, endemic diseases, urbanization, energy cost and climate change.

What knowledge and what view of the world?

Returning to Asian studies one can identify a colonialist/post-colonialist view of the world to the extent that *orientalism,* as defined by Edward Said in his book *Orientalism,* has influenced an endless number of scholars studying Asia. Similar to Africa, Said (1978:10–13) argues that the relationship between Occident and Orient is one of power and domination, to characterize how Europe, in particular Great Britain and France among other European powers, subjugated the Orient from the nineteenth-century until the end of the Second World War. For Said *Orientalism* becomes a term identified with a Western style of colonial and even post-colonial authority, and for that reason he considers that Orientalism is an emblem of European power over the Orient, that it is as a veridical discourse about the orient, which according to him is what the scholarly academia claims to be (ibid.: 14). From an intellectual and theoretical point of view in the post-war period, Western thought continued dominating Asian universities motivated by the need to serve various colonial territories during the 1950s very few Western universities taught courses about Asia or Asian languages (Rozman, 2015a:6). The post-colonial era continued to see scholarship regimes produce research under the Anglo-American academic traditions for most Asian institutions and scholars for the utility of Western knowledge consumers (Tajudeen, 2015:32). In this context, Ngo notes that as a result, of the existing structure of global academic dependency and intellectual division of labour it is not surprising the increasing demand for an alternative scholarship within Asian studies, and the development of 'reverse discourses' in order for non-Western scholarship to theorize back at the West.

(Ngo, 2015:20)

Without question, the rise of capitalism in Asia, much by virtue of the actions of Japan (and recently China) as a leader of Asian industrialization and modernization from the 1960s, turned Japan into the only Asian representative in Western fora and one of the largest foreign aid donors in the world and contributed to this demand for alternative scholarship (Kennedy, 2013:8). Despite the Cold War ideological struggle, Japan's economic miracle centred-theory of 'flying geese' whereby Japan lead the way in labour-intensive exports industries, gave rise to an increased discussion of an alternate East Asian path of modernity (Huat, 2015:68). Here, the dual-role of Japanese economic cooperation (Keizai kyoryoku) was crucial both to Asia's structural development as well as to its own industrial growth (Arase, 2017:106). In other words, a 'new' kind of knowledge production in terms of expertise (economic) and capital accumulation transfer emerged in Asia (ibid.), beyond an epistemological analysis within Asian values and cultural achievements and began shaping international relations. Rozman (2015b:79) points out, 'terms such as *keiretsu, chaebol, and guanxi* suggest that the legalistic ideas of the West were not replicated in the modernization under way in East Asia'. Applied here, Asian worldview implies *knowledge production* that involves not only cultural knowledge (languages, values and traditions) of Asian (African) societies but also other dimensions (economic, political, social and development) of *knowledge produced* both locally and globally. Using the Mackie et al. (2015:12–13) term of 'changing geopolitics of knowledge', one defends that an Afro-Asian view of the world requires an intellectual readiness in terms of accepting other nations views of the world, not only Africa and Asia but also the whole world. Assuming that the rise of Asia in global capitalism can be accepted as the demonstration of its capacity to generate different forms of knowledge in terms of its own model of development of utility to Africa, the question is, what kind of worldview does Africa want? Certainly, African worldview shall be one of economic growth, inclusive sustainable development, peace and prosperity through the prism of democracy and political freedom. However, whether African knowledge can be of utility to Asians only the future will tell. Put differently, before one can ask if Africa's worldview can shape and influence the world (see Moghalu, 2014:16) some may doubt the existence of African knowledge. Smith (2012:25) notes that from a western point of view 'there is no such thing as pure, untainted African knowledge' at least in international relations. According to her this is due not only to the marginalization that African actors and African scholars have been subjected to throughout history, but also the limited access to knowledge production on the basis of gender, class, and ethnicity (ibid.: 33). The object of this Introduction is not to discuss the existence of African knowledge or its possible contribution to Asian (economic or development) 'happiness', rather it attempts to understand the reasons for the neglect of the African/Asian view of scholarship in terms of knowledge production. However, we agree with Moghalu (2014:17) who defends African knowledge, though he admits that the intellectual and outstanding political global leadership of Cheikh Anta Diop, Léopold Senghor, Wole Soyinka, Kwame Nkrumah, Chinua Achebe or even Nelson Mandela is in decline. Similarly, we also do not doubt the existence of culture and economic knowledge in Africa (or Asia) but the capacity to project it. According to Sarr (2015:341) if there is a space where Africa's power of dissemination and irradiation has remained intact, despite the historical convulsions, it is that of culture and its foundations of economic choices. She notes that economic choices are conditioned by culture, and in the

African context this is so true in contemporary African societies, despite traditions it has lost space in the regulation of behaviors the cultural context remains a powerful determiner of the economic choice of its members (ibid.: 343). However, as Monga & Lin (2015:9) observe when African economists, such as Samir Amin and Bernard Founou at the African Institute for Economic Development and Planning (IDEP) in Dakar, Senegal attempted to break the intellectual hegemony of some Western academic institutions their works were rarely accepted. African scholarship and African-based research institutions, such as the African Economic Research Consortium (AERC), the Council for the Development of Social Science Research in Africa (CODESRIA), or the Economic Research Forum (ERF) conflicted with dominant western theories as they are carried out under an Afrocentric perspective that reflected the specific conditions of the continent and yielded new theoretical insights, it was largely ignored (ibid.). The opposite also occurred. When Africans were given the opportunity to study in the West, many, after returning home, used the knowledge acquired in the West to understand the problems in Africa from a western worldview rather than to propose new theories and new answers (ibid.). To create space for an *Africanist or Afrocentrism (Asianist)* view of the world, Africans and Asians must be at the center of societies; ultimately, as Falola (2013:90) notes the traditions and histories independent of each own ideology shall be the pillar of Africanism. However, this requires agency, here understood as the self-reflective social action (both individually and collectively), that produces or is capable of producing knowledge as a result of its action (Poe, 2003:13, 15, 22; Chabal, 2009:7). In sum, the ability of Africans/Asians to decide for their own future (worldview) depends upon their capacity to project their own values and traditions to find equilibrium between the different dimensions of their knowledge.

Having said this, the question of why a Handbook titled Africa–Asia relations is needed is almost tautological. A major reason is to give insight into the most important intellectual, theoretical and empirical developments within the field, drawing on contributions from the leading voices interested in Africa and Asia relations before and beyond the nineteenth and twentieth century and to incorporate African and Asian contemporary studies. With this Handbook, one has a chance to look at the nature of interaction between the African continent and a wider range of Asian countries, and how those interactions are being studied. Given the multifaceted diversity of the two regions, the contributors respond to the growing scholarly interest in Africa–Asia and Asia–Africa relations in terms of its main attributes, significance and their implications by attempting to answer the question,what kind of interactions do these two regions have in historical and contemporary terms? The south–south dimension comes to the fore, as outside of relatively small circles of experts, south–south relations in the pre-colonial period, but also in the modern era have not usually been viewed as critically important and worthy of sustained scholarly attention by mainstream scholarship, which was developed and disseminated in universities of the developed north. In contrast as Peycam (2015) notes there is an over reliance on colonial and post-independence Western categories, such as those of the Nation-State or of neo-imperial geographical ensembles.

To a certain extent Afro-Asian studies are still in the making, as until late 1990s and early 2000s the problem with existing literature was that there was a general tendency toward a particular division of labor among scholars under Cold War ideological thought. This situation began to change in a fundamental way because the global distribution of wealth, power, knowledge and scholarship is spreading more widely from the North's trilateral core of Japan, North America, and Western Europe to adjoining areas of Asia, Latin America, and Africa. These latter areas used to be regarded as the global periphery. They were dependent on the North because of their subordinate position in a vertical international division of labour, their cultural and institutional legacies of colonial or neo-colonial subjugation, and their late accession to international governance regimes authored by an alliance of powerful core Northern and developed states.

Introduction

Despite the commonalities Africa and Asia share by virtue of the manner in which they were incorporated into the modern world through successive waves of globalization, the so-called South is not monolithic. It is only a category created in the sense of being 'late developing' and 'not-North', i.e., not being among the 'First World' advanced, high-income countries in the 1960s–1970s when the North–South discourse took shape between the 'Third World', now the G77 developing countries and the rich OECD countries represented by the G7. Today, formerly 'Second World' (formerly communist bloc countries) have joined the 'not-North' category, and some members, especially the 'emerging aid donors' such as Brazil, China and India, find themselves replicating relations historically associated with North–South relations. But, the 'three worlds' of the cold war era are now merged into one world of economic and internet globalization. Relations between all regions and actors in global society are still far from uniform, but they are on the equal and free footing they have ever enjoyed.

In many respects, the 'renaissance' of Africa since mid 1990s is due to Asian economic growth and development. Because of the increasing diplomatic, trade, investment and development ties between Asia and Africa there has been growing scholarly interest in African and Asian studies with a notable rise in the number of research networks focusing on Asia–Africa and Africa–Asia relations. The actors building these networks are beyond the state level and extend to the academic and civil society domains. Further, the themes, activities and purposes that characterize Africa–Asian relations have diversified beyond political, diplomatic and economic issues. Yet, the study of African and Asian relations would be incomplete without exploring Africa's and Asian historical processes in terms of understanding the impact of earlier connections between the two world regions, and how it stands in current international system.

The book's organization and summary of chapters

This volume divides into three parts, subdivided in nine sections that deal with broad questions about Africa–Asia relations. Given the political, socio-economic, cultural and development diversity of Africa and Asia all together one could say that there are many Africas and Asias. For practical reasons and because it is impossible to examine all countries existent in Africa (54) and Asia (50) the Handbook analysis is confined to the interactions between the most expressive countries in both continents as a whole rather than on the constituent parts of each Africa and Asia sub-regions.

Part One: Africa and Asia Early Contacts has six chapters. It divides into two periods. One comprising the pre-colonial period and early colonialism and the second post-colonialism. The first period is the age of traditional kingdoms and empires of pre-colonial economies; Africa and Asian diaspora and its interactions with Arabs, Islam and Christians and the links with exploration and exploitation, maritime and slavery trade connections. It covers a time before Westernization became synonymous with modernization (Falola, 2013:17) through steam power, chemistry, and electricity empowers the West to subjugate most of Africa and Asia. The second period overall dates from the industrial revolution to the first decolonization until mid 1960s. Contributors are asked to frame their discussions in terms of how the world historical processes have shaped and connected Africa and Asia over time. Themes include implications of the Peace of Westphalia as a means to justify the colonization of Africa and Asia; territoriality defined political units; the role of religion to development within its 'civilizing mission'; anti-colonialism against colonial rulers, institutionalism and nationalism.

In Chapter 1, Samuel Oloruntuba and Sabelo J. Ndlou-Gatsheni address the historical backgrounds of Africa and Asia diaspora with the Indian Ocean as the centre of commercial interactions that brought both continents into contact. They contend that whereas Asians in Africa

11

have achieved significant economic and in some instances, political importance, the same cannot be said of Africans in Asia. Hence, it appears that racial differentiations have given Asian diaspora hegemony over Africans, with the latter having little or no space for social mobility.

In Chapter 2, Daniel Domingues explores how Iberian traders (Portugal and Spain) not only spread Christianity and Western values to Africa and Asia, but also helped connect these regions to the emerging Atlantic economy, further expanding the slave trade in the Indian Ocean and the Far East.

In Chapter 3, Kwame Nimako challenges the false Eurocentric historical narrative that the European colonial enterprise in the Americas, Africa and Asia were justified under the principle that territorial sovereignties and integrity of the peoples of the Americas, Africa and Asia were *not recognized* by European states; therefore, they could be occupied without their consent. As a result, the author argues that the forces that gave rise to the European colonial enterprise/ project and the rise of capitalism in Europe revolved around state formation in Europe, so was the process of decolonization in Africa and Asia.

Iqbal S. Akhtar in Chapter 4, analyses the religious and racial implications of South Asian settlement in East Africa. He demonstrates how Europeans divided Asian communities among European colonial regimes whose policies favoured white settlers in land acquisition, and instituted legal forms of racial discrimination. The author concludes that East African Asian communities have helped to bolster the presence of Muslim communities in public discourse despite the hostile political environment where Islam is increasingly equated with extremism.

In Chapter 5, Jörg Haustein and Emma Tomalin look at the intersection of religions and development practices in Africa and Asia. They argue that the history of European thought about religion and progress served both the Christian missionary efforts through through the colonial 'civilising mission,' and the economic interests of settlers in a common imperial project. As donor agencies increasingly discuss the role of religion in development initiatives, it is instrumental to deconstruct this long history of European interventions, in order to make room for alternative visions of progress and the place of religions in society.

In Chapter 6, Christopher Lee examines the phenomenon of nationalism in Africa and Asia from the colonial into the postcolonial period. He argues that nationalism must be understood as local in orientation, with roots in local political cultures and anti-colonial resistance. While nationalism was reinforced via the United Nations, and conferences, such as the 1955 Asian–African Conference in Bandung, Indonesia, the term *nationalism* became increasingly rhetorical, rather than substantive, in scope during the postcolonial period because most of African and Asian countries maintained relations with imperial powers.

Part Two: Asia–Africa Modern Interactions has eleven chapters that focus on Asia and Africa in the late modern era, covering the period from 1840 to the late Cold War Era in 1989. It contains three sub-sections, as follows: Diplomatic and political exchanges; Political and economic connections; and Societal-level interactions. Agendas in these sub-sections include Asian attempts to rise against Europe after their takeover of the world system around 1800; Third World movements in reaction to the racial European worldview; second decolonization; nation-building (nationalism, state-building, economic development); cold war competition; international development agenda; education and gender; Islam and development; the rise of civil society (gender) and the role of NGOs.

In Chapter 7, Kweku Ampiah discusses how Japan might have responded to the African countries in the Meiji period. The analysis suggests that throughout its modern history Japan tended to view Africa as a region it could afford to ignore, a position it essentially maintained throughout the second-half of the twentieth century. Ampiah concludes that in recent times Japan has attempted to devise a more constructive relationship with the African countries through the Tokyo International Conference on African Development though constrained by the legacy of Japan's aloofness towards the region.

In Chapter 8, Hyo-sook Kim examines South Korean aid to Africa with focus on the second half of the Cold War period. It finds that after the Korean War, aid was used for winning diplomatic recognition in competition with North Korea. Gradually, from the 1980s on South Korea changed its aid approach to Africa from diplomatic purposes to south–south cooperation for sharing its development experience with African countries.

In Chapter 9, Sanjukta Bhattacharya reviews the Africa and Asia journey through independence with emphasis on the 1970–1990 period. The author argues that although Asia and Africa formed shared groupings like the NAM and the G77, to leverage their position vis-à-vis the international community, they have been able to transform common ideological positions into effective South–South cooperation only recently.

In Chapter 10, Seifudein Adem and Darryl Thomas while examining the three inter-related forces (racial solidarity, cultural solidarity, anti-imperial solidarity) that helped to bring Africa and Asia closer together in the twentieth century against their former colonizers, want to understand whether or not after more than 60 years, the Bandung Spirit is being superseded by the BRICS.

In Chapter 11, Alicia Garcia-Herrero and Carlos Casanova analyze the implications of Africa's rising commodity export dependency on China. The authors' argue that since the Maoist era, China's goal has been to promote the advancement of developing country goals into a new world order based on South–South cooperation, with trade as its major pillar. However, a deceleration of China's economy could have negative implications for those countries with higher trade exposure to China. In order to avert further commodity dependency, they advise African economies to diversify and increase their exports to other regions via the implementation of policies that facilitate the integration of regional trade.

Evelyn S. Devadason and Chandran Govindaraju in Chapter 12 evaluate Malaysia–Africa relations during the Cold War. They argue that legacies of colonialism have played out in ways that shape our understanding of modern contemporary relations between the two; and demonstrated that Malaysia–Africa connections originating from early contacts founded loosely on a shared identity of a developing colonial status has evolved into a higher level of strategic partnership within the ASEAN-Africa nexus.

In Chapter 13, Yejoo Kim and Ross Anthony analyze how China's "One" policy affects Taiwan's relationship with South Africa following the latter's diplomatic switch to the PRC. This process is situated within the post-Cold War context of economic pragmatism, in which it is no longer "the state" which solely dictates relations, but rather is included amongst a host of other actors. In other words, diplomatic recognition no longer plays as significant a role as it used to, especially *vis-à-vis* their external counterparts. They conclude that China in exchange for higher economic integration with Taiwan, entails a tolerance of Taiwanese economic engagement in South Africa.

In Chapter 14, Takuo Iwata reviews the process of African studies network formation in Asian countries to reflect on the perspectives on Africa–Asia academic relationship in the twenty-first century. He argues that compared to the Asian situation, Africa has been simply considered and treated as a passive actor or site for Asian scholars to take their research activities. He concludes that though in recent years common interests between African and Asians have brought them together, the different structure of African studies within very different academic disciplines has made it difficult to achieve a consensus among Africanists (and with Asianists) with rivalries and misunderstandings in interdisciplinary communication.

Yoichi Mine in Chapter 15 analyses Africa and Asia as one common geographical entity, which he calls Afrasia. He discusses one of Afrasia's biggest challenges – demography and its implications for development. He concludes that the historical legacy of decentralized democracy in land-abundant parts of the region, may contribute to an egalitarian future of Afrasia.

In Chapter 16, Mayke Kaag highlights the role of Islam in forging linkages between Africa and Asia, by focusing on Islamic relief and development support. She concludes though humanitarianism prospered throughout the 1990s after 9/11, as Islamic relief organisations were accused of supporting Islamic terrorism, seriously hampered their work, and led them to adapt to the new situation in specific ways.

David M. Potter in Chapter 17 examines terminological problems of civil society and the non-profit and voluntary sector in South Asia and Sub-Saharan Africa. He argues that African and Asian civil societies have developed along with the growth of global civil society but have done so through different trajectories. He concludes that structural problems, such as financial dependence on external donors impede cross-regional interaction among NGOs.

In Chapter 18, Emefa Juliet Takyi-Amoako examines North–South and South–South partnerships and their effects on education and gender outcomes in sub-Saharan Africa. She argues that the failure of the global partnership for development to endorse economic progress, generate productive capacities and employment, as well as address income inequalities in SSA undermines efforts to attain gender equality in education in the region. She concludes that without bringing relevant cultural and indigenous knowledge and practices to bear on these processes, the improvement of education and gender policy outcomes in the region will be difficult to attain.

Part Three: *Africa–Asia Contemporary Relations*, consists of twelve chapters, divided in three sections, as follows: Economic and development cooperation; Security and governance, and Migration, environment and politics. Overall, it examines both continents interactions in the post-cold war period, 1989–present. Agendas in these sub-sections include the rise of BRICS economies, new patterns of South–South interactions, rivalry and collaboration between Southern actors, development partnerships, post–2015 development agenda, religious connections to conflicts, production globalization, jihad vs. McWorld responses to globalization, the land-water-food-energy nexus, mineral resources and sustainable development, and geographies of migration and politics.

In Chapter 19, Ian Taylor looks at the role of emerging economies in Africa through the prism of human rights, arguing that the nature of the engagement of the BRICS in Africa is based squarely on capitalism and as a result, the agenda of human rights, inevitably falls below that of capital accumulation and profit.

Chun Zhang in Chapter 20 focuses on mixed feelings and misunderstandings, in particularly those of the West of China's engagement in Africa. He argues that for a true perception of China's role in Africa we ought to understand the whole dimension of their bilateral relations that rests on four distinct but complementary pillars (political, economic, peace and security, and societal relations), without which one cannot envision the "high-speed train" era with new areas of cooperation to strengthen the commitment and confidence on both sides.

In Chapter 21, Carmen Amado Mendes focuses on the bilateral relationship between major Asian powers – Japan, India, South Korea and China – and each of the Portuguese-speaking countries in Africa. She argues that Asian governments are driven by competitive foreign policy strategies, and implement their goals through south–south cooperation rhetoric, which as a result is hampering development interests, wellbeing and good governance in Lusophone countries.

Similarly, Annette Skovsted Hansen in Chapter 22 examines the tensions between cooperation and competition, as they constitute the driving force in Africa–Asia regional partnerships

Introduction

and South–South development cooperation. She concludes that a trend of parallel multiple paradigms and approaches will most likely expand beyond the 2001 New Partnership for African Development (NEPAD), and any current definitions of North, South, Asia – or Africa.

In Chapter 23, Shalini Chawala analyses the inexorable global power shift towards the South and how the emerging powers of Asia within the G20, particularly China, are facilitating the attainment of the Sustainable Development Goals (SDGs) though not without challenges as the growth of Asia–Africa cooperation cannot be isolated from sustainable development and the implementation of the SDGs.

In Chapter 24, Jeffrey Haynes looks at the problem of the ambivalence of religion as a concept and argues that there is no single, elegant theoretical model enabling us to deal with all relevant cases of religious involvement in security and conflict issues in Africa and Asia. He concludes that the influence of religion is said to be increasing in relation to 'good governance' issues in the developing world, often affected by the multiple impacts of globalization with implications to the trajectory of conflict in Africa and Asia.

Larry Swatuk, in Chapter 25 analyses how the complex interplay of the land-water-food-energy nexus, organized along two pathways (one green; the other blue) influences the decisions and actions of elite interests, responding to local, national and global political economic challenges. As a result, given Africa's difficult history of underdevelopment, a significant portion of these activities serve to exacerbate African state pathologies rather than alleviate them.

In Chapter 26, Laura C. Ferreira-Pereira and Alena Vieira examines the evolving EU–Africa relations and argue that the EU's modes of cooperation with Africa have become more extensive over time while incorporating a deeper security dimension and that a similar trend can be seen as regards the Asian continent. They conclude that in parallel there has been a reaching out to Asia accompanied by the advancement of the EU's partnership policy in terms of the development of cooperation in maritime security.

The last section of the handbook looks at the interplay between migration and politics and the second scramble in Africa that involves competition over Africa's natural resources industries.

In Chapter 28, Thomas Feldhoff analyses notions of Asian neo-colonialism in Africa and considers the prospects for the development of a sustainable resource-based economy in Africa. He argues that Asian and Western countries have similar, but competing interests and follows different approaches to their African engagement. Strong regional cooperation with key African and international partners is identified as an important element to strengthen Africa's ownership and position globally as transnational entanglements are becoming ever more complex.

Pedro Amakasu Raposo de Medeiros Carvalho in Chapter 27 and Pablo Shiladitya Bose in Chapter 29 broaden the understanding of migration studies. The chapters though different in context complement each other. While Carvalho's chapter explores the actions of states in voluntarily migration flows in Africa and Asia from pre-modern to contemporary times, Bose's examines the causes and outcomes of forced migration from two of the World's largest refugee-producing regions in Africa and Asia in recent times. Then, Carvalho's argue that throughout time all forms of human mobility share some of the causes of human and forced displacement across and within borders as kingdoms and great powers to attain their geo-strategic, economic; development and trade interests victimized thousands or millions of people in both continents. On his side, Bose's contends that if we are to arrive at lasting solutions to the global refugee crisis we must look beyond forced migration, such as development practices and policies, and environmentally induced displacement; ultimately is due to men actions and inaction upon our responsibility to protect migrants.

Conclusion

Overall, the Handbook reveals that a geopolitical reconceptualization of knowledge production is in fact occurring. This manifests in terms of the following dimensions: political, security, economic, development, environment, cultural, religious, societal, intellectual and academic interconnectedness between Africa and Asia. The following chapters also show there are challenges that hinder the production of a common worldview, which result mainly from a unbalanced knowledge agenda in terms of agency between the two continents in favor of Asia, in particular of China at the expense of Africa, which impel us to rethink and research the state of Africa–Asia relations.

Bibliography

Abrahamsen, R. 2003. 'African Studies and the Postcolonial Challenge', *African Affairs*, Volume 102 (407), pp. 189–210 [online] Available at: https://doi.org/10.1093/afraf/adg001 [Accessed 6 August 2017].

Acharya, A. and Buzan, B. (eds.), 2010. *Non-Western International Relations Theory*, London and New York: Routledge.

Akalu, G. A. 2015. 'Revitalising Higher Education in the Age of Globalisation: The African Dilemma', in E. Shizha and L. Diallo (eds), *Africa in the Age of Globalisation: Perceptions, Misperceptions and Realities*, London: Routledge, pp. 219–234.

Allen, R. C., 2011. *Global Economic History: A Very Short Introduction*, Oxford: Oxford University Press.

Anievas, A. and Nisancioglu, K., 2015. *How the West Came to Rule: The Geopolitical Origins of Capitalism*, London: PlutoPress.

Arase, D., 2017. 'Japanese ODA and the challenge of Chinese aid in Africa', in A. Asplund and M. Soderberg (eds.), *Japanese Development Cooperation: The Making of an Aid Architecture Pivoting to Asia*, London and New York: Routledge, pp. 104–123.

Aryeetey, E. and Nissanke, M., 2003. 'Economic policies and external performance in Southeast Asia and Sub-Saharan Africa', in J. Court, M. Nissanke and B. Weder (eds.), *Asia and Africa in the Global Economy*, Hong Kong: United Nations University Press, pp. 40–87.

Asante, M. K. (ed.), 2015. *The History of Africa: The Quest for Eternal Harmony*, New York and London: Routledge.

Azevedo, M. (ed.), 2005. 'African Studies and the State of the Art', *Africana Studies*, pp. 5–31 [online] Available at: http://pzacad.pitzer.edu/~hfairchi/pdf/Africana%20Studies%20Articles/Acevedo%202005%20Ch%201.pdf [Accessed 16 January 2017].

Chabal, P., 2009. *Africa: The Politics of Suffering and Smiling*, South Africa: University of KwaZulu-Natal Press.

Chakrabarty, D., 2010. 'The Legacies of Bandung: Decolonization and the Politics of Culture', in C. J. Lee (ed.), *Making a World after Empire: The Bandung Moment and its Political Afterlives*, Athens, OH: Ohio University Press, pp. 45–68.

Diarra, M. C., 2009. *Thematic Studies Synthesis: Realized in the Context of the Task Force for Higher Education in Africa*, Paris: United Nations Educational, Scientific and Cultural Organization [online] Available at: www.unesco.org/education/WCHE2009/synthese170609.pdf [Accessed 19 January 2017].

Falola, T., 2013. *The African Diaspora: Slavery, Modernity, and Globalization*, New York: University of Rochester Press.

Fosu, A. K. and Ogunleye, E. K., 2015. 'African growth strategies: The past, present and future', in C. Monga and J. Y. Lin (eds.), *The Oxford Handbook of Africa and Economics*, Volume 2, Policies and Practices, Oxford: Oxford University Press, pp. 23–38.

Goody, J., 2004. *Capitalism and Modernity: The Great Debate*, Cambridge: Polity Press.

Henley, D., 2015. *Asia–Africa Development Divergence: A Question of Intent*, London: Zed Books.

Hobson, J. M., 2012. 'A non-Eurocentric global history of Asia', in M. Beeson and R. Stubbs (eds.), *Routledge Handbook of Asian Regionalism*, USA and Canada: Routledge, pp. 46–57.

Huat, C. B., 2015. 'Inter-Asia referencing and shifting frames of comparison', in C. Johnson, V. Mackie and T. Morris-Suzuki (eds.), *The Social Sciences in the Asian Century*, Australia: Australian National University, pp. 67–96.

Jayasuriya, S. S. and Angenot, J. P. (eds.), 2008. *'General Introduction', Uncovering the History of Africans in Asia*, Leiden: Brill, pp. 1–5.

Kang, D., 2012. 'East Asia when China was at the centre: The tribute system in early modern Asia', in M. Beeson and R. Stubbs (eds.), *Routledge Handbook of Asian Regionalism*, USA and Canada: Routledge, pp. 58–77.

Keita, M., 2005. 'Africans and Asians: Historiography and the Long View of Global Interaction', *Journal of World History*, Volume 16 (1), pp. 1–64.

Kennedy, M., 2013. 'Theoretical Encounters: Postcolonial Studies in East Asia', *The IAFOR Journal of Literature and Librarianship*, Volume 2 (1), pp. 7–15 [online] Available at: https://iafor.org/journal/iafor-journal-of-literature-and-librarianship/volume-2-issue-1/article-1/ [Accessed 20 January 2017].

Khudori, D., 2006. 'Towards a Bandung spirit-based civil society movement: Reflection from Yogyakarta commemoration of Bandung Asian–Africa Conference', *Inter-Asia Cultural Studies*, Volume 7 (1), pp. 121–138.

Lee, C. J. (ed.), 2010. *Making a World After Empire: The Bandung Movement and Its Political Afterlives*, USA: Ohio University Press.

Lumumba-Kasongo, T., 2015. 'Rethinking the Bandung Conference in an Era of "Unipolar Liberal Globalization" and Movements Toward a Multipolar Politics', *Bandung Journal of the Global South*, Volume 2 (9), pp. 3–17.

Mackie, J., 2010. 'The Bandung conference and Afro-Asian solidarity: Indonesian aspects', in D. McDougal and A. Finnane (eds.), *Bandung 1955 Little Histories*, Caulfield: Monash University Press.

Mackie, V., Johnson, C. and Morris-Suzuki, T. (eds.), 2015. 'Australia, the Asia-Pacific and the social sciences', in *The Social Sciences in the Asian Century*, Australia: Australia National University, pp. 1–15.

McNeil, W. H. and Iriye, M. (eds.), 1971. *Modern Asia and Africa*, New York: Oxford.

Moghalu, K. C., 2014. *Emerging Africa: How the Global's Economy's 'Last Frontier' Can Prosper and Matter*, London and New York: Penguin Books.

Monga, C. and Lin, J. Y. (eds.), 2015. 'Introduction: Africa, the Next Intellectual Frontier', *The Oxford Handbook of Africa and Economics*, Volume 1, Context and Concepts, UK: Oxford University Press, pp. 1–26.

Mullen, B. V., 2003. 'Du Bois, Dark Princess, and the Afro-Asian International', *East Asia Cultures Critique*, Volume 11 (1) Spring, pp. 218–239 [online] Available at: https://readthinkwriteteach.files.wordpress.com/2012/07/11-1mullen.pdf.

Namuddu, K., 1991. *'Educational Research Priorities in Sub-Saharan Africa', Strengthening Educational Research in Developing Countries*, Report of a seminar held at the Swedish Royal Academy of Sciences 12–14 September, Stockholm: Institute of International Education and International Institute for Educational Planning, pp. 39–71.

Ndlovu-Gatsheni, S., 2012. 'Bringing Identity into International Relations: Reflections on Nationalism, Nativism and Xenophobia in Africa', in S. Cornelissen, F. Cheru and T. M. Shaw (eds.), *Africa and International Relations in the 21st Century*, New York: Palgrave Macmillan, pp. 69–86.

Ndlovu-Gatsheni, S., 2014. 'Pan-Africanism and the international system', in T. Murithi (ed.), *Handbook of Africa's International Relations*, London and New York: Routledge, pp. 21–29.

Ngo, T. W., 2015. 'New scholarship from Asia', *The Newsletter: Encouraging knowledge and enhancing the study of Asia*, no. 72, (Autumn), p. 20.

Osborne, M. and Kent, S. K. (eds.), 2015. *Africans and Britons in the Age of Empires, 1660–1980*, London and New York: Routledge.

Patel, S., (2015). 'Beyond divisions and towards internationalism: Social sciences in the twenty-first century', in C. Johnson, V. Mackie and T. Morris-Suzuki (eds.), *The Social Sciences in the Asian Century*, Australia: Australian National University, pp. 51–66.

Peycam, P., 2015. 'Forging new connections', *The Newsletter—Encouraging knowledge and enhancing the study of Asia*, no. 72 (August), International Institute for Asian Studies (IIAS), p. 3 [online] Available at: http://iias.asia/sites/default/files/IIAS_NL72_FULL.pdf [Accessed 6 December 2016].

Poe, D. Z., 2003. 'Method to Examine Nkrumah's Contribution to Pan-African Agency 13 Afrocentricity', in M. Asante (ed.), *Kwame Nkrumah's Contribution to Pan-Africanism: An Afrocentric Analysis*, London & New York: Routledge [online] Available at: https://marxistnkrumaistforum.files.wordpress.com/2013/12/kwame-nkrumahs-contribution-to-pan-african-agency-an-afrocentric-analysis-blackatk.pdf [Accessed 6 August 2017].

Pomeranz, K., 2000. *The Great Divergence: China, Europe and the Making of the Modern World Economy*, Princeton and Oxford: Princeton University Press.

Rozman, G. (ed.), 2015a. 'Introduction', in *Misunderstanding Asia: International Relations Theory and Asian Studies over Half a Century*, New York: Palgrave Macmillan, pp. 1–22.

Rozman, G., 2015b. 'The 1990s: Asia's Transformation and IR Theory', in G. Rozman (ed.), *Misunderstanding Asia: International Relations Theory and Asian Studies Over Half a Century*, New York: Palgrave Macmillan, pp. 107–124.

Saaler, S. and Szpilman, C. W. A., 2011. 'Pan-Asianism as an Ideal of Asian Identity and Solidarity, 1850–Present', *The Asia-Pacific Journal*, Volume 9 (17), no.1 (April), pp. 1–29 [online] Available at: http://apjjf.org/-Sven-Saaler--Christopher-W--A--Szpilman/3519/article.pdf [Accessed 7 January 2017].

Said, E. W., 1978. *Orientalism*, London: Routledge & Kegan Paul.

Sarr, F., 2015. 'Economics and culture in Africa', in C. Monga and J. Y. Lin (eds.), *The Oxford Handbook of Africa and Economics*, Volume 1, Context and Concepts, UK: Oxford University Press, pp. 334–350.

Smith, K., 2012. 'Africa as an agent of international relations knowledge', in S. Cornelissen, F. Cheru and T. M. Shaw (eds.), *Africa and International Relations in the 21st Century*, New York and London: Palgrave Macmillan, pp. 21–35.

Tajudeen, I., 2015. 'Old and new knowledge regimes and the public milieu', *The Newsletter—Encouraging knowledge and enhancing the study of Asia*, no. 72 (August), International Institute for Asian Studies (IIAS), pp. 32–33 [online] Available at: http://iias.asia/sites/default/files/IIAS_NL72_FULL.pdf [Accessed 18 January 2017].

UNESCO, 1995. *Education Strategies for the 1990s: Orientations and Achievements*, Report on the State of Education in Africa, Dakar: UNESCO Regional Office for Education in Africa (BREDA) [online] Available at: http://www.unesco.org/education/pdf/15_58.pdf [Accessed 18 January 2017].

UNESCO, 2009. *Thematic Studies Synthesis: Realized in the Context of the Task Force for Higher Education in Africa*, Paris: United Nations Educational, Scientific and Cultural Organization [online] Available at: www.unesco.org/education/WCHE2009/synthese170609.pdf [Accessed 19 January 2017].

World Bank, 2010. *Directions in Development: Financing Higher Education in Africa*. Washington, DC: The World Bank [online] Available at: http://documents.worldbank.org/curated/en/497251467990390368/Financing-higher-education-in-Africa [Accessed 18 January 2017].

Zeleza, P. T. 2006. 'The Inventions of African Identities and Languages: The Discursive and Developmental Implications', in F. Arasanyin and M. A. Pemberton (eds.), *Selected Proceedings of the 36th Annual Conference of African Linguistics*, Sommerville, MA: Cascadilla Proceedings Project, pp. 14–26.

PART I

Africa and Asia early contacts

Early colonialism

1

AFRICA AND ASIA DIASPORA

Reconstructing a neglected history

Samuel Ojo Oloruntoba and Sabelo Ndlovu-Gatsheni

Introduction

Africa and Asia have a long history of contacts. The Indian Ocean is one centre of commercial interactions that brought Africa and Asia into contact. Besides the Indian Ocean being a commercial hub, the ocean facilitated rather than inhibited movement of people. People moved and continue to move for various reasons under different conditions. Human movement is fundamentally a way of life and a human trait. But the cartographic interventions cascading from Euro-North American modernity in the last five hundred or so years, which resulted in the drawing of continental and national boundaries, tended to seek to control human movement and even criminalise it.

Consequently, transnational identities re-emerged within the modern era as an exception, rather than part of long-standing human interactions. Perhaps this is why not much has been done on African diaspora in Asia and vice versa. The most popular literature in this emerging and dynamic area of study include, *The African Presence in Asia: Consequences of the East African Slave Trade* by Harris (1971), *Africa Diaspora in the Indian Ocean,* edited by Jayasuriya & Pankhurst (2003), *African Identity in Asia: Cultural Effects of Forced Migration*, by Jayasuriya (2008) and *Indians in Kenya: The Politics of Diaspora,* by Aiyar (2015). A special issue of the *Journal of African and Asian Studies* was dedicated to African–Asian Diaspora in 2006. These works provide interesting entry points to the study of Africa and Asia diaspora. Even though the studies cover various aspects of diaspora studies such as the history, origin, cultural distinctiveness and identities of Africans in Asia, they say little about Asians in Africa. The relevance of these diasporas in the contemporary, political economy of their countries of residence has not been fully discussed.

This chapter makes a modest attempt to frame historically, the realities of Africa and Asia diaspora and in the process pay attention to the long-standing interactions between Africa and Asia. Perhaps more than any other people, Africans are found in different parts of the Asian world, in what today constitutes what might be called the neglected minority. While some of the encounters between Africans and Asians were borne out of voluntary interactions in which the former sought economic opportunities in marine operations, such boat making and repairs, for example, others were involuntary, through Arab and Portuguese slave trades. For example, Africans of Ghanaian origin were also drafted into Dutch military to fight in Indonesia. Still some people migrated on account of religious identity, especially to the Arab world and settled there permanently. The search for knowledge and career opportunities has led to a new wave of African diaspora to Asia in the twenty-first century. It is not clear if there is any relationship between the new immigrants and old immigrants.

On the other hand, Asians of Indian origin have been found in Africa through the instrumentality of the British imperial adventure in which Indians were brought to Africa as indenture workers. In countries like Kenya, Uganda and South Africa, there are relatively big populations of Indians, who today constitute a sizeable proportion of Asian diaspora in Africa. The search for economic opportunities in the form of access to raw materials and markets for manufactured goods have led to an increase in the number of Asians in Africa, to the extent that today, China has become the biggest trade partner with Africa (Brautigam, 2009).

Basically, this chapter is a historical narrative of the forces and factors that led to the movement of Africans to Asia as well as Asians to Africa. The chapter also contains an analysis of the socio-economic and political positions of Africans in Asia within the context of larger groups with distinct identities. In this regard, we note that whereas Asians in Africa have achieved significant economic and, in some instances, political importance, the same cannot be said of Africans in Asia. Over the last five centuries of interactions and engagements, it would appear that that racial differentiations have ensured that Asians, especially those of the Arab stock have maintained domination and hegemony over Africans, with the latter having little or no space for social mobility. What are the forces that led to the movement of Africans to Asia and how did Asians find themselves in Africa, at least on a permanent basis? How have racial differences affected the socio-economic and political positions of the two racial minorities in their locations of residence? What are the forms of relations that exist between the diasporas of Africa in Asia and Asia in Africa? These questions are discussed and interrogated both in their historical and contemporary contexts in the succeeding sections. But before then, we provide a conceptual clarity on what is meant by diaspora, their characteristics, dimensions and the debates that have framed its studies.

Diaspora: a conceptual interpretation

Diaspora studies is an important part of the study of transnational identities, which was informed by the need to understand the experiences of migrant groups in other social formations away from their homelands. Diaspora formation is a global phenomenon, which encompasses the search for understanding of both racial and non-racial groups in foreign lands. This aspect of socio-cultural studies emerged out of international migration, which is as old as human existence. Hence we have delineated diaspora according to national distinctive groups and identities such as Jewish diaspora (the most prominent), Chinese diaspora, Africa diaspora, Spanish diaspora, Asia diaspora and so on. Despite the previous neglect of this important area of social organisation, Zeleza (2005:35) opines that, 'diaspora is now increasingly invested with new possibilities as a harbinger of globalised futures'. Its relevance to knowledge about the experiences of migrants and non-migrants alike is underpinned by the interrelated conjunctures of history, modernity, globalisation of culture, increasing importance of transnational identities, which in itself is informed by imperatives of the search for better economic opportunities, escape from wars and conflicts as well as from natural disasters.

While migration has been part of human history from time immemorial, globalisation has intensified the ease, as well as the scope, of movement of people from one part of the world to another. To elaborate, the revolution in information communication technology (ICT) and the development of all manners of instant communication devices and social media provides opportunity for people in distant lands to know what is happening in other parts of the world.

Although there is a rise of neoconservative elites and political parties, especially in developed countries, that are increasingly campaigning against the influx of migrants from less developed countries, the reality of an ageing workforce has forced some developed countries to compromise and welcome new migrants.

There are no easy answers as to what constitutes a diaspora. The difficulty in arriving at a conceptual clarification is informed by the multidimensionality of the concepts, including multiple identities, formations and disappearance or re-emergence of diaspora groups, variations in terms of locations, forms, causes and in particular, its fluidity as in cases of circular migration, where those who were once considered as diaspora returned to settle permanently in their countries of origin. In this context, Falola (2013:12) argues that, 'Diasporic identity can be part of the "condition" of living and surviving in other people's lands'. This identity is not uniform as the conditions and status of the migrants differs. For instance, while some African diasporas in a given country can be said to be settled, that is, profitably engaged in one profession or the other, some could be new arrivals who may be struggling to get their feet in terms of having legal residence or finding jobs. It is within the context of this complexity in the discourses on diaspora that Zeleza observes that,

> In many cases, the term 'diaspora' is used in a fuzzy, ahistorical and uncritical way in which all manner of movements and migrations between, and even within, countries are embraced in its generous conceptual bosom, and no adequate attention is paid to the historical conditions and experiences that produce diasporic communities and consciousness . . . not all dispersals result in the formation of diasporas.
>
> *(Zeleza, 2005:39)*

Butler (2000, cited in Zeleza, 2005:40) provides a five dimensional schema through which diaspora can be effectively studied. These include:

- reasons for, and conditions of, the dispersal;
- relationship with homeland;
- relationship with host lands;
- interrelationships within diaspora groups;
- comparative study of different diasporas.

In the same vein, Cohen (1997, in Zeleza, 2005) distinguish various types of diaspora to include 'victim diasporas' (Africans and Armenians), labour diaspora' (Indians), 'imperial diasporas' (British), 'trade diasporas' (Chinese and Lebanese), or 'cultural diaspora' (the Caribbean). Although these schemas and categorizations could provide some understanding, they are not without limitations. For instance, two categorizations by Cohen are not exhaustive. Apart from Africans and Armenians, there are other diaspora groups, such as the Jewish diaspora, which can be correctly labelled as 'victim diaspora'. Also, the movement of highly skilled professionals from the developing to developed countries could well constitute another labour diaspora group other than the Indians (Falola, 2013).

Campbell (2006:305) identifies six characteristics of any dispersed groups of people that can be rightly described as a diaspora. These include:

- displacement from a homeland to two or more peripheral or foreign regions;
- the formation of a 'relatively stable community in exile';
- social rejection by, and alienation from, the locally dominant society;

- an awareness, real or imagined, of a common homeland and heritage, and of the injustice of removal from it;
- efforts to maintain links with, and improve life in, that homeland and a desire to ultimately return permanently to the homeland;
- the formation of a diasporic 'consciousness' for which there are three prerequisites: geographic concentration; common living and working conditions markedly different from the politically dominant group, and a leadership which articulates the diaspora's interests-defined in opposition to those of the dominant group.

Again, while this categorisation may apply to some diasporic situations, it is too general to be analytically useful. For instance, it is not in every instance that a diaspora group will be in opposition to the politically dominant group in a country, especially where the latter is liberal enough to recognise the distinct identity and the contributions of the former to the development of the country.

Given the multiple identities that any given diaspora groups may share, it is difficult to agree with Campbell that diaspora groups share similar working conditions. As noted above, the experiential conditions of diaspora groups are different and reflect largely on the conditions under which they arrive in their host countries.

Diaspora, according to Zeleza,

> Simultaneously refers to a process, a condition, a space and a discourse: the continuous processes by which a diaspora is made, unmade and remade, the changing processes by which it lives and expresses itself, the places where it is moulded and imagined, and the contentious ways in which it is studied and discussed. It entails a culture and a consciousness sometimes diffuse and sometimes concentrated, of a 'here' separate from a 'there', a 'here' that is often characterised by a regime of marginalisation and a 'there' that is invoked as a rhetoric of self-affirmation, of belonging to 'here' differently.
>
> *(Zeleza, 2008a:41)*

He elaborates that,

> Diaspora is simultaneously a state of being and a process of becoming, a kind of voyage that encompasses the possibility of never arriving or returning, a navigation of multiple belongings. It is a mode of naming, remembering, living and feeling group identity moulded out of experiences, positioning, struggles and imaginings of the past and the present, and at times, the unpredictable future, which are shared across the boundaries of time and space that frame 'indigenous' identities in the contested and constructed locations of 'there' and 'here' and the passages and points in between . . . Diaspora are complex social and cultural communities created out of real and imagined genealogies and geographies (cultural, racial, ethnic, national, continental, transnational) of belonging, displacement, and recreation, constructed and conceived at multiple temporal and spatial scales, at different moments and distances from the putative homeland.
>
> *(Zeleza, 2008a:41)*

This comprehensive conceptualisation helps us in our own understanding of diaspora as a distinct social formation within another group, possessing certain characteristics that define them in terms of origin, culture, language, lifestyle, music, religion, worldview and aspirations. The need to preserve these distinct characteristics informs the continuation of many of the practices that they bring from their homelands. For instance, in an edited volume on, *Religion Crossing Boundaries: Transnational Religious and Social Dynamics in Africa and the New African Diaspora,* Adogame & Spickard (2010) show how the New African diaspora in North America instrumentalises religion both as a means of migration and as a practice in the new abode of settlement. Many diaspora groups have been able to maintain their distinct attributes and identities over the cause of many generations as they pass down the cultural practices to their successors.

African diaspora in Asia: a historical narrative

Before we delve into the historical forces that informed the movement of Africans to Asia, it is important to echo the voice of previous scholars who have noted the neglect of the study of Africa diaspora in Asia. Scholars like (Falola, 2013; Zeleza, 2005, 2008a; Jayasuriya, 2006; Campbell, 2006) noted the indifference of scholars to the study of Africans in Asia. This neglect was partly a function of the dominance of the study of Africans in the Americas, especially the United States of America and to a certain extent, Africa diaspora in Europe. This dominance, as Zeleza would argue was attributable to the expressive culture of the United States in which the massive resources of the country predispose it to champion and pursue knowledge production in its area of interest. Said Zeleza (2008:5), 'the field of African diaspora studies is largely framed by the Atlantic model in which the patterns of dispersal are reduced to the slave trade and the process of diasporiszation to racialization'. As if to give vent to this expression, Campbell (2006) dismisses the notion of Africa diaspora in Asia because they did not meet one of his criteria for forming a diaspora, that is, the ultimate desire to return permanently to the homeland. Given the absence of this condition in the framing of Africa diaspora in Asia, he contends that, 'the pre-conditions for an African–Asia diasporic consciousness did not exist in most of Asia, which in turn undermines the argument for the existence of an African–Asia diaspora'. He also argue that Africans who were sold into slavery in Asia, 'possess no common centre of origin as they came from many different regions of Africa and the islands, and represented widely varying ethnicities and cultures'. This argument is specious for various reasons, not the least the use of language and the description of Africans in the discourses of Africa diaspora. Zeleza captures this so vividly when he notes the racialisation and the general use of Africans as a homogenous group, especially by scholars of Atlantic studies (Zeleza, 2005).

Campbell's argument also falls flat in the face of the historical evidences of the different routes that Africa followed to arrive in Asia. As Jayasuriya & Pankhurst (2003) show us, 'the African diaspora has very old roots in the Indian Ocean, which are not entirely the consequences of slave trade'. They note that Africans went to India as policemen, traders, bureaucrats, clerics, bodyguards, concubines, servants, soldiers and sailors from the thirteenth century onwards' (Zeleza, 2008b:46). Many of these diaspora population actually settled in India centuries before the slave trade started (Jayasuriya, 2006). The mobilisation of all Africans for independence, struggles under the banner of Pan-Africanism. Diaspora figures such as William Blyden, Du Bois and Casely Hayford also controvert the argument that Africans in Asia cannot be referred to as a diaspora group because they did not emanate from the same geographical area. It should be noted that Pan-Africanism movement cuts across all the locations where Africans are domiciled. Additionally, the shared experience of oppression, torture and exploitation which forced African slaves in Asian countries, such as Iran and India, to revolt against their masters in the third and ninth centuries, also invalidate the argument of Campbell.

The settlement of African populations in different parts of Asia such as India, Japan, Sri-Lanka, China and Arab countries was informed by various distinct but interrelated forces. Early African explorers engaged in marine activities both on the African Ocean, (which for some curious reasons is generally known as Indian ocean) and the Atlantic Ocean. Many of these seafarers settled in parts of India and Pakistan, and constitute the Sidis diaspora population in India today. As was typical of most migrants of early periods of human existence, these migrants made their new destinations theirpermanent homes and to some extent, they were integrated to their various communities, albeit in a lower status than the indigenes.

Notwithstanding, historical evidences suggest that by far the most important and significant factor responsible for the movement of Africans to Asia was the Trans-Saharan Slave Trade (Campbell, 2006). This trade was particularly brutal and inhumane in nature as most African men that were sold into slavery were castrated to avoid the possibility of procreation. Historical accounts show that millions of Africans were uprooted and sold into slavery to serve as soldiers and courtiers in Asian countries such as India, Iran, Iraq and Pakistan, among others, over several centuries. According to Jayasuriya (2006:277) 'the largest number of black slaves were in Iraq in the ninth century and this resulted in the Revolt of the *Zaaj*, a major episode in Iraqi history, which occurred from 883 AD'. Although the spread of Islamic religion accentuated the trans-Saharan slave trade, in which Muslim merchants served as middlemen in gold and slaves, the presence of Africans in Asia predated Islam on the continent (Jayasuriya, 2006). Ethiopians and other Africans, who were bought as slaves, were used for various purposes such as defence, courtiers in palaces as well as domestic workers in many Asian countries, especially Arab countries.

Imperialism also played a significant role in the forceful movement of Africans to Asian countries. Imperial powers such as Belgium, Britain, France and Portugal, at different times, moved Africans into their Asian territories to serve either as soldiers or as workers. From various historical accounts, this dislocation covers virtually all parts of Africa, but especially Eastern and Southern Africa. Economic benefit and empire building underpinned imperialism. The slave trade contributed significantly to the economic benefits that the imperialists derived from the ignoble trade. In her seminal book on African identity in Asia, Jayasuriya observes, rather poignantly, that:

> The economic importance of slavery was tied to the paths on which slaves were taken. Slaves added value to the commercial operations of colonisers. Since they were cost-less or lowly paid workers, they enhanced the profit margins by enormous amounts. Slaves built fortresses for the Europeans in Asia and worked the fields as well . . . The slave route show the pattern of movement; it shows the vital role that Africans played in the maritime activities in the East. It also reveals where economic power-indigenous as well as imperial-lay.
>
> (Jayasuriya, 2008:43)

Until the British Parliament passed the law that made slavery a criminal action in 1833, the imperialist forcefully removed millions of Africans from the continent and sold them as commodities to different parts of the world (Rodney, 1972). The population of African slaves constituted a huge proportion of the population, especially in the coastal areas. According to Campbell (2006:309), 'slaves in Asia often comprised 20 to 30 percent of the population (rising to 50 percent and over in the Indonesian ports)'.

Jayasuriya (2006) provides a detailed account of the names that Africans in Asia diaspora are generally called. Although some of the names are general, it is not uncommon to find names that identify Africans on the basis of which part of the continent they came from. Depending on the conditions under which they were taken to the various locations, and the roles that they perform, such names include, Baburu, Takruni, Abid, Mawalid, Kaffir, Sidi and so on. The degradation of Africans continues to have effects on their placement in the various Asian societies today.

We elaborate on this aspect of African social status in the penultimate section (see page 29). The next section examines Asians in Africa.

Asian diaspora in Africa

Although the population may be small, the Asia diaspora in Africa constitutes a vital force for economic activity. Like the study of Africans in Asia, not much has been done to study this important segment of the African population. Rather than studying them in relation to their existence in Africa, recent scholarship has been focused on how the presence of Asian countries on the continent (especially China), threaten or undermine the interests of the West (Brautigam, 2009). The presence of Asian diaspora in Africa also has both historical and contemporary imports. Like their African counterparts, the movement of Asians to Africa is both voluntary and involuntary. The involuntary movement can be located within the context of imperial ambition and expansions of world powers such as the, Portuguese, Dutch and the British, in the 17th and 18th centuries. The Dutch in particular was responsible for the movement of Asians to Africa in the seventeenth century (Jayasuriya, 2008). She notes that, 'The Portuguese ushered the Dutch, French, and British into the Asian trade networks-and this led to further movements of Africans across the Indian Ocean'. In the late nineteenth century, the British Empire has consolidated its dominion both in the Indian Ocean and parts of Africa.

In its desire to leverage on its political control for economic advantage, the British Empire exported millions of indenture workers to Africa. These indenture workers, made up mostly of Indians, were found in the Southern and Eastern African countries such as South Africa, Mauritius, Madagascar, Kenya and India (Aiyar, 2015). It is interesting that in most of the countries where Asians were located in Africa, a settler form of colonialism was established, with various implications for the organisation of the society. The case of South Africa was particularly illustrative of how the colonisers adopted a racist approach to delineate the society on the basis of skin colour, in which the Europeans occupied the highest echelon, followed by the Indians, Coloured and the Africans. In his book, *Citizen and Subject: Contemporary Africa and the Legacy of Late Colonialism*, Mamdani (1996) provides a detailed narrative of how the colonial governments in Africa destroyed the indigenous systems of government, altered the pattern of social relations and redirected economic activities to advance the interests of the home governments. Although most of the indenture workers in Africa opted to remain even after colonialism, many of them still maintain circular migration flows in which they travel to and return from India, on a regular basis. In keeping with one of the formulations of Campbell (2006) on what constitutes a diaspora population, Asians in Africa have continued to maintain closer links with their counterparts in the home countries.

The voluntary movement of Asians to Africa predates the imperial intrusion into the Indian Ocean. Indians have been trading with people in the East African coast long before the era of the slave trade and well before the imperial forces moved them to work in the plantations in Southern Africa. The voluntary movement continues today as many Asians from China to India, as well as the Arabs are in different parts of Africa for economic reasons. In many parts of Africa such as Sierra Leone, Kenya, Uganda, Mauritius, Zimbabwe and Nigeria, sizeable numbers of Lebanese, Indians, Chinese and Arabs are found who are engaged in economic activities such as retailing, manufacturing and mining.

Despite many years of their existence in Africa, the Asian diaspora maintain their cultural and linguistic distinctiveness. In the case of China, an extra touch of new imperial importance has been seen in the way in which Chinese Towns, akin to the Government Reservation Towns of the colonial era, are constructed in the major commercial cities in Africa. Although the population of the Asian diaspora in Africa are very small compared to the indigenous Africans, their economic power makes them a strong force to be reckoned with in the political economy of most of the countries, they are located in.

African and Asian diaspora: contextualising locations and influence

The positions that the diaspora populations occupy in the social hierarchies of their countries of abode reflect both historical and emergent conditions. Whereas the African diaspora in Asia constitute a very minute proportion of the population and continue to occupy the lower rung of the ladder, the same cannot be said of the Asian population in Africa. One of the reasons for this continuity in marginality is the nature of the conditions under which the African diaspora settled in Asia. As noted earlier, most Africans found themselves in Asia as slaves, in a context in which the social structure of interactions, as well as the cultural practices, supported social segregation. In other words, no conscious effort was made by the host countries to ensure that Africans were integrated into the society on equal terms with the hosts. The only exception to this was the case of Arab slaves, who on account of religious provisions are accepted as equal citizens when they convert to Islam. Notwithstanding this otherwise generous provision in the Islamic religion, segregation on account of skin colour is a normal everyday experience of the African diaspora in the Arab world.

The possibility that education provides for social mobility has not been totally explored as many Africans are excluded from such opportunities. The disconnection that exists between continental Africa and the Africans in the diaspora could constitute another reason for the lack of influence in the Asian countries. Perhaps as a result of the challenging conditions that continental Africa has had to contend with since gaining independence, many Africans in Asia appear not to have a desire to connect or return to the continent (Campbell, 2006). This is in contrast with Africans in North America, the Caribbean and Latin America who have, to a significant extent, maintained a relationship with the Africans in the homeland. Although there have been a few Africans who have assumed some level of importance in the Asian countries, these are few and far between.

On the contrary, the Asian population in Africa have been integrated to a great extent in the various countries of their sojourn. As mentioned, the differences have to do with the historical conditions that led to their settlement in the African countries. Although Aiyar (2015) argues that in the case of Indians in Kenya, they are treated as minorities, the economic power that many of the Indians possess predisposes them to positions of relevance in the country. Ownership of vast areas of land, as well as businesses which have continued since colonial times, continues to confer material advantages on the Indians in Kenya and elsewhere in Africa. In the case of Mauritius, where Indians constitute about 68 per cent of the population, they control both economic and political power. South Africa presents another scenario in which the Indian population of over one million have equal citizenship rights with all others as guaranteed by the constitution. Access to citizenship rights ensures that they also hold prominent political positions in the country.

One interesting aspect of the diaspora experiences of both Africans and Asians in their respective locations is the proclivity to maintain their cultural distinctiveness, though to varying degrees. For instance, despite many centuries of their relocation from Africa to Asia, the African diasporas in the various Asian countries like Sri Lanka, Japan, India, Pakistan and so on continue to exhibit their cultural practices in the form of music, dance, forms of worship and to a certain extent, even dress. The Asian population in Africa, especially the Indians, have also maintained their cultural practices through intra-marriage, food, religion and dress. This continuity poses the question, how have such cultural practices been sustained over many centuries? In the absence of what one could regard as formal education, it would appear that oral history has played an important part in passing down the culture and lifestyles of the various groups to their successive generations.

Conclusion: towards a Sino-centric world

While this chapter has emphasised the long-standing historical links and interactions between Africa and Asia that are often ignored in existing Diaspora Studies, it seems the future world is a Sino-centric one, in which increased interactions between Africa and Asia are assuming a new and high level of importance. The re-emergence of China as a centre of power as well as formations such as BRICS (Brazil, India, China and South Africa) are poised to galvanise greater interactions and exchanges. Already the Chinese are becoming an important part of the population across the continent of Africa. One can perhaps also reflect on what an emerging de-westernisation, which has the potential to contribute immensely to the re-crystallisation of Africa–Asia relations and the consolidation of Afro-Asian diasporas, holds for the future of Afro-Asian relations. The need to reshape, reform and redirect the global order to serve a more inclusive global society makes closer relations between Asia and Africa particularly compelling. The two regions are host to the largest populations of human beings on earth as well as large deposits of natural resources. Although the pursuit of national interest may undermine the collective efforts of the regions to significantly alter the current global order (see Taylor, 2014), there are indications that a closer cooperation between them can force the much needed reform of the global governance architecture. The declining economic growth in the West, as well as its ageing population, portends a bright prospect for Asian and African countries to take the lead in the coming decades. This is especially true in light of the relatively youthful and highly educated population of African and some Asian countries. Turning the new dynamism in cooperation between Asia and Africa into significant benefits both at regional and global levels will require the adoption of new and pragmatic social-economic and political frameworks for the organisation of the global society.

The radically different approach in the way in which Asian countries, such as China and India, relate to Africa in terms of trade and investment, through the policy of 'no interference' (in the case of China), appears to allow some sense of dignity and autonomy for the latter. Rather than setting or perhaps violently forcing the terms of engagement as the West has a penchant for doing in its relationship with Africa, the Asian countries appear to engage on the basis of mutual respect and equality. As Brautigam (2009) notes in respect of China in Africa, consultation with African leaders on their areas of priority, such as investment in hard infrastructure like railways, roads and dams among others, appears to be working in the interest of these countries. This is different from the approach of the West in which the preferences of Africans are not given due consideration when granting development aid.

Over the past one and a half decades, the relationship between Asia and Africa has grown deeper as higher trade and investment volumes have been recorded (Oloruntoba & Akinboye, 2013). The high volume of economic exchanges have been complemented by a high level of diplomatic relations. Asian countries such as India, Japan and China have also established various technical aid schemes to assist African countries with scholarships for students, technical training exchange programmes and training centres in technology. These multi-dimensional exchanges have potential to further increase the diaspora populations of both Africans in Asia and vice versa. However, the challenge of integrating the diaspora populations in both regions remains crucial. The task of fostering an inclusive society is one to which all modern states should aspire. With the exception of Uganda, where the military government of Idi Amin forcefully ejected thousands of Indians, it would appear that other Asian nationalities in Africa have been integrated into the various societies.

The social system in Africa has also created the right conditions for their mobility both economically and in a few instances, politically. As part of the new engagement of African political and business elites with their Asian counterparts, it will be necessary to make the plight of the African diaspora in Asia an agenda for consideration. In this connection, African leaders should demand reciprocity in the ways in which Africans are treated in Asia by making a demand for an elaborate programme that will culminate in social, economic and political integration of the people to the society. Rather than continuing with the old pattern of social segregation, the people should be given all the necessary support to develop their potentials. The African Union Programme on diaspora should include this important issue in order to foster the integration of the African diaspora in Asia. Educational institutions in Africa should also seek to offer scholarships to indigent students of African descent in Asia to study in African universities. Cultural exchanges should be organised which seek to rediscover the ties that bind homeland Africa with the diaspora in Asia.

While the contemporary African diaspora in North America maintains close relations with their home base through regular visits and remittances, there is an increasing engagement of the old African diaspora in North America and to a large extent Latin America, in which many of them are trying to trace their places of origin. Such interests could be a reflection of many factors, not least the availability of ample studies on the history, experiences and activities of the diaspora population in those regions. Thus, in order to promote a better understanding of the situation of the African diaspora in Asia, greater research interests should be stimulated through more funding, conferences and symposia. Establishment of research Chairs and centres of African diaspora studies in various universities and research institutes, in both in Africa and Asia, will contribute to the further understanding of the conditions and experiences of the diaspora populations in both regions. As Zeleza (2008b) notes, the research funding provided by the Ford Foundation enabled him to conduct research on the African diaspora in about 15 countries, which resulted in the book *Africa and its Diasporas: Dispersals and Linkages*, (2008). Historical and contemporary African diaspora continue to be shaped by new dynamics such as racism and revival of neoconservative and nationalist parties in Europe and elsewhere. In the same way, the new wave of Asians in Africa has a tendency to redefine what we already know about Afro-Asian relations. These dynamics require new scientific enquiries at various levels.

References

Adogame, A. and Spickard, J. (eds.), 2010. *Religion Crossing Boundaries: Transnational Religious and Social Dynamics in Africa and the New African Diaspora*, Leiden and Boston: Brill.

Aiyar, S., 2015. *Indians in Kenya: The Politics of Diaspora*, Cambridge, MA: Harvard University Press.

Brautigam, D., 2009. *The Dragon's Gift: The Real Story of China in Africa*, Oxford: Oxford University Press.

Campbell, G., 2006. 'The African–Asian Diaspora: Myth or Reality?', *African and Asian Studies*, Volume 5 (3–4), pp. 305–324.

Falola, T., 2013. *The African Diaspora: Slavery, Modernity, and Globalization*, Rochester, NY: University of Rochester Press.

Harris, J., 1971. *The African Presence in Asia: Consequences of the East African Slave Trade*, Evanston, IL: Northwestern University Press.

Jayasuriya, S., 2006. 'Identifying Africans in Asia: What's in a Name?', *African and Asian Studies*, Volume 5 (3–4), pp. 275–304.

Jayasuriya, S., 2008. *African Identity in Asia: Cultural Effects of Forced Migration*, Princeton, NJ: Markus Wiener Publishers.

Jayasuriya, S. and Pankhurst, R. (eds.), 2003. *The African Diaspora in the Indian Ocean*, Trenton, NJ: Africa World Press.

Mamdani, M., 1996. *Citizen and Subject: Contemporary Africa and the Legacy of Late Colonialism*, Princeton, NJ: Princeton University Press.

Oloruntoba, S. O. and Akinboye, S. O., 2013. 'Global Trade Governance and Economic Development in Africa: Exploring Opportunities in South–South Cooperation', *Nigerian Journal of International Affairs (NJIA)*, Volume 39 (2), May–August, pp. 93–113.

Rodney, W., 1972. *How Europe Underdeveloped Africa*, 2nd ed., London and Dar-Es-Salaam: L'Ouverture Publications.

Taylor, I., 2014. *Africa Rising? BRICS–Diversifying Dependency*, London: James Currey.

Zeleza, P., 2005. 'Rewriting the African Diaspora: Beyond the Black Atlantic', *African Affairs*, Volume 104 (414), pp. 35–68.

Zeleza, P., 2008a. 'The Challenges of Studying the African Diasporas', *African Sociological Review*, Volume 12 (2), pp. 4–21.

Zeleza, P., 2008b. *Africa and Its Diasporas: Dispersals and Linkages*, Dakar: CODESRIA.

2
IBERIAN TRADE AND SLAVE CONNECTIONS

Daniel B. Domingues da Silva

Iberian traders, mainly from Portugal, played a key role in the relationship between Africa and Asia in the early modern era. They not only spread Christianity and Western culture to these regions, but they also connected them to the emerging Atlantic economy, established new trading patterns in the Indian Ocean, and further expanded the slave trade between Africa and Asia. Africa and Asia have long been in contact with one another. Since the first century, Greek, Roman, and Egyptian traders sailed across the Indian Ocean through the Red Sea in search of exotic commodities produced in India and the Far East (Anonymous, 1912). After the rise of Islam, in the beginning of the seventh century, Arabs and Persians, especially from Yemen and Shiraz, spread their influence in the region. They developed new navigation skills and established commercial centers on both sides of the ocean, where they organized their expeditions and intermingled with the local population. Perhaps, the Swahili city-states of East Africa are the most important example of such centers. Arab and Persian traders married into local Bantu families and transmitted their religion and maritime skills to their descendants, who developed a new language – Swahili – and built fleets of *dhows* and *sumbuks* that crossed the Indian Ocean following the Monsoon, a seasonal variation in the ocean's wind regime that allowed traders to sail between Africa and Asia (Middleton, 1992:10–23).

The Indian Ocean trade was among the wealthiest in the world. Arabian horses came through the Persian Gulf. Gold, ivory, skins, and other 'goods' flowed from East Africa. Colorful Indian cottons came mainly from Gujarat, the Coromandel Coast, and Bengal. Silks, silver, and porcelain emanated from China and Japan. Finally, spices of several kinds – cloves, nutmeg, pepper, etc. – came mainly from the Indonesian archipelago. Traders shipped these goods through a series of strategic ports: the Swahili city-states along the East African coast, especially Zanzibar and Kilwa, which had direct access to Sofala, the port through which most of the East African gold entered the Indian Ocean; Socotra in the strait of Bab-el-Mandeb at the southern end of the Red Sea; Hormuz at the entrance to the Persian Gulf; Surat, Daman, and Diu in Gujarat; Canton and Nagasaki in the Far East; and Malacca in the Indonesian archipelago (Russell-Wood, 1992:123–47). Muslims from different cultural backgrounds controlled many of these ports. Muslims claiming Bantu, Persian, and Yemeni ancestry ruled the Swahili city-states. Muslims from Mamluk Egypt and the Ottoman Empire controlled the Red Sea. Most if not all of the trade in the Persian Gulf was in the hands of Persian Muslims. Even in India and the Indonesian islands Muslims played an important role in the Indian Ocean trade. Nevertheless,

33

other religious and ethnic groups were also active, including Hindus and Buddhists from India, China, Sri Lanka, and Japan (Boxer, 1969:41–46; Russell-Wood, 1992:41).

Enslaved Africans also featured among the 'goods' carried across the Indian Ocean. They were by no means the only people enslaved in the region. Asians probably made up the largest share of the slaves or people living under similar conditions in Asia (Campbell, 2004; Pinto, 1992; Watson, 1980). However, Africans did comprise the majority of the slaves carried across the ocean. Ethnonyms associated with Africans forced into the traffic suggest that the earliest populations transported consisted of Nubians and Ethiopians. Persians, Hindus, and other Asians called them 'Nuba,' from the Greek for Nubia, 'Sudan,' from the Arabic *as-sudan* for blacks, or 'Habasha,' a corruption of *Habesha* or *Abesha*, how the Ethiopians referred to themselves (Jayasuriya, 2006:276–77). However, Africans from regions further south in the continent were gradually pulled into the traffic. They were initially called 'Zanj,' possibly from the Amhara for barbarize, prattle, or stammer, or from the Persian for black. Most of them came probably from the coast of present-day Kenya and Tanzania (Jayasuriya, 2006:277). In the ninth century, their reputation spread in the Indian Ocean world, as many of them, including slaves, joined a group of rebels in a huge uprising against the authorities of Basra, an important salt mining center in Samanid Persia (Popović, 1999). The rebels ultimately failed and enslaved Zanj continued to be transported from East Africa, along with others, who Asians called 'Kaffir,' from the Arabic *qafir* for unbeliever, and 'Sidi,' also from the Arabic *saydi* for captive or prisoner of war (Jayasuriya, 2006:281–91). The documents rarely indicate the actual linguistic or ethnic origins of these Africans.

Iberian conquerors and traders arrived in the Indian Ocean shortly after the Portuguese navigator Bartolomeu Dias rounded the Cape of Good Hope in 1488 (Boxer, 1969:33). As pioneers in maritime exploration, and in view of the diplomatic agreements Portugal and Spain signed, the former Iberian nation assumed a more prominent role in Asia. Portugal was the first to find a sea route to Asia by sailing eastwards. The Spanish favored a westward approach, which culminated with Christopher Columbus's 1492 landfall in the Americas. In 1494, Portugal and Spain signed the Treaty of Tordesillas, which divided the globe between themselves. Portugal would be free to act in Asia, while Spain would have most of the Americas. Eventually, they trespassed on each other's domains. Portugal captured a huge portion of South America, while Spain extended its power to the Far East through the Manila fleet, which connected that Indonesian port to the Spanish colonies in Central America. Similar to Portugal, Spain justified its expansion and economic exploitation in Indonesia by spreading Christianity to the islands and bringing the local population to the 'Kingdom of God' (Andaya, 2014:236). However, this was an uneven arrangement. Although Portugal carved a large colony in what became Brazil, Spanish influence in Asia was small, indirect, and unrelated to Africa. The Manila fleet connected Asia to other Spanish colonies and not Spain (Parry, 1966:132–35). Moreover, Spanish merchants operated in Asia through Portuguese brokers, including the brief period when the Hapsburgs united the crowns of Portugal and Spain (1580–1640) (Boxer, 1969:64).

How did the European presence, particularly the Iberian presence under the Portuguese, change the power balance in the Indian Ocean? How did it affect the slave trade between Africa and Asia? What are the legacies of the Portuguese involvement? Historians of Portugal, like A.H.R. de Oliveira Marques, Joel Serrão, Charles Boxer, and A.J.R. Russell-Wood, refer to this era as the Portuguese Eastern or Oriental Empire (Boxer, 1969; Russell-Wood, 1992; Serrão & Oliveira Marques, 1986). They stress the Portuguese conquests and achievements in the Indian Ocean, but only briefly remark their participation in the slave trade. Similarly, historians of the African diaspora in Asia, such as Joseph Harries, R.W. Beachey, Gwyn Campbell, W.G. Clarence-Smith, and others, have only scratched the surface of the problem

(Beachey, 1976; Campbell, 2006; Clarence-Smith, 1989; Harris, 1971; Talib & El Samir, 1988). As Richard Allen, José Capela, Rudy Bauss, and others have shown, Portuguese merchants and slave traders played a significant role in the traffic, as investors, slave suppliers, and shippers (Allen, 2015; Bauss, 1997a; Capela, 2002; Pinto, 1992). The size of their operations was not the same as in the Atlantic, but neither was the Indian Ocean slave trade similar in size to its Atlantic counterpart. In fact, the lower number of slaves forced into the Indian Ocean, and the seemingly higher degree of integration into their host societies, led some to believe that Africans in Asia never wanted to know their origins, or that affirmative action policies for descendants of enslaved Africans would cause more harm than good (Campbell, 2006:317–18; Harris, 1971). However, without a clear understanding of the size, evolution, and distribution of the Indian Ocean slave trade and of the participation of the different parties involved, including the Portuguese, no one will ever be able to determine its impact on Africa or Asia.

This chapter shows that, once in the Indian Ocean, the Portuguese quickly tapped into the existing commercial networks, emerging as the dominant power in the region. Portuguese dominance lasted for about a century, but it contributed significantly to the spread of Africans in Asia and to reinforcing prevalent racial, ethnic, and religious prejudices and stereotypes in the Indian Ocean. This chapter is divided into two sections. The first examines the establishment of the Iberian, mainly Portuguese, presence in the Indian Ocean from the late fifteenth to the early nineteenth century. The second analyzes the Portuguese participation in the slave trade between Africa and Asia by comparing its size, evolution, and distribution with that of other carriers, especially other European carriers. Thus, this chapter provides a broad approach to the Iberian trade and slave connections in the Indian Ocean. Hopefully, it will encourage other researchers to expand that history and provide additional details of the relationship between the Portuguese and the local population of the various ports and cities of the Indian Ocean, the challenges of the increasing European competition in the region, and the fate of the Africans transported and of their descendants in India, China, Japan, the Middle East, and other areas of Portuguese presence in Africa and Asia.

The Iberian presence in the Indian Ocean

Iberian conquerors and traders established their presence in the Indian Ocean through violence, intimidation, and political maneuvering. In 1497, Vasco da Gama departed from Lisbon to India at the head of a three-ship fleet. He carried a cargo of European goods, such as woolen textiles, glass beads, and metal utensils, in addition to samples of the commodities that the Portuguese were looking for, that is, gold, silver, pearls, spices, and precious stones. After rounding the Cape of Good Hope, Gama went from port to port asking whether any of these goods were available there, or whether the local population knew where he could find them. When he reached Calicut in 1498, an important port in the spice trade between Indonesia and the Persian Gulf located on the Malabar Coast, he realized he had stumbled on to a node of a wide commercial network connecting Asia to Africa and beyond (Velho, 1998:67–100). He also realized that the goods he had brought to trade were inadequate, but that the local population belonged to a mosaic of peoples often in conflict with one another (Boxer, 1969:34). He further noticed that the maritime and military technology of the Portuguese *naus* and *caravelas* were superior to the *dhows*, *sumbuks*, and other ships crossing the Indian Ocean (Boxer, 1969:44). If the Portuguese entertained any ideas of capturing the ocean's trade, the strategy was clear: offer protection to those willing to submit to their rule and destroy any maritime and religious competition (Boxer, 1969:37; Russell-Wood, 1992:20–23).

In the following years, the Portuguese quickly set this strategy into motion. In 1502, King Manuel sent a powerful fleet to seize control of the spice trade on the Malabar Coast (Axelson, 1973:31). In the following year, he dispatched another fleet of seven ships in two divisions, one, under Afonso de Albuquerque and the other, under his cousin Francisco de Albuquerque. They secured Portuguese control over the spice trade on the Malabar Coast and settled a base at Cochin, establishing the basis for the *Estado da Índia* or Indian State, as the Portuguese referred to their possessions in Asia (Axelson, 1973:34). In the subsequent years, the Portuguese turned their attention to the western side of the ocean. In 1505, they captured Sofala, in Southeast Africa, in the expectation of controlling the gold exports from that port (Axelson, 1973:38, 41; Boxer, 1969:47). In 1507, they built a fort in Mozambique Island and, in the following year, another in Hormuz, in the Persian Gulf, after its ruler submitted himself to Portuguese suzerainty by paying, as a tribute, 15,000 xerafins annually (Axelson, 1973:61; Boxer, 1969:47). In 1509, Tristão da Cunha captured Socotra Island at the entrance of the Red Sea and Duarte de Lemos established a factory in Malindi, in East Africa (Axelson, 1973:70–71). The Portuguese also sought to control the sea by destroying shipping competition. In 1509, for example, Francisco de Almeida captured a makeshift Egyptian–Gujarati fleet off Diu, in the Kathiawar peninsula (Boxer, 1969:46).

In the second decade of the sixteenth century, the Portuguese consolidated their conquests in the Indian Ocean and sought to expand their power in the Far East. In 1510, Afonso de Albuquerque captured Goa, north of Cochin, with the support of the local Hindu population, and from 1530 this served as the seat of the *Estado da Índia* (Boxer, 1969:46; Jayasuriya, 2008:175). In 1511, he seized Malacca, the source of most spices entering the Indian Ocean (Boxer, 1969:46; Jayasuriya, 2008:175). Two years later, the Indonesian population tried to resist foreign rule by dispatching a Javanese war fleet of large junks, but the Portuguese crushed the fleet off Malacca (Boxer, 1969:48). Albuquerque then further strengthened the Portuguese position in the ocean by taking Aden, in the Red Sea, in 1513 and reconquering Hormuz in 1515 (Boxer, 1969:46–47). However, control over the Red Sea proved elusive. In 1518, the Ottomans spread their power in that region and took Aden from the Portuguese (Boxer, 1969:47). The latter then tried to take the South China Sea by force in 1521-22, but the Chinese coastguard fleet managed to block them (Boxer, 1969:49). In the 1530s, the Portuguese incorporated Diu and Daman, both in Gujarat, India, to the *Estado* (Jayasuriya, 2008:174, 181). Although they failed to capture the South China Sea by force, Portuguese merchants penetrated the region and managed to establish an *entrepôt*, a city, town, or village to which goods are brought for import and export, in Macau in 1557. The *entrepôt* came to Beijing's attention only some twenty years later and, in view of its long presence, the Chinese government decided to tolerate its activities (Boxer, 1969:51). Portuguese traders at Macau profited significantly from this strategic position, intermediating the trade in silks, silver, spices, cottons, and other valuable goods with China, Japan, India, Indonesia, Portugal, and the Spanish colonies in the Americas via the Manila fleet. As a Dutch visitor noted in 1610, Portuguese traders at Macau 'take no heed of what they spend and nothing is too costly for them' (Boxer, 1969:64).

The *Estado da Índia* reached its peak in the 1560s. It extended from East Africa to the Far East. It was mainly a maritime empire. The Portuguese controlled only small stretches of land. The king appointed a viceroy to govern this huge region from Goa, in India. From 1570, the Portuguese connected Goa to Lisbon through the *Carreira da Índia* or the Indian fleet (Jayasuriya, 2008:173). The king auctioned the right to organize and command the fleet to the highest bidder. Given the size of the enterprise and the goods that these ships carried, only wealthy merchants participated in the auction. Every year, dozens of armed ships departed together from Lisbon on a voyage that could take two to three years to complete (Lapa, 2000:140–41; Russell-Wood, 1992:35–40;

Teles da Cunha, 2006:166–69). On the outbound voyage, they often stopped at Cape Verde, off the West African coast, and called at Bahia, in Brazil, before rounding the Cape of Good Hope. Once in the Indian Ocean, they called at Mozambique Island or sailed straight to Goa. The inbound voyage followed a similar route, except that, instead of calling at Bahia, or before doing so, the ships often called at Luanda, Angola (Boxer, 1969:219–22; Lapa, 2000:140–41; Teles da Cunha, 2006:176–77).

Ships leaving Lisbon carried a variety of goods produced in Europe and the Americas, mainly wine, sugar, and tobacco. Portuguese traders transported these goods to Lisbon in vessels sailing in other routes. These goods were then loaded on the *Carreira*'s ships and transported to Goa, from where they were subsequently transshipped on smaller vessels to other destinations in the Indian Ocean (Russell-Wood, 1992:126–28). Similarly, traders operating from different ports in the Indian Ocean brought their goods to Goa, where they were loaded on the *Carreira*'s ships and transported to Lisbon (Boxer, 1969:44, 58, 120; Pinto, 1994:9–12; Teles da Cunha, 2006:202–20). The merchandise shipped from Goa to Lisbon included a variety of goods, mainly colorful cottons, silks, spices, and Chinese porcelain (Boxer, 1969:59–62; Russell-Wood, 1992:126–28). In addition to collecting tributes from local rulers, Portuguese officials stationed at the *Estado*'s various ports taxed the goods imported to, and exported from, each port. This not only provided the Portuguese with an important source of revenue, but it also allowed them to control the trade more efficiently. Nevertheless, smuggling and corruption among state officials never ceased to be a problem in the *Estado*.

Portuguese dominance in Asia began to change between the late sixteenth and early seventeenth centuries. In 1580, during a succession crisis in Portugal, King Philip II of Spain managed to seize the Portuguese throne and create the Iberian Union. Portuguese traders in Asia worried that they would lose their privileges and position to Spanish merchants, but Philip II decided not to interfere (Boxer, 1969:107–08). Very different was the growing resistance to Portuguese rule in the Indian Ocean. As early as 1512, the Swahili expelled the Portuguese from Kilwa (Axelson, 1973:59). In 1518, the Ottomans captured Aden (Boxer, 1969:47). Not long after that, in 1551-52, an Ottoman admiral, Piri Reis, sacked Muscat and besieged Hormuz with 23 galleys from the Red Sea (Boxer, 1969:57). As previously mentioned, Portugal was never able to assert its power in the South China Sea. Finally, between 1585 and 1586, Mir Ali Bey swept the Portuguese from the whole of the Swahili Coast, apart from Malindi, with a single ship, making 20 Portuguese prizes (Boxer, 1969:57).

Growing competition in the Indian Ocean waters also challenged Portuguese rule. Besides the increasing presence of the Ottomans, especially out of the Red Sea, Maratha, Omani, and Angria seamen extended their activities across the northern section of the ocean, threatening Portuguese trade as far as the Malabar Coast (Boxer, 1969:136–37; Teles da Cunha, 2006:165). More preoccupying, however, was the growing presence of European competitors, especially the Dutch. In 1602, a group of merchants from the United Provinces organized a company, the East India Company (VOC, in the Dutch acronym), which launched one of the largest and finest commercial fleets the world has ever seen, to break into the Asian trade. The Dutch quickly made their way into the Indian Ocean and captured the spice trade from Indonesia (Boxer, 1965:23–24; Teles da Cunha, 2006:165–66). The British and later the French also organized similar companies, further increasing the competition against the Portuguese in the Indian Ocean (Boxer, 1969:146–47; Teles da Cunha, 2006:166). The British were particularly active in the textile and, later, in the opium trade from India and China, establishing important *entrepôts* in Mumbai and Hong Kong. The French settled in the Indian Ocean islands, including Mauritius, Seychelles, and Réunion, where they developed sugar plantations rivaling those in the Americas.

As competition grew, Portuguese dominance in Asia declined and the *Estado*'s power dwindled. The *Estado* depended significantly on the revenue generated from taxes levied on goods imported to and exported from ports in the Indian Ocean. As Portuguese competitors captured many of these ports and opened new commercial routes, the *Estado*'s power shrunk. Increased Portuguese interest in the Americas was another important factor leading to the decline of the *Estado da Índia*. Since the 1530s, Portuguese colonizers in Brazil experimented with sugarcane plantations. Such plantations involved high risks and large investments. The Portuguese started the enterprise by using indigenous slave labor, but towards the end of the sixteenth century, when the activity became highly profitable, they switched to African slave labor. The Portuguese familiarity with the African coast and the establishment of *entrepôts* or factories, as they were called, in the continent during the fifteenth and sixteenth centuries greatly facilitated that transition (Boxer, 1969:30–33, 136–37). By the end of the sixteenth century, one third of the slave population of Bahia and Pernambuco, the leading sugar-producing captaincies of Brazil at the time, was made up of African slaves (Schwartz, 1985:65–72). As a consequence, Portuguese attention gradually shifted from the *Estado da Índia* to Brazil or, as some historians prefer to call it, the Luso-Brazilian Empire (Paquette, 2013; Serrão & Oliveira Marques, 1986).

From the seventeenth century, the Portuguese presence in Asia was never the same. British, Dutch, and French traders increasingly dominated the Indian Ocean. The Portuguese lost ground to these newcomers and other Asian traders, but they managed to keep important strategic positions, remaining active in the Indian Ocean trade well into the nineteenth century. In the seventeenth and eighteenth centuries, Portuguese trade shifted from the Far East and Goa to Diu and Daman, in Gujarat, and to the Portuguese possessions in Southeast Africa, such as Sofala, Mozambique Island, Quelimane, and Inhambane. Although the number of the *Carreira*'s ships declined over the years, these traders operated mostly in secondary routes as shippers, investors, and commercial partners to indigenous traders, especially the Hindu Vaniyas (alternatively spelled Baniyas, Banyans, or Baneanes) from Diu and Daman (Machado, 2014:18–24; Pinto, 1994:51–61). Consequently, it is extremely difficult to estimate the size of Portuguese trade. Viewed from Lisbon, it did not seem very significant, but this may have been an illusion. Trade reports from Goa for the early nineteenth century indicate that over half of all goods imported there came from Surat, in Gujarat, alone. Most of these goods were made up of cottons, paid for in silver and gold brought from China, Portugal, and Brazil (Bauss, 1997b:275).

However thriving this trade was, it did not last for too long. In 1807, in the wake of Napoleon's occupation of Lisbon, the Portuguese royal family decided to move to Brazil. Given Portugal's long commercial relationship with Britain, and the fact that the two nations had repeatedly bypassed Napoleon's continental blockade to trade, the Portuguese royal family sailed across the Atlantic escorted by a British fleet (Manchester, 1969; Paquette, 2013:85–89; Schultz, 2001:68–74). In the following year, upon arriving in Bahia, the Prince Regent, Dom João, opened the Brazilian ports for trade with friendly nations and, under a special agreement signed in 1810, taxed British imports at a lower rate than imports originating from other countries (Paquette, 2013:67–68). This gave British goods an advantage over other goods sold in the Brazilian market. It also allowed them to penetrate Asia in Portuguese ships leaving Brazil. Meanwhile, the British were pursuing a free-trade policy agenda in the Indian Ocean, which harmed Portuguese interests in Asia (Bauss, 1982:82–84). Over time, British textiles replaced Indian cloth in the Portuguese and, after independence in 1822, the Brazilian international trade; Indian manufacturers gradually shifted their economy to commercial and subsistence agriculture; and Portugal lost further ground to Britain and other powers in Asia and East Africa.

Africa–Asia slave connections

Iberian traders pioneered the transatlantic slave trade, but in the Indian Ocean they were merely newcomers to an already long-established activity. The slave trade to Asia differed from its American counterpart in many ways. First, it started much earlier, certainly before the rise of Islam, and continued well into the late nineteenth and early twentieth centuries. Second, although Africans made up the largest contingent of people transported, Asians, especially Indians, Indonesians, and some Chinese, were also forced into the traffic. Third, except perhaps towards the second half of the nineteenth century, the transportation of slaves and other coerced migrants to and from Asia was intermittent and small compared with the Atlantic. In other words, slaves did not cross the ocean every year and, when they did, traders normally carried dozens of slaves per ship (Austen, 1989; Collins, 2006; Larson, 2013; Lovejoy, 2000:24–26). The transatlantic slave trade was a far more systematic enterprise, involving the annual transportation of thousands of slaves in ships, carrying captives in the hundreds. Nevertheless, given the duration of the traffic, historians believe that the African slave trade to Asia moved about the same number of people as the traffic to the Americas, some 12 million people (Collins, 2006:326–37; Larson, 2013:56–76; Lovejoy, 2000:24–26, 47, 142).

Several reasons exist to explain why the slave trade to and from Asia could never reach the same size, in terms of annual average number of people transported, as the traffic to the Americas. After the Europeans arrived in the Indian Ocean, neither Asians nor East Africans experienced anything like the demographic catastrophe that the indigenous populations of the Americas suffered following Columbus's arrival in the Caribbean. Also, slavery and other forms of coerced labor already existed in both Africa and Asia. Although the rise of cash crop plantations accounted for many of the slaves brought to the Americas, there was no shortage of labor-intensive activities in Africa and Asia. Slaves in Africa and Asia dove for pearls, mined salt, and grew dates, cloves, spices, and other plants. They also dug canals, built walls, erected castles, palaces, fortresses, and other buildings. Different from the Americas, slaves were often trained as soldiers and deployed in combat (Harris, 1971:77–90; Talib & El Samir, 1988:721–26). All in all, there were plenty of labor-intensive and life-consuming activities that created a significant demand for slaves in Africa and Asia but, because of internal sources of slaves and other forms of coerced labor, the external slave trade to and from Asia could never really match its Atlantic counterpart.

Enslaved Africans transported to Asia were shipped through three routes. The Red Sea was the earliest route in the African slave trade to Asia. Ethiopians and Nubians are among the earliest African slaves mentioned anywhere in Asia and they came mainly from ports located in the Red Sea, such as Adulis and Massawa, or in the African Horn, like Mogadishu (Austen, 1989:32–35; Collins, 2006:335–40; Lovejoy, 2000:61–62). East Africa, including Madagascar Island, was probably the largest source of slaves to Asia. Swahili city-states, such as Kilwa, Mombasa, and Zanzibar, as well as the Merina Empire in Madagascar supplied slaves to several ports in the Indian Ocean. Most of them headed to the Persian Gulf and India but, in the late eighteenth and early nineteenth centuries, East African slaves were increasingly shipped to sugar plantations located in the Indian Ocean islands, mainly Mauritius, Réunion, and Seychelles (Allen, 2015:3–7; Austen, 1989:22–27; Collins, 2006:335–40; Lovejoy, 2000:61–62). Finally, another route included the trans-saharan trade from West to North Africa. Since the ninth century, slaves from south of the Sahara were shipped across the desert to markets in Fez, Tunis, and Tripoli, from where they were transshipped to Cairo, in Egypt, and then to the Middle East and other regions of western Asia (Austen, 1979; Collins, 2006:330–34; Lovejoy, 2000:61–62).

Europeans engaged in this trade only from the sixteenth century. Estimates of the slave trade to and from Asia are rare, in part because of the lack of sources, especially for the non-European trade.

However, for the European traffic, historians have made some important progress. As previously mentioned, the size of the African slave trade to Asia and other Old World regions was about the same as the traffic to the Americas, 12 million people. Some 5 million of these were transported between the sixteenth and mid nineteenth centuries, with a little over 1 million of them shipped from East Africa alone, where Europeans were active (Lovejoy, 2000:47, 142). Recent estimates indicate that Europeans transported a minimum of 449,800 to 565,200 slaves from Mozambique, the Swahili Coast, Madagascar, India, Sri Lanka, and Southeast Asia to destinations within the Indian Ocean during the same period (Allen, 2015:15). Compared with what they carried across the Atlantic, this figure does not seem significant, something in the order of 4 to 5 percent, but measured against the number of Africans forced into the Indian Ocean from East Africa, and assuming that Africans made up the bulk of slaves Europeans transported, this percentage would increase to 43 or 54 (Lovejoy, 2000:47, 142). In other words, Europeans may have started late, but they were by no means small players in the slave trade to and from Asia.

The European slave trade peaked in the eighteenth century, when they shipped an average of approximately 2,200 slaves per year to and from Asia. Throughout this period, they competed with Omani, Swahili, Chinese, and other Asian traders (Allen, 2015:19, 25). In fact, the distribution of captives transported indicates that Europeans were able to attend only their own markets, which, depending on the agreements they made with other nations in the region, were also supplied with slaves transported in non-European vessels. Moreover, after 1807, when the British abolished their own slave trade and started a campaign to suppress the entire traffic, European activity in the Indian Ocean was further limited. In any case, of all the European nations, the French were the chief carriers, transporting about 71 percent of the slaves shipped in European vessels between the sixteenth and mid nineteenth centuries, mainly from East Africa, Madagascar, and India to the Mascarene Islands, notably Mauritius, Seychelles, and Réunion. The Dutch were the second largest carrier, shipping about 16 percent of the slaves. They were particularly active in the transportation of Indian slaves or coerced laborers to South Africa and the Indonesian archipelago. The Portuguese, the principal Iberian nation involved, were not far behind the Dutch, transporting approximately 12 percent of the slaves, mainly from Mozambique to India. The British and other European nations shipped the remaining slaves, most of them from East Africa and Madagascar to India and South Africa (Allen, 2015:16–18).

Portuguese involvement in the trade started as early as the sixteenth century, and it extended from East Africa to the Far East. Japanese folding screens from the sixteenth and early seventeenth centuries depict scenes of Portuguese traders and missionaries on the coast showing black figures manning Portuguese ships, unloading commodities, and shading traders from the sunrays with large parasols (Carr, 2015:22–23). Since the Portuguese sometimes referred to Indians as 'blacks,' it is not clear whether these figures were in fact Africans. If they were, it is also unclear whether they were East Africans or Africans from the Atlantic coast, or had simply been born in Portugal (Bauss, 1997a:22; Teles da Cunha, 2006:191). However, Jesuit correspondence and Japanese sources do refer to black, African men working in Japan at that time. A popular example is Yasuke, a black man, possibly from Mozambique, who arrived in Japan in 1579 in the company of Jesuits and who later joined Lord Oda Nobunaga's entourage, rising through the ranks of Japanese society to the position of *samurai* (Lockley, 2016:5–7). Another example is of a black, African gunner who worked in the service of Lord Arima Harunobu in 1584 (Lockley, 2016:3).

However, most of the Portuguese slave trade revolved around the transportation of enslaved Africans from Mozambique to India and Macau. This trade also started in the sixteenth century and extended well into the nineteenth but, given the scarcity of sources as well as the fact that the Portuguese did not always clearly identify Africans and their descendants, it is extremely difficult to measure its impact and extent. Nevertheless, estimates based on censuses and customs records show that the number of Africans transported from Mozambique to Portuguese Asia averaged approximately 200–250 slaves annually from the 1770s to 1830. A significant share of these, probably between 50 and 100 Africans per year, was carried to Goa alone (Bauss, 1997a:21; Machado, 2014:249–52). The combined trade to Diu and Daman totaled about 100 slaves per year (Bauss, 1997a:23; Machado, 2014:249–52). However, many of these slaves were transshipped to the hinterland of Goa, beyond the western Ghats, to the Deccan as well as to ports as far as Pondicherry, in southeast India, and Macau, in China (Bauss, 1997a:22). In fact, the number of slaves dispatched from Goa to Macau approximated 20 to 25 Africans annually between 1800 and 1830, making the black population of that port account for some 25 to 35 percent of the total Macanese population of the same period (Bauss, 1997a:23).

Details about the life of these Africans have yet to come to light. Although Africans made up a significant percentage of the population of some ports of Portuguese Asia, this was not the norm, neither in the *Estado*, nor in other regions of the continent. Given the small numbers transported, and their distribution over a vast territory, Africans faced huge challenges to raise families and build communities that would allow them to reproduce part of their culture and traditions in Asia. As slaves, family members could be easily separated through sale and transported to distant lands. Moreover, many of them were engaged in dangerous or labor-intensive activities, which could seriously reduce their life span. As previously mentioned, slaves dove for pearls, mined salt, and grew cash crops. These activities were often reserved for slaves and lower-class subjects, who were further discriminated against according to their race, ethnicity, and religion. However, they also worked in less labor-intensive activities, for instance as domestic servants, porters, craftsmen, concubines, and bureaucrats. Indeed, depending on their numbers, such occupations allowed them to bond and create communities. One example, though from a life-threatening occupation, is the Siddi Risala community of Hyderabad, in the heart of the Deccan. The Siddi Risala community emerged in the mid nineteenth century, when the Hyderabad military forces became part of the British Indian army, but it traces its origins to centuries earlier, when Muslim Bahmani princes recruited African slaves to serve in the military of medieval Hyderabad. After the Mughals conquered the Deccan between 1626 and 1675, several Hindu rulers retained African contingents (Harris, 1971:102–03). These Africans came from different regions, some of them probably shipped in Portuguese vessels, but the bonds they created as comrades-in-arms allowed them to establish a sense of community rooted in their cultural background (Harris, 1971:110–14).

Conclusion

From the sixteenth century, Iberian traders, especially the Portuguese, helped connect Africa to Asia. They tapped into long-established commercial networks, including the slave trade, and rushed the region into a new era of political, economic, and social developments. Although the Portuguese pioneered the slave trade in the Atlantic, in the Indian Ocean they were merely newcomers. Omani, Swahili, Chinese, and other Asians had been trading slaves across the ocean for centuries. Moreover, since slavery and other forms of coerced labor existed in Africa and Asia, the Indian Ocean trade never reached the same size of its Atlantic counterpart. Nevertheless, when Europeans arrived in the region, they captured almost half of that trade, with the French, Dutch, and Portuguese as the leading carriers. The Portuguese, in particular, focused their activities on Mozambique, shipping slaves mainly to Goa, Daman, Diu, and Macau. Some of these slaves were transshipped to other destinations in the interior of India and China, where they worked in a variety of activities, including serving in the militaries of different rulers. Although details about the lives of these individuals have yet to come to light, whenever they could, Africans strove to bond and create communities, which depended in part on the variations in the slave trade between Africa and Asia. This significant migration helped perpetuate prevailing patterns of racial, ethnic, and religious discrimination in the Indian Ocean. Governments and citizens of Europe as well as of modern-day countries like China, India, Iran, Japan, Kenya, Tanzania, and Yemen, to name a few, have yet to reckon with this history and address the socioeconomic disparities that emerged as a result of centuries of forced migration and economic exploitation.

Bibliography

Allen, R. B., 2015. *European Slave Trading in the Indian Ocean, 1500–1850*, Athens, OH: Ohio University Press.

Andaya, B. W., 2014. 'Christianity in modern Southeast Asia', in N. G. Owen (ed.), *Routledge Handbook of Southeast Asian History*, New York: Routledge, pp. 235–245.

Anonymous, 1912. *The Periplus of the Erythræan Sea: Travel and Trade in the Indian Ocean by a Merchant of the First Century*, London: Longmans, Green, and Co.

Austen, R. A., 1979. 'The trans-Saharan slave trade: A tentative census', in H. A. Gemery and J. S. Hogendorn (eds.), *The Uncommon Market: Essays in the Economic History of the Atlantic Slave Trade*, New York: Academic Press, pp. 23–76.

Austen, R. A., 1989. 'The nineteenth century Islamic slave trade from East Africa (Swahili and Red Sea coasts): A tentative census', in W. G. Clarence-Smith (ed.), *The Economics of the Indian Ocean Slave Trade in the Nineteenth Century*, London: Frank Cass, pp. 21–44.

Axelson, E., 1973. *Portuguese in South-East Africa, 1488–1600*, Johannesburg: C. Struik.

Bauss, R., 1997a. 'The Portuguese slave trade from Mozambique to Portuguese India and Macau and comments on Timor, 1750–1850: New evidence from the archives', New York: *Camões Center for the Portuguese-Speaking World Quarterly*, Volume 6/7 (1–2), pp. 21–26.

Bauss, R., 1997b. 'Textiles, Bullion and Other Trades of Goa: Commerce with Surat, Other Areas of India, Luso-Brazilian Ports, Macau and Mozambique, 1816–1819', *Indian Economic and Social History Review*, Volume 34, pp. 275–287.

Bauss, R., 1982. 'A Legacy of British Trade Policies: The End of Trade and Commerce between India and the Portuguese Empire, 1780–1830', *Calcutta Historical Journal*, Volume 6 (2), pp. 81–115.

Beachey, R. W., 1976. *The Slave Trade of Eastern Africa*, New York: Barnes & Noble.

Boxer, C. R., 1965. *The Dutch Seaborne Empire, 1600–1800*, New York: Alfred A. Knopf.

Boxer, C. R., 1969. *The Portuguese Seaborne Empire, 1415–1825*, New York: Knopf.

Campbell, G. (ed.), 2004. *Structure of Slavery in Indian Ocean, Africa, and Asia*, Portland: Frank Cass.

Campbell, G., 2006. 'The African–Asian Diaspora: Myth or Reality?', *African and Asian Studies*, Volume 5, pp. 305–324.

Capela, J., 2002. *O Tráfico de Escravos nos Portos de Moçambique 1733–1904*, Porto: Editora Afrontamento.

Carr, D., 2015. 'Asia and the new world', in D. Carr (ed.), *Made in the Americas: The New World Discovers Asia*, Boston: Museum of Fine Arts, pp. 19–37.

Clarence-Smith, W. G., 1989. 'The economics of the Indian Ocean and Red Sea slave trades in the nineteenth century: An overview', in W. G. Clarence-Smith (ed.), *The Economics of the Indian Ocean Slave Trade in the Nineteenth Century*, London: Frank Cass, pp. 1–20.

Collins, R. O., 2006. 'The African Slave Trade to Asia and the Indian Ocean Islands', *African and Asian Studies*, Volume 5, pp. 325–346.

Harris, J. E., 1971. *The African Presence in Asia: Consequences of the East African Slave Trade*, Evanston, IL: Northwestern University Press.

Jayasuriya, S. de S., 2006. 'Identifying Africans in Asia: What's in a Name?', *African and Asian Studies*, Volume 5, pp. 275–303.

Jayasuriya, S. de S., 2008. *The Portuguese in the East: A Cultural History of a Maritime Trading Empire*, London: Tauris Academic Studies.

Lapa, J. R. do A., 2000. *A Bahia e a Carreira da Índia*, São Paulo: Hucitec, Unicamp.

Larson, P. M., 2013. 'African slave trades in global perspective', in R. Reid and J. Parker (eds.), *Oxford Handbook of Modern African History*, Oxford: Oxford University Press, pp. 56–76.

Lockley, T., 2016. 'The Story of Yasuke: Nobunaga's Black Retainer', *Ohmonronso*, Volume 91, pp. 1–39.

Lovejoy, P. E., 2000. *Transformations in Slavery: A History of Slavery in Africa*, 2nd ed., New York: Cambridge University Press.

Machado, P., 2014. *Ocean of Trade: South Asian Merchants, Africa and the Indian Ocean, c.1750–1850*, Cambridge, UK: Cambridge University Press.

Manchester, A. K., 1969. 'The transfer of the Portuguese court to Rio de Janeiro', in H. H. Keith and S. F. Edwards (eds.), *Conflict and Continuity in Brazilian Society*, Columbia, SC: University of South Carolina Press, pp. 148–183.

Middleton, J., 1992. *The World of the Swahili: An African Mercantile Civilization*, New Haven, CT: Yale University Press.

Paquette, G., 2013. *Imperial Portugal in the Age of Atlantic Revolutions: The Luso-Brazilian World, c.1770–1850*, New York: Cambridge University Press.

Parry, J. H., 1966. *The Spanish Seaborne Empire*, New York: Knopf.

Pinto, C., 1994. *Trade and Finance in Portuguese India: A Study of the Portuguese Country Trade, 1770–1840*, New Delhi: Concept Pub. Co.

Pinto, J., 1992. *Slavery in Portuguese India, 1510–1842*, Bombay: Himalaya Pub. House.

Popović, A., 1999. *The Revolt of African Slaves in Iraq in the 3rd/9th Century*, Princeton: Markus Wiener Publishers.

Russell-Wood, A. J. R., 1992. *A World on the Move: The Portuguese in Africa, Asia, and America, 1415–1808*, New York: St. Martin's Press.

Schultz, K., 2001. *Tropical Versailles: Empire, Monarchy, and the Portuguese Royal Court in Rio de Janeiro, 1808–1821*, New York: Routledge.

Schwartz, S. B., 1985. *Sugar Plantations in the Formation of Brazilian Society, Bahia, 1550–1835*, New York: Cambridge University Press.

Serrão, J. and Oliveira Marques, A. H. R. de, 1986. *Nova História da Expansão Portuguesa*, Lisbon: Editorial Estampa.

Talib, Y. and El Samir, F., 1988. 'The African diaspora in Asia', in M. El Fasi (ed.), *General History of Africa*, London: Heinemann, pp. 704–733.

Teles da Cunha, J. M., 2006. 'Economia e Finanças', in M. de J. dos Mártires Lopes (ed.), *Nova História da Expansão Portuguesa: O Império Oriental, 1660–1820*, Lisbon: Estampa, pp. 162–536.

Velho, Á., 1998. *O Descobrimento das Índias: O Diário da Viagem de Vasco da Gama*, Rio de Janeiro: Objetiva.

Watson, J. L. (ed.), 1980. *Asian and African Systems of Slavery*, Berkeley, CA: University of California Press.

Late colonialism

3

LOST AND FOUND

Sovereignties and state formations in Africa and Asia

Kwame Nimako

Introduction

This chapter contributes to and addresses some of the questions related to the colonization of Asia and Africa by European states and the mobilization of the populations of Africa and Asia to end European colonialism. The notion of sovereignty serves as a thread throughout this chapter because colonization constitutes a loss of sovereignty to the colonized. Since it is European states that colonized Asia and Africa it is essential that we bring state formation in Europe into the equation because colonization requires a colonizer and the colonized. Thus, I emphasize and analyze the processes that informed both the loss and the reclamation of sovereignty in nations across Asia and Africa. Although the focus of this chapter is Africa and Asia it is important to first note that the colonization of Asia and Africa by European states was preceded by, and overlapped with, the expropriation of land and colonization of the Americas by the same nations. In fact the link between the colonization of the Americas, Asia and Africa created the world economy, as we know it today. For instance, the Dutch established the Dutch East India Company which operated in Asia and the Dutch West India Company which operated in Africa and the Americas in the chattel slavery enterprise. The economic activities of each one complemented the other; African captives were forcibly transported to the Americas to work under coercion in order to extract minerals such as gold and silver, and produce goods such as cotton, sugar, coffee and tobacco, for European consumption, as well as to facilitate European trade with Asia. Thus, it is important to remember that while this chapter focuses primarily on Africa, the Americas and Asia, Europe remained a pivotal fulcrum in all the activities (Nimako & Willemsen, 2011).

The revolts of the Americas and establishment of independent states, first, the United States (1776), then Haiti (1804), and later the rest of Latin America, were followed by the intensification of the control of Asian trade and the imperialist scramble for Africa. The subjugation of the Americas is attributed to the arrival of Christopher Columbus in 1492. From the vantage of the emergence of a world economy this was eventful but I have argued elsewhere that navigation does not necessarily lead to colonization (Nimako, 2011). This is all the more so since humans have been navigating and travelling from time immemorial. The colonization of the Americas by some European states, and the use of 'race' as the organizing principle of the enslavement of Africans, to extract wealth from the Americas to Europe, strengthened European states. This in turn made it feasible for some of the European states to colonize much of Asia and Africa. The forces that gave rise to the European colonial enterprise/project revolved around state formation in Europe; so it was for the process of decolonization in Africa and Asia. Bearing this in mind, this chapter also sheds light on why colonization of Asia and Africa took place in the nineteenth century and why decolonization took place in the second half of the twentieth century. Not only was the colonization of the Americas qualitatively different from that of Asia but also, qualitatively, was the colonization of Asia and Africa. In Asia, the European states inserted themselves in existing trade networks and took them over, but their capacity to significantly expropriate land and totally control populations and cultures was less successful. In Africa between the sixteenth and the nineteenth century existing trade networks, such as the Trans-Sahara route, had been interrupted during the Atlantic slave trade and slavery; some lands were expropriated in the southern part of Africa and new trade routes, through the Atlantic and Europe, were created. I use the concept of sovereignty in three ways, namely, territorial, citizenship and 'international law'. First, territorial sovereignty is used as an instrument to delineate the boundaries of nations and states. This became more pronounced in Europe after the Peace of Westphalia in 1648 and laid the institutional foundations for the inter-state system around which European states built a world order, and the very one under which we currently live in the twenty-first century. The Peace of Westphalia provided the signatories a framework for coordinated competition and cooperation and an institutional framework of reciprocity. It also provided a 'legal' mechanism under which they competed for trade and waged wars; thus it regulated both trade and war at the same time; it also facilitated a state monopoly of violence (Nimako & Willemsen, 2011). Second, I use the concept of sovereignty in relation to citizenship; this is tied to the French Revolution in 1789 (Wallerstein, 2004), as a consequence of which, in France, and later in other European countries, citizenship in Europe was elevated to the level of sovereignty; citizens were considered sovereign in relation to rulers and government. Sovereign citizenship undermined the authority of European monarchs but did not change the direction of European colonial ambitions. On the one hand sovereign citizenship increased freedom and so trade unions and affiliated political parties emerged, as did universal voting rights for men, and later, for women. On the other hand, citizens shared in the booty of colonial enterprise as entrepreneurs, soldiers, police, lawyers, civil servants, academics, and in justified colonial projects. Flowing from this not only did the notion of European expansion and discoveries emerge as part of an academic narrative to justify colonialism but also the narrative gave the false impression that the peoples of the world did not know of each other's existence until European navigators brought them together in the sixteenth century (Nimako, 2011; Araujo & Maeso, 2015b). Third, the concept of sovereignty is used in the context of 'international law', in particular within the United Nations framework. The United Nations inherited colonies through the Trusteeship arrangement under its precursor, the League of Nations; this obliged the UN to ponder on colonialism and decolonization and made it a benevolent imperialist. In other words decolonization became an international issue; not just between the colonizer and the colonized. Whereas the colonization of the Americas strengthened European states' ability to colonize Asia and Africa, the Second World War weakened European states and strengthened national liberation movements in Asia and Africa (Amin et al., 1990).

These three forms of sovereignties are essential to understanding this chapter whose central thesis is that, wherever there is domination, one should expect resistance; colonization (domination) and decolonization (resistance) is no exception. People have resisted the encroachment on their territories and persons from time immemorial, and colonization was also resisted and the outcome of the resistance was decolonization, which in turn requires a new vision of the world. The loss and the reclamation of sovereignties constitute a contestation of sovereignties from without, that is foreign aggression and occupation; nationalist movements emerged out of the desire to reclaim sovereignty. The first part of this chapter focuses on the process of colonization, followed by an analysis of decolonization in the second part. Hopefully, the sequence of analysis will shed some light on the relationship between nationalism, nationalist movements and political parties in state formations in Africa and Asia.

On Afro-Eurasia and the European colonial enterprise

The landmass that constitutes Afro-Eurasia connects Africa, Asia and Europe and it is there that trade links have extended back for millennia. Within the Afro-Eurasian world economy, Africa was an important producer of gold, the bulk of which was from West Africa; other supplies of gold came from Nubia, which exported gold via Egypt to Constantinople/Istanbul and from Ethiopia to Egypt, the Red Sea, and India. Another source was Zimbabwe, 'which for a millennium had been important sources of gold for the world, reached its peak production of one ton during the fifteenth century' (Frank, 1998:149–150). Both Christopher Columbus and Vasco da Gama wanted to find an alternative route to Asia partly because Asia was then, as it is now, 'the world factory'; Asian production, competitiveness and trade dominated the world economy. China produced and exported silk, ceramics, some gold, copper, and later tea. India produced and exported cotton and silk textiles. After Columbus and Vasco da Gama led the way, the Portuguese and the Dutch, and later the English and the French, stepped up their involvement in East Asia, seeking a role in the trade between China and other Asian countries. By the end of the sixteenth century, the Afro-Eurasia landmass had been delineated; and the politics underlying the trade links were becoming separate from the geography. Europe had turned to the West in order to reach the East and the idea of Euro-America or the Western world was born out of this constellation. At the broader world level,

> the incorporation into this Old [Afro-Eurasia] World economy of the New [Atlantic] World in the Americas and their contribution to the world's stocks and flows of money certainly gave economic activity and trade a new boost from the sixteenth century onward.
>
> *(Frank, 1998:56)*

This released demographic pressures on Europe through emigration to the Americas; it also released pressure on European lands because Europeans expropriated the lands of the native populations of the Americas. This, de facto, made the Americas an extension of the European world; thus for more than two hundred years the Americas served as farms and mines for Europe. The entire process made race and racism an organizing principle of slavery and called into being an international division of labor, shaped primarily by Western politics, in which enslaved Africans were forced to occupy the lowest level. The geopolitics that emerged from this gave the appearance that Europe no longer formed part of an Asian peninsula. Several important and overlapping economic activities emerged. Minerals acquired in the Americas through the use of enslaved African labor, including silver and gold, were traded in Asia. For example, the Spanish galleon trade directly linked the Spanish Caribbean with the Philippines. European traders also brought extensive crops from across the Americas to Europe. And some of these crops – such as maize and tobacco – were also sent to China (Frank, 1998). The addition of the Americas to the Afro-Eurasia trade networks expanded, strengthened and enriched European states (Nimako, 2011). The Peace of Westphalia resolved the Thirty Years' War, a religious war among Christians who had been ruled from Roman Catholic Rome; this in turn gave rise to religious states, namely, Protestant-led monarchs and states in the northern part of Europe and

Catholic-led monarchs and states and the southern part of Europe (Nimako & Willemsen, 2011). We take this a step further because the Treaty of Westphalia did more than resolve religious conflict. It provided the modalities for the signatories to compete and cooperate; but it also delineated the limits of recognition of the territorial integrity of the states of the signatories by preventing one from swallowing the other. This was one side of the sovereignty coin from the European perspective. The other side of the coin is that the Peace of Westphalia territorial sovereignty arrangement went hand in hand with the non-recognition of the territorial sovereignties of other peoples in the Americas, Asia and Africa. In other words the territorial sovereignties and integrity of the peoples of the Americas, Africa and Asia were not recognized and were trampled upon by European states. In practical terms this meant that European states could occupy the territory of people deemed non-Europeans in the Americas, Asia and Africa and claim it, with or without the consent of the natives, by raising a national flag of a European state on the territory. It is important to note that even if contemporary academia fails to observe the link between Afro-Eurasia and the Americas in their analysis, the European rulers who had colonial ambitions were conscious of the fact that there was a link between developments in Africa, the Americas and Asia. This is all the more so since in 1751 the British Board of Trade ordered the governor of Cape Castle (on the coast of present Ghana) to stop cotton cultivation among the Fante people, because:

> The introduction of culture and industry among the Negroes [i.e. Africans] is contrary to the known established policy of this country [i.e. Britain], there is no saying where this might stop, and that it might extend to tobacco, sugar and every other commodity which we now take from our [Caribbean and American slave] colonies and thereby the Africans, *who now support themselves by wars,* would become planters and their slaves be employed in the culture of these articles in Africa, which they are employed in America.
> *(Boahen, 1966, p. 113 cited in Nimako & Willemsen, 2011:57; emphasis added)*

This quote illustrates that there was a conscious and deliberate effort to interrupt the production and economies of Africa and encourage wars in favor of kidnapping Africans and transporting them to the Americas for enslavement. In other words, Africans had to be restrained from using their labor productively in Africa so it could be used as enslaved African labor in the Americas. This quotation also indicates that there was no laissez-faire or free trade in the way we have been given to understand in economics textbooks. Thus, the epistemology of laissez-faire is misleading and the underlying thesis is false because the world economy, as we know it now, was built neither on free trade nor on free labor. The links between Africa, the Americas and Asia can also be illustrated by considering the ways in which various European states responded to the revolts of the subjugated populations of the Americas against direct European rule. After the British colony in North America revolted and established an independent state of the United States of America (USA) in 1776, Britain intensified its trade activities in Asia. Thus, not only did the British state take the lead to curtail some of the activities of the British East India Company at the end of the eighteenth century, but also when the first consignments of sugar from Bengal started to arrive in Britain in 1793, Mr. Randle Jackson, Director of the East India Company, informed his shareholders that, 'It seemed as if Providence, it took from us America, who should say that Providence had not taken from us one member, more seriously to impress us with the value of another?' (James, 1980 [1938]:52). Less than two decades later, on 5 May 1812, Mr. Jackson informed his shareholders, 'We need to invest in conquest before we can reap the advantages in revenue and trade' (Houghton, www.houghton.hk). After suffering several defeats in Canada and Haiti in the eighteenth century, France intensified its activities in Asia in what it then called Indo-China; and as if that was not enough, France, under the leadership of Napoleon, turned its attention to Europe in an attempt to prevent Britain from trading in continental Europe. Napoleon was not only defeated but France became bankrupt which led to the sale of its territorial control in North America, known as the Louisiana Purchase of 1803. The aftermath of the Napoleonic wars (1799-1815) led to the reconstitution of boundaries in Europe (Wallerstein, 1990); this found its expression in the Congress of Vienna (1815). By the turn of the nineteenth century not only did revolts in Asia against European operatives make it difficult for the European chartered companies to operate profitably but also the end of the Napoleonic wars gave rise to reconstitution of boundaries, first in Europe and later Africa and Asia. In practice this implied the replacement of the chartered monopoly companies by the state and granted European citizens of all classes and gender more access to the colonial booty. For instance, when the Dutch regained their territorial sovereignty from France in 1815 they formed a unitary nation-state and formally moved to colonize Indonesia. According to Legene and Waaldijk, in Indonesia the Dutch 'Simultaneously . . . introduced *forced labour* and large-scale exploitation of natural resources. After the 1860s, *free enterprise* was allowed in, and a growing number of colonial entrepreneurs and officials with their families settled in Indonesia' (Legene & Waaldijk, 2007:189; emphasis added). The reader should take note of our emphasis on the words *forced labour* and *free enterprise* because it reminds us that as Europeans increasingly gained more freedom as sovereign citizens to join the colonial enterprise, the colonized peoples in Asia and Africa increasingly lost their territorial sovereignty and collective freedom.

According to Legene and Waaldijk,

> It was only towards the end of the nineteenth century that the Dutch introduced a more intensive and 'enlightened' mode of colonial rule, which they named the 'Ethical Policy'. It sought to achieve political commitment to the colonial system among the Dutch and the Indonesia population. On both sides of colonial rule, ever more people had to participate in the implementation of colonial rule, under the guidance of an elite of politicians and administrators.
>
> *(Legene & Waaldijk, 2007:189)*

Just as the colonization of the Americas facilitated Europe to trade with Asia, so the colonization of the Indian sub-continent facilitated British aggression towards China. Britain recruited Indians to fight in China on behalf of Britain in the so-called Anglo-Chinese Wars (also referred to as the Opium Wars) between 1839 and 1842, which ended with the Treaty of Nanking. Another war involving France and the United States on one side and the people of China on other took place between 1856 and 1860 and ended with Treaty of Tientsin. This was followed by the implosion of China through the Taiping Rebellion (1850–1864). Recall that the people of China were defending their territorial sovereignty from foreign encroachment and their failure led to the classification of the nineteenth century, in Chinese historiography, as the century of humiliation (Sachs, 2009). By the turn of the twentieth century the Chinese state had been weakened and after the First World War, civil war broke out, followed by the occupation by Japan of the eastern part of China. Within Europe, as a consequence of the Napoleonic Wars and reconstitution of European territories and boundaries, Belgium emerged as an independent country in 1830 (Mommen, 1982). As a latecomer to colonialist intrusions, the Belgian elite went to look for a king and found one in Germany in the person of King Leopold. To count as a relevant king in Europe at the time King Leopold II went to look for a colony and after studying the world map and trying in vain to find a colony in the Americas and the Pacific, he spotted a location in Africa called the Congo that was not yet contested by European states. As if that was not enough King Leopold II of Belgium was able to appeal to his European ruling cousins for part of the colonial booty and he formulated his colonial ambitions and strategies in the following words:

> I'm sure if I quite openly charge [Henry Morton] Stanley [the explorer] with the task of taking possession in my name of some part of Africa, the English will stop me. If I ask their advice, they'll stop me just the same. So I think I will just give Stanley some job of exploration which would offend no one [i.e. European rulers], and will give us the bases and headquarters which we can take over later on.
>
> *(Hochschild, 2006:58)*

He went on to say, 'I do not want to risk . . . losing a fine chance to secure for ourselves a slice of this magnificent African cake' (Hochschild, 2006:58). The slice of magnificent African cake he spoke of is the country now known as the Democratic Republic of Congo. After persuading the British, the French and Americans to give him a role in Africa, he persuaded Germany to organize a conference to implement it. The conference is now recorded in history textbooks as the Berlin Conference 1884/1885 or the Scramble for Africa. Before the Berlin Conference some European nations considered certain geographical locations in Africa as their spheres of influence. The Berlin Conference transformed the idea of 'spheres of influence' into 'effective occupation' (Araujo & Maeso, 2015b:154–177). The occupation had its own logic, namely, occupation, expropriation, appropriation and justification. First, colonialism is not only about the occupation of foreign lands. It required the construction of a state to manage the land and control the colonized. Recall that European citizens had claimed to be sovereign and thus independent since the nineteenth century. But this did not prevent the active mobilization of the citizens in the colonial enterprise. European citizens joined the colonial enterprise as entrepreneurs, soldiers, civil servants, police, academics and missionaries. The colonial state became the extension of European sovereignty and epistemologies emerged to justify it; the territories acquired were branded as British India, Indo-China, British Africa, French Africa, Belgian Congo and Portuguese Africa. Second, the colonial state became a reconstitution and re-construction of African and Asian borders; different ethnic borders were brought under one colonial territorial and administrative roof and referred to the people as natives; and there were specific laws for the natives. The world is more familiar with South African apartheid laws such as the Group Areas Act, the Separate Amenities Act, the Immorality Act and the Population Registration Act than with other colonial administrations; but their variants existed elsewhere. Citizenship, trade unions, political parties and voting rights for both men and women did not exist in the colonial project (Nimako, 1991; Mamdani, 1999).

Recall that during the period of Atlantic slavery the enslaved Africans chopped, planted, picked or harvested, carried, cooked, served, washed and cleaned, so that the enslavers on the plantations could pursue their non-menial activities – reading, writing, sport and so on (Nimako & Willemsen, 2011:52). After the legal abolition of Atlantic slavery Asians (from India, Indonesia, China) were recruited as indentured laborers to work in the Americas to compensate for the loss of enslaved African labor. After the colonization of Asia and Africa colonial subjects from the Indian sub-continent were sent to South Africa to work as indentured laborers on sugar cane fields; they were also sent to various African countries to construct railways; Africans were also recruited as soldiers to fight in Asia and Europe for the colonizers. The division of labor during slavery and the colonial period remained racialized and in Malaysia the colonial authorities were proud to justify this practice in the following words:

The function of the white man in a tropical country is not to labour with his hands, but to direct and control a plentiful and efficient supply of native labour, to assist in the Government of the country, or to engage in opportunities offered for trade and commerce, from an office desk in a bank or mercantile firm.

(*British Malaya, May 1926, cited in Amin & Caldwell, 1977:5*)

Third, native rulers did not only become colonial subjects, they became instruments of colonial rule and control, also known as indirect rule. The native rulers were held hostage by the colonizer on the principle of 'when persuasion fails, force must apply'. It implied that native rulers who did not subscribe to the indirect rule principle were overthrown in favor of rival groups prepared to play second fiddle to the colonizer. But resistance continued and there were numerous revolts against colonial rule: some of the revolts revolved around specific laws, forced labor, imposition of taxes, land expropriation and identification passes.

Not only did the British give new names to the territories they occupied but also they convinced themselves that the territories belonged to them. Let us take one example from Malaysia:

It should be made clear that the Authorities will not tolerate anything that savours of organized agitation. This is British territory, and the men concerned in the strikes are aliens. They [i.e. the indentured laborers from India] come here because the inducements held out appeared good to them, and once here they have to conduct themselves with the circumspection expected of any alien in a foreign country.

(Malaya Tribune, *September 21, 1936, quoted in Amin & Caldwell, 1977:5*)

Clearly, this is a world upside down; the British did not consider themselves as aliens in foreign lands: it was others who were aliens. Thus, as European states and their citizens emerged from the Napoleonic Wars and gained more freedoms and rights, especially the so-called working class, women and children, they joined the colonial enterprise to take away the freedoms and rights of Africans and Asians by convincing themselves that they were on a civilizing mission for the progress of mankind (and why not womankind?). However, unlike in the Americas, the European colonizers in Asia and Africa bit off more than they could chew. Unlike Africa, the colonization of Asia was not authorized at a European conference. Fifteen years after the Berlin Conference a group of people of African descent organized a Pan-African Conference to challenge the outcome of the Berlin Conference. The communiqué of the Pan-African Conference, titled 'Address to the Nations of the World', included the following words: 'The problem of the twentieth century is the problem of the colour-line – the relation of the darker to the lighter races of the men in Asia and Africa, in America and the islands of the sea' (Du Bois, 1960 [1903]). Colonial subjects were ready to mobilize for decolonization, a subject to which we now turn.

On decolonization: from offensive to defensive imperialism

The European colonial enterprise was a violent and oppressive system with an offensive and defensive component (Nimako, 1991). The nineteenth century was the offensive phase of imperialism and involved the signing of dubious treaties with native rulers, waging wars, plundering, occupying foreign lands and the justification of such activities at home as a 'civilizing mission' (Davidson, 1992). Colonialism also constituted an extension of European wars. Thus, unlike previous European wars, by the turn of the twentieth century, such wars became world wars since European states could draw their colonial territories/subjects into them. At the turn of the twentieth century all nationalist movements in Africa and Asia emerged to reclaim territorial sovereignty and this put the European colonizers on the defensive; hence the term defensive imperialism. The essence of defensive imperialism is that it adopts a mechanism of progressive control, a dynamic process that continuously moves to newer forms of control in response to the resistance and revolts of colonized subjects (Nimako & Willemsen, 2011). The colonizers controlled the colonized not only through violence but also through the institution of the colonial education system; academics, media, novelists and missionaries emerged among the colonizers to produce knowledge and discourse for the justification of colonialism. By the second half of the twentieth century the colonial project had produced urban workers and unemployed, teachers, priests and professionals in the colonial territories. It appears contradictory, but it was those who had been born under colonial rule, and trained to support colonial domination, who used the memory of colonial occupation to revolt against colonial rule and mobilized for decolonization. The leaders who led the efforts to regain territorial sovereignty in the twentieth century were not the same native rulers who had lost it to European states in the nineteenth century.

Fast forward to the Second World War which weakened European states and strengthened the United States of America and nationalist movements in Asia and Africa. It was out of this constellation that the United Nations (UN) emerged (Schlesinger, 2003). The UN became an organ of international legal framework through which territorial sovereignty could be reclaimed by colonial subjects. But nationalist claims for territorial sovereignty were usually met with violence by the colonial authorities. From Indonesia, India, Vietnam through Algeria, Madagascar, Ghana, Kenya, Cameroon to Zimbabwe, Angola, Guinea-Bissau, South West Africa and South Africa, legitimate nationalist claims were met with intimidation, arrests and imprisonment, violence and in some cases the assassination of its leaders by the colonizers.

To illustrate the impact of the Second World War on decolonization let us start with Dutch-controlled Indonesia. During the Second World War, not only were the Netherlands occupied by Nazi Germany but also Japan occupied the Dutch colony of Indonesia, pulling the rug from under Dutch colonial feet and holding Dutch colonial authorities as war prisoners. When the US forced Japan to capitulate in 1945 and ended the Second World War in that part of the world, the Indonesian nationalists, led by Sukarno, declared Indonesia an independent nation on August 17, 1945; but the Dutch state that emerged after the Nazi occupation in Europe contested the claim of sovereignty by Indonesian nationalists in Asia, and war broke out between the Indonesian nationalists and the Dutch. But the Dutch did not succeed in returning to the colonial status quo, partly because Indonesia had the United Nations on its side and Indonesia became an independent nation under UN recognition on December 27, 1949. After Indonesia led the way, in the context of UN sovereignty arrangements, India followed; but Indian nationalists could not hold on to the colonial boundaries the British constructed; British India disintegrated into three countries, namely, India, Pakistan and Bangladesh. Like Indonesia, the eastern part of China was occupied by Japan amid civil war before and during the Second World War. In 1949 after more than a decade of struggle, under the leadership of Mao Zedong, the People's Liberation Army emerged victorious and the Communist Party of China gained control of China and the People's Republic of China was proclaimed (Arrighi, 1990).

Like Indonesia and China, Korea was also occupied by Japan.

> In 1945 the Korean people regained their independence from Japan, only to have their country cut in half by foreign intervention. In 1950 a civil war broke out only to be internationalized and conducted (under the flag of the 'United Nations') with all

the brutality that would later accompany American aggression in Vietnam – but without any of the publicity or protest.

(McCormack & Gittings, 1977:7)

The Viet Minh defeated the French at the Battle of Dien Bien Phu in 1954; this was followed by the Geneva Accords in the same year which attempted to make Vietnam an independent nation within the UN framework. But the United States would not let Vietnam go. This led to the division of Vietnam between North and South. The now famous Vietnam War ended in 1975 and, unlike Korea, broke down the north–south divide. Unlike Asia, the decolonization of Africa has to be placed in the context of Pan-Africanism. Ghana led the way in Africa and became the first country in the continent to achieve political independence through conscious mass mobilization within the United Nations self-determination framework. The focus of the Fifth Pan-African Conference in Manchester (UK) in 1945 was the decolonization of Africa; by that time Kwame Nkrumah had relocated from the US to England, and was one of the organizers of the conference. When he returned to Ghana in December 1947 he engaged in the difficult process of decolonizing the country politically, culturally and economically. This was particularly difficult since the colonizers sold the anti-colonial movements to their populations as a fight against communism. Thus the 'civilizing mission' in the offensive phase of imperialism became 'anti-communism mission' in the defensive phase of imperialism; and it was designed to pave the way for the colonizer to use violence to contain nationalist movements. An example of this was the Watson Commission, instituted by the British government to investigate 'disturbances' in Ghana in 1948, three months after the arrival of Nkrumah in the country. Not only were Nkrumah and others arrested by the colonial authorities as a consequence of the 'disturbances' but also the Watson Commission noted in its report that Nkrumah

> [a]ppears while in Britain to have had Communist affiliations and to have become imbued with a Communist ideology which only political expediency has blurred. In London he was identified particularly with the West African National Secretariat, a body which still exists. It appears to be the precursor of a Union of West African Soviet Socialist Republics.
>
> *(Watson Commission 1948, quoted in Nimako, 1991:46)*

To counter colonial misinformation, at a rally in the north of the country on 5 March 1949 Nkrumah stated,

> This country is ours. This land is ours. It belongs to our chiefs and people. It does not belong to foreigners, but we don't say that all foreigners should pack up and go. They can stay as traders, and work with us not us masters and rulers . . .
>
> *Nimako (1991)*

These were the parameters used to undo decades of colonial indoctrination. But the challenge for Nkrumah would be to wake-up Ghanaians into action while not also awakening colonial violence. To achieve this he added,

> The age of politics of words is gone. This is the age of politics of action. We don't have *guns*. We don't have ammunition to fight anybody. We have a great spirit, a great national soul which is manifest in our *unity* . . .

Wherefore my advice is, 'Seek ye first the political kingdom, and all things will be added unto you.'

(Nimako, 1991:45)

I have emphasised the words *guns* and *unity* because colonial rule rested on violence and on divide and rule tactics. In plain language what he meant by 'seek ye first the political kingdom, and all things will be added unto you' was that the economic development of Ghana required Ghanaian agency, and in the colonial context it meant self-determination and political independence. After failing to suppress the nationalists, territorial sovereignty claims, the British Governor in Ghana, Sir Arden-Clarke, when handing over sovereignty to the elected leader for independent Ghana on 6 March 1957, made the following statement:

Nkrumah and his party had the mass of the people behind them and there was *no other party with appreciable public support to which one could turn*. Without Nkrumah, the Constitution would be stillborn and if nothing came of all the hopes, aspirations and concrete proposals for a greater measure of self-government, there would no longer be any faith in the good intentions of the British Government and the Gold Coast [i.e. Ghana] would be plunged into disorders, violence and bloodshed.

(Nimako, 1991:79, emphasis added)

This statement is included to highlight one of the under-theorized issues in political conflict in Africa and Asia, namely, the relation between nationalism, nationalist movements and political parties. As a result of the pattern of mobilization, Ghana had become a de facto one-party state upon the achievement of political independence. The Communist Party of China emerged victorious in the civil war and has been in power since; the Congress Party of India also ruled without interruption for nearly 50 years; we can add developments in Algeria, Tanzania, South Africa and Zimbabwe to these political cultures (Chikane, 2012). Nationalist leaders do not just mobilize to reclaim territorial sovereignty; they also envision a new state and society after the end of colonial rule and once in power, they act upon this vision (Sian, 2014). These new visions found their expression in the design of new national flags to replace colonial flags, national anthems, new names for the country, new development plans for the future society and new political alliances for international relations. Independence struggles in Asia and Africa became mutually reinforcing. Thus before African countries gained their independence, India had already put the issue of apartheid in South Africa on the agenda in the UN. The newly independent Asian and African countries supported China to claim a UN Security Council seat in 1971. Several efforts were made to consolidate political independence within Asia and Africa. Some of these found their expression in conferences such as the Asian People's Conference in New Delhi in 1947 and the Asian–African Conference, also known as the Bandung Conference, in Indonesia in 1955, organized by Indonesia in collaboration with Burma, Pakistan, Sri Lanka and India (Bhasin, 2007). The Bandung Conference culminated in the Non-Aligned Movement (NAM) in 1961. Pan-Africanism moved to Africa when Ghana achieved political independence. The First Conference of Independent African States was held in Accra in April 1958, and the All-African Peoples' Conference was held in December of the same year, also in Accra. These initiatives gave birth to the formation of the Organisation of African Unity (OAU), now the African Union (AU) (Nimako, 2010). Not only did African countries become independent within the UN and Pan-African framework, they also renamed their countries, for example, Nkrumah changed the colonial name Gold Coast to Ghana. Haiti first began the process of adopting its new name in 1804 when it dropped its colonial name, San Dominique. After Ghana, by accident or design, many other African countries followed this tradition when they too became independent including Zambia, Zimbabwe, Malawi, Botswana, Namibia and Burkina Faso (Nimako, 2014). The new reality of decolonization led the British Prime Minister, Harold Macmillan, to note that,

> The wind of change is blowing through the [African] continent, and, whether we like it or not, this growth of national consciousness is a political fact. We must all accept it as fact, and our national policies must take account of it.
>
> *(Speech made to the* South African parliament,
> *on 3 February 1960, African Yearbook of Rhetoric)*

Where colonial policies did not provide the space for mass mobilization, armed struggle was applied. This became the lot of territories like Algeria, Angola, Guinea-Bissau, Mozambique, South Africa, South West Africa, Zimbabwe and Vietnam; and those countries received moral, political and material support from independent states in Africa and Asia within the NAM/OAU as well as the UN framework. Every revolution has its counter-revolution and counter-revolution found its expression in neo-colonialism, which in turn is part of defensive imperialism. A neo-colony is in theory independent and has all the trappings of international sovereignty, but in reality its economic system and political policy are directed by states external to it. I have argued elsewhere that neo-colonialism has three elements, namely, trade, military force and corruption (Nimako, 2011). The US leadership did not find it feasible to, or could not, control the new world order alone and thus turned to its ethnic cousins in Europe to reconfigure the Euro-American alliance that has existed since the sixteenth century. The new world order was now led by the US with (West) Europe as a junior partner and everyone else as real or potential enemy. This found its expression in multilateral institutions like the North Atlantic Treaty Organization (NATO), the World Bank and the International Monetary Fund (IMF); this became the structural context in which Asian and African peoples reclaimed their sovereignties. Thus from China to Africa, trade regimes have been devised (by a Western alliance) to control economies via outright economic sanctions or unfair trade practices (Subramanian, 2011). Corruption was part and parcel of the colonial enterprise, sometimes in the form of a divide and rule policy, but this strategy did not end with decolonization, it just took new forms. In other words, as part of defensive imperialism, the colonial powers found ways to maintain control by inserting themselves into local politics through the support of various political factions. Thus two decades after Indonesia and Ghana led the way in the decolonization project in Asia and Africa respectively, the governments of Sukarno in Indonesia and Nkrumah in Ghana were overthrown in military coups with the tacit support of the former colonizers. But the institutions that both Sukarno and Nkrumah played critical roles in bringing about, such as the Non-Aligned Movement (NAM) and the Organization of African Unity (OAU), survived and continued to support decolonization and economic development of their societies.

Recall that trade unions, political parties and citizenship hardly existed in the colonies during the heyday of colonialism and the newly independent countries had difficulty in making citizens out of colonial subjects. As political independence approached, political parties mushroomed and some ambitious local colonial students like Dr. K. A. Busia, a British-trained anthropologist and the first Ghanaian professor of sociology, emerged as politicians. The political parties Dr. Busia affiliated to lost three general elections (in 1951, 1954 and 1956) prior to the independence of Ghana but he ended up as leader of the opposition parties in parliament. Busia refused to accept his defeat and appeared honest enough to tell us something about his trajectory in politics. Not only did Busia advocate against the granting of independence to Ghana by the British, he also called on the United States government to 'impose economic sanctions' against Ghana in order to bring down the Nkrumah regime. On 3 December 1962 Dr. Busia appeared before a Congressional Committee to plead for the overthrow of Nkrumah by stating

> that politics isn't [his] career, but what made [him] go into politics is the fact that [he] saw right at the beginning, as far back as Nkrumah's return [to Ghana]. . . . That we had there all the makings, all the ingredients of revolutionary communism.
>
> *(Nimako, 1991:91)*

The political irony of people like Busia is that they were educated to support the colonial regime, they were discriminated against and could not explore their professions and talents fully under the colonial regime, but they became defendants of colonialism after the end of colonialism. Thus as nationalist movements emerged to oppose colonialism, other 'political parties' emerged to oppose nationalist movements. As if that was not enough, six months after the official launch of the Organisation of African Unity in Addis Ababa in Ethiopia, the British Ambassador to Ethiopia, J.W. Russel, filed the following report to his government on 31 December 1963.

> Nkrumah's 'political kingdom' seems irreconcilable with the independence, prosperity or unity of others. How then is this lethal rogue to be contained?
>
> Would it not be more logical, and in every way more profitable, to align ourselves according to our interests and our principles? The proposition seems to me a simple one. Nkrumah is our enemy, he is determined to complete our expulsion from an Africa which he aspires to dominate absolutely,
>
> *(quoted in* New African Magazine, *3 May 2013)*

In conclusion, the formation of the OAU/AU has created a framework for Africa within the Non-Aligned Movement and between African and Asian states, the latter symbolized by Africa–China relation (Nimako, 2007). As a gesture of solidarity China built the African Union Headquarters, and by accident or design took the initiative and placed Nkrumah's statue in front of the African Union Headquarters in Addis Ababa, Ethiopia, in 2012. Recall that Nkrumah, the initiator of the OAU, was overthrown on 24 February 1966 while in China on his way to Vietnam. The gesture of the Chinese, to place his statue in front of the AU building, demonstrates that the Chinese government has memory and the memory of colonial humiliation remains an important force in Africa–Asia political and economic relations now.

Conclusion

The central thesis of this chapter is that domination goes hand in hand with resistance; colonization and decolonization are no exception. Over the past 200 years, African and Asian societies and countries have lost their sovereignties to European nations in the process of colonization and they regained them, albeit in modified form, in the process of decolonization, also referred to as national liberation. The colonization of Asia and Africa by European states was preceded by, and overlapped, the colonization of the Americas. The continuous resistance by peoples of Africa and Asia to the European colonial enterprise and domination gave rise to decolonization and continues to this day because neo-colonialism is the half-way stage between colonialism and envisaged political independence. If the process of colonization can be classified as offensive imperialism, the process of decolonization can be classified as defensive imperialism. Thus, we live in the age of defensive imperialism and the memories of these two processes of lost and found sovereignties are major driving forces in state formation and global political economy. More importantly, the reorientation of the world economy to the Orient is not a result of any innate quality of Asians; rather it is challenging the false Eurocentric historical narrative that has been forced through as a result of European colonial enterprise. Asia is the largest continent and has the largest population in the world; they are getting their due because they have regained their sovereignties and their rise is reconnecting Afro-Eurasia and beyond.

Bibliography

African Yearbook of Rhetoric. 2011. Available at: www.africanrhetoric.org.

Amin, M. and Caldwell, M. (eds.), 1977. *Malaya: The Making of a Neo-Colony*, Nottingham: Spokesman Books.

Amin, S., 1990. 'The social movements in the periphery: An end to the national liberation?', in S. Amin et al. (eds.), *Transforming the Revolution: Social Movements and the World System*, New York: Monthly Review Press, pp. 96–138.

Amin, S., Arrighi, G., Frank G. and Wallerstein, I., 1990. *Transforming the Revolution: Social Movements and the World System*, New York: Monthly Review Press.

Araujo, M. and Maeso, S. R. (eds.), 2015a. *The Contours of Eurocentrism: Race, History, and Political Texts*, London: Lexington Books.

Araújo, M. and Maeso, S. R., 2015b. *Eurocentrism, Racism and Knowledge: Debate on History and Power in Europe and the Americas*, New York: Palgrave Macmillan.

Arrighi, G., 1990. 'Marxist century – American century: The making of the world labor movement', in S. Amin et al. (eds.), *Transforming the Revolution: Social Movements and the World System*, New York: Monthly Review Press, pp. 54–95.

Bhasin, H., 2007. 'India and South Africa: Ties that bind', in A. Sinha and M. Madhup (eds.), *Indian Foreign Policy: Challenges and Opportunities*, New Delhi: Academic Foundation.

Chikane, F., 2012. *Eight Days in September: The Removal of Thabo Mbeki*, Johannesburg: Picador Africa.

Davidson, B., 1992. *Africa: The Politics of Failure*, New York: The Socialist Register.

Du Bois, W. E. B., 1960 [1903]. *The Souls of Black Folk*, New York: Faucet World Library.

Frank, A. G., 1998. *ReORIENT: Global Economy in the Asian Age*, Berkeley, CA: University of California Press.

Frank, A. G. and Fuentes, M., 1990. 'Civil democracy: Social movements in recent world history', in A. Samir et al. (eds.), *Transforming the Revolution: Social Movements and the World System*, New York: Monthly Review Press, pp. 139–180.

Hochschild, A., 2006. *King Leopold's Ghost: A Story of Greed, Terror and Heroism in Colonial Africa*, London: Pan Books.

Houghton, R. 2011. Available at: www.houghton.hk.

James, C. L. R., 1980 [1938]. *The Black Jacobins: Toussaint L'Ouverture and the San Domingo Revolution*, London: Alison & Busby.

Legene, S. and Waaldijk, B., 2007. 'Mission interrupted: Gender, history and the colonial canon', in M. Greve and S. Stuurman (eds.), *Beyond the Canon: History for the Twenty First Century*, New York: Palgrave Macmillan.

Mamdani, M., 1999. 'Historicizing Power and Response to Power: Indirect Rule and Its Reform', *Social Research*, Volume 66 (3), pp. 859–886.

McCormack, G. and Gittings, J., 1977. *Crisis in Korea*, Nottingham: Spokesman Books.

Mommen, A., 1982. *De Teloorgang van de Belgische Bourgeoisie*, Leuven: Kritak.

Nimako, K., 1991. *Economic Economic Change and Political Conflict in Ghana*, Amsterdam: Thesis Publishers.

Nimako, K., 2007. 'African regional groupings and emerging Chinese conglomerates', in B. Hogenboom and A. E. Fernandez Jilberto (eds.), *Big Business and Economic Development: Conglomerates and Economic Groups in Developing Countries and Transition Economies under Globalization*, London: Routledge.

Nimako, K., 2010. 'Nkrumah, African Awakening and Neo-colonialism: How Black America Awakened Nkrumah and Nkrumah Awakened Black America', *The Black Scholar: Journal of Black Studies and Research*, Volume 40 (2), pp. 54–70.

Nimako, K., 2011. *Reorienting the World: With or Without Africa?*, MnM Working Paper No. 5, University of South Australia.

Nimako, K., 2014. 'Location and social thought in the black: A testimony of Africana intellectual tradition', in S. Broeck and C. Junker (eds.), *Postcoloniality–Decoloniality–Black Critique*, Frankfurt: Campus Verlag.

Nimako, K. and Willemsen, G., 2011. *The Dutch Atlantic: Slavery, Abolition and Emancipation*, London: Pluto.

Sachs, W., 2009. *The Development Dictionary: A Guide to Knowledge as Power*, 2nd ed., London: Zed Books.

Schlesinger, S. C., 2003. *Act of Creation: The Founding of the United Nations: A Story of Superpowers, Secret Agents, Wartime Allies and Enemies, and Their Quest for a Peaceful World*, Cambridge, MA: Westview Press.

Sian, K. P., 2014. *Conversations in Postcolonial Thought*, New York: Palgrave Macmillan.

Subramanian, A., 2011. *Eclipse: Living in the Shadow of China's Economic Dominance*, Washington, DC: Peterson Institute for International Economics.

Wallerstein, I., 1990. 'Antisystemic movements: History and dilemmas', in S. Amin et al. (eds.), *Transforming the Revolution: Social Movements and the World System*, New York: Monthly Review Press, pp. 13–53.

Wallerstein, I., 2004. *World System Analysis: An Introduction*, Durham, NC: Duke University Press.

4

SOUTH ASIAN MUSLIMS IN EAST AFRICA

Iqbal Akhtar

Introduction

This chapter[1] aims to answer the question, how have Asian[2] Muslims transformed the religious geography of East Africa[3] over the past two centuries? The history of Asian Muslims in East Africa is one of transition from traditional Indic religions to modern Islam through colonization. The place of Asians in East African society so drastically deteriorated with the end of colonization that many became dispossessed and were forced to migrate to Western Europe and North America. Their legacy in East Africa is the social institutions they have developed, such as the Aga Khan Hospital in Dar es Salaam, and their affect on religious demographics, such as the Bilal Muslim Mission's conversion of thousands of Africans to Twelver Shiism. This chapter is organized sequentially, beginning with current scholarship, continuing on to mapping the demographics of the communities differentiated by creed and caste, highlighting the discontinuities of the postcolonial experience, and finally assessing the legacy and extrapolating future trajectories based on past experiences. The legacy of millennia of classical Asian contact with East Africa is sparse.[4] The current Asian communities of Eastern, Central, and Southern Africa originated with a trickle of permanent migration to the Swahili coast at the turn of the nineteenth century. By the 1830s there were established coastal settlements in Bagamoyo, Kilwa, Lamu, Malindi, Mombasa, Pangani, and Zanzibar among others (Ghai & Ghai, 1960:3). Zanzibar, part of the Omani empire, was the centre of East African trade and in 1840 Sultan Seyyid Said transferred the capital from Muscat to Zanzibar. The sultan understood the need for Asian mercantile skills and created an environment conducive to immigration from the Subcontinent. Asians formed an economic class which financed Arab plantations and trading caravans to the interior of the continent (Delf, 1963:1–4). By the turn of the twentieth century, there were 7,000 Asians in Zanzibar alone, 5% of the population (Appletons, 1903:225). For Asian Muslims, being in Sultanate territories brought these communities in contact with Arab forms of Islam, such as Sufism and Ibadism, that began to change their own understandings of an Islamic identity in praxis.

The arrival of Europeans into East Africa with the Scramble for Africa divided Asian communities among European colonial regimes whose policies favoured white settlers in land acquisition, particularly in the highlands, and instituted legal forms of racial discrimination. Despite these handicaps, their laissez-faire economic policies allowed Asians to develop the region economically. It was partially through asserting control over Asian merchants that the British asserted increasing economic control over East Africa (Sheriff, 1987; Bhacker, 1992). Apart from the great Muslim Asian traders and philanthropists of the earlier period, such as Nasser Nurmohammed, Alidina Visram, Tharia Topan, and Karimjee Jivanjee (Gregory, 1992; Oonk, 2014), the majority of Asians in East Africa who remained until the postcolonial period were working-class traders. These small traders, known in Swahili as *dukawalla* (from *dukān*, Gujarati for shop), pioneered the general store and developed supply lines for the importing of finished manufactured products and the exporting of raw materials in trilateral trade among South Asia, the Near East, and East Africa (Nicolini, 2004). As Gregory summarizes regarding their colonial success, Asian 'industry, ingenuity, thrift, and education were bound eventually to bring wealth' (Gregory, 1971:21).

Scholarship

The majority of scholarship in English[5] on Asians in East Africa develops during the period of decolonization and after the 1972 Asian expulsion from Uganda. It is during this period that the Asians were problematized as a remnant of European colonization. Asian economists from East Africa, such as Dharam Ghai (Ghai & Ghai, 1970) and Yash Tandon (Tandon, 1973a, 1973b), as well as Indian journalists such as Prem Bhatia, brought attention and rigour to understanding their dilemma. European-Kenyan Cynthia Salvadori captured the last memories and documents from the descendants of the pioneering generation of Asians who left the Subcontinent in the nineteenth century in *Through Open Doors* (Salvadori, 1983), *We Came in Dhows* (Salvadori, 1996), *Two Indian Travellers: East Africa, 1902–1905* (Salvadori, 1997), and *Settling in a Strange Land* (Salvadori, 2010). Rigorous academic research of colonial archives by scholars such as Robert Gregory (Gregory, 1971) and J.S. Mangat (Mangat, 1969) explored the complex economic and racial interests that were being negotiated in the colonial period with the development of Asian communities in East Africa. Decisive anthropological work by Agehananda Bharati (Bharati, 1972), Hatim Amiji (Amiji, 1975), and Richa Nagar (Nagar, 1998) has described the negotiation of nineteenth-century mercantile caste identity, religion, and social mores with postcolonial African nationalism and globalization in the twentieth century. The development of Indian Ocean Studies has reinvigorated the field in reframing Asian East Africans as inhabiting fluid geographies of commerce and identity (Sheriff, 1987; Bertz, 2015).

While tremendous work has been done to record and theorize the Asian experience in East Africa, gaps remain in fully assessing the Asian influence on East African Islam as vernacular languages and publications have not been used in the writing of Asian African history. Much of the focus of detailed Asian histories centres on a limited reading of colonial and postcolonial archives in European languages which privileges materials from the colonial encounter. Intra-caste Indic language materials are almost completely ignored and only cited in translation. Throughout East Africa there are hundreds of folios of untranslated *hūṇḍīpatrī* (bills of exchange and ledgers). Books and pamphlets were published in East Africa in Kacchī, Punjabi, Gujarati, and Urdu over the past century documenting religious rites, polemics, histories, and political plat-forms. In South Asia, Indic vernacular histories, such as *Khōjā Vṛttānt* (Annals of the Khōjā), document the Khōjā migration to East Africa. Dialects, such as Zanzibari Kacchī-Swahili and Luwati, are functionally extinct and have not been systematically recorded, much less studied. Either scholars do not have the linguistic expertise to engage with the materials or do not see the materials as having value for the questions they are asking about African–Asians. This is in contrast to Arabic and Swahili manuscripts from the coast, which have been meticulously gathered and translated, and are seen as authoritative in their historical telling.

Also, community historians and the average experiences of Asians, particularly the poor and women, are not always engaged with on an equal level to the grander narratives of the great Asian merchants. Families in these countries have photographs, legal documents, and oral histories that create richer stories about the African–Asian experience. Asian exiles and immigrants in North America and Western Europe, such as Zanzibaris and Ugandans, have numerous websites (Fazal, n.d.) and listservs (electronic mailing lists) (Manek, 2000) that document their family stories. While Asians were connected to their caste communities and had a share in communal goods and institutions, the African experience was also one marked by the oppression of poverty and caste elites, particularly for widows and orphans. Popular African–Asian writers, such as M.G. Vassanji and Yasmin Alibhai-Brown, reinforce narratives of alienation and culpability that reduce the multitude of experiences across class, caste, and gender. Microhistories focusing on families, locales, and castes using a combination of European and Indic materials can open new avenues for research that is sensitive to these particularities.

Demography

Who were the Asians that settled in East Africa? They could be historically classified into three main categories: labour, professionals (civil servants/soldiers), and merchants. Professionals comprised the smallest category and brought with them skills necessary for the administration of the colonies. The push factor for labour and merchant castes in the nineteenth century included famines and droughts throughout South Asian, particularly in Kacch and Kathiawar in 1812–1813, 1838–1839, 1869 (Balfour, 1885:1139), and 1899–1900. Colonial schemes of agricultural and railroad labour promoted immigration to Uganda and Kenya from the Punjab. Of the 32,000 indentured labourers brought to build the Uganda Railroad, only 6,724 remained after its completion, the plurality having returned to India and the rest having died during construction (Ghai & Ghai, 1960:4). The majority of Asians in East Africa, unlike most colonial indentured labour emigration from the Subcontinent, were free traders from the region of present-day Gujarat. Sultanate and early colonial policies imposed minimal restrictions on the migration of Gujarati[6] Asian merchant caste members to East Africa. These kinship networks allowed Asians to emigrate with minimal means to East Africa; they were then put to work on arrival in family businesses until they were able to accumulate capital to open their own businesses. Similarities can be seen between East African Asian merchant networks and those of Fujian-Chinese communities in Malaysia.

The Sunni

Caste membership was the historical determinant for communal success in East Africa. Muslim Asians can be divided into five regional and three sectarian categories: Balochi, Konkani, Punjabi, Sindhi, and Gujarati as well as Sunni, Shia, and Aḥmadiyya. The Balochis are the smallest Sunni community and have their origins as mercenaries of the Omani and Zanizbari sultans and traders. There is a strong connection with the Omani empire as Makran was part of this trilateral trade network. The port of Gwadar was part of Oman from 1797 to 1958, when it was incorporated into Pakistan. Their private language in Balochi is an Iranian tongue. The Konkani Muslims are from the coastal part of the state of Maharashtra, which includes Bombay. Their history also includes both mercantile connections to the oceanic economy and technical skills that were useful in colonial projects, such as the railways. Unlike the Goans who have forsaken an Indic identity for a paradoxically local African and European (Portuguese) identity, Kŏṅkaṇī Muslims still speak their ancestral language, though, as with all Asian Muslims in Anglophone Africa, the Indic tongues are giving way to English. The Punjabi Muslims are predominantly

Sunni, though there are Shia Punjabis who are connected to the Khōjā Ithnā 'Asharī community in Kenya. Punjabis primarily came as cultivators, some indentured, and as artisans.

There are also Kacchī and Suratī Muslim communities that are primarily mercantile (Salvadori, 1983:133–195).[7] There is a smaller community of Suratī and a larger Kacchī Sunni Muslim community. For locale grouped Muslim communities, such as Kacchī Sunni Muslims, there are many labour and artisan castes represented, including Sōnāra (goldsmith), Hajām (barber), Kumbhār (potter), Junējā (herdsman), and Bhaḍālā (seaman). In contrast to geographical groupings of Muslim communities, the transnational castes represented have a higher degree of organization and commercial success.

The most significant transnational Asian Sunni Muslim caste, by far, are the Mēmaṇ. Their homeland is the geographic stretch between modern Sindh and Gujarat, which was partitioned in 1947. The majority of Mēmaṇ in the Subcontinent now reside in Karachi. Their language is based on dialects of Sindhi and Kacchī. The term Mēmaṇ comes from their conversion to Islam, from the Arabic *mu'min* 'believer' (Poonawala, 1997) and, as with most Asian Muslims, their conversion is believed to be attributed to Sufi saints, in this case Syed Usaf. Their origins are connected to the conversion to Islam from the Lōhāṇā castes of Sindh, Kacch and western Saurashtra. For all these Sunni groups, there are various sub-caste, regional, and familial identities within the larger ethnic and linguistic category. For example, among the African Mēmaṇ the majority's origins lay in Nasserpur, Sindh, hence Nasserpurias, with a minority of Halais, Akais, Dhokas, Dhoraji Bhavnagari, and Veravadas from Kathiawar and Dhokas from Ahmedabad (Koga, 1991). Mēmaṇ dominance and organization of Sunni Hanafi Islam in East Africa can be seen in their construction and leadership of Asian mosques. Other Sunni communities do have mosques but fewer institutions, and apart from the Mēmaṇ, Sunni Asian Muslims are much less cohesive than Asian Shias, perhaps due to the oppositional identity of Shiism.

The Shia

Shias differ from Sunni in their approach to Islam, with a greater focus on the family of the Prophet in the transmission of religious authority. As such, Shiism tends towards a more defined hereditary religious hierarchy. The two main Shia communities in East Africa are the Khōjā and Bōhrā.

The Khōjā originated, according to tradition, from medieval Punjab and Kashmir, then migrated down the Indus valley and eastward to what is now Gujarat. As with the Mēmaṇ, their conversion is attributed to a Sufi, in this case Pīr Sadaradīn whose shrine is in the city of Ucch in lower Punjab. The arrival of the Aga Khan I in the early nineteenth century created a foundational schism in the Khōjā community. The first group to reject the Aga Khan's leadership and claim of community's property and tithings were the *bārbhā'ī*[8] (twelve brothers) who refused to pay the 12.5% tithing to the mother of Aga Khan I in 1828–1829. The issue reached a crisis in the famous 1866 case in which the Bombay High Court sided with the Aga Khan (Purohit, 2012). The dissenters were *jñātibahār* (outcastes)[9] and formed the core of a nascent Sunni Khōjā community in Bombay. In Zanzibar, there were about five documented Sunni Khōjā families at the time the schism officially reached the shores of East Africa during the visit of Aga Khan III in 1899.

By the late nineteenth century another schism developed among the Āgākhānī Khōjā, the Khōjā majority followers of the Aga Khan. Aside from taxation, control of community assets, and what was perceived as rule by diktat, this group objected to the westernization of Khōjā religion. Edicts by Aga Khan III coalesced religious identity around his orders and the vernacular *jñān* literature. More normative Islamic practices, such as *namājh* (ritual prayers) and *majlīs* (ritual commemorations), were banned. The outcastes embraced a normative Ithnā 'Asharī identity, whereas the Aga Khan and his followers defined a novel, modern Ismailism (Boivin, 2003; Green, 2013). In East Africa, the Khōjā Ismaili and Ithnā 'Asharī communities established parallel institutions that developed and served their community as well as that of Africans, such as the Aga Khan University Hospital and Al Muntazir Academy respectively, in Dar es Salaam. Their primary languages of personal communication in Anglophone East Africa are Kacchī, Gujarati, Swahili, and English (Akhtar, 2015).

The Bōhrā are an Ismaili community whose religious leadership has roots in medieval Yemen, where the Fatimid community there sided with al-Ṭayyib in the succession dispute of 1132. The majority of Bōhrā are of the Dā'ūdī branch, within the Ṭayyibī community whose headquarters are in India, with a population of approximately one million.[10] As with many of these Asian castes in East Africa, their community straddles Kacch and Kathiawar, particularly the cities of Mumbai, Surat, Ahmadabad, Ujjain, Jamnagar, Indore, Dohad, Nagpur, Udaipur, Rajkot, Pune, Kolkata, Chennai, and Karachi (Qutbuddin, n.d.). It is said that whereas the Khōjā originate from the *vaiśya* (merchant) class (Nānajī'āṇī, 1892:1–5), the Bōhrā, as per their namesake (Gujurati. *vōrō* 'trader', Sanskrit *vōhaharō*, a mixed tribe) (Belsare, 2002:1074), are traders that are, primarily, descendants of the Brahmin priestly class and of cultivators (Rāndērī, 1925:42–43). The written legacy of Arabic Bōhrā manuscripts and their aesthetics hint at this high caste theory, though a systematic study of Bōhrā Indic origins is not available.[11] The community's conversion was also impacted by the Mughal Emperor Awrangzīb who forced members to convert to Sunni Islam, creating the Sunni Bōhrā known as the (Ja'farī) Vōhrā. The Bōhrā, similar to the Ithnā 'Asharī Khōjās, believe that their Imam of the age is concealed. Therefore, the Imam's representative, *dā'ī*, continues the Imam's mission on earth and he should be obeyed (Blank, 2001).

The extent of that obedience was in dispute in East Africa, as its development was outside of the direct control of the leader, who resided in Surat during the nineteenth century and then in Bombay from the mid twentieth century until today. As with the Khōjā before the assertion of control by the Aga Khan, the geographic distance from the central authority in colonial India meant that the wealthy merchants of East Africa organized community affairs, built mosques, and established charitable institutions for their caste (Gregory, 1992). For the Africa Bōhrā, one important clan was the Karimjee Jivanjee family (Oonk, 2014). The mid twentieth century saw a reassertion of control by the leader in Bombay, Mohammed Burhanuddin. Burhannuddin increased direct control over Bōhrā properties in East Africa and the collection of tithings, and instituted conservative Islamic requirements, such as the imposition of the veil in 1977 (Ghadially, 1989). Reformist Bōhrā thinkers, such as Ali Asghar Engineer, were outcast because they attempted to weaken the power of the leadership and institute liberal reforms, such as public accountability, through polemics, lawsuits, legislative lobbying, and public agitation (Wright, 2003). Ultimately, both in India and East Africa, these efforts failed to weaken control over the community or create a mass movement for reform and financial transparency from within. Throughout East Africa the result can be seen in Bōhrā mosques, which were founded by local Bōhrā merchants in the nineteenth and twentieth centuries. Burhannuddin instituted a removal of the traditional East African mosque façade for a neo-Fatimid exterior. As of 2012, the last traditional façade on the metropolitan coast was that of the Bōhrā mosque in central Dar es Salaam.

The Aḥmadiyya

The Aḥmadi movement holds that Mīrzā Ghulām Aḥmad (d. 1908) was a reviver of Islam as per a traditional saying of the Prophet which holds that each century a reviver is sent to invigorate Islam. The majority Ahmadiyya Muslim Community (AMC) also believe that Aḥmad was the foretold Mahdi and promised messiah. The minority Lahori community only believe the former. Pakistani Ordinance XX passed in 1984 essentially criminalized the practice of the religion as a form of Islam and there is hostility to the community in many Muslim majority countries because of an apparently etic belief that the Ahmadi believe in Ahmad as a prophet after Muhammad. This is viewed as a heterodox position by the majority of Muslims who believe Muhammad was the final prophet.

The first Ahmadi to settle East Africa were Munshi Muhammad Afzal and Mirza Abdullah in 1896; they were followed by Dr. Muhammad Ismail Giryanwi, who was a military doctor brought to the Sultan of Zanzibar (Ahmadiyya Muslim Community of Tanzania, 2015). The community was also an early translator of the Quran into Swahili, for mass distribution. The 1953 translation riled the Sunni authorities in the region, such as Shaykh al-Fārsī, the *qāḍī* of Zanzibar after the revolution of Kenya (Khan, 1987). The Ahmadi community of East Africa, as in most communities in the developing world, is dominated by the AMC, engaged in pros- elytization and development, and can be seen as a threat by other Asian Sunni leaders. This is the case in Eastern and Southern Africa. Perhaps because of the religious, cultural, and settle- ment histories of West Africa, Ghana is perhaps the largest AMC community in East Africa with official recognition by the state.[12] Whereas the Shia Muslim communities tend not to engage with the Ahmadi, it is Sunni Asians who take umbrage at their presence and prosely- tization in East Africa, based on modern Pakistani religio-political polemics. From 1982 to 1985, there was an unsuccessful case[13] in South Africa that tried to do in South Africa what was ultimately successful in Pakistan, the official denouncement of the Ahmadi as non-Muslim and official ostracism. The modernization of South Asian Islam brought with it ideological exclusivity, as evidenced by the Deobandis, which has had an impact even on the pragmatic mercantile Mēmaṇ.

Caste communities and colonial success

South Asian Muslim institutions in the East African littoral begin to develop in the early and mid nineteenth century in ports such as Bagamoyo, Lamu, Kilwa Kivinje, and Zanzibar. From the littoral, settlements expanded up-country, into the interior, so that by the mid twentieth century hundreds of Asian communities could be found in urban and rural communities in the heart of Africa. The colonial regimes and demographics differed from what are now Uganda, Kenya, and Tanzania. Kenya and Uganda are heavily Christian, with Muslims concentrated on the Swahili coast. Tanganyika and Zanzibar had a much greater concentration of Muslims and fewer European settlers. Uganda differed somewhat in that Asians were also substantial land- owners. In Tanganyika, approximately 98% of buildings were owned by Asians before independence (Aminzade, 2014:226). In Zanzibar, the plantation and trade economies were financially dominated by Asian merchants.

Muslims were among the most successful Asian communities in East Africa, and among the Muslims, it has been caste communities that have benefited the most from the sultanate and colonial periods by acquiring new skills and languages, sharing risk, and wealth redistribution. Endogamy played an important part in creating reciprocal trust relationships for long-distance financing. While there have been successful merchants in all the Asian communities of East Africa, the Mēmaṇ, Khōjā, and Bōhrā have been among the more organized in ensuring the development of institutions, endowments, and welfare for the poorer members of their com- munity. By their nature, merchants are pragmatic and tend towards an apolitical identity that is aligned to state loyalty, in the case of the British, loyalty to the crown and its courts. As an ethnic minority, they were all the more aware of their minority status and that their security was based upon carving a niche between colonial regimes and the local population through the creation of social and religious institutions. By doing so, these communities were able to establish *jamātkhānā* (caste halls), charitable dispensaries, and schools. Institutions founded with Khōjā money and leadership, such as the Aga Khan hospitals and schools, are still today the premier institutions in postcolonial Africa.

The sultanate and colonial periods did not demand assimilation into a larger national identity, simply loyalty to the crown. Asian communities, Muslims, Hindus, Sikhs, and Jains, lived parallel lives in which there was public commercial interaction and private insularity. And yet, British colonization ultimately alienated Asians from their own heritages, languages, and cultures. Technically, British rule was 'strongly anti-assimilationist and guided by Lord Lugard's theories on indirect rule through existing indigenous institutions', whereas the French pursued 'a policy of direct rule of their colonial subjects and their assimilation into the French way of life' (Crowder, 1967:1). And yet the overall impact of colonial rule on Asian languages in East Africa and thereby the preservation of ancestral culture, mores, and distinct identities was quite the opposite. Latin colonization (Belgian, French, Italian and Portuguese) in East Africa allowed Asians to better preserve their languages, such as Gujarati, as private and mercantile languages. The power of colonial English on the Asian psyche as evinced by Macaulay's 'Minute on Indian Education' combined with the ascendency of English as the global language has meant that Indic ancestral languages that have millennia of provenance have essentially died out among Anglophone Muslim Asians in the past 30 years. The Hindu castes of the Bhāṭiyā and Lōhāṇā, among others, have better maintained Gujarati because it is tied to religious rituals and devotion. Notwithstanding, even among them the decline in competency among the youth has been dramatic and apparently irreversible despite attempts by communal leaders to invigorate interest in language and heritage as a way of preserving a distinct identity and morality.

Postcolonial loss

The end of colonization represented a discontinuity with the sultanate and colonial periods in which Asian communities were able to develop economic and social institutions largely free of state coercion. By the mid twentieth century Asian populations had been dispersed throughout eastern, central, and southern Africa. While these societies did not have the same level of multiracial populations as those of contemporary North America or Western Europe, there was a sufficient penetration of non-black populations into the continent for the coast to already have an ancient heritage of multicultural assimilation. As in the Transvaal, the East African Asians became the 'Indian problem' (Pillay, 1976:i–xvii). The forms of African nationalism that developed accorded little space for the multiculturalism of the Swahili experience. To be indigenous meant to be black, and Asians were associated with agents of colonialism even though colonization discriminated, de facto and de jure, against Asians and some even pushed for independence, such as Pio Gama Pinto. Continuing colonial policies, Asian Muslims were categorized by the postcolonial state primarily as Asians. Muslim solidarity with black African coreligionists vis-à-vis Islam and the *umma* was largely irrelevant in communal relations and state policies.[14] They are seen as Asian first and Muslim second, if at all, for communities such as the Ahmadiyya.

The 'Indian problem' was an etic view of Asians as foreigners who were exploiting Africa and the Africans for their own wealth and refusing to assimilate. This meant three things. First, there was the charge that Asian merchants, particularly in the interior where there was little competition, would overcharge at the expense of the African farmer or labourer – that Asian merchants were selling African resources for their own gain and then depositing their wealth abroad. Second, Asians held better government and professional positions than did many Africans.[15] Their institutions, such as schools, and mercantile knowledge, such as accounting and English, made them more useful for colonial and European mercantile endeavours. Third, Asians have historically tended towards endogamy. While biracial Afro-Asian children were borne, mainland Asian Muslims tended to marry within caste and certainly race. In Zanzibar and other port cities in the littoral, such as Zanzibar (Akhtar, 2014) and Muscat, there was more of a possibility of liaison or marriage with Swahili,[16] Arab, and Iranian women. The lack of assimilation charge meant that Asians not marrying Africans was seen as an Asian sense of superiority over the African. These tropes are still revived and suppressed today against Asians; the most recent in Tanzania was Idi Simba's calls for indigenization of the Tanzanian economy (Aminzade, 2014:334–335).

The language of 'problem' is reminiscent of the development of European nationalism in which the development of states encompassed more than an idealized monolithic nation. There is a sense of this in Julius Nyerere's Swahili translation of the *Merchant of Venice* (*Mabepari wa Venisi*). Antonio is equated with Shylock as a capitalist and translated as *mabepari* (Gujarati, *vēpārī* meaning merchant).

> The East African Indian, then, is evoked through a series of displacements, both within the play and without it, by the figure of a European Jew, and this in a way that ends up problematising East Africa itself as a context for his subjectivity.
>
> *(Devji, 2000:182)*

The Asian is framed as the existential other, reviled for his supposed exploitation and perpetually the outsider. This is a common pattern among majoritarian attitudes towards 'middlemen minorities' (Bonacich, 1973), such as Jews in Europe and the Chinese in Southeast Asia.

Each of the three postcolonial countries, Kenya, Tanzania, and Uganda, pursued policies that changed a century of coexistence in which African-born Asians and Europeans lived. Tanzania's Arusha Declaration of 1967 began the process of state control of commerce and nationalizing all the land and property, which made paupers of Europeans and Asians. So hostile was the government that there are few, if any, indigenous Europeans in Tanzania who pre-date independence. For example, there was a thriving Greek agricultural community but the well maintained St. Paraskevi Orthodox Cathedral in Dar es Salaam is a now hollow vestige. The postcolonial state was seen as undermining the rule of law–property rights, control over religious endowments, and capricious enforcement of rules and regulations.

The greatest urban concentration of Asian communities and institutions was in Zanzibar. The Zanzibar revolution on 12 January 1964 forced an almost immediate depopulation of the non-black population and is regarded by the majority of Tanzanians as wholly positive. Other narratives were not publicly tolerated; there was less support for the genocide of between 3,000 and 11,000 Zanzibar Arabs and their exile of almost 30% of the population (Sheriff, 2001:314). Additionally, four Iranian women were forced into marriage with revolutionary leaders in an attempt to forcibly assimilate the non-black population. On the mainland, both men and women were forced into mandatory national service in order to continue their education, which was traumatic for many (Bhikhabhai, 2014). Beyond the loss of patrimony, the perceived loss of power and female autonomy affected the confidence Asians had in an African future.

Kenya, while suffering more violence in the colonial and postcolonial periods, is the only country of the three that has retained a substantial European population from the colonies, though even in Kenya, state policies almost eliminated Asians in government positions and focused on weakening Asian business interests. This anti-Asian sentiment of similar threads throughout East Africa reached its logical conclusion with the expulsion of Asians from Uganda in 1972 by Idi Amin. The impact of the Ugandan exodus reverberated within Asian communities throughout East Africa. From the Zanzibar revolution to the expulsion, the families of talented professionals, shopkeepers with connections abroad, and the wealthy from East Africa left en masse. This period provided an opening for migration to Western Europe and North America before the era of increasing restrictions on migration to the Global North. Asians had no military power in East Africa and yet, remarkably, were not targeted for genocide in Zanzibar and were not among the approximately half a million killed during Amin's rule. It is possible that a combination of the image of newly independent postcolonial African states on the international stage, the reluctant connection of Britain to the fate of Asians, and the role of India as leader of the non-aligned movement helped to resolve the 'Indian problem' through expulsion, emigration, and integration.

For those unable to leave, most lost a century of resources that had been accumulated individually and communally. Essentially, the advantage that Asian communities had in commerce was lost and perhaps that was the point. The collapse of both the Zanzibari and Ugandan economies with the exodus of minorities sent a strong message to future postcolonial African leaders of the cost of such policies. The economic integration of East Africa into the global economy and international commitments since the 1990s make the possibility of such policies in the future remote. Regardless, the era of East Africa as the pioneering frontier for the merchant communities of Gujarat and Sindh has come to a close.

To survive economically in postcolonial East Africa, Asian merchants have had to get involved in the informal economy, work with unsavoury regimes, and overall survive in very challenging conditions in which African state officials see Asian businesses as extractive for bribes and a challenge to the black African bourgeoisie (Trovão & Batoréu, 2013). The economies of Sub-Saharan Africa have great potential for future growth and development, much more than developed economies, but there is a high cost in doing business, from lack of infrastructure and basic utilities to corruption and graft at all levels. Throughout East Africa with the abandonment of the parastatal model, South African multinationals and Chinese entrepreneurs have been able to bring sufficient capital and political power to increase their share of the economy. Asian industrialists such as the Khōjā Ithnā 'Asharī of Tanzania Mohammed Dewji (Forbes.com, 2015), have been able to achieve success based on local knowledge and relationships that hinder foreign investors. But the colonial economy was one that was relatively open to all members of the caste. Merchants would pool start-up capital for entrepreneurs and spread risk among family members. Those basic entrepreneurial skills are no longer sufficient for economic success. Asians have abandoned the hinterland for major metropolises where technical skills and professionalism are rewarded in the twenty-first-century economy. Caste connections are more important than ever in helping to fund university education through student loans, business connections for employment, and emigration by marriage to caste members in the Global North. Ultimately, there are too many people to successfully emigrate to Western Europe and North America in an era of increasing immigration restrictions for Muslims. Other options are emigration to other developing countries such as Malaysia and the UAE or to more fully integrate to the local economy. For well-resourced business people, East Africa can yield great opportunities for profit not available in developed economies. But for the average trader, the cost of maintaining a middle-class lifestyle is a hand-to-mouth existence. Despite postcolonial successes in the aftermath of nationalisation and exodus, there is a sense that the future of Asians in East Africa lies westward. Ironically, educated Asians from South India are recruited on term contracts by Asian and African firms to bring education and technical expertise lacking in the local labour market.

Conclusion: the legacy and future

The legacy of the African experience for Asians has been positive on the whole. It cemented caste organizations and allowed a Pan-Asian ethos of cooperation and mutual respect to develop that would be very difficult to envision in the megacity of Karachi or 'shock city' of Ahmedabad (Spodek, 2011). While caste organization became increasingly hierarchical and organized among the Shia communities, it came at the cost of Islamic religious diversity and Indic culture. The downside of a highly organized caste is that dissent and alternative human experiences are marginalized for an increasingly conservative and ideological vision of the community's past and present. East African Asian communities have helped to bolster the presence of Muslim communities in public discourse in a hostile political environment where Islam is increasingly equated with extremism.

The ideological uniformity of Islam, shared rituals, avowed egalitarianism, and communal identity transformed certain Indic merchant castes into cohesive communally driven economic communities, such as the Bōhrā and Khōjā, which ensured social welfare for their members. On balance, the Asian Muslim experience in East Africa was different from that of Hindus, Sikhs, and Jains in that for Muslims there was a greater degree of cultural assimilation. Whereas the other Indic communities saw the Subcontinent as their spiritual home and anchored themselves thus, Asian Muslims of the western Indian Ocean littoral were within an Arabic and Persian cultural sphere that allowed their religious identity to strengthen at the expense of their Indic heritage. At its most developed, it meant cultural and linguistic assimilation as with the Sunni and Khōjā communities of Oman and Zanzibar. Africa became a new home, no longer a place of temporary settlement awaiting the end of exile and return to an ancestral land. The Asian Muslims of today are caught in the battle for the soul of Africa between Christian and Muslim missionary movements. Of course, puritanical Sunni missionaries see the Khōjā Ithnā 'Asharī and Ahmadiyya as heretical, but their institutions and communal wealth have gained thousands of converts through development and education.

The future of Asian Muslims in East Africa is likely to continue on the current trajectories established in the postcolonial period. The wealthiest and most qualified who can migrate to Western Europe and North America will continue to do so. Wealthy industrialists contribute to their communities by maintaining institutions and assisting their poorest members. Transnational linkages, such as the Aga Khan Development Network of the Khōjā Ismaili, provide political and economic clout for domiciled communities. The East African state is at best benignly negligent and at worst extractive and punitive towards Asians. The larger trends of global Islam, such as Salafism and pan-Shiism, shape the identity of communities as they identify themselves as primarily Islamic at the cost of Kacchī and Kāṭhiyāvāḍī ethnic identities. Because there is no official multicultural vision for East Africa, in contrast to South Africa, East African Asian Muslims will be at best endured for the foreseeable future.

Notes

1 I am indebted to Abdul Sheriff for recommending me for this volume and to Tehsin Takim, Alia Paroo, Zafreen Jaffery, and Zahir Bhalloo for their useful comments in completing this chapter.
2 The term Asian is used both as an emic category and as a way to refer to the peoples of the Subcontinent without the connection to the postcolonial national project that 'Indian' implies. Asian Muslim communities in East Africa, particularly, do not necessarily see themselves as Indian, which is commonly understood to refer to Hindus, and find a closer affinity to Pakistan as an Islamic homeland encompassing part of the these communities' ancestral home. In Swahili, the term *mhindi* (pl. *wahinidi*) is etic and refers to all Asians without religious, regional, or caste distinction. While it can be descriptive, *wahindi* can also be pejorative, similar to the historical use of 'Jew' in English.

3 East Africa is defined here as present-day Kenya, Uganda, and Tanzania – the core of the Swahiliphone and historically greater Zanzibar. This is also the region that was colonized by the British and shares commonalities of that experience, particularly their connection to the Anglophone world. The issues faced by Asians in surrounding nations were similar but had different outcomes due, among other things, to postcolonial warfare – such as in Burundi, Congo, Mozambique, Rwanda, and Somalia.

4 Future research on uncovering the considerable gaps in knowledge of Asian settlement prior to the nineteenth century, as compared with Southeast Asia, could include land and marine archaeological surveys, botanical sampling, genetic testing of populations, and other forms of anthropological research.

5 Because this region of East Africa was mostly under British rule, Anglophone scholars have dominated the scholarship of the region. Most French and German scholars working on the region have published in English. French scholars have demonstrated expertise on Asians in Francophone regions, such as Madagascar (Gandelot, 2014), and Germans on Deutsch-Ostafrika, and of course across European academia there is an unending fascination with Gandhi in South Africa.

6 The term Gujarati here is used for convenience. The idea of a Gujarati identity is a twentieth-century construct for these African communities. The Asian trading castes of East Africa were historically divided both linguistically, Kacch (Western Sindhi) and Kathiawar (Gujarati), as well as by city or village of origin, such as Bhuj or Bhavnagar.

7 The deepest division of Asians in East Africa within castes was the Kacch/Kathiawar divide and also subdivisions based on ancestral place of origin. After about the second generation, African localities replaced or augmented these divides.

8 Transliterated terms are generally from Gujarati, except for Arabic Islamic terminology referring to Near Eastern categories.

9 The early development of these mercantile caste identities is unclear. The majority of transnational Sindhi and Gujarati mercantile communities, such as the Bōhrā, Khōjā, Lōhāṇā, and Mēmaṇ, are amalgamations of communities that were brought into a larger identity that facilitated trade and transnational communal organization. Caste, historically, was linked and also above creed. Consequently, members of a caste could have various creedal practices. For modern Asian Muslims, this became less possible as creedal identities, rituals, and allegiances were standardized and tied to modern hierarchies of power. Hence, a Khōjā, by definition, is Muslim.

10 There are smaller communities of 'Alawī and Sulaymānī Bōhrā.

11 Alternative narratives of Bōhrā origins include Rājpūt, trading castes, and untouchables. The majority of materials on Bōhrā origins both in English and Gujarati focus on Bōhrā origins from the succession dispute during the Fatimid decline. The majority of Shia Asian communities view their pre-Islamic Indic origins as peripheral to their identity, focusing on their Near Eastern spiritual origins as central to their communal narrative. Rāndērī draws upon British scholarship on the Aryan theory to argue racial distinctions for origins of the Bōhrā and other Muslim communities in Gujarat.

12 During the main *jalsa* ('gathering') at London in 2015, the Ashanti King Osei Tutu II visited as an official honoured guest of Khalifa Mirza Masroor Ahmad.

13 The case *Ahmadiyya Anjuman Ishaat Islam Lahore (SA), Ismaili Peck v. The Muslim Judicial Council and Others* was tried in the Supreme Court of South Africa, Cape of Good Hope Provincial Division case number 10058/82 (Mohammad, 1987).

14 In Kenya and Tanzania, communities such as the Khōjā Bilal Muslim Mission (Bilal Muslim Mission of Tanzania, 2015) have increased intrafaith and interfaith meetings in response to perceptions of Christian hostility to Muslim personal law (Lodhi & Westerlund, 1997) and the rise of Salafism in the region.

15 Certain black African tribes were also successful in carving out an economic niche. The Chagga are an example of an African tribe that also benefited from capitalist opportunities in the colonial and postcolonial periods (Fisher, 2012).

16 The category of Swahili is a complex one. Here it is refers to coastal peoples who were Muslim, spoke local dialects of Swahili, and were racially different from the peoples of the interior.

Bibliography

Adamji, E. N. and Darookhanawala, S. M., 1997. 'Being accounts of journeys made by Ebrahimji N. Adamji, a very young Bohra merchant from Mombasa & Sorabji M. Darookhanawala, a middle-aged Parsi engineer from Zanzibar', in C. Salvadori and J. Aldrick (eds.), *Two Indian Travellers: East Africa, 1902–1905*, Mombasa: Friends of Fort Jesus.

Ahmadiyya Muslim Community of Tanzania, 2015, May 24. 'A brief history', Available at: http://ahmadiyyatz.org/a-brief-history [Accessed 12 January 2016].

Akhtar, I., 2014. 'Negotiating the Racial Boundaries of Khōjā Caste Membership in Late Nineteenth-Century Colonial Zanzibar (1878–1899)', *Journal of African Religions*, Volume 2 (3), pp. 297–316.

Akhtar, I., 2015. *The Khōjā of Tanzania: Discontinuities of a Postcolonial Religious Identity*, Leiden: Brill.

Alpers, E. A., 2009. *East Africa and the Indian Ocean*, Princeton, NJ: Markus Wiener Publishers.

Amiji, H., 1975. 'The Bohras of East Africa', *Journal of Religion in Africa*, Volume 7 (1), pp. 27–61.

Aminzade, R., 2014. *Race, Nation, and Citizenship in Postcolonial Africa: The Case of Tanzania*, Cambridge: Cambridge University Press.

Appletons, 1903. *Appletons Annual Cyclopædia and Register of Important Events of the Year* 1902 (Vol. XLII), New York: A. Appleton and Company.

Balfour, E., 1885. *The Cyclopædia of India and of Eastern and Southern Asia*, 3rd ed., London: Bernard Quaritch.

Belsare, M. B., 2002. *Etymological Gujarati–English Dictionary*, 2nd ed., New Delhi: Asian Educational Services.

Bertz, N., 2015. *Diaspora and Nation in the Indian Ocean: Transnational Histories of Race and Urban Space in Tanzania*, Honolulu: University of Hawaii Press.

Bhacker, M. R., 1992. *Trade and Empire in Muscat and Zanzibar: The Roots of British Domination*, Abingdon and Oxford: Routledge.

Bharati, A., 1972. *The Asians in East Africa: Jayhind and Uhuru*, Chicago: Nelson-Hall Co.

Bhatia, P., 1973. *Indian Ordeal in Africa*, Delhi: Vikas Publishing House.

Bhikhabhai, R., 2014, May 8. 'Life at national service camp', Available at: www.tanzaniatoday.co.tz/news/life-at-national-service-camp-by-rama-bhikhabhai [Accessed 8 January 2016].

Bilal Muslim Mission of Tanzania, 2015, June 29. 'BMM Tanzania head office organizes interfaith iftar', Available at: www.bilaltz.org/2015/06/29/bmm-tanzania-head-office-organizes-interfaith-iftar/ [Accessed 17 Jaunary 2016].

Blank, J., 2001. *Mullahs on the Mainframe: Islam and Modernity Among the Daudi Bohras*, 1st ed., Chicago: University of Chicago Press.

Boivin, M., 2003. *La Renovation du Shi'isme Ismaelien en Inde et eu Pakistan: d'après les Ecrits et les Discours de Sultan Muhammad Shah Aga Khan*, Abingdon and Oxford: Routledge.

Bonacich, E., 1973. 'A Theory of Middleman Minorities', *American Sociological Review*, Volume 38 (5), pp. 583–594.

Brennan, J. R., 2006. 'Blood Enemies: Exploitation and Urban Citizenship in the Nationalist Political Thought of Tanzania, 1958–75', *The Journal of African History*, Volume 47 (3), pp. 389–413.

Crowder, M., 1967. *Senegal: A Study of French Assimilation Policy*, 2nd ed., London: Methuen and Co. Ltd.

Delf, G., 1963. *Asians in East Africa*, London: Oxford University Press.

Desai, G., 2013. *Commerce with the Universe: Africa, India, and the Afrasian Imagination*, New York: Columbia University Press.

Devji, F., 2000. 'Subject to Translation: Shakespeare, Swahili, Socialism', *Postcolonial Studies*, Volume 3 (2), pp. 181–189.

Don Nanjira, D., 1976. *The Status of Aliens in East Africa: Asians and Europeans in Tanzania, Uganda, and Kenya*, New York: Praeger.

Fazal, M. H., n.d. 'The Dewani family tree', Available at: www.dewani.ca [Accessed 18 January 2016].

Fisher, T. J., 2012. 'Chagga Elites and the Politics of Ethnicity in Kilimanjaro', *Tanzania*, Edinburgh: Ph.D. Thesis, University of Edinburgh.

Forbes.com. 2015. 'Forbes: Africa's 50 richest: #21 Mohammed Dewji', Available at: www.forbes.com/profile/mohammed-dewji [Accessed 21 January 2016].

Frenz, M., 2014. *Community, Memory, and Migration in a Globalizing World: The Goan Experience, c. 1890–1980*, Oxford: Oxford University Press.

Gandelot, L., 2014. 'Les khojas Ismaïlis Agakhanis de Madagascar: des Gujaratis de l'Océan Indien (1885–1972): Communauté religieuse, politique et territoires', Paris: Ph.D. Thesis, Sorbonne Paris Cité – Université Paris Diderot-Paris 7.

Ghadially, R., 1989. 'Veiling the Unveiled: The Politics of Purdah in a Muslim Sect', *South Asia: Journal of South Asian Studies*, Volume 12 (2), pp. 33–48.

Ghai, D. P. and Ghai, Y. P., 1970. *Portrait of a Minority: Asians in East Africa*, Nairobi: Oxford University Press.

Ghai, Y. P. and Ghai, D. P., 1960. *Asians in East and Central Africa*, Nairobi: Oxford University Press.

Green, N., 2013. *Bombay Islam: The Religious Economy of the West Indian Ocean, 1840–1915*, Cambridge: Cambridge University Press.

Gregory, R. G., 1971. *India and East Africa: A History of Race Relations Within the British Empire*, Oxford: Clarendon Press.

Gregory, R. G., 1992. *The Rise and Fall of Philanthropy in East Africa: The Asian Contribution*, New Brunswick: Transaction Publishers.

Gregory, R. G., 1993. *South Asians in East Africa: An Economic and Social History, 1890–1980*, Boulder: Westview Press.

Joalahliae, R. M., 2010. *The Indian as an Enemy: An Analysis of the Indian Question in East Africa*, Bloomington: AuthorHouse.

Kabwegyere, T., 1976. 'The Asian Question in Uganda, 1894–1972', in W. Arens (ed.), *A Century of Change in Eastern Africa*, The Hague: Mouton Publishers, pp. 47–64.

Khan, M. H., 1987. 'Translations of the Holy Quran in the African languages', *The Muslim World*, Volume 77 (3–4), pp. 250–258.

Kiem, C. G., 1993. *The Asian Minority in East Africa: A Selected Annotated Bibliography*, Bielefeld: Forschungsschwerpunkt Entwicklungssoziologie, Universität Bielefeld, Fakultät für Soziologie.

Koga, M., 1991. *South Asian Community Organisations in East Africa, the United Kingdom, Canada & India*, Tokyo: ILCAA, Tokyo University of Foreign Studies.

Kusimba, C., Killick, D. and Cresswell, R., 1994. 'Indigenous and Imported Metals at Swahili Sites on the Coast of Kenya', *MASCA Papers in Science and Archaeology*, Volume 11, pp. 63–77.

Lodhi, A. and Westerlund, D., 1997. 'African Islam in Tanzania', in *Majoriteten Islam/Islam for the Masses*, London: Curzon Press, pp. 349–372.

Macaulay, T. B., 1835. 'Minute on Indian education', Available at: www.columbia.edu/itc/mealac/pritchett/00generallinks/macaulay/txt_minute_education_1835.html.

Manek, J., 2000. 'East Africa circle', *Yahoo Groups*. Available at: https://groups.yahoo.com/neo/groups/EAcircle/info [Accessed 18 January 2016].

Mangat, J. S., 1969. *A History of the Asians in East Africa, c.1886 to 1945*, Oxford: Clarendon Press.

Mohammad, M. S., 1987. *The Ahmadiyya Case* (Z. Aziz, Trans.), Newark: Ahmadiyya Anjuman Isha'at Islam Lahore Inc.

Nagar, R., 1998. 'Communal Discourses, Marriage, and the Politics of Gendered Social Boundaries Among South Asian Immigrants in Tanzania', *A Journal of Feminist Geography*, Volume 5 (2), pp. 117–139.

Nānajī'āṇī, S., 1892. *Khōjā Vṛttānt*, Amdāvād: Dhī Amarsinhajī Prī. Prēs.

Nicolini, B., 2004. *Makran, Oman, and Zanzibar: Three-Terminal Cultural Corridor in the Western Indian Ocean, 1799–1856*, Leiden: Brill.

Oonk, G., 2014. *The Karimjee Jivanjee Family: Merchant Princes of East Africa 1800–2000*, Amsterdam: Pallas Press.

Pillay, B., 1976. *British Indians in the Transvaal*, Bristol: Longman.

Poonawala, I., 1997. 'Memon', in P. Bearman, T. Bianquis, C. E. Bosworth, E. van Donzel and W. Heinrichs (eds.), *Encyclopaedia of Islam*, Leiden: Brill.

Purohit, T., 2012. *The Aga Khan Case: Religion and Identity in Colonial India*, Cambridge, MA: Harvard University Press.

Qutbuddin, T., n.d. 'Bohras', in K. Fleet, G. Krämer, D. Matringe, J. Nawas and E. Rowson (eds.), *Encyclopaedia of Islam, THREE*, 3rd ed., Leiden: Brill.

Rai, K., 1979. *Indians and British Colonialism in East Africa*, Patna: Associated Book Agency.

Rāndērī, M. Ā., 1925. *Gujarāt prāntnā sunni tathā śī'ā vōharā'ōnuṁitihāsik varṇan* (Pahēlī ed.), Sunrat: Ambikā Vijaya Prī. Prēs.

Salvadori, C., 1983. *Through Open Doors: A View of Asian Cultures in Kenya* (A. Fedders, ed.), Nairobi: Kenway Publications Ltd.

Salvadori, C., 1996. *We Came in Dhows*, Nairobi: Paperchase Kenya Ltd.

Salvadori, C., 1997. *Two Indian Travellers: East Africa, 1902–1905: Being Accounts of Journeys Made by Ebrahimji N. Adamji, a Very Young Bohra Merchant from Mombasa & Sorabji M. Darookhanawala, a Middle-Aged Parsi Engineer from Zanzibar*, Mombasa: Friends of Fort Jesus.

Salvadori, C., 2010. *Settling in a Strange Land: Stories of Punjabi Muslim Pioneers in Kenya*, Nairobi: Park Road Mosque Trust.

Sheriff, A., 1987. *Slaves, Spices, and Ivory in Zanzibar: Integration of an East African Commercial Empire into the World Economy, 1770–1873*, Athens, OH: Ohio University Press.

Sheriff, A., 2001. 'Race and Class in the Politics of Zanzibar', *Africa Spectrum*, Volume 36 (3), pp. 301–318.

Somia, V. J., 2001. *The Ancient History of the Solar Race: A History of the Indians of East Africa*, Bakewell, UK: Country Books.

Spodek, H., 2011. *Ahmedabad: Shock City of Twentieth-Century India*, Bloomington: Indiana University Press.

Tandon, Y., 1973a. *Problems of a Displaced Minority: The New Position of East Africa's Asians*, London: Minority Rights Group.

Tandon, Y., 1973b. *The Future of the Asians in East Africa*, London: Rex Collings.

Trovão, S. S. and Batoréu, F., 2013. 'What's New About Muslim Ismaili Transnationalism? Comparing Business Practices in British East Africa, Colonial Mozambique and Contemporary Angola', *African and Asian Studies*, Volume 12, pp. 215–244.

Vaudeville, C. and Mallison, F., 1994. 'Histoire et philologie de l'Inde médiévale et moderne', *Livret*, Volume 118 (4), pp. 157–158.

Waiz, S. A. (ed.), 1927. *Indians Abroad*, Bombay: Imperial Indian Citizenship Association.

Wright, Jr., T. P., 2003. 'Competitive modernization within the Daudi Bohra sect of Muslims and its significance for Indian political development', in *Competition and Modernization in South Asia*, New Delhi: Abhinav Publications, pp. 151–178.

Postcolonial interactions

5

RELIGION AND DEVELOPMENT IN AFRICA AND ASIA

Jörg Haustein and Emma Tomalin

Since the turn of the century, the religious dimension has been heralded as something of a new discovery in development practice and development studies. Secular donors have channelled increasing amounts of their budgets through so-called faith-based organisations (FBOs), a term which has itself emerged only in the past couple of decades to designate religious organisations working in the field of development. Governmental development offices have sought dialogue with religious communities, such as the UK's Department for International Development (DFID), which recently laid down its 'Faith Partnership Principles' (DFID, 2012). DFID has also funded a large-scale research project on Religions and Development, which was conducted at the University of Birmingham between 2005 and 2010 and continues to provide major resources on this subject.[1] Moreover, there has been a flurry of publications on the subject of religions and development in the past couple of decades (Salemink et al., 2004; Bornstein, 2005; Tyndale, 2006; Haynes, 2007; Clarke & Jennings, 2008; Deneulin, 2009; ter Haar, 2011b; M. Clarke, 2013a; Tomalin, 2013, 2015b; Rakodi, 2014).

The question we would like to pose in this chapter is whether religion really is a new dimension in development practice. In doing so, we seek to highlight, by way of a long history of religion and development engagement, how colonial and post-colonial powers have mapped their ideas about religion on to the so-called developing world in the name of the betterment of those countries. This long history, we argue, is crucial in enabling development theorists and practitioners to offer a critical and constructive perspective on this latest 'turn to religion' in development. Most publications place the origins of the development project with US President Harry S. Truman's second inaugural address in 1949, and go on to assert, more or less explicitly, that at the outset, development and religion were 'regarded in the West as emphatically separate concerns' (Haynes, 2007:1; cf. M. Clarke, 2013b; Deneulin, 2009; Korff & Schrader, 2004). From this vantage point, development appears as a secular project, which now has to accommodate the contemporary 'return of religion' to the public sphere. The problem with this approach is that it neglects the quintessential contribution of colonialism to the history of development thought and practice, and how early notions of development in Africa and Asia were linked to Christian missions and certain perceptions of other religions. Only a few scholars have pointed to a longer history of development and religion (ter Haar, 2011a; Tomalin, 2013; Deacon & Tomalin, 2015), but the details remain to be spelled out. There are also some publications which quite helpfully uncover the ideological roots of development thinking in the eighteenth and nineteenth centuries, but these do not sufficiently consider the colonial or religious dimensions (Cowne & Shenton, 1996; Preston, 1996).

In offering a long history of religion and development, we aim to better understand the ideological justification and practical limitations of various development regimes imposed on Africa and Asia from the nineteenth to the twenty-first century. Colonialism and its legacy thereby serve as our comparative bracket for understanding the relationship between Africa and Asia, as similar ideas and concepts were imposed on both continents. For Africa, the rather concentrated imperial phase of European colonialism, and the fairly homogeneous views it engendered on religion and development, make it possible to address this continent as a whole, despite its wide-ranging diversity in culture, geography, and political history, which is hardly properly acknowledged in most of our sources. For Asia, we have chosen the Indian subcontinent or South Asia as our main point of comparison, since it was the most intensively colonised region of Asia over several centuries, making it an appropriate case study with which to explore continuities and disjunctures between religion and development at different periods in time.

We begin our account with the colonial 'civilising mission', which created a platform for combining Christian missionary efforts and economic interests in a common imperial project, despite their at times diverging interests. Other religions were displaced or marginalised by a narrative of modernity and 'civilising' religion, unless they managed to adapt their religious outlook to the modernising project, like some Islamic, Hindu and Sikh reform movements in South Asia managed to do. The transformation of the global economy after the Second World War marked the next important transition, which we analyse in our second section. Decolonisation and the rise of the USA as a major global player was marked by the emergence of an optimistic vision of progress for 'underdeveloped' countries, imbued by notions of a modernity governed by science and rational macro-economic principles. This vision was compatible with both the emerging nationalist governments in the former African and Asian colonies and containing a feared Soviet ideological hegemony in the Cold War era. However, as we will show, it was not as immediately and fully secular as some have suggested, especially as this new development project did not fundamentally displace religious interests and organisations in development practice. Rather, the Western tendency to relegate religion to the 'private sphere' disabled donors and development strategists in accounting for religious interests and dynamics in the various factors influencing their work. Finally, the re-emergence of religion in development reasoning was closely related to the end of the Cold War and the rise of the religious right in the USA, as we show in our third section. Tracing the emergence and the limits of the category of FBO, we argue that the 'rediscovery' of religion in 'development' follows its colonial and post-colonial predecessors insofar as it parochialises religion and is only interested in its subsidiary functions for a development project whose ethos and aims are defined elsewhere. This latest 'turn to religion', therefore, emerges to be part of a longer history of projecting Western visions of society, religion and progress on to Africa and Asia – a common history which is at the core of the Africa–Asian relationship in religion and development.

The colonial 'civilising mission'

Religion and development as agents of empire

The nineteenth century marked a decisive shift in European colonialism, as the system of charter companies and trading outposts changed into one of imperial expansion and European control over almost all of Africa and large parts of Asia. Christian missions and advocacy groups were instrumental parts of this change as they infused the emerging imperial colonialism with religious sentiment from the start. How precisely was the relationship between Christian missions and colonial development efforts configured? What perceptions of development and religion did it produce and with what effects? And how did the colonised engage with these perceptions?

In Africa, this process had an important root in the British antislavery movement, which celebrated its first significant success in the Abolition of the Slave Trade Act of 1807. This fundamental political turn against the slave trade had been made possible, if not advantageous, by the larger geopolitical context of the time, most importantly the loss of the American colonies and the Napoleonic Wars. However, its passage would have been unlikely had it not been for the campaigns of the antislavery movement, a 'curious alliance of Enlightenment humanism and evangelical outrage'. (Reid, 2012:28; cf. Drescher, 2009:205–241). In 1833, the antislavery movement celebrated its second major victory when Britain abolished slave ownership altogether throughout the Empire.

However, despite these successes and the considerable British efforts in disrupting slavery transport through maritime raids and pressuring other countries to adopt similar policies, it had become clear by the late 1830s that slave raiding and trading in Africa had not diminished, but had actually increased. A new generation of antislavery advocates took on this cause. Amidst their brittle political alliances and theological differences, 'commerce and Christianity' emerged as a new guiding slogan, wrapped in a providentialist theology about the God-given British mission to the world (Stanley, 1983; Porter, 1985; Follett, 2008). The idea of 'commerce and Christianity' was to establish a 'legitimate trade' in Africa and Asia through a combination of entrepreneurial and missionary effort. If successful, this would end the detrimental practice of the slave trade and its related ailments and improve the respective countries by providing an economic alternative and incentive – a development thought to the core. Thomas Fowell Buxton (1768–1845), Quaker, abolitionist, member of parliament, and cofounder of the Anti-Slavery Society, provided the founding manifesto for this idea in his 1840 publication, *The African Slave Trade and Its Remedy* (Buxton, 1840). Contending that any effort to advance 'civilisation' and commerce in Africa must fail without the aid of Christianity, Buxton saw a necessary conflation of religion and development:

> Let missionaries and schoolmasters, the plough and the spade, go together, and agriculture will flourish; the avenues to legitimate commerce will be opened; confidence between man and man will be inspired; whilst civilization will advance as the natural effect, and Christianity operate as the proximate cause of this happy change.
>
> *(Buxton, 1840:511)*

Buxton's programmatic suggestions were put into action in the following years. The first attempt was spearheaded by Buxton himself, who founded a society to equip and organise the Niger Expedition of 1841. The society's aims read like a modern development programme: enable literacy (by introducing scripts for local languages), provide medical education to prevent diseases, improve agricultural methods, and end human trafficking (Buxton, 1840:7–10; cf. Táíwò, 2010:64). The Niger Expedition, a government-funded conglomerate of missionaries, linguists, explorers, military commanders, and craftsmen, failed spectacularly, mostly due to tropical diseases. However, the Expedition's most prominent African member, Samuel Ajayi Crowther, became the embodiment of Buxton's vision of development and Christianity. He went on to receive education in England, was ordained in the Anglican church, and finally became the first African to be crowned bishop when he was put in charge of the church in 'the countries of Western Africa beyond the limits of the Queen's dominions'. Arguably the most famous proponent of Buxton's strategy was David Livingstone, who echoed his call of 'commerce and Christianity' in the 1850s and 1860s. His cause inspired the Universities' Mission to Central Africa, which initially failed to make significant inroads into the East African slavery economy (Anderson-Morshead, 1909). However, the lofty humanitarian rhetoric of the 'Scramble for Africa' in the late 1880s would have been impossible without references to moral figures like Livingstone and the missionary–colonial alliance they engendered. This was not only a British construction; Germany likewise relied on a missionary–colonial, antislavery platform to enable its conquest of East Africa, albeit in a much more calculated political move (Haustein, forthcoming; Bade, 1977).

With the post-'Scramble' establishment of colonial governance in the early 1890s, the common platform of 'commerce and Christianity' was gradually replaced by a complex field of diverging interests between colonial governments, settlers, and economic interest groups (Porter, 2002). Depending on local circumstances, this led to cooperation, competition, or conflict, and the ideological configuration of religious and developmental aims in the 'civilising mission' became more fluid. However, regardless of this new complexity, missionaries remained a central and complementary part of colonialism due to the many and increasing developmental services they delivered in the African colonies. Their enterprise was professionalised in the beginning of the twentieth century. Medical missionaries, already prefigured by Livingstone himself, now became an established profession, embodied perhaps most famously by Albert Schweitzer in Gabon or Thomas Lambie in Ethiopia. Mission stations regularly provided vocational training and employment opportunities, and they engaged with aspects of traditional culture and beliefs they saw as detrimental to societal progress. In remote regions they functioned as vital trade links and a primary source for cultural imports – and vice versa; missionaries were a major source of geographical, biological, and anthropological knowledge, even as the respective sciences professionalised and increasingly replaced missionary sources. Most importantly, missions had an unchallenged monopoly on education in most African colonies, as the colonial governments established only few schools, and the traditional education systems were not compatible with colonial and capitalistic employment needs. In British tropical Africa, 96 per cent of pupils were attending a mission school at the end of the Second World War (Hastings, 1994:542).

In Asia the trajectories were similar, although in South Asia the devastating impact of the Indian Mutiny in 1857 played a decisive role in the emergence of the close relationship between 'commerce and Christianity' (Stanley, 1983). The Mutiny led to the demise of the British East India Company, which had existed since 1600, and to the establishment of the so-called British Raj in 1858, as well as a renewed role for Christian missionaries in the region (Stanley, 1983; Erickson, 2014). Resentment against the Company had been building amongst the *sepoys*, the local soldiers recruited into the Company's army, and between May 1857 and June 1858, a rebellion was staged (Hibbert, 1978; Dalrymple, 2006). The reasons for the Mutiny were complex but had a particular link to the Company's orientation towards religion. Being a trading company, interested in making a profit rather than claiming souls, the East India Company had tried to remain neutral towards religion and had discouraged the presence of missionaries in India. Until the 1813 Charter Act, which renewed the Company's rule in India but at the same time granted sovereignty of its territory to the British Crown and ended its trade monopoly, Christian missionaries had been unable to officially spread their faith. However, with the passing of this Act they became more prominent in the subcontinent. Another important feature of the 1813 Charter Act was the introduction of Western education into India, and while this was to be provided by the East India Company, Christian missionaries played an increasingly important role as a means of imparting knowledge about Christianity as well as about Western values (Bellenoit, 2007;

Sengupta, 2011). This marks a shift from the earlier days of the Company when interference in local customs and traditions was avoided in case it got in the way of trade, to a situation where pressure from evangelicals and Anglicists gave rise to a new climate of engagement that sought to educate and civilise Indian nationals, heralding the growth of mission schools, hospitals, and clinics, many of which survive to this day (Fischer-Tiné & Mann, 2004).

By the time the 1857 rebellion took place there was a creeping suspicion that the Company was becoming more interested in religion and would eventually seek to convert its employees to Christianity. While from the Indian perspective there were concerns that Christianity was gaining too strong a foothold in the region, as Stanley tells us, the missionary lobby in Victorian England felt the opposite and 'immediately hailed the Mutiny as divine retribution for the East India Company's compromising religious policy', whereby Britain had given India 'too little' Christianity (Stanley, 1983:85). The East India Company was perceived by evangelical Christians in England as not being explicitly supportive of their activities in India and as accommodating local religions in its activities, including Hinduism and Islam (Alavi, 1995). Between 1857 and 1858 there was a marked increase in donations to missionary societies and in the recruitment of missionaries where 'it was perfectly clear that the road back to imperial prosperity followed the path of Christian duty, that a Christian government of India was "the only safe policy"' (Stanley, 1983:87). However, of importance to our interest, Stanley also makes it clear that, 'Christian government was not, however, the only constituent of the Indian insurance policy: economic development was equally indispensable' (1983:87). Evangelicals in England supported the construction of India's rail network at this time, with an aim to grow the cotton industry and thereby undercut the slavery-reliant US cotton farms, as well as to provide a means for the spreading of Christianity into remote and isolated areas. Thus, 'many Christian observers . . . yoked together commerce and Christianity in their remedies for India's malaise' (Stanley, 1983:89).

While the appetite for the 'alliance between commerce and Christianity gradually fell apart' in the course of the 1860s (Stanley, 1983:91), Christian missionaries in India also had a wide-ranging impact upon indigenous religious actors who also became key players in the colonial modernising project and development narrative. As van der Veer states:

> Although the legitimizing rituals and discourses of the colonial state were those of development, progress, and evolution and meant to be secular, they could easily be understood as essentially Christian. The response both the state and the missionary societies provoked was also decidedly religious. Hindu and Islamic forms of modernism led to the establishment of modern Hindu and Muslim schools, universities, and hospitals, superseding or marginalizing precolonial forms of education. Far from having a secularizing influence on Indian society, the modernizing project of the secular colonial state in fact gave modern religion a strong new impulse
>
> *(van der Veer, 2002:179)*

Various forms of religious reform emerged in Islam, Hinduism, and Sikhism, including a tendency to draw clearer boundaries between those traditions in order to match the categories favoured by the colonial state, as well as to define and justify their integrity in the face of Christianity's influence (Oberoi, 1994; van der Veer, 2001). For instance, the failure of the 1857 Mutiny led to the suppression of many Muslim leaders by the colonial state and gave rise to a number of reform movements within Islam as both a response to British cultural and political hegemony and a reaction to Christian missionary criticism of Islam. The Deobandi was one of the most significant movements and emerged following the setting up of the Darul Uloom Deoband Madrasa in 1866. This madrasa became an important centre for both learning and political organisation during the independence struggles, and under its administrative and ideological guidance a network of madrasas was forged across the subcontinent (Metcalf, 1978; Qasmi, 2001:17). These madrasas catered to the needs of the poor, who could not afford education, especially in rural areas, thus contrasting with the role of madrasas in Muslim India as elite, higher learning establishments producing civil servants and judicial officials (Nair, 2009). Other important Islamic movements of the period were the Firangi Mahal (Robinson, 2001) and Aligarh (Lelyveld, 1994).

In a similar fashion, Hindu groups became more politicised and clearly defined during this period, through the emergence of reform movements such as the Brahmo Samaj (established in 1828), Arya Samaj (1875), Ramakrishna Mission (1897), Satyashodhak Samaj (1873), and Indian National Social Conference (1887). For instance, in 1828 Ram Mohan Roy founded the Brahmo Samaj and, in response to Christian criticism of Hinduism, outraged 'orthodox Hindus by writing against idolatry, sati, child-marriage, and caste, and in favour of education for women' (Knott, 1998:71). However, he not only wanted social reform within Hinduism, but also to mould the tradition into something that more closely resembled a 'religion' (i.e. following the Christian model). In particular, as Knott explains, he stressed that the Upanishads were the 'authentic' Hindu text and promoted a 'reasoned, ethical monism' rather than the perceived idolatrous polytheism typical of much popular Hindu practice (1998:72). These movements were not just confined to the religious realm, but importantly to forms of developmental progress and also nationalism in the bid to free India from British rule. In particular, the example of Christian missionaries' activities in education, health, relief, and the welfare of poor and neglected sections of society was catalytic in spurring development-related activities by some of these Hindu groups. Swami Vivekananda and Mahatma Gandhi are also important to mention here. Vivekananda marketed a style of monotheistic neo-Vedanta philosophy in both India and the West and also founded the Ramakrishna Mission (named after his Bengali teacher), a socio-religious welfare organisation that is still active in development and humanitarian work in India today. He was not only interested in attracting Westerners to Hinduism but also in gaining their financial support for development work back home. Mahatma Gandhi was similarly concerned with social and religious reform, and while his activities were more clearly political than the other reformers discussed, it is apparent that they went hand in hand with his modernist approach to Hinduism and Christianity, which had emerged from his engagement with Orientalist and Theosophist discourse (Bergunder, 2014). Above all, Gandhi was concerned to rid India of British rule and also to improve conditions for marginalised groups, such as dalits and women. Equally important to mention here are Sikh reformist groups, such as the Ad Dharm movement (representing dalit Sikhs), which were largely confined to the Punjab (Oberoi, 1994; Mahajan & Jodhka, 2009; Jodhka & Kumar, 2010) and must also be seen against this Christian/ colonial backdrop.

Two main points follow from the colonial period with regard to religions and development in Africa and South Asia. Firstly, religions were invoked as an ally or even central ideological justification for the colonial 'civilising' project. Christian missions and abolitionist activists were at the root of this configuration, and later conflicts and diverging interests notwithstanding, colonial missions did not question the perceived necessity of the European input for the betterment of African and Asian societies. Moreover, other religions were judged on their compatibility with this 'civilising' project, which sparked 'modernising' movements within some religions, asserting their reformist potential and compliance with European social and economic visions. Secondly, religious institutions became key providers of the welfare services which functioned as crucial indicators of the 'civilising' project, providing health care, education, vocational training, as well as local information and advocacy. Complementing the failures and needs of the colonial economy in rapidly transitioning contexts, they in many ways occupied the same structural position that non-governmental organisations (NGOs) have today (Manji & O'Coill, 2002). This was not only limited to Christian actors; local religious institutions occupied similar spaces in their engagement with colonial religion as the South Asia example shows.

Decolonisation and underdeveloped states

The marginalisation of religion in development

The emergence of a new bipolar world order after the Second World War brought about fundamental changes in the configuration of the global economy and its narratives about inequality, especially as the USA and its competition with Russia displaced the waning colonial powers. The erstwhile partition of the world into colonisers and colonised was relabelled to 'developed' and 'underdeveloped' countries and the Gross Domestic Product became the main measure of inequality among formally equal states (Rist, 2014:73–76). Truman's Marshall Plan and his global development programme, announced in his second inaugural address of 1949, became the new hallmarks of economic and military interventionism in the name of human progress, framed in a modernist language of prosperity, which was based on scientific and economic rationality. Given that this new world order inherited the legacy of colonialism, were there any echoes of the Christian missionary idea of progress and development? And if this was the case, where did the secularism of the development project come from, and how was it linked to sociological theorisation of secularisation? Finally, how did this new secularism in development theory impact Africa and South Asia? Were religious actors and perspectives forced out of development programmes or did they more or less continue in their role?

Truman's programmatic invocation of a 'bold new program . . . for the improvement and growth of underdeveloped areas' in his second inaugural address certainly echoed the earlier colonial rhetoric and structures of the 'civilising' mission, a point which is often lost in the various introductions to development studies. After spelling out the necessary development efforts in a modernist language evoking scientific progress, Truman quickly turned to a more lofty and idealistic rhetoric to conclude his speech and justify its outlook. He now invoked the Biblical Sermon on the Mount ('Our allies are the millions who hunger and thirst after righteousness' (Truman, 1949, cf. Matthew 5:6)), which was also one of the two Biblical texts he had rested his hand on when taking the oath of office. Moreover, his closing remarks exhibited a considerable measure of providentialism:

> Steadfast in our faith in the Almighty, we will advance toward a world where man's freedom is secure.

> To that end we will devote our strength, our resources, and our firmness of resolve. With God's help, the future of mankind will be assured in a world of justice, harmony, and peace.

> *(Truman, 1949)*

While these remarks have to be placed in the context of the American 'Civil Religion' (Bellah, 1970) rather than be read as a mere continuation of Victorian sentiment, it is still noteworthy that Truman's modernism is far removed from a fully secular development agenda, as the political mobilisation for his Point Four Programme did not rest in scientific progress alone but drew heavily on Christian views of social justice and eschatology.

Religion and development in Africa and Asia

Development theory did not immediately push aside religion. The Princeton economist and Nobel prize laureate, W. Arthur Lewis, who was influential in shaping development policy at the UN, in Ghana, and in the Caribbean, discussed religion in some detail in his *Theory of Economic Growth* (1955:101–107; cf. Deneulin, 2009:30–37). Discussing the stimulating and stymieing effects of religious beliefs on economic growth, Lewis importantly rejected the view that religious sentiments merely followed economic factors. Rather, religion appears as a fundamental factor in economic development:

> After all, social change results mainly from what people do, and this in turn is mainly the result of what they believe. Religion permeates our beliefs because religious instruction (whether formal or informal) begins while we are still on our mother's knees. What we learn late in life for ourselves we can often unlearn by argument or demonstration, but what we have absorbed in childhood is much harder to cast out
> *(Lewis, 1955:106)*

In the same way as the post-war development agenda did not immediately discount religion in political rhetoric and economic theory, religion also remained a significant practical factor in the continued presence of Christian missions in Africa and Asia. The charitable monopoly they had built in social care, education, and poverty alleviation made it exceedingly difficult to let go of their 'mission fields'. Rather, the foreseeable impact of national independence on defining working areas, retaining staff, and upholding fundraising causes led to various tactical responses for ascertaining a continued influence (Kalu, 2003). As the different post-colonial scenarios unfolded in Africa, key missionary industries, especially in education and health, were nationalised rapidly or gradually, but in all cases, missions managed to retain or regain a significant presence. The moratorium debate of the 1970s was a clear expression of this, when Africans voiced their unease with how the missionary presence and their financial aid mirrored a continued dependence of Africa on the West (Sundkler & Steed, 2000:1027–1029), and it was estimated that by 1995 there were still 30,000–40,000 Western missionaries working in the continent (Isichei, 1995:327). In South Asia, the legacy of partition shaped both religious and developmental dynamics during the post-independence period (Tomalin, 2015a). Partition resulted in the separation of West Pakistan and East Pakistan from India, renamed Pakistan and Bangladesh, in 1971, after the Bangladesh Liberation War. Both India and West and East Pakistan were initially established as secular states, but by 1956 Pakistan had become an Islamic state, with India retaining its officially 'secular' status to this day. In both settings Christian missionaries were allowed to continue operating openly for several decades after independence and remained engaged in maintaining the infrastructure of Christian institutions. However, the situation became increasingly tense from the 1980s onward when the rise of Hindu nationalism in India brought new laws and restrictions on missionary activity, and in Pakistan 'newly aggressive Islamic communal politics placed Christians in . . . danger, and placed new obstacles in the path of foreign missionaries' (Cox, 2008:245). Nonetheless the legacy of Christian social welfare activities continues in both settings, for instance, in Christian schools and hospitals, alongside numerous social welfare and developmental projects sustained by local indigenous religious actors.

Despite these clear indications of a continued participation of religious actors in development 'on the ground', religion did largely disappear from Western development theory in the following years. A clear and frequently cited example of this is Rostow's influential *The Stages of Economic Growth: A Non-Communist Manifesto* (1960). His high-modernist, universal theory of economic development marginalised the role of religion, most importantly by rejecting the Weberian sense of religion as a singular or primary influence on the development of economic

83

systems (cf. Deneulin, 2009:36). However, when Rostow explained why his model would be the only adequate one for human development as opposed to the historical determinism and ruthless utilitarianism of Marxism, he suddenly fell back on the Christian religion as a fundamental expression of democratic values and a sustainable social system (Rostow, 1960:165). Religion was also featured in his speculative outlook beyond the age of mass consumerism, when he mused whether humanity would be able to overcome the ensuing 'spiritual stagnation' or 'spiritual boredom' (Rostow, 1960:92). So even for Rostow, there seemed to have been a fundamental religious dimension to human societies and development, which informs the ethics of economic progress and simultaneously acts as an uncertain horizon for the age of mass consumption.

The point of these observations is not to argue that religion had an invariable presence in development thought throughout the twentieth century, but rather to draw out more precisely the continuities and changes to this relationship in Western thought about societal development and religion. Rostow's evolutionary system of development fundamentally rested on Talcott Parsons' modernisation theory (Gilman, 2007:163). Parsons, in turn, continued Weber's thinking of modernity as grounded in the Reformation, but provided a more optimistic view of modern capitalism than Weber had, a vision which was 'perfectly suited . . . for development crusaders trying to sell the American version of modernity to postcolonial regions' (Gilman, 2007:93). Moreover, Parsons' thought was also influential for the emerging secularisation theories of the twentieth century. While he ascribed religion with central integration and legitimisation functions, these were impeded by processes of differentiation and pluralisation that necessarily followed with modernisation. As a result, he saw religion retreating from the public sphere through privatisation, leaving behind a moral community built around value-generalisation (Parsons, 1966). This is the core of the neo-classical theory of secularisation, which was worked out in the following years by sociologists like Peter Berger, Thomas Luckmann, and Niklas Luhmann. Their theories of secularisation were mirrored by Christian theologies as well, most famously perhaps in Harvey Cox's *The Secular City* (Cox, 1965) or the Death of God theology of the 1960s and 70s.

The inability of Western political theory, sociology, and theology to account for religion in the public sphere certainly impacted donors, development theory, and programmes, but it should not be confused with an absence of religion in development thought and processes in the global South. Latin American Liberation Theology (Gutiérrez, 1974) and its many adaptations in Korean Minjung Theology, Dalit Theology, Black Theology, and South African Liberation Theology became major amplifiers of the anti-modernist Dependency Theory of development (Preston, 1996:179–195) and provided religiously inspired visions of development and social organisation that ran counter to the narrative of the privatisation of religion. Alongside the already mentioned continued presence of missions and their development work, new religious organisations and networks arose and equally compensated for the failures of post-colonial states, for example, in the form of Pentecostal and Charismatic churches in Africa (cf. Freeman, 2012), as well as in the various reform movements in India stemming from Islam, Hinduism, and Sikhism. Arguably, development played an even greater role in the different Islamic reform movements in Africa and Asia. Organisations like the Muslim Brotherhood in Egypt and their sister organisations elsewhere have always conducted relief and development activities in close proximity to their religious and political aims. Saudi Arabia has had a considerable impact on Muslim education in Africa by bringing African students to Saudi Arabian universities and funding schools in various countries. This helped to strengthen the religious hegemony of Wahhābism over Muslim Reformist thought in Africa, in a process that already began in the 1920s (Lauzière, 2010). And even the socialist autocrats of African Muslim countries, like

Mu'ammar Qaddāfī in Libya, Ja'far al-Numayrī in the Sudan, and Siad Barre in Somalia, regularly invoked Islamic principles for justifying not just political, but also developmental aims, such as greater gender equality or economic progress. In South Asia, madrasas constitute the largest part of the Muslim faith-based sector and play an important role in education of the poor. Although Muslim involvement in health care is virtually non-existent, many prominent madrasas also undertake philanthropic and humanitarian work through associated charities, trusts, or relief organisations (Iqbal & Siddiqui, 2008:28). Similarly, Hindu and Sikh organisations are also involved in education and health services across India, and play an important role in relief and humanitarian work.

Thus, in contrast to much of Western post-colonial development thought, religious organisations and articulations retained an important role in the provision of welfare services and the imagination of social progress in Africa and South Asia. Even post-war development as such did not begin with a pronounced confession of secularism, but rather continued the eschatological vision of progress articulated by the Christian 'civilising mission' of colonialism. The ideological roots of the secular development project are rather to be found in the sociological theories of secularisation of the 1960s, which sought to account for the gradual disappearance of religion from the public sphere in many Western European countries, and more or less relegated religion to the cultural roots of a society's value system. What emerged, then, was a disconnect between secular development theory and donor preference and the continued presence and role of religious actors in developing countries, rather than a universally secular development project.

Faith–based organisations (FBOs) and non-governmental organisations (NGOs)

The 're-discovery' of religion in development thought

Arguably then, the recent re-emergence of religion in Western development thought had more to do with an intellectual reassessment and a changed political and sociological conversation, than with changes on the ground. An example of this is the emergence of the term faith-based organisations (FBOs) or faith-based initiatives, which spearheaded the emergence of the new literature on religion and development. While there is a tendency within this literature to view FBOs as a subset of a broader category NGO, we will argue that the situation is actually more complex and that this way of articulating faith-based development activity is rather narrow and fails to capture the diverse ways that religion and development are intertwined in contemporary settings in Africa and Asia. So how did this new category of FBO emerge and in what political circumstances? How adequate is this category and the related re-discovery of religion in development theory and practice? What effects has this theoretical reorientation had on the so-called developing world via donor preferences and research?

The so-called NGO-isation of development began in the 1980s with 'NGOs fill[ing] gaps left by the privatization of state services' (Desai & Potter, 2008:500) following the rolling back of the state that accompanied the neo-liberal structural adjustment programmes (SAPs) implemented by the World Bank and the IMF to reform governments in developing countries (Simon, 2008:87). Donors have increasingly directed their funds via NGOs rather than national governments and while most are secular, others are linked to religious traditions in different ways, and are today commonly referred to as faith-based organisations (FBOs) (although different terms have been used to describe them, including, religious NGOs or faith-based development organisations). Over the past decade or so, development donors have increasingly chosen to support the work of FBOs and have also played a role in defining the category and spurring on their proliferation. While we are focusing here on the newfound interest in FBOs within development practice and studies since the turn of the century, it is important to also emphasise that FBOs have been funded by donors for decades. However, because of the explicit secularism of development donors, and their dislike of evangelism in particular, FBOs have tended to downplay their religious identities and motives (especially in Europe). It is also important to highlight that religious actors have been involved in various types of charitable, philanthropic, humanitarian, and development work far longer than since the turn of the century, either as formal NGO-like organisations since the 1980s or as far older traditional social welfare actors at the heart of most, if not all, religious traditions. However, part of the re-emergence of religion in Western development has been an explicit recognition of the faith-based dimension of the NGO sector, alongside a tendency to increasingly seek engagement with it. Yet, this is done in a way that is based on a series of assumptions about its presumed advantages, which are often asserted without substantial evidence as to their validity (Tomalin, 2012). This owes much to broader global shifts around the so-called resurgence of religion as well as specific attempts in the USA to regulate the rise of religion in the public sphere within a secular form of politics guided by the First Amendment to the US Constitution, which requires that religion is separate from the state (Tomalin, 2012).

In the USA in particular, the rise of the so-called religious right since the 1980s and reactions after 9/11 have both contributed to a greater focus on the role of faith in society, including increased funding for FBOs. The 1996 charitable choice provision of the new Welfare Act enabled faith-based organisations in the USA to apply for federal funding to support welfare projects, and in 2002, George W. Bush established the Center for Faith-Based and Community Initiatives at USAID in order 'to create a level playing field for faith and community based organisations to compete for USAID programs' (USAID, n.d.; Stambach, 2015; Adkins et al., 2010; Cooper, 2014). During his presidency, Bush almost doubled funding to faith-based groups, from 10.5 per cent of aid in 2001 to 19.9 per cent in 2005 (James, 2009:5) with 'much of this increase going to evangelical Christian organizations' (Occhipinti, 2015:332; Hackworth, 2012). However, this turn towards religion was not only confined to the USA; governments in the UK, Switzerland, the Netherlands, Denmark, and Sweden, as well as the World Bank, also channelled attention and funding to FBOs for both domestic and international projects (Marshall, 2001; Jones & Petersen, 2011:1294–5; G. Clarke, 2013; Haynes, 2013; Deacon & Tomalin, 2015).

A sizeable amount literature has now emerged which seeks to define what an FBO is, or attempts to develop typologies for classifying them. Much of this has developed in the USA with regard to domestic policy about FBOs and how to accommodate them whilst maintaining the First Amendment (Dionne & Chen, 2001; Solomon, 2003). Thus, in North America some argue that definitions of the term FBO should not include places of worship or congregations but instead the term FBO should only be used to refer to separately incorporated organisations which are used for development, charity, or service provision. This is because the First Amendment requires the separation of church and state (Tomalin, 2012:693; Jeavons, 2004:144). However, over the past decade or so a literature has emerged that examines FBOs in developing settings, drawing upon and reworking the USA literature, while at the same time seeking to complicate and challenge it (Clarke, 2008; Tomalin, 2012; Berger, 2003).

Defining what an FBO is has proved challenging in a number of ways, and one issue to consider is what to include and what to leave out. While Jeavons, for instance, argues that the US domestic definition should be exclusive, leaving out places of worship/congregations and only including formal organisations (Jeavons, 2004), other definitions have been more inclusive, bringing in places of worship and congregations, as well as numerous organisations that are not affiliated with a larger faith community or formally registered like NGOs (Clarke &

Jennings, 2008; Occhipinti, 2015; Tomalin, 2013). While widening the definition allows us to bring in a broader range of faith actors with which donors and other NGOs can engage, it is not always clear that these faith actors use the term FBO in self-reference. For example, Kirmani & Zaidi (2010) found that Islamic charities in Karachi did not identify themselves as FBOs for complex reasons that reflected the lack of relevance in that setting of distinguishing between 'faith-based' and 'non-faith-based' organisations, since religion was relevant across social domains, as well as the desire to avoid the political sensitivity of issues of faith and religion (Occhipinti, 2015:334). This suggests that the apparent need to isolate a specific set of faith-based as opposed to secular organisations makes more sense from a Western perspective. Another approach to thinking about FBOs in developing settings has involved a typological approach that places organisations along a spectrum representing the extent to which faith is manifest in different aspects of their work, from faith permeated, or saturated, to secular (Berger, 2003; Sider & Unruh, 2004; Hefferan et al., 2009). Sider and Unruh (writing about the US setting) for instance argue that 'whether an organization is faith-based cannot be answered with a simple yes or no. The faith nature of organizations is multidimensional, requiring a range of types' (Sider & Unruh, 2004:116).

Thus, there are doubts about whether the term FBO is wholly useful in developing contexts in terms of its ability to capture the broad range of organisational contributions from religious traditions to service delivery, advocacy, welfare, or disaster relief. However, it is now widely used by development donors and other development actors, in both the Global North and the Global South, and despite its particular origin within the USA, is increasingly adopted by religious actors across the globe in order to tap into funding streams and beneficial partnerships specifically aimed to include the faith sector. It is also important to remember the colonial dynamics that laid the foundations for the emergence of the contemporary FBOs and NGOs. The emergence of voluntary organisations involved in social welfare and development activities can again be traced back to the colonial periods in Africa and Asia. During the period of British rule in India, 'voluntary organizations were institutionalized and laws regarding the registration and regulation of philanthropic and voluntary organizations passed in order to formalize, legalize and control their activities' (Tomalin, 2015a:185). For instance, the Societies Registration Act was passed in 1860, primarily to regulate the associations blamed for the Mutiny. Thus, during the British Raj, there was a proliferation of both religious and secular non-profit organisations, a good number of which aimed to protect the interests of different religious and cultural groups in the face of colonialism, and many of which are still active today. In Africa, numerous development organisations originated from the colonial missionary projects mentioned earlier in the chapter, which were handed over (voluntarily or involuntarily) either to national governments or to newly independent churches in the aftermath of decolonisation. Another type of religious organisation important for development in Africa, especially with regard to education and economic sustenance, was the various Sufi orders in Islam. Though many have a longer history in Africa, they became very important during the imperial colonial and post-colonial phase, offering alternative political and economic networks. For example, the Qādirīyya arrived in mainland Tanzania in about 1905 and was connected to new forms of social and economic mobility from the start, going on to form an alliance with Julius Nyerere in post-colonial Tanzania as an important local ally in his political and developmental aims (Nimtz, 1980).

Thus, the 'turn to religion' in development policy, practice, and studies and its increased interest in FBOs in some ways only sanctions already established practice in Africa and Asia. Even before the emergence of the FBO terminology, religious actors had functioned as gatekeepers to local communities to facilitate the entrance of NGOs, helping to establish contacts and legitimise given NGO objectives. In other instances they have made important modifications to gain NGO funding, by founding development wings or adjusting their project plans and funding applications to the required language. The borderline between NGOs and FBOs is accordingly fluid in many contexts. A recent testing of the FBO/NGO distinction in Nigeria provides some instructive details about this problem (Davis et al., 2011; cf. also Leurs, 2012). The study compared three organisations classified as NGOs and five classified as FBOs in three districts of Nigeria (two in Kano state, one in Lagos state), all of which were engaged in HIV/AIDS related work. While respondents and the organisations themselves were typically able to identify whether an organisation had a religious or secular background, the overlap between both was substantial, given the strongly religious background they operate in. They pursued the same development aims, and though FBOs would tend to frame this in more religious language, the intensity and relevance of religion for defining these aims varied strongly. Like FBOs, many NGOs were led by highly religious individuals, who justified their motivations and plans in religious language. Both types served various religious constituencies, with FBOs being generally closer to the members of their faith communities, whereas NGOs would also serve those considered to be living against the rule of a given religion (e.g. prostitutes). All organisations, whether Christian, Muslim, or secular, were engaged in similar activities, which in turn were defined by local expectations and customs. Differences emerged only with regard to some beliefs, for instance with regard to acceptable preventative methods. Both were held in high praise by their local constituents and were similarly poor in systematically measuring their outcomes and impact. FBOs were generally more financially independent, and more discriminatory in their hiring practices, but the latter was not consistent even within a given organisation. The study therefore presented a rather fluid and inconclusive result, and one of the project coordinators argued as a result that 'a standardised donor preference for FBOs is inappropriate', since the distinction between religious and secular organisations is difficult to uphold, outcomes are insufficiently measured in all cases, and the organisations' 'effectiveness is influenced not only by their characteristics and strategies but also by the context in which they operate' (Leurs, 2012:704).

All of this would indicate that the distinction of FBOs and NGOs, or more generally the question of the presence of religion in a given development organisation or collaboration, is much too blunt an instrument for an adequate assessment. Rather, like any contextual variable, donors and practitioners would have to assess how specific beliefs, religious organisation, and moral communities impact a given project in terms of organisation, legitimacy, constituents, accepted practices, and achievable outcomes. This requires a good amount of religious literacy and signals the end of rather blunt and unspecific approaches to religions and development.

Conclusion

Deconstructing religions and development

As we have argued, religions and development may be a recent discovery in development studies, but they are actually part of a longer history of the European and North American engagement with the rest of the world, simultaneously seeking to define progress and the role of religious beliefs, organisations, and practices therein. The imperial phase of colonialism was marked by the joint impetus of 'commerce and Christianity', and despite the at times diverging interests between missionaries and other colonial advocates, Christianity retained an important place in the justification and implementation of the colonial project in Africa and Asia, as other religions were forced to answer and adjust to the colonial narrative of modernity. The emergence of the development/underdevelopment rhetoric after the Second World War can initially be seen as a continuation of this colonial vision of the world, especially as the established colonial structures in Africa and Asia, like the role of missions or financial dependence, proved fairly resilient to the dawn of formal independence. In focusing on economic indicators only, in answering the Soviet ideological challenge, and in adapting to the emerging neo-classical sociology of secularisation, development thought increasingly ignored or criticised religion as irrelevant or obstructive to the envisioned progress. However, this hardly matched the continuing role of religions in Africa, Asia, and elsewhere in the developing world, and religions (now including the increasingly indigenised Christianity) were again found to be incompatible with what modernity required. The recent turn to religions in parts of development studies seems to be aimed at correcting some of these misrecognitions, but the categories employed as well as the genesis of this field of study rather point to changing perceptions and political ideas about religions in the West. Their adequacy for describing, understanding, and incorporating religions in Africa and Asia in sustainable development processes has yet to be proved. Given the long-standing ideological relations between narratives about religion and those about development that we have highlighted in this chapter, we would like to suggest that the generalised debate about the benefits or dangers of religions in development or about the suitability of FBOs to development does little more than continue an essentially Western debate about the role of religion in society.

In the study of religions, it is an established insight that the application of the originally Western category of religion to Africa and Asia cannot be understood properly apart from the colonial and post-colonial history of the past two centuries (Chidester, 1996, 2014; King, 1999; Fitzgerald, 2000; Masuzawa, 2005). As we have shown, narratives about development are an important part of this history, and their relationship with ideas about religion needs to be deconstructed in this larger context. This should help to offer critical reflection on the current rediscovery of religion in development studies, laying bare some of the ideological configurations behind this issue and rendering moot some of the more general discussions about the benefits or dangers of religion in fostering development. What we would advocate instead is a contextually sensitive approach to development and religion that highlights local histories and conceptual frameworks in assessing societal progress and the role of religions therein. While this would mean a more fragmented approach to the issue, as Africans and Asians need to explore these in dialogue their widely varying local cosmologies and ritual practices, they have a common interest in such a post-colonial deconstruction of the dominating ideas and generalisations about religion and development. Constructing alternatives to the offered dichotomies, concepts, and visions about the role of religion in development may thus be an important part of an emancipatory endeavour. After all, the most difficult and contested category of development is that of ownership.

Note

1 http://www.birmingham.ac.uk/schools/government-society/departments/international-development/rad/index.aspx

Bibliography

Adkins, J., Hefferan, T. and Occhipinti, L. (eds.), 2010. *Not by Faith Alone: Social Services, Social Justice, and Faith-Based Organizations in the United States*, Lanham, MD: Lexington Books.

Alavi, S., 1995. *The Sepoys and the Company: Tradition and Transition in Northern India, 1770–1830*, Delhi: Oxford University Press.

Anderson-Morshead, A. E. M., 1909. *The History of the Universities' Mission to Central Africa 1859–1909*, new and revised, London: Office of the Universities' Mission to Central Africa.

Bade, K. J., 1977. 'Antisklavereibewegung in Deutschland und Kolonialkrieg in Deutsch-Ostafrika 1888–1890: Bismarck und Friedrich Fabri', *Geschichte und Gesellschaft*, Volume 3, pp. 31–58.

Bellah, R. N., 1970. *Beyond Belief. Essays on Religion in a Post-Traditional World*, New York: Harper & Row.

Bellenoit, H. J. A., 2007. *Missionary Education and Empire in Late Colonial India, 1860–1920*, London: Routledge.

Berger, J., 2003. 'Religious Nongovernmental Organizations: An Exploratory Analysis', *Voluntas: International Journal of Voluntary and Nonprofit Organizations*, Volume 14 (1), pp. 15–39.

Bergunder, M., 2014. 'Experiments with Theosophical Truth: Gandhi Esotericsim, and Global Religious History', *Journal of the American Academy of Religion*, Volume 82 (2), pp. 398–426.

Bornstein, E., 2005. *The Spirit of Development: Protestant NGOs, Morality, and Economics in Zimbabwe*, Stanford, CA: Stanford University Press.

Buxton, T. F., 1840. *The African Slave Trade and Its Remedy*, London: John Murray.

Chidester, D., 1996. *Savage Systems. Colonialism and Comparative Religion in Southern Africa*, Charlottesville, VA: University Press of Virginia.

Chidester, D., 2014. *Empire of Religion: Imperialism & Comparative Religion*, Chicago, IL: University of Chicago Press.

Clarke, G., 2008. 'Faith-based organizations and international development: An overview', in G. Clark and M. Jennings (eds.), *Development, Civil Society and Faith-Based Organizations: Bridging the Sacred and the Secular*, Basingstoke: Palgrave Macmillan, pp. 17–45.

Clarke, G., 2013. 'The perils of entanglement: Bilateral donors, faith-based organisations and international development', in G. Carbonnier (ed.), *International Development Policy: Religion and Development*, Basingstoke: Palgrave Macmillan, pp. 65–78.

Clarke, G. and Jennings, M. (eds.), 2008. *Development, Civil Society and Faith-Based Organizations: Bridging the Sacred and the Secular*, Basingstoke: Palgrave Macmillan.

Clarke, M., 2013a. *Handbook of Research on Development and Religion*, Cheltenham: Edward Elgar (Elgar original reference).

Clarke, M., 2013b. 'Understanding the nexus between religion and development', in M. Clarke (ed.), *Handbook of Research on Development and Religion*, Cheltenham: Edward Elgar, pp. 1–13.

Cooper, M., 2014. 'The Theology of Emergency: Welfare Reform, US Foreign Aid and the Faith-Based Initiative', *Theory, Culture and Society*, Volume 32 (2), pp. 53–77.

Cowne, M. P. and Shenton, R. W., 1996. *Doctrines of Development*, London: Routledge.

Cox, H., 1965. *The Secular City. Secularization and Urbanization in Theological Perspective*, London: SCM Press.

Cox, J., 2008. *The British Missionary Enterprise since 1700*, London: Routledge.

Dalrymple, W., 2006. *The Last Mughal: The Fall of a Dynasty, Delhi 1857*, London: Bloomsbury Publishing.

Davis, C., Jegede, A., Leurs, R., Sunmola, A. and Ukiwo, U., 2011. *Comparing Religious and Secular NGOs in Nigeria: Are Faith-Based Organizations Distinctive?*, Birmingham: Religions and Development Research Programme (Religions and Development Working Paper; 56).

Deacon, G. and Tomalin, E., 2015. 'A history of faith-based aid and development', in E. Tomalin, (ed.), *The Routledge Handbook of Religions and Global Development*, London: Routledge, pp. 68–79.

Deneulin, S., 2009. *Religion in Development: Rewriting the Secular Script*, London: Zed Books.

Department for International Development (DFID), 2012. *Faith Partnership Principles. Working Effectively with Faith Groups to Fight Global Poverty*, London: Department for International Development, Available at: www.gov.uk/government/uploads/system/uploads/attachment_data/file/67352/faith-partnership-principles.pdf [Accessed: 28 December 2015].

Desai, V. and Potter, R. (eds.), 2008. *The Companion to Development Studies*, 2nd ed., London: Hodder Education.

Dionne, E. J. and Chen, M. H. (eds.), 2001. *Sacred Places, Civic Purposes: Should Government Help Faith-based Charity?*, Washington, DC: Brookings Institute Press.

Drescher, S., 2009. *Abolition: A History of Slavery and Antislavery*, Cambridge: Cambridge University Press.

Erickson, E., 2014. *Between Monopoly and Free Trade: The English East India Company, 1600–1757*, Princeton, NJ: Princeton University Press.

Fischer-Tiné, H. and Mann, M., 2004. *Colonialism as Civilizing Mission: Cultural Ideology in British India*, London: Anthem Press.

Fitzgerald, T., 2000. *The Ideology of Religious Studies*, New York: Oxford University Press.

Follett, R. R., 2008. 'After Emancipation: Thomas Fowell Buxton and Evangelical Politics in the 1830s', *Parliamentory History*, Volume 27 (1), pp. 119–129.

Freeman, D. (ed.), 2012. *Pentecostalism and Development. Churches, NGOs and Social Change in Africa*, Basingstoke: Palgrave Macmillan.

Gilman, N., 2007. *Mandarins of the Future: Modernization Theory in Cold War America*, Baltimore, MD: Johns Hopkins University Press.

Gutiérrez, G., 1974. *A Theology of Liberation: History, Politics, and Salvation*, London: SCM Press.

ter Haar, G., 2011a. 'Religion and development: Introducing a new debate', in G. ter Haar (ed.), *Religion and Development: Ways of Transforming the World*, New York: Columbia University Press, pp. 3–25.

ter Haar, G. (ed.), 2011b. *Religion and Development: Ways of Transforming the World*, New York: Columbia University Press.

Hackworth, J., 2012. *Faith Based: Religious Neoliberalism and the Politics of Welfare in the United States*, Athens, OH: Ohio University Press.

Hastings, A., 1994. *The Church in Africa 1450–1950*, Oxford: Oxford University Press.

Haustein, J. (forthcoming). 'Strategic Tangles: Slavery, Colonial Policy, and Religion in German East Africa, 1885–1918'.

Haynes, J., 2007. *Religion and Development. Conflict or Cooperation?*, Basingstoke: Palgrave Macmillan.

Haynes, J., 2013. 'Faith-based organizations, development, and the World Bank', in G. Carbonnier (ed.), *International Development Policy: Religion and Development*, Basingstoke: Palgrave Macmillan, pp. 49–64.

Hefferan, T., Adkins, J. and Occhipinti, L. (eds.), 2009. *Bridging the Gaps: Faith-Based Organizations, Neoliberalism, and Development in Latin America and the Caribbean*, Lanham, MD: Lexington Books.

Hibbert, C., 1978. *The Great Mutiny: India 1857*, London: Allen Lane.

Iqbal, M. A. and Siddiqui, S., 2008. *Mapping the Terrain: The Activities of Faith-Based Organisations in Development in Pakistan*, Birmingham: International Development Department, University of Birmingham (Religions and Development Research Programme Working Paper; 24).

Isichei, E., 1995. *A History of Christianity in Africa: From Antiquity to the Present*, London: SPCK.

James, R., 2009. *What is Distinctive About FBOs? How European FBOs Define and Operationalise Their Faith*, Oxford: INTRAC (INTRAC Praxis Paper; 22), Available at: www.intrac.org/data/files/resources/482/Praxis-Paper-22-What-is-Distinctive-About-FBOs.pdf [Accessed 4 January 2016].

Jeavons, T. H., 2004. 'Religious and Faith-Based Organizations: Do We Know One When We See One?', *Nonprofit and Volunteer Sector Quarterly*, Volume 33 (1), pp. 140–145.

Jodhka, S. S. and Kumar, A., 2010. *Religious Mobilizations for Development and Social Change: A Comparative Study of Dalit Movements in Punjab and Maharashtra, India*, Birmingham: International Development Department, University of Birmingham (Religions and Development Research Programme Working Paper; 47).

Jones, B. and Petersen, M. J., 2011. 'Instrumental, Narrow, Normative? Reviewing Recent Work on Religion and Development', *Third World Quarterly*, Volume 32 (7), pp. 1291–1306.

Kalu, O., 2003. 'Passive revolution and its saboteurs: African Christian initiative in the era of decolonization, 1955–1975', in B. Stanley (ed.), *Missions, Nationalism, and the End of Empire*, Grand Rapids, MI: Eerdmans, pp. 250–277.

King, R., 1999. *Orientalism and Religion. Postcolonial Theory, India and 'The Mystic East'*, London: Routledge.

Kirmani, N. and Zaidi, S., 2010. *The Role of Faith in the Charity and Development Sector in Karachi and Sindh*, Birmingham: International Development Department, University of Birmingham (Religions and Development Research Programme Working Paper; 50).

Knott, K., 1998. *Hinduism: A Very Short Introduction*, Oxford: Oxford University Press.

Korff, R. and Schrader, H., 2004. 'Does the end of development revitalise history?', in O. Salemink, A. van Haarskamp and A. K. Giri (eds.), *The Development of Religion/The Religion of Development*, Delft: Eburon, pp. 9–17.

Lauzière, H., 2010. 'The Construction of Salafiyya: Reconsidering Salafism from the Perspective of Conceptual History', *International Journal of Middle East Studies*, Volume 42, pp. 369–389.

Lelyveld, D., 1994. 'The fate of Hindustani. Colonial knowledge and the project of a national language', in C. A. Breckenbridge and P. van der Veer (eds.), *Orientalism and the Postcolonial Predicament. Perspectives on South Asia*, New Delhi: Oxford University Press, pp. 189–214.

Leurs, R., 2012. 'Are Faith-Based Organisations Distinctive? Comparing Religious and Secular NGOs in Nigeria', *Development in Practice*, Volume 22 (5–6), pp. 704–720.

Lewis, W. A., 1955. *The Theory of Economic Growth*, Homewood, IL: Richard D. Irwin.

Mahajan, G. and Jodhka, S. S., 2009. *Religion, Democracy and Governance: Spaces for the Marginalized in Contemporary India*, Birmingham: International Development Department, University of Birmingham (Religions and Development Research Programme Working Paper; 26).

Manji, F. and O'Coill, C., 2002. 'The Missionary Position: NGOs and Development in Africa', *International Affairs*, Volume 78 (3), pp. 567–583.

Marshall, K., 2001. 'Development and Religion: A Different Lens on Development Debates', *Peabody Journal of Education*, Volume 76 (3–4), pp. 339–375.

Masuzawa, T., 2005. *The Invention of World Religions. Or, How European Universalism Was Preserved in the Language of Pluralism*, Chicago, IL: University of Chicago Press.

Metcalf, B. D., 1978. 'The Madrasa at Deoband: A Model for Religious Education in India', *Modern Asian Studies*, Volume 12, pp. 111–134.

Nair, P., 2009. *The State and Madrasas in India*, Birmingham: International Development Department, University of Birmingham (Religions and Development Research Programme Working Paper; 15).

Nimtz, A. H., 1980. *Islam and Politics in East Africa: The Sufi Order in Tanzania*, Minneapolis, MN: University of Minnesota Press.

Oberoi, H., 1994. *The Construction of Religious Boundaries. Culture, Identity and Diversity in the Sikh Tradition*, Delhi: Oxford University Press.

Occhipinti, L. A., 2015. 'Faith-based organisations and development', in E. Tomalin (ed.), *The Routledge Handbook of Religions and Global Development*, London: Routledge, pp. 331–345.

Parsons, T., 1966. '1965 Harlan Paul Douglass Lectures: Religion in a Modern Pluralistic Society', *Review of Religious Research*, Volume 7 (3), pp. 125–146.

Porter, A., 1985. '"Commerce and Christianity": The Rise and Fall of a Nineteenth-Century Missionary Slogan', *Historical Journal*, Volume 28 (3), pp. 597–621.

Porter, A., 2002. 'Church History, History of Christianity, Religious History: Some Reflection on British Missionary Enterprise since the Late Eighteenth Century', *Church History*, Volume 71 (3), pp. 555–584.

Preston, P. W., 1996. *Development Theory: An Introduction*, Cambridge, MA: Blackwell Publishers.

Qasmi, M. B., 2001. *Darul Uloom Deoband: A Heroic Struggle Against the British Tyranny*, Mumbai: Markazul Ma'arif India.

Rakodi, C. (ed.), 2014. *Religion, Religious Organisations and Development: Scrutinising Religious Perceptions and Organisations*, London: Routledge.

Reid, R., 2012. *A History of Modern Africa: 1800 to the Present*, Chichester: Wiley-Blackwell.

Rist, G., 2014. *The History of Development: From Western Origins to Global Faith*, London: Zed Book.

Robinson, F., 2001. *The Ulama of Farangi Mahall and Islamic Culture in South Asia*, London: C. Hurst & Co Publishers.

Rostow, W. W., 1960. *The Stages of Economic Growth: A Non-Communist Manifesto*, Cambridge: Cambridge University Press.

Salemink, O., van Haarskamp, A. and Giri, A. K. (eds.), 2004. *The Development of Religion/The Religion of Development*, Delft: Eburon.

Sengupta, P., 2011. *Pedagogy for Religion: Missionary Education and the Fashioning of Hindus and Muslims in Bengal*, Berkeley, CA: University of California Press.

Sider, R. J. and Unruh, H. R., 2004. 'Typology of Religious Characteristic of Social Service and Educational Organizations and Programs', *Nonprofit and Voluntary Sector Quarterly*, Volume 33 (1), pp. 109–134.

Simon, D., 2008. 'Neoliberalism, structural adjustment and poverty reduction strategies', in V. Desai and R. Potter (eds.), *The Companion to Development Studies*, 2nd ed., London: Hodder Education, pp. 86–92.

Solomon, L. D., 2003. *In God We Trust? Faith-Based Organizations and the Quest to Solve America's Social Ills*, Lanham, MD: Lexington Books.

Stambach, A., 2015. 'Development organizations' support for faith-based education: Recent turns toward ethics and dialogue', in E. Tomalin (ed.), *The Routledge Handbook of Religions and Global Development*, London: Routledge, pp. 109–134.

Stanley, B., 1983. '"Commerce and Christianity": Providence Theory, the Missionary Movement, and the Imperialism of Free Trade, 1842–1860', *Historical Journal*, Volume 26 (1), pp. 71–94.

Sundkler, B. and Steed, C., 2000. *A History of the Church in Africa*, Cambridge: Cambridge University Press.

Táíwò, O., 2010. *How Colonialism Preempted Modernity in Africa*, Bloomington, IN: Indiana University Press.

Tomalin, E., 2012. 'Thinking About Faith-Based Organisations in Development: Where Have We Got to and What Next?', *Development in Practice*, Volume 22 (5–6), pp. 689–703.

Tomalin, E., 2013. *Religions and Development*, Abingdon: Routledge.

Tomalin, E., 2015a. 'Religion and development in India and Pakistan: An overview', in E. Tomalin (ed.), *The Routledge Handbook of Religions and Global Development*, London: Routledge, pp. 183–199.

Tomalin, E. (ed.), 2015b. *The Routledge Handbook of Religions and Global Development*, London: Routledge.

Truman, H. S., 1949. 'Second inaugural address, 20 January 1949', Available at: www.trumanlibrary.org/whistlestop/50yr_archive/inagural20jan1949.htm [Accessed 17 December 2015].

Tyndale, W. R., 2006. *Visions of Development. Faith-Based Initiatives*, Aldershot: Ashgate.

USAID, n.d. 'Center for Faith-Based and Community Initiatives: History', Available at: www.usaid.gov/faithbased-and-community-initiatives/history [Accessed: 4 January 2016].

van der Veer, P., 2001. *Imperial Encounters. Religion and Modernity in India and Britain*, Princeton, NJ: Princeton University Press.

van der Veer, P., 2002. 'Religion in South Asia', *Annual Review of Anthropology*, Volume 31, pp. 173–187.

6

NATIONALISM IN AFRICA AND ASIA

Christopher J. Lee

In October 1945 the United Nations (UN) was officially established following the devastation of the Second World War, which had engulfed much of the world in conflict. The principal purpose of the organization was to prevent such a global conflagration from happening again. Indeed, tentative negotiations for the establishment of the UN as a replacement for the failed League of Nations had been initiated early on in the war with the Atlantic Charter agreed to by President Franklin Roosevelt of the United States (US) and Prime Minister Winston Churchill of Great Britain. Based on meetings held on August 9 and 10, 1941, off the coast of Newfoundland, the Atlantic Charter set out to define the intentions of the US and Britain in the face of war, going so far as to outline eight shared principles for a postwar order. Though largely speculative in scope, given that the war in Europe, Asia, and Africa was still ongoing, the Atlantic Charter reinforced in particular the idea of popular self-determination, albeit intended for Europe alone, that had served as a founding principle of the League of Nations as articulated by US President Woodrow Wilson (Mazower, 2012: 250). Self-determination as an idea was not exclusive to Wilson, having been embraced by other political figures such as the Soviet leaders Vladimir Lenin and Joseph Stalin (Lenin, 2004 [1914]; Stalin, 2013 [1913]). But Wilson's advocacy proved particularly influential during the period after the First World War, with Wilsonianism providing an international ethos that rationalized and legitimated nationalist struggles for self-determination across the world, especially those located in territories under colonial control (Manela, 2007). Through the influence of thinkers such as Wilson and Lenin, as well as institutions such as the League of Nations and the United Nations, nationalism became the dominant force in the shaping of global politics during the twentieth century.

This chapter examines the emergence of nationalism in Africa and Asia and its maturation during the postcolonial period. Given the magnitude of the topic, this brief overview does not pursue comprehensive geographic coverage or historical accounting, nor does it propose a single framework for interpreting nationalism as a phenomenon. Indeed, the problem of nationalism as a subject of study rests precisely in the diversity of forms it has taken dependent on interactive factors of demography, geographic space and location, cultural dynamics, class differences, and historical timing, among many features. Put simply, though nationalism has become a 'modular' form in world politics, to cite an influential argument by Benedict Anderson, it is nevertheless a specific historical formation and thus shaped by a range of contingencies, whether in terms of international shifts in institutions and ideologies or through fluctuating grassroots conditions, which typically shape the local meanings of nationalism (Anderson, 2006: 137). Nationalism is at once imagined and concrete, specific and comparable, local and global. It is also interconnected in different ways, being the product of shared experiences of colonialism, circulating ideologies between Africa and Asia, and institutional fora and routines, such as the UN and the Non-Aligned Movement (NAM).

This chapter takes account of this political range, scale, and interaction. The first section begins by charting the origins, contexts, and reasons for the emergence of nationalism in Africa and Asia. Nationalism across these continents must be understood in the first instance as primarily the outcome of Western imperialism and a dialectical logic of anti-colonialism that responded to political and economic measures which not only denied popular will and sovereignty as a result of foreign conquest and rule, but also placed increasing strain on local communities over time. Forms of collective resistance were gradually articulated and justified in different ways by activist-intellectuals who frequently described and promoted its 'national' content, thus positioning this strengthening political agency as qualitatively different from purely reactionary measures that sought to restore an earlier precolonial political order. The second part of this chapter examines how nationalism in Africa and Asia must also be comprehended as an ongoing process *after* political independence. Nation-building typically could only take place post-independence, often consolidating political interests and consent after decolonization and thus averting possible counter-revolutionary measures. This postcolonial maturation of nationalism at times stabilized chaotic political situations in beneficial ways. At other times, it hardened the position of ruling elites to the detriment of popular interests. This chapter consequently concludes that nationalism must be situated in time and place in order to grasp both its wide-ranging significance and its complex—and at times malevolent—meanings.

Anti-colonial nationalism

Nationalism as both a concept and a historical formation has experienced considerable debate across a number of academic fields, due to varying circumstances of time period and political geography, among many factors. It has been commonly understood as a modern invention, particularly in Africa and Asia, given its emergence under colonial rule. Yet it also draws upon preexisting communities, cultural practices, and histories, thus complicating this assumption vis-à-vis these continents and elsewhere. Ernest Renan's classic essay, 'What is a Nation?' (1882), is one early example of the challenges involved in defining nations and nationalism as distinct from racial, linguistic, religious, and other communities (Renan, 1990 [1882]). Renan famously remarked that a nation survives by way of a 'daily referendum' that is perpetually reinforced on a daily basis, thus highlighting both its priority and its relative instability compared with other political communities. Postcolonial countries in Africa and Asia have been prone to this weakness. The term nationalism has subsequently been qualified with prefatory descriptions such as 'civic' nationalism versus 'ethnic' nationalism, the former expression identifying a nationalism based on the acceptance of shared laws, citizenship qualifications, and political practices, while the latter expression defining nationalism as membership in a particular social group by birth or descent, not political agreement or recognition (Brubaker, 1992; Brown, 2000). Civic nationalism in turn has often been viewed as a reflection of modern political values, while ethnic nationalism has been interpreted as consisting of premodern, primordial sentiments that draw from a deeper, and more deeply felt, history of shared symbols and traditions (Greenfeld, 1992; Smith, 1986, 2004). These two forms of nationalism present a provisional framework for approaching nationalism in Africa and Asia.

In actual fact, however, these two versions of nationalism have frequently co-existed with one another. Modern civic-oriented nationalism has not superceded premodern forms of political community predicated on origin and sentiment. Indeed, presumably premodern social customs have often been invented or refurbished for contemporary purposes (Hobsbawm & Ranger, 1983). Ernest Gellner, Benedict Anderson, and Eric Hobsbawm, among other scholars, have addressed these seemingly incongruous aspects of nationalism in different ways, though with relative agreement that nationalism itself is a modern phenomenon motivated by a need for common identification in the face of large-scale political and economic change. As Hobsbawm writes, albeit somewhat tautologically, 'The basic characteristic of the modern nation and everything connected with it is its modernity' (Hobsbawm, 2012 [1990]: 14). Gellner and Hobsbawm have stressed the roles of industrialization and urbanization in particular as encouraging the rise of national identities that transcended local divisions and identities based upon descent. However, they did so from different angles, with Gellner taking a more elitist or statist view and Hobsbawm undertaking a popular, class-based approach (Gellner, 1983; Hobsbawm, 2012 [1990]). Working against Eurocentric histories and their assumptions, Anderson has separately emphasized the role of creole elites located in colonial peripheries, as well as modern media and language, in the formation of nationalism, each of which enabled national political communities to be 'imagined' into being (Anderson, 2006 [1983]).

Following Anderson, whose work concentrated on Southeast Asia, postcolonial countries in Africa and Asia have experienced tensions between local traditions and the promise and challenges of modernity similar to those found in Europe. Like countries elsewhere, they continue to endure such frictions between indigenous culture and global political norms and practices. However, similar to the Americas, modernity, at least in the Western sense, must be understood as having been introduced in the context of Asia and Africa through European imperialism and capitalist expansion (Appadurai, 1996; Wallerstein, 2004). While alternative forms of cultural modernity have existed and continue to persist, as examined in different ways by Dipesh Chakrabarty, Engseng Ho, and Wang Hui, the political modernity embodied in the nation-state introduced by Western imperialism and later reinforced by the Cold War has been hard to elude (Chakrabarty, 2000; Ho, 2006; Hui, 2014). Embracing modern political values and institutions proved to be a starker choice than in Europe, involving the acceptance of ideas that were not only foreign, but imposed by force. In an edited book particularly relevant to this chapter, titled *Nationalism in Asia and Africa* (1970), Elie Kedourie presented such political and economic factors as important for understanding the widespread adoption of nationalism as a political concept and form outside Europe (Kedourie, 1970). But he also disagreed that these foreign elements alone could explain the ubiquity of nationalism. Kedourie placed additional emphasis on the role of history and its capacity to give 'coherence and significance' to institutions, political practices, and beliefs. As a tool for nationalist sentiment, history could explain and legitimate the present, while also providing a sense of direction and progress for the future (Kedourie, 1970: 36–37). In this sense, Kedourie drew upon earlier arguments by Wilson, Lenin, and Stalin which formulated nationalism as an ideology of self-determination, comparable to socialism and other political ideologies that had emerged during the modern period (Kedourie, 1960).

These observations by Kedourie—who, it must be noted, was a critic of nationalism—form a useful backdrop to the later and more influential arguments of Anderson, Gellner, and Hobsbawm, especially regarding historicism. If defining nationalism has been approached through factors of culture, class, labor, language, and descent, among other features, the factor of history provides a fundamental means for bringing these different elements together. Historicism is essential in terms of understanding national identities as socially created formations, as well as addressing the utility of history in drawing broader comparisons across geographic space and time. The histories of colonialism and postcolonialism in Africa and Asia by a mutual set of European powers—Great Britain, France, and Portugal in particular—allow for similarities and contrasts to be drawn regarding the conditions for the emergence of modern nationalism, whether in Senegal, India, or South Africa. Though parts of Africa and Asia did escape formal colonial control, such as Thailand and Ethiopia for a time, the broader imperial world nevertheless informed political conditions across these two continents, as did decolonization after the Second World War. These common experiences allow for themes to emerge, particularly the role of anticolonial resistance as an indispensable aspect in the rise of nationalism.

Yet anticolonialism and nationalism must be treated as separate phenomena, even if they informed and often conjoined with one another eventually. Anticolonialism as a political action was typically confined, at least initially, to smaller-scale regions and provincial communities. A national outlook as such was not immediately articulated, let alone embraced. Understanding anticolonialism has therefore meant engaging with the social, political, and ethical life of local states and indigenous societies. Geography could be beneficial in providing enclaves for resisting colonial intrusion. However, it frequently presented a tactical challenge for activists seeking broader alliances of solidarity, with the spatial scale from local politics to national politics posing a considerable obstacle. Furthermore, if we accept a definition by V. Y. Mudimbe that colonialism and colonization derive from the Latin root word *colĕre*, meaning to design or cultivate, the social range and cultural magnitude of anticolonialism becomes even greater, extending well beyond formal politics to resistance in realms of language, faith, and culture more generally (Mudimbe, 1988: 1). The effects of colonialism were multiple, requiring a range of tactics that, in turn, informed the nature of anticolonial nationalisms.

Nonetheless, local responses to foreign intrusion and colonial rule were immediate, frequent, and ongoing. The fact of armed resistance generated constant anxiety for colonial states and European settlers in locales throughout Asia and Africa. These acts of indigenous opposition are too numerous to list, but can include such varied examples as the Indian Mutiny of 1857, the Battle of Isandlwana in 1879 in colonial KwaZulu Natal, and the Igbo Women's War of 1929 in Nigeria, to offer several well-known case studies (Pati, 2007; Falola & Paddock, 2011; Matera et al., 2012). These episodes of revolt were defined by specific circumstances of mistreatment, military incursion, and patriarchy, yet they share a common agenda of colonized people defying state power that was deemed unjust. The political legitimacy of foreign rule was constantly questioned. It was protected at times by self-validating ideologies of racial and cultural superiority, but just as easily contested if deteriorating social, political, or economic conditions warranted criticism. Terence Ranger captured the proto-nationalist importance of such resistance in his first book, *Revolt in Southern Rhodesia, 1896–97* (1967), a study of the First Chimurenga ('struggle' in the Shona language) between the Shona and the Ndebele against encroaching British settlers in what would become colonial Rhodesia and, later, independent Zimbabwe in 1980. Ranger's text blends historical analysis with an African nationalist sensibility that acknowledged the political uncertainties and ambitions of Southern Rhodesia and Southern Africa more generally, which, during the 1960s, were still experiencing political struggle and decolonization (Ranger, 1967). Though focused on the past, Ranger viewed this early anticolonialism as anticipating the nationalism that later took hold during the 1960s. An understanding of anticolonial efforts, even those dating from a century prior, was seen as essential for comprehending nationalisms of the late twentieth century.

Ranger was not alone. Allen Isaacman, for example, applied similar techniques to understand the complexity of peasant consciousness and agency in rural Mozambique and sub-Saharan Africa more generally and to identify the local sources of nationalism (Isaacman, 1993). Jean Allman has similarly tracked the interaction between rural bases and broader nationalist political parties in Ghana, examining more specifically the tensions between the Ghanaian National Liberation Movement party and the Convention People's Party led by Kwame Nkrumah (1909–1972) (Allman, 1993). Susan Geiger has applied a vital gender focus to such activism in a study of the Tanganyika African National Union in late colonial and early postcolonial Tanzania (Geiger, 1997). In urban areas, Frederick Cooper has detailed how economic development— the cherished ambition of many imperial powers—introduced a set of growing tensions between colonial policies and emerging African working classes in the colonies, resulting in unionization, labor strikes, and eventually moves toward decolonization (Cooper, 1996). This research on the emergence of anticolonialism in West, East, and Southern Africa points to the diverse circumstances and origins of colonial and postcolonial nationalisms, but also a common pattern of grievance and political ambition across sectors of African society.

Arguably the most prominent historiography to emerge from anticolonialism and the conceptualization of resistance has been the Subaltern Studies collective which published a series of anthologies on local colonial histories in South Asia. Drawing initially from the ideas of the Italian communist Antonio Gramsci, from whom the term subaltern (a subordinate) derives, this group of historians not only sought to articulate the perceptions and agency of common people against the British Raj, but positioned these experiences as a critique against a postcolonial historiography that neglected these populist stories in favor of elitist national narratives—a notable example of why anticolonialism and nationalism should not be conflated. These subaltern histories not only demonstrated how workers, peasants, women, and religious minorities challenged the hegemony of British colonial rule, but they equally confronted postcolonial conditions that continued to ignore the political aspirations and needs of such communities. As Ranajit Guha, the leader of this group of historians, wrote in the first volume of the collective's writings, a key motivation of Subaltern Studies was to understand the 'historic failure of the nation to come to its own . . . it is the study of this failure which constitutes the central problematic of the historiography of colonial India' (Guha, 1982: 7). This group of historians, involving such scholars as Dipesh Chakrabarty, Gyanendra Pandey, and Gayatri Chakravorty Spivak, consequently pursued this agenda, encountering deeper questions of epistemology as a result—for example, how the possibilities of restoring the past were structured and limited by both the colonial archive and the postcolonial political present (Guha & Spivak, 1988). Other scholars of Asia, notably James Scott, have similarly taken resistance not as a reductive sign of the nation, but as a critique of it, through careful attention to the moral economies, hidden transcripts, and 'weapons of the weak' employed by peasants, thus enabling a diversification of how the political and social life of colonial and postcolonial societies can be understood (Scott, 1976, 1985, 1990). Prasenjit Duara has summarized these efforts by applying a proximate approach to China to argue that too often a linear nationalist narrative has been applied to the histories of postcolonial nation-states—a methodological technique that oversimplifies the political complexities of the past (Duara, 1997).

Yet, despite this complexity of circumstance, anticolonial resistance did gradually transform into nationalist sentiment, especially through the work of intellectuals. It is essential to grasp the critical philosophies and moral rationales behind activism that popularized anticolonialism and eventually nationalism. Postcolonial nationalism was not simply the outcome of civil disobedience, armed struggle, and similar tactics of political agency. Figures such as Mohandas K. Gandhi (1869–1948), Ho Chi Minh (1890–1969), Patrice Lumumba (1925–1961), Frantz Fanon (1925–1961), and Nelson Mandela (1918–2013) not only served as political leaders in varying capacities, but they also explained, and at times critiqued, anticolonial activism and nationalism. They became emblematic symbols and speakers for the political struggles they represented. Consequently, anticolonialism must be examined for its philosophical content—the articulation of oppositional views and their basis in social grievances, as well as the complex interplay of local traditions and foreign ideas introduced by imperialism. Anticolonial resistance did not only take form through public social protest or cultural expression—it had an intellectual basis. Its militancy took textual form through the writing of manifestos, the establishment of newspapers, the publication of subversive fiction, and the embrace of revolutionary ideologies more generally. These sources illuminate once more the diverse origins of nationalism and the consequent challenges of consensus that postcolonial nationalists would face.

By extension, it is important to distinguish the assorted and frequently dissimilar attributes of such intellectual production to avoid a tendency toward monolithic definition, as cited earlier. Anticolonial thought encompassed a range of topics, at times concerned with the individual and his or her health and wellbeing, as discussed by Gandhi and Fanon, while on other occasions it focused on larger communities and group strategies in order to expel foreign rule. It is critical to emphasize the variety and complexity of intellectual life among the colonized, which was at times accommodating and reform-minded in relation to colonialism (Higgs, 1997; Kwon, 2015; Robinson, 2000). It was not always directed toward political overthrow and decolonization per se. Furthermore, anticolonial thought did not necessarily conceive of national self-determination. Organized religions such as Islam, for example, played a significant role in rationalizing and coalescing anticolonial resistance in such varied locales as Senegal, Algeria, and Afghanistan (Babou, 2007; Brower, 2009; Dalrymple, 2013; Sessions 2011). The idea of jihad (holy war) was invoked and often pursued. Christian thought was also mobilized against colonial rule, with its principles used as an ethical basis for criticizing social inequality and economic exploitation. John Chilembwe (1871–1915), the pastor of an independent church in Nyasaland (present day Malawi), famously led a short-lived revolt against British rule in central Africa. Despite its brevity, the 1915 Chilembwe uprising attained legendary status, demonstrating the capacity of Christian converts among the colonized to turn literacy and Western ideas into political expression—a pattern repeated elsewhere in Africa (Shepperson & Price, 1958; Fields, 1985; Gordon, 2012; Peterson, 2012).

Still, secular notions of individual rights, suffrage, economic justice, and national self-determination proved to have greater influence on anticolonial thought than either religious ideals or preexisting local traditions. The postcolonial world that came into being after the Second World War signaled this effect by embracing a nation-state model of constitutional governance based on citizenship rights. The mainstreaming of these ideas and the opening of new political possibilities depended on the intellectual work of individual thinkers, many of whom blended different strands of thought filtered through their own life experience to rationalize different strategies of resistance. Comparing Frantz Fanon with Aimé Césaire (1913–2008) is a useful illustration. Césaire and Fanon were both from the island of Martinique, a French *département d'outre-mer* (overseas department) in the Caribbean. Fanon in fact studied under Césaire, who taught at his secondary school in Fort-de-France. Yet both carved distinct political paths. Césaire is famous for being one of the founders of Négritude, along with Léopold Senghor (1906–2001) and Léon-Gontran Damas (1912–1978), during the interwar period—a popular literary movement that was critical of French racism. Yet Négritude was not entirely critical of French rule as such. Césaire and Senghor both served in the French National Assembly after the Second World War and sought, for a time, a federal model of decolonization that would keep their respective countries of Martinique and Senegal within a broader French community (Cooper, 2014; Wilder, 2015). As demonstrated in his first book, *Black Skin, White Masks* (1952), Fanon was also keenly critical of French racism and the impossibility of equal citizenship, despite French claims to the contrary (Fanon, 2008 [1952]). He ultimately pursued total decolonization as the only possible option for a complete political and social revolution, as outlined in his final book, *The Wretched of the Earth* (1961) (Fanon, 2004 [1961]). Fanon's ideas were more radical than Césaire's, which is not to say that the latter was entirely compliant with French rule—he did publish the fierce polemic *Discourse on Colonialism* (1955)—but it is essential to differentiate between critical internal views and calls for complete decolonization (Césaire, 2000 [1955]). Using the terms anticolonial or nationalist gratuitously can smooth over nuances and differences of opinion like those that existed between Césaire and Fanon. Such intricacies persistently raise fundamental questions about how broadly or narrowly these terms should be defined.

These differences were often informed by personal experience. Césaire was a poet, teacher, and, ultimately, a lifelong politician, who was mayor of Fort-de-France for a remarkable period from 1945 until 2001, with only one short break during this time. He also served in the French National Assembly for an equally extraordinary tenure from 1946 to 1993. Fanon, on the other hand, worked as a staff psychiatrist at a French hospital in Blida, Algeria, where he witnessed firsthand the trauma of the Algerian War (1954–1962). Though he was a veteran of the Free French during the Second World War—an experience that taught him of the use of violence as a technique for fighting power—Fanon never became a combatant during Algeria's revolution. His immediate experiences within the revolutionary context of Algeria centered on his medical work treating a range of patients who had suffered the consequences of war. He later continued this work in Tunisia. His additional diplomatic efforts for the anticolonial National Liberation Front (FLN) in Ghana, Mali, and elsewhere undoubtedly shaped his belief that complete decolonization was the only option to end the dehumanization of Western colonialism.

Intellectual differences of this kind can be found elsewhere. As a leader of India's nationalist struggle, Mohandas Gandhi pursued a philosophical agenda, anticolonial in scope, which proved far different from the diplomatic pragmatism of his compatriot Jawaharlal Nehru (1889–1964). Gandhi's *Hind Swaraj* (1909) offers a critique of British rule in India from the individual to the civilizational level, framing the problem of colonialism and the question of decolonization as not simply political issues, but matters of personal conduct. *Satyagraha in South Africa* (1928) and *An Autobiography, or The Story of My Experiments with Truth* (1927 and 1929) similarly accent individual ethics as the starting point for broader struggle through non-violent anticolonial resistance (Gandhi, 1983 [1927 and 1929], 2008 [1928], 2009 [1909]). In contrast, Nehru's *The Discovery of India* takes a civilizational point of view like Gandhi—as did Césaire and Senghor with Négritude—but he positions this backdrop as providing a historical rationale, rather than a purely philosophical one, to make a specific political claim for India's right to sovereignty. India was a historical nation, similar to European nations (Nehru, 2004 [1946]).

These different arguments underscore once more the need to resist any essentialized understanding of anticolonial nationalism. The long history of insurgent thought is one defined by internal tensions between different thinkers responding to one another along generational and experiential lines. Furthermore, this intellectual history of nationalism is a history of entanglement with the frequent use and incorporation of Western and non-Western ideas together, as seen in the work of such varied thinkers as Muhammad Iqbal (1877–1938) of Pakistan, Abdulrahman Mohamed Babu (1924–1996) of Zanzibar, M. N. Roy (1887–1954) of India, and B. R. Ambedkar (1891–1956) also of India, each of whom explored Islam, Maoism, Marxism, and Buddhism both with and against Western political ideas (Ambedkar, 2014 [1936]; Burgess, 2009; Manjapra, 2010; Sevea, 2012). But, to conclude this section, it is important to stress how, through such methods of borrowing and bricolage, these thinkers themselves consciously sought to reinvent nationalism and ideas of the nation-state that reflected local popular interests. Nationalism in Africa and Asia, as both a political and intellectual project, sought to invoke and reflect local cultural priorities rather than simply be a received, derivative discourse as critiqued by

Chatterjee (1993). As a result, it is essential to grasp the complexity and precision of anticolonial nationalism in order to understand the predicaments established by colonialism as well as the challenges of national consensus that the postcolonial leaders of Africa and Asia faced.

Postcolonial nationalisms

From April 18 to 24, 1955, twenty-nine countries from Africa and Asia convened in the city of Bandung, Indonesia, to address pressing issues their continents faced during the early Cold War period. Formally called the Asian–African Conference, the Bandung conference, as it is more commonly known, was the largest diplomatic meeting of its kind up to that point, ostensibly representing 1.4 billion people or almost two-thirds of the world's population by some estimates. Only the UN, which had seventy-six members in 1955, was larger in numeric representation and in terms of geographic and political magnitude. The Indonesian conference offered a stage for the rise of such statesmen as Sukarno (1901–1970) of Indonesia, Nehru of India, Gamal Abdel Nasser (1918–1970) of Egypt, and Zhou Enlai (1898–1976) of the People's Republic of China (PRC), all of whom promoted personal, national, and international interests. Sponsored by Indonesia, Burma (present day Myanmar), Ceylon (present day Sri Lanka), India, and Pakistan, official delegations in attendance came from the PRC, Egypt, Turkey, Japan, Libya, Lebanon, Jordan, Syria, Iran, Iraq, Saudi Arabia, Yemen, Afghanistan, Nepal, Laos, Cambodia, Thailand, North and South Vietnam, the Philippines, Ethiopia, the Gold Coast (present day Ghana), Sudan, and Liberia. Though regional conflict in Southeast Asia between North and South Vietnam provided the catalyst for holding the conference, the program ultimately included broader issues regarding American and Soviet influence in Asia and Africa, the consequent importance of post-colonial sovereignty, and remaining questions over the surge of decolonization then occurring, particularly in Africa. The origins and purposes of the meeting were ultimately multifaceted, geographically and politically, reflective of the expansive continental representation at hand and the political changes then occurring across the world (Abraham, 2008; Acharya & Tan, 2008; Ampiah, 2007; Lee, 2010; McDougall & Finnane, 2010).

The Bandung meeting also reflected the transformation of anticolonial nationalism in Africa and Asia from a type of insurgent politics to a method of statecraft. Indeed, the continuation of anticolonial politics after political independence is important to grasp, particularly as many of the first generation of postcolonial leaders, like Nehru, Sukarno, and Ahmed Ben Bella (1916–2012), for example, held leadership roles in national liberation struggles. Anticolonial nationalism as a political sentiment and worldview did not quickly subside, but instead took a new shape to inform the international politics of the postcolonial period. The reasons are self-evident. Diplomatic occasions like that at Bandung took place during a critical period of transition between colonial and postcolonial periods, amid a passing era of modern European imperialism and a new era of Cold War rivalry and intervention—a type of informal imperialism, if often denied as such. Furthermore, global decolonization was an uneven process, with many national liberation movements, like those in Southern Africa, continuing for decades. Postcolonial diplomacy and statecraft as political practices consequently emerged during a time of both uncertainty and opportunity. These conditions perpetuated the continuation of nationalism as part of a need for Asian and African countries to secure sovereignty, resist foreign intervention, and participate in the global politics then taking shape. The threat of neocolonialism through trade agreements, security arrangements, and other political alignments with Western powers encouraged the persistence of anticolonial nationalist rhetoric to protect the meaning of political independence.

Diplomacy was vital in this regard. The thesis of this section is that diplomatic conferences and alliances were essential to postcolonial nationalisms in Africa and Asia. They marked a decisive change in scope from a grassroots political orientation to a global one based on international recognition. Unlike internal forms and practices of nationalism, which addressed local concerns and popular needs, these international venues connected postcolonial nation-states and their concerns to one another. They allowed for the mutual constitution of postcolonial nationalisms. International meetings like that at Bandung and membership of broader institutions like the UN presented public occasions for reiterating national self-determination and the right to sovereignty. The rapid emergence of the conference format among newly independent countries after the Second World War can be understood through these motivations, given the relative weaknesses that countries in Africa and Asia individually maintained as new nation-states and the immediate possibilities of collective strength through group alignments. Postcolonial diplomatic meetings of the Non-Aligned Movement (NAM), the Organization of African Unity (OAU), and the Arab League, among others, provided alternative venues for affirming political recognition and strengthening relationships among peers, beyond the immediate purview of former colonial powers. Summitry—defined as the institutionalized practice of heads of state meeting on a routine basis—legitimized postcolonial national autonomy, reinforced the principle of non-interference by external powers, and, in a number of ways, continued the ethos of anticolonial nationalism by asserting self-determination as not simply a right justifying pre-independence struggles, but as an abiding rule and technique of governance against present and future territorial threats (Dunn, 1996; Groom, 2013).

Indeed, despite its importance, the 1955 Asian–African Conference was far from isolated. To list a few examples, preceding meetings include the 1947 Asian Relations Conference in Delhi, the 1953 Asian Socialist Conference in Rangoon (present day Yangon), and the 1956 Asian Socialist Conference in Bombay (present day Mumbai). In the context of Africa, the 1958, 1960, and 1961 All-African People's Conferences in Accra, Tunis, and Cairo, respectively, enabled new patterns of political networking among states and remaining national liberation movements, such as those in Southern Africa, during the early postcolonial period (Ahlman, 2010; McCallum, 1947; Jack, 1959; Houser, 1961; Jansen, 1966). The location of these conferences in cities in Asia and Africa strikingly indicated a new political geography that had emerged from the shadows of Western colonial rule. Yet these postwar meetings also continued a chronology of conferences during the early twentieth century, including such precursors as the Pan-African Congresses and the 1927 League Against Imperialism meeting held in Brussels, Belgium, sponsored by the Soviet Union's Communist International (Comintern). While these preceding efforts failed to achieve many of their goals, their historical significance persisted due to their enabling geographically dispersed people to meet, converse, and produce political solidarities, anticolonial in orientation. Attended by persons without official capacity, they nonetheless engaged with national self-determination and acquired symbolic value through broadly conceived political imaginations anchored in shared experiences of racial discrimination, cultural prejudice, and political repression.

Postwar diplomacy highlighted a fundamental shift from these earlier events, given that attendees represented sovereign nation-states rather than national liberation movements and like-minded intellectuals. Still, struggles for national self-determination remained in parts of Africa and Asia circa 1960, which is why anticolonial nationalism continued, as cited before. But the growing involvement of autonomous states facilitated a set of different possibilities that reflected political independence and the resources that went with it, in contrast to previous conferences where those gathered had little actual political power to draw upon. Postwar conferences like the Bandung meeting proved to be generative in scope. If the geographic balance of the 1955 meeting tilted toward Asia, the future of Asia–Africa relations soon shifted to the African continent, fostering Asian and African nationalisms in a different context. Nasser positioned himself as a leader of the 'Third World', a status enhanced by the support Egypt garnered during the 1956 Suez Crisis. In December 1957, the Afro-Asian Peoples' Solidarity Organization (AAPSO) was established in Cairo, marking a new intercontinental endeavor in the wake of Bandung. AAPSO had wider involvement, including a range of cultural and professional organizations, rather than solely official state delegations, from Asian and African countries. The conferences it organized during the late 1950s and 1960s continued the 'Bandung spirit' through professional exchange, cultural promotion, women's coalitions, and youth participation. Furthermore, its meetings were held within an expanding range of locales including Ghana, Guinea, and Tanzania—a clear signal of the wave of decolonization occurring and the promotion of Asian and African nationalisms.

Arguably the most significant outcome of this set of alliances, however, was the birth of the Non-Aligned Movement. The Belgrade Conference of Non-Aligned States that convened in Yugoslavia in September 1961 formalized this political coalition. Key figures included former Bandung participants such as Nehru, Nasser, and Sukarno, along with new figures like Kwame Nkrumah of Ghana and Josip Broz Tito (1892–1980) of Yugoslavia. Zhou and the PRC were notably absent—an indication that political solidarities did not necessarily persist. In this case, tensions and eventually war—specifically, the 1962 Sino-Indian War—put an end to good relations between India and the PRC. A second NAM conference was held in Cairo in October 1964 with delegations from forty-seven states in attendance, a numeric growth assigned to the wave of decolonization in sub-Saharan Africa. The NAM ultimately superseded the 1955 Asian–African Conference—drawing upon it symbolically in different respects, but marking a different configuration of nation-states that would meet routinely in the decades ahead (Lüthi, 2016).

The idea of non-alignment also signaled a broader convergence of postcolonial nationalism, statecraft, and emergent transnational communities. In addition to Afro-Asianism, ideologies of Pan-Africanism, promoted by Nkrumah, and Pan-Arabism, promoted by Nasser, marked different efforts to unite nation-states under the banner of broadly construed identities, geographic and cultural in scope, positioned against the Euro-American West. The 1963 founding of the OAU (later reorganized as the African Union in 2001) and the establishment of the United Arab Republic (1958–1961), which briefly unified Egypt and Syria, manifested these ideas institutionally and territorially. Leaders such as Nkrumah, Julius Nyerere (1922–1999) of Tanzania, and Léopold Senghor, then president of Senegal, further articulated forms of African socialism that blended local ideas with introduced ideologies like Maoism, as in the case of *ujamaa* ('family-hood') in Tanzania, which aimed to make their respective countries economically independent from former colonial powers (Bjerk, 2015; Lal, 2015; Schneider, 2014). The ideology of non-alignment itself had circulated earlier as an idea before it became a state practice, specifically through the diplomatic efforts of India's UN ambassador V. K. Krishna Menon, who started the term. It also originated from the anticolonial strategy of non-cooperation before India's independence.

Yet these developments that indicate the continuation of anticolonialism as a defining feature of postcolonial Asian and African nationalisms must be understood as more limited and complex than public diplomatic rhetoric might suggest. Despite claims of neutrality or non-alignment, a number of NAM members had formal relations with the United States and the Soviet Union. In fact, such alignments had developed prior to the Bandung meeting, underscoring once more the need to avoid oversimplified views and definitions of either anticolonialism or postcolonial nationalism in Africa or Asia, which would have its proponents share a uniform view or even political consistency. Indeed, though both terms would continue to be applied to politically fraught situations like that in South Africa during the 1970s and 1980s, the term nationalism became increasingly rhetorical, rather than substantive, in scope during the postcolonial period—a tool for marking a critical position, citing a patriotic history, and creating both political solidarity and exclusion, rather than identifying any immediate threat or galvanizing a revolutionary movement as such. The emergence of postcolonial ethnic violence in countries such as Rwanda and Zimbabwe and communal violence in India points to challenges that postcolonial nationalism has faced internally (Das, 2006; Mamdani, 2002; Pandey, 2002). Though such divisions often reflect local colonial legacies, these unresolved differences have nonetheless remained, and at times been exploited by postcolonial leaders, to stress forms of ethnic, rather than civic, nationalism, to the detriment of a greater public good.

Conclusion

This chapter has briefly examined the origins and trajectories of nationalism in Africa and Asia during the colonial and postcolonial periods. It has argued for the importance of understanding the genealogies of nationalism and its postcolonial forms as deriving from sources of anticolonial activism and thought. This chapter has also promoted the need to think laterally about Asian and African nationalisms during the postcolonial period and specifically the role of international diplomatic conferences in crystalizing political recognition and sovereignty. Postcolonial national identities took form horizontally, through such formal occasions of mutual acknowledgement, in addition to vertical connections from below based on local ambitions and cultural norms. Nationalism has had internal effects in all countries, an issue that scholars have widely addressed and as touched upon at the start of this chapter. Political exclusion, economic corruption, and genocide have been unfortunate outcomes of nationalist politics in a number of countries. The Subaltern Studies collective is the best known recent example to confront these present problems, having set out during the late 1970s and early 1980s with the intention of not only decentering Western perspectives on South Asian history, but equally challenging nationalist visions of India's long anticolonial struggle that had privileged the role of elites and 'great men' such as Gandhi and Nehru. The critical views and political agency of non-elites would be foregrounded instead, as stated in the agenda presented in Guha's opening chapter of the first volume, titled 'On Some Aspects of the Historiography of Colonial India'. Mounting a sharp critique of both 'colonialist elitism and bourgeois-nationalist elitism', Guha called upon historians to restore the 'politics of the people', which he viewed as 'autonomous' (Guha, 1982: 1, 4). That Guha's call for a new postcolonial history in India has resonated widely among scholars working in other parts of Asia and Africa highlights the importance of this populist agenda—that diplomatic conferences are not the only means of connection between African and Asian nationalisms. Academic exchange and the circulation of knowledge more generally are also crucial, promising continued forms of fruitful criticism of the past, as well as the present and future.

Bibliography

Abraham, I., 2008. 'From Bandung to NAM: Non-Alignment and Indian Foreign Policy, 1947–65', *Commonwealth & Comparative Politics*, Volume 46 (2), pp. 195–219.

Acharya, A. and Tan, S. S. (eds.), 2008. *Bandung Revisited: The Legacy of the 1955 Asian–African Conference for International Order*, Singapore: National University of Singapore Press.

Ahlman, J., 2010. 'The Algerian Question in Nkrumah's Ghana, 1958–1960: Debating "Violence" and "Nonviolence" in African Decolonization', *Africa Today*, Volume 57 (2), pp. 67–84.

Allman, J. M., 1993. *The Quills of the Porcupine: Asante Nationalism in an Emergent Ghana*, Madison, WI: University of Wisconsin Press.

Ambedkar, B. R., 2014. *Annihilation of Caste: The Annotated Critical Edition*, S. Anand (ed.), London: Verso.

Ampiah, K., 2007. *The Political and Moral Imperatives of the Bandung Conference of 1955: The Reactions of the US, UK and Japan*, Leiden: Brill/Global Oriental.

Anderson, B., 2006. *Imagined Communities: Reflections on the Origin and Spread of Nationalism*, rev. ed., London: Verso.

Appadurai, A., 1996. *Modernity at Large: Cultural Dimensions of Globalization*, Minneapolis, MN: University of Minnesota Press.

Babou, C. A., 2007. *Fighting the Greater Jihad: Amadu Bamba and the Founding of the Muridiyya of Senegal, 1853–1913*, Athens, OH: Ohio University Press.

Bjerk, P., 2015. *Building a Peaceful Nation: Julius Nyerere and the Establishment of Sovereignty in Tanzania, 1960–1964*, Rochester, NY: University of Rochester Press.

Brower, B. C., 2009. *A Desert Named Peace: The Violence of France's Empire in the Algerian Sahara, 1844–1902*, New York: Columbia University Press.

Brown, D., 2000. *Contemporary Nationalism: Civic, Ethnocultural and Multicultural Politics*, London: Routledge.

Brubaker, R., 1992. *Citizenship and Nationhood in France and Germany*, Cambridge, MA: Harvard University Press.

Burgess, G. T., 2009. *Race, Revolution, and the Struggle for Human Rights in Zanzibar: The Memoirs of Ali Sultan Issa and Seif Sharif Hamad*, Athens, OH: Ohio University Press.

Césaire, A., 2000. *Discourse on Colonialism*, trans. J. Pinkham, New York: Monthly Review Press.

Chakrabarty, D., 2000. *Provincializing Europe: Postcolonial Thought and Historical Difference*, Princeton, NJ: Princeton University Press.

Chatterjee, P., 1993. *Nationalist Thought and the Colonial World: A Derivative Discourse*, Minneapolis, MN: University of Minnesota Press.

Cooper, F., 1996. *Decolonization and African Society: The Labor Question in French and British Africa*, Cambridge: Cambridge University Press.

Cooper, F., 2014. *Citizenship Between Empire and Nation: Remaking France and French Africa, 1945–1960*, Princeton, NJ: Princeton University Press.

Dalrymple, W., 2013. *Return of a King: The Battle for Afghanistan, 1839–42*, New York: Knopf.

Das, V., 2006. *Life and Words: Violence and the Descent into the Ordinary*, Berkeley, CA: University of California Press.

Duara, P., 1997. *Rescuing History from the Nation: Questioning Narratives of Modern China*, Chicago, IL: University of Chicago Press.

Dunn, D. H. (ed.), 1996. *At the Highest Level: The Evolution of International Summitry*, New York: St. Martin's Press.

Falola, T. and Paddock, A., 2011. *The Women's War of 1929: A History of Anti-colonial Resistance in Eastern Nigeria*, Durham, NC: Carolina Academic Press.

Fanon, F., 2004. *The Wretched of the Earth*, trans. R. Philcox, New York: Grove Press.

Fanon, F., 2008. *Black Skin, White Masks*, trans. R. Philcox, New York: Grove Press.

Fields, K. E., 1985. *Revival and Rebellion in Colonial Central Africa*, Princeton, NJ: Princeton University Press.

Gandhi, M. K., 1983. *Autobiography: The Story of My Experiments with Truth*, Mineola, NY: Dover Publications.

Gandhi, M. K., 2008. *Satyagraha in South Africa*, Ahmedabad: Navajivan Publishing House.

Gandhi, M. K., 2009. *'Hind Swaraj' and Other Writings*, ed. A. J. Parel, Cambridge: Cambridge University Press.

Geiger, S., 1997. *TANU Women: Gender and Culture in the Making of Tanganyikan Nationalism, 1955–1965*, Portsmouth, NH: Heinemann.

Gellner, E., 1983. *Nations and Nationalism*, Ithaca, NY: Cornell University Press.

Gordon, D. M., 2012. *Invisible Agents: Spirits in a Central African History*, Athens, OH: Ohio University Press.

Greenfeld, L., 1992. *Nationalism: Five Roads to Modernity*, Cambridge, MA: Harvard University Press.

Groom, A. J. R., 2013. 'Conference Diplomacy', in A. F. Cooper et al. (eds.), *The Oxford Handbook of Modern Diplomacy*, Oxford: Oxford University Press.

Guha, R., 1982. 'On Some Aspects of the Historiography of Colonial India', in R. Guha (ed.), *Subaltern Studies I: Writings on South Asian History and Society*, New Delhi: Oxford University Press.

Guha, R., and Spivak, G. C. (eds.), 1988. *Selected Subaltern Studies*, Oxford: Oxford University Press.

Higgs, C., 1997. *The Ghost of Equality: The Public Lives of D. D. T. Jabavu of South Africa, 1885–1959*, Athens, OH: Ohio University Press.

Ho, E., 2006. *The Graves of Tarim: Genealogy and Mobility Across the Indian Ocean*, Berkeley, CA: University of California Press.

Hobsbawm, E., 2012. *Nations and Nationalism Since 1780: Programme, Myth, Reality*, Cambridge: Cambridge University Press.

Hobsbawm, E. and Ranger, T. (eds.), 1983. *The Invention of Tradition*, Cambridge: Cambridge University Press.

Houser, G. M., 1961. 'At Cairo: The Third All-African People's Conference', *Africa Today*, Volume 8 (4), pp. 11–13.

Hui, W., 2014. *China from Empire to Nation-State*, trans. M. G. Hill, Cambridge, MA: Harvard University Press.

Isaacman, A. F., 1993. 'Peasants and Rural Social Protest in Africa', in F. Cooper et al. (eds.), *Confronting Historical Paradigms: Peasants, Labor, and the Capitalist World System in Africa and Latin America*, Madison, WI: University of Wisconsin Press.

Jack, H. A., 1959. 'Ideological Conflicts', *Africa Today*, Volume 6 (1), pp. 11–17.

Jansen, G. H., 1966. *Nonalignment and the Afro-Asian States*, New York: Praeger.

Kedourie, E., 1960. *Nationalism*, London: Hutchinson & Co.

Kedourie, E. (ed.), 1970. *Nationalism in Asia and Africa*, New York: New American Library.

Kwon, N. A., 2015. *Intimate Empire: Collaboration and Colonial Modernity in Korea and Japan*, Durham, NC: Duke University Press.

Lal, P., 2015. *African Socialism in Postcolonial Tanzania: Between the Village and the World*, Cambridge: Cambridge University Press.

Lee, C. J. (ed.), 2010. *Making a World after Empire: The Bandung Moment and Its Political Afterlives*, Athens, OH: Ohio University Press.

Lenin, V., 2004. *The Right of Nations to Self-Determination*, ed. J. Katzer, trans. B. Isaacs and J. Fineberg, Honolulu: University Press of the Pacific.

Lüthi, L. M., 2016. 'Non-Alignment, 1946–1965: Its Establishment and Struggle Against Afro-Asianism', *Humanity: An International Journal of Human Rights, Humanitarianism, and Development*, Volume 7 (2), pp. 201–223.

Mamdani, M., 2002. *When Victims Become Killers: Colonialism, Nativism, and the Genocide in Rwanda*, Princeton, NJ: Princeton University Press.

Manela, E., 2007. *The Wilsonian Moment: Self-Determination and the International Origins of Anticolonial Nationalism*, New York: Oxford University Press.

Manjapra, K., 2010. *M. N. Roy: Marxism and Colonial Cosmopolitanism*, New Delhi: Routledge.

Matera, M., Bastian, M. L. and Kent, S. K., 2012. *The Women's War of 1929: Gender and Violence in Colonial Nigeria*, New York: Palgrave Macmillan.

Mazower, M., 2012. *Governing the World: The History of an Idea*, New York: Penguin.

McCallum, J. A., 1947. 'The Asian Relations Conference', *The Australian Quarterly*, Volume 19 (2), pp. 13–17.

McDougall, D. and Finnane, A. (eds.), 2010. *Bandung 1955: Little Histories*, Melbourne: Monash Asia Institute.

Mudimbe, V. Y., 1988. *The Invention of Africa: Gnosis, Philosophy, and the Order of Knowledge*, Bloomington, IN: Indiana University Press.

Nehru, J., 2004. *The Discovery of India*, New York: Penguin.

Pandey, G., 2002. *Remembering Partition: Violence, Nationalism and History in India*, Cambridge: Cambridge University Press.

Pati, B. (ed.), 2007. *The 1857 Rebellion*, New York: Oxford University Press.

Peterson, D. R., 2012. *Ethnic Patriotism and the East African Revival: A History of Dissent, c. 1935–1972*, Cambridge: Cambridge University Press.

Ranger, T. O., 1967. *Revolt in Southern Rhodesia, 1896–97: A Study in African Resistance*, Evanston, IL: Northwestern University Press.

Renan, E., 1990. 'What is a Nation?', in H. K. Bhabha (ed.), *Nation and Narration*, New York: Routledge.

Robinson, D., 2000. *Paths of Accommodation: Muslim Societies and French Colonial Authorities in Senegal and Mauritania, 1880–1920*, Athens, OH: Ohio University Press.

Schneider, L., 2014. *Government of Development: Peasants and Politicians in Postcolonial Tanzania*, Bloomington, IN: Indiana University Press.

Scott, J. C., 1976. *The Moral Economy of the Peasant: Rebellion and Subsistence in Southeast Asia*, New Haven, CT: Yale University Press.

Scott, J. C., 1985. *Weapons of the Weak: Everyday Forms of Peasant Resistance*, New Haven, CT: Yale University Press.

Scott, J. C., 1990. *Domination and the Arts of Resistance: Hidden Transcripts*, New Haven, CT: Yale University Press.

Sessions, J. E., 2011. *By Sword and Plow: France and the Conquest of Algeria*, Ithaca, NY: Cornell University Press.

Sevea, I. S., 2012. *The Political Philosophy of Muhammad Iqbal: Islam and Nationalism in Late Colonial India*, Cambridge: Cambridge University Press.

Shepperson, G. A. and Price, T., 1958. *Independent African: John Chilembwe and the Origins, Setting and Significance of the Nyasaland Native Rising of 1915*, Edinburgh: Edinburgh University Press.

Smith, A. D., 1986. *The Ethnic Origins of Nations*, Oxford: Blackwell.

Smith, A. D., 2004. *The Antiquity of Nations*, Cambridge: Polity.

Stalin, J., 2013. *Marxism and the National Question*, New York: Prism Key Press.

Wallerstein, I., 2004. *World-Systems Analysis: An Introduction*, Durham, NC: Duke University Press.

Wilder, G., 2015. *Freedom Time: Negritude, Decolonization, and the Future of the World*, Durham, NC: Duke University Press.

PART II
Asia–Africa modern interactions

Diplomatic and political exchanges

7

THE DISCOURSE OF 'DATSU-A RON'

Japan and Africa in the network of modern history and contemporary politics

Kweku Ampiah

In attempting to map out the relations between Africa and Japan, this chapter takes its cue from history, and its inspiration from Michel Foucault's exhortation to go 'beneath the great continuities of thought, beneath the solid, homogenous manifestation of a single mind or of a collective mentality, to . . . try to detect the incidents of interruptions' that may illuminate the 'new search for rationality and its various effects' (1972: 4). The intention is not so much to break away from tradition as to try to specify and understand the different concepts that enable us to conceive of discontinuity (threshold, the phenomenon of rupture) in the flow of historical events (Foucault, 1972: 4). It is also to acknowledge that although 'historical descriptions are necessarily ordered by the present state of knowledge, they increase with every transformation and never cease, in turn, to break with themselves' (Foucault, 1972:5).

This chapter, in the first instance, assesses the positions of Japan and Africa in the context of the Euro-American hegemony throughout the late nineteenth and first half of the twentieth century. Using Japan's attitudes towards its neighbours (with the inception of the Meiji Restoration from 1868) as a basis for inductive analysis, this chapter attempts to bring into perspective how, placed in the same set of circumstances within an African context, Japan might have responded to its neighbouring African countries. The discussion uses as its frame of reference the infamous newspaper editorial with the striking title *Datsu-A ron*[1] (the proposal that Japan depart from Asia), which was published in the Meiji period, to interrogate Japan's evolving identity in the context of its modernisation, and attempts to articulate the stance Japan might have adopted towards Africa.

The chapter then traces some of the causes of tension between Japan and the major powers in the interwar era, including policies enacted against Japanese exports to Africa in the context of European colonialism in the region. This is followed by an assessment of Japan–Africa relations in the post-World War II era, which examines Japan's economic and political responses to postcolonial Africa. The final section of this chapter reflects on the dynamics of the relationship since the end of the Cold War, and in the context of the emergence of East Asia as a competing force in the newly forming geo-political world.

The analysis suggests that throughout its modern history Japan has tended to view Africa as a region that it could afford to divorce itself from and ignore, and that the popular Japanese conception of Africa as 'distant', not necessarily in a spatial sense, makes it difficult for Japan to bond with Africa in the way that China, for example, seems to currently be doing with the region, or indeed the manner in which Japan has bonded with the West. In essence, while the recent economic transformation of Africa has ignited a developmentalist reaction and a more proactive attitude on the part of Japan towards the region, as is evident in the Tokyo International Conference on African Development (TICAD) process, there is a vacuum in Japan's relations with Africa, which could be put down to Japan's lack of public diplomacy with African countries. The analysis suggests that this is attributable to the sources of Japan's ambitions as inspired by its modernisation from the nineteenth century, including the injunctions in *Datsu-A ron*, which may be seen as encompassing policy recommendations for Japanese diplomacy.

Modernisation, imperialism and the aspiration of national dignity

This discussion demands a reflection (by way of introduction) on the issue of national dignity in Japan's modern history, and an evocation of the relevance of the problematic of dignity to the colonial history of Africa. There are two primary concerns that should be highlighted under the theme of national dignity, which can be understood as the self-proclaimed right of a people to be valued and respected in all manifestations of human relations. Starting from the late nineteenth century, this chapter will attempt to identify common areas of interest between the African countries and Japan with regard to the issue of national dignity and how this manifested in international politics and diplomacy. Secondly, it will attempt to show where the Japanese and the Africans might have diverged in their respective pursuance of this ideal in a world dominated by European imperialism. Thus the analysis in this section will include an assessment of Japanese experiences abroad in the face of Euro-American hegemony in the late nineteenth century and the first half of the twentieth century.

Datsu-A ron: Japan's enlightenment movement, and estrangement from its neighbours

As nineteenth-century Japan discovered the material value of Western civilisation, and deemed it the epitome of human achievement, this automatically devalued, in Japan's estimation, all other forms of culture and civilisation, including those of its neighbours, and to some extent even its own traditional values, because they are inherently related to those of its neighbours. What to do about its 'failed' neighbours therefore preoccupied the minds of Japan's new leaders right from the beginning of the Meiji Restoration, following the end of the ancien régime. The opium wars of the 1840s, leading to China's defeat by the British, had weakened the coherence and security of East Asia, a factor partly responsible for the upheavals that led to the 'Restoration' of imperial rule in Japan and its decision to modernise. Embracing modernisation was a strategic necessity for Japan, but it also confirmed Japan's submission to, and identification with, the new hegemonic powers of East Asia, Europe and the USA. And it confirmed Japan's recognition of its future as being with the affluent and powerful West, which implied Japan's rejection of its weak and immobile neighbours. It was in that context that the enigmatic missive, *Datsu-A ron*, the proposal for Japan to 'abandon Asia', arose as an expression of the appreciation of the proven strength of the West in relation to the weak and failed countries of East Asia. It was a binary format that preoccupied Meiji Japan, and which served as the basis for the proposal for Japan to decamp and embrace Western civilisation. The piece was first published in the Japanese newspaper *Jiji Shipō* on 16 March 1885 and is attributed to Fukuzawa Yukichi, Japan's foremost enlightenment figure.

The first sentence of *Datsu-A ron*, on what clearly concerned Japan's quest for dignity refers to the winds of Western civilisation blowing to the East as a result of the fluidity of modern communications, and didactically suggests the need to submit to the currents of those winds. 'The blade of grass should bend in the direction of the wind,' it exhorts. It further notes that should Japan attempt to stand in the way of change it would end up losing its sovereignty, since the forces of change would not permit Japan to exist in isolation. The article affirms that Japan had already embraced Western civilisation and detached itself from Asia's narrow-mindedness, and laments Japan's close proximity to failed states like China and Korea, 'who unlike Japan lack[ed] the ability to progress' because they were shackled to ancient traditions and practices such as Confucianism. Fukuzawa was clearly ashamed of Japan's historical and cultural associations with its neighbours, which he saw 'as superstitious, devoted to a belief in Yin and Yang, and lawless', and lamented that Westerners might think the Japanese were no different because of their geographical proximity to these countries. Thus he recommended that Japan should abandon Asia, and not treat its neighbours any differently from how Westerners would treat them. The final statement of the treatise pronounces that 'those who keep bad company cannot avoid being labelled as bad either', and affirms a 'heartfelt resolve to decline any association with the bad companions in East Asia'[2] (Fukuzawa, 1885).

The exhortation that Japan should abandon Asia is indeed evocative, not least because it affirms frustrations with Japan's circumstances, and the determination to see Japan improve its standing in relation to the West. But *Datsu-A ron* was not about isolating Japan from the rest of Asia; instead, Fukuzawa seemed determined that a modern Japan with a new political system, divested of the (old) Asian values and practices that held it back, would help revive the region from its slumber by disinheriting it from antiquated values such as Confucianism, which Fukuzawa saw as a source of its failure. Reinventing the region was necessary because there was concern that the current circumstances of Japan's neighbours would be a drawback to its own standing in the eyes of the civilised West, which saw the countries of East Asia as culturally homogeneous.

Rather than divorce itself from the region, Japan, according to Fukuzawa's treatise, would serve as the axle[3] of the region and 'liberate' East Asia from its malaise, but in that role Fukuzawa was firm in his recommendation that Japan should not treat the countries in the region any differently from how Western countries treated them. Consequently, Japan embarked on imperialist missions against its neighbours in a fashion that ultimately, if ironically, led to its further estrangement from the region as it assumed the mantle of the villain, an imperial power that disrespected the dignity of the nations it dominated. In essence, by dint of geographical proximity, Japan initiated a form of continental imperialism, but initially in collaboration with Western countries. It subsequently turned its back on the West and assumed a unilateral, if desperate, mission to free East Asia from Western domination, through the East Asia Co-prosperity Sphere.

The idea of the Co-prosperity Sphere was a product of Japan's estrangement from the West as the imperialist struggle in East Asia intensified from the 1930s. Essentially, the more Japan found itself divorced from its Western collaborators, the more it found it necessary to commit itself to creating an enclave within its immediate surroundings, not through alliances with its neighbours but by means of a system of aggressive expansionism that further isolated it in the region.

The Co-prosperity Sphere, as declared by the Japanese government in June 1940 (which was enlarged from its predecessor, New Order in East Asia[4]), was designed to ensure two mutually

The discourse of 'Datsu-A ron'

reinforcing objectives, one economic and the other political. Economically, East Asia, Southeast Asia and Oceania, with Japan at its centre, would be a single economic bloc; this would be complemented by political unity of the countries in the region, excluding Western countries, an idea reminiscent of the Monroe Doctrine of 1823 by which the United States excluded the European powers from Latin America in order to ensure its hegemony in the region (Chomsky, 1969; Perkins, 1960).

It is clear from Japan's relations with its neighbours since 1885 that it managed to establish itself as the axle of East Asia, as predicted in *Datsu-A ron*, and proceeded to treat the countries in the region with reckless abandon, and in a manner that undermined, according to historical accounts, the dignity of those countries, even while Japan itself was resisting indignities Western powers were attempting to impose. Fukuzawa expected modern Japan to treat its neighbours as aggressively as Western countries treated them. But why was there such urgency on the part of Japan to behave, as *Datsu-A ron* divined it would, in such an aggressive manner towards its neighbours? Michel Foucault's dichotomy of the idea and organisation of a pastoral type of power, as opposed to the government of a city-state, might be a useful point of reference in attempting to understand Japan's attitude. Based on this dyadic configuration of power, pre-World War II Japan emerges as the equivalent of a Greek city-state whose primary concern was ensuring the security of the nation. Thus, like the ancient Athenians, 'the object or target of the government [was] the city state in its substantial reality' (Foucault, 2004: 123–25). In that regard, 'power [was] defined by its ability to triumph over enemies, defeat them, and reduce them to slavery', and as much 'by the possibility of conquest' and territorial aggrandisement (Foucault, 2004: 126). Consequently, imperial Japan was devoid of what Foucault (2004: 126) refers to as 'pastoral power', which is 'fundamentally a beneficent power . . . a power of care' (Foucault, 2004: 126–27), the source of which Foucault attributes to the Abrahamic God who serves as a shepherd (*pasteur*) to his flock 'to avoid the misfortune that may threaten the least of its members' (Foucault, 2004: 127). *Datsu-A ron*'s prescriptions regarding the power relationship between modern Japan and its neighbours excluded the positive valuation of the theme of beneficence (Foucault, 2004: 147) towards its weak neighbours. Indeed, as early as 1876 Japan had imposed unequal treaties on Korea, copying the Ansei Treaties that had been forced upon it by the major powers in 1858. Subsequently it took Taiwan as a colony following war with China in 1895, colonised Korea in 1905, and progressed across East Asia in aggressive leaps to expand its sphere of influence in the region.

In their urgency and desperation to anchor the state, the leaders of early modern Japan simply dismissed empathy (pastoral care) towards their neighbouring failed states as a luxury Japan could not afford, for it would have limited Japan's own ambitions and development, as argued by Fukuzawa in *Datsu-A ron* But while Foucault suggests that 'the spread of the pastorate as the source of a specific type of power over men, as a model and matrix of procedures for the government of men, really only begins with Christianity' (2004: 147–48), we cannot overlook the fact that Japanese imperialism was essentially a copy of what the Christian countries were doing in the nineteenth and early twentieth century. As with Western imperialism, Japan's actions were about the political domination of 'others' without the 'power of care' (2004: 127), as Foucault might say.

Placing Japan in the context of colonial Africa

Transposing the East Asia scenario to Africa, it is tempting to suggest that Japan would have behaved no differently towards its African neighbours, not least because Japan's perception of Africa was easily discernible from the comments about Japan's neighbouring countries in

Datsu-A ron. Like East Asia, Africa was backward and bankrupt, and from Japan's perspective should, at best, serve as an example of what Japan should not become in the context of its evolving modernisation process. In that regard the region did serve as a reference point for Japan's own progression into a modern state, not least through how, based on the outcomes of the Berlin Conference of 1884–85, European colonialism played out in Africa, and the economic implications of that for the colonisers and the colonised alike. In essence, it is no exaggeration to assume that, if what happened in East Asia in the nineteenth century as a result of European imperialism had been replicated in sub-Saharan Africa, placed in the context of Africa in the mid nineteenth century, Japan would have embarked on a similar spree of imperialist expansionism in Africa as it carried out in East Asia. In other words, it would have found it strategically necessary to 'distance' itself from its 'backward' neighbours, as *Datsu-A ron* exhorted Japan to do with regard to the East Asian countries. Distancing itself from its neighbours, as suggested, amounted, in fact, to getting embroiled in territorial expansion in the region.

Africa and Japan in pursuance of national dignity

Although Japan was never colonised as most African countries were, the Japanese sense of inferiority with regard to America and Europe was palpable from the second half of the nineteenth century through to the interwar period, and remained so for a very long time. In that regard, Japan's diplomatic initiatives as a fledgling modern state in the nineteenth century revolved around two main ambitions: firstly, to snatch back its dignity in response to the Ansei Treaties and the extraterritorial rights imposed on it by Western countries in 1858; and secondly, to attain prestige in world affairs in the interwar period, and following its defeat in World War II.

Meanwhile, sub-Saharan Africa, which had been disembowelled by the slave trade, and subsequently by agreements among the world powers following the Berlin Conference, remained traumatised by different sets of indignities. As such, the African countries continued to strive to attain a semblance of dignity for themselves, albeit through formulae not necessarily always identical to Japan's, as shown by the following examples. The Zulus of South Africa fought the British in 1879, and the four Anglo-Ashanti wars between 1824 and 1901 were fought to defend the Ashanti kingdom from British encroachment. The Treaty of Addis Ababa of 23 October 1896 was also the culmination of a war between Ethiopia and Italy, in which Emperor Menelik II overcame the technological might of the Italian army with the result that Ethiopia emerged victorious in the famous battle of Adwa. These examples of African resistance were in pursuance of political autonomy, the maintenance of territorial integrity, and indeed national dignity.

On the other hand, in striving for these two ambitions, Japan initially purposefully submitted itself to Euro-American domination and systematically copied the practices of the Western imperial powers from the latter part of the nineteenth century. The basis of this non-confrontational approach to combating external threats was presumably the belief among Japan's leaders that for their country to attain dignity and prestige in world affairs it would have to copy, and behave like, the imperialist powers. Consequently, as discussed above, Japan embarked on a road show of imperialism, taking colonies here and there, in what is referred to as 'continental imperialism'. In essence, Japan colonised its neighbours, people whose racial appearance matched that of the Japanese themselves. But it is clear in the historiography that without Britain's support and assistance Japan might conceivably not have emerged successful in its earlier imperialist ambitions. A crucial case in point is the Russo-Japanese war of 1905, in which Japan emerged seemingly victorious, and which facilitated Japan's colonisation of Korea. That crucial victory over Russia also made possible Japan's advance into Manchuria to dominate the region from 1931.

The discourse of 'Datsu-A ron'

Despite Japan's achievements as an imperial power and its resounding diplomatic successes, such as the Anglo-Japanese Alliance and its contributions towards World War I on the side of the Allies, by 1919 it felt it was being deprived of the dignity and prestige it desperately desired. This was strikingly evident in certain crucial decisions taken at the Paris Conference of 1919, and Japan's subsequent reactions. Accounts of the lives and ambitions of Japanese nationals who lived and circulated in different parts of Africa in the nineteenth and early twentieth centuries, as chronicled in Aoki's (1993) monograph and Kitagawa's (2014) article, affirm some of the indignities Japan and its nationals were confronted with, despite the prestigious place the country already occupied as an imperial power and in international affairs. Kitagawa chronicles the concerns of Japanese travellers in Southeast Africa, such as Captain Katsue Mori and the writer Ikai Shirakwa, among others, about discriminatory practices against Japanese nationals in the region. For our purposes, this chapter will reflect on the informative case of Mr Komahei Furuya, a Japanese merchant who settled in Cape Town in the final moments of the nineteenth century, and who, as will be discussed, felt that he was not respected as a Japanese national. The discussion is sourced from the Colonial Office files of the British National Archives.

It seems that Mr Furuya was a successful merchant, but his race and nationality were hindrances to both his life and his business in South Africa because of the restrictive legislation regarding Asians in the country. He settled in South Africa in 1898, and ran a successful import and retail business in Japanese and Chinese sundry goods, with the sphere of his wholesale trade extending over most of South Africa. He was confronted with discriminatory laws and practices in parts of the country, pertaining in particular to the Asiatic Law Amendment Act of 1908 (Section 14), which stunted the expansion of his business. Exasperated, in 1909 Mr Furuya wrote a letter to the Japanese Ambassador, His Excellency Mr Takaaki Kato, complaining about the special Immigration Act that forbade all Asians to enter or reside in the Transvaal and Orange River colonies. In particular, the legislation made it impossible for him to establish a branch of his business in Johannesburg, and he lamented that 'this is indeed one of the great drawbacks under which we, the Japanese merchants, are struggling'. Consequently he appealed to the Ambassador, 'I beseech your Excellency to induce the Transvaal Government to extend to the Japanese subjects the privilege of *exemption* from the . . . special laws aimed at Asians.'[5]

In fact, the Japanese were faced with cases like this in different parts of the world controlled by Western powers, including California and the Dutch East Indies, where they were apparently treated in the same manner as the Chinese, and by which they felt appalled, a point which underlines Fukuzawa's concern as expressed in *Datsu-A ron*, namely discomfort that Western countries would be inclined to lump the Japanese together with their neighbours[6] because of their cultural similarity and geographical proximity.

When Japan's attempts to be fully accepted and treated as a European nation by the Western powers failed, it proposed a 'racial equality clause' in the Covenant of the League of Nations, at the Paris Conference in 1919, in a desperate attempt to snatch dignity for Japanese people outside of Japan. As Shimazu's (1998) monograph, *Japan, Race and Equality*, confirms, the racial equality clause was not designed with universal rights in mind; however,understandably, Africans associated themselves with it, and attempted to deploy the Japanese proposal to gain dignity for Africans. But when the Liberian delegate, who supported the Clause, approached Makino Nobuaki about collaborating on the issue of racial equality, the Japanese Foreign Minister is reported to have told him to go and see Georges Clemenceau, the Chief French delegate at the conference and an architect of the Treaty of Versailles, about the matter (Shimazu, 1998: 114). At any rate, the proposal was rejected by the League, and the Japanese Foreign Minister stated at a press conference, 'we are too proud to accept a place of admitted inferiority in dealing with one or more of the associated nations. We want nothing but simple justice' (Shimazu, 1998).

From then on, Japan's responses to and attitude towards the West became progressively more critical, as it felt it was unfairly made to constantly negotiate from a position of weakness in international affairs.

As Japan's elected governments gradually lost ground to the military and nationalists following the invasion of Manchuria in 1931, Tokyo finally withdrew from the League of Nations on 24 February 1933. Yosuke Matsuoka, the Chief Japanese delegate, said, 'we are not coming back' and led the Japanese delegation out of the conference hall in Geneva, apparently out of frustration in the face of international criticism of Japan's occupation of Manchuria.

This account shows that the Africans and the Japanese were both struggling for racial equality – what Makino referred to as 'simple justice'. Their respective narratives about the quest for dignity were indeed pregnant with the ignominy of racial discrimination. Yet there was a divergence in how the problem was approached from the respective positions of the Africans and the Japanese. As indicated, the Japanese government was alarmed by the 'universalist' interpretation that was attached to its 'nationalistic' proposal; after all, assessed in the context of *Datsu-A ron*, it was better for Japan to disassociate from failed countries such as African nations. Consequently there was no hesitation on the part of Makino to *Datsu-A* (depart from Africa), as it were, a response that confirmed the lack of a sense of pastoral power on the part of imperial Japan with regard to its weak neighbours. The Africans, on the other hand, took the universalist nature of the proposal for granted. As noted, a Liberian delegate was enthusiastic about the proposal. The Pan-African Congress, whose members included the American scholar and pan-Africanist W.E.B. Du Bois and Blaise Diange, the first black African elected to the French Chamber of Deputies, also invoked the clause in the interest of Africans and people of African origin, wherever they were.

Meanwhile, as Japanese exports expanded into the British colonies in Africa from the late 1920s and the early 1930s, the Colonial Office instituted higher tariffs and taxes on Japanese cotton exports to East and West Africa (Ampiah, 1991), essentially to stem Japanese economic inroads into African markets. This was detrimental to the interest of African consumers as it denied them access to cheap Japanese exports, but it also undermined the economic interests of Japan, whose exports to both East and West Africa were smothered, essentially to protect cotton exports from Lancashire. This was the context of the brewing geo-political tensions between Japan and the imperial powers of the West, and indeed in the context of the world economic depression.

The post-World War II discourse about Japan's relations with Africa

The discourse about Africa–Japan relations following the end of World War II tends to concentrate on events from the 1970s, ignoring the early postwar period. The discussions ponderously leapfrogged the 1950s and early 1960s. However, Japan's attitude towards Africa is meaningfully observable from the mid 1950s at the very least, especially in relation to the Japanese government's responses to the unfolding discourse about decolonisation. In this regard it is perhaps convenient for our purposes to focus on the position of the Japanese Ministry of Foreign Affairs (MoFA) on decolonisation in relation to the Bandung Conference of 1955 (Ampiah, 2007). What emerged from the MoFA's position was that Japan should be sensitive to the concerns of the colonial powers about the anticolonial movement, and that as a participant in the conference it should not express a position on the issue of decolonisation. In essence, Japan did not support the anticolonial movement, a position that incidentally fits within its matrix of non-association with weak countries and the theme of pastoral power, although there was no indication that it opposed the cause. Given Japan's circumstances as a villain of the war, a defeated country stealthily making its way back into international politics after the war, 'Aspiring sincerely to an international peace based on justice and order' (as stipulated in Article 9, the Peace Clause, of the postwar Constitution), perhaps staying neutral on the issue of the volcanic decolonisation process was strategically sensible.

Moreover, Japan's burgeoning economic relations with South Africa in the 1960s made it difficult for it to support any radical measures the United Nations General Assembly (UNGA) adopted against the apartheid regime. Consequently, Japan became estranged, following our *Datsu-A ron* matrix, from the Afro-Asian (AA) group of states at the General Assembly on the issue of apartheid, and also on questions about decolonisation. The situation was such that as early as 1963, British policymakers realised Japan was the 'odd man out' within the AA Group and that such an 'odd position' had 'conditioned' as well as 'limited the role it could play within the UN' (Pan, 2005: 99–108). Thus, despite its ambitions to serve as a bridge between the AA Group and the West, in fact, as the British noted, 'Japan had little moral influence' within the group (Pan, 2005: 109). This was compounded by the fact that despite the growing expanse and depth of its economy globally, Japan's interest in the African political-economy was wholly insignificant throughout the Cold War era, perhaps a testament to the historical distance Japan insisted on maintaining between itself and the poorer countries.

The post-Cold War era and the TICAD process

Since the end of the early 1990s, however, there has been a tremendous shift in Japan's attitude towards Africa, and the discourse about Japan–Africa relations reflects this. The emphasis of the discussions since 2000 has been on Japan's contributions to Africa's economic development, exemplified by the Tokyo International Conference on African Development (TICAD) process. While the discussions have tended to address generalities without much concern with specific themes, or an attempt to deal with concepts, they overwhelmingly note the trend in terms of Japan's attitude towards Africa since the early 1990s, and confirm the motivation on the part of Japan to apply pastoral power, in the form of economic assistance, in its relations with African countries. Through TICAD, Japan has been contending with the African development problems, specifically through the activities of the Japan International Cooperation Agency (JICA).

The TICAD initiative is conceivably the most comprehensive and, so far, consistent development aid package ever designed for Africa, although, as it stands, it serves essentially as development software that minutely assesses and pieces together strategies to bring to bear remedies for the structural problems hindering Africa's development. Broadly speaking, TICAD (Ampiah, 2012; Ampiah & Rose, 2012) seems designed to link the separate components of a range of development essentials – education (capacity building), infrastructure, health, agriculture, industrial policy – to harness the possibilities for sustainable economic growth. It has also led the way for the African countries to seek economic and development partners beyond their traditional partners, the European countries and the US, and such institutions as the World Bank.

Although TICAD began as a foreign policy initiative by the MoFA, with an emphasis on economic assistance as a palliative for the impoverished African countries, it was hoped that the initiative would evolve into a strong economic partnership between Japan and the African countries, reminiscent of Japan's own conception of aid as economic cooperation (*keizai kyōryoku*). Indeed, the African partners in the TICAD process have insisted on trade and investment as the primary basis for the TICAD initiative, and as the ingredients for economic growth. Consequently, since TICAD IV (2008) Japan has attempted to encourage the process towards the direction of PPP (Public–Private Partnership) to attract the participation of the Japanese private sector, the vanguards of the economic development of Southeast Asia from the 1950s to the 1980s. There is an awareness among the Japanese development community, including academics and bureaucrats, that Africa needs a long lifeline of concentrated support in terms of knowledge and capital (Nihon Keizai Shinbun, 2008: 2) in order to revitalise its economy. As such, for the first time, the Japanese business magazine *Tōyō Kezia*, as part of the drive to entice the private sector to engage more proactively with the TICAD process, devoted an issue in January 2010 to Africa, proclaiming it as the last new market in the world. In the introduction to his 2013 monograph, Hirano Katsumi of the Institute of Development Economies noted that Africa was certainly and steadily going through an economic transformation, not least because, while the region had not experienced any growth for over 20 years, the reverse is now the case, with Africa achieving high growth that has attracted much commendation (Hirano, 2013: i). As such, there is now a general awareness among Japanese policymakers of the need for Japan to approach TICAD as a partnership with potential economic benefits for the relevant stakeholders.

But TICAD is not sustainable in the long term if it does not yield tangible economic gains for Japan, and given the country's attempts to find correctives for its stifled economy, perhaps the African countries might proactively emphasise the potential mutual benefits the initiative promises. The fifth TICAD summit in 2013 indeed emphasised, in principle, the importance of the private sector in Africa's economic development. This was based on the proposals of the high profile Public–Private Council for the Promotion of TICAD V,[7] which was chaired by the Minister of Foreign Affairs and the Vice Chairman of the Keidanren, Mr Masahiro Sakane, representing the private sector. The Council met four times between August 2012 and April 2013, prior to TICAD V, during which time officials of the Ministry of Finance, Ministry of Economy, Trade and Industry (METI), and representatives of development agencies including JICA, Japan External Trade Organization (JETRO) and the Japan Bank for International Cooperation (JBIC), along with 20 private sector representatives, hammered out recommendations for a robust involvement of the private sector in the TICAD process. Among the recommendations was that funds should be provided towards assisting the economic and business environment of Africa, as well as maintaining the industrial base of the region to attract Japanese private sector investments to the region (Keizai Dōyūkai, 2013: 8). As the title of the Japanese version of the document containing the recommendations affirmed, TICAD V was seen as an opportune moment for Japan to make a strategic commitment towards Africa's development. The subtitle is equally positive (A New Horizon for Japan's Trailblazing Economy with Dynamic Africa); it suggests constructive relations between Japan and Africa. Yet even after TICAD VI, which took place in August 2016, Japanese private sector involvement in the TICAD process is still work in progress.

Public diplomacy in Japan–Africa relations

Much of the recent discussions about Africa's economic transformation include an assessment of the dimensions of China's influence in the region, both economically and diplomatically. Indeed, China is currently Africa's major trading partner, which raises the question of how China has managed to establish such a significant presence in Africa while Japan's relations with the African countries still remain to be fully formed. The answer may lie partly in the fact that the Forum on China–Africa Cooperation (FOCAC), which was established in 2000 (seven years after the inception of TICAD), operates primarily as a forum for business deals (trade and investment) between China and Africa (Hirano, 2013: 2), whereas TICAD largely exists as a forum for the discussion of minute policy details about development and the provision of

The discourse of 'Datsu-A ron'

mostly grant and technical aid, seemingly as an end in itself without the incentives, trade and investment for sustainable economic growth. As noted, Japanese development assistance to the region has lacked Japanese private sector investment and commitment to trade relations with the region (Hirano, 12), essential components of the Japanese economic assistance to East Asian countries from the 1950s to the present. This is indeed a crucial difference in the manner in which the two countries, Japan and China, operate in Africa, but there are also other fundamental differences.

China has a working public diplomacy towards Africa, which Japan lacks. China's approach towards postcolonial Africa (for ideological reasons) has been proactive, and the ideological content of the relationship continues, covertly, to influence China's dealings with the region. In contrast, the lack of public diplomacy on the part of Japan towards Africa has not helped in ameliorating, and in fact has contributed to, Japan's reticent relations with Africa.

It is tempting to view Japan's continued lack of public diplomacy towards Africa as a legacy, if not a by-product, of its historical aloofness towards the region, itself a product of the *Datsu-A ron* principle from the nineteenth century. As argued, Japan found it strategically useful to distance itself from what it saw as failed states. While Japan's circumstances in the post-World War II era necessitated and enforced a more reformed Japanese attitude towards its neighbours, the distance (both spatial and imagined) between Japan and Africa has not really been bridged, and the depressed economic circumstances of most of Africa have not helped. Consequently, despite Japan's grand and commendable initiatives through TICAD, and the fact that the forum celebrated its twentieth anniversary in 2013, the average person in Japan, including university graduates and university students, knows almost nothing about the forum. In contrast, a Chinese university graduate or university student seems reasonably informed about China's relations with the African countries, and conceivably about FOCAC.

In that respect, the official Chinese position has proved to be more proactive and dynamic in China's public diplomacy towards Africa. An understanding of public diplomacy would be useful here. It is conceived as 'one of the most important facets of foreign policy . . . and often takes the form of broadcasting, exchanges, and outreach with foreign populations . . . to help promote greater understanding' between a government and the international community (Committee on Foreign Relations, 2010: 1). As a foreign policy tool, 'it is distinguished from the exclusive contact with foreign governments that has characterised traditional diplomacy' (Committee on Foreign Relations, 2010: 4). Thus public diplomacy is about reshaping traditional diplomacy, to take it beyond the formal setting and exchanges between elites in closed rooms. It is also about ensuring a horizontal, as opposed to a top-down, approach to diplomacy. Public diplomacy can be formulated into five broad categories (Cull, 2008: xv; Committee on Foreign Relations, 2010: 16–17):

1   Communication, with an emphasis on listening and responding accordingly;
2   Advocacy through education;
3   Cultural diplomacy, which is designed to enlighten the foreign public about the actor's core values and aesthetics in a manner that would promote the actor's interests;
4   Exchange diplomacy, to enable direct interaction between foreign audiences and citizens in order to nurture mutual interests between people of different cultures, a good example of which is the exchange of college students;
5   International broadcasting, in particular the transmission of news.

Examples of a useful public diplomacy tool are the national organisations for educational and cultural relations with foreign countries, such as the British Council, the Alliance Française, the

Japan Foundation, and more recently the Confucius Institute (CI). Using these organisations as a medium for assessing how affluent countries engage with the African public, it would seem that Japan has neglected this tool in its diplomacy towards Africa. A comparison between China and Japan in this regard further highlights the point, not least because although the Confucius Institute, which began in 2004, is a relatively new institution, it has been far more proactive in Africa than the Japan Foundation, which was founded in 1972, as an agency of the Ministry of Foreign Affairs (MOFA), but since 2003 exists as an independent institution under the jurisdiction of MoFA.

Since the first CI was established in Africa in December 2005, 31 CIs are currently operating in the region. There are also five Confucius Classrooms (teaching Chinese language and culture at local schools). In contrast, there is no Japan Foundation office anywhere in sub-Saharan Africa, and only one in all of Africa, based in Egypt. Conversely, there are six Japan Foundation offices in Europe, two in the US, and five in Southeast Asia alone. As it stands, East Asia has seven Japan Foundation offices. If we use this as a basis for assessing Japan's public diplomacy we would have to conclude that in regard to Africa it has failed miserably, especially since the Foundation aims towards comprehensive and effective development of its international cultural exchange programmes in the following categories:[8]

- Promotion of (Japanese) arts and cultural exchange;
- Promotion of Japanese-language education overseas;
- Promotion of (overseas) Japanese studies and intellectual exchange.

But the correlation between Japan's economic and diplomatic interests and the location of a Japan Foundation office does not have to be scientifically proved; it is obvious. All the same the question has to be posed: Why would Japan, through its most powerful medium for public diplomacy, the Japan Foundation, promote Japanese studies in, and intellectual exchange with, for example France and Canada, but not do the same with regard to Nigeria and Tanzania?

Conclusion

The editorial board members of *Jiji Shipō*, including Yukichi Fukuzawa, were very alert to the dynamics of global affairs, particularly those involving the major powers. They were journalists and scholars with much interest in the political economy and diplomacy of the European countries and the United States. It is highly plausible then that they, and Fukuzawa in particular, attentively, if not zealously, followed the proceedings of the Berlin Conference. Incidentally, *Datsu-A ron* was published less than two weeks after the Conference, which ended on 26 February. If Fukuzawa followed the Conference's proceedings as suggested, he would have carefully noted its outcomes, which might have informed him of how an imperial power should deal with its dominions. The proposal in *Datsu-A ron* for Japan to distance itself from its weak neighbours might have served as a blueprint for Japan's foreign policy behaviour towards weaker nations and cultures. To put it another way, in so far as historical moments evoke the past and filter through to the future, Korhonen's (2014) point that *Datsu-A ron* appeared just once in the 1880s, implying that it was not part of the popular debate about Japan's relations with its neighbours until it was resurrected and problematised in the post-World War II era, is neither here nor there. What is important is how the idea might have impacted on policymaking in the Meiji era and indeed in the long term. While Kitaoka (2011, 34) argues that 'at the time [the editorial] failed to draw much attention', certainly the Meiji elite and policymakers would have read the piece and reflected on its content, if only because it appeared in the most important newspaper at the time and, as is popularly believed, was written by Fukuzawa. At any rate the idea might have been conceived to legitimise, by signalling support for, the government's imperialist ambitions, which policymakers would have found difficult to dismiss. What is not in doubt is that the jingoistic tone of the *Datsu-A ron* largely reflected modern Japan's attitude towards its neighbours until the end of World War II.

This chapter, taking its cue from Michel Foucault's concept of pastoral power, argues that Japan's aggressive behaviour towards other East Asian countries, as recommended by the *Datsu-A ron*, meant that Japan's relations with its weak neighbours were devoid of a sense of pastoral care. Japan chose instead to question and undermine their dignity; ironically this was in Japan's attempts to assert its own dignity in a world dominated by Western imperialist powers. The discussion in this chapter attempts to identify possible common areas of interest between African countries and Japan on the issue of national dignity, how this manifested itself in international politics, and where the Japanese and the Africans might have diverged in their respective pursuance of this ideal as they contended with Euro-American imperialism. The assessment of the interwar period shows how Japan's triumphs as an imperial power did not yield the prestige it craved in international affairs, forcing it to initiate policies that further alienated it from its neighbours, and indeed from Western powers.

The analysis suggests a correlation between the proposals in the editorial *Datsu-A ron* for Japan to remain aloof towards its weak neighbours, and Japan's reticent attitude towards African countries, which continued in the post-World War II era, as demonstrated by its reserved responses to the aspirations of postcolonial African countries. The MoFA's policy brief concerning how Japan should deal with questions about anticolonialism at the Bandung Conference is indicative of Japan's estrangement from the primary concerns of the decolonisation movement in Africa, and the Asia–Africa bloc at the UN as a whole. Essentially, Japan's relations with the postcolonial African countries remained stunted throughout the era of the Cold War, plagued by questions about Japan's expanding economic relations with South Africa.

Japan's responses towards Africa were, however, transformed from the early 1990s through the TICAD process. Since then Japan has systematically and constructively contributed to the discourse about Africa's economic development by endeavouring to find ways to deal with some of the region's structural economic problems. Despite these recent developments, Japan–Africa relations remain encumbered by the metaphorical distance between Japan and Africa. The Japanese obsession with the idea that Africa is too distant,[9] which constantly appears in discussions and narratives about the region, has not helped to mediate the gap. In relation to TICAD IV in 2008, for example, the popular Japanese newspaper *Nihon Keizai Shinbun* (2008: 2) repeated the phrase, albeit in a much wider context. In the main, the distance alluded to does not seem to be quantifiable, because it refers as much to a virtual gap in regard to culture, mutual understanding and affinity between Africa and Japan, which might have been fomented by Japan's earlier *Datsu-A ron* attitude towards weak nations, and sustained indeed by geographical distance. The lack of public diplomacy on the part of Japan towards the African countries, which is possibly a legacy of the above principle, has not helped. But the gap is also attributable to the postcolonial African countries' lack of vision in terms of diversifying their international partners; until quite recently they tended to stick with their traditional Western partners, despite these partners' overt demonstrations of fatigue in their relations with Africa.

In the early part of the discussion I noted that the opportunities for modernisation promised by Western civilisation forced Japan's leaders in the late nineteenth century to embrace European ideals of modernisation. Perhaps it is now time for African countries to wake up to the fact that the world has experienced a seismic shift in the past 30 years, in the resounding performance in economic development in East Asia, and that instead of continuing to follow the old ideas of development from the West that have not worked for the African countries, it is imperative they start learning from the countries currently transforming the parameters of the debate about development, the East Asian countries. The most auspicious way to do this would be to start teaching East Asian history in secondary schools in Africa, and East Asian Studies should be introduced and incorporated into higher education; this should include the teaching of East Asian languages such as Chinese and Japanese, which would also help to bridge the gap between African countries and East Asian countries and mitigate the proverbial distance between Japan and Africa, for example. Perhaps the Japan Foundation would find it useful, as part of Japan's public diplomacy, to contribute to this.

Notes

1 Pekka Korhonen, 'Leaving Asia? The Meaning of *Datsu-A* and Japan's Modern History', *The Asia-Pacific Journal*, Volume 12, Issue 9, No. 3, March 3, 2014.
2 悪友を親しむ者は共に悪友を免かる可らず。我は心に於て亜細亜東方の悪友を謝絶するものなり。
3 「。。。亜細亜全州の中に在て新に一機軸を出し。。。」
4 This was announced on 22 December 1938 by Prime Minister Fumimaro Konoe.
5 My emphasis. 'Mr Komahei Furuya to the Japanese Ambassador', South Africa, Questions Affecting Coloured and Native Races, Further Correspondence (1910), CO 879/104.
6 Mr J. A. C. Tilley (Foreign Office) to Mr H. C. M Lambert (Colonial Office), 20 January 1910, South Africa, Questions Affecting Coloured and Native Races, Further Correspondence (1910), CO 879/104; Sir Richard Solomon to Sir Francis Hopwood, 10 March 1910, South Africa, Questions Affecting Coloured and Native Races, Further Correspondence (1910), CO 879/104; Mr G. R. Clerk (Foreign Office) to Mr H. C. M Lambert (Colonial Office), 4 March 1919, South Africa, Questions Affecting Coloured and Native Races, Further Correspondence (1910), CO 879/104.
7 Public–Private Council for the Promotion of TICAD V, Proposal by the Public–Private Council for the Promotion of TICAD V: A New Horizon for the Japan's Trailblazing Economy with Dynamic Africa (Provisional Translations, May 16 2013.
8 www.jpf.go.jp/e/about/outline/img/Pamphlet_e.pdf Accessed 17 July 2014.
9 アフリカは遠い.

Bibliography

Ampiah, K., 1991. 'British Commercial Policies Against Japanese Expansionism in East and West Africa, 1932–1935', *International Journal of African Historical Studies*, Volume 23 (4), pp. 619–641.
Ampiah, K., 2007. 'Japan's journey back to Asia and the new foreign policy of independence', *The Political and Moral Imperatives of the Bandung Conference of 1955: The Reactions of the US, UK and Japan*, Folkestone: Global Oriental, pp. 166–202.
Ampiah, K., 2012. 'The Discourse of Local Ownership in Development: Rhapsodies about Self-Help in Japan's Economic Assistance to Africa', *Japanese Studies, Special Issue*, Volume 32 (2), pp. 161–182.
Ampiah, K. and Rose, C. 2012. 'The Evolving Relations between Japan and Africa: The Discourse of the Tokyo International Conference on African Development', *Japanese Studies, Special Issue*, Volume 32 (2), pp. 153–159.
Aoki, S., 1993, *Afurika ni Watatta Nihonjin*, Tokyo: Jiji Tsushinsha.
Chomsky, N., 1969. 'The revolutionary pacifism of A. J. Muste on the back ground of the Pacific War', in N. Chomsky (ed.), *American Power and the New Mandarins: Historical and Political Essays*, New York: Pantheon Books.
Committee on Foreign Relations, 2010. 'The future of US Public Diplomacy: Hearing before the sub-committee on International Operations and Organizations, Human Rights, Democracy, and Global Women's Issues of the Committee of Foreign Relations', *United States Senate, One Hundred and Eleventh Congress, Second Session*, Washington: US Government Printing Office, March 10 2010. Available at: www.gpo.gov/fdsys/pkg/CHRG-111shrg63020/pdf/CHRG-111shrg63020.pdf [Accessed 10 October 2013].

Cull, N. J., 2008, *The Cold War and the United States Information Agency: American Propaganda and Public Diplomacy, 1945–1989*, Cambridge: Cambridge University Press.

Foucault, M., 1972. *The Archaeology of Knowledge and the Discourse on Language*, New York: Pantheon.

Foucault, M., 2004. *Security, Territory, Population: Lectures at the Collège de France, 1977–1978*, New York: Palgrave Macmillan.

Fukuzawa, Y., 1885. 'Datsu-a Ron', *Jiji Shimpo*, 16 March.

Hirano, K., 2013. *Keizai Tairiku, Shigen, Shokuryō Mondai Kara Kaihatsu Seisaku Made*, Tokyo: Chuo Kōron Shinsha.

Keizai Dōyūkai, 2013. 'TICAD V o keiki ni, afurikia no seichōni muketa senryakuteki komitomento o: minori aru nichi-afurika kankei no kōchiku ni mukete', 15 February. Author has a copy of the paper. The English version of the paper is available at: www.mofa.go.jp/mofaj/files/000007221.pdf.

Kitagawa, K., 2014. 'The relationship between Japan and South Africa before World War II', *Kansai University Review of Economics*, 16 March.

Kitaoka, S., 2011. 'The inception of a modern relationship', *Japan–China Joint Historical Research Report (Provisional Translation), Modern and Contemporary History*, Volume I, March. Available at: www.mofa.go.jp/region/asia-paci/china/pdfs/jcjhrr_mch_en1.pdf.

Korhonen, P., 2014. 'Leaving Asia? The Meaning of *Datsu-a* and Japan's Modern History', *The Asia-Pacific Journal*, Volume 12 (9), pp. 1–18.

Nihon Keizai Shinbun, 2008. 'Shasetsu', 26 May.

Pan, L., 2005. *The United Nations in Japan's Foreign and Security Policymaking, 1945–1992: National Security, Party Politics, and International Status*, Cambridge, MA: Harvard University Press.

Perkins, D., 1960. *A History of the Monroe Doctrine*, London: Longmans.

Shimazu, N., 1998. *Japan, Race and Equality: The Racial Equality Proposal of 1919*, New York, Routledge.

Tōyō Kezia, 2010. 'Afurika no Shōgeki, Chikyūjō Saigo no Shin Ichiba', 9 January.

8

THE ROLE OF AID IN SOUTH KOREA'S RELATIONS WITH AFRICA DURING THE COLD WAR

Hyo-sook Kim

Introduction

South Korea has been increasing its aid to the African region rapidly in recent years. In 2013, South Korea committed US$567.76 million in aid to African countries in the form of grants and loans; ten years ago, the commitment was only US$5.2 million. In gross disbursement, the proportion of aid to Africa jumped from 6.62 percent in 2003 to 18.34 percent of South Korea's bilateral aid in 2013. In 2014, it was recorded as 21.51 percent; the last time that the proportion of aid to Africa in bilateral aid exceeded 20 percent was 1995.

In March 2006, President Roh Moo-hyun visited three African countries (Egypt, Nigeria and Algeria), the first South Korean head of state to do so in 24 years. This visit was a turning point in South Korean diplomacy towards Africa. In Nigeria, Roh announced 'Korea's initiative for Africa's development', and the first meeting of the Korea–Africa Forum (KAF) was held in Seoul in November 2006 as a part of this initiative. The KAF was developed as a regular meeting at the ministerial level 'to serve as a mechanism for substantive cooperation' (Ministry of Foreign Affairs and Trade of South Korea (MOFAT), 2006) between South Korea and Africa.[1] After the initiation of the KAF, the South Korean government opened or reopened embassies in six African countries—Angola in 2007, Cameroon and the Democratic Republic of Congo in 2008, Rwanda and Uganda in 2011 and Mozambique in 2013. At the same time, seven African countries—Senegal and Kenya in 2007, Angola in 2008, Rwanda in 2009, Ethiopia in 2012 and Sierra Leone and Zambia in 2014—opened or reopened embassies in Seoul.

As a major tool in its foreign policy, aid has contributed to South Korea's current cooperative relations with Africa. Therefore, the question of why South Korea provides aid to Africa is relevant to understanding Seoul's foreign policy and its bilateral relations with Africa. In contrast to China, which began to make inroads into Africa in the early 1950s, South Korea only started its aid programme to developing countries in 1963 in the form of training programmes funded by the United States Agency for International Development. In 1965, the South Korean government for the first time launched a programme to accept trainees, and the country started dispatching experts overseas in 1967. Grant aid was initiated in 1977. Nevertheless, like other Asian donors (China and Japan), South Korea has a more than 50-year history of aid to African countries. During the Cold War, Africa became a priority region for South Korean aid. This raises several questions: Why did South Korea provide aid to Africa during the Cold War?

To what extent did South Korean aid contribute to establishing cooperative bilateral relations with Africa during that period? And what does this suggest for understanding the current South Korea–Africa relations?

To answer these questions, this chapter aims to examine South Korean aid to Africa with a focus on the second half of the Cold War period, from 1970 to the early 1990s (i.e. the late modern era). The key findings in this chapter can be summarized as follows. First, during the late modern era, South Korea provided aid to Africa, aiming not only to win its diplomatic competition with North Korea, but also to advance its historical and economic goals. Particularly noteworthy was South Korea's emphasis in the 1980s on south–south cooperation in building cooperative relations with other Asian and African countries. Second, although South Korea's aid in this period did not successfully contribute to diplomatic and economic relations with African countries, it nevertheless evolved into the current aid efforts in sharing development experience with African countries. This chapter argues that studying South Korean aid to Africa in the late modern era is essential for better understanding South Korea–Africa relations because South Korea's attempts to strengthen south–south cooperation and its own development experience in this period paved the way for the today's cooperative South Korea–Africa relations.

This chapter begins with a brief survey of South Korean aid to Africa and its motivations through a review of the major literature. The second section analyses from three perspectives (historical, political/diplomatic and economic relations) why South Korea provided aid to Africa in the late modern era. The third section examines how South Korea's south–south cooperation has evolved towards establishing the current cooperative relations with African countries. The conclusion summarises the findings above and considers their implications for understanding current South Korea–Africa relations.

South Korean aid to Africa and its motivations

With the rise of Africa's profile in South Korea, studies of South Korean aid to Africa have accumulated in recent years. Emphasising the role of aid as a tool for foreign policy, Kim noted that 'aid to Africa is a mirror that shows the relation between the foreign policy and foreign aid in Korea explicitly' (H. S. Kim, 2013b: 26). K. S. Kim (2013a) focuses on the engagement of aid to Africa with resource development, foreign direct investment and trade. Yoon & Moon (2014) empirically proved that South Korea's own economic interests in oil and potential markets motivated South Korean aid to Africa. By focusing on ideational factors in determining South Korean aid to Africa, Hwang (2014) argued that South Korea, as a middle power, has been using aid to Africa to develop its soft power strategy. Other Asian donors, especially China, have also been urging South Korea to cultivate cooperative relations with African countries. In East Asia, 'competitive' (Carvalho et al., 2012) relations and a sense of 'rivalry' (Iwata, 2012) among East Asian countries resulting from 'regional geopolitics' (Watson, 2014) affected their aid behaviours towards Africa.

In spite of the differences in their arguments, these studies have contributed to capturing the essence of South Korea's motivations—South Korea's economic interests—for providing aid to Africa. However, most of them analysed South Korean aid to Africa since 1991, after the South Korean government had established its aid organisations and began providing bilateral aid in earnest, or since the middle of the 2000s, when the ODA (official development assistance) volume to the African region started to increase rapidly.

As noted, Africa was one of the priority regions for South Korean aid, especially grant aid, during the Cold War. Aid to Africa accounted for 31 percent of its grant aid from 1977 to 1987, the largest proportion of grant aid during that period, whereas technical cooperation concentrated on Asia. Through to 1987, South Korea provided grants to 37 out of 50 African countries, including some in North Africa. During the 1977–1987 period, Ethiopia received US$2.96 million and was the top African recipient of South Korea's grant aid, followed by Senegal, Guinea-Bissau, the Central African Republic, Liberia, Ghana, Côte d'Ivoire, Zaire, Comoros and Sierra Leone, in that order (Park, 1989: 112–114).

Park (1989) found that trade and diplomatic relations between South Korea and African countries did not consistently determine South Korea's aid allocation in Africa. Apart from Park, however, scholars have only shared a general understanding that South Korea provided aid to Africa in the Cold War era to gain international recognition in an ideological confrontation with North Korea. What factors, then, drove South Korea to provide aid to African countries during the Cold War? Since the literature is lacking, the motivation for South Korean aid to Africa during the Cold War remains somewhat puzzling.

To fill the gap in the literature, this chapter analyses South Korean aid to Africa focusing on the period from 1970 to the early 1990s. The late modern era provides valid answers about the role of aid in South Korea's relations with Africa for the following reasons: first, South Korea's diplomacy towards Africa became active in the 1970s and 1980s. South Korea began its diplomatic initiatives towards Africa in 1961 under the Park Chung-hee regime, but did not establish diplomatic relations with African countries that had already established diplomatic relations with North Korea. South Korea expanded its diplomatic network in Africa in earnest after 1973 when the government officially abandoned this policy. In 1982, President Chun Doo-hwan visited Africa for the first time as the head of South Korea. Second, during this period, the central motivation behind South Korean aid to Africa shifted from diplomatic imperatives to economic ones. In the 1980s in particular, South Korea recognised the importance of economic cooperation including south–south cooperation with African countries. Therefore, studying the late modern era is important because South Korea laid the groundwork in this period for the current aid to Africa and the sharing of its development experience.

Drivers of South Korean aid to Africa in the late modern era

This section analyses and investigates why and what drove South Korea to provide aid to Africa during the late modern era. It proposes three major factors: historical relations during the Korean War, the political/diplomatic competition with North Korea for international recognition and support regarding the Korean question in the United Nations, and economic cooperation through south–south cooperation.

Historical relations in the Korean War

South Korea began its diplomatic initiatives towards Africa during the 1960s as part of the diplomacy towards the Third World regions including Asia, the Middle East and Latin America. In fact, the geographic distance between South Korea and Africa had strained attempts at mutual contact. The participation of Ethiopia and South Africa in the United Nations forces in the Korean War comprised the first official contact between South Korea and Africa (Ha, 1988: 302).

South Korea was liberated from Japanese colonial rule in 1945 and established its own government in 1948. Meanwhile, South Korean politics and society were divided over the issues of trusteeship, enacted by the United States and the Soviet Union, and the implementation of a general election on the Korean Peninsula. In these circumstances, on 25 June 1950, 'the Korean War was started by North Korea with the support of Soviet Union, who intended to communise and sovietise the Korean Peninsula' (Ministry of Patriots and Veterans Affairs of South Korea (MPVA), 2012: 41).

After the outbreak of the war, the Security Council decided to dispatch the United Nations forces; 16 member states sent their fighting forces and 5 states supported medical teams. 'Ethiopia was the only African country whose ground army participated in the Korean War' (Ministry of Patriots and Veterans Affairs of South Korea (MPVA), 2012: 51). In August 1950, Haile Selassie, Emperor of Ethiopia, made the decision to enter the Korean War, and the Ethiopian Expeditionary Forces to Korea landed at the port of Pusan on 6 May 1951. Ethiopia sent more than 6,000 soldiers to the war. Among these, 121 soldiers died and 536 were wounded. For this reason, the South Korean government came to view its relationship with Ethiopia as a 'blood pledge (*hyeolmaeng*)' meaning a solid alliance (Ministry of Patriots and Veterans Affairs of South Korea (MPVA), 2012: 165).

This historical connection motivated the South Korean government to maintain friendly relations with Ethiopia and to provide aid following the establishment of diplomatic relations in 1963. However, the reasons why South Korea and Ethiopia took until 1963 to establish diplomatic relations should be noted. After the Korean War Armistice in 1953, the South Korean government made national survival and security against North Korea its highest priority along with promoting economic development. Thus, South Korea concentrated its diplomatic efforts on building a bilateral alliance with the United States. Furthermore, the Lee Seung-man regime (1948–1960) 'adopted three negative foreign policy doctrines: no contact with the communist bloc, no contact with North Korea and no contact with the Third World' (Park, 1978: 76). Thus, the Lee regime did not establish diplomatic relations with any African country. Notably, there were only six independent states in Africa until the 1950s. After the Lee regime collapsed following the revolution on 19 April 1960, the Chang Myun administration came into power in August of the same year. This administration shifted South Korean foreign policy to positive interactions with the Third World and sent goodwill missions to 13 African countries. However, the Chang administration was ended by Park's coup d'état on 16 May 1961, and thus was too short-lived to implement this policy (Jeong, 1988: 51–52). It was the Park Chung-hee regime in 1961 that launched South Korean diplomacy towards Africa. The details of this policy are given in the next section.

In the early years after the establishment of diplomatic relations with Ethiopia, South Korea dispatched experts to that country including teachers and urban planners, inviting trainees and providing medicines. The South Korean government maintained cooperative relations by providing aid even when Ethiopia was governed by a communist regime from 1974 to 1991, during which time it shifted to a pro-North Korea policy. South Korea began providing equipment, such as tillers, water pumps, sewing machines, trucks, minibuses, cars, televisions, military uniforms and medicines in the amount of an average of US$350 million per year. Trainees also continued to be invited (Ministry of Patriots and Veterans Affairs of South Korea (MPVA), 2012: 158–159). In 1987, the cumulative amount of grant aid to Ethiopia was US$2.96 million, accounting for the largest part of South Korea's grant aid, as previously noted (Park, 1989: 112). The relations between the two countries were normalised after the collapse of the communist regime in Ethiopia in 1991. In 1995, the Korean International Cooperation Agency (KOICA) opened an overseas office in Addis Ababa, for the first time in the African region.

Based on this historical relationship, South Korea has continued to advance its contemporary relations with Ethiopia. In July 2011, President Lee Myung-bak visited Ethiopia, and the South Korean government signed a new basic contract for the Economic Development Cooperation Fund (EDCF) with the Ethiopian government. In 2013, US$100 million for the Modjo-Hawassa Highway Project was committed as the first loan to Ethiopia. In May 2016, President Park

Geun-hye visited three African countries including Ethiopia. During her visit to Addis Ababa, she attended the ceremony to mark the 65th anniversary of Ethiopia's participation in Korean War, and she pledged to continue South Korea's support for Ethiopia's development. In addition, the South Korean government has continued support for Ethiopian veterans and their descendants through grants. The support includes projects for building elementary schools, vocational training and scholarships.

Political/diplomatic competition with North Korea

More generally, the reason why South Korea provided aid during the Cold War was that the government aimed to ensure its dominance over North Korea in international prestige by establishing cooperative relations with non-aligned countries (Ministry of Finance and Economy and Export-Import Bank of South Korea, 2007: 35–36). Towards this end, the Park Chung-hee regime began to expand South Korea's diplomatic network to the Third World after it came into power in 1961. However, the Park regime's diplomacy towards Africa was limited since it did not extend to pro-communist African governments. In addition, the importance of a bilateral alliance with the United States in South Korea's foreign policy did not change under the Cold War structure.

Furthermore, diplomacy towards the United Nations became a top priority in South Korea's foreign policy during the Cold War because the Korean question (*hanguk munje*) shifted to the General Assembly of the United Nations following the breakdown of the Geneva political conference in 1954. The Korean question addressed the continuation of the United Nations Commission for the Unification and Rehabilitation of Korea and the implementation of a simultaneous general election under the supervision of the UN in South–North Korea in proportion to the population. Later, the Korean question brought about an east–west confrontation related to procedural issues of whether representatives of South or North Korea should participate in discussing the problem (Ban, 1995: 34).

A representative aid programme resulting from these concerns was the dispatch of teams of doctors to African nations. The South Korean government had received requests from African countries to dispatch medical teams since 1964. However, budget limitations prevented South Korea from sending them. Additionally, seven African countries—Cameroon, Upper Volta (Burkina Faso), the Democratic Republic of Congo, Chad, Lesotho, Liberia and Sierra Leone—abstained or did not participate in the resolution on the Korean question at the 22nd General Assembly of the United Nations in 1967. The South Korean government realised the necessity of cooperating with neutral African countries and decided to dispatch medical teams (Korea International Cooperation Agency (KOICA), 1992: 50). The aid programme began in 1968 and ended in 2008. During those 40 years, 115 doctors were sent to developing countries, and 85 of those were dispatched to 26 African countries. They not only contributed to preventing diseases and improving the health of the local population, they also helped to promote friendly and cooperative relations with African countries and improve South Korea's image abroad. Thus, they played a role as diplomatic missions on a personal level (Shim & Kim, 2011).

On 23 June 1973, Park announced the 'Special Statement on Foreign Policy for Peace and Unification', declaring that South and North Korea would not intervene with each other, and both could belong to the same international organisations including the United Nations, and South Korea would open its door to all countries (Ministry of Foreign Affairs and Trade of South Korea (MOFAT), 2009: 133). However, confrontation with North Korea continued at the conference of non-aligned countries until 1983, when neutral opinions on the Korean question were adopted (Ban, 1995: 35). After 1983, South Korea still needed to gain the support of non-aligned countries for simultaneous South–North membership in the United Nations to occur (Shim & Park, 1989: 152).

Under these circumstances, by 1987, South Korea distributed aid in kind to 37 African countries including North African countries. However, 13 African countries did not receive any aid (Park, 1989). Of these 13 countries,

> Eleven countries had diplomatic relations with North Korea, and two had relations with both the South and North. This meant that establishing diplomatic relations was an important condition for providing development assistance. Although Egypt, Zambia and Tanzania received aid and exports [from South Korea], they had diplomatic relations only with North Korea. In addition, the Seychelles, Congo, Angola, Mozambique, Benin, Guinea and Togo also received either aid or exports [from South Korea], so it can be assumed that diplomatic relations were not a necessary condition [for receiving South Korea's aid]. [translated by the author]
>
> *(Park, 1989: 127)*

The South Korean government had rejected the use of 'aid as a pre-condition for establishing diplomatic relations (*seonkyeonghyeop-husugyo*)'. When South Korea established diplomatic relations with Sudan in 1977, it maintained its policy of 'political relations as a pre-condition for economic cooperation' against the May regime, the Sudanese government in power at the time. The South Korean government signed agreements on culture, trade, the economy and technical cooperation with the May regime, and economic cooperative relations between South Korea and Sudan developed rapidly (Kim, 2002).

In spite of these efforts, South Korea fell behind North Korea over the Korean question in the United Nations in the 1970s. Park (1978) found that in the 1960s and 1970s, African countries were not ideologically cohesive in their voting on the Korean question in the United Nations, nor in establishing diplomatic relations with divided countries, including China and Taiwan and East and West Germany. For example, some countries with diplomatic relations with South Korea opposed the pro-western resolution, although all of the countries that had diplomatic relations with only North Korea voted for the pro-eastern resolution. In addition, some maintained their foreign policy postures, but others changed their positions on the Korean question.

President Roh Tae-woo's Special Declaration in the Interest of National Self-Esteem, Unification and Prosperity on 7 July 1988 was a turning point in South Korea's diplomacy towards Africa. This declaration was prepared to ensure the peaceful coexistence of South and North Korea in the Korean Peninsula. As part of the policy, Northern Diplomacy was introduced. This diplomacy aimed to normalise and promote relations with communist countries (Ministry of Foreign Affairs and Trade of South Korea (MOFAT), 2009: 141–142). South Korea expanded its diplomatic network under this policy, and it completed the establishment of diplomatic relations with all African countries by reopening relations with the Seychelles in January 1995 (Ministry of Foreign Affairs and Trade of South Korea (MOFAT), 2009: 103).

Economic cooperation via south–south cooperation

As previously noted, the disadvantageous situation for South Korea in the United Nations began to improve in the 1980s, bolstered by an issue of economic cooperation based on pragmatic policy in both South Korea and Africa. In 1982, President Chun Doo-hwan visited four African countries—Kenya, Nigeria, Gabon and Senegal—for the first time as the head of South Korea. During his visit, he suggested strengthening economic cooperation between Asia and Africa (*a-a hyeopryeok*), including south–south cooperation. He said that many Asian and African countries had experienced colonial rule and had been marginalised in international politics in the past. He emphasised that south–south cooperation based on a spirit of collective self-help between Asian and African countries could form a 'development front (*gaebal jeonseon*)' that would serve as a new basis for cooperation among developing countries (Presidential Secretariat, 1982: 183–184, 259–260). Indeed, President Chun and Nigerian President Shagari agreed to exchange development experience and made agreements on economic, scientific and technical cooperation during President Chun's visit to Nigeria. They discussed the exchange of managers, experts and engineers in the fields of agriculture, science and technology; the participation of South Korean companies in Nigeria's development plan; and the acceleration of both countries' business activities through the formation of a joint corporation (Presidential Secretariat, 1982: 112–113).

In the 1970s and 1980s South Korea's economic growth made many African countries attractive to South Korea for economic development. Park (1989) noted the following:

> With its rapid economic development since the late 1970s, South Korea has received various aid requests from many least-developed countries [LDCs] to share its development experience and provide technical and financial support. This is because of the LDCs' . . . desire to promote their development plans efficiently through technology and financing aid at appropriate levels, neither too advanced nor too basic, by forerunners such as South Korea. In addition, because South Korea had experienced the challenges of colonial rule, war, a military coup d'état and dictatorship that developing countries suffered or are suffering, the idea of achieving remarkable development under the worst conditions of resource poverty and disorder [as did South Korea] resonates with LDCs. [translated by the author]
>
> *(Park, 1989: 101–102)*

To respond to the increase in aid requests by developing countries, the South Korean government established the EDCF, a south–south cooperation mechanism, in 1987, and the first EDCF project provided US$10 million for the Passenger Coach Purchase Project in Nigeria. It was expected that this loan aid/project would activate South Korea's aid to Africa (Park, 1989: 95). Indeed, some loan/aid projects were implemented in African countries such as Nigeria, Ghana and Uganda by the early 1990s.

The South Korean government became pragmatic in its engagements with African countries in the 1970s. In the 1980s, South Korea took concrete actions to strengthen economic relations with African countries through south–south cooperation. Therefore, the late modern era is an important period for better understanding South Korean aid to Africa, since its central motivation shifted from diplomatic to economic interests.

Nevertheless, economic relations, especially export relations, were not a decisive factor in South Korea's provision of aid during the Cold War (Park, 1989). President Chun's visit to Nigeria was evaluated as the first diplomatic consequence of the South Korean government's emphasis on South Korea's economic interests such as securing natural resources (Lee, 2009: 349). Until the 1990s, however, South Korea did not recognise African countries as economic partners. The reasons South Korea failed to strengthen south–south cooperation with African countries in this period are the following. First, political, economic and social instability in many African countries prevented South Korea from recognising African countries as potential economic partners until the 1990s. Africa's economy stagnated in the 1980s when structural adjustment programmes were adopted due to debt crises. In addition, regional instability due to conflict was relatively high in the 1990s; between 10 and 15 conflicts took place per year in Africa from 1989 to 2002. This conflict and political instability not only led to the loss of human resources, but also made investors perceive Africa as a risky environment (United Nations Economic Commission for Africa, African Union, African Development Bank and United Nations Development Programme, 2014: 2–4).

Second, South Korean and African countries' attempts to separate politics from economics also damaged South Korea's relations with Africa (Park, 1978: 86). South Korea had trade relations with a few African countries, whose diplomatic relations and voting in the United Nations were mostly pro-eastern and pro-North. South Korea's major trading partners were Nigeria, Liberia, Kenya, Ghana, Ethiopia, Niger, Tanzania and Uganda. These countries were all larger and richer than other African countries (Park, 1978: 83). South Korea's economic relations with Africa were not directly related to its political relations. However, for both South and North Korea, Africa was more important politically than economically (Park, 1978: 86).

Third, the influence of former colonial powers in Africa also constrained South Korea's involvement in the continent (Lee, 1999). Fourth, South Korea did not yet have a specific policy or established aid model for sharing its development experience with other developing countries. However, attempts to enhance economic cooperation with African countries in the 1980s created the foundation for current cooperative relations between South Korea and Africa.

South Korea's development experience and aid to Africa

South Korea's unique development experience enabled it to succeed in transforming itself from one of the world's poorest states to a DAC (Development Assistance Committee) donor in a short period. South Korea's gross national income (GNI) per capita was only US$120 in 1963 when it began its aid programme to developing countries. In 2014, South Korea's GNI per capita was recorded as US$27,090.[2] On 25 November 2009, South Korea's membership of the Development Assistance Committee of the Organisation for Economic Development and Cooperation was approved at a special session held for that purpose.

Meanwhile, the South Korean government gradually built up its aid organisations. In 1987, EDCF was founded as an implementation agency for loan aid, as previously noted. KOICA was established in 1991 to unify the government's fragmented implementation of grant aid and technical cooperation. By the early 2000s, South Korea had recovered from the financial crisis that had struck its economy in 1997 and began to make efforts to globalise its development experience and contribute to reducing global poverty.

Byung-se Yun, the Minister of Foreign Affairs of South Korea, identified 'taking ownership and successfully mobilising development resources through the catalytic use of ODA' (OECD, 2014: 30) as key elements of South Korea's experience. The South Korean government asserts that South Korea can play 'a bridging role between developed and developing countries' (The Republic of Korea Permanent Mission to the United Nations, 2014: 6) in reducing global poverty, and its ODA 'can guide other countries in their development' (OECD, 2014: 30). To embody these ideas, the Committee for International Development Cooperation, which has the authority to adjust, deliberate and resolve major ODA policies in South Korea, adopted the *Research on Establishing a Korean ODA Model* (hereafter, the *Research*) at its thirteenth meeting held in 2012. The Korean ODA Model Task Force of the Prime Minister's Office supervised this research (Joo et al., 2012: 20).

According to the *Research*, the South Korean development process had five distinctive features: strategic concentration, a result-based management system, private-public partnerships, an open-door policy and infrastructure construction. Effective policies and institutions brought about the growth of both material and human resources and technological R&D, and South Korea succeeded in expanding exports, advancing its industrial structure, developing scientific techniques, constructing a social safety net and establishing social development policies. The government has intervened in the economy when necessary (Tcha et al., 2012a). South Korea's ODA Model, which was proposed by the *Research*, is based on the country's unique development experience and, fundamentally, on respect for universal values, ideas and objectives in international society. The model represents the basic spirit and objective of the South Korean ODA prescribed in the Framework Act and emphasises the concept of ownership (Tcha et al., 2012b).

In the 2000s, Africa began to maintain high GDP growth, and poverty also declined more quickly in the late 2000s; improved governance in many African countries and the implementation of social protection mechanisms contributed to this decline (United Nations Economic Commission for Africa, African Union, African Development Bank and United Nations Development Programme, 2014: 12). With economic and political conditions improving, many African countries began to move towards national development. And a number of leaders of African countries have looked to South Korea's development experience as their model.

However, Igbafen (2014) noted that there are several difficulties in applying the South Korean development model to African countries. Both South Korea and African countries have experienced colonial rule in the past; however, over both the colonial and postcolonial era, many African countries have depended on foreign ideas based on neoliberalism and the political system characterised by neopatrimonialism for their development. This tendency has constrained their development, while South Korea's industrialisation, initiated under Japanese colonial rule, established the basis for its development. Furthermore, the cohesive state structure and strong leadership that drove South Korea's development is lacking in most African countries (Igbafen, 2014). In addition, applying the South Korean developmental model to other developing countries, especially under the Park authoritarian regime, has been difficult for present-day ODA recipients due to fundamental transformations in global politics and economics (Kim et al., 2013). Kim et al. (2013) suggest that the South Korean strategy of economic liberalisation and democratisation during the period from 1982 to 2002 can offer several lessons for currently developing countries. They further emphasised that this framework should be considered a South Korean alternative rather than a one-size-fits-all model.

Still, South Korea's experience provides several useful lessons for developing countries, especially in Africa. Kim (1995) argued that South Korean development through industrialisation from the 1960s to the 1980s resulted from 'active state intervention within a market framework' (Kim, 1995: 88). During this period, the South Korean government guided the direction of national economic development, participated in economic activities and cooperated with the private sector. The interaction between the government and markets in South Korea provides an especially good example for future development in Africa, since such interactions have often resulted in bureaucratic corruption and mismanagement in the region. In order to establish a macroeconomic environment that contributes to the efficient use of resources, the South Korean government established several new public enterprises in key-sector industries and utilised these for infrastructural development. Public enterprises contributed to capital formation and technical development and generated forward and backward linkages. Price-setting for resources such as exchange and interest rates by the government promoted efficient resource utilisation. Another relevant feature in South Korean development was its dynamic policy formation for structural transformation from labour-intensive light industry to heavy and chemical industries and for targeting strategic sectors. There is no doubt that investment in human capital through the improved quantity and quality of education has also served as a foundation for South Korean development (Kim, 1995).

However, the South Korean development model does not ignore other areas. For example, the government also promoted agricultural development to avoid urban–rural income disparities (Kim, 1995: 136–137). Saemaul Undong (the New Community Movement) ODA is a representative aid project that aims to share South Korea's experience of this type. It is a rural development project aimed at reducing poverty and increasing income by promoting ownership, improving living environments and expanding infrastructure in local communities (Government of South Korea, 2014: 3). It emphasises the values of diligence, self-help and cooperation, the three core values of traditional Saemaul Undong in South Korea in the 1970s. (Sharing, volunteering and creating were additional important values.) Since 2011, Saemaul Undong pilot ODA projects, such as the establishment of a Saemaul complex centre, joint product cultivation and improvement of farmland, have been implemented in Myanmar, Laos and Rwanda, respectively (Government of South Korea, 2014: 10).

It is also noteworthy that South Korea launched the Knowledge Sharing Programme (KSP) in 2004. The KSP is an aid programme for sharing South Korea's development experience with developing countries by supporting detailed policy formation and institutional capacity building, although aid for policy consultation had already been in place since the mid 1980s. In addition, the KOICA has also dispatched experts to developing countries for policy consultation, especially in Africa (Hwang, 2013: 222–224).

Hwang (2013) agreed that the South Korean development experience is relevant as a development model and applicable to African countries. Among them, in particular, Rwanda 'has potential to replicate what South Korea has experienced in the path of rapid development' (Hwang, 2013: 215). The economic circumstances of Rwanda in the early 2000s are similar to those of South Korea in the early 1960s. Moreover, Rwanda shares with South Korea several non-economic traits affecting its development: both nations are small, mountainous and densely populated. Both have experienced division and conflicts in the past. The current president of Rwanda, Paul Kagame, also shares a military background with Park Chung-hee (Hwang, 2013: 213–215).

President Paul Kagame of Rwanda is known to be a supporter of South Korea's development experience. When he visited Seoul for the first time as president of Rwanda in March 2008, he said that he considers South Korea 'a role model for the development of Rwanda' (Cheong Wa Dae, 2008). In particular, he focused on South Korea's IT-based economy. During the fourth Development Assistance Committee High Level Forum on Aid Effectiveness in November 2011, held in Busan, he met President Lee again and said that he hoped to make Rwanda an IT hub in East Africa, modelling it after South Korea (Cheong Wa Dae, 2011). Indeed, South Korea has implemented ICT projects such as the Projects for the Establishment of the School of ICT at the National University of Rwanda (2008–2011) and Capability Building for ICT Innovation (2013–2015). Rwanda is also one of the African countries in which South Korea is implementing a pilot project of Saemaul Undong ODA.

South Korea established diplomatic relations with Rwanda in 1963, but it stopped all relations from 1975 to 1987. Meanwhile, the South Korean government repeatedly opened and closed its embassy in Rwanda. Most recently, Rwanda opened an embassy in Seoul in 2009, and South Korea reopened its embassy in Kigali in 2011. South Korean aid to Rwanda had been under US$1 million until 2007. In 2013, South Korea committed US$79.99 million aid to Rwanda.

Conclusion

Since the establishment of its government in 1948, South Korea has placed its diplomatic priorities on a bilateral alliance with the United States and relations with three other major powers close to South Korea (China, Japan and Russia and previously, the Soviet Union). Needless to say, North Korea has been the most important country in its national security and foreign policy. Africa, as a Third World region, has been marginalised in its foreign policy. Economic relations between South Korea and Africa have also been limited; trade with Africa has never exceeded 3 percent of South Korea's total trade volume. In these contexts, African studies have fallen into 'a status of marginalisation in Korean academia' due to the 'government's indifference and public ignorance' (Chang, 2014: 10).

In the first section, this chapter noted the lack of literature on aid to Africa as well as the general agreement that the diplomatic imperative to gain international predominance over North Korea motivated South Korea's aid to Africa during the Cold War era. The second section found that historical connections to the Korean War and economic cooperation through south–south cooperation, as well as diplomatic relations, motivated South Korean aid to Africa during the Cold War. In particular, South Korea's attempts at south–south cooperation with Africa already began in the 1980s. During the Cold War, however, aid did not play a sufficient role in increasing South Korea's focus on African countries' foreign policy and failed to strengthen economic cooperation with Africa. The third section indicated that for the past decade, South Korea promoted aid in the form of sharing its development experience, a strategy that offers several useful lessons for Africa's development. Today, such aid plays a role as a mediator in connecting South Korea and African countries such as Rwanda.

This chapter has argued that studying the late modern era is imperative for better understanding South Korea–Africa relations because South Korea's aid efforts and development experience in the late modern era prepared the way for the current mutually beneficial relations between South Korea and Africa. The arguments suggest the importance of a shared interest in promoting cooperative bilateral relations between South Korea and Africa. To see whether and how aid contributes to such shared interests, a variety of research approaches from several policy areas are needed, as this chapter emphasised.

Notes

1   All citations of Korean-language sources in this chapter were translated by the author into English.
2   The data of GNI per capita comes from World Bank (2015).

Bibliography

Ban, K. M., 1995. 'Dae Yuen Oegyo Reul Jungsim Euro (Focusing on Diplomacy Towards the United Nations)', *Oegyo (Diplomacy)*, Volume 35, pp. 32–41.
Carvalho, P. A. R., Kim, H. S. and Potter, D. M. 2012. 'Aid to Africa from Japan, Korea, and China: Ideology, economic interests, and poverty reduction', in H. S. Kim and D. M. Potter (eds.), *Foreign Aid Competition in Northeast Asia*, Sterling, VA: Kumarian Press, pp. 129–157.
Chang, Y. K., 2014. 'African studies and its discontents: Facing with academic marginalisation and public ignorance', Paper Presented at Commemorative International Conference for the 50th Anniversary of Japan Association for African Studies, Kyoto University, Japan, 23 May 2014.
Cheong Wa Dae (Blue House), 2008. 'Korea and Rwanda hold their first summit ever', *Summit Diplomacy*, 31 March 2008. Available at: http://17cwd.eng.pa.go.kr/pre_activity/summit/diplomacy_view.php?uno=656&board_no=E05&search_key=&search_value=&search_cate_code=&cur_page_no=1&code=17 [Accessed 20 April 2015].

Cheong Wa Dae (Blue House), 2011. 'Busan segye gaebal chonghoi gyegi han-ruwanda jeongsang hoidam (Korea-Rwanda summit at the fourth DAC High Level Forum on Aid Effectiveness)', *Cheong Wa Dae News*, 30 November 2011. Available at: http://17cwd.pa.go.kr/kr/president/news/news_view. php?uno=1693&article_no=45&board_no=P01&search_key=&search_value=&search_cate_ code=&order_key1=1&order_key2=1&cur_page_no=1&cur_year=2011&cur_month=11 [Accessed 20 April 2015].

Government of South Korea, 2014. 'Jiguchon Saemaul Undong jonghap chujin gyehoik, an (a comprehensive plan for Saemaul Undong, proposal)', Proposal Reported at the 18th Meeting of Committee for International Development Cooperation, 14 March 2014.

Ha, K. K., 1988. 'Hankuk gwa Apurika (South Korea and Africa)', in J. G. Choi (ed.), *Hankuk Oegyo Jeongchaek (South Korea's Foreign Policy)*, Seoul: Hankuk Kukje Gwangye Yonguso, pp. 302–333.

Hwang, K. D., 2014. 'Korea's Soft Power as an Alternative Approach to Africa in Development Cooperation', *African and Asian Studies*, Volume 13 (3), pp. 249–271.

Hwang, W. G., 2013. 'Modeling and sharing Korean development expertise for African growth' in K. Ohno and I. Ohno (eds.), *Eastern and Western Ideas for African Growth: Diversity and Complementarity in Development Aid*, London: Routledge, pp. 204–228.

Igbafen, M. L., 2014. 'South Korea's development experience as an aid recipient: Lessons for sub-Saharan Africa', in E. M. Kim and P. H. Kim (eds.), *The South Korean Development Experience: Beyond Aid*, London: Palgrave Macmillan, pp. 111–135.

Iwata, T., 2012. 'Comparative Study on "Asian" Approaches to Africa: An Introductory Reflection', *African Study Monographs*, Volume 33 (4), pp. 209–231.

Jeong, Y. T., 1988. 'Hanguk Gwa Apurika Gukka Gan Gwange Baljeonui Jedangye (The Stage of Friendly Relationship Development Between South Korea and Africa)', *Apurika Yeongu (African Affairs)*, Volume 4, pp. 49–72.

Joo, D. J., Tcha, M. J. and Kwon, Y. (eds.), 2012. *Hangukhyeong ODA Model Surip Chongron [The Research on Establishing Korean ODA Model]*, Seoul: Korean Institute for Industrial Economics & Trade.

Kim, E. M., Kim, P. H. and Kim, J. K., 2013. 'From Development to Development Cooperation: Foreign Aid, Country Ownership, and the Development State in South Korea', *The Pacific Review*, Volume 26 (3), pp. 313–336.

Kim, H. S., 2013. 'Korean Foreign Aid and Foreign Policy: Dynamism of Aid to Africa and Its Objectives', *Kukje Gaebal Hyeopryeok Yeongu (International Development and Cooperation Review)*, Volume 5 (2), pp. 1–36.

Kim, J. D., 2002. 'Korea–Sudan Relations during the May Regime', *Journal of the Korean Association of African Studies*, Volume 16, pp. 5–36.

Kim, K. S., 1995. 'The Korean miracle (1962–80) revisited: Myths and realities in strategies and development', in H. Stein (ed.), *Asian Industrialization and Africa: Studies in Policy Alternatives to Structural Adjustment*, London: Macmillan Press, pp. 87–143.

Kim, S. Y., 2013. *Korea in Africa: A Missing Piece of the Puzzle?* London: The London School of Economics and Political Science. Available at: www.lse.ac.uk/IDEAS/publications/reports/pdf/SR016/SR-016-Kim.pdf [Accessed 26 August 2015].

Korea International Cooperation Agency (KOICA), 1992. *Hankuk Kukje Hyeopryeokdan Yeonbo (Annual Report of KOICA)*, Seoul: Korean International Cooperation Agency.

Lee, H. Y., 1999. 'Hanguk Ui Dae Apurika Oegyo: Apurika Ui Jaepyeonga Wa Baljeon Banghyang (South Korea's Diplomacy Towards Africa: Re-estimation and New Direction)', *Korean Political Science Review*, Volume 33 (3), pp. 371–390.

Lee, H. K., 2009. 'Hankuk Ui Dae Apurika Jeongchaek Ul Tonghaeseo Bon Magurebu E Daehan Oegyo Jeonryak Gwa Gwaje (Diplomatic Strategy and Tasks of Maghreb Through South Koran Policy Towards Africa)', *Kukje Jiyeok Yeongu (Journal of International Area Studies)*, Volume 13 (3), pp. 343–366.

Ministry of Foreign Affairs and Trade of South Korea (MOFAT), 2006. 'Seoul Declaration on the Korea–Africa Forum', *Press Release*, 9 November 2006. Available at: www.mofa.go.kr/ENG/press/ pressreleases/index.jsp?menu=m_10_20 [Accessed 18 August 2015].

Ministry of Foreign Affairs and Trade of South Korea (MOFAT), 2009. *Hankuk Oegyo 60 Nyeon (South Korean Diplomacy 60 Years)*, Seoul: Ministry of Foreign Affairs and Trade of South Korea.

Ministry of Finance and Economy and Export-Import Bank of South Korea, 2007. *Daeoe Gyeongje Hyeopryeok Gigum 20-Nyeonsa (Economic Development Cooperation Fund 20 Years)*, Seoul: Export-Import Bank of Korea.

Ministry of Patriots and Veterans Affairs of South Korea (MPVA), 2012. *Yeongwonhan Donbanja Hankuk Gwa Etiopia (The Eternal Partnership: Ethiopia and South Korea)*, Seoul: Ministry of Patriots and Veterans Affairs of South Korea.

OECD, 2014. *Development Co-operation Report 2014*, Paris: Organisation for Economic Co-operation and Development.

Park, S. S., 1978. 'Africa and Two Koreas: A Study of African Non-Alignment', *African Studies Review*, Volume 21 (1), pp. 73–88.

Park, W. T., 1989. 'Hankuk Ui Dae-Apurika Geabal Wonjo (South Korea's Development Assistance to Africa)', *Journal of the Korean Association of African Studies*, Volume 4 (1), pp. 93–136.

Presidential Secretariat, 1982. *Segye Rul Hyanhan Geobo: Chun Doo-Hwan Daetongryeong Naeoebun Apurika Kanada Sunban (Big Start Towards the World: President Chun Doo-Hwan and the First Lady Visit Africa and Canada)*, Seoul: Presidential Secretariat.

Shim, U. S. and Kim, H. G., 2011. 'Hankuk Ui Apurika Jeongbu Pagyun Uisa Jeongchaek Ui Seonggwa E Daehan Dochal (Review for the South Korean Medical Doctors Dispatched by Government in Africa)', *Journal of the Korean Association of African Studies*, Volume 34, pp. 3–23.

Shim, U. S. and Park, J. K., 1989. 'Hankuk Ui Tai Apurika Oegyo Jeongchaek Banghyang [Direction of South Korea's Foreign Policy Towards Africa]', *Journal of the Korean Association of African Studies*, Volume 4 (2), pp. 145–155.

Tcha, M. J., Kang, W. J., Kim, J. W., Lee, J. H. and Jung, S. I., 2012a. 'Hankuk ui baljeon gyeongheom [South Korea's development experience]', in D. J. Joo, M. J. Tcha and Y. Kwon (eds.), *Hangukhyeong ODA Model Surip Chongron [The Research on Establishing Korean ODA Model]*, Seoul: Korean Institute for Industrial Economics & Trade.

Tcha, M. J., Kang, W. J. and Woo, H. Y., 2012b. 'Hankukhyeong ODA model kibon gyehoek [Basic plan for Korean ODA model]', in D. J. Joo, M. J. Tcha and Y. Kwon (eds.), *Hangukhyeong ODA Model Surip Chongron [The Research on Establishing Korean ODA Model]*, Seoul: Korean Institute for Industrial Economics & Trade.

The Republic of Korea Permanent Mission to the United Nations, 2014. 'Address by H. E. Park Geun-Hye President of the Republic of Korea at the 69th Session of the General Assembly of the United Nations', 24 September 2014. Available At: www.un.org/en/ga/69/meetings/gadebate/pdf/KR_en.pdf [Accessed 28 June 2017].

United Nations Economic Commission for Africa, African Union, African Development Bank and United Nations Development Programme, 2014. *MDG Report 2014: Assessing Progress in Africa toward the Millennium Development Goals*, Addis Ababa: Economic Commission for Africa.

Watson, I., 2014. *Foreign Aid and Emerging Powers: Asian Perspectives on Official Development Assistance*, New York: Routledge.

World Bank, 2015. 'Korea, Rep.', *Data*. Last updated 28 July 2015. Available at: http://data.worldbank.org/country/korea-republic [Accessed 26 August 2015].

Yoon, M. Y. and Moon, C. S., 2014. 'Korean Bilateral Official Development Assistance to Africa Under Korea's Initiative for Africa's Development', *Journal of East Asian Studies*, Volume 14, pp. 279–301.

9

ASIA–AFRICA POLITICAL AND DIPLOMATIC INTERACTIONS: 1970–1990

Sanjukta Banerji Bhattacharya

More than two years ago twenty-nine governments of independent states convened together at the Bandung Conference to declare to the world at large that the tide of history has changed its course, and that Asia and Africa . . . have now become free world powers . . . with a decisive role in shaping the future of the whole family of Nations. The Conference of Bandung was likewise convened to stress to the peoples of Africa and Asia the great importance of solidarity and the great weight they would have on the trend of world affairs when united.

(Sadat, 1957)

The Bandung Conference of 1955 that Anwar el Sadat, later to become President of Egypt and one of the founders of the Non-Aligned Movement, speaks so promisingly of in his address to the first Afro-Asian People's Solidarity Conference (1957), marked the emergence of the ideas of 'Asia' and 'Africa' in a context very different from the Western conceptualization of these regions, which had grown and persisted from the early years of mercantilism and colonization as areas to be subordinated and exploited. Since the state system of Africa was, for the most part, the outcome of the Berlin Conference (1884–1885), the idea of Africa, let alone the concept of the state, could only have emerged during colonial times, among a few educated elite with visions of a 'united' Africa; the vast majority of Africans had little idea of their continent. Independence, for the most part, came in the 1960s, but a number of countries remained under colonial rule until the 1970s, 1980s and even 1990s. Therefore, many states could not have autonomous relations with other states for parts of the period discussed in this chapter. Further, the states that became independent in the 1960s were embroiled in power struggles, civil wars, economic dislocation and adjusting to international political and economic trends, where former metropolitan countries and the two antagonistic superpowers, the United States (US) and the Soviet Union, enjoyed a privileged place. In this context, political or economic relations with countries in Asia could only be of a limited nature.

Much of Asia too had been under the yoke of imperialism for around 200 years or more. However, not all Asian colonized countries had been uniformly subjugated by colonial powers. Many regions in Asia had verifiable histories/civilizations, organized polities and administrative systems going back much further than the recorded histories of the imperialist powers that colonized them. Therefore, the post-World War II emerging political scenario in Asia was very different from the African one. What was common was that both lacked any decision-making role in international relations and were, therefore, peripheral in international affairs.

It must also be emphasized that while the idea of Africa was institutionalized, first in the Organization of African Unity (OAU) and later in the African Union (AU), it is perhaps not possible to speak of Asia in the same manner. The continent is too economically, politically and culturally diverse for any continental grouping to emerge. To speak of Africa–Asia relations in general terms is an impossible task. What is possible is to discuss bilateral relations between some important countries in Asia and Africa or to examine the degree of compatibility/community of ideas and actions between African and Asian countries in international organizations of the period, like the Non-Aligned Movement (NAM), the G-77 and the United Nations (UN).

The main hypothesis of this chapter is that the mid-twentieth century was the seed-time of relations between Africa and countries of Asia, especially India and China, which are now bearing fruit in the twenty-first century. This chapter will try to answer the question, why did Africa–Asia relations not flourish despite both regions facing similar political constraints in international relations in the second half of the twentieth century? Why particularly did India, a leader of the NAM and the G-77 and a champion of anticolonialism and anti-racism, have only limited relations with African countries? What constraints prevented African and Asian countries, lumped together as the Third World, from coming together in a more politically cohesive manner? The answers can be found in the prevailing conditions of the time, where African and Asian countries, equally, had little say in determining the course of international politics and were too weak to go beyond expressing a wish for south–south cooperation. This chapter will explore these issues to explain why the period 1970 to 1990 can be seen as the seed-time for future relations.

Brief literature review

There are almost no books or articles on Asia–Africa political or diplomatic relations between 1970 and 1990, although newspaper reports on events are many. Both continents were under intense scrutiny amid the prevailing political conditions of the Cold War and major upheavals including decolonization wars, civil wars, coups, inter-state conflicts, the Vietnam war and the Soviet intervention in Afghanistan. None of these events could occur in isolation and they were either supported or condemned in international forums that included African and Asian countries. Views/writings on such matters will be mentioned here along with studies on bilateral relations between African and Asian states, especially India and China.

The *Journal of Asian and African Studies* (published since 1966) contains some articles that discuss Asia and Africa separately (Fatton, 1989; Kapur, 1990) and some that analyse bilateral relations (Hofmeyr & Williams, 2009); there are no broad articles on Africa–Asia relations. *African Affairs* of the Royal African Society, published from 1901, has many scholarly articles on African politics and contemporary foreign relations but very few on bilateral relations with Asian countries of the period under study. Ampiah (2005) argues that Japan had limited relations with Sub-Saharan Africa between 1960 and 1990 because Japanese policy makers felt no historical guilt of a colonial past in Africa. Another article on Japan–South Africa relations in the post-apartheid period (Alden, 2002) mentions bureaucratic and institutional hurdles in both countries.

Other journals on both Asia and Africa include the *International Journal of African and Asian Studies* published from 2013 (Zurich), *African and Asian Studies* published from 2002 (New York), *African Journal of International Affairs and Development* published from 1995, *African Journal of*

Political Economy (1986–1990), *African Studies Quarterly* (from 1997, University of Florida, Gainesville), *African Studies Review* (University of Cambridge), to mention a few. All of them contain mainly country-specific or issue-oriented articles on Africa. One area that has seen some study is the African-Asian Diaspora, especially in *African and Asian Studies* (Campbell, 2006; Collins, 2006).

In India, the Indian Council for Africa, New Delhi, published *Africa Quarterly: A Journal of African Affairs* from 1961 and books like *India and Africa: Perspectives of Cooperation*. Tabassum Jamal's *Economic and Technical Co-operation between India and Africa* and R. R. Ramchandani's *India–Africa Economic Relations in the Context of Economic Co-operation among Developing Countries* may be mentioned. But there is a general dearth of in-depth research given the lack of access to primary African sources.

A recent publication by Antoinette Burton, *Africa in the Indian Imagination: Race and the Politics of Postcolonial Citation*, re-thinks post-Bandung Afro-Asian solidarity. It critiques the Indian view of a sentimentalized, nostalgic and fraternal history of Afro-Asian solidarity and presents an alternative view of colonial racial hierarchies echoed in the subordination of Africans and blackness (Burton, 2016). While this argument cannot be discounted, it is incomplete and grounded in only a partial historical understanding of India's growth trajectory with the author looking at only selected texts.

There is little scholarship on China–Africa relations in this period. China's economic relations with Africa took off from the late 1970s, though they began to flourish from the 1990s. Shinn and Eisenman's *China and Africa: A Century of Engagement* may be mentioned for its insights into China's political support of African countries that accepted China's 'One China' policy (Shinn & Eisenman, 2012). Several articles discuss China's attempts to wean African states away from Taipei (Wu & Longenecker, 1994; Taylor, 1998; Payne & Veney, 2001), and some research has been done on the attraction of the Chinese model and its provision of foreign aid as an alternative to Western imperialistic models (Ismael, 1971; Poole, 1966; Brautigam, 1998).

A few books with divergent views discuss Chinese foreign policy towards Africa. Larkin contextualizes China's Africa policy in the broader background of China's foreign policy with an emphasis on ideological factors (Larkin, 1971). Ogunsanwo speaks of China's 'revolutionary pragmatism' as the driving factor behind China's interest in Africa (Ogunsanwo, 1974). Another view is that of Hevi, a Ghanaian student in China, who warned that Nkrumah's favouring of the Chinese model would lead Africa down a dangerous road (Hevi, 1967).

An informative article by Chinese author Li Anshan, 'African Studies in China in the Twentieth Century: A Historiographical Survey' gives an insight into how scholarship of Africa was built in China, mentioning foreign language articles on Africa that were translated into Chinese (Li, 2005: 59–87). The Chinese Association of African Studies (1979) and the Chinese Society of African Historical Studies (1980) were formed following the Cultural Revolution to promote knowledge of Africa. Li mentions important Chinese publications, which give an idea of the extent of Chinese scholarship on Africa prior to the 1990s. No such systematic study of Africa was undertaken anywhere else in Asia in this period, although university departments in Africa studies did spring up in countries like India.

Africa: domestic politics and international relations (1970s–1990s)

Western and Third World scholars have suggested that Africa was peripheral to global politics. The literature survey suggests that this was reflected in academia. This peripherality may be partially explained by Africa's 'insecurity dilemma' (Job, 1992) in the immediate post-colonial period, which may have impeded Africa–Asia relations. While African states, post-independence, accepted the legitimacy of colonially created states and claimed sovereignty over their people, the state's authority was not unchallenged. Colonial rule had not lasted long enough in Africa for nationalism to penetrate. Further, the colonial state was the antithesis of the nation state with little power being devolved to the 'natives'. Most African states were, therefore, not prepared for independence, with successor elites having little experience of governance. The result was intra-state and inter-state conflicts that included civil wars, border and other conflicts, military coup d'états and authoritarian rule (Marshall, 2005; Aremu, 2010). Insecurity in Africa can also be traced to famine, disease and pestilence, the horrors of which were further exacerbated by corruption, inefficient governments, and a high level of indebtedness and poverty. Poverty was further embedded through refugee flows, humanitarian crises and malgovernance.

Africa's insecurity dilemma gave both the US and the Soviet Union space to play out their rivalries in areas of relative strategic importance. Although conflicts had domestic roots, the superpowers became heavily involved in supporting respective client states in the Horn of Africa in the 1970s and 1980s, with the US trying to prevent Soviet expansionism through an 'encirclement strategy' of military alliances and the Soviet Union focusing on Ethiopia. The full impact of the resulting militarization of the region was perceivable after the Cold War (Lyons, 1996: 85–99). In southern Africa too, while the power struggles between various nationalist guerrilla groups in Angola and Mozambique were inevitable, the respective proxy forces of and arms supplies from the superpowers helped to intensify the violence and prolong the wars (Minter, 1994). The net result was that most countries in Africa were engulfed in conflict with no resources for growth or trade, making them unattractive destinations for developing Asian countries.

According to one analysis, 'If the 1960s and 1970s marked the consolidation of authoritarian dispensations in Africa, the 1980s marked their unravelling, while the 1990s was the decade of subaltern revolt' (Hutchful & Aning, 2004). Wars, corruption, bad governance, famines, etc. caused severe economic compression. By the late 1970s, Africa's development along with donor aid had begun to stall. While African leaders suggested inter-African trade and investment for Africa's growth in the Lagos Plan of Action (1980), the World Bank's response was the Berg Report (World Bank, 1981), which blamed malgovernance and state control over market forces for Africa's predicament. It prescribed a dual strategy of liberalization and privatization, the basis of Structural Adjustment Programmes (SAPs), which often became new sources of largesse for supporters and clients. A series of UN reports then debated what was needed for Africa's growth (UNECA (United Nations, Economic Commission for Africa), 1990; World Bank, 1989). SAP may not have succeeded as expected as thirty-one sub-Saharan countries are still marked as 'heavily indebted poor countries' (World Bank, 2015).

Under the then prevailing political and economic conditions in Africa, the scope for having energetic African-Asian relations was limited, particularly because Asian countries also had no control over the terms of economic and political engagement, which had been set decades earlier by countries now known as 'developed'. Interestingly, no mention was made of Asia's role in the debate on Africa's development. Yet, similar experiments were being undertaken in different forms in some Asian countries while others were already liberalizing their economies. Yet others were framing nationalization policies on the basis of various dependency theories and the call for a New International Economic Order (NIEO) and south–south cooperation stemmed from a particular reading of Third World, particularly Afro-Asian, unity.

The next section will point out that the situation in Asia, though not similar, was also not conducive to meaningful African–Asian partnership, despite rhetorical solidarity expressed by leaders in both continents.

Asia: political conditions (1970s–1990s)

Political conditions in Asia in the 1970s and 1980s were a mixed bag. According to Robert Scalapino, political scientist and analyst, 'Asian states run the gamut from high levels of economic growth and political tranquillity to conditions of economic stagnation or retrogression, and perennial conflict' (Scalapino, 1979). While Taiwan, Singapore and Malaysia had GNP growth rates of 7 to 8 percent by 1979, Japan's growth rate averaged 6 percent. In India and China, the rates were lower in 1979, India's being less than 4 percent. Scalapino also speaks of mid-level states whose poor performances he blamed on leaderships committed to earlier forms of socialism. Vietnam's communist government and Pol Pot's extremist experiments in Kampuchea isolated both countries. Much of Asia remained dependent on individuals or small oligarchies for decision-making; durable institutions were yet to be built and many countries were plagued by succession crises. While Japan had a successful parliamentary democracy, the imposition of the state of emergency in India caused a short democratic setback; Pakistan and the new state of Bangladesh had intermittent rollbacks to military rule.

However, spaces appeared for cooperation in the Third World in view of the common power-impotency of the postcolonial period, perhaps more at the ideological than the practical level, despite the problems of nation-building. In Southeast Asia, US withdrawal was followed by Sino-Soviet rivalry reflected more directly in the region's wars (Chanda, 1986). Cold War politics were deeply entrenched as the Southeast Asia Treaty Organization continued to safeguard the West's interests. States that were not 'frontline' had their own problems: for instance, Indonesia faced civil war in East Timor. Singapore and Malaysia, despite high growth rates, faced the challenges of political and socio-economic consolidation. In South Asia, the India–Pakistan war of 1971 resulted in the emergence of the state of Bangladesh. Pakistan faced a huge refugee crisis after the Soviet invasion of Afghanistan, causing the Cold War to enter directly into the region. Sri Lanka faced an insurgency in the north which grew incrementally in ferocity. India's embroilment in the issue, with the Indian Peace Keeping Force (IPKF) being sent to Sri Lanka, resulted in the assassination of an Indian Prime Minister. The Middle East was in turmoil right through this period: the 1973 Yom Kippur war was followed by the OPEC (Organization of the Petroleum Exporting Countries) oil price hike, leading to depression and stagflation in many Western as well as Third World non-oil producing countries. The 1979 Khomeini revolution in Iran and the Iran–Iraq war (1980–1990) had grim consequences that became evident in the 1990s. Egypt became sidelined in regional politics after it signed the Camp David Agreement in 1979 with Israel. In the Far East, although China began to open up economically towards the late 1970s, it remained a closed system politically. The period can best be explained by the *fang* (letting go)/*shou* (tightening up) cycle, with phases of reform alternating with periods of relative restraint (Baum, 1994).

Thus, all Asian countries faced the challenges of nation building and were fragile. Relations with equally (if not more) fragile states of Africa could, therefore, only be limited. Apart from the numerical strength of African states in international forums, there was little to attract Asian countries to Africa in the 1970s or the 1980s. However, as mentioned, Cold War politics and state fragility did provide some common grounds for cooperation.

Ideological associations and organizations

The League against Imperialism and Colonialism Conference in Brussels (1927) first brought nationalist and anti-imperialist leaders from colonized and Latin American countries together. Prior to India's independence, India's visionary Prime Minister-to-be, Jawaharlal Nehru, realizing the need for unity among Asian nations, had called the Asian Relations Conference (1947). Following that, the Colombo Conference (1954) decided on a political meeting of heads of state from Africa and Asia. At the Bandung Conference in 1955, the first two-continent meeting, Indonesia's President Sukarno's inaugural speech summed up the aspirations of these newly independent countries:

> We are of many different nations . . . But what does that matter? . . . We can inject the voice of reason into world affairs. We can mobilise all the spiritual, all the moral, all the political strength of Asia and Africa on the side of peace . . . We, the peoples of Asia and Africa, 1,400,000,000 strong . . . can mobilise what I have called the Moral Violence of Nations in favour of peace . . .

> . . . This Conference is . . . [one] of brotherhood . . . it is a body of enlightened, tolerant opinion which seeks to impress on the world that all men and all countries have their place under the sun . . . and to develop a true consciousness of the interdependence of men and nations for their well-being and survival on earth
>
> *(The Ministry of Foreign Affairs, Republic of Indonesia, 1955)*

Post-independence Asia and Africa shared hopes of the dividends of peace but were aware that 'colonialism is not yet dead . . . so long as vast areas of Asia and Africa are unfree' (The Ministry of Foreign Affairs, Republic of Indonesia, 1955). 'Unfree' did not imply colonialism alone, but the bondages of poverty, instability and underdevelopment. Moreover, the new states had little control over international relations then infused by the Cold War. As Sukarno pointed out, 'We cannot indulge in power politics. Diplomacy for us is not a matter of the big stick' (The Ministry of Foreign Affairs, Republic of Indonesia, 1955.). The Final Communiqué, therefore, contained sections on economic and cultural cooperation, political issues and world peace. Interestingly, it noted

> that the representation of the countries of the Asian-African region on the Security Council, in relation to the principle of equitable geographical distribution, was inadequate [and] . . . as regards the distribution of the non-permanent seats, the Asian-African countries . . . should be enabled to serve on the Security Council, so that they might make a more effective contribution to the maintenance of international peace and security
>
> *(The Ministry of Foreign Affairs, Republic of Indonesia,*
> *1955, Final Communiqué)*

It also called for total disarmament and prohibition of the use or testing of nuclear weapons. While the Panchsheel Treaty is touted as the main outcome of the Bandung Conference, the Final Communiqué gives an insight into the shared thinking of a number of African and Asian leaders about the fragile position of their countries in the international state system and their common interest in avoiding the wars of the great powers, since 'freedom and peace are interdependent'. Their collective interest in social and economic progress was reflected in the section on 'Economic Cooperation', which included suggestions for stabilizing commodity prices and trade in primary products, and stated that cooperation among participating countries did not 'preclude either the desirability or the need for co-operation with countries outside the region, including the investment of foreign capital' (Final Communiqué). These ideas later developed into the Non-Aligned Movement, the Group of 77 and the demand for NIEO.

The NAM was formed in 1961. The vast majority of member states were from Africa and Asia with few representations from Latin America and only Yugoslavia from Europe.

All African states were members because the OAU was an institutional member. Although the NAM preferred to call itself a 'movement' and did not have any strict organizational structure, it provided a forum for African and Asian states to raise their concerns on racism, colonialism, apartheid and underdevelopment. The NAM began the AFRICA Fund in 1986 to assist states facing oppression from minority regimes. Member states contributed generously even though they themselves faced fund crunches. Many resolutions were passed in the UN General Assembly against apartheid and in favour of people struggling against racism and colonialism in its various forms. India accorded diplomatic status to the African National Congress (ANC) in 1967 and the South West African People's Organization (SWAPO) in 1985. In fact, with regard to the Namibian issue, the NAM played a key role in internationalizing it and in advancing the legitimacy of SWAPO, both in the UN General Assembly and the Security Council (Saunders, 2015:145–147). An extraordinary meeting of the NAM's Coordinating Bureau in Maputo in 1979 included members of Southern African liberation movements and representatives of international organizations and thereby helped the frontline states, the liberation movements and the NAM to develop a common position on the struggles in Rhodesia, Namibia and South Africa (Thomas, 1995).

However, while the NAM provided a forum for ideological cooperation among like-minded states, it took an activist role only in the passage of pertinent resolutions in inter-governmental organizations on issues like racism and colonialism. Perhaps a closer Afro-Asian affinity can be found in organizations that took up politico-economic issues of developmental inequality resulting from structures constructed during colonial times. Countries of both continents faced similar challenges of being on the periphery of political and economic decision-making. Dependency theorists blamed the international economic order created in the age of imperialism for the persistence of underdevelopment in modern times. This idea resulted in the demand for NIEO and the organization of the G-77. According to Julius Nyerere, speaking at the fourth ministerial meeting of the G-77, 'It was practical understanding of the fact that legal independence did not mean economic freedom which made most of us think of cooperating with others similarly placed' (Nyrere, 1979). Out of such thoughts of collective interdependence, the idea of south–south cooperation was born. The cooperation of Asian and African member states led to the passage of a resolution at the UN (A/RES/S-6/3201) at the sixth special session on the establishment of NIEO, to remove 'disequilibrium' through 'international economic co-operation on a just and equitable basis' (UN Documents, 1974). However, neither Asian (except perhaps Japan) nor African countries had the economic capacity to change the terms of trade or enough capital to invest in each other's countries. Both Asian and African countries were mainly commodity producers, which meant demand for each other's products was minimal. Of necessity, their trade was directed to the north. South–south cooperation was further hampered by the protectionist policies followed by most countries of the south at the time.

Interestingly, it was a politico-economic matter which had led to the enthusiasm behind the demand for NIEO: the effective use of oil as a weapon by Middle Eastern countries following Western military support of Israel in the 1973 Yom Kippur war. The Organization of Arab Oil Exporting Countries subsequently decided to increase the posted price of oil by 70 percent and cut production by a minimum of 5 percent every month until Israeli forces vacated occupied Arab territory, and also announced an oil embargo on 'hostile' (pro-Israel) countries. The OAU fully supported the Arab stand at the sixth special session of the UN General Assembly which passed the resolution on NIEO; the oil embargo was hailed as a practical example of what developing countries were capable of if they could manage their natural resources in the 'proper way'. However, the oil price rise also affected the developing countries of Asia and Africa and the euphoria subsided as foreign exchange reserves depleted. The response of the West Asian states is worth mentioning: Algeria started an oil price discount scheme for neighbouring oil importers and diverted 3 percent of its crude to West African states. This goodwill gesture was partly the cause of the formation of the Economic Organization of West African States (ECOWAS). The Organization of Petroleum Exporting States (OPEC) also set up a Special Fund of US$800 million, which was in addition to US$200 million that was to be disbursed through the Arab Fund and the Arab Bank for Economic Development in Africa (Corradi, 1979; Namboodri, 1983). These efforts at cooperation were not enough and contributed to the debt problem of both Asian and African countries in the 1980s. But what is important is that these Asian countries did try to ease the burden on other developing countries, particularly African ones.

Two other areas of political cooperation developed from the ideological ferment of the Cold War period. The first was the Afro-Asian Peoples' Solidarity Organization, begun in 1957 as the Solidarity Council of Afro-Asian Peoples' Solidarity Conference at Cairo. Its aim, according to its by-laws of 1974, was to coordinate and strengthen the liberation struggles of the people of Asia and Africa against imperialism, colonialism, neo-colonialism, racism, Zionism and fascism and further their socio-economic and cultural development. It was left-leaning at the time but lost its leftist orientation and now has consultative status with the UN Economic and Social Council (ECOSOC), the UN Educational, Scientific and Cultural Organization (UNESCO), the UN Industrial Development Organization (UNIDO) and the UN Conference on Trade and Development (UNCTAD) and observer status at the NAM and the African Committee for Human Rights and Peoples, which implies developmental cooperation between African and Asian people (AAPSO, Afro-Asian Peoples' Solidarity Organization, 2008). In response to this organization, which was considered too Soviet-oriented, the Organización de Solidaridad con los Pueblos de Asia, África y América Latina (OSPAAAL) was started in 1966 as a Cuban initiative on a tricontinental basis to promote socialism and communism of the Cuban variety in the Third World. It attracted leftist Latin American, Asian and African leaders, but gave verbal support to the struggle against colonialism and apartheid (Valdes, 1979). It is better known for its poster art supporting political causes in the three continents and these are still available.

Another offshoot of the Bandung Conference was the Asian–African Legal Consultative Organization (AALCO), an international governmental organization formed in 1956. Initially it advised member states on matters of international law, for instance, extradition treaties and mutual assistance in criminal matters, but began focusing on issues like an Afro-Asian view of the UN Charter, regional cooperation and the NIEO, and the Indian Ocean as a zone of peace. It continues to function, has a standing invitation to participate as an observer in the UN General Assembly and focuses on matters of common contemporary interest to Asia and Africa like the working of the International Criminal Court (ICC), the World Trade Organization (WTO), the international protection of folklore and human rights in Islam.

While these are areas where political space was utilized for cooperation at a collective and even continental level, bilateral political relationships, though limited, were also growing between individual African and Asian states. The two countries worth mentioning here are India and China, although there were fears of a Japanese 'yellow peril' in the 1930s (Bradshaw & Ransdell, 2011). By the 1970s, however, Japan's economic focus was on the US.

China: political relations (1970–1990)

India–China friction regarding leadership of the developing world became particularly marked after China's incursion into India in 1962, and this was reflected in the tone of reporting on

Political and diplomatic interactions

each other's activities in Africa in their respective print media. Both India and China spoke of south–south cooperation, but while India had little money to back up its verbal posture, China had a definite political bent in its relations with Africa. Chinese premier Zhou En-Lai and vice-premier Chen Yi visited ten African countries in 1963–1964, where Zhou spoke extensively on opposing imperialism, colonialism, racism, expansionism, safeguarding world peace, strengthening unity among Asian and African countries and promoting friendly relations between China and other Asian and African countries (Adie, 1964). Robert Scalapino, who was in Africa at the time, analysed the tour thus:

1   China was attempting to sell the idea of Afro-Asian solidarity under Chinese leadership as opposed to NAM's, that is, they were trying to oppose a 'Yugoslav–India pincer movement' against them;
2   it was trying to recast the image of China which may have been tarnished because of Soviet propaganda that it was a 'left-deviationist' society;
3   Zhou was seeking to get across the impression that China was a major power;
4   the premier was in Africa to get a first-hand impression of Africa itself for long-term planning.

Scalapino believed that China gave small amounts of aid for selected purposes and focused on the poorest (Mali, Guinea) rather than the richest, and its influence was likely to be more in countries at the pre-independence revolutionary phase (Scalapino, 1964).

In the next two decades, Chinese interest in getting a political base in Africa was evident in several projects that it financed, most importantly, the 1,860 km long Tan-Zam railroad connecting Dares Salaam to Kapiri Mposhi in Zambia. China gave an interest-free loan of around US$450 million, its largest foreign aid project at the time. The *New York Times* claimed that the railway was 'only one element of China's overall foreign policy' (Graham, 1974). China was obviously interested in gaining Africa's goodwill especially in the context of its 'One China' policy. Tanzania's Julius Nyerere was so happy with China's terms of friendship that he called on the UN to accept the People's Republic as a member (Nyerere, 1966). China also funded industrial and other projects in Tanzania, Kenya, Sudan, Sierra Leone, Liberia, Zambia, Equatorial Guinea, Somalia, Burundi, Somalia, Congo, to mention a few countries, and gave selective military assistance to Zanzibar, Congo-Brazzaville and Tanzania. It supplied arms to the UNITA (National Union for the Total Independence of Angola) and the FNLA (National Front for the Liberation of Angola) who were fighting the Soviet-backed MPLA (People's Movement for the Liberation of Angola) in Angola. At the end of the civil war, Angola's infrastructural needs were helped through its oil-for-loan deal with China instead of condition-based structural adjustment assistance from Western institutions and governments (Aidoo, 2013). Interestingly, despite its talk of anticolonialism, it had relations with South Africa and Rhodesia through Macao (Mukherjee, 1970). What is being emphasized here is that the impact of China in Africa did not depend on the volume of assistance, which, compared with Western aid, was negligible, but on the politically apt choice of projects.

Chinas willingness to use the veto in support of an African candidate, Tanzanian foreign minister Salim Salim, for the post of secretary-general of the UN was widely appreciated by African countries. Again, there was a visit by a Chinese premier, Zhou Ziyang, in 1983, to ten African countries during which there was no policy or ideological statement on either South Africa or Namibia, the focus of NAM at the time. Zhou reiterated repeatedly during his tour that the task ahead in Africa was 'to consolidate political independence by strengthening the national economy', which was a far cry from the theme of Zhou En-Lai's tour that Africa 'was ripe for revolution' (Editorial, *The Statesman,* 1983). Perhaps this was the beginning of China's enhanced politico-economic role in the continent that became evident in the 1990s.

India: political role (1970–1990)

India's role in Africa at this time focused on its ideological commitment to non-alignment and the principles of anti-racism and anticolonialism. It therefore gave strong verbal support to the anti-apartheid movement in South Africa and diplomatic recognition to the ANC in 1967 and SWAPO in 1985. At the eighth NAM summit at Harare, Prime Minister Rajiv Gandhi was chiefly credited with setting up the Africa Fund. India was also one of the main contributors to UN peacekeeping troops in Africa beginning with the Congo in 1961, where an Indian, Major-General Dewan Prem Chand, was in command. Other important missions were Angola (1989–1999), Mozambique (1992–1994), Somalia (1993–1994), to mention a few. These initiatives helped to promote India's diplomatic position in Africa. In fact, India's general stand in Africa was an amicable solution to problems through cooperation and negotiations. To cite an example, while sympathizing with the cause of the Sahrawi Arab Democratic Republic (SADR), which was continuing its fight with Morocco for independence, India's stand was that SADR's and Morocco's leaders should negotiate an amicable settlement in cooperation with the NAM and OAU. However, India's stance against the use of force was not always appreciated by countries trying to free themselves.

India's long-term policy in Africa always included economic cooperation and building Africa's human resources through educational and training programmes in India through the Indian Technical and Economic Cooperation (ITEC) programme, which since its inception has trained around 25,000 Africans in engineering, agriculture, medicine, the social sciences, etc. Several bilateral cooperation programmes were also taken up, like a credit agreement for ₹ 50 million (Indian rupees) with Tanzania (1972) and a cultural exchange programme of artists, teachers and scientists (1975), when the Indo-Tanzanian Joint Commission was set up to ensure follow-up of programmes. In 1977, India was the fourth largest supplier of goods to Tanzania and played an important role in offshore oil explorations in Songo Songo.

India had and continues to have a large diaspora in Africa, many of whom are industrialists and businesspeople. However, this very fact, added to the relative prosperity of Indian people as well as the reluctance of people of Indian origin (PIO) to integrate into their adopted countries, made them targets of 'Africanization' programmes in the post-independence period. Post-independence (1963), Kenya gave non-Kenyans two years to acquire Kenyan citizenship. Many Indians were dismissed from the civil service for non-compliance and faced incremental discrimination. The Kenyan Immigration and Trade Licensing Acts of 1967 required them to acquire trade licences and limited the areas where they could do business. In Uganda, President Idi Amin expelled around 50,000 Asians in 1972, although a kind of 'Indophobia' existed even during his predecessor's time. It is interesting that there was little press coverage of this event in India. In 1987, there were riots against the Indian community (locally called Karanas) in Malagasy, one reason being the prosperity of an alien community that refused to integrate. Indians also faced problems in Ghana for activities 'not in the interests of the country' (*The Hindu,* 1987). However, the Indian government never seems to have taken up the cause of the Indian diaspora in Africa. In fact, Nehru had categorically stated that Indians who chose to stay abroad should consider themselves nationals of their host countries, integrate with the host culture and fight for the liberation of their adopted countries. This seems to have been the trend of India's diaspora policy till the 1990s, when economic compulsions resulted in a marked shift. However, since the Indian government took up the cause of expelled Indians only half-heartedly in the

Political and diplomatic interactions

early 1970s, the Indian diaspora in Africa that has been there much over 100 years is not as responsive to India's change in policy as PIOs elsewhere (Bhattacharya, 2014).

Another issue that needs to be highlighted is that even though India wooed Africa with words and some aid, Africa was never a priority in its foreign relations in the period under study. While high dignitaries from Africa like President Julius Nyrere of Tanzania, President Moi of Kenya, President Nkrumah of Ghana and Sam Nujoma, leader of SWAPO, visited India, Prime Minister Nehru's short trip to Nigeria was followed by Rajiv Gandhi's visit to Zimbabwe, Zambia, Angola and Tanzania twenty years later in 1986. Even today, India has only ten embassies, fifteen high commissions and six consulates in Africa's fifty-four countries. This emphasizes that despite the increasing level of economic relations, it may be surmised that India's political relations with African states may not have the significance that needs to be given at the governmental level, despite the India–Africa forum summits, for sustained robust economic relations.

The question is why did India, considered to be a beacon of anti-racism and anticolonialism and a founder of the NAM, mainly resort to rhetorical support in important forums and not take a more positive political role in Africa's nation-building process or have a more vibrant political relationship with African countries? The answer may be found in a counter-question: would African leaders have appreciated this or considered it as interference, since they were themselves emerging from colonial subjugation? The NAM, in fact, emphasized peaceful coexistence and non-aggression. Moreover, India's early policy was shaped by Gandhian idealism based on non-violent direct action, which was re-shaped by Nehruvian ideological underpinnings of non-alignment, both focusing on moral rather than physical force. Incidentally, Gandhi began his anti-racial sojourn in South Africa, which developed into nationalism in India, and his as well as Nehru's legacy is well recognized in that and other African states.

Further, India did not have the political capacity to initiate activism against colonialism and racism in a world where the major powers set the rules. It could only resort to condemnatory resolutions, rhetorical support and recognition of banned freedom-fighting organizations. India was also a new state facing major internal and external challenges, both threatening the integrity of the state. At the time that Idi Amin was expelling Asians, India was just recovering from a war with Pakistan which it helped to divide, thus inviting severe criticism internationally along with a threat of reprisal from Pakistan's supporters. It also faced incremental internal challenges of sub-nationalism and extremist ideologies forcing it to intensify its energies within its borders as well. Under the circumstances, India–Africa relations were not a priority despite India's commitment to freedom and democracy. However, the goodwill that it built up with its strong, unstinted and unconditional stand in favour of freedom in Africa, and the leadership it provided through NAM and other similar groupings and its contribution to UN peacekeeping forces, is paying dividends today.

India's external challenges from neighbours modified Nehruvian ideology, and a more realistic stance began to re-shape it after China's incursion in 1962, followed by wars with Pakistan in 1965 and 1971. Even though non-alignment continued to be the articulated cornerstone of India's foreign policy till the 1990s, the reality was slightly different as India sought support against perceived and real external threats. India was also a poor country at the time, with foreign exchange reserves of only US$0.97 billion in 1970–1971, which increased to US$5.81 billion in 1990–1991 (*The Economic Times*, 2011). Given its population of 868.9 million in 1990, it could not afford to go beyond the rhetoric of south–south cooperation. It is because of its poverty and limited resources that India's economic policy, along with its foreign policy, began a drastic transformation in the 1990s, towards liberalization and pragmatism and away from state control over the economy and ideological non-alignment. While Gandhi had once spoken of a 'commerce' only of 'ideas and services' and not of 'manufactured goods' and 'raw materials' between India and Africa, India now sees Africa as a partner in its development and holds out a promise of growth to African countries based on its own model. South–south cooperation has become a reality and has found a politico-economic base in the India–Africa Forum Summits that have been held regularly since 2008 (Bhattacharya, 2010). But this might not have been possible without the grounding of India–Africa relations in the goodwill of the earlier period.

Conclusion

The 1970s to the 1990s is a different world from that of today; the Cold War and its indirect impediment of independent political interactions in the Third World are over. Today, a vibrant relationship is growing between Asian and African states. The seeds of this relationship were, however, laid in the disturbed decades between 1970 and 1990. The very factors that made these decades troubled created areas of convergence among developing countries. Most countries of Africa and Asia had emerged from varying years of colonialism and wanted political independence in world affairs. This created space for the Non-Aligned Movement, which implied independent decision-making, particularly on issues concerning the developing world. While none of these countries could afford to cut off economic relations with developed countries, they could call for different, beneficial terms of trade and talk of south–south cooperation. This led to the demand for NIEO and the formation of G-77. There was cooperation on issues like racism and apartheid in inter-governmental organizations, which created a community of ideas and confidence-building. Having undergone periods of imperialist oppression, Asian and African countries wanted a different kind of relationship with each other, one that entailed partnership and mutual benefit. It was in the period under study that future relations were taking shape, that is taking different forms today like the New Asian-African Strategic Partnership (NAASP) at one level, and the India–Africa Forum Summit, the Tokyo International Conference on African Development (TICAD) or the Forum on China–Africa Cooperation, at another. The present relationships have their roots in the past: the vibrancy that we see today might not have been possible without the groundwork that had been laid in the latter half of the twentieth century.

References

AAPSO, Afro-Asian Peoples' Solidarity Organization, 2008. Constitution of the Afro-Asian Peoples' Solidarity Organization, 1958, as re-framed in 1988, and Final Communiqué. Available at: www.aapsorg.org/en/aboutus/arconstitution.html [Accessed 13 December 2015].

Adie, W. A. C., 1964. 'Chou En-lai on Safari', *The China Quarterly*, Volume 18, pp. 174–194.

Aidoo, R., 2013. 'China and Angola: The "True Dynamic Duo" in Sino-Africa Relations', *Foreign Policy*, 20 June. Available at: www.foreignpolicyjournal.com/2013/06/20/china-and-angola-the-true-dynamic-duo-in-sino-africa-relations/ [Accessed 1 November 2015].

Alden, C., 2002. 'The Chrysanthemum and the Protea: Reinventing Japanese–South African Relations after Apartheid', *African Affairs*, Volume 101 (404), pp. 365–386. doi:10.1093/afraf/101.404.365.

Ampiah, K., 2005. 'Japan and the Development of Africa: A Preliminary Evaluation of the Tokyo International Conference on African Development', *African Affairs*, Volume 104 (414), pp. 97–115. doi:10.1093/afraf/adi005.

Aremu, J. O., 2010. 'Conflicts in Africa: Meaning, Causes, Impact and Solution', *African Research Review*, Volume. 4 (4), Serial No. 17, pp. 549–560.

Baum, R., 1994. *Burying Mao: Chinese Politics in the Age of Deng Xiaoping*, Princeton, NJ: Princeton University Press.

Bhattacharya, S. B., 2010. 'Engaging Africa: India's interests in the African continent, past and present', in F. Cheru and C. Obi (eds.), *The Rise of China and India in Africa: Challenges, Opportunities and Critical Intervention*, London: Zed Books, pp. 63–76.

Bhattacharya, S. B., 2014. 'The role of the Indian diaspora in Africa', in R. Beri (ed.), *India and Africa: Enhancing Mutual Engagement*, Delhi: IDSA, pp. 142–149.

Bradshaw, R. and Ransdell, J., 2011. 'Japan, Britain and the Yellow Peril in Africa in the 1930s', *The Asia-Pacific Journal*, Volume 9 (44), p. 2. Available at: http://apjjf.org/2011/9/44/Richard-Bradshaw/3626/article.html [Accessed 31 October 2015].

Brautigam, D., 1998. *Chinese Aid and African Development: Exporting Green Revolution*, London: Macmillan Press, p. 4.

Burton, A., 2016. *Africa in the Indian Imagination: Race and the Politics of Postcolonial Citation*, Durham, NC: Duke University Press.

Campbell, G., 2006. 'The African–Asian Diaspora: Myth or Reality?', *African and Asian Studies*, Volume 5 (3–4), pp. 305–324. doi:10.1163/156920906779134795.

Chanda, N., 1986. *Brother Enemy – The War After the War: History of Indo-China After the Fall of Saigon*, San Diego, CA: Harcourt Brace Jovanovich.

Collins, R. O., 2006. 'The African Slave Trade to Asia and the Indian Ocean Islands', *African and Asian Studies*, Volume 5 (3–4), pp. 325–346. doi:10.1163/156920906779134821.

Corradi, A. Q., 1979. 'Energy and the Exercise of Power', *Foreign Affairs*, Volume 57 (5), Summer.

Editorial, *The Statesman,* 1983. *Zhou's Quiet Safari*, Calcutta, 29 January.

Hevi, E., 1967. *The Dragon's Embrace: The Chinese Communists and Africa*, London: Pall Mall Press.

Fatton, R., Jr., 1989. 'The State of African Studies and Studies of the African State: The Theoretical Softness of the "Soft State"', *Journal of Asian and African Studies*, Volume 24, pp. 170–187. doi:10.1177/002190968902400302.

Final Communiqué of the Asian-African Conference of Bandung, 1955. Available at: http://franke.uchicago.edu/Final_Communique_Bandung_1955.pdf.

Graham, J. D., 1974. 'The Tanzam Railway: Consolidating the People's Development and Building the Internal Economy', *Africa Today*, Volume 21 (3), p. 27. Available at: www.jstor.org/stable/4185423 [Accessed 1 February 2016].

Hofmeyr, I. and Williams, M., 2009. 'South Africa–India: Connections and Comparisons', *Journal of Asian and African Studies*, Volume 44, p. 517. doi:10.1177/0021909608098674.

Hutchful, E. and Aning, K., 2004. 'The political economy of conflict', in A. Adebajo and I. O. D. Rashid (eds.), *West Africa's Security Challenges: Building Peace in a Troubled Region*, London: Lynne Rienner, Chapter 9.

Indian Council for Africa, 1967. *India and Africa: Perspectives of Cooperation*, New Delhi.

Ismael, T., 1971. 'The People's Republic of China and Africa', *Journal of Modern African Studies*, Volume 9 (4), p. 527.

Job, B. L., 1992. *The Insecurity Dilemma: National Security of Third World States*, Boulder, CO; Lynne Rienner.

Kapur, A., 1990. 'Introduction: An Overview of Asia', *Journal of Asian and African Studies*, Volume 25, pp. 3–8. doi:10.1177/002190969002500102.

Larkin, B. D., 1971. *China and Africa 1949–1970: The Foreign Policy of the People's Republic of China*, Berkeley, CA: University of California Press.

Li, A. 2005. 'African Studies in China in the Twentieth Century: A Historiographical Survey', *African Studies Review*, Volume 48 (1), pp. 59–87.

Lyons, T., 1996. 'The international context of internal war: Ethiopia/Eritrea', in E. J. Keller and D. Rothchild (eds.), *Africa in the New International Order: Rethinking State Sovereignty and Regional Security*, London: Lynne Rienner.

Marshall, M. G., 2005. *Conflict Trends in Africa, 1946–2004: A Macro-Comparative Perspective*, Report Prepared for Africa Conflict Prevention Pool (ACPP), Government of the United Kingdom, October 14, Center for Systemic Peace, available at http://www.systemicpeace.org/africa/AfricaConflictTrendsMGM2005us.pdf [Accessed 20 January 2016].

The Ministry of Foreign Affairs, Republic of Indonesia, Djakarta, 1955. President Sukarno of Indonesia, Speech at the Opening of the Bandung Conference, April 18, 1955, *Asia–Africa Speaks from Bandong*, pp. 19–25, text reprinted in the *Internet Modern History Sourcebook*, available at http://sourcebooks.fordham.edu/halsall/mod/1955sukarno-bandong.html [Accessed 15 December 2015].

Minter, W., 1994. *Apartheid's Contras: An Inquiry into the Roots of War in Angola and Mozambique*. London: Zed Books.

Mukherjee, D., 1970. 'China in Africa: A New Friendship Drive', *Times of India,* New Delhi, 30 September.

Namboodri, P. K. S., 1983. 'Politics and Economics of Oil Prices', *Strategic Analysis*, Volume 7(4), pp. 339–342.

Nyrere, J. K., 1966. *Freedom and Unity: A Selection from Writings and Speeches, 1952–65*, Dar es Salaam: Oxford University Press, pp. 323–325.

Nyrere, J. K., 1979. 'Unity for a New Order, Speech at the 4th Ministerial Meeting of the G-77, Arusha, Tanzania, February 12, 1979. Available at: www.gov.go.tz/egov_uploads/documents/unity_for_a_new_order_1979_sw.pdf [Accessed 19 January 2016].

Ogunsanwo, A. 1974. *China's Policy in Africa, 1958–71*, Cambridge: Cambridge University Press.

Payne, R. and Veney, C., 2001. 'Taiwan and Africa: Taipei's Continuing Search for International Recognition', *African and Asian Studies*, Volume 36 (4), pp. 437–450.

Poole, P. A., 1966. 'Communist China's Aid Diplomacy', *Asian Survey*, Volume 6 (11), pp. 622–629.

President Sukarno of Indonesia: Speech at the Opening of the Bandung Conference, 1955. *Internet Modern History Sourcebook* (Sourced from *Africa–Asia Speaks from Bandong*, Djakarta, Indonesian Ministry of Foreign Affairs, 1955, pp. 19–29). Available at: http://sourcebooks.fordham.edu/halsall/mod/1955sukarno-bandong.html [Accessed 4 July 2017].

Sadat, A. E., 1957. *Address Delivered by Mr. Anwar el Sadat at the First Afro-Asian People's Solidarity Conference, December 26*, Internet Modern History Sourcebook: Anwar el Sadat: Afro-Asian Solidarity and the World Mission of the Peoples of Africa and Asia, 1957, *The First Afro-Asian Peoples' Solidarity Conference, 26 December 1957 to January 1*, 1958, 2nd edition (Cairo), pp. 7–12. Available at: https://legacy.fordham.edu/halsall/mod/1957sadat-afroasian1.html [Accessed 24 November 2015].

Saunders, C., 2015. 'The Non-Aligned Movement, the neutral European countries and the issue of Namibia's independence', in S. Bott, J. S. Hanhimaki, J. Schaufelbuehl and M. Wyss (eds.), *Neutrality and Neutralism in the Global Cold War: Between or Within the Blocs?* London: Routledge.

Scalapino, R. A., 1964. *On the Trail of Chou En-Lai in Africa, Memorandum RM-4061-PR, April 1964, Prepared for the US Air Force Project Rand*, Santa Monica, CA: The Rand Corporation. Available at: www.rand.org/content/dam/rand/pubs/research_memoranda/2009/RM4061.pdf [Accessed 1 February 2016].

Scalapino, R. A., 1979. 'Asia at the End of the 1970s', *Foreign Affairs*, America and the World 1979 issue. Available at: www.foreignaffairs.com/articles/asia/1980-02-01/asia-end-1970s [Accessed 1 March 2016].

Shinn, D. H. and Eisenman, J., 2012. *China and Africa: A Century of Engagement*, Philadelphia: University of Pennsylvania Press.

Taylor, I., 1998. 'Africa's Place in the Diplomatic Competition Between Beijing and Taipei', *Issues and Studies*, Volume 34 (3), pp. 126–143.

The Economic Times, 2011. *How the Indian Economy Changed in 1991–2011*. Available at: http://economic-times.indiatimes.com/news/economy/indicators/how-the-indian-economy-changed-in-1991-2011/articleshow/9339258.cms [Accessed 1 August 2016].

The Hindu, 1987. Madras, India, 26 November.

Thomas, S. M., 1995. *The Diplomacy of Liberation: The Foreign Relations of the ANC Since 1960*, London: I. B. Tauris, pp. 107–108.

UN Documents, 1974. UN General Assembly, Sixth Special Session, 1 May 1974, Resolution adopted by the General Assembly, 3201 (S-VI). Declaration on the Establishment of a New International Economic Order, A/RES/S-6/3201. Available at: www.un-documents.net/s6r3201.htm [Accessed 26 January 2016].

UNECA (United Nations Economic Commission for Africa), 1990. *African Alternative Framework to Structural Adjustment Programmes for Socio-Economic Recovery and Transformation (AAF-SAP), Addis Ababa*. Available at: http://hdl.handle.net/10855/5670 [Accessed 15 January 2016].

Valdes, N. P., 1979. 'Revolutionary solidarity in Angola', in C. Blasier and C. Mesa-Lago (eds.), *Cuba in the World*, Pittsburg, PA, University of Pennsylvania Press, p. 89.

World Bank, 1981. 'Report of the African Strategy Review Group', in E. Berg (coordinator), *Accelerated Development in Sub-Saharan Africa: An Agenda for Action*, Washington, DC, World Bank. Available at: www-wds.worldbank.org/external/default/WDSContentServer/WDSP/IB/2000/04/13/00017883 0_98101911444774/Rendered/PDF/multi_page.pdf [Accessed 15 January 2016].

World Bank, 1989. *From Crisis to Sustainable Growth – Sub Saharan Africa: A Long-Term Perspective Study*. Washington, DC: The World Bank. Available at: documents.worldbank.org/curated/en/1989/11/439705/crisis-sustainable-growth-sub-saharan-africa-long-term-perspective-study [Accessed 15 January 2016].

World Bank. 2015. *World Bank List of Economies*. Available at: http://siteresources.worldbank.org/DATA-STATISTICS/Resources/CLASS.XLS [Accessed 2 February 2016].

Wu, G. T. and Longenecker, D. J., 1994. 'The Beijing–Taipei Struggle for International Recognition: From the Niger Affair to the UN', *Asian Survey*, Volume 34 (5), pp. 475–88.

10

FROM BANDUNG TO BRICS

Afro-Asian relations in the twenty-first century

Seifudein Adem and Darryl C. Thomas

Introduction

The purpose of this chapter[1] is to examine four generations of developing solidarity among Third World states comprising the global South, with a greater emphasis on the coalition between global Africa and global Asia, in the twenty-first century. First, Afro-Asianism emerged in the 1950s as the Third World reaction to the racial order in the world system. Second, nonalignment developed as a response by Third World leaders to the Cold War and the bipolar power structure of the world system. Third, the East–West conflict was replaced by the North–South conflict as the most salient issue confronting the global South in the 1970s. The quest for a new international economic order (NIEO) became the raison d'être for Third World solidarity from the 1970s to the 1980s. Fourth, dialogue among these actors developed in the 1980s as an important catalyst for community building in the global South during this period of global restructuring. Collective self-reliance in the South had possibilities of degenerating into sub-imperialism within the global South as the semi-periphery or the newly industrializing countries sought to carve out their own niches in the changing international division of labor. During the 1980s South Africa was the only state in the South pursuing a sub-imperial role. Until very recently, most of the other semi-peripheral states, Brazil, South Korea, Turkey, etc., sought access to the lucrative markets in the United States, Europe and Japan rather than launching a sub-imperialist project (Thomas, 2001:xi). We are now witnessing a resurrection of a fifth generation of Afro-Asian solidarity with the growing political, economic and cultural collaboration and cooperation between global Asia and global Africa in the twenty-first century. This chapter poses the following question: does the new and developing friendship between Africa and China (and the rest of Asia) epitomize a manifestation of the Bandung Spirit or a facade of neocolonialism (Quan, 2012; Thomas, 2013)?

We contend that African and Asian leaders were responding to the construction of the post-World War II new world order that was organized around the conflict between the United States and the Soviet Union, as these superpowers competed for influence over the newly independent states of Africa and Asia, attempting to reduce these actors to mere pawns on the chessboard of international relations. The Cold War became the new modus operandi for integrating Afro-Asian states into the new global order. The question which arises now is whether or not we are witnessing the birth of a new system, even as we also recognize that the Bandung Spirit will continue to frame the discourse surrounding the Afro-Asian relationship and as the frame of reference for drawing the balance sheet of the relationship. However, the spirit may cease to serve as the source of inspiration of the relationship. Indeed, what one calls this emerging pattern of relationships may matter less for the time being, whether one calls it neoimperialism or neodependency or neocolonialism, than the fact that it is indeed emerging and it is new.

This is how the chapter is structured. The next part juxtaposes the Bandung Conference of 1955 against the Berlin Conference of 1884–1885. It also recounts the recurrent and changing themes of the Bandung Spirit which, going back to the Korean War in 1953, might even pre-date the Bandung Conference itself. The third part examines the relationship between Japan, China, and Africa in the wider context of global power transitions before it zooms in on one aspect of China's policy in Africa: the principle of non-intervention. The fourth part carefully analyzes not only what the Bandung Spirit means today but also whether we are entering the era of what may be called the BRICS (the association of five major emerging national economies: Brazil, Russia, India, China, and South Africa) Spirit.

The Cold War and the new terms of order

Cedric J. Robinson observes that the Cold War was believed to have subsumed all other conflicts; yet it was possible to cast the competition between the two imperial hegemonies, the USA and the Soviet Union, as a historical sidebar to the struggle to either obtain or vanquish racial domination. Indeed, two of the most intensive sites of the war were the USA and the Republic of South Africa. Contrary to the colossal cultural, political, technological, military and propaganda industries contrived on behalf of the Cold War obsession for the past 50 years, the awe-inspiring and longer-lasting dualism has been what Franz Fanon recognized as the racial order of a Manichaean colonial domination: 'The cause is the consequence: you are rich because you are white: you are white because you are rich.' From there he calculated, 'It was not the *organization of production* but the *persistence and organization of oppression* which formed the primary social basis for revolutionary activities' (Fanon, 2005:22–23). In addition, the West's political leaders gave secondary significance to the driving forces of racial supremacy so central to the imperial wars of the nineteenth century and the global wars of the twentieth century, masked as they were beneath the discursive veil of inter-nation (international) conflict. Corporate and political elites/leaders ratcheted up the clash with the Soviet Union and China, providing them with an ideological apparatus with which to preserve imperial and colonial 'adventures' among 'darker peoples', and to keep in check democratic movements at home (Robinson, 1997:135).

Cedric Robinson's scholarship transcends the nation-state as the unit of analysis and performs an archaeological dig that uncovers the hidden elements within racial capitalism that influence the development and trajectory of the capitalist world system. His first efforts to establish the theoretical architecture of political authority began with *Terms of Order: Political Science and the Myth of Leadership* (Robinson, 2016). In this text, he probes those intellectual traditions in Western political thought that have contributed to the illusion of social order. Robinson seeks to remove the veil of legend, myth and belief—a kind of folklore—in which authority and order in the West are cloaked and which form the Western political sensibility. We operationalize terms of order at the international level, drawing attention to global power systems such as the Great Power System, multipolar and unipolar balance of power systems, the Cold War, the North and South, Core, semiperiphery and periphery, global North and global South.

H. L. T. Quan observes that the mainstream comparative method employed by political scientists and area studies specialists angles a US-centered foundational status, by which all nations are compared and measured (Quan, 2012:15). Hence, a methodological US-centrism is employed in order to compare and contrast nations and peoples revolving around American experiences and values, e.g., individualism, white supremacy, Protestantism, etc., that serve as a code for understanding the non-Western other. Quan notes that this exercise in white privilege, this US-centricity, results in a type of reaction to hegemonic-subject position. Additionally, Quan observes that this hegemonic presumption is part and parcel of Western imperial science, and the comparative method thus becomes part of the function of centralizing US hegemonic status, even as it peripheralizes all others (Mignolo, 2000). This practice essentializes the foundational status of the US, often omitting and/or obscuring the relationships between other nations, particularly among the subordinate nations, that is, the nations of the Third World. As Quan also observes: 'the search for counter-narratives must include the "decolonizing" of methodology as part of the larger process of democratizing knowledge. Decolonizing knowledge, according to Fanon, requires at a minimum, bringing into question dominant episteme' (Quan, 2012:15).

Roderick Bush states that if the cultural hegemony of a European-based world economy relied in part on the social glue of Pan-European social solidarity as a moral rationalization for and justification of Euro-North American world hegemony, then the subordinate populations of the non-European world and their descendants experience this point of view as a system of oppressive humiliation that denied their humanity, intelligence, and dignity. Nevertheless, people of African descent, who were at the bottom of the global hierarchy, were actively engaged in constructing dreams of freedom and liberation, which in the post-slavery twentieth century were often captured in the slogan 'The Rise of the Dark World' (Bush, 2009:6). Since radical Black Nationalism had little confidence in a strictly nationalist answer, it has long hung its hope on an internationalist solution. African American interest in world affairs can be traced back to the American Revolutionary War, the Haitian Revolution, and the Abolition Movement in the pre-Civil War era. New World Africans' interest in influencing international affairs took on a new life when the USA established its overseas empire and Europe divided Africa and Asia into spheres of influence. At this critical juncture, when much of the world came under the control of Europe or its descendants in the USA, African Americans developed a view of world affairs that drew connections between the discrimination that they faced at home and the expansion of empire abroad. Black internationalism, as a worldview, was an ideology that stressed the role of race and racism in world affairs drawing attention to the linkages, interconnections, and interrelationships between racial capitalism and the color line in world affairs. As a consequence of the main principle, black internationalism believed that, as victims of racial capitalism and imperialism, the world's darker races, a term they employed to describe the non-European world, shared a common interest in overthrowing white supremacy and creating a new world order based on racial equality and social justice (Thomas, 2013:133).

At the turn of the twentieth century, examples abound of this move towards black internationalism including Ida B. Wells-Barnet's appeals against lynch mob violence at the end of the nineteenth century. Du Bois at the turn of the last century used his speeches at the Pan African Congresses to challenge the global problems of the color line. The New Negro Movement; Du Bois, Graham, and Robeson during the popular front era; and Malcolm X, Dr. Martin L. King, Jr., the Student Nonviolent Coordinating Committee (SNCC), Angela Davis, Robert F. Williams and the Revolutionary Action Movement (RAM), and the Black Panther Party during the 1960s and the 1970s, followed a similar trajectory (Bush, 2009:15). Malcolm X captured the critical importance that the Bandung Conference represented to the Dark World, that is, Africa, Asia, and the Middle East, but also to black populations scattered through North America and Europe.

At this critical juncture, Malcolm X and the Nation of Islam defined all non-white people as Black, thus enlarging the global majority. Initially, Malcolm's response to the Bandung Conference was cast within the Nation of Islam's prophetic tradition. Later, Malcolm's position would be more nuanced and encompass a broader canvas that transcended the position of the Nation of Islam and emphasized critical elements of black internationalism. Malcolm stated:

> The time is past when the white world can exercise unilateral authority and control over the dark world. The independence and power of the dark world is on the increase; the dark world is rising in wealth, power, prestige, and influence. It is the rise of the dark world that is causing the fall of the white world.
>
> As the white man loses his power to oppress and exploit the dark world, the white man's own wealth (power or "world") decreases . . . You and I were born at the turning point in history; we are witnessing the fulfillment of prophecy. Our present generation is witnessing the end of colonialism, Europeanism, Westernism, or "White-ism" . . . the end of white supremacy, the end of the white man's unjust rule.
>
> *(Malcolm, 1971:130)*

Malcolm made his observation during the era of decolonization in Africa and Asia when the Spirit of Bandung was the underlying set of ideas for what he referred to as the worldwide revolution. The 1955 Bandung Conference was the most important international gathering of the twentieth century, and it had ramifications for the Third World, Europe, and the Cold War, but also for black people in the United States. Occurring a mere decade after the end of World War II and in the middle of enormous political turmoil, the 29 countries that came together represented half of the world's population at that time (Daulatzai, 2012:26). In the shadows of the United States and Soviet interference in the affairs of the newly independent countries, the stated position of Bandung was a call for an end to colonialism and neocolonialism from European powers, the United States, and the Soviet Union. It vowed to support the anticolonial struggles of countries still under colonialism and the eventual creation of a non-aligned movement as the new base for Third World solidarity, a third path that refused entanglement with either the US or USSR credo (Daulatzai, 2012:26; Thomas, 2001).

Third World solidarity pre-dates the Cold War conflict between the United States and the Soviet Union and it is born out of a legacy of actual struggles for political, economic, and cultural independence within the larger global context of racial capitalism. Racial capitalism is one of several critical factors that promote Third World solidarity and it first evolved as an issue of race, progressed to a shared determination to avoid Cold War alliances, and is now based on a shared interest in terminating poverty and inequality (Thomas, 2001:29–30).

Indonesian President Sukarno, in his opening speech to the Bandung Conference, outlined the hopeful tone of the Conference when he declared, 'Let a New Asia and a New Africa Be Born,' and 'the nations of Asia and Africa are no longer the tools and playthings' of Europe, the United States, and the Soviets (Marable & Agard-Jones 2008: 153; Daulatzai, 2012:26). The Bandung Conference recognized that despite the diverse variations of Western imperialism, it was characterized by its allegiance to a hierarchical racial structure (Ledwidge, 2012:128).

The Bandung Conference

The Bandung Conference of 1955 was the antithesis of the Berlin Conference of 1885, which ushered in a second wave of colonialism for Africa and the rest of the Third World. The Berlin

Conference of 1885, hosted by Bismarck, was an assembly of imperial powers of the West planning to partition Africa. The Bandung Conference of 1955 (70 years after the Berlin Conference) was, as indicated, an assembly of the colonized countries and formerly colonized, not only plotting how to defeat the remnants of colonialism but also deliberating the postcolonial period. In 1855, most of Africa was still free—but about to be subjected to colonialism. In 1955, most of Africa was subjugated—but about to experience the winds of liberation.

The four years from 1953 to 1957 had wider implications concerning relations between the West and the Developing World. First, 1953 witnessed the end of the Korean War—with a stalemate between the mighty power of the United States leading a United Nations 'coalition of the willing,' on one side, and communist North Korea supported by so-called 'volunteers' from the People's Republic of China, on the other.

That the Korean War resulted in a stalemate and a ceasefire rather than the defeat of North Korea was one of the early shifts in power between the mighty global North and the much less developed global South. The following year witnessed another great indicator that developing countries need not necessarily be on the losing side of North–South conflicts. Events were unfolding which would constitute more than just the wind of change. A benign hurricane was about to shift the chapter of history.

The Vietnamese in the Battle of Dien Bien Phu defeated the French colonizers in 1954. The days of a French Empire in Asia were coming to an end. The Vietnamese militarily defeated the French 20 years before they defeated the Americans. The Algerian War of Independence broke out in 1954, that is, the same year that the French were defeated in Vietnam. Once again, France, which had been humiliated by the Vietnamese, now faced a similar challenge from North African nationalists in Algeria. But 1954 was also a year expectant with fundamental changes for the African Diaspora. In Washington, DC the US Supreme Court handed down its momentous decision regarding Brown versus the Board of Education of Topeka. The old Jim Crow racial doctrine of separate but equal was abandoned.

But these three winds or hurricanes of change in 1954 had divergent consequences.

In the US, Brown vs. Board of Education of Topeka signified the beginning of the end of overt racial segregation in the country. The changes that followed freed Black people from second class citizenship, but also enhanced the image of the United States internationally as a more democratic society.

For Algeria, 1954 turned out to be truly ironic. The Algerian struggle for independence (1954–1962) not only helped Algeria to attain sovereignty but also enabled France to achieve greater stability. Three years after Bandung (in 1958), France faced the risk of a civil war on the streets of Paris – not because Algerian nationalists had come to France, but because the war in Algeria had precipitated a colossal crisis. The crisis eventually had far-reaching consequences for the domestic politics and foreign policies of France. By fighting for their independence, Algerians changed more than the history of Algeria—they changed the history of France and Europe.

The Vietnamese triumph at Dien Bien Phu in 1954 defeated France, but did not reunite Vietnam. By the time of its conclusion in the 1970s, the Vietnam War cost at least 3 million Vietnamese lives and nearly 60,000 American lives. But Vietnam in the end illustrated that a poor and underdeveloped Asian country could militarily defeat a superpower—the United States.

Afghanistan a decade later illustrated that an even poorer underdeveloped country could defeat another superpower—the Soviet Union. Indeed the USSR's defeat in Afghanistan may have been the most important cause of its collapse.

British Prime Minister Harold Macmillan addressing the white-only South African parliament in February 1960 was another signature event evoking global change; he could not have known the historical and political impact of his speech years later. During this same year at least 17 African countries achieved independence, with many others to follow. Macmillan's words were visionary:

> The wind of change is blowing through this continent, and whether we like it or not, this growth of national consciousness is a political thought. We must all accept it as a fact, and our national policies must take it into account.
>
> *(Macmillan, 1960)*

Those remarks became an epigraph of both European colonialism and white minority rule in Africa. African decolonization confronted setbacks in the Portuguese colonies (Angola, Cape Verde, Guinea-Bissau, and Mozambique) and the white minority regimes in Rhodesia (eventually gaining independence and renamed Zimbabwe), Apartheid South Africa and South African-control led Southwest Africa (which eventually became independent Namibia), as these actors resisted the 'wind of change' blowing across the continent. By the end of the long campaign against Portuguese colonialism and white minority rule in Southern Africa, in 1974 and 1994 respectively, Africa's struggle had gone global. The anticolonial struggles in the Portuguese colonies ended in the mid-1970s, followed by years of international conflict. It was one of the most ruthless episodes of the Cold War, as decisive as Vietnam and Afghanistan and involving such actors the US, South Africa, Cuba, the Soviet Union (Harding, 2016), the national and transnational anti-Apartheid movements, and the frontline states comprising Tanzania, Zambia, Zimbabwe, Botswana, and Mozambique. The frontline states responded to South Africa's retaliatory strategy of destabilization in the face of the loss of the Portuguese colonies and Rhodesia, and launched the Southern African Development Coordination Conference (SADCC) which morphed into the Southern African Development Community (SADC) 12 years later.

Asia in 2015 was significantly different from Asia in 1955; and so is Africa to some extent. The change is highlighted by the growing power and influence of China, Japan, and India in the global political economy. Let us now explore the implications of this dynamic change for Afro-Asian solidarity. Would the Bandung Spirit survive the rise of the BRICS?

Emerging Africa, rising Asia, and Afro-Asian solidarity

Recently, there has been a proliferation of studies examining hegemonic transition from an American–European world to China and the Group of 20 projecting the economic, financial, and potential military power of an ascending China (Shambaugh, 2013; Nye, 2015; Dyer, 2014; French, 2014; Kissinger, 2015; Christensen, 2015). However, most of these studies have neglected the role of the African continent in providing both human capital and natural resources in hegemonic transitions in the past, and the critical role the continent is playing today. Similarly, the focus and usage of Afro-Asian solidarity captured today in the usage of the 'trope of Third World solidarity' has also been neglected or ignored altogether. First, let us examine the Afro-Asian solidarity in relation to China's, Japan's, and India's interactions with Africa. Let us examine these overlapping relationships between Asia's leading economic and political actors and their African partners.

At least three distinct phases can be identified in the history of China's diplomacy in Africa. Ideologically oriented, the first phase (1955–1978) began in Bandung (Indonesia) at the conference in 1955. In the subsequent years, China supported national liberation movements in Africa.

It then forged relations with independent African countries, so long as those countries were not close friends of the US. Later, the ideological litmus test became the Soviet Union. This phase of China's diplomacy was conducted in the shadow of Mao's ideologically inspired experiments at home, too, including the Hundred Flowers Experiment (1956), the Great Leap Forward (1958–1960), and the Cultural Revolution (1965–1967). After Mao's death in 1976, the role of ideology in China's diplomacy and domestic politics waned, running its course around 1978.

Deng Xiaoping's 'Four Modernizations' heralded the beginning of the second phase of China's diplomacy in Africa (1979–1989). This phase coincided with the end of the liberation project in the continent, except for Southern Africa. Ideology ceased to be a major consideration. China thus forged relations with countries like Zimbabwe, Angola, and Ivory Coast. The Tiananmen Square incident in 1989 sealed the fate of the second phase of China's diplomacy in Africa, while heralding the third phase. The incident brought China and many African countries closer, even as it led, for a while, to China's global isolation (Anshan, 2008:28).

The third phase (1990–present) of China's diplomacy in Africa is marked by the end of the Cold War globally and the triumph of market socialism in China. This period saw accelerated economic and diplomatic interactions between China and African countries. China's trade with Africa grew by leaps and bounds, and its leaders became frequent guests of their African counterparts.

The trajectory of Japan's diplomacy in Africa has been different from that of China. Beginning in 1961, when the Africa Division was created in the Ministry of Foreign Affairs, Japan's diplomacy in Africa has passed through five or six phases. In the first phase (1961–1972), Japan seriously took on the role of supporter of America, vowing to curb the spread of communism in the continent by ensuring its diplomacy was in lockstep with America's overall Cold War strategy. But Japan's 'Cold War' diplomacy in Africa ended long before the Cold War ended. The former came to an end in 1973 when the Organization of Petroleum Producing Countries (OPEC) decided to raise the price of oil. One effect of the OPEC decision was thus to usher in the second phase of Japan's Africa diplomacy (1973–1992) in which the nation realized more than ever before that it must diversify sources of energy and other raw materials critical to its industries. Japan paid attention to Africa, too, sending for the first time its Foreign Minister (Toshio Kimura) to visit the continent in 1974 (Ochiai, 2001:39).

In the third phase (1993–2006), Japan showed greater independence than ever before in its Africa diplomacy (Adem, 2001; Cornelissen, 2012). It became a leading Official Development Assistance (ODA) donor globally, also taking certain initiatives in its African diplomacy, such as the launching of the Tokyo International Conference on African Development (TICAD) in 1993. Generally, Japan's diplomacy in this period reflected the nation's international status as well as its global aspirations. The first ever visit to Africa by a sitting Japanese Prime Minister took place when Yoshiro Mori visited Kenya, South Africa, and Nigeria in 2001. Prime Minister Mori's successor, Junichiro Koizumi, continued this policy by making visits to Ghana and Ethiopia in 2006.

In its fourth phase (2007–2013), Japan's diplomacy in Africa looked less vigorous. This phase also coincided with drastic changes to the conditions that had inspired a vibrant diplomacy previously. China became the largest trading partner of Japan in 2008 and of Africa in 2009. China overtook Japan as the second largest economy globally in 2010. No Japanese Prime Minister visited Africa in this period, including Mr. Aso (2007:251–253) who had lived in Sierra Leone for two years when he was younger.

Questions have now arisen as to whether or not the fifth phase of Japan's diplomacy has begun with Prime Minister Shinzo Abe's visit to Africa in January 2014, and whether or not the visit was partly a reaction to the growing influence of China in Africa.

It is generally believed that China had a greater soft power in Africa than Japan had, partly because of China's longer and deeper involvement in Africa. But how do China and India compare on a similar scale? Which country has a greater soft power in Africa? Some observers have suggested that in the long run India will have a greater soft power than China in Africa. In this vein, for instance, the distinguished Kenyan political scientist Mazrui (2012) observed a few years ago:

> China and India are two emerging superpowers on the global stage. India's influence in Africa already includes the influence of 'Bollywood', Indian music, South Asian cuisine, and the legacies of Gandhi, Nehru and nonalignment from the 20th century onwards. India's cultural power is much older than China's. However, Beijing's involvement in Africa's liberation wars, oil exploration, investments, arms sales and infrastructural projects have begun to deepen China's penetration of postcolonial Africa. India has greater softer power than China; China is evolving harder forms of leverage.
>
> *(Mazrui, 2012)*

But at least one recent study suggests otherwise. It is China rather than India that will probably come to enjoy greater soft power in Africa:

> Mahatma Gandhi and Jawaharlal Nehru were prominent in helping South Africa's struggle against apartheid and the continent's struggle to sever its colonial bonds. But Indo-Afro solidarity was put to the test during the 1962 border war between India and China; many African countries did not provide the political support New Delhi had hoped for. While the peaceful ideals of non-violent resistance and cultural co-existence expressed by Gandhi and Nehru fell easily on the ears of African leaders, they could not match China's more tangible military, political and financial support.
>
> *(Patey, 2014:145)*

On non-interference

One of the key principles that the participants in the Bandung Conference endorsed enthusiastically was non-interference in the internal affairs of another country. Has this principle stood the test of time in Afro-Asian relations? How is it being practiced by Asia's major powers in their dealings in Africa? In order to elucidate these principles let us return to the 2005 declaration by the New Asian–African Strategic Partnership (NAASP). This declaration preserved the Spirit of Bandung while simultaneously also provoking an entirely different discourse of Third World relations, namely, one that is state-driven, pre-occupied with order, and structurally compromised (Quan, 2012:133). Nevertheless, this approach to growth and development is a reiteration of what Quan refers to as 'savage developmentalism,' which underscores modern development's proclivity to secure order and capitalist expansion, while simultaneously fostering antidemocratic social and political forms (Quan, 2012:133). The parties to this framework effectively stated that the purpose of NAASP was to 'ensure peace, stability, and security in the two continents by boosting trade and stepping up cooperation in the war against terrorism and transnational organized crimes' (NAASP, 2005). Still, an intellectual debt is owed to Third World thinkers beyond the ghost of Mao including Franz Fanon, Amilcar Cabral, Walter Rodney, Fidel Castro, Carlos Marighela, and Che Guevara to name a few (Quan, 2012:134). Let us briefly look, for example, at a key dimension of China's non-interference posture in the Sudan and its ramifications for order.

'Darfur is a part of Sudan, and you have to resolve this problem.' This was what President Hu Jintao of the People's Republic of China reportedly told President Bashir of Sudan in February 2007 (Patey, 2014:175). In addition, the major opposition movements in the Sudan, both armed and unarmed, do not seem to believe that China follows the principle of non-interference in the Sudan (as well as in other parts of Africa). As one Sudan People's Liberation Army (SPLA) commander put it, 'The suffering of the people is on the hands of the Chinese' (Patey, 2014:222). What these observations suggest is that the principle of non-interference, which China promotes, was hardly followed in practice. And this raises one intriguing question. It is not whether China interferes in the domestic affairs of African countries or not: we know it does, despite the narrative otherwise (Lee, 2010:2). The question instead is, what forms does this interference take? Let us probe further into the distinction among various types of China's interference in the domestic affairs of African countries.

If China's interventionist behavior is obvious, then, how can we explain the broad consensus to the contrary? One source of this confusion may be the tendency to view the absence of conditionality attached to China's trade with, aid to, and investment in Africa as, ipso facto, proof of China's adherence to the principle of non-interference in the internal affairs of African countries. We may also be taking too much for granted in assuming that China has such a desire. But, even if the desire was there on the part of China, does that mean China could control the nature and outcome of its activities in Africa?

It is safe to conclude that China, too, interferes in the domestic affairs of African countries even if the effects of its interference could sometimes take a long time to mature. Furthermore, we can assume, given the historical patterns in the behavior of great powers, that China's natural impulse towards interference would become stronger as its power and interests expand, prompting it to brand itself as more and not less interventionist in African affairs, not only because that is what it would be doing in any case, but also because the principle of non-interference is no longer cherished even by Africans. The question which thus arises is, is China's diplomatic rhetoric lagging behind the principle of African diplomacy as it is practiced today?

From Bandung to BRICS

It is perhaps fair to say that Afro-Asian solidarity came into being in 1955. The solidarity was nevertheless the effect rather than the cause of the Bandung Conference. There were major disagreements among the leaders of Asian and African countries who arrived in Bandung. As Chakrabarty (2010:49) observed, '[the leaders] were not of the same mind on question of international politics, nor did they have the same understanding of what constituted imperialism.' Lee (2010:3) has also argued that 'Bandung contained both the residual romance of revolution, as well as the realpolitik of a new world order in the making.' We should not therefore overstate the sense of solidarity among states that gathered in Bandung. The Bandung meeting was intended as much to manage the growing divergence among those states, as it was to draw on shared concerns and common objectives.

Sixty years later, in 2015, Africa and Asia, miracles of diversity in their own right, are no less divided between and among themselves. Africa today has 54 states of unequal size, a total population larger than those of the USA and EU put together; it has a landmass bigger than those of China, USA, the EU, and India combined, and it boasts today 10 out of the top 20 fastest growing economies in the world. Perhaps the description of Africa by Bright and Hruby is more comprehensive:

> The climates and landscapes of [Africa's] 54 countries (48 in SSA) are diverse and highly unique in the world. There are jungles in Sierra Leone; rainforests in Cote d'Ivoire; and deserts, such as the Danakil in Ethiopia and the Kalahari in Botswana, Namibia and South Africa. Then, of course, there's Africa's unique wildlife and geographical wonders ... Known for its red earth in places such as Tanzania's Serengeti National Park, Africa also gets snow on Mount Kilimanjaro (its highest peak) and in South Africa's Drakensberg and Lesotho's Maluti Mountains ... Africa is the most diverse continent on the planet by numbers of linguistic and ethnic grouping (more than 2000 in each). When it comes to population, Africa is surging forward on four global demographic milestones. It has the world's fastest-growing population (surpassing a billion in 2009), largest youth population (200 million between the ages of 15 and 24), most rapidly urbanizing population (3.09 percent going rural to urban annually), and the globe's fastest growing consumer class, in terms of expanding individual spending power.
>
> *(Bright & Hruby, 2015:25)*

Asia surpasses Africa in landmass and population size. Focusing on East Asia alone, Buzan and Zhang have observed the following about the rich diversity of the region:

> Cambodia and Laos feel more like Africa; Burma and Vietnam feel like the Middle East; Thailand, the Philippines, Indonesia and Malaysia feel like Latin America; Japan, South Korea, Taiwan and arguably Singapore feel more like Europe, although without the element of security community. If North Korea has any comparators they might be found in Russia and Belarus. China likes to think of itself as sui generis, and perhaps it is, combining a singular *mix of communist government and capitalist economy* with massive size and unique civilizational heritage.
>
> *(Buzan & Zhang, 2014:8; italics added)*

Particularly relevant for understanding the future of the Bandung Spirit is perhaps the deeper meaning of China's 'mix of communist government and capitalist economy,' or the transformation of China from a member of the Third World into what Khanna (2008:300) called the Second World, 'combining third-world feudalism, a massive industrial base, and a first-world elite.' What does this mean for Afro-Asian solidarity? This question must have specially confounded those who had in the past suggested, for instance, that Africa should de-link itself from the global capitalist system.

There had been, on the one hand, the view held by some intellectuals that global capitalism has the propensity to under-develop Africa and that the solution was for Africa to disengage itself from the world capitalist system. On the other hand, there were also those who saw the process of economic exchange between Africa and the West as a positive-sum game, beneficial to both sides, even if the benefit was never equal (Leys, 2009:3–43). Subsequent to China's renewed interest and increased activities in Africa since the 1990s, however, some intellectuals are reversing their position by advocating Africa's deeper engagement with China and suggesting that this could accelerate Africa's own development. But why would the logic of capital change when the Chinese, as opposed to Europeans, are in the driver's seat? Could capitalism be de-occidentalized? These are intriguing questions.

In the 1990s, the rise of the newly industrialized countries in the global South, often referred to as the semiperiphery, also prompted a new discourse on the potential role of this part of the Third World exploiting the peripheral sector of the Third World. Most of the newly industrialized countries—Brazil, South Korea, Singapore, Malaysia, and Turkey—sought markets in the United States, Europe, or Japan rather than their fellow Third World states in the periphery, and South Africa was the lone exception to this earlier pattern (Thomas, 2001:137–180). Since the 1990s many of these actors, including China, India, and Brazil, have acquired capabilities to project economic, financial, and political power on both regional and global levels.

Although Asian countries have on balance done better in economic terms than African countries, it is also true that Africans, too, are generally better off today than they were in the middle of the last century (Henley, 2015:5). If the shared indigence were one of the factors that made the Bandung Spirit possible, would the shared wealth steadily erode that spirit? This seems to be a logical scenario, at least from the perspective of the sociology of inter-state disparity.

> First, rich countries have more potential areas of disagreement in the economic field than poor countries. Second, if one world power has troubles in a distant part [of the world], the chances are that there is at least one other world power, which stands to benefit by those troubles. Third, being under privileged is a condition of greater revolutionary potential than being privileged. The poor are more likely to be aroused into joint indignation than the rich. By being potentially revolutionary a state of relative deprivation is also potentially more unifying.
>
> *(Mazrui, 1972:290–291).*

The rise of China and India is a mixed blessing so far for Africa. In the long term, too, the situation would not be much different as far as potential consequences are concerned. As Nayyar put it,

> The consequences could be positive if China and India provide markets for exports, resources for investment, and finances for development, which would stimulate the process of growth in Africa. On the other hand, the consequences could be negative if growth in China and India is competitive rather than complementary to growth in Africa. The economic engagement of the Asian giants with Africa, through trade and investment, may also perpetuate traditional patterns of specialization, which inhibit rather than foster industrialization in African countries. The impact, on balance, will depend upon how reality unfolds. It will depend on the nature of China and India's interactions with Africa. Even more so, it will depend on what African countries do, in terms of initial conditions, better bargaining, and appropriate policies, to maximize the benefits and minimize the costs associated with the process of increasing economic interaction with China and India.
>
> *(Nayyar, 2012:559)*

The anticapitalist critique of capitalism has been pivotal to the theory and practice of Third World solidarity, particularly when it is employed as a counterweight or challenge to global capitalism, neoliberalism, and other models of development that continue to rely on antidemocracy and racial capitalism as critical dimensions of capital accumulation. In other words, contemporary China–Africa relations do not counteract capital expansion or the neoliberal world order (Steinfeld, 2012). More precisely, they serve as a system that reinforces its trajectory. Regardless of its trading partners, so long as Africa remains a market outpost for foreign manufactured goods, accumulation by dispossession persists, and the possibility of economic democracy remains postponed, if not exiled (Quan, 2012:143).

Conclusion

We have sought to demonstrate in this chapter that the future of the Bandung Spirit, if it has any future, largely depends on the relationship between China, India, and Japan. At least on three levels Sino-Japanese relations are uniquely more complex than it is sometimes assumed. In their respective long histories, this is the first time when the two countries have both acquired the status of major power at the same time, making it difficult for us to look back at history for clues about the future (Hsiung, 2007:1–21). The second uniqueness of Sino-Japanese relations is captured by the catchphrase used to refer to it, 'hot economics and cold politics,' or *seirei keinetsu*. In other places, one witnesses just the reverse of seirei keinetsu—hot politics and cold economics, because industrially advanced countries that are also on friendly terms politically sometimes declare trade wars on each other. Japan and China are also unfriendly towards each other. It must be pointed out that this description is literally true, unlike in some other cases, where states are often personified for analytical convenience. Japan and China appear to have little affection for each other even at the grassroots level. This is the third, and probably most worrisome aspect of the uniqueness of Sino-Japanese relations.

Both China and Japan could each make positive contributions to Africa's efforts to modernize, if they wish to do so, as they also help themselves to Africa's vast resources. In this case, Africa becomes an arena of Sino-Japanese cooperation rather than conflict, with all sides benefiting in the process, including Africa. This would amount to the fulfillment of the Bandung Spirit in the twenty-first century.

The emerging relationship between China and India may also have an impact on Africa, positively or negatively. Positively, they could, for instance, articulate, with African countries, a collective position for Afrasia in such multilateral institutions as the World Trade Organization. But if the two Asian powers get embroiled in an adversarial relationship, Africa could easily become an arena of confrontation rather than cooperation.

We have indicated that one of the bonds which brought Africa and Asia together in 1955 was that of being fellow victims of European racial arrogance and racial solidarity. A related question which now arises is this, is the era of Afro-Asian solidarity that was based on 'pigmentational solidarity' coming to an end? Is the Bandung Spirit suffering from a crisis of ultimate purpose? Contrary to logic and conventional wisdom, the answer to both questions must be no. Again, as Ali Mazrui has observed,

> this is the third round of racial devastation. The First Round of modern racial catastrophes led to genocide in the Americas and the trans-Atlantic slave trade. (This was the era of the West on the ascendancy.) The Second Round of modern racial catastrophes was the period of colonialism and imperialism through which my generation lived. (This was the era of the West triumphant.) Both these rounds were hot wars of race, rather than cold wars. As for what is now unfolding, it could be the Third Round of modern racial catastrophes. It is the period of racism by neglect of the weakest . . . racism by military containment of the darker races . . . (This is the era of the West on the defensive.)
>
> *(Mazrui, 1997)*

Note

1 A section of this chapter draws upon a draft paper written by the late Ali A. Mazrui, 'From Bandung to Baghdad: Africa and Asia in the Postcolonial Experience' (2006). It was his wish expressed in writing that his draft paper be expanded, revised and published.

Bibliography

Adem, S., 2001. 'Emerging Trends in Japan–Africa Relations', *African Studies Quarterly*, Volume 5 (2). [Online] Available at: http://asq.africa.ufl.edu/adem_summer01/.

Anshan, L., 2008. 'China's New Policy toward Africa', in R. I. Rotberg (ed.), *China into Africa: Trade, Aid and Influence*, Washington, DC: Brookings.

Aso, T., 2007. *Arc of Freedom and Prosperity: Japan's Expanding Diplomatic Horizon*, Tokyo: Gentosha.

Bright, J. and Hruby, A., 2015. *The Next Africa: An Emerging Continent Becomes a Global Power House*, New York: St. Martin's.

Bush, R. D., 2009. *The End of White World Supremacy: Black Internationalism and the Problem of the Color Line*, Philadelphia, PA: Temple University Press.

Buzan, B. and Zhang, Y., 2014. 'Introduction: Interrogating Regional International Society in East Asia', in B. Buzan, and Y. Zhang (eds.), *Contesting International Society in East Asia*, Cambridge, UK: Cambridge University Press.

Chakrabarty, D., 2010. 'The Legacies of Bandung: Decolonization and the Politics of Culture', in Christopher J. Lee (ed.), *Making a World after Empire: The Bandung Moment and its Political Afterlives*, Athens, OH: Ohio University Press.

Christensen, Thomas J., 2015. The *China Challenge: Shaping the Choices of a Rising Power*, New York: W.W. Norton and Company.

Cornelissen, S., 2012. 'Japan's Role in Africa: Principle, Pragmatism and Partnership', *African East Asian Affairs*, Available at: http://aeaa.journals.ac.za/pub/article/view/87.

Daulatzai, S., 2012. *Black Star, Crescent Moon: The Muslim International and Black Freedom Beyond America*, Minneapolis: University of Minnesota Press.

Dyer, G., 2014. *The Contest of the Century: The New Era of Competition With China and How America Can Win*, New York: Alfred A. Knopf and Company.

Fanon, F., 2005. *The Wretched of the Earth*, New York: Grove Press.

French, H. W., 2014. *China's Second Continent: How a Million Migrants are Building a New Empire in Africa*, New York: Vintage Books.

Harding, J., 2016. 'Apartheid Last Stand', *London Review of Books*, Volume 38 (6), pp. 9–21.

Henley, D., 2015. *Asia–Africa Development Divergence: A Question of Intent*, London: Zed Books.

Hsiung, J. C., 2007. 'Introduction: Theory and the Long-Running Tussle', in Jams C. Hsiung (ed.), *China and Japan at Odds. Deciphering the Perpetual Conflict*, New York: Palgrave.

Khanna, P., 2008. *The Second World: Empires and Influence in the Global Order*, New York: Random House. [Advance Reader's Edition.]

Kissinger, H. 2015. *World Order*, New York: Penguin Books.

Lee, C. J., 2010. 'Introduction: Between a Moment and an Era: The Origins and Afterlives of Bandung', in Christopher J. Lee (ed.), *Making a World after Empire: The Bandung Moment and its Political Afterlives*, Athens, OH: Ohio University Press.

Ledwidge, M., 2012. *Race and US Foreign Policy: The African American Foreign Affairs Network*, London: Routledge.

Leys, C., 2009. *The Rise and Fall of Development Theory*, Bloomington: Indiana University Press.

Macmillan, H., 1960. Available at: www.un.org/africarenewal/magazine/august-2010/'wind-change'-transformed-continent.

Malcolm, X., 1971. *The End of White Supremacy: Four Speeches*, New York: Merlin Press.

Marable, M. and Agard-Jones, V., 2008. *Transnational Blackness: Navigating the Global Color Line*, New York: Palgrave MacMillan.

Mazrui, A. A., 1972. 'The Political Economy of World Order: Modernization and Reform in Africa', in Jagdish N. Bhagwati (ed.), *Economics and World Order: From the 1970s to the 1990s*, London: Macmillan.

Mazrui, A. A., 1997. 'A Racial Paradigm of World Order: From the Cold War of Ideology to the Cold War of Race'. Institute of Global Cultural Studies, Binghamton University, New York. Unpublished paper.

Mazrui, A. A., 2012. 'Are China and India Rivals for Influence in Africa? Afro-Asian Interaction in the Post-Cold War Era', unpublished paper, Institute of Global Cultural Studies, Binghamton University, New York.

Mazrui, A. A. and Seifudein A., 2013. *Afrasia: A Tale of Two Continents*, Lanham: University Press of America.

Mignolo, W., 2000. *Local Histories/Global Designs: Coloniality, Subaltern Knowledges, and Border Thinking*, Princeton Studies in Culture/Power/History, Princeton, NJ: Princeton University Press.

Nayyar, D., 2012. 'The Emerging Asian Giants and Economic Development in Africa', in Akbar Noman, Kwesi Botchwey, Howard Stein, and Joseph E. Stiglitz (eds.), *Good Growth and Governance in Africa. Rethinking Development Strategies*, Oxford: Oxford University Press.

New Asian-African Strategic Partnership (NAASP), 2005. Summit declaration, Jakarta—for a full discussion see Quan, 2012: 128–133.

Nye, J. S., 2015. *Is the American Century Over?* Malden, MA: Polity.

Ochiai, T., 2001. 'Beyond TICAD Diplomacy: Japan's African Policy and African Initiatives in Conflict Response', *African Studies Monographs*, Volume 22, pp. 37–52.

Patey, L., 2014. *The New Kings of Crude: China, India, and the Global Struggle for Oil in Sudan and South Sudan*, London: C. Hurst & Co.

Prashad, V., 2006. 'Bandung is Done: Passages in AfroAsian Epistemology', in H. Raphael-Hernandez and S. Steen (eds.), *AfroAsian Encounters: Culture, History, Politics*, New York: New York University Press.

Quan, H. L. T., 2012. *Growth Against Democracy: Savage Developmentalism in the Modern World*, Lanham, MD: Lexington Books.

Robinson, C. J., 1997. *Black Movements in America*. New York: Routledge.

Robinson, C. J., 2016. *Terms of Order: Political Science and the Myth of Leadership*, Chapel Hill, NC: University of North Carolina Press.

Shambaugh, D., 2013. *China Goes Global: The Partial Power*, New York: Oxford University Press.

Steinfeld, E., 2012. *Playing Our Game: Why China's Rise Doesn't Threaten the West*, New York: Oxford University Press.

Thomas, D. C., 2001. *The Theory and Practice of Third World Solidarity*, Westport and London: Praeger Publishers.

Thomas, D. C., 2013. 'Cedric Robinson and Racial Capitalism: Africana Liberation Resistance Structures and Black Internationalism in the 21st Century', *African Identities*, Volume 11 (2), pp. 133–147.

Wright, R., 1956. *The Color Curtain: A Report on the Bandung Conference*, Cleveland, OH: World Pub. Co.

Political-economic connections

11
AFRICA'S RISING COMMODITY EXPORT DEPENDENCY ON CHINA

Alicia Garcia-Herrero and Carlos Casanova

Introduction

China has gone from being a supporter of fringe Maoist regimes in the 1960s to providing more financial assistance to the region than the World Bank (Cheng, 2015). But the idea that China would be crucial to African development is neither new nor accidental. In fact, Chinese policy-makers have been aware of this notion for quite some time. China's Ya–Fei–La Strategy, literally meaning Asia–Africa–Latin America, was conceived during the Maoist era in the 1960s (Myers, 2012) in an attempt to promote the advancement of developing country goals in a new world order. Since then, China has played an active role in promoting South–South cooperation, Africa–China cooperation being an important part of that equation.

While the economic relationship between Africa and China has been characterized by many aspects in the past years, bilateral trade is perhaps the one area that has garnered the most attention, and understandably so. China's double-digit growth rates and thirst for natural resources drove it into relatively unexplored frontiers in search of natural resources, a quest of Homeric proportions which helped to fuel trade with commodity exporters in Africa and beyond (Casanova et al., 2015). As a result of this expansion, trade between China and Africa surged to USD 207 billion in 2013, growing by an average of approximately 30% per year compared with a decade earlier. The 'Chinese engine of growth', as it has come to be known amongst commodity exporters in the emerging world, provided a much-needed spare wheel at a time when traditional sources of demand faltered, as the developed world was struggling to get to grips with a financial crisis. However, China has started to slow down as a result of its rebalancing towards a more sustainable direction, which involves shifting away from investments and towards domestic consumption. Inevitably, this will have consequences for African exporters. A slowing China, particularly in the context of its economic rebalancing, will lead to a fall in demand for much valued African commodities such as copper, iron ore and oil – vital inputs in the construction of China's gleaming new airports, railway stations, bourgeoning housing complexes and boundless highways.

But will this drop in demand affect all countries in the region equally? Not necessarily. Countries which benefited the most from China's expansion should, logically, feel the impact more strongly; whereas countries which have not increased their trade links with China as much should be less affected. The basis of this relationship may seem obvious, but quantifying this impact is not a straightforward task. In order to prove which countries will be affected the most by a slowdown in China, it is important to understand bilateral trade links in the context of Africa's trade dependency on China. In other words, the implications of a slowdown will be felt most strongly among those countries and commodities which are more dependent on China and/or have seen the fastest increases in recent years.

Consequently, in this chapter we will analyze the implications of Africa's rising commodity export dependency on China. The structure of this chapter is as follows. In the first section, we analyze the historical backdrop of China–Africa trade links. In the second section, we look at the development of bilateral trade ties to date in more detail. In the third section, we will elaborate on our definition of commodity export dependency and examine the levels of dependency of African commodity exports to China, focusing on a number of key commodities. In the fourth section, we look at the implications of increased dependency on China; and lastly, we will offer some conclusions and policy implications in the fifth section of this chapter.

A final note of caution before we delve deeper into this topic: bilateral trade may have played a pivotal role in defining economic relations between China and Africa, but these are by no means the only significant flows. In addition to being a key trading partner, China has risen very quickly to become one of Africa's largest sources of development assistance (Bräutigam, 2011), foreign direct investment (Chen et al., 2015) and financing (Gutman et al., 2015). Having said that, these flows are many orders of magnitude smaller than bilateral trade, so while they do constitute a welcome addition to the region's economic development, it is unlikely that growth in this area will be sufficiently robust to substitute for trade as a major revenue source in the short term. This is especially worrisome for African governments that depend on incomes from commodity exports, but have not done enough to build up their fiscal buffers over the years, as falling demand from China could escalate the risk of a full-fledged fiscal crisis taking place.

Changing dynamics: the backdrop of China–Africa trade links

China has maintained contact with the African continent since antiquity, with the first records of bilateral ties between Africa and China dating back to the Tang Dynasty (618–907). During the Song Dynasty (960–1279), the transit of Chinese vessels across all corners of the Indian Ocean intensified remarkably, which explains why Chinese objects of this period can nowadays be found in regions from Somalia to Mozambique. But it wasn't until the twelfth century that recognized naval routes for the trade of ivory, precious woods, myrrh and tortoise shell were established between the east coast of Africa and the south coast of China. Between 1417 and 1431, various emperors of the Ming Dynasty (1368–1644) sent trade missions to East Africa, which returned to China with cargoes of exotic gifts, including a number of mythological creatures – in reality giraffes, zebras, lions and other African wildlife – which were offered to the Ming court as proof of the empire's 'celestial sovereignty' (Rotberg, 2008).

China's modern economic relations with Africa started shortly after the founding of the People's Republic of China in 1949. During this period, China pursued the advancement of Chinese-style communism in the region by supporting independent movements in Africa, primarily by providing military equipment and training (Bräutigam, 2009). Later on, China also sent doctors, nurses and technicians to provide assistance to African nations and funded numerous infrastructure projects, including the colossal 1860km Tanzania–Zambia railway, which is now considered a monument to China–Africa friendship (Yu, 2011). What's more, at first most of this aid was granted for free. Many considered this free aid to have come at a great cost for China, especially during the 1960s, when the country was experiencing a famine and domestic turmoil (Peng, 1987). However, these efforts paid off, as they enabled China to garner the support of African nations in multilateral forums. Let's not forget that the support from African nations was instrumental in granting China a permanent seat at the United Nations (UN) General Assembly in 1971 – 26 of the 76 votes in favor came from African nations (Chau, 2014).

Contrary to popular belief, political ideology per se was never a consideration for China when dealing with Africa, or any of its emerging market peers. On the contrary, Beijing has readily engaged with both rightist and leftist regimes in the past. Taiwan, on the other hand, played a decisive role in defining relations. For example, Seko Mobutu, who ruled the Democratic Republic of Congo from 1965 to 1997, shifted his allegiance from Taipei to Beijing in 1972, upon receiving USD 100 million in technical aid from Beijing. This was in spite of opposing China at the UN a year earlier, and notwithstanding his strong reservations towards Beijing. These reservations were understandable, given China's support of Maoist rebels during the Simba Rebellion in 1964 (Leslie, 1993).

Taipei and Beijing have been competing for the allegiance of the small states that sustain diplomatic relations with Taiwan to date. They do this by providing substantial grants and technical assistance as well as in a stratagem that has been referred to as 'checkbook diplomacy'.[1] While this is still an important constituent of relations between China and other emerging markets such as Latin America and the Caribbean, checkbook diplomacy has lost some of its weight in Africa. Only 3 of the 22 countries that still have full diplomatic relations with Taiwan are in Africa, namely Burkina Faso, Sao Tome and Principe, and Swaziland. Notwithstanding these caveats, as the incentive to compete with Taiwan for the allegiance of African nations dwindled, relations evolved to satisfy the pragmatic economic interests of both sides (Meidan, 2006).

With the 'opening and reform' led by Deng Xiaoping starting in 1978, the tone of China's economic policy shifted in a more pragmatic direction. As a result, relations with Africa were put on a second plane, as Chinese foreign diplomacy focused on redeploying efforts towards advanced economies. This would quickly change following the diplomatic vacuum left by the Tiananmen Square protests of 1989, which drove China to seek political support from its African allies in multilateral forums, as well as, of course, alternative market opportunities. This new direction is exemplified by Jiang Zemin's 'Five Points Proposal' for the development of a long term relationship between China and African nations, which was announced during an address to the Organization of African Unity in 1996 (Sithara, 2007). It was following this address that China's relations with Africa took a markedly commercial twist. Diplomatic efforts focused on bilateral trade while moving away from interest rate free loans. Development aid and assistance also developed a commercial focus, by enabling bilateral trade links through, for example, better infrastructure and technological know-how, thereby generating win-win opportunities for African exporters and China. This turning point constitutes a very clear break from its strategy in the 1960s.

This trend was further reinforced by China's 'going-out policy', an initiative established in 1999 by the Chinese government to promote the expansion of Chinese enterprises internationally. Going abroad was seen as a priority for China as it would enable it to tap into new opportunities, securing access to resources to fuel its investment boom, but also creating new markets for its manufactured goods and services overseas. This led to a surge in Chinese foreign direct investments (FDI) in Africa, which increased from USD 1.5 billion in 2001 to USD 26 billion in 2013, according to official statistics compiled by China's Ministry of Commerce (Ministry of Commerce of the People's Republic of China (MOFCOM) Database, 2014).

China's 'going-out' coincided with a new period of unprecedented development in China, particularly during 2000–2013, when GDP grew by an average annual rate of 10% per year

(National Bureau of Statistics of China, 2014). During this time, economic relationships with Africa intensified tremendously, as rising demand for resources drove China into relatively unexplored frontiers. Going back to the point on checkbook diplomacy, whatever attractiveness diplomatic relations with Taiwan still had was quickly eroded by the appeal of China's double-digit growth rates and soaring demand for commodities.

This new approach suited the strategic interests of China in Africa and so has prevailed, until not so long ago. However, China's economy has started to slow, exposing some of the uglier aspects of the surge in bilateral trade links, as we shall explore in the following section of this chapter.

Delving deeper: burgeoning bilateral trade links remain unbalanced

China's demand for resources took off a decade ago, as the country's economic model shifted towards heavy industrial production, the private property market exploded, and wealthier citizens demanded a richer diet, boosting imports of agricultural commodities as well as raw materials. As a result, bilateral trade between China and Africa grew exponentially during this period. Trade between China and Africa reached USD 207 billion in 2013 (United Nations COMTRADE Database, 2014) and China now accounts for almost 20% of Africa's total bilateral trade flows, although this figure is much higher for some countries (Angola 40%, Republic of Congo 41%, and Sierra Leone 53%). Trade flows with China are an important vital source for Africa, especially if we consider that total bilateral trade with the world accounts for approximately 50% of Africa's GDP. In other words, the continent's relatively small GDP (USD 2.30 trillion in 2013) relative to its trade openness make it quite vulnerable to shifts in external demand. China, being one of the largest partners, is an important strategic priority for Africa.

To some extent, this is also true for China. Trade is also an important growth driver for the Asian giant's economy (43% of its GDP in 2013). However, Africa only accounts for a reduced proportion of the country's total trade with the world, equivalent to approximately 10% (Garcia-Herrero & Casanova, 2014).

The asymmetries don't stop here. Many African countries have already accrued trade deficits with China, while the region as a whole had a questionable trade surplus with China in 2013.[2]

This pattern may be explained by different relative comparative advantages and Purchasing Power Parity (PPP) of both regions. Many African countries enjoy rich natural resource endowments, which grant the continent a certain competitive advantage in commodity exports. On the other hand, cheap Chinese imports may be more appropriate for the purchasing power of emerging economies in Africa compared with imports from other regions. For example, Chinese apparel is now commonplace in African markets and it is not unusual to see it being sold at a discount compared with second-hand clothes originating from Europe and North America. In addition, anybody who has visited the region will be aware of the important contribution that Chinese-made (as well as Indian) vehicles and bikes have made in improving mobility in the region, with huge gains for its economic development.

Having said that, this message may be bad news for Africa as it points towards a significant degree of import substitution. In other words, cheap Chinese imports of manufactured goods are used to substitute for (less competitive) domestic manufactures. In fact, excluding exports of unclassified goods from South Africa, trade data reveals that a 'substitution effect' may have already started to take place in Africa, particularly amongst the more advanced economies, despite having lower PPP levels than other emerging markets in Asia and Latin America (Garcia-Herrero & Casanova, 2014).

Table 11.1 Trade with China versus trade with the US

Country	Trade with China as a % of total trade	Trade with the US as a % of total trade
Algeria	8.3	6.2
Angola	40.2	8.6
Benin	8.2	5.0
Burkina Faso	6.8	2.4
Burundi	7.7	1.3
Cabo Verde	5.9	1.0
Cameroon	20.6	3.8
Central African Rep.	6.0	6.4
Chad	10.7	52.6
Comoros	14.5	1.8
Congo, Dem. Rep.	30.0	2.5
Congo, Rep.	40.5	4.9
Cote d'Ivoire	4.7	6.2
Djibouti	26.1	2.8
Equatorial Guinea	24.1	6.3
Ethiopia	19.0	10.5
Gabon	14.4	8.8
Gambia	31.7	3.5
Ghana	20.8	5.7
Guinea	13.8	1.7
Guinea-Bissau	8.7	0.4
Kenya	11.9	9.7
Liberia	15.8	2.0
Libya	8.4	2.2
Madagascar	15.6	4.1
Malawi	7.5	4.3
Mali	8.8	1.0
Mauritania	29.0	3.9
Mauritius	11.1	4.5
Morocco	5.4	5.9
Mozambique	20.8	2.9
Niger	13.6	2.8
Nigeria	12.2	6.3
Reunion	0.0	0.0
Rwanda	10.8	3.1
Sao Tome & Principe	4.8	1.6
Senegal	5.9	1.9
Seychelles	2.8	1.0
Sierra Leone	52.6	3.7
Somalia	7.8	1.2
South Africa	12.8	3.6
Sudan	0.0	0.4
Tanzania	23.9	2.1
Togo	21.3	4.6
Tunisia	3.8	3.4
Uganda	9.7	2.0
Zambia	8.7	1.0
Zimbabwe	15.8	1.5

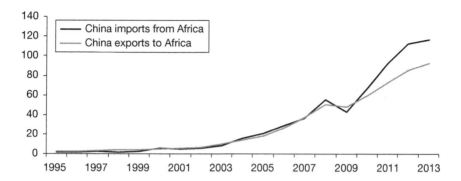

Figure 11.1 Bilateral trade links

This is not favorable for countries trying to build up their manufacturing capacity. It is especially worrisome for resource-rich economies, as it increases the risks of 'Dutch Disease' (Zafar, 2007). The Dutch Disease refers to a mechanism by which increases in revenues from natural resources make an economy's currency stronger, resulting in the nation's other exports becoming more expensive and imports becoming cheaper. The consequences include a less competitive manufacturing sector and increased exposure to commodity price volatility.

Trade relations with China are skewed both on a market and product basis, particularly with regard to Africa's exports to China. For instance, a reduced number of countries account for the bulk of total exports to China. These are led by Angola, South Africa and Republic of Congo. The situation is even more pronounced if we look at exports as a percentage of GDP, where it is in fact the smaller, export-oriented economies that are the most exposed to China. The most prominent examples are Angola and Zambia

Moreover, exports to China are remarkably concentrated around a limited number of products, all of which are classified as commodities according to the Organization for Economic Cooperation and Development (OECD) database. In line with the extractive nature of China's trade links with Africa and Latin America, mineral products and base metals feature most prominently. Mineral products and base metals account for approximately 65% of total exports to China, with crude oil accounting for a bigger chunk than base metals. Iron ores follow in third place (Tralac (Trade Law Center), 2013). In addition to mineral products and base metals, other unclassified goods accounted for 26% of Africa's exports to China in 2013.

In stark contrast to exports, African imports from China are somewhat more diversified on a country and product basis. Five countries accounted for 50% of all imports from China in 2013, led by South Africa, Nigeria, Algeria, Angola and Kenya. Meanwhile, on the product front, transportation equipment, textiles and clothing, machinery, footwear and plastics accounted for just over 50% of Africa's total imports from China. All of these products fall into the manufacturing category (Tralac (Trade Law Center), 2013). In other words, Chinese exports into Africa are much more diversified than those of Africa into China, which means that bilateral trade between the two remains very unbalanced. As of today, there is little hope that this can be corrected very soon.

This detail reveals an important underlying theme in trade relations between China and Africa: China imports primarily raw materials from Africa and exports manufactured goods. One could, thus, argue that Africa's growth resilience during the global crisis put the continent in a position to act as a limited – but still welcome – spare wheel for China's huge export capacity. At the same time, it also benefited from China's huge stimulus package, intended to buffer the

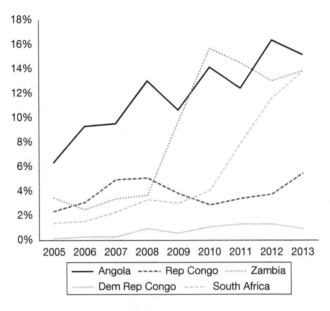

Figure 11.2 Exports to China as a percentage of GDP for key African countries
Source: Author's calculations based on data by International Monetary Fund.

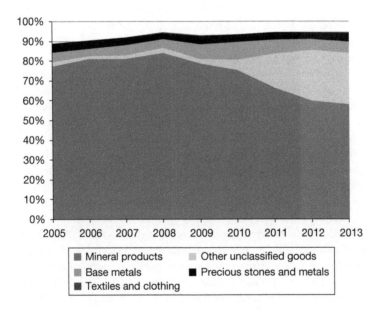

Figure 11.3a Exports by commodity
Source: Author's calculations based on data by UN COMTRADE and Tralac.

economy from an ailing external demand during the global crisis. The resulting investment-led growth model helped to fuel a commodity super-cycle, which inexorably favored exports from Africa.

Commodity export dependency on China

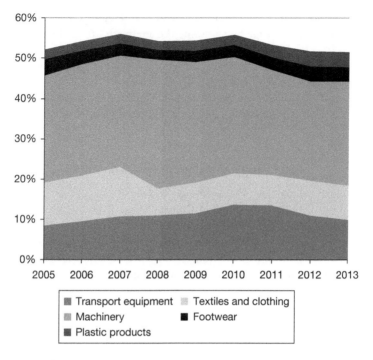

Figure 11.3b Imports by product

Source: Author's calculations based on data by UN COMTRADE and Tralac.

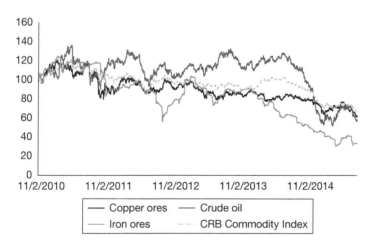

Figure 11.4 Commodity price index

However, the nature of bilateral trade flows raises some alarms. At this juncture, China's growth momentum has begun to dwindle and, more importantly, the growth model is being geared from investment towards consumption. For this reason, it is unlikely that the pace of growth in bilateral trade can continue, at least as concerns Chinese commodity imports from Africa. In fact, this may have already started. Bilateral trade links between China and Africa fell by 2.9% in 2013, the second time trade links between both regions experienced negative growth since 1990 – the first time being during the aftermath of the global financial crisis in 2009. Falling trade volumes in combination with lower commodity prices (see Figure 11.4) are bad news for many African commodity exporters. In addition to lower government revenues, these economies could experience a deterioration in their terms of trade, leading to widening trade deficits with China unless imports of Chinese manufactured goods can be substituted with local alternatives, which takes time and investment. But which economies are most vulnerable?

Increasing dependency: how to define it?

The extent to which a slowdown in bilateral trade will impact African exports depends on how vulnerable these commodities are to shifts in Chinese demand. To measure this, the authors of this chapter have deployed an export dependency index for the major countries in Africa (Garcia-Herrero & Casanova, 2014). The index measures the relative exposure of Latin American exporters to shifts in demand from China and is scaled from 0 to 1 (the higher the score, the more exposed an exporter is to disruptions of trade with China). The index works as follows:

$$Index_{x,y} = \sqrt[3]{\frac{EXP_{x,y}}{EXP_y} \times \frac{EXP\ to\ China_{x,y}}{EXP_{x,y}} \times avg\left[\frac{IMP_{x\ China}}{IMP_x} \times \left(1 - \frac{EXP_{x,y}}{EXP_x}\right)\right]}$$

Whereby:

$$\frac{EXP_{x,y}}{EXP_y}$$

refers to country y's exports of commodity x as a share of its total exports. This shows how concentrated a country's exports are into one commodity (x);

$$\frac{EXP\ to\ China_{x,y}}{EXP_{x,y}}$$

refers to country y's exports of commodity x to China divided by its total export of that commodity. This shows how dependent the world is on China to sell a particular commodity relative to other export markets. And:

$$avg\left[\frac{IMP_{x,\ China}}{IMP_x} \times \left(1 - \frac{EXP_{x,y}}{EXP_x}\right)\right]$$

is the average of two components: the first half refers to the share of China's imports of commodity x in the global market, while the second half is 1 minus country y's export market share of commodity x. This provides a measure of China's strength as a buyer or pricing power compared with the exporting country's strength as a seller.

To determine the sample, we identified the top five exporters to China and then selected the products that constituted circa 90% of those countries' total exports to China respectively. These included Angola (mineral fuels), Democratic Republic of Congo (mineral fuels, copper and base metals), Republic of Congo (mineral fuels), South Africa (unclassified) and Zambia (copper).

It is important to stress that dependency in the context of this chapter is a relative term, defined as the degree to which the exports of a certain commodity of a particular country will be affected provided there is a shift in demand from China. In other words, the index is a relative measure of export dependence on China for each particular commodity and is therefore not reflective of the impact that a unit shift in demand from China will incur on the economy as a whole. In other words, the higher the score in our commodity index, the more vulnerable any export of a particular commodity will be to a potential disruption of trade with China.

After running our index using aggregates from the United Nations Commerce and Trade Database, we discovered that commodity dependence has increased in Africa between 2005 and 2015

This result is not surprising given China's size and fast pace of growth. Intuitively, in the context of booming bilateral trade links, export dependency on Chinese demand should increase as China takes up a much larger share of total trade.

Looking at commodity dependence on China in absolute terms, it is apparent that the story in Africa is really about Angola and Zambia, which makes sense given that both countries are amongst the most important commercial partners of China in the region, and have been so for quite some time. For example, Sinopec was the first Chinese company to enter the African energy market in 2004, after securing a deal to exploit Angola's Block 18 offshore field in partnership with Sonagol, just months after Beijing approved a USD 2 billion loan to Angola (Levkowitz et al., 2009). However, the largest increases in dependence between 2005 and 2013 can be observed in Democratic Republic of Congo's copper, base metals and mineral fuel exports. Again, this makes sense intuitively. China has greatly increased its economic exposure to the Democratic Republic of Congo and is now a significant source of financing as well as final demand. For example, 2008 saw the announcement of a multi-billion dollar project to grant Sicomines, a consortium of Chinese companies, mineral concessions in Democratic Republic of Congo's Katanga province in exchange for infrastructure investments, funded by China EX-IM bank (Jansson et al., 2009). China takes pride in maintaining a 'non-interference' policy with its commercial partners. Given that the country is not favored by international investors for political risk and humanitarian reasons, this dependence is not surprising.

On a commodity basis, dependence is largest in the case of mineral fuels. China is a huge importer of fuels and minerals, with some authors estimating that the Asian giant accounted for approximately 40% of the world's total market growth since 1995 (Winters & Yusuf, 2007). In fact, according to the US Energy Information Administration (EIA), China overtook the US as the world's largest oil importer in 2013 (US Energy Information Administration (EIA), 2014). But China's imports of this commodity are heavily concentrated among relatively few countries in Africa, which include, primarily, Sudan, Congo, Angola, Zambia and South Africa (Ademola et al., 2015). This concentration is also reflected in the different commodity export dependency levels of the countries in our sample. In the case of Angola – the main mineral fuel exporter – mineral fuels accounted for a very significant proportion of the country's total exports in 2013, or approximately 98%. Furthermore, China has a significant market share of Angolan mineral exports, roughly 50% in the same year. China's sheer size and the fact that Angola focuses so much on one type of commodity export have translated into high dependency levels (see Figure 11.5). Democratic Republic of Congo is a different story.

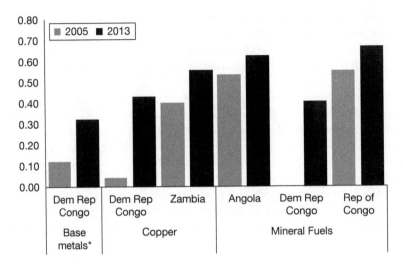

Figure 11.5 Commodity dependence increase: Africa
Source: Author's calculations based on data by UN COMTRADE and Tralac.

Mineral fuels account for a much more modest 15% of its total exports, which makes sense as the country (unlike Angola) is not an established producer. However, as we mentioned previously, China is Democratic Republic of Congo's top buyer, accounting for 90% total mineral fuel exports, which explains the high dependence.

Zambia stands out for the case of copper. Zambia is one of Africa's largest copper producers and copper exports account for a large chunk of the country's total exports, equivalent to 60% in 2013. In addition, the metal is an important source of government revenue and foreign exchange earnings for Zambia, underpinning the importance of copper to the region. China buys approximately 40% of Zambia's copper exports, a significantly large market share. Inevitably, this has translated into a very large dependency on Chinese demand, which isn't surprising given the role that China has played in Zambia in the past. While Zambia benefited greatly from China's economic expansion, it now faces the double constraints of lower exports and worsening terms of trade from falling copper prices.

Implications of Africa's export dependency on China

Bilateral trade links reveal the unbalanced nature of China–Africa trade relations. China is importing raw commodities and exporting manufactured goods. Furthermore, the dependence on Chinese demand for these exports has increased, making the growing trade deficit harder to reverse. This may have three important implications, which we will analyze in more detail below.

Manufacturing substitution

One of the most worrisome implications is that of manufacturing substitution, or the degree to which cheaper Chinese manufactures are displacing local production. A simple measure of import penetration can be used to gauge the incidence of Chinese imports in apparent consumption (Melguizo, 2016):

$$I_{it}^{j} = \frac{M_{it}^{jc}}{AC_{it}^{j}} \star 100$$

I = import penetration of commodity j in country i; M = country i's imports of commodity j from China; and AC = Apparent consumption of commodity j in country i. Apparent consumption is defined as:

$$AC_{it}^{x} = NS_{it}^{j} + M_{it}^{j} - X_{it}^{j}$$

NS = country i's national supply of commodity j; M = country i's imports of commodity j from the world; and X = country i's exports of commodity j to the world.

In Figure 11.6, we can see that import penetration increased considerably between 2000 and 2010 for China's main export markets in Africa.[3] Machinery, textiles and transportation equipment, which together accounted for approximately 50% of Africa's imports from China, all experienced increases, meaning that locally manufactured goods were being substituted by cheap Chinese imports, particularly in the lower value segment. This is in line with Africa's increasing commodity export dependency on China.

In the absence of policies that generate employment, import substitution could lead to higher income inequality and social unrest. Extractive sectors are less labor intensive than manufacturing, which benefits capital at the expense of labor. During a commodity boom, a commodity exporter will see its terms of trade improve, exerting upward pressure on the country's currency and relative wages. Skilled workers, or those employed in the extractive sectors, benefit from higher wages and cheaper imports. However, as is the case in many African commodity exporters, a preponderance of unskilled workers will find it hard to find a job as the labor-intensive sectors of the economy struggle to absorb the excess employment.

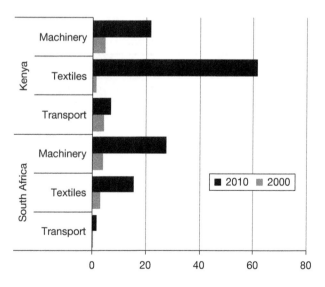

Figure 11.6 Chinese import penetration

Source: UNIDO, UNCOMTRADE and author's calculations.

This situation may be sustainable during the good years, but a turn of the tide could really throw the system into turmoil. As commodity prices relapse, exporters will see their terms of trade worsen, putting downward pressure on the exchange rate and wages. Given that manufacturing capacity is something that cannot be built overnight, this would leave the country with a vast pool of unskilled and unemployed workers with an eroded purchasing power. To make things worse, as the price elasticity of consumer goods is very high, commodity exporters, who have experienced significant increases in manufacturing substitution, would have to continue importing manufactured products which are more expensive in relative terms, leading to a widening of the trade deficit and a worsening of the current account. Given Africa's relatively low industrial base, there is room to develop policies that boost manufacturing and downstream processing capacity, but this is something that requires proactive policymaking. It might be harder to overturn the trade deficit with China.

The need to boost interregional trade

One of the main implications of trade dependency on China is that it may have played a role in reducing the potential for interregional trade. Interregional trade as a percentage of total trade is much lower in Africa compared with other emerging economies, a trend which can be explained by inadequate infrastructure levels in the continent. For example, while Latin America is by no means the poster child of connectivity, it does enjoy better overall infrastructure levels than Africa; this may have facilitated closer trade links within the region but also with the United States, which makes sense given Latin America's geographic proximity to the United States.

Dependence on demand from the United States may therefore have played a role in muting the impacts of growth in Chinese demand. Likewise, in the case of Africa, in the absence of a trade hegemony like China, the region may have otherwise been forced to invest in projects that enable better links within the region but also with neighboring markets in the

Table 11.2 Intraregional exports and imports as a percentage of total exports and imports

	Exports			Imports		
	1996–2000	*2001–2006*	*2007–2011*	*1996–2000*	*2001–2006*	*2007–2011*
Developing Africa	9.7	9.8	10.9	13.3	13.5	12.7
Eastern Africa	12.4	14.1	13.9	8.8	9.3	7.1
Central Africa	1.2	1.0	1.3	2.6	2.5	3.1
Northern Africa	3.2	2.9	3.9	2.8	3.7	3.8
Southern Africa	4.4	2.1	2.1	11.9	10.7	7.9
Western Africa	10.2	10.0	9.0	11.3	12.5	10.2
Developing America	19.1	17.6	20.6	17.6	19.0	21.1
Developing Asia	41.5	45.1	50.1	40.6	49.3	53.0
Developing Oceania	1.3	3.0	3.3	0.9	2.3	2.7
Europe	67.3	71.4	70.0	68.3	67.0	64.4

Source: UNCTAD Statistical Database.

Diversification of exports in order to capture a larger share of value added

Trade in Value-Added (TiVA) describes a statistical approach, developed by the OECD in conjunction with the WTO, which is used to estimate the source of value that is added in producing goods and services for export and import. As can be observed from Figure 11.7, both trade in nominal terms and trade in value added terms have grown significantly between 2000 and 2009.

However, growth rates seem smaller when looking at value added data rather than raw data, indicating that bilateral trade flows may have been overestimated. In addition, notwithstanding fast growth patterns in nominal terms and somewhat humble growth rates in TiVA, the ratio of exported value added relative to gross exports is lower in 2009 compared with 2000

This hints towards a more complex pattern, namely that China has shifted from importing commodities to meet domestic demand, to exporting value added via global value chains.

Value retention lies ahead as a big challenge for trade relations between Africa and China unless good policies are put in place. The good news is that China's rebalancing towards consumption and away from investment (Pettis, 2013) could spur the inflow of much needed Chinese investments, particularly in sectors with overcapacity. These include low value-added manufacturing such as textiles and apparel, but also basic processing of natural resources, non-metallic mineral products, smelting and processing of ferrous metals, smelting and pressing of non-ferrous metals and raw chemical materials are amongst the sectors with the most significant overcapacity concerns in China (Casanova et al., 2015).

An example of how China can export low value-added manufacturing in sectors with overcapacity can be seen in Africa's textile industry. This industry remains very fragmented and has experienced significant losses stemming from intense competition from cheaper Chinese manufactures. However, there is recent evidence that points towards an inflow of Chinese investment into the sector, as Chinese companies try to take advantage of preferential trade agreements between Africa and the United States and Europe, such as AGOA and the European Neighborhood Policy (ENP) (Tang, 2014).

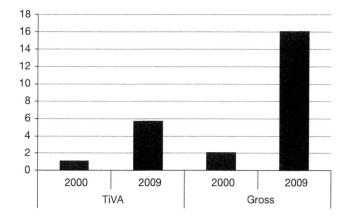

Figure 11.7 TiVA has not grown as fast as gross trade

Source: Author's calculations based on data by the OECD.

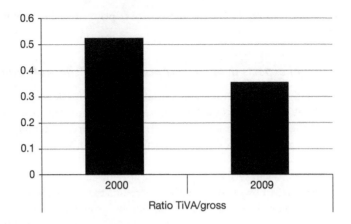

Figure 11.8 The ratio of TiVA/gross fell significantly
Source: Author's calculations based on data by the OECD.

Conclusion

China is seen by ally regimes of both ends of the spectrum as an emerging power in the South and therefore closer to the problems of the South. While booming trade links have definitely contributed to the fast growth of Africa in the past decade, shielding the continent from a collapse of traditional sources of demand stemming from the global financial crisis, this trend has started to slow.

African commodity exports are very dependent on China. This dependency has increased overall since 2005, which is not surprising given the size of China's economy as well as rapid growth in the past decade. China's thirst for natural resources enabled it to become a key engine of growth for emerging commodity exporters in Africa and beyond, elevating South–South trade links to a new level. Not surprisingly, this dependency was more striking amongst traditional trade partners in the continent.

As China's economy starts to slow, following its restructuring away from investments towards more domestic consumption, we expect the pace of bilateral trade with Africa will moderate, on the back of falling commodity exports. This will impact African countries tremendously, particularly those with a high exposure to China (higher dependence) and those where growth is more reliant on external demand. On a commodity basis, dependency on China increased overall for the three major exports to China: iron ore, copper and oil. Having said that, the impact of a Chinese deceleration will be felt most strongly amongst exporters of metals (not so much mineral fuels or agricultural commodities), as increases in these flows have been for the most part associated with China's investment binge.

Furthermore, bilateral trade patterns are becoming increasingly unbalanced. China imports raw materials and exports manufactured goods to Africa. In addition, we have evidence pointing towards a substitution of African manufacturing with cheap Chinese substitutes, which will make the trade deficit that many nations already have with China more difficult to reverse. As Africa's average income levels increase, it is likely that the trend will be exacerbated and the extent to which this scenario is sustainable in the midterm remains unclear.

In order to avert further commodity dependency increases, African economies need to do more to boost their exports to other regions as well as within the continent. This could be done via implementing policies that facilitate the integration of regional trade, for example by increasing investments in transportation infrastructure. African economies could also leverage their preferential geopolitical position by boosting their share of exports to the developed world via AGOA and the ENP. Another option would be to implement policies that enable the region to move up the global value chains by retaining more value added and promoting downstream refining and processing capacity.

All in all, China remains a strategic priority for Africa. While the story will continue to center around the region's exposure to a Chinese deceleration, the Asian giant's rebalancing towards consumption also offers some opportunities. Specifically, Africa could be strategically positioned to benefit from the offshoring of this excess capacity from China. It could also benefit from China's demand for other products that enable it to diversify its export basket. FDI and lending are picking up, providing a different and welcome dimension to China–Africa economic relations, particularly if they help the region to become more globally integrated. However, some pain in the short term may be inevitable for countries that haven't developed fiscal buffers over the years.

Notes

1 Checkbook diplomacy was put on hold after Taiwanese President Ma Ying-jeou was elected in 2008, following his announcement of Taiwan's 'no reunification, no independence, and no war' strategy. It is unclear whether the results of the recent Presidential election in Taiwan will worsen cross-strait relations, in turn reigniting the incentives to engage in checkbook diplomacy.
2 Africa would have a trade deficit with China if we exclude South Africa's exports of unclassified goods to China. It is unclear what these goods are, as they appear reported by the China customs side but not by South Africa's customs. For the second part of this chapter, we will use trade flows as reported by China to the United Nations Commerce and Trade Database. These constitute actual flows according to this methodology, meaning Africa still has a surplus with China on an aggregate level.
3 Our calculations are based on data from UNCOMTRADE and UNIDO. China's largest export markets in Africa were South Africa, Nigeria, Algeria and Kenya in 2013. However, the UNIDO database does not contain comprehensive data for Nigeria and Algeria, so our analysis is confined to two countries.

References

Ademola, O. T., Bankole, A. S. and Adewuyi, A. O., 2015. 'China–Africa Trade Relations: Insights from AERC Scoping Studies', *European Journal of Development Research*, Volume 21, pp. 485–505.
Bräutigam, D., 2009. *The Dragon's Gift: The Real Story of China in Africa*, Oxford: Oxford University Press.
Bräutigam, D., 2011. 'Chinese development aid in Africa: What, where, why and how much?' in J. Golley and L. Song (eds.), *Rising China: Global Challenges and Opportunities*, Canberra: Australia National University Press, pp. 203–223.
Casanova, C., et al., 2015. 'Measuring Latin America's export dependency on China', *BBVA Working Paper 15/26*. Available at: www.bbvaresearch.com/en/publicaciones/measuring-latin-americas-export-dependency-on-china/ [Accessed November 2015].
Chau, D. C., 2014. *Exploiting Africa: The Influence of Maoist China in Algeria, Ghana, and Tanzania*, Annapolis: Naval Institute Press.
Chen, W., et al., 2015. *Why is China Investing in Africa? Evidence from the Firm Level*, Washington, DC: Brookings Institution Press.
Cheng, C., 2015. 'Official development with Chinese characteristic: Development cooperation between China and Africa', in C. P. Freeman (ed.), *Handbook on China and Developing Countries*, Washington, DC: Edward Elgar, pp. 193–226.
Garcia-Herrero, A. and Casanova, C., 2014. 'China's trade relations with the South: What can Africa learn from the Latin American case?', *BBVA Research*. Available at: www.bbvaresearch.com/en/publicaciones/chinas-trade-relations-with-the-south-what-can-africa-learn-from-the-latin-american-case/ [Accessed November 2015].
Gutman, J., et al., 2015. *Financing Africa's Infrastructure: Can the World Deliver?*, Washington, DC: Brookings Institution Press.

Jansson, J., Burke, C. and Jiang, W., 2009. *Chinese Companies in the Extractive Industries of Gabon and DRC: Perceptions of Transparency*, Stellenbosch: University of Stellenbosch.

Leslie, W. J., 1993. 'Zaire in the international arena', in W. J. Leslie (ed.), *Zaire: Continuity and Political Change in an Oppressive State*, Boulder, CO: Westview Press.

Levkowitz, l., McLellan Ross, M. and Warner, J. R., 2009. 'A Case Study in Chinese Inverstors' Operations in Angola and Beyond', *US–China Economic and Security Review Commission Working Paper*.

Meidan, M., 2006. 'China's Africa Policy: Business Now, Politics Later', *Asian Perspective*, Volume 30 (4), pp. 69–93.

Melguizo, A., 2016. *Latin American Outlook 2016: Towards a New Partnership with China*, Paris: OECD Development Center.

Ministry of Commerce of the People's Republic of China (MOFCOM) Database. 2014. Available at: http://english.mofcom.gov.cn/article/statistic/ [Accessed November 2015].

Myers, M., 2012. *China's Engagement with Latin America: More of the Same?* Washington, DC: Inter-American Dialogue.

National Bureau of Statistics of China, 2014. *China Statistical Yearbook*, Beijing: China Statistics Press.

Peng, X. Z., 1987. 'Demographic Consequences of the Great Leap Forward in Chinese Provinces', *Population and Development Review*, Volume 13 (4), pp. 630–670.

Pettis, M., 2013. *The Great Rebalancing: Trade, Conflict and the Perilous Road Ahead for the World Economy*, Princeton, NJ: Princeton University Press.

Rotberg, R. I., 2008. *China into Africa: Trade, Aid and Influence*, Washington, DC: Brookings Institution Press.

Sithara, F., 2007. 'Chronology of China–Africa Relations', *China Report*, Volume 43 (3), pp. 363–373.

Tang, X.Y., 2014. 'The impact of Asian investment on Africa's textile industries', *Carnegie-Tsinghua Center for Global Policy*. Available at: http://carnegieendowment.org/files/china_textile_investment.pdf [Accessed November 2015].

Tralac (Trade Law Center), 2013. 'Africa–China trade data'. Available at: www.tralac.org/resources/our-resources/4795-africa-china-trade.html [Accessed November 2015].

US Energy Information Administration (EIA), 2014. 'China is now the world's largest new importer of petroleum and other liquid fuels'. Available at: www.eia.gov/todayinenergy/detail.cfm?id=15531 [Accessed on November 2015].

United Nations COMTRADE Database, 2014. Available at: http://comtrade.un.org/ [Accessed November 2015].

United Nations Conference on Trade and Development (UNCTAD), 2015. *World Investment Report 2015: Reforming International Investment, Governance*. Geneva: United Nations Press.

Winters, L. A. and Yusuf, S., 2007. *Dancing with Giants: China, India, and the Global Economy*, World Bank and Institute of Policy Studies.

Yu, G., 2011. 'Working on the Railroad: China and the Tanzania–Zambia Railway', *Asian Survey* Volume 11 (11), pp. 1101–1117.

Zafar, A., 2007. 'The Growing Relationship between China and Sub-Saharan Africa', *World Bank Observer*, Volume 22 (1), pp. 103–130.

12
BRIDGING ASIA WITH AFRICA
The case of Malaysia

Evelyn S. Devadason and V.G.R. Chandran Govindaraju

Introduction

South–South cooperation (SSC), defined as 'the processes, institutions and arrangements designed to promote political, economic and technical cooperation among developing countries in pursuit of common development goals' (UNCTAD, 2010), was put on the international agenda with the establishment of the Non-Aligned Movement (NAM) in 1961, and the United Nations Conference on Trade and Development (UNCTAD) and the Group of 77 (G77) in 1964. The rhetoric of SSC, however, was lost for several decades thereafter, as it did not yield the sort of economic self-reliance and political independence that developing countries had sought. It was not until the 1990s (Hamidin, 2003) that SSC regained some renewed interest. In the Asia–Africa context, the hallmark of SSC, inter-regional links, began with Japanese aid to Africa in 1993, and subsequently the rise of new donors and/or actors from other parts of Asia, China, India, and including Malaysia.

SSC is also integral to Malaysia's foreign policy (Hazri, 2011), and has shaped the government's strategy for engagement with Africa. Underlying SSC, early contacts were established between Malaysia and Africa, during the late Cold War period, largely built around the axis of shared legacies of colonialism. Charting diplomatic history, the core argument forwarded in this chapter is that the development of relations between Malaysia and Africa since the 1970s has gone through a number of stages, oscillating from a common identity of a 'developing South' (Mawdsley, 2012) in the late Cold War era, to the outright hostility of Malaysia towards apartheid in South Africa, and finally the establishment of diplomatic ties in the post-apartheid era. Following this, full diplomatic relations between Malaysia and Africa were delayed until the 1990s. The connections between the two leading up to the establishment of full diplomatic relations were also sporadic.

It can be construed that the intermittent connections between Malaysia and Africa from the 1970s to 1990s may not have contributed much to the contemporary bilateral commercial relationship that has been developing through a strong trade–investment nexus since the beginning of the 1990s (UN, 2013). This chapter however argues that the present relationship between Malaysia and Africa is inextricably connected to the past. Specifically, legacies in colonialism have played out in ways that challenge and shape our understanding of modern contemporary relations between Malaysia and Africa, particularly South Africa. It can therefore be hypothesized

185

that early (historical) contacts and diplomacy have laid the foundations for the establishment of commercial links between the two.

Underlying SSC is also the idea that Malaysia and some African states have similar development policies. This is because Malaysia was appropriated as a developmental model for Africa, as it was one of the fastest growing economies in the world in the 1970–1990 period, while effecting wealth redistribution (Snodgrass, 1995). The defining characteristics of Malaysian policies that brought the country into focus in that period include the affirmative action programme under the New Economic Policy (NEP) for the period 1971–1990 (Lee, 2010), the push for export-oriented industrialization in the 1970s (Henley, 2015), and the embrace of privatization policy in 1983 together with public–private cooperation under the 'Malaysia Incorporated, approach to development. Much of this attention, it seems, was not substantially informed. Manifestations of divergence in development between Malaysia and Africa, despite following the Malaysian template, provoked debates as to whether the former is an appropriate comparator and developmental model for the latter. In the wake of these debates, which dominated scholarly writings, a new role emerged for Malaysia as a partner to development, with the establishment of commercial links with Africa in the 1990s. Taken together, it can be hypothesized that Malaysia may be redefining its position, not just as a role model for policy emulation, but as a partner to development with the continent.

These contentions, related to the influence of historical connections and the relevance of the role model story for contemporary Malaysia–Africa relations, give rise to several important questions:

- What constrained early diplomatic ties between Malaysia and Africa and how do past connections relate to modern diplomacy between the two?
- Why did a privileged relationship develop between Malaysia and South Africa in a comparative context, particularly with that of the African continent as a whole?
- Is Malaysia still relevant as a developmental role model for contemporary Africa?
- Does Malaysia hold the potential within Asia, namely the Association of Southeast Asian Nations (ASEAN), to pave the way as a partner to development?

This chapter provides an overall picture and evaluates the relationship between Malaysia (a 'second wave' SSC actor[1]) and the African states. Two dimensions are considered: diplomatic relations and commercial links through trade and investment. This chapter proceeds as follows. The next section reviews literary works on Malaysia–Africa that are shaped by the narrative of SSC. This is followed by an assessment of the political and economic engagement between Malaysia and Africa from the late Cold War era to the present context. The final section summarizes the core arguments related to the evolution of diplomacy between Malaysia and Africa, and concludes with the opportunities presented for Malaysia, within the ASEAN–Africa nexus, to push ahead with its engagement in the continent.

Previous literary works

Despite the growing diplomatic and commercial ties between Malaysia and Africa, there is a dearth of documented research between the two. Only a coterie of scholars analysed Malaysia (Southeast Asia[2]) and Africa (Henley, 2015, 2012, 2007; Lee, 2010, 2014, 2015; Van Donge, 2012; Van Donge et al., 2012; Dadzie, 2011; Haron, 2007; Muda, 1996; Hart, 1994) in the context of Asia–Africa, while the research on the relations between Northeast Asia (Japan, China, South Korea) and South Asia (India) with Africa is fairly documented (Rampa et al., 2012).

The following review of previous studies on Malaysia–Africa gives some credence to arguments about the South–South development linkages.

Early comparative studies between Malaysia with Ghana (Chhibber and Leechor, 1995), Cote d'Ivoire (Harrold et al., 1996) and Tanzania (Nyagetera, 1998) suggest some important policies for economic performance of the three African economies. In the case of Ghana, the applied lessons were higher spending for basic education and maintaining macroeconomic stability. The issues of macroeconomic stability, low inflation for encouraging saving and investment, and low exchange rates for maintaining exports were also emphasized for Cote d'Ivoire in the comparative analysis with Malaysia. The Malaysian experience was also considered relevant for creating an enabling investment environment for Zambia and managing diversity and governance for Tanzania. For that, Malaysia has provided development expertise for Zambia under the Japan International Cooperation Agency (JICA) (Jegathesan and Ohno, 2013), and for Tanzania as part of its own Malaysia Technical Cooperation Programme[3] (MTCP) initiative. Tanzania has adopted the Malaysian model of development, and has consulted Malaysian policymakers under the 'Big Results Now (BRN)'[4] 2013/2014 initiative (World Bank, 2014b) to transform the country into a middle-class economy (*The Citizen*, 12 April 2013).

Though many of the early comparative studies were policy-centric and provided lessons of experience, some contemporary works have been more critical in addressing the diverging paths of both regions. More recently, Van Donge (2012) and Kinuthia and Murshed (2015) examine the context of Kenya and Malaysia, two countries that embarked on similar development trajectories in the 1960s, but produced radically different outcomes. They argue that the divergent outcomes, comparatively, are the result of Malaysia's better access to development finance from national resources, better management of long-term financing and better capture of investment flows, relative to Kenya. Van Donge further qualifies that though both countries had similar governance problems, related largely to rent-seeking activities, better access to financing allows Malaysia to overcome governance matters. Henley (2015) further extends Van Donge's (2012) argument of divergent growth outcomes between Malaysia and Kenya. He agrees with Van Donge (2012) that though the two countries sought the 'capitalist road' to development, the stalled growth in Kenya relates to its constrained access to credit financing. However, he also stresses that policy failures in Kenya, in the form of the lack of investments in broad-based rural development and over-regulation of the economy, have contributed to its lacklustre performance.

Dadzie (2011) also takes on the issue of divergent growth trajectories between Malaysia and Ghana. Beyond political instability, Dadzie attributes the divergence to the absence of a connection between savings, investment and exports, poor investment in human development, a lack of diversification in economic activities, an absence of an entrepreneurial class, and the role of external capital in Ghana. He draws on the role of the developmental state in agricultural transformation (see also Van Donge et al., 2012) in Malaysia, more specifically, as a policy lesson for Ghana. Drawing on the transformation to the competition state model, instead, van der Westhuizen (1999) makes the case for patron–client rentierism (instead of corporatism as commonly perceived) in Malaysia and societal corporatism in South Africa as different tactical responses to conflicting pressures of international expectations (globalization) and domestic demands (growth with equity).

The general conclusions reached from previous comparative work between Southeast Asia and Africa (Harrold et al., 1996; Dibie, 1998; Nyagetera, 1998; Zeufack, 2002; Karshenas, 2001; Ansah, 2006; UNCTAD, 2007; Dadzie, 2011; David and Asuelime, 2015) are that many policy lessons can be derived from the former, for the latter. They include outward looking and market friendly trade and investment policies, prudent fiscal (low budget deficit) and monetary policies (low inflation, stable exchange rates), and other issues related to governance, transparency and accountability. Insofar as these comparative works continue in academic literature, they have become less popular, as there is much debate on replicating the Asian model, coupled with transferability of developmental lessons, given the constraints in Africa.

For example, Hart (1994) and Simpson (2005) contest the invocation of the Malaysian model on affirmative action as a case for post-apartheid South Africa to emulate, especially in a decontextualized or ahistorical fashion. Hart bases her argument on the divergent and problematic outcomes[5] of socially constructed racial classes that developed in Malaysia through aggressive state intervention. Lee (2014) concurs with Hart that a transferability of policies in this case is limited, since the context of affirmative action in Malaysia is led by a strong executive with minimal parliamentary accountability, while the regime in South Africa is more palatable as it is embedded in a democratic system. Following which, Lee opines that Malaysia could instead look at South Africa as a reference. Alternatively, Hart maintains that instead of a model, Malaysia could serve as a set of lenses, which can help to clarify the possibilities and limits of transformation in South Africa, through which debates on comparative models and international experience can be brought into sharper focus.

Soludo (2003) also questions the replicability of the Asian model of export-oriented industrialization and foreign direct investment (FDI) led growth to Sub-Saharan Africa (SSA), where infrastructure and institutional arrangements are relatively underdeveloped. Faced with different initial conditions and industrial challenges from developing Asia (see also Page, 2012), Soludo underscores the importance of fundamental transformations for this outlying region of SSA, namely through state intervention in industrial policy (see also Edwards, 1995) to create a conducive environment for business and investment. The failure of Africa to industrialize after several decades brought with it new thinking in Africa. The refrain is that 'African problems require African solutions'. Following which, the initial focus on modelling Africa after Southeast Asia has partly given way to attention on the constraints on Africa and understanding the implementation of Asian policies under those conditions (see also Henley, 2007, 2015).

From late Cold War connections to today's realities

Diplomatic bonds: historical context

Malaysia's contact with Africa during the late Cold War era remained limited because of the turmoil in the latter. The 1970s and 1980s marked a period of catastrophe for Africa, as it was saddled with major economic problems, such as declines in growth, dwindling production and trade, widening poverty and burgeoning foreign debt (Hamidin, 2003). Despite that, Malaysia followed closely the developments in Africa throughout the 1970s and 1980s, as it viewed Africa as a natural ally in its policy drive for cooperation within the global South. Their common identity as 'developing' nations, built on common experiences of 'colonial exploitation (or suppression), post-colonial inequality (see also Lee, 2010) and present vulnerability to uneven neo liberal globalization' (Mawdsley, 2012: 152) drew both parties together. Both states shared similar concerns that North–South relations were not working in the favour of the South, thereby leading to severe imbalances in the South. Malaysia firmly advocated for 'win-win' relations in the South–South context. Considering Africa's large presence in the developing South, it was therefore not surprising that Malaysia asked Mwalimu Julius Nyerere, the former President of the United Republic of Tanzania, to be the first chair of the newly established independent South–South Commission[6] (succeeded by the South Centre) in 1986.

Malaysia's engagement with Africa thereon was mostly through their joint participation in international organizations such as the Group of 15 (G15) and G77. Government-to-government level connections were strongly forged under the leadership of the then Prime Minister, Tun Dr Mahathir Mohamad, in the vanguard of South–South relations throughout the 1990s. Mahathir was active through the G15, to voice the concerns of the developing world. Interestingly, the G15 was another platform for Malaysia to engage with Sub-Saharan Africa, namely Zimbabwe, Kenya, Nigeria and Senegal, to jointly voice similar instances of discontent towards the West. In the Second Summit of the G15 in 1991, Mahathir and the Zimbabwe President jointly denounced the discriminatory trade tactics used by rich countries against the developing countries. Subsequently, in the Seventh Summit in 1997, where national priorities took centre stage, Mahathir voiced his displeasure towards foreign speculators, while Zimbabwe's President deplored the issue of destabilizing FDI flows (Sridharan, 1998).

On the national front, diplomatic links between Malaysia and Africa began in the early 1990s, as it was only at the end of the 1980s that Africa conceded to democratic rule following mounting pressures from domestic opposition and global influence. Specifically, the special partnership established between Malaysia and South Africa since the post-apartheid democratic era of the latter would not have emerged if not for the unique (and different) experiences of a shared oppressive colonialized history which brought both nation states together. The then Malaya was drawn into the political domain of pre-democracy South Africa's oppressive state from the 1960s, as it stood firmly against the latter's espoused apartheid doctrines. Malaya, under the first Prime Minister Tunku Abdul Rahman (1957–1970), strongly supported international action to end apartheid, and played a pivotal role in the withdrawal of South Africa from the Commonwealth in 1961 (Muda, 1996). Malaysia's vehement opposition to apartheid in the 1960s continued into the 1970s and 1980s under the premierships of Tun Abdul Razak (1970–1976), Tun Hussein Onn (1976–1981) and particularly Tun Mahathir Mohamad (1981–2003), who was exceptionally vocal about racial policies in South Africa during the transition period. Mahathir followed Tunku's aggressive approach and took up the apartheid issue at many international fora, including several Commonwealth Heads of Government Meetings (CHOGM) in 1985, 1987 and 1989, and was subsequently appointed to a committee to oversee South African matters. South Africa embraced democracy and this represented a turning-point in Malaysia–South Africa relations. Formal contacts were established with South Africa in 1991, ending the 30-year (1961–1990) adversarial (Haron, 2007) behaviour of Malaysia towards the apartheid state. Full diplomatic relations were then established between Malaysia and South Africa in 1993.

After the African National Congress (ANC) was unbanned in the early 1990s, the Malaysian ruling party, the United Malays' National Organization (UMNO) (and the Barisan Nasional or the National Front, successor to UMNO in 1974), promoted its initial interest in South Africa. The driving force of the inter-state links was the fact that UMNO shared a warm relationship with the liberation movement of the ANC; underlying this was also the strong bond of friendship that had developed between Mahathir and Mandela on a personal dimension. Malaysia's business or investment interests in South Africa in the immediate post-apartheid era (1993–1996) were therefore politically guided (Padayachee and Valodia, 1999). In turn, the Malaysian experience was used as a model for South African transformation[7] (Southall, 1997) in terms of racial reconciliation, affirmative action and economic reconstruction (Hart, 1994; Haron, 2007; Lee 2010, 2014, 2015). The ANC, in efforts to redress the apartheid legacy, was drawn to Malaysia's experience of *Bumiputra* (Malays and indigenous groups) empowerment under the NEP (1971–1990) to promote its own version of black economic empowerment (Ponte et al., 2006).

To further promote a bumiputra class with overseas ventures (or acquisitions), Mahathir articulated a framework for building political and economic relations between Malaysia and African countries, known as the Smart Partnership, launched in 1995. Consequently, bumiputra investments were promoted in Ghana in mid 1995, which Ansah (2006) refers to as the beginning of the era of the 'Rawlings–bumiputra' alliance. The 1997–1998 Asian Financial Crisis (AFC), however, was somewhat of a turning-point, as it created setbacks for some overseas ventures. It also raised questions about the sustainability of Malaysian investments in Africa. With the exception of Petronas, major investors such as Renong and Sime Darby (diversified conglomerates) reported huge losses in their investments in South Africa. The aftermath of the crisis clearly marked the dawning of economic and risk-based considerations for investments in the continent. Having said that, investment ties were not broken, as the internationalization of Malaysian businesses to the continent continued even in the aftermath of the crisis. This is because Malaysian companies that ventured overseas, including to Africa, were firms that had developed their capabilities over a long period and had established themselves in the local market.

During the onset and immediate aftermath of the AFC, Malaysia became preoccupied with its own internal affairs, namely the sacking of Deputy Prime Minister Anwar Ibrahim, the rift in the ruling party with the Mahathir–Anwar debacle, and finally the 1999 elections. Notwithstanding the chaotic developments in Malaysia between 1997 and 1999, for South Africa, Malaysia continued to be a good role model in ASEAN as it was able to weather both the internal and external problems and get the economy back on track (David & Asuelime, 2015).

Hence, Mahathir's successors, namely Abdullah Badawi (2003–2009) and (current) Najib Razak, have both maintained Malaysia's commitment to the developing South. In 2009, Najib launched a UNESCO–Malaysia trust fund to enhance SSC. This new initiative was focused on capacity building in education and science for the benefit of the least developed countries and small island states and in support of the Priority Africa agenda. Despite the lack of state-level visits, Najib's 2012 visit to South Africa to witness the hundredth anniversary of the ANC was considered significant for both countries. It is a reflection of Malaysia's continued support for the ANC since the post-apartheid era. Table 12.1 traces some of the developments between Malaysia and South Africa since the 1990s.

The historical diplomatic ties between Malaysia and Africa appear sporadic and erratic, as they were founded loosely on a shared identity of a developing status and common experiences of colonialization. This clearly was not sufficient to upgrade those relations into a strategic partnership. Despite the awareness of the importance of integrating with Southern partners, it was not until the past decade that weight was accorded to this relationship when economic considerations, apart from political direction, began to play a decisive role in the Malaysia–Africa connection. It is from this commercial context that some have begun to question whether the close partnership that had developed between both Malaysia and the continent throughout history can mature into a strategic relationship.

Commercial connections: changing landscape

The turn of the twenty-first century saw trade patterns shifting even more towards South–South trade[8] to address global imbalances. In 2005, the New Asian–African Strategic Partnership (NAASP) was established, with three core principles guiding the relationship: solidarity,

Table 12.1 Progressive developments between Malaysia and South Africa

Year	Event
May-90	Meeting between Mahathir Mohammad and Nelson Mandela in Nigeria.
Nov-90	BN hosted dinner for Nelson Mandela in Malaysia.
1991	Malaysia lifted people-to-people sanctions against South Africa.
1992	Malaysia set up a liaison office in Johannesburg.
Jan-93	Air Services Agreement signed between both states.
Nov-93	Full diplomatic ties established with South Africa.
Jan-94	South Africa established an Embassy in Malaysia (subsequently became a High Commission).
Aug-94	Malaysia bestowed the Tun Razak International Award on Nelson Mandela in Kuala Lumpur. MOU on concluding agreements that enhance trade and investment between Malaysia and South Africa.
Aug-95	Mahathir Mohammad visited South Africa.
Jul-96	First official visit of *Bumiputra* business elite to Ghana.
Nov-96	Memorandum of Understanding (MOU) on Defence Cooperation signed between both states.
Mar-97	Nelson Mandela visited Malaysia. Official launching of the Malaysia–South Africa Business Council (MSABC).
Mar-97	Trade Agreement and Agreement on Merchant Shipping and Related Maritime Matters signed between both states.
May-97	Mahathir Mohammad received the Order of the Cape of Good Hope from Nelson Mandela in Cape Town.
Jun-97	Agreement Governing the Exchange and Protection of Classified Information in the Field of Defence signed between both states.
Jun-99	South Africa appointed honorary consuls in the states of Penang and Sarawak.
May-00	The Asia–Africa Investment and Technology Promotion Centre (AAITPC) was established in Kuala Lumpur.
Sept-03	MOU concerning the Establishment of a Joint Commission for Economic, Scientific, Technical and Cultural Cooperation signed between both states.
Nov-04	Joint mission with Japan to South Africa (and other states) to study possibilities of new cooperation activities.
Jun-05	Abdullah Badawi visited South Africa.
Jul-05	Agreement for the Avoidance of Double Taxation and the Prevention of Fiscal Evasion with Respect to Taxes on Income signed between both states.
Jul-07	MOU on Agricultural Cooperation signed between both states.
Apr-11	Protocol Amending the 2005 Agreement between the states for the Avoidance of Double Taxation and the Prevention of Fiscal Evasion with Respect to Taxes on Income.
Jan-12	Najib Tun Razak's visit South Africa to witness the hundredth anniversary celebration of the ANC.
Sept-13	Jacob Zuma's visit to Malaysia to provide the keynote address at the Malaysia–South Africa Business Forum and to accept a Lifetime Campaigner for Peace and Freedom Award by the Mahathir Global Peace Foundation, on behalf of Nelson Mandela.

Sources: (1) Haron (2007). (2) Updated from media releases.

friendship and cooperation. The need to become less reliant on developed markets, apart from harnessing comparative advantage within the South–South untapped opportunities, was among the reasons for the this new wave of cooperation (Régnier, 2009). The South–South connection is also considered important for the transfer of appropriate, adaptable and affordable technology (World Bank, 2014a). This explains the sharp rise in trade between Asia[9] and Africa, rising from US$2.8 billion in 1990 to US$270 billion in 2012 (*The Straits Times*, 22 April 2015).

Africa is also becoming an important investment destination for ASEAN (Hutt, 2014). Malaysia has already emerged as the third largest investor (behind the United States and France) in Africa in 2011, with 24 per cent of its outward foreign direct investment (OFDI) or US$19.3 billion destined to the latter (UNCTAD, 2013). Surprisingly, Malaysia went ahead of China and India in terms of its size of OFDI to Africa. With its heavy investment footprint in the continent, MacPherson (2015a) argues that Malaysia is establishing an important dynamic in the ASEAN–Africa nexus. In fact, bilateral investment relations between Malaysia and Africa are long established, with the former being one of the first countries to invest in South Africa in 1994. In 1994, Malaysia's investment in South Africa stood at US$4.5 billion or 8 per cent of total OFDI to Africa (Padayachee and Valodia, 1999). Bilateral trade and investment in South Africa is poised to grow even further as South Africa considers Malaysia a hub for Southeast Asia (Farhaanah, 2015), while Malaysia looks to South Africa to make further inroads into Southern Africa. A commitment by both parties to push bilateral cooperation is reflected in the recent announcement to re-launch the South Africa–Malaysia Business Council, which was previously established in 1997.

Malaysian investments into the African continent transcend traditional North–South FDI patterns. It is strongly aided by the government to enhance political and economic diversification, to increase the resilience of the economy and reduce its dependence on traditional markets, under the promotion of SSC and mutual benefits. As recent as the run-up to the sixtieth anniversary of the 1955 Bandung Asia–Africa Summit in 2015, the government continued to express its commitment towards the SSC. Consequently, the Malaysian agenda has also been strongly driven by 13 diplomatic missions[10] on the continent and 16 African embassies and diplomatic missions in Malaysia (UN, 2013), which is robust compared with many of its ASEAN counterparts (MacPherson, 2015a, 2015b).

The case of Petronas's (wholly government-owned oil and gas company) investments in the oil fields of Sudan and Egypt and that of Telekom Malaysia's (government-linked telecommunications company) (divested) information and communication technology (ICT) operations in Malawi, Guinea and Ghana (UN, 2013) illustrate the support of the Malaysian government for its multinational corporation (MNC) ventures into Africa. Private entities have also followed suit to tap into the burgeoning investment opportunities on the continent, namely in sectors such as manufacturing and commodities trading, oil, gas and telecommunication, palm oil plantations, hotel and leisure, shipping, broadcasting and financial services.

FDI[11] relations between Malaysia and Africa are however unidirectional (as OFDI of Africa to Malaysia is limited), with Malaysian investors targeting African markets, mainly motivated by trade and demonstrating a strong trade–investment nexus. Though Malaysia's OFDI to Africa has fluctuated over the past two decades, it has generally trended upwards (Figure 12.1). While OFDI flows to Africa declined in 2012, Malaysia is still considered the largest developing country investor in Africa, ahead of China, when measured by OFDI stock (UNCTAD, 2014).

There has been some diversification of Malaysian investments in Africa, in terms of markets and types of investments. In 2004, the African host countries that had the largest OFDI stock

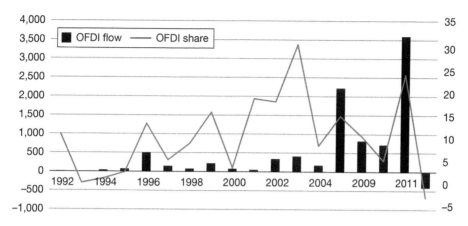

Figure 12.1 OFDI flows of Malaysia in Africa (US$ millions)

Notes: (1) Data is not available for 2005–2007. Latest data available is 2012. (2) Right axis: share of OFDI in total OFDI of Malaysia (%).

Source: UNCTAD (2014).

from Malaysia were Mauritius, followed by South Africa and Sudan (UNCTAD, 2007). Recent statistics show that Malaysia has expanded its investments into 6 of the 15 SSA (Sub-Saharan Africa) countries in the past three years. Now, Malaysia's FDI is highly dispersed geographically throughout Africa, including the less developed countries such as Chad, Guinea, Malawi, Mozambique and Tanzania. This stands in sharp contrast with the other major investors of Southeast Asia, namely Singapore, whose FDI in Africa is highly concentrated. Notably, recent investments by Malaysia into Africa are also largely infrastructure investments into the Eastern and Southern African sub-regions. MacPherson (2015b) points out that the rising infrastructure investments in Africa further open up a new wave of opportunity, as there are possibilities for linking Kuala Lumpur's Islamic finance community with the sponsors of these projects.

Table 12.2 shows some of the major Malaysian companies that have invested in Africa.

Petronas and Telekom Malaysia were responsible for more than 24 per cent of the total number of Southern mergers and acquisitions (M&As) purchases in the continent during the period 1987–2005 (UNCTAD, 2010). The involvement of Petronas in infrastructural projects in Africa was wholly linked to resource extraction (UN, 2013). For that same period, Malaysia recorded the largest number of M&As (57 per cent) by Southeast Asian economies. For the period 1991–2008, in cumulative terms, Malaysia recorded a lower contribution of 10 per cent of total cross-border M&As in African countries concluded by developing economy transnational corporations (UN, 2013).

Sime Darby was the first private Malaysian firm to venture into Africa, namely Liberia, in 2007. It invested in land for the oil palm sector. Other private companies have also ventured into the plantation sector in Africa for the following reasons: adequate land and labour availability to sustain new plantations; large market for edible oil selling at a premium; rising demand for palm oil from local biodiesel sector and for industrial use. The Malaysian private sector supports SSC within the framework of the National Chambers of Commerce and Industry (NCCIM) and has undertaken various initiatives to promote South–South cooperation. These activities are implemented through two South–South organizations set up by the private sector, namely, the Malaysian South–South Association (MASSA) and the Malaysian South–South Cooperation (MASSCORP).[12]

Table 12.2 Selected Malaysian companies in Africa

Companies	Type of Investment	Country
Petronas	oil and gas/infrastructure	Sudan, Egypt, Guinea, Mozambique, Niger, Somalia, South Africa Chad, Cameroon
Telekom Malaysia	telecommunications	Malawi, Guinea, Ghana
Malaysian Resources Corporation Bhd. (MRCB)	broadcasting	Ghana
Peremba Construction	infrastructure	Sudan
MMC Corporation Bhd.	infrastructure	Sudan
Nam Fatt Corporation	infrastructure	Sudan
Ranhill International Inc.	infrastructure	Tanzania, Sudan
Probase Manufacturing Sdn. Bhd.	infrastructure	Kenya
Pacific Inter-Link Sdn. Bhd	manufacturing/commodities trading	Ethiopia, Nigeria, Ghana
Wan's Gem Stones	semi-precious gemstones	South Africa
INS Trading	biotechnology	South Africa
Mitrajaya Development SA (Pty) Ltd	real estate/property	South Africa
Genting	hotels and leisure/ plantation/infrastructure	Mauritius, South Africa
Sime Darby	oil palm	Egypt, Tanzania, Tunisia, Liberia
IOI Corporation	oil palm/property/trading	Mauritius
ATAMA Plantations	oil palm	Congo
Kuala Lumpur Kepong	oil palm	Liberia
Malaysia International Shipping Corporation (MISC) Bhd.	shipping	Nigeria
Opus International	asset management	South Africa
Putera Capital	financial services	Ghana, Mozambique, Tanzania

Sources: (1) UN, 2013. (2) UNCTAD, 2007. (3) Compiled from media release.

Relations with Africa are undeniably driven by strictly commercial imperatives as Malaysia does not have a significant aid programme with the continent (UN, 2013). Market-seeking FDI (in countries with sizeable domestic markets such as Nigeria, South Africa and Egypt), apart from resource-seeking (extractive) FDI, is now driving the state and private sector to increase engagement with Africa. There is also a shift from just M&As to greenfield investments. The diversification is also observed in the sectors of investment and geographical dispersal of investments in the continent.

Similar to that with FDI, the trade relationship between Malaysia and Africa is highly imbalanced. Africa accounts for only 2 per cent of Malaysia's total trade. The asymmetric trade relations between Malaysia and Africa mirror those between Asia and Africa. Africa accounts for 3 per cent of Asia's trade flows, whereas Asia is 26 per cent of Africa's flows. Notwithstanding that, Malaysia's total trade with Africa had grown to a healthy 16 per cent for the period 1992 to 2013. Trade balances are in favour of Malaysia for the entire period of review (see Figure 12.2).

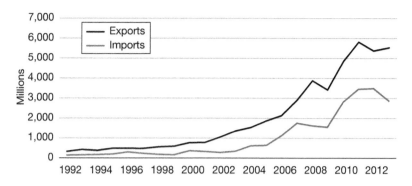

Figure 12.2 Malaysia–Africa trade, 1992–2013 (in US$ millions)
Source: UN COMTRADE.

Malaysia's trade with the continent is concentrated in certain markets.

South Africa is also both an important export destination and import source for Malaysia in manufactures. This is not surprising as within Southeast Asia, South Africa has built its strongest ties with Malaysia. South Africa is also recognized as the second largest developing country investor, after Malaysia, in Africa (UNCTAD, 2014). Another key point to note from Table 12.3 is that, though import sourcing was less geographically concentrated in the 12 major export partners of the continent in 1992 (20 per cent of total imports from Africa), now there is more import sourcing from the latter. This suggests greater two-way trade flows between Malaysia and its 12 top trading partners in Africa.

The composition of bilateral trade in Table 12.4 shows that Malaysian exports to Africa are dominated by agricultural commodities (47 per cent) and manufactures (38 per cent), while its imports from Africa constitute minerals (35 per cent). Palm oil dominates exports to Africa, while crude petroleum comprises the major import from the continent. Trade with the continent provides Malaysia with the opportunity to expand the variety of manufactured exports.

Conclusion

This chapter assessed Malaysia–Africa relations since the late Cold War. This chapter has demonstrated that historical precedents in Malaysia and Africa are important for understanding what drew Malaysia to the continent, the context in which initial contacts were established between the two, before blossoming into formal diplomatic relations and extending to economic diplomacy. The key findings of this chapter are summarized herein.

First, though Africa was featured prominently in Malaysia's foreign affairs agenda through its advocacy for SSC since the 1970s, contacts with Africa up to the 1990s were largely constrained by internal challenges in the continent and the apartheid rule in South Africa. Second, through the passage of time, Malaysia and South Africa enjoyed a special relationship. Relations between both nation states have their roots in a discordant relationship during the apartheid rule and strong party-to-party ties between UMNO and the ANC since the 1990s, followed by significant growth in bilateral trade and investments. The strengthening of economic ties, anchored in flows of trade and investment since the 1990s, appears to have found its beginnings in political diplomacy that is maturing into the next stage of economic diplomacy. Both findings support the first hypothesis formulated in the introductory section, that diplomatic history laid the foundation for commercial engagement between Malaysia and Africa.

Table 12.3 Malaysia–Africa: market concentration of trade (%)

Region	1992			2000			2005			2013		
	X	M	Total	X	M	Total	X	M	Total	X	M	Total
North	63.69	3.87	45.22	35.86	14.55	28.93	32.09	10.67	26.64	23.45	18.79	21.86
Central	2.24	3.60	2.66	1.64	0.94	1.41	3.58	5.10	3.97	12.37	14.24	13.01
West	17.33	16.27	17.01	13.10	11.29	12.51	21.37	24.94	22.28	31.20	28.88	30.41
South	0.00	0.00	0.00	33.41	60.68	42.28	30.69	45.52	34.46	15.78	29.97	20.61
East	16.54	76.26	34.98	13.95	11.45	13.14	10.24	12.90	10.92	13.51	7.84	11.58
Northeast	0.19	0.00	0.13	2.04	1.07	1.72	2.02	0.87	1.73	3.69	0.27	2.53
Major Partners												
South Africa	0.00	0.00	0.00	32.63	60.56	20.38	30.14	44.94	33.91	15.55	29.72	20.38
Nigeria	13.77	4.28	10.84	6.40	2.07	8.22	9.84	2.05	7.86	7.00	10.59	8.22
Egypt	46.47	0.66	32.32	29.32	4.21	12.47	24.57	5.78	19.78	15.55	6.50	12.47
Benin	0.88	0.06	0.63	0.21	0.21	0.21	1.41	0.14	1.09	9.29	0.14	6.17
Angola	8.73	0.00	0.02	0.24	0.00	0.16	1.23	0.00	0.92	8.42	1.75	6.15
Kenya	0.70	3.40	1.54	4.05	1.92	3.36	2.77	1.05	2.33	5.04	0.18	3.39
Togo	0.07	2.46	0.81	0.81	0.73	0.79	2.69	0.22	2.06	6.05	0.00	3.99
Cote d'Ivoire	0.85	5.92	2.41	1.16	3.22	1.83	0.32	5.22	1.57	1.79	11.85	5.22
Libya	2.67	2.83	2.72	0.58	4.33	1.80	0.87	1.76	1.09	0.69	7.80	3.11
Congo	0.06	0.00	0.04	0.77	0.00	0.52	0.89	0.00	0.66	1.33	7.52	3.44
Ghana	0.82	0.45	0.70	3.12	0.97	2.42	3.60	7.74	4.65	3.16	4.88	3.75
Algeria	8.73	0.00	6.03	2.57	1.43	2.20	2.74	0.12	2.08	2.59	3.38	2.86
Total	83.75	20.06	58.06	81.87	79.64	54.36	81.07	69.02	78.00	76.47	84.31	79.15

Notes: (1) X – exports; M – imports. (2) Only the 12 top countries are considered of the 53 countries in the continent.

Source: Calculated from UN COMTRADE.

Table 12.4 Malaysia–Africa: product concentration of trade (%)

		X	M	X	M	X	M	X	M
South Africa	**Agri**	**0.00**	**0.00**	**24.64**	**14.04**	**19.14**	**14.53**	**16.77**	**11.77**
	Mining	**0.00**	**0.00**	**0.04**	**2.10**	**0.36**	**8.29**	**9.33**	**29.02**
	Manu	**0.00**	**0.00**	**75.33**	**83.85**	**80.50**	**77.18**	**73.90**	**59.21**
Nigeria	**Agri**	**41.21**	**0.07**	**54.47**	**1.51**	**1.42**	**68.84**	**37.95**	**13.60**
	Mining	**0.00**	**7.56**	**12.15**	**92.32**	**0.00**	**6.45**	**19.14**	**82.50**
	Manu	**58.79**	**92.37**	**33.38**	**6.18**	**98.58**	**24.71**	**42.92**	**3.91**
Egypt	**Agri**	**78.80**	**45.59**	**65.80**	**19.42**	**55.30**	**17.27**	**50.81**	**12.04**
	Mining	**0.03**	**0.76**	**0.00**	**11.23**	**0.02**	**24.41**	**4.77**	**53.87**
	Manu	**21.17**	**53.65**	**34.20**	**69.35**	**44.68**	**58.32**	**44.42**	**34.09**
Benin	Agri	35.35	0.00	78.70	0.00	94.91	0.00	95.59	1.03
	Mining	0.00	0.00	0.00	0.00	0.00	0.00	0.00	0.00
	Manu	64.65	100.00	21.30	100.00	5.09	100.00	4.41	98.97
Angola	Agri	0.00	100.00	33.01	0.00	52.83	82.73	39.46	0.11
	Mining	0.00	0.00	0.00	0.00	0.00	0.00	34.42	88.47
	Manu	100.00	0.00	66.99	0.00	47.17	17.27	26.12	11.42
Kenya	Agri	7.33	0.86	53.69	30.90	49.84	28.58	29.35	82.66
	Mining	0.00	0.00	0.00	0.00	4.20	14.49	45.21	0.08
	Manu	92.67	99.14	46.31	69.10	45.96	56.93	25.44	17.26
Togo	Agri	9.76	0.00	94.42	0.00	96.47	32.76	43.40	85.11
	Mining	0.00	0.00	0.00	0.00	0.00	0.00	53.90	0.00
	Manu	90.24	100.00	5.58	100.00	3.53	67.24	2.70	14.89
Cote d'Ivoire		5.23	1.57	62.17	7.41	13.56	85.77	54.97	43.87
	Mining	0.00	0.78	0.00	1.80	0.00	0.00	0.01	0.00
	Manu	94.77	97.65	37.83	90.78	86.44	14.23	45.03	56.13
Libya	Agri	0.45	0.00	3.40	0.00	16.63	0.00	12.92	0.00
	Mining	0.00	0.00	0.00	0.00	0.00	0.00	0.21	99.81
	Manu	99.55	100.00	96.60	100.00	83.37	100.00	86.87	0.19
Congo	Agri	41.36	0.00	0.88	0.00	60.99	0.00	76.11	0.30
	Mining	0.00	0.00	0.00	0.00	0.72	0.00	1.97	96.42
	Manu	58.64	0.00	99.12	0.00	38.29	100.00	21.92	3.28
Ghana	Agri	0.91	1.87	5.09	95.88	75.79	99.18	72.36	98.45
	Mining	0.00	47.42	0.00	0.00	0.05	0.00	0.01	0.00
	Manu	99.09	50.72	94.91	4.12	24.16	0.82	27.63	1.55
Algeria	Agri	97.47	0.00	67.45	0.00	42.18	7.77	43.62	0.02
	Mining	0.00	0.00	0.00	61.10	0.00	0.00	0.00	99.98
	Manu	2.53	0.00	32.55	38.90	57.82	92.23	56.38	0.00
Total	Agri	56.91	2.26	41.24	13.37	38.06	24.65	46.95	19.27
	Mining	0.02	9.68	1.36	7.07	1.05	9.98	14.60	45.94
	Manu	43.07	88.05	57.39	79.56	60.89	65.37	38.45	34.78

Source: Calculated from UN COMTRADE.
Notes: (1) Agri – agriculture; Manu – manufacturing. (2) HS – Harmonized System. (3) HS01-HS24 – Agriculture; HS25-HS27 – Mining; HS28-HS99 – Manufacturing. (4) Only the 12 top countries are considered of the 53 countries in the continent.

Third, in the process of this evolving relationship, Africa, which was initially inspired by the Malaysian developmental model of the 1970s and 1980s, is now engaging with Malaysia more as a development assistance provider and partner to trade and investment. Discourses on the Malaysian developmental model have also come into sharp focus, that it cannot be fully mimicked, nor fully discarded. Malaysia therefore still remains relevant to Africa in as much that experiences in state-led economic development continue to provide some policy relevance to the latter. The evidence is in favour of the second hypothesis that Malaysia is defining its initial position as a role model for emulation to new partnership for Africa's development.

Fourth, Malaysia is already establishing itself as an important player in the ASEAN-Africa nexus. The pursuit of economic diplomacy is directing the Malaysia–South Africa relationship to a level of a strategic partnership, as explained below:

- Malaysia has established the strongest distinctive ties with South Africa, a major player in the continent. The South Africa connection is important for Malaysia to make further inroads into the southern region, which is also the largest regional import source of Malaysia within the continent, and an important link with ASEAN through the Southern Africa Development Community (SADC).
- South Africa retains a special position in Malaysia's bilateral trade with the continent because of its high concentration of manufactured exports to Malaysia. The prominence of two-way trade in manufactures with South Africa holds the potentials for Malaysia to balance trade with its largest trading partner, relative to that with the other African countries. This will certainly pave the way for deeper integration between the two.
- Malaysia's recent emergence as the largest investor from developing Asia in the continent is only half the story of its engagement with Africa. More importantly, the sectoral and geographical diversification of its investments in the continent reflects the growing interest of the private sector in exploring markets beyond ASEAN. It also puts Malaysia ahead of the other major ASEAN investors, such a Singapore, that are no match for its diverse undertakings in the continent.

Notes

1 De Renzio and Seifert (2014) distinguished SSC actors into SSC leaders and second wave of SSC actors. The latter refers to 'a set of smaller middle-income countries with a more recent engagement in development activities; they remain more limited in size and scope when compared to the former'.
2 In fact, Henley (2015) argued for comparative work between Southeast Asia and Africa relative to other parts of Asia, given their important similarities and relevance of the policy experience of the former for developing economies in Africa. However, the emphasis has been on Indonesia (Dibie, 1998), Thailand (Chhibber and Leechor, 1995; Harrold et al., 1996) and Vietnam as comparators for Africa.
3 Malaysia's major initiative for SSC was through the establishment of the MTCP in 1978, officially launched in 1980. The programme was established to provide support through training and assistance in institutional development, particularly planning and financial skills.
4 The BRN initiative is the proverbial leaf taken out of the Malaysian book entitled 'Big Fast Results (BFR)'.
5 The divergence refers to the contrasting mechanisms for affirmative action (Lee, 2015), while the problematic outcomes include rent seeking behaviour and political patronage (van der Westhuizen, 1999).
6 A commission of independent high-level experts from the South set up by developing countries to review the South's development experience and make recommendations on the development strategy for developing countries in the post-Cold War era.

7 Many questioned the application of the Malaysian model to the South African context given the huge differences in terms of the following: growth with redistribution and transformation of the economy; revenue from natural resources; policies related to growth; role of civil society (Padayachee and Valodia, 1999).

8 In 2013, South–South trade accounted for US$5 trillion, a magnitude close to that of North–North trade (UNCTAD, 2015).

9 The source of Southern FDI is dominated by Asia (World Bank, 2014a).

10 This includes 8 embassies (Algeria, Guinea, Egypt, Libya, Morocco, Senegal, Sudan, Zimbabwe) and 5 consulates (Ghana, Kenya, Namibia, Nigeria, South Africa).

11 Worth noting here is that FDI data by origin, destination and sector is not readily available (see also World Bank, 2014a).

12 MASSA's main objective is to promote economic and trade relations between Malaysia and other developing countries while that of MASSCORP, as MASSA's investment arm, is to develop investment linkages with countries of the South.

Bibliography

Ansah, E.S. (2006). Close encounter between Africa and Asia: Ghana's look East policy and the making of Malaysia's overseas investors, unpub. PhD thesis, University of Amsterdam.

Chhibber, A. and Leechor, C. (1995). From adjustment to growth in Sub-Saharan Africa: the lessons of East Asian experience applied to Ghana, *Journal of African Economies*, 4(1): 83–114.

Dadzie, R.B. (2011). Developmental State and agriculture for development: Lesson for Ghana from East Asia, unpub. PhD thesis, University of Missouri-Kansas City.

David, O.J. and Auselime, L.E. (2015). The theory and practice of the developmental state: a comparative assessment of South Africa's and Malaysia's development, paper presented at the Regional Conference on Building Democratic Development States for Economic Transformation in South Africa, 20–22 July, Pretoria.

de Renzio, P. and Seifert, J. (2014). South–South cooperation and the future of development assistance: mapping actors and options, *Third World Quarterly*, 35(10): 1860–1875.

Dibie, R. (1998). Cross-national economic development in Indonesia and Nigeria, *Scandinavian Journal of Development Alternatives and Area Studies*, 17(1): 65–85.

Edwards, C. (1995). East Asia and industrial policy in Malaysia: lessons for Africa?, in H. Stein (ed.), *Asian Industrialization and Africa: Studies in Policy Alternatives to Structural Adjustment*, Basingstoke: MacMillan, pp. 239–256.

Hamidin, A.H. (2003). In pursuit of equality Malaysia–Africa relations in the 1990s, *Jati*, 8: 67–84.

Haron, M. (2007). South Africa and Malaysia: Identity and history in South–South relations, unpub. PhD thesis, Rhodes University.

Harrold, P., Jayawickrama, M. and Bhattasali, D. (1996). Practical lessons for Africa from East Asia in industrial and trade policies, World Bank Discussion Paper No. 310, World Bank: Washington, DC.

Hart, G. (1994). The new economic policy and redistribution in Malaysia: a model for post-apartheid South Africa? *Transformation*, 23: 44–59.

Henley, D. (2007). Chalk and cheese? Africa and the lessons for Asian development, paper presented at the Fifth International Convention of Asian Scholars, 2–5 August, Kuala Lumpur.

Henley, D. (2015). *Asia–Africa Development Divergence: A Question of Intent*, Zed Books: London.

Jegathesan, J. and Ono, M. (2013). Strategic action initiatives for economic development: trade and investment promotion in Zambia, in K. Ohno and I. Ohno (eds.), *Eastern and Western Ideas for African Growth: Diversity and Complementarity in Development Aid*, London and New York: Routledge, pp. 205–228.

Karshenas, M. (2001). Agriculture and economic development in sub-Saharan Africa and Asia, *Cambridge Journal of Economics*, 25: 315–342.

Kinuthia, B.K. and Murshed, S.M. (2015). FDI determinants: Kenya and Malaysia compared, *Journal of Policy Modeling*, 37: 388–400.

Lee, H-A (2010). Racial inequality and affirmative action in Malaysia and South Africa, unpub. PhD thesis, University of Massachusetts Amherst.

Lee, H-A (2014). Affirmative action regime formation in Malaysia and South Africa, *Journal of Asian and African Studies*, DOI: 10.1177/0021909614550895.

Lee, H-A (2015). Affirmative action in Malaysia and South Africa: contrasting structures, continuing pursuits, *Journal of Asian and African Studies*, 50(5): 615–634.

MacPherson, R. (2015a). Malaysia's economic push in Africa: pathfinder for ASEAN? RSIS Commentary 196, Singapore: Rajaratnam School of International Studies (RSIS), Nanyang Technological University.

MacPherson, R. (2015b). Malaysia ramping up in Africa, ISEAS Perspective No. 54, Singapore: ISEAS Yusof Ishak Institute.

Mawdsley, E. (2012). *From Recipients to Donors: Emerging Powers and the Changing Development Landscape*, London and New York: Zed Books.

Muda, M. (1996). Malaysia–South Africa relations and the commonwealth, 1960–95, *The Round Table*, 85(340): 423–439.

Nyagetera, B.M. (1998). Malaysian economic development: some lessons for Tanzania, *UTAFITI*, 4: 1–30.

Padayachee, V. and Valodia, I. (1998). Malaysian investment in South Africa: some initial observations, *Economic and Political Weekly*, 33(38): 2435–2437.

Padayachee, V. and Valodia, I. (1999). Malaysian investment in South Africa: South–South relations in a globalizing environment? *Journal of Contemporary African Studies*, 17(2): 287–297.

Page, J. (2012). Can Africa industrialize? *Journal of African Economies*, 21(2): ii86–ii125.

Ponte, S., Roberts, S. and van Sittert, L. (2006). To BEE or not to BEE? South Africa's Black Economic Empowerment (BEE), corporate governance and the state in the South, DIIS Working Paper No. 2006/27, Copenhagen: Danish Institute for International Studies.

Proksch, M. (2008). Asian-African trade and investment cooperation, *Asia-Pacific Trade and Investment Review*, 4: 141–153.

Rampa, F., Bilal, S. and Sidiropoulos, E. (2012). Leveraging South–South cooperation for Africa's development, *South African Journal of International Affairs*, 19(2): 247–269.

Régnier, P. (2009). New development of agro-food small business linkages between Southeast Asia and Western Africa, *Journal of the Asia Pacific Economy*, 14(3): 227–245.

Sesay, A., Olusola, O.K. and Omotosho, M. (2013). Africa and South–South cooperation: opportunities and challenges, in J. Dargin (ed.), *The Rise of the Global South: Philosophical, Geopolitical and Economic Trends of the 21st Century*, Singapore: World Scientific, pp. 95–123.

Simpson, R.A. (2005). Government intervention in the Malaysia eonomy, 1970–1990: lessons for South Africa, unpub. Master of Public Administration thesis, University of the Western Cape.

Snodgrass, D.R. (1995). Successful economic development in a multi-ethnic society: the Malaysian case, Development Discussion Paper No. 503, Cambridge, MA: Harvard Institute for International Development (HIID), Harvard University.

Soludo, C. (2003). Export-oriented industrialization and FDI in Africa, in E. Aryeetey, J. Court, M. Nissanke, and B. Weder (eds.), *Asia and Africa in the Global Economy*, Tokyo, New York, Paris: United Nations University Press, pp. 247–281.

Southall, R. (1997). Party dominance and development: South Africa's prospects in the light of Malaysia's experience, *Commonwealth & Comparative Politics*, 35(2): 1–27.

Sridharan, K. (1998). G-15 and South–South cooperation: promise and performance, *Third World Quarterly*, 19(3): 357–374.

UN (2013). *Infrastructure Development within the Context of Africa's Cooperation with New and Emerging Development Partners*, Ethiopia: United Nations.

UNCTAD (2007). *Asian Foreign Direct Investment in Africa: Towards a New Era of Cooperation among Developing Countries*, Geneva: United Nations Conference on Trade and Development.

UNCTAD (2010). *South–South Cooperation: Africa and the New Forms of Development Partnership*, Geneva: United Nations Conference on Trade and Development.

UNCTAD (2013). *World Investment Report 2013: Global Value Chains – Investment and Trade for Development*, Geneva: United Nations Conference on Trade and Development.

UNCTAD (2014). *Bilateral FDI Statistics 2014*, Geneva: United Nations Conference on Trade and Development.

UNCTAD (2015). *Key Statistics and Trends in International Trade 2014*, Geneva: United Nations Conference on Trade and Development.

van der Westhuizen, J. (1999). Malaysia, South Africa and the marketing of the competition State: globalization and States' response, unpub. PhD thesis, Dalhousie University, Halifax, Nova Scotia.

Van Donge, J.K. (2012) Governance and access to finance for development: an explanation of divergent development trajectories in Kenya and Malaysia, *Commonwealth & Comparative Politics,* 50(1): 53–74.

Van Donge, J.K., Henley, D. and Lewis, P. (2012). Tracking development in Southeast Asia and Sub-Saharan Africa: the primacy of policy, *Development Policy Review*, 30(S1): 5–24.

World Bank (2014a). Foreign direct investment flows in Sub-Saharan Africa, March, Washington DC: World Bank.

Zeufack, A. (2002). Export performance in Africa and Asia's manufacturing: evidence from firm-level data, *Journal of African Economies*, 10(3): 258–281.

Magazines, press releases

The Citizen (2013). Tanzania: implementation of Malaysia model "set to start soon", 12 April. Available at: http://www.trademarksa.org/news/tanzania-implementation-malaysia-model-set-start-soon

Farhaanah, M. (2015). S. Africa – Malaysia trade relations show substantial growth over the last 20 years, CNBCAFRICA.com, 12 February. Available at: http://www.cnbcafrica.com/news/southern-africa/2013/08/27/south-africa-malaysia-trade-relations-show-substantial-growth-over-the-last-20-years/

Hazri, H. (2011). Malaysia's South–South Cooperation leaves lasting effects far and wide, The Asia Foundation, 30 November. Available at: http://asiafoundation.org/in-asia/2011/11/30/malaysias-south–south-cooperation-leaves-lasting-effects-far-and-wide/

Hutt, D. (2014). The-not-so-dark-continent, Southeast Asia Globe Magazine, Ocotber 8. Available at: http://sea-globe.com/dark-continent-africa-asean-trade-southeast-asia-globe/

The Straits Times (2015). New council to boost trade between Asia and Africa, 22 April. Available at: http://www.straitstimes.com/asia/new-council-to-boost-trade-between-asia-and-africa

World Bank (2014b). How Tanzania plans to achieve "Big Results Now" in education, 14 July. Available at: http://www.worldbank.org/en/news/feature/2014/07/10/how-tanzania-plans-to-achieve-big-reforms-now-in-education

13

NAVIGATING THE ONE CHINA POLICY

South Africa, Taiwan and China

Ross Anthony and Yejoo Kim

Introduction

A crucial aspect of sovereign state identity is official recognition from other states. Over the past half century, Taiwan has witnessed a massive decrease in international recognition. The end of the Cold War and the rise of China played an important role in Taiwan's losing of official alliances. Taiwan's status in the international arena has become increasingly limited along with the rise of China as a global superpower. Beijing's One China policy has now gained international acceptance and is embedded as a norm. Worldwide, Taiwan only has official political relations with 21 countries (although Taipei has over 100 overseas offices, acting as de facto embassies, around the world). In Africa, diplomatic competition has led to an obvious victory for the People's Republic of China (PRC). For instance, when China and Taiwan variously hosted consultative forums with African states, 48 African countries' presidents attended the PRC-held 2006 Forum on China–Africa Co-operation (FOCAC), as opposed to 5 African heads of state for the 2007 Taiwan–Africa Summit.

At the time of writing, in 2017, Taipei maintains diplomatic relations with only Burkina Faso and Swaziland; even amongst these countries, the relationship is fragile; for instance in December 2016, São Tomé and Príncipe switched allegiance to the Republic of China.[1]

One of Taiwan's strongest allies on the continent, through the 1970s, 80s and 90s, was South Africa, an equally outcast state. However, with the fall of apartheid and the takeover by the socialist-leaning African National Congress (ANC) government, ties with the PRC were established – a prerequisite of which was the severing of diplomatic relations with Taiwan – and the two parties have drawn even closer through bilateral as well as multilateral mechanisms. Both China and South Africa have strengthened their common identity as representatives of the Global South. Nevertheless, South Africa has continued to engage with Taiwan on a number of levels. While both numbers of Taiwanese in South Africa, as well as economic engagement between the two entities, decreased in subsequent years, Taiwan has nevertheless managed to maintain a working relationship with South African officials and business community. Pre-existing relations are mobilised in order to continue trade and investment activities in South Africa. In fact, Taiwan has been able to maintain robust trade relations with many countries while quietly scaling back on diplomatic efforts to win recognition.

The primary question which this chapter seeks to address is what kind of relationship Taiwan has had with South Africa following its diplomatic switch to the PRC. In addressing the question, the work is situated within the context of an increasingly economically liberal global context in which issues of state sovereignty and economic realism are decoupled. This relationship can be situated within the broader, post-Cold War phenomenon of economic pragmatism, in which it was no longer solely 'the state' which dictated relations but rather a host of other actors. The persistence of Taiwanese engagement has stemmed not only from pragmatism on the South African side, but also from the Mainland itself: its integration into global markets over the past several decades has witnessed a parallel degree of economic integration with Taiwan (which far surpasses any equal achievement in the political realm). This increasing economic interdependency, which overlooks political constraints, is echoed in China's foreign policy regarding Taiwan. In South Africa, the PRC and the Republic of China (ROC) are agencies of economic statecraft which effectively derive from growing liberalised cross-strait economic relations. As such, South Africa's relationship with Taiwan is demonstrative of how transitional market economies, both in Africa and East Asia, are adept at side-stepping political issues when engaging in economic activity.

This chapter begins by situating the relationship within the broader geopolitical context of the 1980s and 1990s, in which several East Asian countries (the East Asian Tigers) became formidable economic powerhouses and China increasingly began to integrate itself into the global market economy. Simultaneously, it traces South Africa's transition from the isolated apartheid regime into a constitutive democracy which was also integrating itself into the global economic market system. Within this context, it then moves on to outlining the Taiwan–South Africa relationship and then examining the transition which South Africa underwent in terms of switching recognition from Taiwan to the PRC; South Africa's post-1997 relationship with the PRC is also discussed. The work then goes on to examine the afterlife of the Taiwan–South Africa relationship, through highlighting in particular the sustained economic engagement between the two entities, despite political non-recognition. Here, it is highlighted that the PRC permits this interaction insofar as it poses no penalties on the South African government for doing so. The final section reflects on this kind of economic pragmatism within the broader context of global market actors generally but with specific reference to the China–Taiwan relationship, which, in effect, is not that different from the Taiwan–South Africa relationship: namely, a robust attitude to trade and investment despite virtually irresolvable political issues. Thus, the pragmatism of Taiwan–South African relations is a manifestation of the kind of economic pragmatism that China exerts on a more global scale.

South African–East Asian liberalism

Francis Fukuyama (1989) famously declared that, following the end of the Cold War, the vast majority of nation states would embrace the norms of democracy and capitalist economies. Within Asia, China was one of the major global countries rolling back on communist ideology and embarking on a series of economic reforms. When post-apartheid South Africa, itself integrating into the global economic sphere, reached out for new development partners, East Asia was one of the recipients. A series of high level visits took place during the 1990s. President Mandela visited Japan and South Korea in July 1995, after diplomatic relations with Japan, which had started in January 1992, had become full relations in 1994 after the lifting of UN sanctions against apartheid South Africa. Then Deputy President Thabo Mbeki visited Japan and South Korea in 1998, explicitly speaking of the inspiration the African Renaissance gained from the Meiji Restoration in Japan (Alden, 2002), which triggered Japan's modernisation in the late nineteenth century. East Asia, with its flourishing economies and rapid economic development, promised to offer insights which would generate broad-based economic development. After the Cold War, and at a time when the African continent sought growth models after depressing experiences with (failed) structural adjustment dictates in the 1980s, East Asia and its 'Tiger states' clearly were en vogue in the 1990s. This interest was somewhat interrupted by the Asian Financial Crisis in 1997, yet saw a new surge with a China-specific focus in the first decade of the twenty-first century.

Along with the economic interest from South Africa, political developments were a crucial backdrop to the interest in East Asia. The change towards democracy in South Africa happened a few years after Asian people power movements led to a surge in democratisation in Asia in the late 1980s (e.g. Taiwan, South Korea, the Philippines). Additionally, this happened only a few years after the Tiananmen Square protests in Beijing and the crackdown of 1989. The PRC had resisted the global fall of communist political systems by violent means while liberalising its economy, making it a difficult partner for cooperation. In this context, in the mid-1990s, the first post-apartheid South African government under President Nelson Mandela did not immediately recognise the PRC. Rather, as a continuation of past policies, it initially maintained linkages with Taiwan, which – similar to other Asian countries – had become a multi-party democracy in the 1980s. This continuation was despite early contacts with Beijing already by the then-apartheid regime in 1991 (Shelton, 2008), but in line with a rather idealist new South African foreign policy, stipulating 'that just and lasting solutions to the problems of humankind can only come through the promotion of democracy worldwide' (Mandela, 1993). A realignment of South Africa's foreign policy in East Asia became increasingly unavoidable for realist reasons; China, whose economic clout was growing dramatically, was one of the veto powers in the United Nations Security Council (UNSC). China reported an unprecedented growth in its economy and great progress in reducing absolute poverty, making the country an indispensable regional – and also global – power. Reasons for and against diplomatic recognition of the PRC were thus a focal point of obvious tension between idealist goals and realist demands in South Africa's nascent foreign policy during the Mandela government. South African post-apartheid foreign policy has been viewed in some quarters as overtly idealistic and inflexible (Le Pere & van Nieukerk, 2004).

Taiwanese recognition

The literature on Taiwan's relations with Africa is comparatively thin, including work on Taiwan's, 'dollar diplomacy' in its diplomatic tug of war with the PRC (Taylor, 2002). More recently Rich & Banerjee (2015) reaffirm this, by arguing that economic factors have, at least in the post-World War II era, trumped political factors in establishing diplomatic relations. Within the context of South Africa–Taiwan relations, Pickles & Woods (1989) offer an overview of Taiwan's economic engagements in South Africa in the 1980s and how this dovetailed with the South African domestic policy of industrialisation in the 'homelands'. One of the most comprehensive volumes on Taiwan–Africa relations is an unpublished Doctoral thesis by San-shuin Tseng which covers the various African regions, examines the various types of diplomacy and scrutinises different political periods up until 2004, with a detailed narrative on the trajectory of Taiwan–South Africa relations. Taylor (2006) includes a history and analysis of Taiwan–South African relations in his monograph 'China and Africa: engagement and compromise', while Alden (1997) has written on the transition period in South Africa from 1994 onward, in which South Africa embarked on the lengthy process of switching diplomatic recognition from Taiwan to the PRC. There has been very little written on Taiwan–South African relations following South Africa's switch of allegiance (Davies, 1998; Grimm et al., 2014).

Competition for international diplomatic recognition between the PRC and Taiwan has been ongoing, with the position of Taiwan becoming increasingly marginalised on the international stage compared with Taipei's 'golden era' (1950–1971) when Taipei could maintain 197 bilateral treaties (Van Vranken Hickey, 2007). The diplomatic battle between the two Chinas entered a critical phase when the UN General Assembly passed UN Resolution 2758 which stated that the PRC is the only legitimate government of China on 25 October 1971. Afterwards the PRC became a permanent member of the Security Council of the UN. China's return to the UN resulted in a setback for Taipei in that a number of countries immediately severed diplomatic relations with the ROC: it experienced 40 cut-offs by 1975 and eventually lost its seat in a number of international bodies. Finally, the competition seemingly ended in favour of the PRC when the United States switched official bilateral ties to Beijing in 1979 (Van Vranken Hickey, 2007).

Africa, one of the largest voting blocs in the UN, became a diplomatic battleground for both sides during the Cold War. In the 1990s, along with the end of the Cold War, African leaders, who suddenly lost support from both the West and the East, saw the competition between the PRC and the ROC as a good opportunity to enhance their bargaining power. Most African countries preferred to maintain relations with both the PRC and the ROC, as they did not view legitimacy as a critical matter. Beijing strictly followed the principle of One China; however some African leaders realised that they could 'play off' the two Chinas against one another (Taylor, 2002). In this context, the foreign policies of the two Chinas were labelled as 'dollar diplomacy' or 'checkbook diplomacy', and was often linked to funding corrupt leaders (Taylor, 2002).[2]

Diplomatic relations between the ROC and South Africa, starting in 1949, were strengthened by the common stance of being staunchly anticommunist in their foreign policy. Apartheid South Africa was suspicious of the encroachment of the PRC and Soviet-backed socialist states in Southern Africa. This was matched by Nationalist Taiwan's sustained vigilance against the Communist Mainland (Pickles & Woods, 1989). From the early 1980s onwards, the relationship developed rapidly, based on the economic interests of both countries. Up until this time, Taiwan, as was the case with other East Asian developmental states such as South Korea, coupled intensive state funding on education, agriculture and infrastructure, with cheap, labour-intensive manufacturing of goods such as textiles and toys and later heavy industry, infrastructure and advanced electronics.

Over time, the relationship between the ROC and South Africa was strengthened by both parties' political and economic interests. The growing international isolation of both countries in the 1970s became the political catalyst which reinforced the diplomatic relations. Major blows, namely the international de-recognition of Taiwan and the growing international condemnation of the despised apartheid regime, further strengthened the relationship between the two, which was upgraded to full diplomatic relations with full embassies (Alden, 1997). From the early 1980s onwards, the economic interests of the ROC and South Africa further cemented their relationship. Then Taiwan started losing its competitive edge in the light manufacturing sector at home, Taiwanese investors sought a new production base with low labour wages as well as a new market and South Africa became one of their destinations (Pickles & Woods, 1989). The concurrent economic liberalisation of Mainland China during this period also played a role insofar as Taiwanese entrepreneurs began moving their manufacturing bases across the strait, due to lower wages. At this stage, China was but one geographical location, with Taiwan also moving its businesses to other low-cost countries; as such South Africa became an attractive destination (Pickles & Woods, 1989).

South Africa, on the other hand, urgently needed foreign investment in the wake of increasing and economically painful international sanctions. In the 1980s, the government embarked on an industrial decentralisation policy to further their aims of segregation: the policy was designed to attract labour-intensive industry to the region's African 'homelands'; in doing so, it sought to limit the growth of the black population in metropolitan areas. While the policy attracted a number of investors from Hong Kong, South Korea and Israel, it was the Taiwanese investors who ranked first in terms of the amount of investment and job creation they could provide (Pickles & Woods, 1989). The South African government offered additional support to the Taiwanese by easing immigration procedures and providing them with tax exemptions (Pickles & Woods, 1989). Taiwan's influence on South Africa's industrial development and the local economy became considerable. For instance, prior to 1998, Taiwanese entrepreneurs invested in 620 businesses in South Africa, spending a total amount of US$ 1.5 billion, and employed approximately 45,000 local people (Interview with an official of the Taiwanese Liaison Office in Cape Town, South Africa, May 2013).

In the 1990s, when it became evident that South Africa was on the path to democratisation and regime change, the South African-Taiwanese relationship increasingly came under strain. As South Africa's international relations started to normalise, Beijing intensified the race between the two Chinas for recognition from the new South African political leadership. Taiwan also went through the democratisation process; however, it was still considered a pariah state (Taylor, 2006). The South African government under Nelson Mandela did not initially regard the issue of choosing one of the two Chinas as a top priority, as it had to resolve various urgent domestic issues such as rampant inequality, poverty and social unrest inherited from the apartheid government. Additionally, Taipei still had relatively strong bargaining power with the ANC, since it had supported the ANC's 1994 electoral campaign financially (Davies, 1998; Shelton, 2008). It also supported the ANC's Reconstruction and Development Programme (RDP), which required massive finance from outside. Thus, Taipei's economic influence was still substantial (Tseng, 2008).

The rise of China

Despite declarations of unity in the days of struggle, interactions between the ANC and China did not share much in the way of a united struggle history. While during the Cold War the Global South's liberation movements drew on support from the socialist bloc countries, the Sino-Soviet split (1959), and their hostility towards each other during the Cold War, meant that African liberation groups supported by the Union of Soviet Socialist Republics (USSR) could not receive simultaneous support from Beijing. This led China to take some strange bed-fellows, seen in the PRC's support for Jonas Savimbi's Union for the Total Independence of Angola (UNITA), in their struggle against the Communist-inspired People's Movement for the Liberation of Angola (MPLA), supported by the USSR. With regards to South Africa, Beijing supported the Pan-African Congress (PAC); this was because the USSR had already secured relations with the ANC, thus precluding closer ANC–China relations. Despite this, China was never a supporter of the apartheid regime. Beijing's foreign policy was, and continues to be, dictated by an 'anti-hegemonic' approach, particularly with regard to African states (Taylor, 2006). This dovetailed with the general ethos of the ANC as a party of liberation, not to mention that both countries' ideologies were informed by strong socialist traditions.

Nevertheless, with the economic rise of Mainland China, the potential was overwhelmingly obvious. China as a permanent member of the UNSC and having a population of 1.3 billion, was ranged against Taiwan which was internationally marginal and had a population (and hence: market) of 23 million. Additionally, Mandela was under pressure from his own party and its allies, the South African Communist Party (SACP) and the Congress of South African Trade

Unions (COSATU), the government, businesses and academia, as well as the PRC which was fervently against the continuity of the diplomatic relationship with Taiwan. Mandela's dual approach thus did not succeed and the diplomatic relationship between South Africa and Taiwan ended in January 1998, opening up a new era for South Africa's relationship with the PRC (Lin, 2001:300). The looming handover of Hong Kong, from British colonial rule to a Special Administrative Region (SAR) of the PRC in 1997, provided good enough reasoning for the overdue realignment of policies, despite intense lobbying by Taipei. At the time, most South African business interests were located in Hong Kong. The changes in Hong Kong's status allowed South Africa – despite its idealist policy – to follow the realist move towards recognising Beijing that had already been undertaken by most of the African continent and the entire Organisation for Economic Co-operation and Development (OECD) world in the early 1970s.

In 1999, Mandela made the first state visit to China after the formal diplomatic relationship had begun. In 2000, President Jiang Zemin visited South Africa. At that time, the two heads of state signed the Pretoria Declaration on the Partnership between the People's Republic of China and the Republic of South Africa, which, for the first time, enhanced the partnership from both sides (Chinese Embassy, 2013). Highly visible diplomatic visits to South Africa have taken place since, the most recent of which were President Zuma's visit to Beijing in 2010 and President Xi Jinping's visit to South Africa in 2013 during the BRICS summit. South Africa and China have successfully co-hosted the 2015 summit-level China–Africa Co-operation Forum. In addition to visits by the heads of state, high-level officials such as Chinese foreign ministers, Chinese special envoys to Africa and party members' visits have reinforced the symbolic value. Another important aspect of official visits is that they are accompanied by business delegations, which makes networking with key decision-makers possible, as well as the effective promotion of businesses (Grant, 2011). Currently, official interaction with the PRC is done through the Department of International Relations and Cooperation- (DIRCO-) driven Bi-National Commission, which is held at deputy presidential level. It is led by the Joint Economic Trade Committee at ministerial level. South Africa is of strategic importance to China. For the PRC, diplomatic and political support from South Africa is important; the support from South Africa has provided China with a base in the international community and amongst international organisations and agencies. In the international community, South Africa has often assumed a (somewhat self-declared) role of spokesperson for the African continent. This burgeoning South Africa–China relationship formed a contrast to the declining relationship between South Africa and Taiwan. South Africa and China's bilateral trade started in earnest in 1992 when China's Ministry of Foreign Trade and Economic Cooperation opened an office in Johannesburg, South Africa. In 2012, trade volume was approximately US\$ 250 million (Shinn & Eisenman, 2012:345). Since South Africa announced that it would recognise the PRC, the trade volume has rapidly increased to US\$ 3 billion. In 2011, the trade volume stood at ZAR 85 billion, roughly US\$ 11 billion. China has been South Africa's largest trading partner since 2010, with a total trade volume of ZAR 270 billion in 2013 and pledging a further ZAR 90 billion to South Africa in 2015.

The Taiwan–South Africa afterlife

In 1998 South Africa cut official ties with Taiwan, having decided in favour of Beijing's One China doctrine. It seems that forging economic interests within the foreign policy arena became significant for decision-makers. While the ANC leadership was likely to look unfavourably upon countries which were supporters of the apartheid regime, the issue of economic gains became a fairly important determinant. China offered a potentially massive economic windfall by means of long-term economic ties if Pretoria were to switch recognition. Besides, Mainland China had a market of 1.3 billion, while Taiwan had a population of only 23 million. Taiwan was one of South Africa's largest trading partners during the 1980s and 1990s, but trade with Taiwan was already about to reach a peak (Tseng, 2008). South Africa's big businesses were already showing an interest in the huge untapped Chinese market, which they entered following the end of apartheid in 1994 (Tseng, 2008). In addition, the return of Hong Kong to China considerably strengthened the PRC's economic influence in South Africa, providing a gateway for South African businesses to the Mainland (Taylor, 2002).

While it is obvious that the economic aspect became the main driver of South Africa's decision to stop recognising Taipei, South Africa did not completely sever relations with Taiwan. Despite the diplomatic cut off which included, for example, the cancelling of preferential permits to investors (Tseng, 2008), the transition was mostly smooth, with the Taiwanese side viewing the gradual transition as a generous gesture by the South African government. Beijing did not object to continuing economic relations between South Africa and Taiwan during the process of South Africa's diplomatic switch from Taiwan to the PRC (Shelton, 2012). That there was to be non-interference was confirmed during interviews with officials from all three sides, (These interviews with officials from Taipei, Beijing and South Africa took place in May and June 2013.) South Africa and Taiwan have maintained unofficial relations through the Taipei Liaison Offices in both Pretoria and Cape Town; South Africa also has a Liaison Office in Taiwan. These offices are in charge of consular services as well as promoting economic, trade, cultural, educational, scientific, financial, and other exchanges and cooperation between Taiwan and South Africa, in order to expand Taiwanese influence in non-diplomatic and non-political areas (Interviews, 5 June 2013 and 7 June 2013). Taiwanese diplomats at representative offices seem to have experienced hardship in terms of making contact with their South African counterparts. However, the limited access to the South African government does not mean that no communication exists between the two sides; both parties have maintained working-level relations through Liaison Offices.

Beijing does not, in principle, oppose unofficial relations between South Africa and Taipei, so long as Taipei does not raise the issue of sovereignty. Beijing, for instance, did not object to continuing economic relations between South Africa and Taiwan during the process of South Africa's diplomatic switch from Taiwan to the PRC (Shelton, 2012). According to interviewees, the consideration shown was derived from the close relationship inherited by the ANC from the former National Party government. This is in stark contrast to the Taiwanese experience with other countries which derecognized relations with Taiwan. The one-year grace period granted by the South African government gave Taiwanese expatriates in South Africa sufficient time to consolidate property. During this period, Taiwanese people could sell their businesses and properties in South Africa without huge haste and incurring losses. Interestingly, some former diplomats have become politicians-turned-business people and have stayed on in South Africa, utilising their knowledge of and networks in the country, engaging in fishery, forestry and information and communications technology (ICT). A number of high-profile Taiwanese diplomats studied for degrees in South Africa while they served there and then continued their service at the Ministry of Foreign Affairs in Taiwan. Other former diplomats who left South Africa have moved to neighbouring countries like Lesotho and Swaziland, and continue to serve their country.

At government level, various interactions still occur at director-general level instead of ministerial level, as was the case before 1998. Even though the discussion level between the two countries has been downgraded, both sides have tried to make cooperation more workable and practical. For example, South Africa and Taiwan have held a 'South Africa and Taiwan Dialogue

Forum' annually since 2002. One of the most notable results is that South Africa and Taiwan have agreed on a memorandum of understanding (MoU) in various areas including agriculture, fisheries and forestry. These sectors play an important role in the economic development of Taiwan, providing capital, labour and a market for industrial development as well as laying the foundation of Taiwan's economy. Based on its competitive edge in these areas, Taiwan has sought to deepen cooperation with South Africa. Also, South Africa's exports to Taiwan in these primary production sectors are seen as having potential. Taiwan has engaged with South Africa through various types of international cooperation, such as medical assistance, agricultural cooperation, and training programmes which include scholarships for government officials.

Even though Taiwan is a de facto autonomous actor in international relations, it has limited diplomatic relations and cannot function as effectively as it used to. Taiwan and South Africa are only able to co-host at director-general level consultation meetings. South Africa's Department of Trade and Industry deals with Taiwan under the auspices of a 'special administrative province'; an interviewee at the department claimed that they do not sign agreements with Taiwan but rather have 'arrangements' signed with the Taiwan Liaison Office. The South Africa–Taiwan Consultation is led by the DTI and, from the Taiwanese side, by the Ministry of Economic Affairs; the consultation is chaired at the chief director level, with director-general level officials participating on the South African side. Considering the hierarchical organisational structure of government, it thus takes longer to implement decisions made during discussions than it would have done during the previous era of a formal diplomatic relationship. All issues discussed now need to go through a minister who finally confirms the agendas discussed at director-general level. Another problem is that, while the Taiwanese side only holds director-general level meetings with South Africa, too many high-level government official visits from the PRC indirectly put pressure on the Taiwan–South Africa relationship. In fact, the Taiwanese government has experienced similar problems in other countries. Even though there seems to have been no intervention so far when the Taiwanese government advances its relationship with other countries, many countries, especially those which need China's development assistance, appear wary of evoking rejection if they build a relationship with Taiwan.

Under the circumstances, an obvious side channel which has emerged is the use of non-state actors, which can engage with various actors without having to tip-toe around China. For instance, because Taiwan sees itself as a world leader in science and technology, cooperation in the health sector has become a new frontier. Climate change is seen as another key area for collaboration. This cooperation, which involves aid, functions as a pivotal instrument of Taiwan's economic diplomacy towards South Africa. It will help boost the image of the country and may yield opportunities for the donor country in terms of trade and investment. Additionally, the role of non-state actors as facilitators has been significant. In addition to the diplomatic channel, namely, ministries and embassies, the roles of the Africa Taiwan Economic Forum (ATEF) and the Taiwan African Business Association (TABA) have become significant in promoting trade and investment. These actors have become one of the elements which are treated seriously within the multifaceted contemporary foreign policy towards South Africa.

Woolcock & Bayne (2007) argue that from the late 1990s to the 2000s, a noticeable shift occurred in forms of international engagement. Whereas prior to this period, global economic diplomacy was dominated by permanent officials from a few powerful countries, we now see a process which is shaped, not only by diplomats, but also by business, civil society, non-government organisations and international organisations (Hill, 2003:8). This multi-actor approach to international relations signifies a more general turn in the field of international relations. Another advocate of this expanded field can be found in the work of Susan Strange, who highlights the formidable power of business interests in the shaping of global affairs

(Strange, 1988). In many respects, it is true that shifts in the global economy have precipitated this new multiplicity of actors, although one wonders whether such plurality has not always been the case and that its recent recognition reflects more a shift in analytical methods, as opposed to any shift in political reality.

However, the change in diplomatic relations with South Africa is noticeable when looking at the current Taiwanese population in South Africa. Without formal diplomatic relations, Taiwanese people were left more vulnerable insofar as they had no official authorities who could protect or represent them in South Africa (Interview, 2 May 2013). At the height of this relationship, 50,000 Taiwanese people resided in South Africa; in 2013, the population was less than 10,000 (Interview, 2 May 2013). Interviewees pointed out that the exodus of Taiwanese investors had already started in the late 1980s, and South Africa's increasing crime level, strong trade unions and threats to physical safety were listed as the top reasons why Taiwanese nationals returned to Taiwan or headed for other countries (Interviews, 5 June 2013 and 7 June 2013). The Taiwanese population in South Africa has dramatically decreased since the diplomatic switch; this is due to South Africa's own deteriorating business environment.

Cross-straits pragmatism

The economically pragmatic relationship which Taiwan has developed with South Africa is more broadly reflective of its relationship with the PRC itself. Although holding unwavering pro-independence views, and causing tension in the relationship between Taiwan and China, under the Chen Shui-bian administration (2000–2008), economic interdependence was deepened as Chen's main economic policy was to normalise cross-strait economic relations. Chen opened direct trade with China in 2001. Both parties also became members of the World Trade Organisation (WTO) and ceased discriminating practices towards each other's products. Under Ma Ying-jeou, the establishment of the Economic Cooperation Framework Agreement (ECFA), signed in 2010 and aimed at reducing tariffs and commercial barriers, is regarded as one of the significant signs of the coming-to-terms of cross-strait relations. Also, Taiwan's broader global strategy has been to move away from winning new diplomatic allies. Rather, the ROC is now focussing on strengthening its trade and investment links with other nations. The Taiwanese do not bring up politically sensitive issues but concentrate on maintaining the relationship in general.

By 2006, cross-strait trade had already reached US$ 100 billion. Although there were no official travel links during this period, 4.4 million Taiwanese people visited China; 600,000 businesspeople invested in the Mainland; and half a million Taiwanese people already lived in Shanghai and adjacent areas. It has been argued that this shift was a natural one, insofar as cultural and linguistic links facilitated the ease of migration and trade (Deng, 2008). Mainland Chinese tourists in Taiwan totalled 2.8 million in 2014. Cross-strait trade rose to US$ 197 billion in 2013 and Taiwan's trade surplus with China was US$116 billion (*The Economist*, 2014). The number of investment permits to mainlanders also rapidly grew from 23 cases in 2009 to 138 cases in 2012 (Ministry of Economic Affairs, interview, 13 June 2013). This massive transfer of economic know-how has led to a series of bilateral economic agreements and frameworks between the two territories. There is the Straits Exchange Foundation, used to handle technical and business matters between the two territories (its counterpart on the mainland is the Association for Relations Across the Taiwan Straits). Another significant example is the first ever talks between China and Taiwan which were held in November 2015. This was the first official meeting between the two sides since 1949. The relationship between the PRC and the ruling party KMT (Kuomintang) might result in Taiwan having more room to manoeuvre when approaching other countries without causing conflict with the PRC. Under the banner of pragmatic diplomacy, Taiwan could still enjoy limited but numerous diplomatic benefits such as resuming or attaining observer status at various international organisations. Based on this, the Taiwanese have put emphasis on the fact that engagement with Taiwan will not cause trouble for South Africa and its relationship with the PRC (Interviews, 5 June 2013 and 7 June 2013).

The former president of the ROC, Chen Shui-bian, an ardent supporter of Taiwan's independence, came to power in 2000 and since then has attempted to resume Taipei's international standing, stressing the importance of Taiwan's national identity. Consequently cross-strait relations deteriorated under his administration and this affected Taiwan's diplomatic relationships. Taiwan maintained diplomatic relations with 29 countries in 2000; however, when Chen Shui-bian stepped down in 2008, it had 23 left. Under the Ma administration, cross-strait relations have become more open, stable and predictable than ever (Interviews, 5 June 2013 and 7 June 2013). President Ma Ying-jeou's administration, aiming at reducing tension, restarted dialogue, and the improving economic relations brought about a thaw in cross-strait relations even though they resulted in intense domestic debate and a further divide in domestic politics. During Ma Ying-jeou's term Beijing relaxed its policy towards Taipei. Glaser (2013:12) argues that the PRC realises that interference in Taiwan's international relations will negatively affect Beijing by undermining Ma's domestic support for his policy towards the PRC and therefore lead to the deterioration of cross-strait relations. Taiwan has never experienced such a strong wave of nation building and national identity. This might reverse the current stability between the two Chinas.

Conclusion

This chapter highlights two seemingly different processes occurring. On the one hand, a general shift towards global economic competitiveness has ushered in an almost laissez-faire form of economic activity between South Africa, China and Taiwan. Taiwan's growing economic dependence on the Mainland has been more successful in integrating Taiwan and China than any other measure taken since their split in 1949.

As economic realism has largely prevailed in the Taiwan–China relationship, cross-strait relations have remarkably improved in an organic fashion. In comparison with the hard politicking involved in the symbolic acknowledgement of Taiwan as a sovereign entity, interference or overriding in the political economic domain has been comparatively minimal. The return of political power to the KMT under Ma Ying-jeou since 2008 has moved Taiwan closer to the Mainland in political terms. The economic pragmatism employed between the PRC and Taiwan sets the tone for Taiwanese interests elsewhere, including in South Africa. In other words, diplomatic recognition no longer plays as significant a role as it used to, especially vis-à-vis their external counterparts. Rather increased trade and trade dependence between states produce foreign policy convergence. From this perspective, Taiwan's economic engagement with South Africa is perfectly acceptable to the PRC – and in fact, many Taiwanese companies whose goods are sold in Africa run their manufacturing bases in China. This highlights an economic pragmatism shared on all three sides; this situation looks set to increase as Taiwan abandons its pursuit of trying to win over foreign states to officially recognise its sovereignty. On the other hand, the spectacular economic growth of Mainland China has sucked South Africa into its orbit to such a degree that Taiwan, despite its best efforts to the contrary, has been economically marginalised by South Africa. Additionally, de-recognition has weakened Taiwanese avenues of influence on South African government. Thus, despite the shift of all three entities towards an economic pragmatism, the power of political influence still exerts its effects on economic influence. For the South African government, the promotion of economic interests is one of the most important parts of foreign policy. South Africa has become increasingly enthralled with the vast Chinese market and the opportunities it offers for both institutional and personal business interests. This has resulted in a sidelining of more serious economic engagement with Taiwan.

Taiwan's increasing isolation in the international community led to its pushing a policy of flexible diplomacy in order to avoid unnecessary confrontation with Beijing over the sovereignty issue (Kan, 2012). This shifting terrain is evident in Africa, where Taiwan maintains three diplomatic relationships. The PRC's package for economic development entailing infrastructural development has lured more and more of Taiwan's diplomatic allies on the continent away from it.

Along with Beijing's strong presence on the continent and its pledges to assist African counterparts' development through various mechanisms including the FOCAC, the ROC has gradually lost ground on the continent. The current relations between Taipei and the three remaining allies is not a guarantee that their relationship will be sustained in the future.

In the era of global capitalism, economic pragmatism finds a way around diplomatic restrictions. During the Mandela administration, relations with other nations were motivated by a rather idealistic philosophy, and the notion of foreign policy shifted towards a more developmental agenda in which economic interests have come to the fore. When South Africa recognised the PRC, there was criticism on both national and international levels: South Africa has been criticised for seeking economic benefits at the expense of democracy and human rights. However, as far back as 1997 and 1998, the ANC noted that human rights should be understood in the various contexts (Barber, 2005). South Africa's foreign policy was a developmental foreign policy concerned with financing development (Landsberg, 2005). The strategic partnership with Beijing is significant in this context. The shift to a more realpolitik-driven agenda has occurred in tandem with the global phenomenon of China's rise and its particular economic focus on the African continent. The economic pragmatism which is evident between China, Taiwan and South Africa is reflective of an economic rationality which exists in spite of the charged political dimensions of the relationship.

Notes

1 In November 2013, Gambian president Yahya Jammeh declared that the country would side with Beijing. At that time, the Gambia overlooked the fact that Beijing and Taipei were adhering to an undeclared 'truce' and not actively seeking to win-over states' recognition from each other. Burkina Faso's recent ongoing political turmoil before the transition to democratic rule in 2015 has already signalled uncertainty regarding whether a new leader will be on Taipei's side or whether the country will move into the orbit of the PRC (Yen, 2015). Despite Taipei's unprecedented financial support, São Tomé and Príncipe have indicated that they may realign themselves with Mainland China. In June 2014, President Manuel Pinto da Costa visited the Mainland (Atkinson, 2014). The most recent interaction between the PRC and São Tomé and Príncipe is an MoU with China's state-owned enterprise, China Harbour Engineering Company (CHEC), scaling up its deep water port infrastructure (Dos Santos, 2015).

2 For example, Benin, Burkina Faso, the Central African Republic, Chad, the Gambia, Lesotho, Liberia, Niger and Senegal all used the diplomatic recognition card more than twice in order to maximise financial support, switching between the PRC and the ROC.

Bibliography

Alden, C., 1997. 'Solving South Africa's Chinese Puzzle: Democratic Foreign Policy Making and the "Two China" Question'. *South African Journal of International Affairs*, Volume 5 (2), pp. 80–95.

Alden, C., 2002. 'The Chrysanthemum and the Protea: Reinventing Japanese–South African Relations after Apartheid', *African Affairs*, Volume 101, pp. 365–386.

Atkinson, J., 2014. 'Time for Taiwan to Rethink Its Diplomacy'. *The Diplomat*. [online] Available at: http://thediplomat.com/2014/06/time-for-taiwan-to-rethink-diplomacy/ [Accessed 17 December 2015].

Barber, J., 2005. 'The New South Africa's Foreign Policy: Principles and Practice', *International Affairs*, Volume 81, pp. 1079–1096.

Chinese Embassy, 2013. *China–South African Relations on Fast Track*. [online] Available at: http://www.chinese-embassy.org.za/eng/zngx/gk/t942572.htm [Accessed 17 December 2015].

Davies, M., 1998. *South Africa and Taiwan: Managing the Post-diplomatic Relationship*. Witwatersrand: East Asia Project (EAP), International Relations Department and University of the Witwatersrand.

Deng, Y., 2008. *China's Struggle for Status: The Realignment of International Relations*. Cambridge: Cambridge University Press.

Fukuyama, F., 1989. 'The End of History?' *National Interest*, Volume 16, pp. 3–18.

Glaser, B.S., 2013. *Taiwan's Quest for Greater Participation in the International Community*, Lanham, MD: Rowman & Littlefield.

Grant, C., 2011. *State Visits as a Tool of Economic Diplomacy: Bandwagon or Business Sense?*, South African Institute of International Affairs, Occasional Paper, No. 87.

Grimm, S., Anthony, R. and Kim, Y., 2014. *South Africa's Relations with China and Taiwan: Economic Realism and the 'One China' Doctrine*. CCS Research Report. Stellenbosch University, Centre for Chinese Studies.

Hill, C., 2003. *The Changing Politics of Foreign Policy*, 1st ed., New York: Palgrave Macmillan.

Kan, F.Y., 2012. *Taiwan's New Foreign Relations and National Security*, Taiwan: Centre for Security Studies.

Landsberg, C., 2005. 'Toward a Developmental Foreign Policy?: Challenges for South Africa's Diplomacy in the Second Decade of Liberation', *Social Research: An International Quarterly*, Volume 72(3), pp. 723–756.

Le Pere, G. and van Nieukerk, A., 2004. 'Who Made and Makes Foreign Policy?', in E. Sidiropoulous (ed.), *South Africa's Foreign Policy 1994–2004: Apartheid Past, Renaissance Future*, Johannesburg: South African Institute of International Affairs, pp. 119–134.

Lin, S., 2001. 'The Relations between the Republic of China and Republic of South Africa, 1948–1998'. Doctoral Dissertation. Pretoria: University of Pretoria.

Mandela, N., 1993. 'South Africa's Future Foreign Policy'. *Foreign Affairs*, Volume 72 (5), pp. 86–97.

Pickles, J. and Woods, J., 1989. 'Taiwanese Investment in South Africa'. *African Affairs*, Volume 88 (353), pp. 507–528.

Rich, T. and Banerjee, V., 2015. 'Lesotho's 2015 Legislative Election: Providing or Undermining Stability?' *Journal of Asian and African Studies*, Volume 49 (6), pp. 637–653.

Shelton, G., 2008. *The Forum on China–Africa Cooperation: A Strategic Opportunity*, Pretoria: Institute for Security Studies.

Shelton, G., 2012. *Hong Kong–South Africa's Gateway to China*. South African Institute of International Affairs. Occasional Paper, No. 108.

Shinn, D. and Eisenman, J., 2012. *China and Africa: A Century of Engagement*, Pennsylvania: University of Pennsylvania Press.

Strange, S., 1988. *States and Markets*, New York: Continuum.

Taylor, I., 2002. 'Taiwan's Foreign Policy and Africa: The Limits of Dollar Diplomacy'. *Journal of Contemporary China*, Volume 11 (30), pp. 125–140.

Taylor, I., 2006. *China and Africa: Engagement and Compromise*, 1st ed., London: Routledge.

The Economist. 2014. 'Symbolism as Substance'. [Online] Available at: http://www.economist.com/news/china/21596555-chinese-and-taiwanese-government-officials-meet-first-time-china-still-worries-about [Accessed 17 December 2015].

Tseng, S., 2008. 'The Republic of China's Foreign Policy towards Africa: The Case of ROC–RSA Relations'. Doctoral Dissertation. Johannesburg: University of Witwatersrand.

van Vranken Hickey, D., 2007. *Foreign Policy Making in Taiwan: From Principle to Pragmatism*, London and New York: Routledge.

Woolcock, S. & Bayne, N., 2007. *The New Economic Diplomacy: Decision-Making and Negotiation in International Relations*. 2nd ed., Aldershot: Ashgate.

Yen, C., 2015. *Taiwan Wary of Burkina Faso's Political Turmoil*, Stellenbosch: Centre for Chinese Studies.

Societal-level interactions

14

AFRICA–ASIA RELATIONS IN ACADEMIC NETWORK FORMATION

Takuo Iwata[1]

Introduction

This chapter aims to reflect on the African studies network formation process in Asian countries.[2] In Asia, the academic exchanges and interactions among scholars and institutes of African studies have accelerated in recent years. Institutes of African studies in Asian countries, such as China, India, Japan, and South Korea, have increasingly organized international conferences, workshops, and seminars, and not only invited African and Western scholars but also other Asian scholars. Since the international conference on African studies successfully organized in South Korea in April 2012,[3] the academic exchanges among Chinese, Indian, Japanese, and Korean Africanists have been expanding. Now, closer collaboration is required in these Asian countries to globalize African studies, while respecting each country's background and contexts. How can the academic network be established in African studies in Asian countries? What challenges do Asian scholars and research institutes face when trying to develop international research networks in African studies?

Compared with the Asian situation, Africa has been considered and treated as a passive actor in, or site for, Asian scholars' research activities. Indeed, African scholars have not been considered leading academic stakeholders in Asian studies. However, we have recently observed a remarkable change in the academic landscape in African countries: the Asian studies network has started to sprout through intercontinental cooperation among African, Asian, and Western scholars and institutes.

This change in the academic landscape not only affects the Asian and African academic worlds; it affects the Western one as well. In the context of global competition, Western institutes need more academic cooperation with non-Western partners. Thus, it is crucial that Western institutes and universities promote closer relationships with their Asian counterparts.

This chapter examines the African studies network formation process in Asian countries compared with the networking trials for Asian studies in African countries and then reflects on the perspectives on Africa–Asia research cooperation. First, this chapter draws on the history and contemporary situation of African studies in Asian countries to provide an image of its genealogy. Then it moves to focus on the African studies network formation in Asia in comparison with the international networking process that was earlier established in Europe and the nascent network for Asian studies in African countries. Finally, this chapter considers the linkage among these new international networks in Africa and Asia as both sides of the same coin. By comparing these academic networks that have been developing in Africa and Asia, this chapter seeks to understand the potentialities and challenges of newly forming international academic networks for area studies.

Genealogy of African studies in Asian countries

This section aims to examine the genealogy[4] of African studies in Asia. First, it traces the history of African studies in Japan. Then it compares this with the progress of African studies in other influential Asian countries in Asia, such as China, India, and South Korea.

Japan

In 1984, the Japan Association for African Studies (JAAS) celebrated its twentieth anniversary. JAAS organized a roundtable talk to retrace its 20 years of activities with its executive members. JAAS published the minutes of the roundtable in a special issue of its main journal, *Journal of African Studies (JAS-JAAS)*,[5] and reviews by specialists from different academic fields (geology, geophysics, physical geography, animal ecology, primatology, physical anthropology, ecological anthropology, cultural anthropology, study on crafts, sociology, medical science, archaeology, history, literature, linguistics, law, political science, international relations, economics, and economic history) in another special issue of *JAS-JAAS* (No. 25, 1984). These issues of *JAS-JAAS* enable us to trace the history of African studies in Japan. What follows briefly discusses the history of African studies in Japan, in reference to these special issues of *JAS-JAAS*.

JAAS was founded in April 1964 in Tokyo. After its 20 years of existence, JAAS had about 400 members who had majored in various academic disciplines, from natural to human and social sciences. However, the history of African studies in Japan is short compared with that in Western countries. In general, Japanese academia began to establish an academic relationship with Africa only after the Second World War. A Japanese research team conducted its first fieldwork only in 1958. The Japan Monkey Center sent a research team from Kyoto University to study the origin and evolution of human beings through fieldwork on gorillas and primitive hunting tribes in Congo (Zaire) (Matsuzawa, 1983: 1). Hence, in the early years, African studies in Japan focused on primatology, and then cultural anthropology (Miyamoto, 1984: 121).

After Imanishi's Kyoto University team conducted this research, sponsored by the Japan Monkey Center (JAS-JAAS 1983: 6), a research group from Nagoya University conducted archeological field research in Kenya and Tanzania in 1968 (Omi, 1984: 107). Researchers would begin to conduct physical anthropological fieldwork in Africa in the late 1960s (Ishida, 1984: 50).

For the first generation of Japanese Africanists, raising the funds was the most difficult part of conducting their research in Africa, before the Ministry of Education began according research subsidies (*Kakenhi*, Japan Society for the Promotion of Science). Research groups had received funds ad hoc from Japanese enterprises. At that time, Japan was still classified as a developing country in the recovery process after having been defeated in the Second World War. During this initial period, JAAS received financial support from Tenri-kyo,[6] a religious organization (JAS-JAAS 1983: 5). Tenri was a temporary center for African studies in the Kansai region.

In the 1960s, the field research was principally conducted by teams. However, some researchers individually visited Africa. In the early 1960s, Kawada stayed in Upper Volta

(Burkina Faso) to carry out his research on the Mossi society. Yamaguchi conducted his research in Nigeria as a visiting lecturer at the University of Ibadan (Yoneyama, 1984: 72). These two Japanese anthropologists would become internationally renowned scholars. Cultural anthropology became one of the most representative disciplines of African studies in Japan. The Foundation of the National Museum of Ethnology[7] contributed to the development of anthropological studies in Japan (Yoneyama, 1984: 75).

In the field of medical studies, Japanese medical researcher Hideyo Noguchi[8] would come to symbolize the bridge between Japan and Africa. Noguchi was the first Japanese medical researcher to conduct research in Africa in the 1920s, with the support of the Rockefeller Foundation. Noguchi dedicated his life to infectious disease studies and died in Ghana due to yellow fever, which he had studied. To honor Hideyo Noguchi's legacy, the Japanese government founded the Noguchi Memorial Institute of Medical Research[9] at the University of Ghana (Otatsume & Minami, 1984: 100, 102).

History studies were begun in the translation of works of Western scholars, such as Basil Davidson. While the study of history gradually advanced, there were no courses on African history and no professors who had majored in African history at a Japanese university (Miyaji, 1984: 114). Linguistic studies were beginning to take place through interviews in addition to text-based research (Yukawa, 1984: 128). The studies of political science and international relations focused on issues current during the independence period, such as liberation from colonial rule, nationalism, pan-Africanism, African socialism, and military regime (Oda, 1984: 139–142; Urano, 1984: 147). While African political studies were developing in Japan, it was still the 'time of frontier' (Oda, 1984: 143). Further, for a long time, Japanese Africanists were afflicted with an inferiority complex for being 'latecomers' to the field (Oda, 1984: 138) as compared with Western scholars.

Twenty years later, in 2004, on the occasion of JAAS's fortieth anniversary, President Miyamoto remarked as follows.

> After having started with 200 members, 40 years later, JAAS had about 900 members and had become one of the biggest academic associations of area studies in Japan. JAAS covers almost all disciplines in the human, natural, and social sciences. However, African studies in Japan face the significant challenge to go a step further in its international activities while working with foreign Africanists, particularly with African scholars. Thus, African studies in Japan should be more open to the world.
>
> *(Miyamoto 2004: 1–2)*

In 2004, JAAS organized another special roundtable at its annual academic meeting and then published a report in a special issue of *JAS-JAAS*. There are still very few research institutes in Japan that exclusively conduct research and educational activities in African studies. Two remarkable exceptions that have led African studies in Japan are the Research Institute for Languages and Cultures of Asia and Africa,[10] known as AA-ken, at Tokyo University of Foreign Studies (founded in 1964) and the Center for African Area Studies,[11] known as Africa Center, at Kyoto University (founded in 1986) (*JAS-JAAS* 2004: 133–134). Another remarkable exception is the Institute of Developing Economies (IDE, *Asia Keizai Kenkyu-jo*, founded in 1958),[12] which is one of the most important research institutes to lead African studies in the domain of social science.

In general, the institutes or professors at Japanese universities have individually trained future Africanists scholars in each disciplinary program, such as development studies, international relations, agriculture, anthropological and political studies, etc. Young Africanist researchers are not necessarily trained in African studies in the institutionalized system in Japan.

Before its fortieth anniversary, JAAS published a special issue of its journal, 'African Studies in the Twenty-First Century' (*JAS-JAAS* Nos. 57–58, 2001), which was composed of reviews from the principal fields (international relations, linguistics, literature, economics, medical science, cultural and social anthropology, physical geography, gender, human geography, ecological anthropology, earth science, agriculture, political science, primatology, and history).

Some authors published in *JAS-JAAS* were conscious of the previous special issue of the journal (No. 25, 1984) that reviewed Japan's 40-year history of African studies. In the previous special issue (1984), gender studies within the field of African studies were not on the agenda. However, the gender issue has been considered an important research subject in African studies in Japan. In fact, a women's forum was set up at JAAS (Miyamoto Ritsuko, 2001: 33). However, African history studies currently remain underdeveloped in Japan. African pessimism since the 1980s has denied the value of the history of Africa (Yoshikuni, 2001: 37, 39). In political science, 16 years after Oda's (1984) publication in *JAS-JAAS*, the situation of the political scientist-Africanist did not seem to have drastically improved in Japanese academia. There were still very few universities offering African studies (Toda, 2001: 23). However, after the previous review published in 1984, new research agendas were pursued, such as democratization, civil society, and elections (Toda, 2001: 24).

In physical geography, the researchers' work on Africa was still inferior to that on the Antarctic region (Mizuno, 2001: 30). In primatology, the research activities were affected by conflicts in Congo, and they had to shift from gorillas to chimpanzees, and from Congo to Tanzania in the 1960s. Many gorillas had been eaten as bush meat during contemporary conflicts; therefore, protecting species became an important activity for primatologists (Yamagiwa, 2001: 28–29, 34–35). In ecological anthropology, the approaches have been changing as the changes in the world due to globalization have influenced how nature is perceived. Nature has been established through historical, social, and cultural human activities (Kawai, 2001: 5, 8).

Comparing the two JAAS special issues[13] in terms of how they reviewed African studies in Japan, we can observe the progress in African studies, as well as the many challenges that the field faced. In addition, Japanese Africanists are particularly conscious of the community issue in their studies, because the Japanese people retain their memory of the home village despite the swift disappearance of traditional Japanese society (Yoshida, 2007: 376).

However, we should always be careful not to generalize the trend of African studies in Japan on the sole basis of these reviews, because these publications sometimes reflected each author's individual experiences and opinions. Keeping this in mind, these issues are good resources for obtaining an image of the genealogy of African studies in Japan.[14]

China

This section outlines African studies in other major Asian countries that have established remarkable relationships with African countries and have developed African studies for a long time. It is not only interesting to outline the progress and trend of African studies in Asia in a comparative fashion; this endeavor is also indispensable for understanding the established relationship between Africa and Asia.[15] Here, this section outlines the progress in African studies in China, India, and South Korea.

For the past decade, the Western world has regarded the issue of China in Africa with some fear. Western journalism has focused on economic and commercial issues, but not on the academic activities of Chinese scholars in Africa. I have been keenly interested in how Chinese Africanist scholars have conducted their studies on and in Africa and what their academic interests are.

The Chinese government has rapidly expanded the Confucian institutes throughout the world, including in Africa. These institutes were established not only in order to teach the Chinese language and introduce Chinese culture to the local people, but also to provide young Chinese scholars opportunities to expand their knowledge and research on the country and society they have been dispatched to. Indeed, the Chinese government has sent young Chinese Africanist scholars to these institutes in African countries with the expectation that the Confucian institutes will enhance China's soft power around the world.

The following quotations exemplify the trend of African studies in China:

> In recent years, African studies have gradually become a growing 'new frontier' of China's academic domain . . . We hope more young Chinese scholars would step into African studies to discover academic treasures and create an 'Africology' with Chinese characteristics . . . . . .

> We usually cherish the belief that China is a nation with a great ancient civilization and a big power in the world. Chinese people always have a world-oriented ideology and an idea of universal love with Chinese characteristics.
>
> (Liu, 2009a: 4, 12)

The Beijing Foreign Studies Institute (now Beijing Foreign Studies University) began teaching Swahili in 1961 and Hausa language in 1964, thereby contributing to the Sino-African cultural exchange (Sun, 2009: 270–271). Today, this university offers four African language majors; besides Swahili and Hausa, one can study Zulu and Amharic. This is the richest university in Asia in terms of the variety of the African language teaching.[16]

In the 1970s, ideology was an influential factor in Sino-African relations (Liu, 2009b: 29). Further, it is reasonable to expect that the political situation greatly influenced African studies. Until the end of the Cultural Revolution, African studies were conducted in an ideology-oriented fashion in China.

In the 1980s, after the end of the Cultural Revolution, China initiated its economic reform and decreased the ideological influence over national politics. Moreover, it developed a more practical relationship with Africa, except with regard to the Taiwan issue (see Chapter 13). As China's influence spread across the world, the country started to become more conscious of the great historical legacy of its civilization (Liu, 2009b: 30). However, such Chinese behavior would be more careful due to the Tiananmen Square incident in 1989 and democratization processes in African countries at the beginning of the 1990s.

> Along with the political democratization of African and the deepening of China's reform and opening-up, the domestic situations and foreign relations of both sides have witnessed some changes, which have posed new problems and challenges to the fast-growing China–Africa economic relations.
>
> (Zhang, 2009: 73)

After the Tiananmen Square incident, China needed to establish a closer relationship with Africa. Accordingly, African studies became more important in Chinese academia.

> From an academic perspective, we need to move from the theoretical system dominated by western idea to a new theoretical system based on the experiences of Asian and African development. A new theoretical system is bound to draw lessons from Chinese history and civilization.
>
> (Liu, 2009b: 53)

In the twenty-first century, China's confidence has increased as it becomes a great world power. Consequently, Chinese academia became more influential, launching an alternative academic paradigm reflecting the Chinese perspective, against the criticism from the Western world concerning China's activities in Africa.

Li Anshan, one of the most internationally recognized Chinese Africanists, summarizes African studies in China as follows. For Western researchers, African studies in China have been a mystery. However, China has a long history with Africa (Li, 2005: 59–60). In the period of 1945–65, African studies were encouraged by the Communist Party leader, Mao Zedong, because China was focusing on the nationalist independent movements in the third world and the areas under colonial rule (Li, 2005: 62). In 1961, the Institute of Asian-African Studies was founded under the Central Party External Ministry and the Chinese Academy of Science (Li, 2005: 63).

During the Cultural Revolution (1966–76), African studies had almost ceased due to the political turbulence, except for Marxist-Leninist-Maoist thought related studies (Li, 2005: 64). In tandem with the political and economic reforms initiated under Deng Xiaoping's leadership, African studies restarted in a more academic and practical fashion than an ideology-oriented style. Two nationwide associations of African studies were established: the Chinese Association of African Studies (1979) and the Chinese Society of African Historical Studies (1980). Furthermore, research institutions were reformed to empower African studies. Centers for African Studies were established at Peking University, Xiangtan University, and Zhejiang Normal University (Li, 2005: 66). The principal subjects within this field of study in the 1990s were socialism, ethnic issues, international relations, South Africa, cultural studies, economic studies, Sino-Africa relations, and African democratization (Li, 2005: 69).

Finally, Li points out the crucial challenges of improving African studies in China, such as the overconcentration of research institutes in Beijing and Shanghai, dependence on secondary research resources published in English, insufficient fieldwork experience, insufficient development of anthropological and ethnographic studies, few country-based case studies, and insufficient international communication (Li, 2005: 73–74).

After the publication of Li's article, African studies in China have rapidly progressed. As China became an economic giant, many young Chinese Africanists were sent to African countries to begin their long-term fieldwork. The disciplines within African studies became more diversified to include traditionally unfamiliar majors, like anthropology. Thus, besides the development between Africa and China in terms of business and diplomacy, an academic relationship also flourished. In considering China–Africa relations, we cannot ignore China's academic power, in addition to the economic and diplomatic elements.

India

Indian political leaders, remarkably Mahatma Gandhi and Jawaharlal Nehru, encouraged the establishment of African studies in India. Their idea derived a great deal from Gandhi's personal experiences in South Africa and India's position in the world in its earlier independent years. India was acutely conscious of the African liberation movements. Nehru expected newly independent African states to support his Non-Aligned Movement. Area studies emerged in the 1950s as part of India's world strategy (Biswas, 2007: 305).

The Department of African Studies at the University of Delhi was founded in 1955 in accordance with a proposal by the Ministry of External Affairs (Biswas, 2007: 308). During a speech to inaugurate the department, Nehru emphasized, 'It is therefore necessary for people of India to study Africa not merely as an academic subject but in all its bearings – cultural, political, economic and historical' (*Hindustan Times*, 1955, quoted in Biswas, 2007: 309).

In the 1950s, a small center for African studies was established at the School of International Studies in Delhi. Then the African Studies Division at Jawaharlal Nehru University became a part of the Centre of West Asia and Sub-Saharan African Studies (Biswas, 2007: 310).

The Centre for African Studies at the University of Mumbai was set up in 1971–72 (Biswas, 2007: 308). The remarkable character of this center is that it is one of the few academic institutes in India to focus on policy matters (Biswas, 2007: 311). Moreover, the Universities of Delhi and Mumbai offer a one-year diploma course in Swahili language (Biswas, 2007: 310, 311).

Indian Africanist scholars had sought for decades to establish a nationwide African Studies Association to develop these studies collectively. In 2003, the African Studies Association of India (ASA-India)[17] was established by leading Indian Africanists. Since ASA-India was established, African studies in India have accelerated including the organization of many international academic meetings and the launch of many publications.

In India's African studies, social scientists, particularly political scientists, seem to have occupied an important position.

> *Although area studies in India was established as an inter-disciplinary field of study, the disciplinary profiles of the area specialists betray the marked presence of political scientists. Thus, out of twenty Africanists associated with the Area Studies Programme, fifteen are from the field of political science, two from economics, and one each from history, geography and language, and none from anthropology and sociology . . . The discipline of anthropology has been neglected by African studies programmes in India.*
>
> *(Biswas 2007: 312)*

South Korea

South Korea has also developed its African studies like other influential Asian countries in Africa such as China, India, and Japan.

The Institute of African Studies was established at Hankuk University of Foreign Studies (HUFS) in 1977 as the first institute of African studies in South Korea (Chang, 2014: 2–3). This institute has led African studies in South Korea. The Korean Association of African Studies was established in 1982 with 20 members from universities, government research institutes, and diplomats (more than 100 individual members and 10 institutes in 2014) and South Korea has built up its African studies in this short period (Chang, 2014: 1) and South Korean Africanist scholars have increased their presence internationally. HUFS has repeatedly organized international conferences on African studies and especially became a hub for the international network of African studies in Asian countries. Many Chinese, Indian, and Japanese Africanist scholars have joined in HUFS conferences in recent years. In terms of the education program, HUFS provides African language courses such as Hausa, Swahili, and Zulu.

As with other major Asian countries, African studies has been marginalized in academia in South Korea (Chang, 2014: 1, 4–5). However, there was an explosion in the establishment of research institutes for African studies in South Korea in the twenty-first century (Chang, 2014: 6). The year 2006 was a historical turning point for Korea–Africa relations and African studies in South Korea. In 2006, South Korea organized the first international forum for Africa's development, the Korea–Africa Forum (KAF) in Seoul, and joined the Development Assistance Committee of OECD (Chang, 2014: 5). This diplomatic trend stimulated the environment in African studies which went from a marginalized area of study to the hot topic which attracts research fundraising from the national foundation or Korean foreign aid agency (KOICA).

Chang Yongkyu, the former director of the Institute of African Studies (HUFS), summarizes the character of African studies in South Korea, saying that African studies are dominated by social science disciplines such as political science and economics rather than human science (Chang, 2014: 6–7). Chang believes this character has been brought out as a result of the diplomatic struggle against North Korea (Chang, 2014: 2). He mentions the difficulty in conducting interdisciplinary research (Chang, 2014: 9). He also points out the challenges in overcoming the shortage of material and manpower, to diversify the academic disciplines among Africanist scholars, and to develop the methodology for the further development of African studies in South Korea.

Similar to the case of China's progress, India's rapid economic development has improved the academic environment for African studies. There is a clear contrast between China–India (non-OECD) and Japan–South Korea (OECD). While African studies were principally led by anthropologists and natural scientists in the early years in Japan, the anthropologists have not been influential in China, India, and South Korea. It is historians who have led African studies in China. Furthermore, social science related majors have dominated in India and South Korea, while the social scientists have not been a dominant force in African studies in Japan. Hence, this comparison reveals a stark contrast, despite the quite limited resources on the genealogy of African studies in China, India, and South Korea. Although there are some differences in the character of African studies, Africanist scholars in Asian countries have many areas in which they can work together and learn from their differences in order to enrich African studies.

Networking trials for African studies in Asia

The international exchanges within African studies in Asia have been modest in comparison with Europe. In general, the history of African studies in Asian countries is shorter than that of Western countries, particularly compared with the former colonial master countries. However, certain Asian countries have spent more than half a century conducting African studies. Asian scholars have gradually played an unignorable role in African studies in the world. In the twenty-first century, as the world economic and political order began to change, the relationship between Africa and Asia has become much closer and increasingly diversified.

African studies have progressed with the transformation of the world situation. The need for African studies has been increasing in Asian countries, and particularly in emerging countries, in terms of business interests, and diplomatic and security issues. In emerging countries besides China and India, such as Brazil, Russia, and Turkey, African studies have received more focus as part of their national interests.

In fact, until very recently, African studies had been taking place separately in each Asian country, although these countries were working with African and Western scholars and institutes. However, the lens focused on the relationship between Africa and Asia as the world situation changed. Scholars of African studies in Asian countries need to deepen and widen their knowledge and learn from the research products of African studies conducted in other Asian countries, because Asian countries naturally share similar interests in and challenges with Africa in terms of economic, diplomatic, political, and cultural issues. Therefore, Asian Africanist scholars began communicating to accelerate the academic exchange in African studies.

Each Asian country, institute, and individual scholar involved in networking activities for African studies has worked with different interests, resources, and approaches. However, they keep sharing their minimal and symbolic common interests in order to work together to establish a network for African studies in Asia.

As in European countries, African studies have progressed in Asian countries in terms of the country's unique approach, historical background, academic culture, and national strategy. For example, as mentioned in this chapter, Japanese Africanists launched the first full-scale fieldwork in Africa in primatology studies at the end of the 1950s. Then, natural and cultural anthropologists traveled to Africa to conduct their fieldwork. In general, the arrival in Africa of Japanese researchers in the natural sciences preceded that of the social and human science disciplines. In the 1960s, Africa was still very far away for Japanese social scientists who wanted to conduct fieldwork. Therefore, most of the studies took place using texts introduced from Western countries. However, in the 1970s, social and human science scholars gradually developed African studies through long and frequent fieldwork.

This is just a case in the Japanese context. It can neither be generalized nor considered to be the prototype process of African studies in Asia. The progress of African studies can be traced differently in other Asian countries. However, Africanist scholars in Asian countries can learn from the differences between each country's courses and experiences to enrich African studies as a whole. This networking activity must differ from international cooperation in terms of foreign aid, where the economically 'powerful' side unilaterally supports the 'powerless' with certain conditions. This academic network should be a horizontal partnership.

The author has proposed the creation of an international network for African studies in Asian countries since 2011. I have visited influential institutes of African studies in China (Zhejiang Normal University, Peking University), India (University of Mumbai), South Korea (Hankuk University of Foreign Studies), and Japan (Kyoto University) to share the idea of establishing an Asian Africanists Network (AAN). For the most part, these Asian institutes welcomed this proposition. The Institute of African Studies at Hankuk University of Foreign Studies (IAS-HUFS) organized the international conference 'Africa in Asia, Asia in Africa' in 2012 in South Korea, with Chinese, Indian, Japanese, and Korean Africanist scholars, as well as African and European scholars.

Before this historic conference, we had already held many international meetings on African studies in Asian countries. However, this conference was the first international conference to receive Africanist researchers from all four major Asian countries (China, India, Japan, and South Korea) in the field of African studies, including the current and former presidents of the National Association of African Studies, and with the consciousness of 'Asianness' in African studies. Moreover, this conference might be recognized as the first 'Asian' conference on African studies.

At the closure of this conference, IAS-HUFS, the host institute, organized a business meeting to discuss how to develop future projects of cooperation and to create new exchange opportunities for the younger generation of Asian Africanists (April 28, 2012).

After this historic conference, networking activities gradually but surely advanced. A Memorandum of Understanding was concluded between Korean institutes (IAS-HUFS) and Japanese institutes (Center for African studies, Ryukoku University) in December 2011. Shuttle exchanges and workshops have been repeatedly held between Korean and Japanese scholars. Furthermore, Indian institutes have repeatedly organized international conferences[18] and often invited other Asian scholars to participate. Chinese scholars are the most popular invitees to the conferences organized in other Asian countries.

While we are gradually broadening our horizons through such collaborations among Asian scholars, these stakeholders have been aware of the need to organize the second comprehensive Asian Africanist meeting to share their research results and assess the process of accelerating this cooperation project.

In May 2014, JAAS organized the commemorative international symposium celebrating its fiftieth anniversary. This meeting was titled 'Asian Africanists meet African Asianists,' with the subtitle, 'the "second" Asian conference on African studies.' Besides the networking process among Asian Africanists, other parallel networking processes seem to have been launched under the banner of the 'African network of Asian Studies.' Next, the JAAS's international meeting provided an opportunity for two new networks to meet while considering the academic paradigm shift in the near future.

An idea of an Asian Africanists Network (AAN) may have expanded from China, India, Japan, and South Korea to the Southeast Asian countries. Nanyang Technological University (Singapore) and Singapore Business Federation have jointly established the first Center for African Studies in ASEAN countries in 2014 focusing on trade and business in Africa.[19] University of Malaya (Malaysia) is also interested in the establishment of the new institute for African studies.

Networking process for African studies in Europe

The author has learned from the networking process for African studies in Europe and wishes to apply this example to the Asian network of African studies. This section focuses on the formation of the Africa–Europe Group for Interdisciplinary Studies (AEGIS),[20] one of the biggest and most established international networks of African studies in the world.

AEGIS organizes of the European Conference on African Studies (ECAS), one of the biggest international conferences[21] on African studies in the world, receiving more than 2,000 participants not only from Europe, North America, and Africa but also from Asia and Latin America. The recent conferences, held in Lisbon in 2013 and in Paris in 2015, comprised almost 200 panels over three days. Today, the AEGIS network is recognized as the most successfully organized international network for African studies in the world.

However, this huge international network of African studies was born at a very modest meeting held in Bordeaux, France, in 1991. British, French, and Spanish Africanist scholars discussed the future of African studies in Europe at the time of the end of the Cold War and European integration into the European Union (EU). They agreed to establish closer international communication among European Africanists.[22]

Needless to say, Europe has been at the heart of African studies due to its historical connections with the African continent. During the colonial era, African studies were established and developed, particularly in the United Kingdom and France, which were the biggest colonial master states. Even after the African colonies gained independence, these two countries retained their influence on and superiority in African studies, which continue today. In addition to the United Kingdom and France, other European countries such as Germany, the Netherlands, Portugal, and Sweden founded centers of African studies and developed African studies. However, an international exchange for African studies in Europe had yet to be institutionalized. After the Cold War ended, the academic cooperation would be expected to include former Soviet Union member countries that had developed their different approaches to and histories with African studies. Thus, it was a common challenging objective for European Africanists to establish an internationally institutionalized network for African studies in Europe.

Despite the agreement to accelerate international collaborations, early on, the network activities progressed modestly. This was due to the insufficient financial, human, and logistic resources for carrying out such a groundbreaking project. As all of these scholars had their own jobs at their own organizations and domestic African studies exchanges, it was difficult for them to carry out such an extraordinary task. Hence, in the early years, the network activities slowly and modestly advanced. AEGIS clearly states its objectives on its website as follows:[23]

> AEGIS (Africa–Europe Group for Interdisciplinary Studies) was set up in 1991 in order to build upon the resources and the research potential available within Africanist institutions of the European Union. As the dynamics of contemporary change in Africa and the continent's response to globalisation are intimately linked, understanding the continent's evolution is the major academic and policy challenge AEGIS seeks to address. AEGIS consequently aims to: Share intellectual resources for research and advisory purposes, Conceptualise new research themes, Improve and disseminate knowledge about Africa, Provide academic guidance and foster institutional exchanges of students, senior researchers and academic staff, Promote interdisciplinary approaches to the study of Africa.

In 2011, the author visited some leading European institutes on African studies in France (Bordeaux), Germany (Frankfurt), Sweden (Uppsala), Portugal (Lisbon), and the United Kingdom (Edinburgh) to conduct interviews on the researchers' interests and challenging agendas in this network.[24] The author learned that AEGIS is an academic cooperation platform composed of different actors. Each member institute keeps its different interests, approach, academic tradition, and strategy for African studies, while sharing the common idea that they need to work together in order to globalize their African studies. Even member institutes from the same country keep different objectives and engage in rivalries with each other.

AEGIS has drastically expanded its activities in the twenty-first century. In 2016, AEGIS comprised 28 European full-member institutes from 12 countries (Austria, Belgium, Denmark, France, Germany, Italy, the Netherlands, Norway, Portugal, Spain, Sweden, and Switzerland)[25] and other affiliate memberships. With the support of the EU and other sponsors, AEGIS's meetings became bigger year by year. ECAS, AEGIS's biggest event, has been held every two years since 2005, in London, Leiden, Leipzig, Uppsala, Lisbon, and Paris by different host organizer institutes.[26] The upcoming seventh conference in 2017 is planned for Basel. With every conference, ECAS increases in size. In addition, AEGIS has organized thematic conferences[27] and provided summer schools for students.[28] Today, AEGIS continues to expand with new membership requests.[29]

AEGIS is the institution-based European network on African studies. Therefore, a non-European institute cannot become a full member of AEGIS. However, AEGIS is open to work with non-European actors joining in as affiliate members. After the African studies Association of India (ASA-India), the JAAS became the second Asian member of AEGIS.[30]

Beginning of Asian studies network formation in Africa

In comparison with the networking process for African studies in Asian countries, Asian studies in African countries is still a new frontier in the academic world.

However, the academic trend is not static in Africa. As the relationship between Africa and Asia has strengthened, the need for Asian studies in African countries has emerged in recent years. Nevertheless, there are still few African universities that have a research or educational institute dedicated to Asian studies,[31] due to the limited research interest, and limited human and financial resources. In spite of this, the interest in Asia has been increasing in African countries.

In recent years, Western institutes have shown an interest in bridging the gap between African and Asian academics. With regard to this, there are two remarkable initiatives by Dutch and

German institutes. One initiative is that of the International Institute for Asian Studies (IIAS)[32] at the University of Leiden in the Netherlands. This initiative aimed to establish the Association for Asian Studies in Africa (A-ASIA). This initiative organized the inaugural international conference, African Association for Asian Studies in Africa,[33] in September 2015,[34] in Accra, Ghana after preparatory meetings held in Lusaka (Zambia, in November 2012) and Macau (China, in June 2013). The objective and approach of this international conference are as follows:

> *The Accra conference will inventory the state of Asian studies in Africa by identifying its main gaps and exploring research and other scholarly opportunities for institutional and individual collaboration over the longue durée ... In addressing these kinds of questions, the AASIA Conference will serve as a base-setting forum for deliberating research ideas, discussing findings, and exploring collaborative opportunities by scholars with interest in Asian Studies in Africa and orientations in the social sciences and humanities.*[35]

> *The conference ... will seek to assess the prospects for Asian Studies in Africa in a global context by addressing a number of theoretical and empirical questions that such an enterprise will raise: How should Asian studies be framed in Africa? Is Asian studies relevant for Africa? ... Asian studies dovetail into the broader field of 'Area studies', as it has been developed mainly in Western institutions. Are new narratives required for understanding the very visible contemporary presence of Asia in Africa and Africa in Asia?*[36]

Another initiative is that of the research project, Africa's Asian Options (AFRASO), of Goethe University, Frankfurt (Germany). To this end, Frankfurt University has collaborated with the University of Malaya (Malaysia). An international conference was organized by the Africa–Asia Development University Network (AADUN) of the University of Malaya and the research project (AFRASO)[37] of Frankfurt University in Kuala Lumpur, in March 2014,[38] to reflect the relationship between Africa and Asia.

This conference's aim was stated as follows:

> *The aim of this international conference is to provide a more systematic overview of the empirical dimensions and analytical implications of these multifaceted and conflicting processes. What is new about Asian-African interactions? Do they follow specific patterns? How can they be characterised and analysed? Do they give rise to mutually beneficial modes of cooperation, or do they produce new asymmetries?*[39]

The objectives of this conference were to explore and examine the new opportunities and risks that are brought through African–Asian encounters under four major themes: Markets on the Move; Transnational Civic Networks between Africa and Asia; New Avenues for Civilizational Dialogue between Asia and Africa, and Improving Living Habitats by Africa–Asia University Cooperation.[40]

> The transregional arena constituted by the recent strong growth of African-Asian interactions may well have a decisive impact on the 21st century. .... *At the same time, there has been growing concern (both outside and inside Africa) about new forms of dependency and exploitation – or even a 'new colonialism' – generated by Asia's and especially China's intensified engagement in Africa.*[41]

> *(emphasis added)*

The abovementioned two European initiatives might have been launched for different reasons and interests. However, these initiatives seem to have similar motives. The changes in the global situation have radically affected the academic world. Today, we are used to referring to the century of Africa and Asia as the emerging world order in the beginning of the twenty-first century. Now, universities all over the world are facing a competition to survive on the global stage. Western universities need to establish closer relationships and cooperation with non-Western universities, and especially with Asian universities, as part of their long-term strategy. These two European institutes seem to have tried to promote their global strategy while exploiting their advantages because they have accumulated significant academic resources for African and Asian studies over a long period. These institutes obviously aim to establish a new academic hub while bridging the African–Asian academic network through their initiatives.

Conclusion

Primarily, this chapter attempts to examine the network formation process for African studies in Asian countries. In addition, it traces the genealogy of African studies in Asian countries. While it was possible to consider some trends and progress in African studies in Asian countries, this chapter's reflection remains an introductory attempt to understand the character of African studies in Asian countries. The author should continue to learn from African studies which have been progressing in each Asian country. We, Asian Africanist scholars, need to know more and allow ourselves to know each other, to develop this academic network.

Asian scholars are increasingly conscious of international collaboration and networking with regard to African studies in Asia. In Asian countries, a comprehensive regional integration framework like the EU does not yet exist. However, African studies scholars and institutes in Asian countries share a common interest in exchanging and working together to achieve each stakeholder's interest and strategy. Networking for African studies has been gradually diffusing among Asian institutes and scholars. Asian institutes have recently organized more international conferences, symposiums, and workshops while reflecting the 'Asianness' of their African studies.

Finally, this chapter also considers European networking approaches to African studies and bridging the gap between the African and Asian academic communities. Through learning about the AEGIS formation process, the author learned that European scholars and institutes of African studies have spent decades fostering an international academic network while overcoming problems and challenges. Through the Africa–Asia networking trials, we could learn how Western academia changed its strategy to retain its influence in 'the century of Africa and Asia.'

The author learned two important lessons through this reflection. First, it takes time to establish, drive, and consolidate a regional academic network in area studies. Even in the same country, African studies are structured according to very different academic disciplines. This has made it more difficult to achieve a consensus among Africanists with rivalries and misunderstandings in interdisciplinary communication. Even within the field of African studies, the scholars and institutes in each country have different academic histories, cultures, backgrounds, and strategies. When we work together in the international network, we should pay attention to and respect other's situation. Further, we need to plan and act with the long term in mind – at least two or three decades – so as not to rush to seek a result within a few years, because Asian countries are less integrated politically and economically as compared with Western European countries. Sufficient time is also required to foster trust in each other.

Second, we, Asian scholars and institutes of African studies, need to develop networking in a more horizontal partnership, for long-term, sustainable progress, even though it will take additional time to make decisions. In other words, it is favorable to organize in a more decentralized and rhizomatous fashion. A unilateral approach in a vertical relationship, like the donor–recipient relationship in foreign aid, would not bring sustainable international network development in academia in Asia.

The year 2015 marked the sixtieth anniversary of the Bandung Conference. The relationship between Africa and Asia has developed and changed during these six decades. Academic networking process between Africa and Asia no longer works in the framework based on the nostalgia of egalitarian Third World solidarity, but should shift to a more realistic framework of global competition.

Notes

1 The author has updated and modified his paper ('Network Formation Challenges for African Studies in Asia,' *Ritsumeikan Kokusai Kenkyu* [*The Ritsumeikan Journal of International Relations*], Vol. 27 (1), 2014, pp. 95–115.) for contribution to this *Handbook*. **Note:** according to the author, *The Ritsumeikan Journal* has no stipulation on the reproduction.

2 This chapter outlines the networking process for African studies in Asian countries. Some of this is based on my personal experiences. For its sustainable development, it is favorable to advance such networking in a decentralized and rhizomatous manner.

3 The International Conference of the Institute of African Studies and Humanity Korea, 'Africa in Asia & Asia in Africa: Asian Experiences and Perspectives in African Studies,' was held on 27–28 April 2012, at the Institute of African Studies, Hankuk University of Foreign Studies (IAS-HUFS), Yongin, South Korea. This conference is also recognized as the first Asian conference on African studies.

4 The author can only show certain aspects of African studies in Japan, as this field comprises many academic disciplines, from natural science to human and social sciences. The author's knowledge is too limited to outline the trend of all disciplines. It remains a 'trial' to outline the progress of African studies in Japan. It should be possible to trace this progress in different fashions.

5 The main journal of JAAS, *Afurika Kenkyu* (*Journal of African Studies*), was launched in 1964. It began by publishing one issue annually. Since 1982, it has published two issues per year. Back issues of *Afurika Kenkyu* are accessible on JAAS's website, http://african-studies.com/bak_jaas/index-e.html [accessed 27 December 2013].

6 Tenrikyo website, www.tenrikyo.or.jp/eng [accessed 27 December 2013].

7 National Museum of Ethnology website, www.minpaku.ac.jp/english [accessed 27 December 2013].

8 About the life history of Noguchi, see the Japanese Cabinet Office website 'Hideyo Noguchi Africa Prize,' www.cao.go.jp/noguchisho/english/about/lifehistorydrnoguchi.html [accessed 28 December 2013]. Noguchi's legacy continues in the twenty-first century. The Japanese government established the Hideyo Noguchi prize to celebrate the outstanding contributions of medical researchers to medical studies related to Africa's problems at the Tokyo International Conference for Africa's Development (TICAD). About TICAD, see the Japanese Foreign Ministry website, www.mofa.go.jp/region/africa/ticad/index.html [accessed 28 December 2013].

9 University of Ghana website, www.ug.edu.gh/index1.php?linkid=357&sublinkid=279 [accessed 28 December 2013].

10 The Research Institute for Languages and Cultures of Asia and Africa website, www.aa.tufs.ac.jp/en [accessed 28 December 2013].

11 The Center for African Area Studies website, www.africa.kyoto-u.ac.jp/eng/enindex.html [accessed 28 December 2013].

12 Institute of Developing Economies – Japan External Trade Organization website, www.ide.go.jp/English/Info/index.html [accessed 10 January 2014].

13 J-Stage website (*Journal of African Studies*, JAAS), www.jstage.jst.go.jp/browse/africa/1984/25/_contents,www.jstage.jst.go.jp/browse/africa/2001/57/_contents, www.jstage.jst.go.jp/browse/africa/2001/58/_contents [accessed 29 December 2013].

14 It is something like a meta-study attempt to outline the genealogy of African studies in Asia. However, the author immediately reached an impasse. 'African studies' comprises many varied disciplines.

15 Author's knowledge of African studies in other Asian countries is still limited, as is the access to resources' available in English as compared with those in Japanese, despite the author's five years of

experience of communication to tackle the networking formation for African studies in Asia (which will be argued in the following part).

16 The foremost language university in Korea, Hankuk University of Foreign Studies, provides Swahili, Hausa, and Zulu language courses. In Japan, Osaka University (former Osaka University of Foreign Language) provides a Swahili course.

17 ASA-India website, www.africanstudies.in [accessed 10 January 2014].

18 African Studies Association of India website, www.africanstudies.in/activities [accessed 26 December 2013].

19 Singapore Business Federation website, www.sbf.org.sg/cas [accessed 21 June 2016].

20 About the management of AEGIS, see AEGIS website, www.aegis-eu.org [accessed 23 December 2013]. See also its flier, www.aegis-eu.org/images/AEGIS_flyer_english_march_2011.pdf [accessed 24 December 2013].

21 European Conference on African Studies website, http://cea.iscte.pt/ecas2013 [accessed 1 June 2013].

22 Fortunately, the author was able to learn about the birth of AEGIS from an eyewitness. Three European Africanist researchers held this small meeting in Bordeaux by Donal Cruise O'Brien (the United Kingdom), Christian Coulon (France), Graham Furniss (UK), and Ferran Iniesta (Spain). The author interviewed Prof. Christian Coulon in Bordeaux, April 26, 2011, and Prof. Ferran Iniesta in Bordeaux, June 1, 2011, and Prof. Graham Furniss in Yongin, South Korea, November 29, 2014.

23 AEGIS website, www.aegis-eu.org/index.php/why-aegis.html [accessed 24 December 2013].

24 In 2011, I stayed in Bordeaux during my sabbatical year. It was a great opportunity to learn about two decades of European experience in networking for African studies. AEGIS website,/www.aegis-eu.org [accessed 24 December 2013].

25 Membership institutes are located in Barcelona, Basel, Bayreuth, Birmingham, Bologna, Bordeaux, Cambridge, Cologne, Copenhagen, Edinburgh, Frankfurt, Gent, Hamburg, Leiden, Leipzig, Leuven, Lisbon, London, Madrid, Mainz, Naples, Oxford, Paris (CESSMA), Paris (IMAF), Roskilde, Trondheim, Uppsala, and Vienna. AEGIS website, www.aegis-eu.org [accessed 13 July 2016].

26 AEGIS website, www.aegis-eu.org/index.php/ecas-conferences.html [accessed 24 December 2013].

27 AEGIS website, www.aegis-eu.org/index.php/thematic-conferences.html [accessed 24 December 2013].

28 AEGIS website, www.aegis-eu.org/index.php/summer-schools.html [accessed 24 December 2013].

29 The author attended plenary meetings of AEGIS in Lisbon on June 26, 2013, in Paris on July 7 2015.

30 During the ECAS held in Paris in 2015, AEGIS board members set up a meeting with Asian African-ist participants. They exchanged for further cooperation between European and Asian Africanists in a more institutional way. AEGIS board members honestly talked about cooperation with Asian scholars and institutes became more important for their fundraising even in African studies. After this meeting, JAAS applied for affiliate membership of AEGIS. The author attended this meeting held between AEGIS board members including its President (Clara Carvalho, President, Lisbon, Pierre Boilley, Paris, and Celine Thiriot, Bordeaux) and Asian prominent Africanist scholars (Ajay Dubey, Delhi and Masayoshi Shigeta, Kyoto) on July 9, 2015, at University of Paris (Sorbonne).

31 Stellenbosch University (South Africa) manages the Center for Chinese Studies; and Witwatersrand University (South Africa) founded the Centre for Indian Studies. The Center for Chinese Studies (Stellenbosch University) website, www.ccs.org.za [accessed 2 January 2014]. The Centre for Indian Studies (Witwatersrand University) website, www.cisa-wits.za [accessed 3 January 2014].

32 The International Institute for Asian Studies website, www.iias.nl [accessed 22 December 2013].

33 A-Asia's steering committee is coordinated by the members, Lloyd Amoah (Ashesi University College, Ghana), Thomas Asher (Social Science Research Council, the USA), Scarlett Cornelissen (University of Stellenbosch, South Africa), Webby Kalikiti (Secretary A-Asia/University of Zambia), Liu Haifang (Peking University, China), Yoichi Mine (Doshisha University, Japan), Oka Obono (University of Ibadan, Nigeria), Philippe Peycam (International Institute for Asian Studies, the Netherlands). IIAS website, www.iias.nl/aasia-cfp [accessed 22 December 2013].

34 The inaugural conference was programmed in January 2015. However, it was postponed due to the Ebola outbreak in West African countries.

35 The Association of Asian Studies in Africa website, www.a-asia.org/?page_id=63 [accessed 22 December 2013].

36 IIAS website, www.iias.nl/aasia-cfp [accessed 22 December 2013].

37 The second AFRASO conference was held in Cape Town, South Africa, in March 2015, in cooperation with the Centre for Chinese Studies, Stellenbosch University. The third conference was held in

September 2016 in Frankfurt, Germany. AFRASO website, www.afraso.org/en/content/conference-african-asian-encounters-ii-re-thinking-african-asian-relationships-changing, www.afraso.org/en/content/conference-african-asian-encounters-iii-afrasian-transformations-beyond-grand-narratives-0 [accessed 24 June, 2016].

38 AADUN-AFRASO conference website, http://umconference.um.edu.my/AA2014=7895fc13088ee 37f511913bac71fa66f [accessed 2 January 2014].

39 AADUN-AFRASO conference website, http://umconference.um.edu.my/AA2014=1f3202d820180 a39f736f20fce790de8 [accessed 2 January 2014].

40 AADUN-AFRASO conference website, http://umconference.um.edu.my/AA2014=eaa32c96f620053 cf442ad32258076b9 [accessed 2 January 2014].

41 AADUN-AFRASO conference website, http://umconference.um.edu.my/AA2014=1f3202d820180 a39f736f20fce790de8 [accessed 2 January 2014].

Bibliography

Biswas, A., 2007. 'African studies in India', in T. Z. Paul (ed.), *The Study of Africa – Global and Transnational Engagements*, Dakar: CODESRIA, pp. 305–313.

Chang, Y., 2014. 'African Studies and Its Discontents: Facing Academic Marginalisation and Public Ignorance', Paper presented at Commemorative International Conference for 50th anniversary of Japan Association for African Studies. African Studies meet Asian Studies (May 23, 2014, Kyoto University).

Ishida, H., 1984. 'Physical Anthropology', *Journal of African Studies (Afurika Kenkyu)*, Volume 25, pp. 50–58.

Japan Association for African Studies, 1984. 'Roundtable: Review and Perspectives in 20 Years of African Studies in Japan', *Journal of African Studies (Afurika Kenkyu)*, Volume 25, pp. 138–146.

Japan Association for African Studies, 2004. 'Roundtable Discussion: Commemorating the 40th Anniversary of the JAAS', *Journal of African Studies (Afurika Kenkyu)*, (Supplement), pp. 119–138.

Kawai, K., 2001. 'Ecological Anthropology in Africa for Tomorrow', *Journal of African Studies (Afurika Kenkyu)*, Japan Association for African Studies, Volume 58, pp. 5–9.

Li, A., 2005. 'African Studies in China in the Twentieth Century: A Historical Survey', *African Studies Review*, Volume 48 (1), pp. 59–87.

Liu, H., 2009a. 'African studies and "new frontiers" of China's academic domain', in H. Liu and J. Yang (eds.), *Fifty Years of Sino-African Cooperation: Background, Progress & Significance*, Kunming: Yunnan University Press, pp. 4–23.

Liu, H., 2009b. 'Fifty years of Sino-African cooperation: Background, progress & significance', in H. Liu, and Y. Jiemian (eds.), *Fifty Years of Sino-African Cooperation: Background, Progress & Significance*, Kunming: Yunnan University Press, pp. 24–56.

Matsuzawa, I., 1983. 'A Foreword', *Journal of African Studies (Afurika Kenkyu)*, Volume 23 (Supplement).

Miyaji, K., 1984. 'History', *Journal of African Studies (Afurika Kenkyu)*, Volume 25, pp. 114–120.

Miyamoto, M., 1984. 'Literature', *Journal of African Studies (Afurika Kenkyu)*, Volume 25, pp. 121–127.

Miyamoto, R., 2001. 'A Review and Perspective of Gender Studies by Japanese Researchers', *Journal of African Studies (Afurika Kenkyu)*, Volume 57, pp. 33–36.

Miyamoto, M., 2004. 'A Foreword', *Journal of African Studies (Afurika Kenkyu)*, Volume 23 (Supplement).

Mizuno, K., 2001. 'Physical Geography', *Journal of African Studies (Afurika Kenkyu)*, Volume 57, pp. 29–31.

Oda, H., 1984. 'Political Science', *Journal of African Studies (Afurika Kenkyu)*, Volume 25, pp. 138–146.

Omi, G., 1984. 'Archaeology', *Journal of African Studies (Afurika Kenkyu)*, Volume 25, pp. 107–113.

Otatsume, S., Minami Kazumori, 1984. 'Medical Science', *Journal of African Studies (Afurika Kenkyu)*, Volume 25, pp. 100–106.

Sun, X., 2009. 'Building the bridge of Sino-African cultural exchanges', in H. Liu and Y. Jiemian (eds.), *Fifty Years of Sino-African Cooperation: Background, Progress & Significance*, Kunming: Yunnan University Press, pp. 270–277.

Toda, M., 2001. 'Political Science', *Journal of African Studies (Afurika Kenkyu)*, Volume 58, pp. 23–25.

Urano, T., 1984. 'International Relations', *Journal of African Studies (Afurika Kenkyu)*, Volume 25, pp. 147–151.

Yamagiwa, J., 2001. 'Perspectives of Primatology by Africanists in the 21st Century', *Journal of African Studies (Afurika Kenkyu)*, Volume 58, pp. 27–36.

Yoneyama, T., 1984. 'Cultural Anthropology', *Journal of African Studies (Afurika Kenkyu)*, Volume 25, pp. 71–85.

Yoshida, M., 2007. 'African studies in recent years in Japan', in T. Z. Paul (ed.), *The Study of Africa–Global and Transnational Engagements*, Dakar: CODESRIA, pp. 369–384.

Yoshikuni, T., 2001. 'Studying African History Amidst the Currents of "The End of History"', *Journal of African Studies (Afurika Kenkyu)*, Volume 58, pp. 37–40.

Yukawa, Y., 1984. 'Linguistics', *Journal of African Studies (Afurika Kenkyu)*, Volume 25, pp. 128–133.

Zhang, H., 2009. 'Reflections on promotion of a harmonious and win–win relationship between China and Africa', in H. Liu and Y. Jiemian (eds.), *Fifty Years of Sino-African Cooperation: Background, Progress & Significance*, Kunming: Yunnan University Press, pp. 65–79.

15

DREAMING AFRASIA

An essay on Afro-Asian relations in space–time perspectives

Yoichi Mine

Introduction

In the seminal work that discussed a possibility of non-Western international relations theory, the two leading scholars of the discipline, Amitav Acharya and Barry Buzan, expressed an emphatically cautious view against the advocacy of an exclusively Asian perspective of international relations.

> . . . we are *not, repeat not,* concerned with identifying or advocating an Asian school of international relations. This would link us to constructs (and debates surrounding them) such as Asian values, Asian democracy, Asian way, etc. We want to stay clear of such reifications, which, while they may have their usefulness in building non-Western IRT, are also hugely problematic because of the extent of generalizations they involve, and the suspicions they evoke as an elite-driven and politically motivated exercise.
>
> *(Acharya & Buzan, 2010:229. Italics in original)*

The purpose of this chapter is to consider the relevance of setting uniquely Afro-Asian spatial and historical perspectives (the term *Afrasia*[1] is used hereafter) to contemporary international relations and development. Given the possible danger of elitism and political manoeuvring involved in an exclusively Asian grouping, the proposition of considering international relations in the framework of Afrasia may sound equally problematic. Otherwise, the proposed framework may be too general, broad and abstract to pose a substantial threat to healthy intellectual debate.

However, the political space of Afrasia has been alive since the time of the Bandung Conference. The original Bandung Conference (Asian-African Conference) held in April 1955 was attended by the delegates of 23 Asian and 6 African states, representing more than half the global population at the time. Although the second reunion was not convened for a long time, the original conference affirmed the principle of equal sovereignty of diverse nations in Afrasia and their reciprocal cooperation, opposed all forms of colonial intervention and then gave birth to the Non-Aligned Movement (Ampiah, 2007; Lee, 2010). In the twenty-first century, the spirit of Bandung that has receded into history textbooks is being reactivated. The second Bandung of 106 states was held in 2005, and the third, the 60th Anniversary Conference

Summit of 109 states, took place in April 2015. Now the group of Bandung is deemed the largest regional organization, even though it remains an ad hoc grouping with no permanent secretariat as of 2016.[2]

This chapter does not claim that a selfcontained space of Afrasia as a political and economic entity already exists, but suggests that this broad stretch of land and sea areas is a *potential* region that may be created through active dialogue among those who live there. As a space in which pan-Africanism and pan-Asianism meet, Afrasia is a project in the making rather than an accomplished fact. Therefore, the aim of this chapter is merely to incubate a 'pre-theory' of international relations across Afrasia and indicate new research areas based on some key historical literature; as described by Thomas Kuhn, a paradigm shift may be prepared by 'speculative and unarticulated theories' in face of a crisis of normal science (Kuhn, 2012:61, 87).

In the following sections, this chapter rewinds the time from the future to the past, by discussing the long term projection of Afrasian demography, then examining pan-nationalist ideals propounded by eminent intellectuals in Afrasia in the twentieth century, and finally, describing features of precolonial economic and political orders in the vast region that have cast a long shadow over the present. The biggest challenge Afrasia is expected to face is to find a way to avoid possible bifurcation of development and underdevelopment within the region. The core message of this chapter is that intellectual traditions of universal pan-nationalism in Afrasia, as well as the historical legacy of decentralized democracy in land-abundant parts of the region, bode well for an egalitarian future of the region in the making.

The foreseeable future

According to a projection released by the United Nations Population Division, 4.71 billion people will live in Asia, 4.18 billion in Africa, and about 1.96 billion in the rest of the world in 2100.[3]

This means that more than 80 per cent of the world's population will be either Asians or Africans in the early twenty-second century. Given the democratic principle of equal representation (one person one vote), organising a visionary dialogue between Asia and African, where an absolute majority of people will reside, is critically important in deciding the future shape of the world.

It is no wonder that the presence of Asia in the world will remain significant in terms of population as well as economic power in the coming century. As the population of Asians had already reached 4.17 billion in 2010, however, the major contributing factor of the global population increase will be the continuous demographic expansion in Africa, where the population is projected to quadruple from the baseline of 1.03 billion in 2010. The African continent, the birthplace of humankind, is expected to regain its demographic presence on par with the vastness of its landmass.

This picture of an 80 per cent majority of Asians and Africans requires some caution. First, it must be remembered that the Malthusian assumption (Malthus, 1985), in which the unchecked population increase would eventually lead to a human-environmental catastrophe, has been often narrated with mythophobic perceptions such as 'yellow-peril' and 'black-peril'. In reality, the simple Malthusian scenario conceived in the late eighteenth century has proved to be wrong; the population did not keep growing exponentially in any society, and agricultural production has grown steadily to accommodate the aggregate needs of the global population to date. There is much evidence to show that women's education and their involvement in 'gainful' employment outside the home tends to lower the total fertility rate (TFR), namely, the average number of children a woman in a society is expected to have in her lifetime (Sen, 1999). Rising costs

Dreaming Afrasia

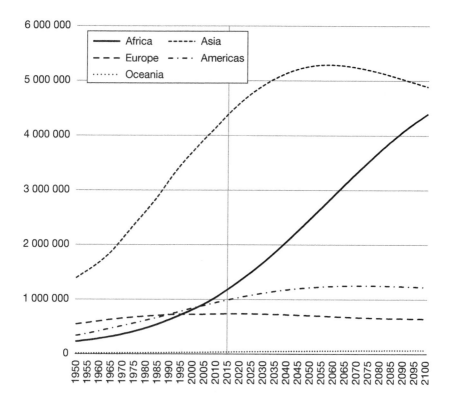

Figure 15.1 Projection of population growth by region

Sources: Based on the medium variant of UNDESA (2015), Population Division, available at https://esa.un.org/unpd/wpp/Download/Standard/Population/

of childbearing concomitant with urbanization, as well as the spread of contraception, also contribute to the decline of TFR. In short, a Malthusian catastrophe is avoidable through the empowerment of women.

Technically speaking, future population is determined solely by the levels of birth rate and death rate. The present pattern of demographic change has a momentum (or inertia), as the TFR of women and the death rate of alive persons do not radically change in the short term in any society. Therefore, it is known that the population projections at least for the next couple of decades are quite accurate, even though a projected state one century later is, more or less, guesswork (Livi-Bacci, 2012:216). The UN population projection is based on an assumption that the trend of declining TFR continues; the TFR of African women already started to decline in the 1980s.

As long as the TFR remains as high as four and five, the absolute size of the population on the African continent will continue to expand. However, in future Africa, just as in the rest of the world in the recent past, the TFR is assumed to drop gradually and settle down to around two, the replacement level. The United Nations projection therefore predicts that the '80 per cent majority' situation in the early twenty-second century will be a sort of stationary state, rather than one stage in an unending crisis of population explosion.

Second, population growth should not be considered an independent variable, as human demography is affected by various factors including policy choices and unfolding events that cannot be foreseen. While China introduced the rigid one child policy in 1979, Indira Gandhi's

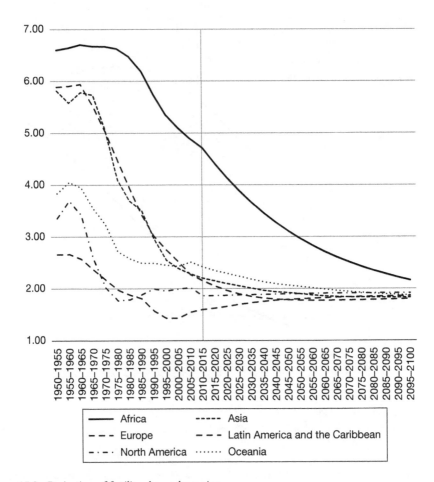

Figure 15.2 Projection of fertility change by region

Source: 15.2 Based on the medium variant of UNDESA (2015 online), Population Division, available at https://esa.un.org/unpd/wpp/Download/Standard/Population/

coercive birth control policy faced intense opposition in India in the late 1970s and was brought to a standstill, and the resultant contrasting population policies of China and India have greatly affected the paths of population transition in the two countries (Livi-Bacci, 2012). Such a divergence between the two countries was completely unpredictable at the time of their independence in the late 1940s. Looking at Africa, in hindsight, the high mobility of people conditioned by low population density was a major factor in the spread of HIV/AIDS, but the epidemic was largely unnoticed in the 1980s (Iliffe, 2006).

Third, the population question is not just about size. The future state of population is changeable in accordance with the choice of policies, which affect not only the absolute number of population of a given society, but also the quality of life of the increasing or decreasing population as well as their relationship with the natural environment. Therefore, it must be emphasized that the real problem lies in the population *structure* rather than in its absolute size. The rapid decline of population growth rate combined with relative longevity enjoyed by Asians means their region faces a drastic ageing of the population, which may entail an acute shortage of a working-age population and the collapse of formal pension systems. In contrast, on the

African continent, the young generation is expected to augment its presence into the twenty-second century. The UN projection shows that the world population will grow from 6.92 billion in 2010 to 10.85 billion in 2100, and as mentioned, this increment is largely attributable to the increase in Africa, which will put an enormous strain on the food security, or food sovereignty, of African nations. Given the prospective population expansion in Africa and global environmental constraints, a soft landing should be managed to ensure a decent life for all, especially the coming generations, who live on the African continent and elsewhere.

Although it is not propitious that the policy-makers in African countries have not been enthusiastic about agricultural reform after independence, compared with their Southeast Asian counterparts (Henley, 2015), radical agricultural modernization may not work in large parts of Africa where communal landholding functions as a last resort of social security. Capital-intensive development of the agrarian sector in Africa would deprive rural people of their more or less equal access to land and bring devastating social consequences. Without taking a labour-absorbing peasant path, the ongoing new 'enclosure' robbing the rural mass in the 'South' of land and jobs would be tantamount to the genocide of half of humanity (Amin, 2011:124). It must also be noted that the enhancement of agricultural production is not necessarily a solution to food shortages by itself. Even when the total food supply surpassed the aggregated demands of society, a lack of effective mechanism of market control and food distribution occasionally led to serious famine crises in both South Asia and Africa, as demonstrated by Amartya Sen's study on famine crises in Bengal, Bangladesh, Ethiopia and the Sahel (Sen, 1981).

In the twenty-first century, we have a plethora of regular Asian-African forums to solve developmental issues faced by contemporary Africa while aiming at ensuring mutual benefit: Tokyo International Conference of African Development (TICAD) started in 1993, Forum on China–Africa Cooperation (FOCAC) started in 2000, Korea Africa Forum started in 2006, and Africa–India Forum Summit started in 2008 (Taylor, 2011; Raposo, 2014; Dubey & Biswas, 2016). At some point in the future, based on a shared historical vision, these country-to-region summits may well be reorganized into a single region-to-region (Afro-Asian or Afrasian) forum, thereby avoiding duplication and unnecessary competition and opening up a way of dynamic mutual learning between Asians and Africans, rather than one-way transfer of knowledge from a big Asian country to dozens of separate African nations.

Pan-nationalist aspirations in Afrasia

Despite the cautions and unpredictability described in the previous section, it is almost certain that people who reside in Afrasia will form an overwhelming majority of the global population in the early twenty-second century. The quality of direct communication between Africans and Asians will therefore greatly influence the future shape of the world, but the opportunities of dialogue and mutual learning between these two regions are still very scant and intermittent at best. Here, the historic symbolism of Bandung stood out as the first instance of the framing of a broad regional group of Afrasia based on a binding spirit of anticolonialism and self-reliance. Despite the shared distance from the socialist bloc at the time, the organizers of the conference, especially Indonesia, were at pains to incorporate Maoist China into the Bandung framework. In this section, let us take a cursory overview of the pan-nationalist ethos propounded by some of the great intellectuals in twentieth-century Afrasia, in order to highlight the keynote aspirations underlying the spirit of Bandung.

It is possible to identify three common threads in their writings and speeches. First, the eminent nationalists in Afrasia protested against the military might and greed associated with the colonial aggression of the West. Their strong anti-Western attitudes may appear too bitter and confrontational today, but that was the reality in the twentieth century, especially for the awakened intellectuals in colonies. Second, the quintessence of their voice was to combine nationalism and humanism with the expectation that an assertion of particular values would ultimately enrich the universal human values. Third, they advocated unifying values of Asia or Africa surpassing parochial national interests, and in this sense, they were not so much nationalists as pan-nationalists. Although reactive nationalism begins with self-assertion of one's own values against the hegemonic powers, the articulation of nationalism often reached beyond a mere expression of narrow territorial identification.[4]

Having witnessed the horrendous violence of World War I, Rabindranath Tagore stated that 'the spirit of conflict and conquest is at the origin and in the centre of Western nationalism' (Tagore, 1917:33) and warned against the assimilation of such a spirit on the part of Japan and India. In one of his lectures, delivered in China in 1924, Tagore referred to an anecdote of British airmen at a crash-landing site being rescued by local people in a Mahsud village in Afghanistan, which had been attacked by the very same British aircraft. Then, comparing the bomber to an expensive 'toy' given to a child, he made the following point:

> Man's ideal has for its field of activity the whole human nature from its depth to its height. The light of this ideal is gentle because diffused, its life is subdued because all-embracing. It is serene because it is great; it is meek because it is comprehensive. But our passion is narrow; its limited field gives in an intensity of impulse. Such an aggressive force of greed has of late possessed the western mind. This has happened within a very short period, and has created a sudden deluge of things smothering all time and space over the earth.
>
> *(Tagore, 2002:133)*

Then Tagore cautioned the Chinese audience, 'I am sure you know that this soulless progeny of greed has already opened its elastic jaws wide over the fair limb of your country, wider perhaps than in any other part of the world' (ibid.: 138). The spirituality of Asian civilizations was accentuated by the Japanese pan-Asianist Okakura Tenshin (Kakuzo), a sworn friend of Tagore and a curator of the Museum of Fine Arts in Boston, the United States (Tankha, 2009). He commenced the first chapter of *The Ideals of the East* with a resounding statement.

> Asia is one. The Himalayas divide, only to accentuate, two mighty civilisations, the Chinese with its communism of Confucius, and the Indian with its individualism of the Vedas. But not even the snowy barriers can interrupt for one moment that broad expanse of love for the Ultimate and Universal, which is the common thought-inheritance of every Asiatic race, enabling them to produce all the great religions of the world, and distinguishing them from those maritime peoples of the Mediterranean and the Baltic, who love to dwell on the Particular, and to search out the means, not the end, of life.
>
> *(Okakura, 1903:1)*

Here, China and India are regarded as the core civilizations of Asia, though Okakura's contempt for 'maritime peoples' sounds somewhat strange because his own Japanese people as well as Southeast Asian and other coastal peoples in Asia are also exemplary 'maritime' peoples with dynamic polytheistic cultures akin to the ancient Greek culture. Still, in the early twentieth century, the idea of pan-Asianism was shared among a number of East Asian key intellectuals including Li Dazhao, one of the founders of the Chinese Communist Party. In 1924, the same year that Tagore visited China, Sun Yat-sen delivered a passionate lecture on pan-Asianism in Kobe, Japan.

Dreaming Afrasia

> Now, what is the problem that underlies Pan-Asianism, the Principle of Greater Asia, which we are discussing here today? Briefly, it is a cultural problem, a problem of comparison and conflict between the Oriental and Occidental culture and civilization. Oriental civilization is the rule of Right; Occidental civilization is the rule of Might. The rule of Right respects benevolence and virtue, while the rule of Might only respects force and utilitarianism. The rule of Right always influences people with justice and reason, while the rule of Might always oppresses people with brute force and military measures.
>
> *(Sun, 1924)*

At the end of his speech, Sun defied the Japanese audience to choose between 'the hawk of the Western civilization' and 'the tower of strength of the Orient', a question that could be potentially posed to any 'successful' nation in Asia. Japan eventually plunged into a complex and destructive war with its neighbours, Korea, China, the Pacific and the Western Allies, as the chimeral imperial power on the Far Eastern front of World War II.

Given the history of the transatlantic slave trade, as well as the depth and length of the Western colonial domination in Africa, the discourse of pan-Africanism was more abundant and articulate than that of pan-Asianism, making meticulous citations almost redundant. The First Pan-African Conference was organized by Henry Sylvester-Williams in London in 1900, then the First Pan-African Congress by W.E.B. Du Bois in Paris in 1919, followed by a series of gatherings that took place in various parts of Western Europe and North America in the 1920s. A galaxy of major advocates of pan-Africanism included Marcus Garvey, C.L.R. James and George Padmore. Though often misunderstood as a banal humanist, due to an out-of-context translation of a part of his poem from French to English, the Martinican poet Aimé Césaire eloquently denounced the evil of colonialism and Eurocentrism in 1955, the very year of Bandung.

> I note . . . that colonial enterprise is to the modern world what Roman imperialism was to the ancient world: the prelude to Disaster and the forerunner of Catastrophe. Come, now! The Indians massacred, the Moslem world drained of itself, the Chinese world defiled and perverted for a good century; the Negro world disqualified; mighty voices stilled forever; homes scattered to the wind; all this wreckage, all this waste, humanity reduced to a monologue, and you think all that does not have its price? The truth is that this policy *cannot but bring about the ruin of Europe itself,* and that Europe, if it is not careful, will perish from the void it has created around itself.
>
> *(Césaire, 1972:75. Italics in original)*

While the Bandung Conference was attended by only 6 African states, 34 states became independent from 1956 to 1965, and 11 more from 1966 to 1975. The gravity of pan-Africanism shifted from the African diaspora world to the continent, and the Caribbean pan-Africanist thinkers such as George Padmore and W.A. Lewis crossed the Atlantic and served as the advisors of Kwame Nkrumah of Ghana. Compared with East Asia where the Cold War confrontation was to manifest in the Korean War and the Vietnam War, Africa seems to have been better positioned to tap into the Non-Alignment Movement to promote African unity. The president of Tanzania, Julius Nyerere, attempted to construct an 'imagined community' of village-based Ujamaa (family-like solidarity), partly inspired by the philosophy of self-reliance in Maoist China.[5]

'UJAMAA', then, or 'familyhood', describes our Socialism. It is opposed to Capitalism, which seeks to build a happy society on the basis of the Exploitation of Man by Man; and it is equally opposed to doctrinaire Socialism which seeks to build its happy society on a philosophy of Inevitable Conflict between Man and Man. We, in Africa, have no more need of being 'converted' to socialism than we have of being 'taught' democracy. Both are rooted in our own past – in the traditional society which produced us.

(Nyerere, 1962)

The pan-African thought nurtured by Africans both in the diaspora world and on the African continent was synthesized by Steve Biko, who advocated Black Consciousness in apartheid South Africa. Inspired by the writings of Frantz Fanon, Sékou Touré, Kenneth Kaunda, Robert Sobukwe and other pan-Africanist thinkers as well as the Hegelian master–servant dialectic, Biko lucidly argued that African humanity would make an immense contribution to the world. He was tortured and killed at the age of thirty.

We reject the power-based society of the Westerner that seems to be ever concerned with perfecting their technological know how while losing out on their spiritual dimension. We believe that in the long run the special contribution to the world by Africa will be in this field of human relationship. The great power of the world may have done wonders in giving the world an industrial and military look, but the great gift still has to come from Africa – giving the world a more human face.

(Biko, 1978:46–7)

Based on the dichotomy between the West and 'us', those pan-nationalist figures of Afrasia exalted a culture and collective dignity of their own, denouncing the Western expansionism accompanied by militarism, and dreamt a contribution of the particular to the universal, and tried to bring forward an alternative humanistic frame of the universal. In the latter half of the twentieth century, pan-nationalist aspirations became more pressing as the liberation wars in Algeria and Vietnam were getting fierce and conclusive.

However, in spite of the concurrence and strong resonance of voices, there was not much literature in which the aspirations of pan-nationalism in Asia and Africa were expressed as the single agency, except for a handful of political tracts written under the influence of Marxism. The role of Islam, which was born in the seventh century after Judaism and Christianity in the knot of Afrasia and then permeated much of the southern belt of Asia as well as the northern and eastern part of Africa, has not been discussed explicitly in the framework of Afrasian politics either, though a pan-Islamic dream nurtured by Jamal ad-Din al-Afghani, who wandered through India, Afghanistan, Persia, Turkey and Egypt in the latter half of the nineteenth century, is still powerfully enticing (Mishra, 2012).[6] Although it is undeniable that the spirit of Bandung embraced both pan-Asianism and pan-Africanism, the group of Bandung was no more than a coalition of newly independent nation-states. The political leaders of post-independent Afrasia were therefore expected to fulfil the roles of benign 'teachers' to guide their peoples within the cages of new sovereign nations (Chakrabarty, 2010).

Beyond the reversal of centre–periphery relations

It was the historian Arnold Toynbee who originally coined the term Afrasia, which signified nomadic grasslands that used to stretch 'from Arabia across Northern Africa', where the Sumerian and Egyptian civilizations were born as responses to gradual desiccation (Toynbee, 1946:57–8, 68–74).

For Toynbee, Afrasia was the space physically connecting Africa and Asia, today's Middle East, that served as a cradle of civilization, from which the geographic cores of Africa and Asia were excluded as its hinterlands.[7] More recently, Jared Diamond (1997) argued that the vast west–east stretch of the temperate zone in the Eurasian continent gave rise to the economic development of Western Europe at the western end of the axis, while the diversity of ecological zones hampered the development of Africa due to the lack of economy of scale. Diamond paid very little attention to the emergence of economic centres at the eastern end of the Eurasian axis; China lost its 'technological lead' after all. In his thesis, the historical experience of Eastern Asia in parallel with Western Europe was sidelined, and the major part of Africa was characterized principally by its geographic inaccessibility. The powerful nomadic civilization in Central Asia that connected both ends of Eurasia also vanished from the scene. Despite the emphasis on the Eurasian axis, the west–east interplay is underrated in the Diamond thesis.

In contrast, the recent key literature in economic history puts a fresh focus on the holistic connectivity of Eurasian, rather than Afrasian, paths of economic development. The centrality of Asia, especially China, in the single world system was elucidated by Andre Gunder Frank (1998) in *ReOrient* and by Kenneth Pomeranz (2000) in *The Great Divergence*. In terms of material wealth, according to these works, the Asian economy had at least stayed on par with its European counterpart until the eighteenth century (or the nineteenth century depending on authors and their definitions), and the European economy started to emerge, or diverge, only since then. The rise of Europe was made possible only through Europe's monopolistic control of the silver flow from Latin America, as well as the benefit Europe received from the coercive transatlantic slave trade. According to Frank, the entire world order had been Sinocentric from 1400 to 1800 with the great exporter, China, functioning as the final 'sink' of the world's silver, while Pomeranz stressed that parts of Western Europe and Eastern Asia revealed 'surprising resemblances' before the great divergence, and urged economic historians to engage in 'reciprocal comparisons'.[8]

From this long term viewpoint, the gravity of economic development is now decisively shifting from the West to the East, pushing China and other Asian nations *back* to their original predominant positions in the world economy. Giovanni Arrighi argued that China and East Asian nations had followed a Smithean 'natural' path of economic development based on inclusive market expansion, while North Atlantic nations had taken an 'unnatural' path of development driven by foreign trade and buttressed by military power. In today's East Asia, the Smithean path manifests its original strength (Arrighi, 2007). Finally, the North Atlantic capital-intensive path of 'industrial revolution' is contrasted with the East Asian labour-intensive path of 'industrious revolution', and the implications of this dual-path model for other regions, especially Africa where land has been abundant while labour and capital have been scarce, are vigorously discussed (Sugihara, 2003; Austin & Sugihara, 2013).

With the re-emergence of Asia, it seems that Sinocentric international relations have been gradually restored. In this light, China is expected to play a major role as a responsible great power, responsible not only for the entire world including the West but also for the rest of Afrasia, including sub-Saharan Africa and Southeast Asia, not as a void of history but as distinctive sub-regions with their own economy and institutions. As the North Atlantic powers gradually retreat from Asia, the question of the Western domination that great pan-nationalists confronted is dissipating, and the peoples of Afrasia are now obliged to address a possible bifurcation of development and underdevelopment within their own region. The exercise of mainstreaming the experience of the 'periphery' of Afrasia will also contribute to recasting the meaning of freedom, defined as the power to act according to one's own will without restraint.

In land-abundant and labour-scarce societies, in abstract terms, political systems tend to be centrifugal and farming methods tend to be extensive. In such conditions, unlike land-scarce and labour-abundant societies, it is meaningless to mobilize labour for collective development because surplus labour does not exist in permanent forms. African precolonial societies were characterized by high mobility of people in unoccupied, boundless land; in case of conflict and natural calamities, groups of disgruntled and stressed people were pushed out of established polities into sparsely populated frontiers as the 'institutional vacuum' and formed new settlements, which eventually grew into new chiefdoms and kingdoms, and the dynamic process of fission and fusion was repeated. The ubiquity of this 'frontier tradition' is supposed to have formed a pan-African political culture (Kopytoff, 1987; Herbst, 2000).

Historical high mobility of people is observed not only among continental Africans but also maritime and mountain peoples in East and Southeast Asia. In Southeast Asia, the power of kings and lords was also limited, because in this part of the world 'where land was abundant, buildings impermanent, and property insecure, it was in followers that power and wealth were primarily expressed' (Reid, 1988:120). It is well known that the widespread tributary networks centring on China greatly contributed to the rise of the East Asian economy before and after Western colonization. While Chinese expatriate merchants and their communities scattered across East and Southeast Asia, their regional movement was largely autonomous, being motivated by trading opportunities rather than unilaterally dictated by the will of the successive central governments of China (Hamashita et al., 2008). When it comes to the mountain peoples, stateless forms of self-government were deliberately chosen by the locals in a vast highland zone of Southeast Asia called Zomia, and it is argued that this 'anarchical' governance was not a residual trait of primitive societies but the manifestations of the agency of people who tried to escape from the authority of the lowlands (Scott, 2009).

Based on his exit-voice model, A.O. Hirschman elucidated the internal logic of constant fission and fusion in land-abundant and labour-scarce societies. In such conditions, the principle of 'voting with one's feet' prevails like in the idealized market economy, where a customer is completely free to switch from one trader to another. However, the mobile societies of the Nuer, Central African peoples, the Khoisan and the Mbuti pygmy in sparsely populated Africa, as well as of the Nambikwara of Central Brazil, had to succumb to 'the perhaps less efficient but more powerful societies – exitless and endowed with a centralized political organization – that arose elsewhere' (Hirschman, 1978:96).

No condition is permanent, indeed. In the process of land dispossession and apartheid social engineering in the twentieth century, people in South Africa started to face acute land shortage and structural unemployment across cities and the countryside. 'Southern Africans began to suffer the land-scarce family poverty long predominant in more densely peopled continents' (Iliffe, 1987:260). Rapid population increase in Africa is certainly expected to change the patterns of factor endowments and affect the modality of political, economic and social institutions on the continent. Sooner or later, population growth and land grabbing on the African landmass will oblige Africans to face developmental challenges similar to those in labour-abundant India and China. If African countries invest sufficiently in health and education, the principal components of human development, however, labour supply will improve in quantity and quality, thereby paving the way for labour-intensive industrialization in Africa (Austin, 2013).

Although a rapid population increase in a relatively labour-scarce economy can be a blessing in disguise, it must also be remembered that institutions have a force of inertia. Institutional norms and practices in a given nation may change in a relatively short time, but once established, they tend to stay constant, resist change and determine long-term paths of development of economy and society (Acemoglu & Robinson, 2012). Therefore, 'Africa had land-rich cultural traditions even where land was scarce' (Iliffe, 2007:4). However, there can be a reverse situation: a centripetal statecraft developed in a land-scarce situation is superimposed on a centrifugal land-abundant society. The following is the famous characterization of Southeast Asian plural society by J.S. Furnivall.

> In Burma, as in Java, probably the first thing that strikes the visitor is the medley of peoples – European, Chinese, Indian and native. It is in the strictest sense a medley, for they mix but do not combine. Each group holds by its own religion, its own culture and language, its own ideas and ways. As individuals they meet, but only in the market-place, in buying and selling. There is a plural society, with different sections of the community living side by side, but separately, within the same political unit.
>
> *(Furnivall, 1948:304)*

In this citation, Furnivall honestly noted that he was a 'visitor'; local people may have interacted with each other in ways unnoticed by outsiders. Still, at least, they did not want to work together for the colonial rule at the time. The founder of social anthropology, A.R. Radcliffe-Brown, characterized the 'composite society' in colonial Africa, most typically in South Africa, in almost the same way as Furnivall (Radcliffe-Brown, 1952:202). Then, what would happen if the European segment lost power in a colonial plural society? The Fabian socialist colonial officer Furnivall argued that Southeast Asian nations should grapple with the challenge of 'reintegration' in order to prepare themselves for future independence. It is in this context that the 'imagined communities' as bonding national artefacts were constructed with zeal in colonial and postcolonial Afrasia, modelling the Western precedents (Anderson, 1983). Nevertheless, the propensity towards power dispersal in land-abundant society in Afrasia seems to affect the organizational ways of the Association of Southeast Asian Nations (ASEAN) and the African Union (AU), which have gradually formed consensus-based political communities without creating pariah members.

Ester Boserup, the development economist renowned for her theory of population growth and agricultural development, pointed out that women in sub-Saharan Africa and Southeast Asia participated fully in shifting agriculture as well as trade activities in cities (Boserup, 1970). Extensive agriculture, which was a reasonable method of farming in a land-abundant society, but is considered a bottleneck of productivity rise in agriculture, functioned as an arrangement conducive to the relative freedom of one half of the population: women. It seems that institutions and practices in Africa and Southeast Asia are more advantageous to women than in hierarchical societies in the rest of Afrasia. Amartya Sen demonstrated that a great number of women were 'missing' in the world. As women tend to outlive men biologically, the female–male ratio (FMR) should be more than one. In reality, however, the FMR is less than one in many countries in South, East and West Asia as well as North Africa, in contrast with those in sub-Saharan Africa and Southeast Asia where women enjoy relative longevity, not least due to their engagement in economic activities outside the home. If the FRM in sub-Saharan Africa is considered a benchmark, we can calculate the 'deficit' of women in other regions, which amounts to 100 million in total (Sen, 1990).[9] They are missing mainly due to the structural neglect of women, selective abortion and even female infanticide.

A reversal of global history heralded by the resurgence of Asia may lead to a bifurcation of Asia and Africa. While the rise of European capitalism was financed by the uncompensated extraction of silver and exploitation of African slaves in the Americas, the economic expansion of China, Japan, the Asian NIEs as well as India is now supported by industrial inputs such as crude oil from Africa. Whether the present patterns of trade boil down to an intra-Afrasian return of macroparasites (McNeill, 1976) or the realization of a new equitable global economic order largely depends on the stability of the world price of primary commodities. In the 1970s, there was a limited scheme to stabilize export earnings of the African, Caribbean and Pacific countries operated by the European Commission, but the voice calling for a global mechanism has lost its momentum due to the breakup of the 'South'. If the growth of the global economy slows down, export-oriented African economies may suffer a devastating blow, while industrialized countries are forced to adjust their already diversified economies. The principle of equal sovereignty, reciprocity and mutual benefit confirmed repeatedly in Bandung will have to go through a serious trial if a global economic crisis should occur.

To sum it up, in the future, the two components of Afrasia may follow divergent paths of development and underdevelopment if African economies remain dependent on exports of a certain set of primary commodities. Another possible scenario is the convergence of patterns of poverty and development across Africa and Asia as discussed earlier. Given a gradual shift of factor endowments in Africa due to a massive increase of population and resultant scarcity of arable land, the shape of African society in the twenty-first century may approach hierarchical societies of populous countries such as India and China. However, the same transformation may open up a possibility for Africa to pursue a labour-intensive development path driven by human capital development. In reality, the forces towards divergence and the forces towards convergence are entangled with each other, and the future course of intra-Afrasian relationships will be determined by the quality of dialogue and mutual learning between Africa and Asia, not only at the diplomatic and academic levels but also in daily encounters of African and Asian transnational migrants who are at the forefront of inter-regional human exchange (Cornelissen & Mine, 2017).

Conclusion

Clifford Geertz described the nature of Bali's political institution like this: 'The political development of precolonial Indonesia does not consist of a relentless unfoldment of a monolithic "Oriental despotism", but of an expanding cloud of localized, fragile, loosely interrelated petty principalities' (Geertz, 1980:4). The democracy of 'voting with one's feet' in smaller communities in Africa and Southeast Asia may function as an antidote to the traditional authorities of big nations in Afrasia. At the same time, it must be remembered that the great pan-nationalists in East and South Asia, Africa and the African diaspora world opposed the 'rule of Might' and military nationalism, advocated wider regional, multilateral frameworks that would accommodate aspirations of both big and small nations, and envisioned the contribution of the particular to the universal. If we return to the supreme writings and eloquent speeches produced by pan-Asianists and pan-Africanists in the twentieth century, an Afrasian unity in diversity seems to be promising without being preoccupied with 'an elite-driven and politically motivated exercise' too much.

In the first section of this chapter, we envisaged a future world in which Asians and Africans would form an 80 per cent majority. While the population theories of Malthus (1985) and Boserup (1965) are often contrasted as the extremes of pessimism and optimism, these two perspectives seem to complement each other in that the former makes much of the long term constraints of resource scarcity, while the latter sheds light upon the possibility of short term innovative responses to population crises, the accumulated effects of which may eventually make a huge difference to outcomes. Capacity development, the enhancement of problem-solving abilities of communities, is the *sine qua non* to address the structural problems such as youth unemployment, ageing, food crisis, deteriorating environment and other pressing issues concomitant with

Dreaming Afrasia

the global population transition. The ideal of Sarvodaya propounded by Mohandas Gandhi (1954) and the concept of intermediate technology presented by E.F. Schumacher (1973) should be revisited, and methods of successful small experiments should be adapted to other conditions and scaled up. University institutions in Afrasia are expected to play significant roles as the sites of innovation, reproduction and diffusion of knowledge to cope with the historic transition.

Politically, it must be stressed that the key to an Afrasian revival is to realize political stability in the joint point of Afrasia, the Middle East and North Africa. This sub-region anguishes in the vortex of wars ignited by the onslaught of military intervention of the West, especially the United States, which the great pan-nationalists of Afrasia should have unanimously condemned. Restoration of peace in the knot of Afrasia is the precondition for eternal peace of the entire human race. The binding frame of Afrasia was justified by the common history of decolonization in the twentieth century; the pan-nationalist aspirations of Asians and Africans were always expressed in relation to the West, with underlying affections of love and hate, in the hope of embracing a provincialized Europe (Chakrabarty, 2000). In today's Afrasia, the major challenge is to find workable ways to realize the coexistence of diverse, both big and small nations within the broad region in a peaceful and consensual way. The Nobel Prize economist of African descent, W. Arthur Lewis, once stated that democracy had two meanings: 'Its primary meaning is that all who are affected by a decision should have the chance to participate in making that decision . . . Its secondary meaning is that the will of the majority shall prevail' (Lewis, 1965:64). Afrasia's denunciation of colonialism is not necessarily anti-Western, but simply means that the 'rule of Might' should not be allowed in the region forever.

Finally, where is the natural place for the Americas outside the historical-political nexus of Euro-Afrasia? In the societal dimension, the Americas are characterized by creolization between indigenous peoples and the diasporas of African, Asian as well as European origins. While Acemoglu & Robinson (2012) accentuated the institutional advantage of North America over Latin America separated by the Mexican border, the historical fact is that Latin America and the Caribbean, especially the large nation, Brazil, were exempt from the rigid racial segregation that was manifest in the American South and apartheid South Africa (Marx, 1998). Probably, the Americas as a combined whole stay one step ahead of Afrasia in terms of diversity of population, as well as their capabilities to accommodate conflicting needs and aspirations of people with a wealth of backgrounds, previsioning an image of a united people on the globe in the future.

Notes

1   The frame of Afrasia has been presented in Mazrui & Adem (2013) with an emphasis on the diversity of Afro-Asian societies, their connectivity and the multiple effects of globalization. There is an 'Afrasian Research Centre' at Ryukoku University, a Japanese Buddhist university in Kyoto. http://afrasia. ryukoku.ac.jp/english/ (last accessed 1 May 2016). I am grateful for the invaluable comments on earlier versions of this chapter given by colleagues and students I have met in places including Accra, Cape Town, Delhi, Beijing, Tokyo and Paris.
2   In 2014, the Asian Infrastructure Investment Bank (AIIB) was launched by 50 mainly Eurasian nations. Several major economic powers like the United States, Canada and Japan did not participate as its founding members.
3   UNDESA (2015). The figures cited here are based on the medium variant. Africa includes Northern Africa, while Asia is composed of Eastern, South-Central, Central, Southern, South-Eastern and Western Asia based on the UN definition of regional boundaries. The estimation and projection are updated every few years, so the readers are advised to consult the latest figures. A few years after 2050, one will be able to see a projection up to 2150 at the UNDESA website (if the network called 'internet' is still in use).

4 According to H.W. Arndt, the notion of 'economic development' had its origins exclusively in the West. It was argued that 'reactive nationalism' fermented by the Western intrusion had played a major role as the catalyst of modernization in Japan, China, India and other non-Western nations (Arndt, 1987).
5 Though Nyerere is widely respected by Tanzanians as Mwalimu (teacher), his bureaucracy failed to 'capture' the Tanzanian peasantry and to rally them to the national socialist cause of Ujamaa (Hyden, 1980).
6 The role of secular pan-Arabism is also beyond the reach of the present discussion. As for an attempt to revitalize the tradition of 'Afro-Asian coalition' in the multi-lateral fora, see Adebajo (2008), which touches upon the roles of the 'Terrible Triplets', Jawaharlal Nehru, Gamal Abdel Nasser and Kwame Nkrumah, in the Non-Aligned Movement. Nelson Mandela's first book, *No Easy Walk to Freedom*, was titled after one of Nehru's writings (Mandela, 1965).
7 There have been Asian and African attempts at claiming the ownership of the motherland of mono-theistic religions. Sun Yat-sen's statement that 'even the ancient civilizations of the West, of Greece and Rome, had their origins on Asiatic soil' (Sun, 1924) is correct as long as the eastern coast of the Mediterranean Sea is accepted as belonging to West Asia. On the other hand, Cheek Anta Diop (1974) emphasized the African origin of the Egyptian civilization.
8 Beyond reciprocity, Hobson (2004) even argues that the overwhelming influence of the East on the West extended over the spheres of technologies, institutions and ideas.
9 If we recalculate the missing women based on the latest UN population estimation (UNDESA, 2015), the number still appears to be hovering around 110 million. In 2015, the FMR of sub-Saharan Africa was 100, while those of West Asia, India, China and Southeast Asia were 92, 93, 94 and 100 respectively.

References

Acemoglu, D. and Robinson, J. A. 2012. *Why Nations Fail: The Origins of Power, Prosperity, and Poverty*, New York: Crown Publishers.
Acharya, A. and Buzan, B. 2010. 'On the possibility of a non-Western international relations theory', in A. Acharya and B. Buzan (eds.), *Non-Western International Relations Theory: Perspectives on and beyond Asia*, London and New York: Routledge, pp. 221–38.
Adebajo, A. 2008. 'From Bandung to Durban: Whither the Afro-Asian coalition?', in S. S. Tan and A. Acharya (eds.), *Bandung Revisited: The Legacy of the 1955 Asian–African Conference for International Order*, Singapore: NUS Press, pp. 105–31.
Amin, S. 2011. *Ending the Crisis of Capitalism or Ending Capitalism?*, Cape Town: Pambazuka Press.
Ampiah, K. 2007. *The Political and Moral Imperatives of the Bandung Conference of 1955: The Reactions of the US, UK and Japan*, Folkestone, Kent: Global Oriental.
Anderson, B. 1983. *Imagined Communities: Reflections on the Origin and Spread of Nationalism*, London: Verso.
Arndt, H.W. 1987. *Economic Development: The History of an Idea*, Chicago: University of Chicago Press.
Arrighi, G. 2007. *Adam Smith in Beijing: Lineages of the Twenty-First Century*, London: Verso.
Austin, G. 2013. 'Labour-intensity and manufacturing in West Africa, c.1450–c.2000', in G. Austin and K. Sugihara (eds.), *Labour-Intensive Industrialization in Global History*, London and New York: Routledge, pp. 201–230.
Austin, G. and Sugihara, K. (eds.) 2013. *Labour-Intensive Industrialization in Global History*, London and New York: Routledge.
Biko, S. 1978. *I Write What I Like: A Selection of His Writings*, London: Heinemann.
Boserup, E. 1965. *The Conditions of Agricultural Growth: The Economics of Agrarian Change under Population Pressure*, London: George Allen & Unwin.
Boserup, E. 1970. *Woman's Role in Economic Development*, London: Earthscan.
Césaire, A. 1972. *Discourse on Colonialism (1955)*, New York: Tr. Joan Pinkham, Monthly Review Press.
Chakrabarty, D. 2000. *Provincializing Europe: Postcolonial Thought and Historical Difference*, Princeton, NJ: Princeton University Press.
Chakrabarty, D. 2010. 'The legacies of Bandung: Decolonization and the politics of culture', in C. J. Lee (ed.), *Making a World after Empire: The Bandung Moment and Its Political Afterlives*, Athens, OH: Ohio University Press, pp. 45–68.

Cornelissen, S. and Mine, Y. (eds.), 2017. *Migration and Agency in a Globalizing World: Afro-Asian Encounters*, Basingstoke: Palgrave Macmillan.

Diamond, J. 1997. *Guns, Germs, and Steel: The Fates of Human Societies*, New York: W.W. Norton.

Diop, C. A. 1974. *The African Origin of Civilization: Myth or Reality*, Chicago: Tr. Mercer Cook, Lawrence Hill.

Dubey, A. K. and Biswas, A. (eds.), 2016. *India and Africa's Partnership: A Vision for a New Future*, New Delhi: Springer.

Frank, A. G. 1998. *ReORIENT: Global Economy in the Asian Age*, Berkeley, CA: University of California Press.

Furnivall, J. S. 1948. *Colonial Policy and Practice: A Comparative Study of Burma and Netherlands India*, Cambridge: The University Press.

Geertz, C. 1980. *Negara: The Theatre State in Nineteenth-Century Bali*, Princeton, NJ: Princeton University Press.

Gandhi, M. 1954. *Sarvodaya: The Welfare of All*, Ahmedabad: Navajivan Publishing House.

Hamashita, T., Linda, G. and Selden, M. (eds.), 2008. *China, East Asia and the Global Economy: Regional and Historical Perspectives*, London: Routledge.

Henley, D. 2015. *Asia–Africa Development Divergence: A Question of Intent*, London and New York: Zed Books.

Herbst, J. 2000. *States and Power in Africa: Comparative Lessons in Authority and Control*, Princeton, NJ: Princeton University Press.

Hirschman, A. O. 1978. 'Exit, Voice, and the State', *World Politics*, Volume 31(1), pp. 90–107.

Hobson, J. M. 2004. *The Eastern Origins of Western Civilisation*, Cambridge: Cambridge University Press.

Hyden, G. 1980. *Beyond Ujamaa in Tanzania: Underdevelopment and an Uncaptured Peasantry*, London: Heinemann.

Iliffe, J. 1987. *The African Poor: A History*, Cambridge: Cambridge University Press.

Iliffe, J. 2006. *The African AIDS Epidemic: A History*, Oxford: James Currey.

Iliffe, J. 2007. *Africans: The History of a Continent*, 2nd ed., Cambridge: Cambridge University Press.

Kopytoff, I. (ed.), 1987. *The African Frontier: The Reproduction of Traditional African Societies*, Bloomington and Indianapolis: Indiana University Press.

Kuhn, T. S. 2012. *The Structure of Scientific Revolutions*, 4th ed., Chicago: University of Chicago Press.

Lee, C. J. (ed.), 2010. *Making a World after Empire: The Bandung Moment and Its Political Afterlives*, Athens, OH: Ohio University Press.

Lewis, W. A. 1965. *Politics in West Africa*, Toronto and New York: Oxford University Press.

Livi-Bacci, M. 2012. *A Concise History of World Population*, 5th ed., Chichester: Blackwell.

Malthus, T. R. 1985. *An Essay on the Principle of Population (1798): And a Summary View of the Principle of Population (1830)*, Harmondsworth: Penguin, 1985.

Mandela, N. 1965. *No Easy Walk to Freedom: Articles, Speeches and Trial Addresses*, New York: Basic Books.

Marx, A. W. 1998. *Making Race and Nation: A Comparison of South Africa, the United States, and Brazil*, Cambridge: Cambridge University Press.

Mazrui, A. A. and Adem, S. 2013. *Afrasia: A Tale of Two Continents*, Lanham, MD: University Press of America.

McNeill, W. H. 1976. *Plagues and Peoples*, New York: Anchor Press.

Mishra, P. 2012. *From the Ruins of Empire: The Revolt Against the West and the Remaking of Asia*, London: Penguin.

Nyerere, J. K. 1962. *'Ujamaa': The Basis of African Socialism*, Dar es Salaam: Taganyika Standard.

Okakura, K. 1903. *The Ideals of the East: With Special Reference to the Art of Japan*, London: J. Murray.

Pomeranz, K. 2000. *The Great Divergence: China, Europe, and the Making of the Modern World Economy*, Princeton: Princeton University Press.

Radcliffe-Brown, A. R. 1952. *Structure and Function in Primitive Society: Essays and Addresses*, London: Cohen & West.

Raposo, P. A. 2014. *Japan's Foreign Aid Policy in Africa: Evaluating the TICAD Process*, New York: Palgrave Macmillan.

Reid, A. 1988. *Southeast Asia in the Age of Commerce, 1450–1680, Volume One: The Lands below the Winds*, New Haven, CT: Yale University Press.

Schumacher, E. F. 1973. *Small is Beautiful: A Study of Economics as if People Mattered*, London: Blond and Briggs.

Scott, J. C. 2009. *The Art of Not Being Governed: An Anarchist History of Upland Southeast Asia*, New Haven: Yale University Press.

Sen, A. 1981. *Poverty and Famines: An Essay on Entitlement and Deprivation*, Oxford: Clarendon Press.

Sen, A. 1990. 'More Than 100 Million Women Are Missing', *New York Review of Books*, 20 December. Available at: http://www.nybooks.com/articles/archives/1990/dec/20/more-than-100-million-women-are-missing/ (Accessed 1 May 2016).

Sen, A. 1999. *Development as Freedom*, New York: Alfred A. Knopf.

Sugihara, K. 2003. 'The East Asian path of economic development: A long-term perspective', in G. Arrighi, T. Hamashita and M. Selden (eds.), *The Resurgence of East Asia: 500, 150 and 50 Year Perspectives*, London: Routledge, pp. 78–123.

Sun, Y.-S. 1924. *'Pan-Asianism'*. Available at: https://en.wikisource.org/wiki/Sun_Yat-sen's_speech_on_Pan-Asianism (Accessed 1 May 2016).

Tagore, R. 1917. *Nationalism*, New York: Macmillan.

Tagore, R. 2002. *Talks in China: Lectures Delivered in April and May, 1924*, New Delhi: Rupa.

Tankha, B. (ed.), 2009. *Okakura Tenshin and Pan-Asianism: Shadows of the Past*, Folkestone, Kent: Global Oriental.

Taylor, I. 2011. *The Forum on China–Africa Cooperation (FOCAC)*, Abingdon, Oxon: Routledge.

Toynbee, A. J. 1946. *A Study of History: Abridgement of Volumes I–VI by D.C. Somervell*, London and New York: Oxford University Press.

UNDESA (United Nations, Department of Economic and Social Affairs) Population Division. 2015. *World Population Prospects: The 2015 Revision*. Available at: http://www.un.org/en/development/desa/population/ (Accessed 1 May 2016).

16

THE ROLE OF ISLAM IN FORGING LINKAGES BETWEEN AFRICA AND ASIA FROM THE 1970S

The case of Islamic relief and development support

Mayke Kaag

Introduction

As a contribution to the discussion of different aspects of Africa–Asia relations over time in this volume, the present chapter aims to highlight the role of Islam in forging linkages between Africa and Asia. Taking as a point of departure that Islam's bridging role has taken on different forms at different times and is constantly evolving, I will analyse a particular form of Islamic 'bridging' that emerged in the 1970s, namely Islamic humanitarianism, relief, and development support. The specific ways in which Islamic relief has nourished African-Asian relations will be discussed as well as its consequences and prospects.

As already shown in preceding chapters in this volume (see Chapters 4 and 5), Islam has been a source, a vehicle, and a purpose for contacts between different parts of Africa and Asia from a very early age. These contacts concerned trade, such as the trans-Saharan trade that developed, in particular, between the eighth and nineteenth centuries, the Sahara constituting part of a much larger world system of exchange centred on the Muslim world, which extended from West Africa across Arabia and central Iran through Central Asia to Inner Mongolia (Ross, 2011: 2). Examples of scholarly exchange also abound, during pilgrimages to Mecca or when studying with a celebrated Muslim *shaykh* (spiritual master). Students from Pakistan, Malaysia, Indonesia, and the Sudan and the Senegambia, for instance, who came to study with Al-Samman (1718–1775) in Medina in Saudi Arabia, took his teachings back with them, thus helping to spread the sufi order of the *Samaniyya* in their home regions. (O'Fahey, 2004; Hunwick, 1984). Some of them, through their teachers, travels, and writings, became a link between Southeast Asia and the Sudan (O'Fahey, 2004).

Colonialism, on the one hand, hampered contacts between different parts of the Islamic World; on the other hand, there are several instances when it also facilitated these contacts. British rule, for example, brought Muslims in South Africa and South Asia together under one empire (Reese, 2014). From the end of the nineteenth century, improved means of communication and the development and expansion of (mass) printing technically facilitated contacts between different parts of the world and dissemination of religious ideas (Green, 2012). After World War II, these contacts continued and intensified beyond colonial control. What was billed as the first Asian-African Conference took place in the Indonesian city of Bandung in 1955. While its explicit purpose was to overcome racial, religious, and ideological divides and to nurture a common voice of anticolonialism, for the Muslim countries participating, their shared religion certainly smoothed the relationships, exchange, and solidarity between them, and Indonesia gained good publicity in the rest of the Muslim world by organising the event (Van Bruinessen, 2012).

In this context of intensifying globalisation in the postcolonial era, the 1970s saw new forms of Islamic connections between Asia and Africa,[1] such as Islamic relief and development support, including providing scholarships for Africans to study in the Middle East and East Asia. It is on this phenomenon of Islamic relief that this chapter will focus. Islamic humanitarianism prospered throughout the 1990s, but became increasingly problematic towards the end of this decade, and particularly after 9/11, as the work of Islamic relief organisations was seriously hampered by accusations of support for Islamic terrorism. As we will see towards the end of this chapter, this led them to adapt to the new situation in specific ways.

This chapter takes as a point of departure that the Middle East is an integral part of Asia, and that North Africa is part of Africa, despite the fact that several strands of Asian and African Studies have for a long time stated otherwise. In this, I am following Green's perspective that it is useful to look at spheres of influence, instead of using fixed (colonially determined) definitions of what constitutes Asia and/or Africa (Green, 2014). From this point of view, we can see that the Middle East and North Africa have been crucial in connecting Muslim communities in Africa and Asia, and that from this centre, influence spread to the larger Asian and African hinterlands, from where Muslims also connected back to the centre. Another old centre of connections between Muslims in Africa and Asia has been the Indian Ocean (Bang, 2003; Green, 2014). It is interesting to note that, in the era that is the focus of this chapter, through Islamic relief, once largely elitist African-Asian Islamic connections – i.e. which primarily connected trading and scholarly elites – came to include poorer segments of African populations, too. We will see, however, that these connections through the charity chain also have repercussions for the mutual perceptions of the different groups on both continents.

I will first describe the emergence of transnational Islamic charities in the late 1970s and explain some of their characteristics. I will then elaborate on how Asian-African connections are being built by the work of these charities, followed by a section on how 9/11 and its aftermath have influenced these organisations' work. The chapter will conclude with a brief reflection on the future of Islamic relief as a bridge between Asia and Africa. Data for this chapter have been collected through literature review and several fieldwork trips to Chad and Senegal in the period 2004–2016, and to Qatar in 2015.

The birth of transnational Islamic relief adding to the humanitarian landscape

The late 1970s saw the establishment of the first transnational Islamic charities. Their emergence was triggered by the war in Afghanistan, while the oil boom in the Arab countries provided the funds for their work (Ghandour, 2002). In the following years, these organisations started to work in other parts of Asia and increasingly also in Africa. The International Islamic Relief Organisation (IIRO), one of the first Saudi transnational charities (created in 1978 by the Saudi government), started its work in Africa in the early 1980s. The Kuwaiti African Muslims Agency (AMA) was another transnational Islamic NGO (Non-Governmental Organisation) that started to work in Africa in the 1980s. This first wave occurred during a period of serious drought in the Sahel. The rise of the mass media in this same period made it possible to globally publicise the ensuing famine, which led to an extensive humanitarian response. Islamic charities also started to offer humanitarian relief in the affected areas.

A second wave of transnational Islamic charities arriving in Africa can be discerned from the mid 1990s onwards. In the mid and late 1990s, Saudi Arabia had seen an upsurge of new NGOs that were more independent from the Saudi state (but often still administered by members of the Saudi elite) and that were looking for an outlet for their funds. Consequently, the group of Islamic NGOs increasingly diversified, not only including GONGOs[2] but also private charities such as the Makka al Mukkarama Foundation, Al Haramain, al Biir, and others. The Red Crescent, the Islamic counterpart of the Red Cross Society, became increasingly visible on the international scene during these years, too, and Red Crescent societies from the Gulf region also started to offer relief in African countries. The Emirate Red Crescent society, for instance, intervened in Somalia in 1992–1993, and in Sudan in 1998 (Ghandour, 2002).

The activities of Islamic charities from the Gulf region in Africa include emergency relief, care for orphans, medical care, and the construction of wells, mosques, and schools. But as Islamic organisations – and not merely organisations run by Muslims – the charities studied also have a missionary function: they are ultimately concerned with the advancement of Islam, be it by deepening people's understanding of Islamic principles and by improving Muslims' religious practices (re-islamisation) or by conversion of non-Muslims (islamisation). This missionary aspect is explicit in their activities in the field of religious education and the promotion of Islam (sponsoring of Quranic teachers, distribution of learning materials, etc.) but, in fact, underlies all other activities as well.

Islamic NGOs from the Gulf countries generally disseminate what is often called a Salafi form of Islam. Salafism is a modernist current that aims to follow the 'pious predecessors' (Arabic, *salaf*); that is, the first generation of Muslims, whose practice of Islam is considered to be the 'purest' form (Ghandour, 2002). Salafis seek an Islamic revival through the elimination of what they consider to be foreign innovations, and the many Sufi orders prominent in Africa are targeted in this way – Salafis aim to 're-educate' African Muslims about Islam and to purify Islam of allegedly un-Islamic practices. The transnational Islamic charities studied also work in zones that are considered fringe regions between Muslim Africa and regions where animist and, more recently, Christian traditions can be found, such as southern Chad and Southern Sudan, and the Casamance region in Senegal. Here, their activities are less geared towards re-education and much more towards conversion.

On the one hand, the emergence of Islamic aid can be related to the competition between the West and the Arab World (Benthall & Bellion-Jourdan, 2003; Kaag, 2008) as well as competition within the Islamic World (Ghandour, 2002; Wright, 2015). The latter can be illustrated, for instance, by King Faysal of Saudi Arabia's decision to establish the World Islamic League (WIL) in 1962. IIRO later became the humanitarian branch of WIL, in a bid to counter the influence of Gamal Abdel Nasser's pan-Arabism (Wright, 2015: 273). Competition between the West and the Arab World is evident in the literature on Islamic charities. Ahmed (2009), for instance, states that for Islamic missionary organisations, Christian missions serve as the main opponent and a role model to be imitated when it comes to methods and strategies of conversion. Benthall & Bellion-Jourdan (2003) also describe the emergence of Islamic NGOs from a competition perspective, as a reaction to the presence of Western NGOs. I also encountered this political view of the humanitarian arena during my own research – especially in transitional zones between Muslim and Christian dominated areas, the competition between Islam and Christian NGOs is quite fierce. During my research in southern Chad in 2004, for instance,

I found that Christian missions and Islamic NGOs were working against one another, albeit with little direct confrontation, by each trying to influence and 'win' the local population (Kaag, 2007). An informant in Chad told me that, in the 1990s, some higher placed individuals had started a lobby in the Gulf states to attract Islamic charities. They organised meetings and conferences in which it was explained that Chad is a poor country in need of material, social, and cultural support. One of the arguments they used was: 'The Christian organisations do not wait until they are invited, so why should you?'[3] and this call had, apparently, been rather effective.

On the other hand, it should be stressed that the emergence of Islamic humanitarianism can also be explained, by looking at internal developments within Islam and the Muslim World, as organically growing out of Islamic history. Charity is one of the pillars of Islam, and therefore, naturally, in a globalised world, this charity takes on a transnational character.

Such a perspective enables us to consider how Islamic NGOs are inspired and led by religious values, traditions, and motivations. Their ideas of 'development' are rooted in and justified by Islam, or, as eloquently put by Juul Petersen (2011: 140), 'the provision of aid is explained and legitimated with reference to Muslim traditions and concepts such as *zakat*, *sadaqa* and the *hadiths*, rather than the Millennium Development Goals, the Universal Human Rights Declaration or the Human Development Index'.

Islamic relief organisations build on Islamic principles of charity, as exemplified by *zakat* and *sadaqa* – zakat being a religious obligation to give alms, while sadaqa is a more voluntary version. Zakat can be considered a kind of 'financial worship', and constitutes both an act of social solidarity and an affirmation of faith ((Benthall & Bellion-Jourdan, 2003: 26).

The Qur'an states who has a right to zakat. In many places, it was traditionally paid to help the needy in one's own community, but it has increasingly been understood that the community can encompass the whole of the *umma* (global Muslim community).This idea took root in rich countries such as Saudi Arabia as Muslims progressively felt that the real poor no longer, or only sporadically, lived in their own countries – a fact highlighted by the mass media, which exposed poverty and disasters worldwide. It is this recognition that has stimulated the foundation of many of today's transnational Islamic NGOs, such as AMA (Association des Musulmans d'Afrique) and Muslim Aid.

A point of contention is whether zakat is directed only towards needy Muslims, or whether it can also be given to non-Muslims. In general, it is considered to be for Muslims alone, but zakat can also be deemed appropriate aid to anyone eligible to become Muslim (Benthall & Bellion-Jourdan, 2003). For many Islamic charities, especially those from the Gulf region, this means that missionary activities or *da'wa* (the invitation or call to Islam) are and should be an important component in their strategy.[4]

While transnational Islamic charities from the Gulf region were the first to set up and to start working in Africa, the field of transnational Islamic relief has been increasingly diversified by, among others, the Pakistani Ahmadiyya movement (Langewiesche, 2016), and by Islamic relief organisations founded by African and Asian Muslim migrant communities in the West. Their approaches are, in some instances, similar to the one described, in other instances they differ – a couple of European-born Islamic charities, such as Islamic Relief, have developed an approach that is similar to European secular relief organisations. I will return specifically to this point towards the end of this chapter.

Forging specific Asian-African linkages through the Islamic charity chain

When establishing what the specificity is of the Asian-African linkages forged through Islamic relief, we can observe that, while earlier Muslim connections involved mainly trader and scholarly elites, now, for the first time, the poor are also directly involved. By receiving aid from these Islamic relief organisations, African target populations are connected to well-doers in Southwest Asia and beyond.

Connections at the practical level are being built, for instance, through the educational programmes taught in schools that are financed and managed by some of these organisations. The curriculum is the official curriculum of the country of intervention, and lessons are often given both in Arabic and in the official language of the country concerned. Wherever possible, however, an explicit Islamic perspective is adopted. History, for example, is taught from an Islamic perspective. This means that students' knowledge and worldview connects them to the Muslim World and its history. The transnational solidarity underlying the projects is represented visually by the boards placed outside the mosque or hospital, stating the name of the Asian donor or of the transnational charity. Foster parents' programmes for orphans link foster children and their families to sponsors in Asia and while the latter tend to remain rather abstract and anonymous to the target group, there is a sense that someone in the wider Muslim World is involved and is paying for them. They are in touch with expatriate staff and have to deal with ways of doing things that often have their roots in Islamic currents and cultures that differ from what is common locally, and what people are used to.

In order to gain a deeper understanding of the character of the connections involved, one must move beyond the practical level and take a closer look at the aforementioned concept of zakat, which is so central in the organisation of Islamic charity. Apart from zakat, other forms of pious gifting exist, such as *hadiya* (Soares, 2005), in which the act of giving is of central importance and confers blessings (*baraka*) on the one who gives. What becomes of the money afterwards is considered less important. In the case of zakat, however, the objective and final destination of the gift are also vital: the wealthy Muslim gives to improve the lives of the poor. Zakat can thus be seen as a means of redistributing wealth in Muslim society (Weiss, 2002). Furthermore, by linking pious givers to needy recipients, zakat can be considered a connection, a bridging device that enables flows of money and baraka, flows through which relationships are established (see also Kaag, 2012): the donor gives, and, by improving the recipients' situation, gets a blessing in return.

In order to show the different layers involved, let us consider the following example: In June 2004, I visited an orphanage in the Chadian capital of N'Djamena, run by the Saudi relief organisation al-Makka al-Mukarrama. It was a festive day because a Saudi representative had come to visit the orphanage and to distribute clothes to the children. The children had been organised in rows and were clearly impressed by their important visitor from the Gulf. One by one, they were called forward to receive their package of clothing. They were told that these had been donated by pious Muslims in Saudi Arabia, and that they should work hard and study well to become good and pious Muslims themselves. The Saudi representative approached the children and, with paternal warmth, gave them their clothes while the whole event was filmed so that it could be shown to the donors back in Saudi Arabia.

This example illustrates how connections are being woven through the work of this Islamic NGO. At one level, a connection is being established by the flow of material aid to target groups and the return of a blessing to the donors. At another level, images and moral messages are transmitted that strengthen the idea, on both the Chadian and the Saudi side, of one Islamic community and the importance of Islamic solidarity.

However, the messages underlying and conveyed through this instance of the Islamic charity chain deserve further attention, as they also influence the ways in which African and Asian target groups imagine each other. Besides the message that Asian donors and African target groups belong to one global Muslim community, the umma, there is another, underlying message that clearly represents Africa as a continent that needs help – materially and spiritually – and Asian actors as powerful doers of good. This evidently mirrors the ways in which Western missionary and development activities have influenced Western ideas of Africa and Africans' perceptions of Europeans. It appears to be a problem inherent to humanitarianism, but one that is often overlooked. Despite the power of these messages, as I have argued elsewhere (Kaag, 2012), the actual reach and influence of these Islamic charities in Africa, including how they are perceived, and the ways in which they are integrated in local African strategies, depends, to a large degree, on the specific political, social, and cultural contexts in which these organisations come to work.

A large part of the work of transnational Islamic charities takes place in the localities of the target groups, as they provide relief and support to the poor on the ground, in African urban centres or refugee camps, for example. Scholarships for studying at Islamic Universities in Asia are a different type of support provided by Islamic relief organisations and Islamic states such as Saudi Arabia and Malaysia. These have offered African students the opportunity to obtain degrees from institutions of Islamic higher learning in the Middle East and East Asia. Reese (2014: 22) underscores that when they return, these students often seek 'the latest trends in scripturalist reform, which often puts them at odds with other elements of society'. However, I also encountered former students who had started to work for transnational Islamic charities after their return and explained their role as justly bridging cultural divides.

Islamic humanitarianism as a bridge between Africa and Asia after 9/11

During my research, I met several African Muslim intellectuals who, initially, had been very enthusiastic about the emergence of Islamic humanitarianism and who had sometimes even worked for these organisations as country or regional directors, but who had become disillusioned over time. A Senegalese Muslim intellectual who I interviewed in 2015, explicitly stated that Islamic relief has become 'a failure', both for internal reasons, such as a lack of professionalism, and for external reasons, the latter related to international reactions after the terrorist attacks on the World Trade Center in New York on 9/11.[5]

The 'War on Terror', instigated by the Bush administration after 9/11, hit the Islamic charity sector hard. While Islamic NGOs had been accused of promoting and supporting terrorism from the early 1990s onwards in countries like Afghanistan, the Palestinian Territories, Pakistan, Bosnia, and Kenya (Benthall & Bellion-Jourdan, 2003), the accusations became more general and serious after 9/11, with transnational Islamic NGOs being accused of providing financial, material, and logistic support to the al-Qaeda network and organisations such as Hamas. A director of a transnational Islamic NGO working in Chad, however, stated that their aim was to take care of the orphans of Hamas and rebuild houses in those Palestinian areas destroyed by the Israeli army. In other words, their support is strictly humanitarian and they are not involved in armed struggle. All the staff of the Islamic NGOs I met stressed the fact that terrorists are not good Muslims and that Islam is a peaceful religion.

In the framework of this chapter, such accusations raise the obvious question of whether these Gulf charities, in addition to building religious and philanthropic connections, may have established terrorist linkages between Asia and Africa, too. In this respect, it should be stressed that there is no direct relation between the Salafi message of these NGOs and religious violence or terrorism, and that these organisations' commitment to da'wa may be considered comparable to those of Western organisations, both Christian and secular, which also propagate their value systems (Kroessin & Mohamed, 2008; Kaag, 2011). One of the reasons that it is difficult to make a general judgement about these NGOs is the fact that they are transnational organisations that, until recently, often did not have a strong central accountability system. That is to say, different strategies and different priorities could be pursued in different countries, while (local) staff dealt with diverse local environments without much guidance. Accusations concerning one branch thus were not necessarily applicable to another branch in another country or continent. It seems that until 2002 such variation was relatively well accounted for in US policy; al-Haramain, for instance, had been closed in only a few countries (Somalia, Bosnia). After that, however, it seems that policies became less differential and entire Muslim organisations became the target of anti-terrorism measures, which, at times, began to look like a witch hunt. Restrictive measures taken by their own and foreign governments have made it increasingly difficult for Islamic charities in the Middle East to execute their work in settings other than in their home countries.

During my fieldwork on transnational Islamic charities in Chad in 2004, the effects of the war on terror were just starting to become visible. A number of charities were preparing to pull out, and the directors told me that they had been called back to Saudi Arabia and would no longer be working in Chad, while one had been dissolved altogether. I then predicted that the war on terror would have direct social consequences, as the dissolution of these charities would result in schools having to close and orphans no longer being supported (Kaag, 2007). When I returned to Chad in 2012, this forecast had become reality: a couple of Saudi charities had indeed left, while others had been forced to severely curtail their activities. The reason behind this was that international money transfers from Arab countries had become more difficult. Such transactions could no longer be made anonymously and, in some instances, not in cash (see also Bokhari, Chowdhury & Lacey, 2014). This meant, for instance, that Islamic relief organisations were obliged to terminate their orphan support programmes. A director told me that they were sometimes still able to give some money, but only irregularly. Another informant reported severe cutbacks in educational funding and well construction projects that used to be carried out by Islamic charities from the Gulf.[6]

The Kuwaiti organisation AMA appeared not to be affected financially. However, the country director told me that the organisation would no longer carry the name African Muslims' Agency, but use the name of its mother organisation, Direct Aid, instead. The phenomenon of Islamic NGOs no longer presenting themselves as Islamic organisations seems to be a trend as it is also observable among other Islamic charities, which tend to transform, at least in name, into more general humanitarian organisations and advertise their Islamic projects as side activities. Another example is provided by Human Appeal International. When I wanted to visit the Senegalese offices of the Emirate NGO Human Appeal International, I had difficulties in gaining access as the director did not want to receive someone doing research on Islamic NGOs. He reiterated that his organisation was just a general humanitarian organisation.

The war on terror has thus limited the number of Asian Islamic charities in Africa and their potential to offer relief and deploy activities on the ground. Furthermore, there is a trend among Islamic charities of becoming less visible as Islamic organisations. Finally, it can also be noted that Islamic charities are increasingly vulnerable at the local level, as accusations of links to terrorism aimed at transnational Islamic charities have become a part of local struggles over political and religious influence (Edwin, 2009; Kaag, 2012).

Conclusion: the future of Islamic humanitarian linkages between Asia and Africa

In this chapter, I have analysed transnational Islamic relief as it emerged in Southeast Asia in the 1970s, as a specific bridging device between Asian and African Muslim communities; a bridging device that changed and diversified over time, but which largely maintained a specific Islamic humanitarian outlook, coupling da'wa and religious education to material support. We have seen that this form of religious humanitarianism has increasingly experienced difficulties, especially after 9/11, due to accusations of contributing to Islamic extremism and the funding of terrorism. The adverse global climate has forced Asian Islamic relief organisations to respond and to adapt. Some have halted their transnational activities, others have adapted by, among other things, changing their explicit Islamic outlook.

But, as has been convincingly shown by many scholars of Islam (Hunwick, 1997; Bang, 2003; Green, 2012; Reese, 2014), Islamic linkages between Asia and Africa have existed since the beginning of Islam and will continue to do so, albeit their forms and contents will evolve and change over time. At the end of this chapter, it therefore appears worthwhile to ask whether transnational Islamic relief, as described in this chapter, has been and/or will be replaced by other forms of Islamic humanitarian linkages between Asia and Africa.

It can indeed be observed that with the decline in the type of transnational Islamic relief described here, other humanitarian linkages between Asian Muslims and African target groups have emerged, in which Islam is still a source of motivation and inspiration, but is more opaque and in which da'wa is less an objective. The schools of the Turkish Gülen movement that have sprung up in many African countries over the past 15 years are a good example of this development. While Islam is their source of motivation and informs their educational programme, they do not explicitly promote Islam, but rather translate their educational engagement in a moral education framed in universal terms. This accent on values and moral education (in contrast to 'just teaching') is coupled with an emphasis on science (Dohrn, 2013; Mohamed, 2007). Another example is provided by the Pakistani Ahmadiyya movement, which created its own humanitarian NGO, Humanity First, in 1994, and while the movement as such is committed to proselytism, its humanitarian branch is explicitly excluded from all missionary activities. The organisation targets non-Muslims and Muslims alike and aims to collaborate with non-secular and secular Western humanitarian organisations, rather than with transnational Islamic charities[7] (Langewiesche, 2016). Asian and African Muslim migrant communities, who until recently used to send money to their countries of origin, are now increasingly committing to sponsoring aid elsewhere in the world, and they do so by setting up their own relief organisations (such as the Turkish Time to Help) or by donating through established transnational Islamic NGOs based in the West like Islamic Relief.

Alongside new forms of institutionalised transnational Islamic aid, transnational Islamic charity has also sought new non–institutionalised channels by way of personal connections and networks. African students who studied in Asia are often instrumental in forging further linkages on their return, and have, for instance, helped to fund mosques or provide educational support for orphans back home. As has been argued by scholars like Roy (2002) and Hackett & Soares (2015), new media has helped to facilitate more individualised linkages between Muslims worldwide, and it remains to be seen how this development will shape Islamic relief in the years to come, including its place in the ever-evolving plurality of connections between Asian and African Muslims.

Notes

1   See also Ellis 2011, who problematises the all-too-common periodisation that divides Africa's history into precolonial, colonial, and postcolonial phases, and who points to the 1970s as a watershed moment for Africa's position in the world.
2   Government Operated Non-Governmental Organisation, such as IIRO.
3   Interview N'Djamena, May 2004.

4   Other Islamic NGOs, such as the UK-based Islamic Relief, take a more neutral stance and provide aid for non-Muslims and Muslims alike, without having *da'wa* as a strategy. See also Petersen (2011) who makes a distinction between transnational Islamic NGOs with a sacralised aid ideology and those with a secularised aid ideology.
5   Interview Dakar, November 2015.
6   Interview N'Djamena, September 2012
7   The latter aspect also has to do with the fact that the Ahmadiyya are often not recognised by other Muslim groups, and often face discrimination or are the object of defamation campaigns (Langewiesche, 2016).

Bibliography

Ahmed, C., 2009. 'Networks of Islamic NGOs in sub-Saharan Africa: Bilal Muslim Mission, African Muslim Agency (Direct Aid), and al-Haramayn', *Journal of Eastern African Studies*, Volume 3 (3), pp. 426–437.

Bang, A. K., 2003. *Sufis and Scholars of the Sea: Family Networks in East-Africa, 1860–1925*, London: Routledge.

Benthall, J. and Bellion-Jourdan, J., 2003. *The Charitable Crescent: Politics of Aid in the Muslim World*, London and New York: I.B. Tauris.

Bokhari, Y., Chowdhury, N. and Lacey, R., 2014. 'A good day to bury a bad charity: Charting the rise and fall of the Al-Haramain Islamic foundation', in J. Benthall and R. Lacey (eds.), *Gulf Charities and Islamic Philanthropy in the 'Age of Terror' and Beyond*, London and Berlin: Gerlach Press, pp. 199–230.

Dohrn, K., 2013. 'Translocal Ethics: Hizmet Teachers and the Formation of Gülen-inspired Schools in Urban Tanzania', *Sociology of Islam*, Volume 1 (2013), 233–256.

Edwin, G. A., 2009. 'Globalization and the assertive Ummah: The case of Islam in Kenya', in A. A. Mazrui, P. M. Dikirr, R. Ostergard, M. Toler and P. Mackaria (eds.), *Africa's Islamic Experience: History, Culture and Politics*, New Delhi: Sterling Publishers, pp. 165–185.

Ellis, S., 2011. 'Africa in the world: A historical view', in T. Dietz, K. Havnevik, M. Kaag and T. Oestigaard (eds.), *African Engagements: Africa Negotiating an Emerging Multipolar World*, Leiden and Boston, MA: Brill, pp. 364–376.

Ghandour, A.-R., 2002. *Jihad humanitare: Enquête sur les ONG Islamiques*, Paris: Flammarion.

Green, N., 2012. *Sufism. A Global History*, Oxford: Wiley-Blackwell.

Green, N. 2014 'Rethinking the "Middle East" after the oceanic turn', *Comparative Studies of South Asia, Africa and the Middle East*, Volume 34 (3), pp. 556–564.

Hackett, R. and Soares, B. F. (eds.), 2015. *New Media and Religious Transformations in Africa*, Bloomington: Indiana University Press.

Hunwick, J., 1984. 'Salih al-Fullani (1752/3–1803): the career and teachings of a West African *'alim* in Medina', in A. H. Green (ed.), *Towards an Islamic Humanism: Arabic and Islamic Studies in Memory of Mohamed al-Nowaihi*, Cairo: American University of Cairo Press, pp. 139–155.

Hunwick, J., 1997. 'Sub-Saharan Africa and the wider world of Islam: Historical and contemporary perspectives', in D. Westerlund & E. E. Rosander (eds.), *African Islam and Islam in Africa. Encounters between Sufis and Islamists*, London: Hurst & Co., pp. 28–54.

Juul Petersen, M., 2011. 'For Humanity or for the Umma? Ideologies of Aid in Four Transnational Muslim NGOs', PhD thesis, University of Copenhagen.

Kaag, M., 2007. 'Aid, *Umma* and politics: Transnational Islamic NGOs in Chad', in R. Otayek and B. Soares (eds.), *Muslim Politics in Africa*, New York: Palgrave Macmillan, pp. 85–102.

Kaag, M., 2008. 'Transnational Islamic NGOs in Chad: Islamic Solidarity in the Age of Neoliberalism'. *Africa Today*, Volume 54 (3), pp. 3–18.

Kaag, M., 2011. 'Connecting to the Umma through Islamic Relief. Transnational Islamic NGOs in Chad'. Special issue on translocal development. *International Development Policy Review*, November 2011, pp. 463–474.

Kaag, M., 2012. 'Comparing connectivities: Transnational Islamic NGOs in Chad and Senegal', in M. De Bruijn and R. van Dijk (eds.), *The Social Life of Connectivity in Africa*, New York: Palgrave Macmillan, pp. 183– 201.

Kroessin, M. R. and Mohamed A. S., 2008. 'Saudi Arabian NGOs in Somalia: 'Wahabi' Da'wah or humanitarian aid?' in G. Clarke and M. Jennings (eds.), *Development, Civil Society and Faith-Based Organizations, Bridging the Sacred and the Secular*, Basingstoke, Hampshire: Palgrave Macmillan.

Langewiesche, K., 2016. 'Missionary Islam and humanitarian engagement: The case of the Ahmadiyya movement'. Oral presentation, African Studies Centre, Leiden University, 25 February 2016.

Mohamed, Y., 2007. 'The educational theory of Fethullah Gülen and its practice in South Africa', Paper presented at the Gülen Conference, held at the London School of Economics, 27 October 2007.

O'Fahey, R. S., 2004. '"Small world": Neo-sufi interconnexions between the Maghrib, the Hijaz and Southeast Asia', in S. S. Reese (ed.), *The Transmission of Learning in Islamic Africa*, Leiden and Boston: Brill, pp. 274–288.

Reese, S. S., 2014. 'Islam in Africa/Africans and Islam', *Journal of African History*, Volume 55 (1), pp. 17–26.

Ross, E., 2011. 'A historical geography of the Trans-Saharan trade', in G. Krätli and G. Lydon (eds.), *The Trans-Saharan Book Trade: Manuscript Culture, Arabic Literacy and Intellectual History in Muslim Africa*, Leiden and Boston: Brill, pp. 1–34.

Roy, O., 2002. *L'Islam Mondialisé*, Paris: Seuil.

Soares, B. F., 2005. *Islam and the Prayer Economy. History and Authority in a Malian Town*, Ann Arbor, MI: University of Michigan Press.

Van Bruinessen, M., 2012. 'Indonesian Muslims and their place in the larger world of Islam', in A. Reid (ed.), *Indonesia Rising. The Repositioning of Asia's Third Giant*, Singapore: ISEAS Publishing, pp. 117–140.

Weiss, H., 2002. *Social Welfare in Muslim Societies in Africa*, Uppsala: Nordiska Afrikainstitutet.

Wright, Z. V., 2015. *Living Knowledge in West-African Islam. The Sufi Community of Ibrahim Niasse*, Leiden and Boston: Brill.

17
CIVIL SOCIETY AND THE RISE OF NGOS IN AFRICA AND ASIA
Parallel trajectories?

David M. Potter

Introduction

The global associational revolution described by Lester Salamon in the mid 1990s has not excluded Africa and Asia. Discussions of the roles of non-governmental organisations (NGOs), and, more recently, as scholarly trends have changed, civil society in both regions have been vigorous and the scholarly literature focused on them is in many ways impressive. The focus, however, has been on the effects of globalisation and the development of global civil society, especially since the 1980s, or on national and sub-national issues facing NGOs. An intermediate region-to-region focus is lacking.

This chapter examines the expansion of voluntary non-profit sectors primarily in East and South Asia and sub-Saharan Africa. This chapter discusses terminological problems of civil society and the non-profit and voluntary sector when analysing the two regions; the historical development of civil societies in each; relations between NGOs and the state, focusing on regulation of NGOs; democratisation and civil society/NGOs; financial dependence on external donors; and whether there is evidence of South–South cooperation across the two regions. This chapter argues that African and Asian civil societies have developed along with the development of global civil society but have done so through different trajectories. As such, a number of structural problems impede cross-regional interaction among NGOs. Evidence of interaction between non-profit and voluntary organisations between the regions remains limited and largely undocumented.

The literature on civil society and the non-profit sector has not focused on Africa–Asia as a regional subset of global civil society. The bulk of the literature on civil society and the non-profit sector has focused on the Global North, especially the United States, as a perusal of *The Nonprofit and Voluntary Sector Quarterly* and *Voluntas* quickly reveals. The unit of analysis for most studies of Africa and Asia follows one of three patterns. One pattern tends to look at NGOs and CSOs (Civil Society Organisations) globally, with individual cases from the two regions in question here. The Johns Hopkins Comparative Nonprofit Research Project and the subsequent CIVICUS project (CIVICUS is an international network of civil society organisations) are outstanding examples of attempts to catalogue and measure the dimensions of the non-profit and civil society sectors of the world (see also Boli & Thomas, 1999). World region is a second unit of analysis. Here important work has been done on Asia (Farrington, 1993; Alagappa, 2004; Schak & Hudson, 2003; Shigetomi, 2002; Lee, 2004) and Africa (Bratton, 1989; Pinckney, 2009; Obudare, 2014). A related group of research examines the non-profit and non-governmental sectors in the developing world (Fisher, 1998; Salamon & Anheier, 1998; Howell & Pearce, 2001). Country studies and case studies located in particular countries comprise a third unit of analysis. This by far is the largest body of research; in fact, much of the global and regional research cited above relies on country case studies. This is also the analytical framework within which most of the burgeoning number of civil society index projects work (Casey, 2016:91–130). This literature is far too abundant to capture here. In sum, the bulk of the research heretofore conducted on civil society and the non-profit sector in Africa and Asia has tended to be conducted in parallel; cross-regional research is rare (Cleary, 1997; Obiyan, 2005).

The largely national character of the research on non-profit and voluntary organisations in these two regions presents daunting methodological problems to the researcher attempting to identify commonalities and make generalisations about civil society. The countries included within the geographic parameters of these two regions include half of the membership of the United Nations and represent a wide array of political, social, religious, ethnic, and economic conditions and developmental trajectories. The Hudson Institute Center for Global Prosperity's recently inaugurated Index of Philanthropic Freedom provides a snapshot of this in the context of the discussion in this chapter. The index measures 64 countries along three dimensions of philanthropic freedom (ease of registering, operating, and dissolving civil society organisations; availability and attainability of tax deductions and exemptions; and ease of engaging in cross-border philanthropy). African and Asian countries can be found across the spectrum. Japan, the Philippines, and Tanzania are ranked among the upper third (ninth, nineteenth, and twenty-third, respectively); Nepal, Qatar, and Saudi Arabia are ranked last (sixty-second through sixty-fourth, respectively) (Hudson Institute, 2015:40–41). Generalisations should therefore be treated with caution.

Civil society, the non-profit sector, and problems of nomenclature

Scholars have debated the existence and parameters of civil society in Africa and Asia. The term is problematic in the case examined here for two reasons. First, as is widely understood, the idea has developed out of Western civilisation and its experience of state–society–market relationships. Whether it is applicable to world regions with quite different traditions of government and state–society relationships is no small question. This is especially the case in sub-Saharan Africa where there is limited history of a central state of any kind against which to juxtapose civil society. Even in Asia trajectories of state development have varied widely: Anthony Reid, for example, contrasts 'enduring states' of Northeast Asia with 'state-averse' Southeast Asia (Reid, 2010:15–23), with the latter likely to bring up problems similar to those of sub-Saharan Africa.

Second, the concept of civil society itself is broad. Summarising this vast literature, which spans centuries, Michael Edwards (2004) identifies three strands in the history of Western political thought: civil society as associational life, civil society as the ideal society to be achieved, and civil society as a form of Habermasian public sphere. All of these share a common commitment to liberal society and some form of democracy. But the objects of discussion in each vary, and edited work especially tends to paint civil society with a broad brush that draws upon all three traditions (see for example Lele & Quadir, 2004; Obudare, 2014).

Third, discussions of civil society and the voluntary non-profit sectors in Africa and Asia are frequently clouded by the varying terminology used to describe organisations and their activities.

Scholars have distinguished between non-governmental organisations (NGOs), understood as intermediary organisations engaged in support of local communities, and local associations themselves, variously labelled as community-based organisations, local organisations, grassroots organisations, people's organisations, and so on. Similarly, a distinction between Northern NGOs and Southern NGOs has been made (Ahmed & Potter, 2006). This terminology has developed as a means to achieve analytical clarity in specific contexts, but the overall effect has been to create a welter of competing and frequently overlapping terms.

Muthiah Alagappa (2004:9) defines civil society in the Asian context as,

> a distinct public sphere of organization, communication, reflective discourse, and governance among individuals and groups that take collective action employing civil means to influence the state and its policies but not capture state power, and whose activities are not motivated by profit. The four aspects of this definition are: a distinct space for organization by nonstate, nonmarket groups; a site for communication and discourse; a site for governance; and a means to influence the structure and rules of the political game.
>
> *(Alagappa, 2004:9)*

This is essentially the definition followed by Lee Hock Guan's (2004) edited volume on civil society in Southeast Asia and in line with Larry Diamond's (1994:5) definition: '[the] realm of organized social life that is voluntary, self-generating, (largely) self-supporting, autonomous of the state, and bound by a legal order or set of shared rules'.

This definition is close to Yamamoto's (1998) concept of the 'broad non-profit sector' in Japan, articulated as a means to encompass the wide array of distinct corporate legal categories as well as the notions of philanthropy that typically constitute discussions of civil society and the non-profit sector. It sees the non-profit sector as comprising more than simply NGOs, an overly restrictive concept that tends to have disparate but specific meanings in national contexts and somehow is supposed to designate a category of associations that has come to be seen as somehow representative of the non-profit sector. The concept also operationalises this broad non-profit sector according to the International Classification for Nonprofit Organisations (ICNPO) developed by the Johns Hopkins Comparative Nonprofit Research Project (Salamon & Anheier, 1997) and serves as the foundation for the rest of this chapter.

This approach is somewhat narrowing. Many understandings of civil society are broader than the notion of the non-profit sector. To borrow from Michael Edwards' (2004) typology of civil society as associational life, civil society as the good society, and civil society as the public sphere, the ICNPO approach leans heavily towards the first. It therefore privileges the institutional aspects of civil society instead of its normative or discursive aspects. This is done at the cost of a full overview of civil society in these two continents but allows scholars to observe and measure institutional aspects of the sector and therefore compare it across regions and countries.

The neoliberal understanding of NGO and the non-profit sector more broadly is of a sector that promotes parliamentary democracy and complements state efforts to provide public goods (notably social welfare services) in an era of restrained government intervention in society and economy. The idea of civil society, however, is broader. It certainly includes social movements that contest politics with the state (Tarrow, 1998) rather than simply complementing it. In the African context civil society has been understood to include media and political parties (Monga, 1995; Mw Makumbe, 1998), blurring the lines between for-profit and non-profit and governmental and non-governmental.

David M. Potter

Civil society since when? Colonialism, nationalism, independence, and civil society

Many scholars have argued that civil society organisations in Africa and Asia pre-date colonialism and the creation of modern nation-states (Sen, 1997, 1998; Atingdui, 1997; Mw Makumbe, 1998; Weller & Hsiao, 2003; Shigetomi, 2002). The implication here is that while civil society and the organized non-profit sector may be newly introduced concepts, the cultural and organisational foundations for them in Africa and Asia are not.

Yet scholars also point to the societal disruptions brought about by Western intrusion. John Mw Makumbe (1998:306) states that

> the colonial governments throughout Africa destroyed most of the civic groups and organizations that existed prior to the advent of colonial rule. These civic groups were viewed with suspicion by the colonial rulers, who feared that they could be instrumental in mobilizing the colonized against the colonizer ... Further, the colonial regimes in most of sub-Saharan Africa actively discouraged the formation of civic groups which could have participated in the political processes in their countries.
>
> *(Mw Makumbe, 1998:306)*

The European colonial interlude and subsequent nationalism surely changed the structure of those civil societies and the voluntary associations that inhabited them. Atingdui (1997) points out that voluntary associations existed in precolonial Ghana, organised along ethnic, kinship, and age group lines, but these adapted to new colonial regimes. Christian missionary organisations followed, bringing with them not only new faith into already complex cultural and religious environments but educational and welfare repertoires that served as models of later relief and development work as well. Transformation of economic production led to the creation of business associations and trade unions.

Colonial administration itself had a variety of impacts on civil society organisation. The evolution of colonial dependencies into nation-states, of course, created the political space for national civil society that transcended older localistic associational forms. This had profound implications for participation in post-independence in international society. U. A. Tar comments that, 'colonialism did not invent civil society in Africa, but it provided a decisive moment in its growth' (Tar, 2014:267). Colonial administrations established legal frameworks for the legal incorporation of non-profit and voluntary organisations that superseded older institutional forms. In the case of the Indian subcontinent and East Africa, for example, British imperial rule also systematised private philanthropy along secular legal lines. The legal foundations of the charitable sector in these countries frequently dates from the colonial period, as Table 17.1 shows in the cases of Bangladesh, India, Pakistan, and Tanzania. Their effect was to help

Table 17.1 Colonial-era legal foundations of non-profit organisations in South Asia and Tanzania

India	Bangladesh	Pakistan	Tanzania
Societies Registration Act (1860)	Societies Registration Act (1860)	Societies Registration Act (1860)	Societies Act (1954)
Trust Act (1882)			Trustees
Cooperatives Act (1904)	Trust Act (1882)	Trust Act (1882)	Incorporation
Charitable and Religious Trusts Act (1920)	Cooperative Societies Act (1925)	Cooperative Societies Act (1925)	Act (1956)
Trade Union Act (1926)			Companies Act (1958)

Sources: Potter & Khondaker, 2015; Mmanda, 2008.

institutionalise a pluralistic, philanthropic, and charitable sector in all four countries with participation by associations both religious and secular. To be sure, each of the former colonies has developed a distinctive non-profit sector profile since independence. Yet they partake of a common colonial history that has left visible legacies for their philanthropic and charitable sectors.

Malaysia provides an interesting case study of the legacy of colonialism for the non-profit and voluntary sector. British immigration policy introduced sizeable populations of Indians and Chinese to the colony, which resulted, after independence, in a multi-ethnic polity with a sizeable, but not necessarily majority, Malay-Muslim population that it nevertheless guaranteed special rights and privileges to under the constitution and subsequent public policies. This has significant consequences for the philanthropic and non-profit sector in Malaysia. The non-governmental sector is relatively small and NGOs and philanthropic organisations have organised largely along communal lines. Elizabeth Cogswell (2002:107) concludes that,

> despite rhetoric and legal requirements that suggest cross-cultural philanthropy, much if not most remains ethnic specific, often targeted to the religious or cultural preservation of the ethnic group of the donor . . . Ethnic-specific philanthropy is reinforced by both internal and external political and economic influences.
>
> *(Cogswell, 2002:107)*

The Mahathir government co-opted Muslim-Malay associations into the politically dominant United Malay Nationalist Organisation as a means to channel and control potential opposition. The result is that Malay-Muslim NGOs are neither independent of the ruling coalition nor have they developed an advocacy orientation. 'Consequently, autonomous NGOs have remained very inactive among Malays' (Kaneko, 2002:191). Moreover, as the *bumiputra* (a Malaysian of indigenous Malay origin) policy favours Malays in government employment, education, and other social services there has been less perceived need for Malay NGOs to fill state gaps.

Colonialism also organised subject societies along lines that would eventually become national states, which in turn raised the possibility of new forms of transnational communication and action. As Boli and Thomas (1999) point out:

> There is a close relationship between INGO [international non-governmental organisation] growth and the expansion of the state system: national independence seems vital to INGO activity. African and Asian INGOs were rare while their continents consisted mainly of colonies; after independence many regional INGOs emerged. Put another way, national citizenship seems to be a precondition for world citizenship.
>
> *(Boli & Thomas, 1999:32–34)*

Independence in Africa and Asia focused attention on nation-building. Concerns with national unity tended to concentrate energies and political power in single overarching political parties, either civilian or military. Post-independence political systems tended to be unfriendly to vigorous and independent civil societies: it is safe to say that Leninist or Maoist variants of national liberation and many military governments were outright hostile to them. Thus, civil societies and their component institutions tended to exist within the shadow of overarching national political projects or were either suppressed or co-opted into them.

The rise of NGOs in Africa and Asia since the 1980s has been due to multifarious reasons. One contributing factor has been the global trend towards a more vigorous civil society sparked by events in former socialist countries, but which also affected Africa (Mw Makumbe, 1998:308) and Asia. The forces of globalisation have no doubt contributed to development in Africa and Asia as they have elsewhere, making communications faster, cheaper, and easier and thereby reducing transaction costs especially for non-profit and voluntary associations. The third wave of democratisation and economic liberalisation clearly also opened political space for the development of civil society in both continents. In Asia, these two trends appear to have been the main catalysts for the rise of civil society after the 1980s (Tandon & Kak, 2008:92–94).

In Africa, on the other hand, the rise of civil society and concomitant attention to and expectations of it have been associated not only with democratisation and a neoliberal policy agenda but with the crisis of the state itself. Michael Bratton (1989:569) characterised the situation thus:

> Under the combined pressure of growing international indebtedness and shrinking government budgets, public services in the African countryside have actually begun to break down. The devastating African famines of 1974 and 1984 emphasized not only the apparent helplessness of some governments in the face of natural calamity, but also the vitality of non-governmental organizations as conduits for relief and development assistance. Especially in the remotest regions of the African countryside, governments often have had little choice but to cede responsibility for the provision of basic services to a church, an indigenous self-help group, or an international relief agency.
>
> *(Bratton, 1989:569)*

Bratton neatly encapsulates the key elements of this process, the weakening and diminution of the state apparatus and the appearance of neoliberal forms of action to compensate. This situation has endured: Gregory Mann (2015) argues, for example, that the African Sahel has seen the development of 'nongovernmentality', a form of governance in which international NGOs are the most visible signs of power in the long intervals between government posts and have increasingly encroached on sovereignty.

There is clearly a normative aspect to the attention paid to the development of African and Asian civil societies. In fact, the expectation that robust civil society institutions will promote and sustain democracy and economic development is widespread not only among scholars but also practitioners. At the same time scholars have pointed to the institutional and political weakness of civil society in Africa and Asia even as their numbers have grown (Michael, 2005; Mw Makumbe, 1998:310–312; Opoku-Mensah, 2008:75–90; Nega & Schneider, 2014; Casey, 2016:123). CIVICUS research points out the relative weakness of civil society in five countries in sub-Saharan Africa, noting that it operates in an environment that 'can at best be regarded as disabling and at worst hostile' (Opoku-Mensah, 2008:81). Among the 34 countries included in the CIVICUS Global Civil Society Index measuring civil society along four dimensions of size, capacity, sustainability, and impact, the countries of Africa and Asia ranked between fifteenth (Tanzania) and thirty-fourth (Pakistan) (cited in Clarke, 2013:40). The non-profit sectors in each region are also relatively small as measured by employment (Salamon et al., 2004:33, 37).

NGOs, civil society, and the state

The postcolonial state in Africa and Asia has alternately been characterised as neo-patrimonial (Clapham, 1984), largely in the African context, or developmental (Woo-Cummings, 1999) in the Asian. Both tend to be authoritarian, the developmental because it seeks to mobilise public resources for national economic ends and the neo-patrimonial because it seeks to capture public resources for private aggrandisement. Alternatively, scholars of sub-Saharan Africa have

Civil society and the rise of NGOs

wondered whether the African state is really either a state or truly indigenous (Englebert, 1997). One-party states or one-party-dominant states have not been uncommon, nor are monarchies unknown in the Middle East and parts of Asia. Thus, one frequently finds statements like the following: 'Thailand's non-profit sector, long viewed by the country's various military governments as a potential if not actual competitor for power' (Pongsapich, 1997:446); Egypt has had 'a state apparatus intensely distrustful of civil society' (Kandil, 1997:350). In modern Japan the idea of civil society has been closely identified, since the Meiji period (1868–1912), with radical democracy and, therefore, opposition to state authority (Najita, 2004).

This does not mean that states have uniformly tried to suppress civil society associations. In fact, one is struck by the great variety of official responses to the development of civil society, not only among countries, but frequently at different times within the same country. To consider polar opposites of the first dimension of this variety, consider that the Philippines has a constitution today that mandates cooperation between local governments and NGOs and guarantees the organisational rights of the latter, while the Kingdom of Saudi Arabia allows practically no independent private associations (Elbayar, 2005:3). On the second point, Taiwan suggests one such complex relationship, with 'no genuine NGO sector that could have engaged in any legitimate or genuine state–civil society dialogue or exchange' characteristic of the period of martial law under the Guomindang, changing to a period of rapid growth leading to a situation in which 'it could be said that Taiwan today has a very robust NGO sector' (Hsiao, 2003:181, 182).

Regulation of CSOs is variable across the two continents. Middle Eastern government regulations tend to be highly restrictive, although Lebanon and Palestine stand out as exceptions (Elbayar, 2005). The Jordanian state, one of the less illiberal in the region, has required registered voluntary organisations to retain state security personnel on their boards and that most NGOs be members of the government-controlled General Union of Voluntary Services (Wiktorowicz, 2002; Benthall, 2009:99). With notable exceptions, like the Philippines, legal frameworks, governing non-profit registration and taxation have tended to be inflexible, usually limiting rather than enabling non-profit activity (Silk, 1999; Sidel, 2010). Cumbersome registration procedures and inefficient bureaucracy in West Africa have similar results on non-profits there (Mamattah, 2014:149–151). The countries of Africa and Asia mostly cluster in the bottom half of the Index of Philanthropic Freedom, in no small part due to lower scores on tax exemption and ease of registration. Available data also suggests that public support for non-profits in Africa and Asia is relatively modest, which makes them reliant on fees to secure revenue (Salamon et al., 2004:33, 37). This likely also limits their scope of activity and renders them vulnerable to changing economic conditions.

Japan provides a good example of civil society in a strong state in Asia. Among the industrial democracies Bloodgood et al. (2014) characterise Japan as a representative case of corporatist regulation, in which the state controls the size and impact of the non-profit organisations, as highly restrictive and rigid, and further notes that the state has generally been suspicious of an independent civil society sector. Categories of legal corporations reflect state priorities and incorporation historically depended upon permission granted at the discretion of the relevant administrative agency (Pekkanen, 2006).

Yamauchi et al. (1999) and Deguchi (2001) describe the Japanese non-profit sector as bifurcated. Similarly, Pekkanen (2006) describes a dual civil society. One group is made up of legally defined non-profits with close links to government, mostly school corporations, religious corporations, social welfare corporations, medical corporations, and neighbourhood associations. Voluntary organisations, including NPOs as a new type of legal corporation by law in December 1998, comprise the second. As a result of high barriers to entry or the desire to remain independent of government regulation, many voluntary associations do not seek legal incorporation, a situation only partially alleviated by the 1998 NPO law.

Salamon et al. (2004:45) identify Japan and South Korea as forming an 'Asian industrialized model' of non-profit and voluntary sector development in which 'government has aggressively promoted rapid industrialization while supplying the bare minimum of social protections and generally discouraging, or at least not actively promoting, the development of civil society institutions'. A modified version of this pattern can be seen in China, where mass organisations and government-organised NGOs have legal status and close relations with government and party officials while most voluntary organisations operate without such sponsorship. Similarly, a dual structure characterises the Malaysian non-profit sector depending upon relations with the ruling United Malay Nationalist Organisation (Kaneko, 2002).

Bangladesh, on the other hand, has had a weak state which has never been 'strong enough to lead economic development in an authoritarian way nor to manage the people as a welfare state' (Nobusue, 2002:36). Along with its South Asian neighbours, India and Sri Lanka, it also has one of the most active and prominent non-profit sectors anywhere. NGOs have been active in Bengali society since independence. In fact, the NGO sector has been characterised by *The Economist* as 'the other government in Bangladesh' (1998:30). The social development sector, it is averred, is dominated by NGOs that compensate for the lack of state capacity; four – Grameen Bank, ASA, Proshika, and BRAC – make up three-quarters of the micro-finance sector (Fernando, 2011:225–227). Jose Fernando (2011:230) characterises the relationship between the non-profit sector and the state thus: 'the ruling party, mainstream NGOs, and Islamic NGOs operate as three parallel states in Bangladesh.' The NGO sector itself is often in contention with state agencies, and Islamic organisations are often in contention with secular NGOs.

Africa and Asia, of course, have been swept up as much as any world region in the waves of globalisation of the past half millennium. With successive waves has come the development of complex trans-regional interactions that have affected not only states but their societies. One trajectory, the most prominent, has occurred along the North–South dimension. For civil society and voluntary non-profit associations the discourse concerning North–South interactions in the past 30 years has focused on local civil society organisations' dependence on international donor largesse (either official or non-governmental) and a corresponding concern about the problem of accountability.

Donor dependence is such an issue that its existence has shaped official and academic discourses on the scope and construction of African and Asian non-profit voluntary sectors. From Beijing to Pretoria government authorities typically classify international NGOs as a separate category of non-profit subject to special rules. They may exist in a national or local milieu but are not necessarily integral to it. In the African context especially, some view them as instruments of neo-colonialism (Manji & O'Coill, 2002; Shivji, 2007). Dependence has stretched traditional norms of accountability not only by increasing the number of stakeholders to which a CSO is responsible, but by rendering significant aspects of accountability transnational and therefore subject to norms and procedures set outside of local and national milieu (Ahmed & Potter, 2006; Stiles, 2002). The dependence on external donors has also raised questions about whether sectoral and geographic development projects are skewed towards donor concerns to the detriment of local needs and priorities (Brass, 2011; Fruttero & Gauri, 2005; Koch, 2009; Morfit, 2010). More to the point here, these NGOs reinforce the geography of North–South power relations, focusing external relations on Europe and North America and away from Afro-Asian connections.

This dynamic is replicated to a certain extent even in African-Asian relations. Japan and South Korea are members of the Organisation for Economic Cooperation and Development and its Development Assistance Committee. Along with government-to-government aid both provide modest amounts of official development assistance through NGOs. NGOs in both countries report carrying out activities in Africa but at lower rates than they do in Asia, a pattern that is repeated with projects subsidised by official funding (Potter & Potter, 2016). In both cases NGOs tend to be small with limited budgets, which constrains the scope of their international activities especially outside of the region. While the rise of non-DAC aid donors in recent years has the potential to augment official resources for cross-regional civil society interactions, it is not clear if this will actually happen. One finds it hard to see China as a major contributor to civil society development in Africa.

Africa–Asia interactions: rise of the Global South?

The research on global civil society interactions between Africa and Asia is also sobering. Boli et al. (1999) point out that membership in INGOs by individuals and organisations increased across all countries and world regions after 1960. European participation, however, was the highest and participation by Africans and Pacific Islanders was the lowest (52–53 per cent). ECOSOC (United Nations Economic and Social Council) data on African and Asian NGOs in consultative status bears out this impression: these regions are underrepresented, with around 11 per cent of all NGOs in consultative status hailing from Africa and about 16 per cent hailing from Asia. The author's own research using the *Yearbook of International Associations* revealed that practically all countries in Africa and Asia are home to at least a few regional and international associations. India is the outstanding example, playing host to a broad range of such institutions.

But there are marked regional differences. When one looks at memberships rather than headquarters, four points emerge. First, citizens and associations in Africa and Asia show a strong tendency to affiliate with INGOs headquartered in the North. Second, colonial ties persist. *La Francophonie* in West Africa and the Commonwealth in East Africa and Asia are well represented among INGO memberships. Third, regional affiliations are also strong. Africans tend to belong to African regional INGOs (and West Africans to West African INGOs, for example), Asians tend to be members of Asian regional organisations. In the latter case the ASEAN (Association of Southeast Asian Nations) countries stand out as an institutional hub for the broader region. Fourth, using a simple measure of headquarters location of associations listed in the 2000–2001 *Yearbook*, the author found cross-regional memberships to be relatively rare. Moreover, ties tend to be among professional associations. In sum, African and Asian transnational civil society ties tend to exist through the medium of international associations headquartered in the North rather than directly between the two regions.

There are two prominent cross-regional links, however. Many INGOs in both regions are tied together by their common faith in Islam. Not all such organisations are religious in nature, but clearly INGOs headquartered in Riyadh, Jedda, and Cairo help link civil societies from Kuala Lumpur to Accra. Akhtar (Chapter 4) explores this linkage in depth. Second, one finds traces of the Non-Aligned Movement in selected countries. India, which hosts a large of number of INGOs anyway, has affiliations with a number of NGOs that carry the 'Afro-Asian' label, reminiscent of official aspirations of newly independent countries during the Cold War.

It is not clear, however, whether Third World solidarity has done much to promote civil society communication The Non-Aligned Movement was predominantly interstate and many of its prominent leaders headed states committed to national unity of the kind not conducive to the growth of vigorous, independent civil societies. Similarly, the renascence of South–South development cooperation is predominantly conducted along official lines. A series of

Asian-initiated conferences promoting cooperation with Africa, the Tokyo International Conference on African Development (TICAD), the Forum on China–Africa Cooperation (FOCAC), the Korea–Africa Forum (KAF), and the India–Africa Forum, are primarily diplomatic fora with varying degrees of participation by civil society organisations. The TICAD, oldest among these, has facilitated and strengthened communication between Japanese NGOs and their African counterparts (Raposo, 2014:81–82). China's growing reach is more likely to undermine civil societies abroad than to support them (Nathan, 2015). A report by the Institute of Development Studies (2015) examining South–South cooperation by Brazil, India, and Mexico found a fresh wave of civil society-based cooperation, most of which was intra-regional (e.g. between Latin American organisations); the report cited only one Indian–South African cooperative project. The report noted that:

> civil society initiatives remain relatively little-known and under-analysed . . . [I]n part this is due to the state-centric approach taken by rising power governments in promoting their South–South Development Cooperation activities. Governments who are now keen to share their development innovations with the world tend not to recognize the role that civil society may have played in generating them.
>
> *(Institute of Development Studies, 2015:2)*

That said, these fora and initiatives may have an indirect effect on cross-regional civil society interactions: a coalition of some 200 African and Indian NGOs used the occasion of the Third India–Africa Forum in 2015, for example, to issue a joint statement on the upcoming World Trade Organisation Ministerial Meeting in Nairobi.

The Indian diaspora may act as yet another trans-regional link. The sub-continent and East Africa have served as nodes of commercial and cultural exchange across the Indian Ocean for centuries. Colonial and post-independence policies deepened the interactions, namely by introducing large numbers of Indians more or less permanently to Africa, but the legacies of these periods may have hindered as much as helped civil society intercourse. Expulsion of Indians from Uganda during the government of Idi Amin and Kikuyu-centred politics in Julius Nyerere's Kenya no doubt disrupted the development of Indian civil society associations and their integration with national polities. So, too, South Africa's colonial and post-independence apartheid policies divided civil and political society along racial lines and therefore compartmentalised civil society (Bhana & Vahed, 2006:242–253). The similarity to Malaysia in this regard bears consideration.

Four South Asian NGOs merit attention in this regard. One is the Aga Khan Development Network, with an Ismaili background but declaring itself non-denominational, which has affiliates across Central and South Asia, Africa (the Maghreb and South of the Sahara), Europe, and North America. Another is the Bangladesh Rural Advancement Committee (BRAC), Bangladesh's largest and one of its most famous NGOs. Since 2000 BRAC has expanded its focus from South Asian development to include projects in Tanzania, Uganda, and South Sudan (Smillie, 2008:237–244). Similarly, Grameen Foundation reports working in Ghana, Kenya, Nigeria, and Uganda. Since 2013 India's Self Employed Women's Association (SEWA) has begun to develop ties with NGOs in Ethiopia and South Africa. All of these organisations boast substantial financial resources and well-developed ties with international NGOs and official development agencies from the Global North. Whether they are representative of broader civil society in Africa and Asia, however, is open to debate; generally, civil society and non-profit voluntary associational narratives are national, global, less trans-regional, at least in the cases of the two regions studied here. Discussions of South–South cooperation, for example, remain focused on official channels.

Conclusion

Africa and Asia present a rich and varied picture of civil society and component non-profit sectors. The issue of whether the concept of civil society is applicable to these two regions has largely been answered in the affirmative. Regardless of alternative conceptions of social system historically, including the relationship between society and the state, scholars have applied the concept with success in analyses of contemporary African and Asian development. The European colonial interlude and the ensuing wave of globalisation no doubt served as catalysts, shaping societies they touched into forms more amenable to state–market–society configurations in which civil society discourse takes place.

At the same time those transformations have occurred through the birth of nationalism and the expansion of a society of national states. Discussions of civil society and NGOs have tended to follow these parameters, leaving the observer with a picture of two continents, the civil societies of which have developed in parallel trajectories. The issues and possibilities they face share common traits but are not necessarily mutually regarding. If anything, the scholarly literature on civil society and non-profits in Africa and Asia tends to examine each region separately. This is in part due to professional research norms but also reflects the preoccupations of states in both regions, where transnational projects have not flourished and regional interstate organisations are not necessarily committed to the idea of a robust and independent civil society (see, for example, Gerard, 2014). It may also be due to the institutional and financial limitations of non-profit and voluntary organisations.

The final section of this chapter briefly examined interconnections between civil society organisations in Africa and Asia. The evidence presented suggests that North–South civil society linkages are more robust than Africa–Asia linkages. The apparent weakness of direct institutional Africa–Asia civil society interaction is no doubt ameliorated in part by participation in global civil society networks and international organisations. In fact, such participation should reduce transaction costs for non-profit and voluntary associations. Consultative status at the ECOSOC and other UN agencies is an example, despite the relatively low rates of registration of African and Asian NGOs. To take another small example, in 2000 the British-based Voluntary Service Overseas began to accept Filipino volunteers for overseas placement, including posts in Africa. One survey of these volunteers' experiences reveals that some of them had backgrounds in NGO work at home (Avila et al., 2004). This kind of volunteering has the potential to foster institutional linkages between African and Asian civil society organisations. Here a great deal of research may profitably be done. The problem, however, is that much of this kind of interaction has not been systematically documented and analysed. The scope of a truly intercontinental research project on the subject is daunting but may well be worth the venture. So, too, the impact of diaspora communities as civil society carriers. To date, diaspora studies focused on Asia, for example, have focused on diaspora philanthropy by Chinese, Indian, and Pakistani emigrant communities in the United States (Geithner et al., 2004; Najam, 2006); the diaspora literature on Asian communities in Africa does not adopt the civil society lens.

Bibliography

Ahmed, S. and Potter, D. M., 2006. *NGOs in International Politics*, Bloomfield, CT: Kumarian Press.
Alagappa, M. (ed.), 2004. *Civil Society and Political Change in Asia*, Stanford, CA: Stanford University Press.
Anheier, H. and Salamon, L., 1998. 'Introduction: the non-profit sector in the developing world,' in H. Anheier and L. Salamon (eds.), *The Nonprofit Sector in the Developing World: A Comparative Analysis*, Manchester and New York: Manchester University Press, pp. 1–50.

Atingdui, L., 1997. 'Ghana,' in L. Salamon and H. Anheier (eds.), *Defining the Nonprofit Sector: A Cross-national Analysis*, Manchester: Manchester University Press, pp. 369–400.

Avila, V. et al., 2004. *Journeys of Filipino Volunteers Overseas*, Quezon City: KEN, Inc.

Benthall, J. and Bellion-Jourdain, J., 2003. *The Charitable Crescent: Politics of Aid in the Muslim World*, London: I. B. Tauris.

Benthall, J. and Bellion-Jourdain, J., 2009. *The Charitable Crescent: Politics of Aid in the Muslim World*, 2nd ed., London: I.B. Tauris.

Bhana, S. and Vahed, G., 2006. 'South Africa,' in L. Brij, P. Reeves and R. Rai (eds.), *The Encyclopedia of the Indian Diaspora*, Singapore, Kuala Lumpur, and Paris: Editions Didiet Miller, pp. 242–253.

Bloodgood, E., Tremblay-Boire, J. and Prakash, A., 2014. 'National Styles of NGO Regulation.' *Nonprofit and Voluntary Sector Quarterly*, Volume 43 (7), pp. 716–736.

Boli, J. and Thomas, G., 1999. 'INGOs and the organization of world culture,' in J. Boli and G. Thomas (eds.), *Constructing World Culture: International Nongovernmental Organizations Since 1875*, Stanford, CA: Stanford University Press, pp. 13–49.

Boli, J., Loya, T. and Loftin, T., 1999. 'National participation in world-polity organizations,' in J. Boli and G. Thomas (eds.), *Constructing World Culture: International Nongovernmental Organizations Since 1875*, Stanford, CA: Stanford University Press, pp. 50–77.

Brass, J., 2011. 'Why do NGOs Go Where they Go? Evidence from Kenya.' *World Development*, Volume 40 (2), pp. 387–401.

Bratton, M., 1989. 'The Politics of Government–NGO Relations in Africa.' *World Development*, Volume 17 (4), pp. 569–587.

Casey, J., 2016. *The Nonprofit World: Civil Society and the Rise of the Nonprofit Sector*, Boulder and London: Kumarian Press.

Clapham, C., 1984. *Third World Politics: An Introduction*, Madison, WI: University of Wisconsin Press.

Clarke, G., 2013. *Civil Society in the Philippines: Theoretical, Methodological and Policy Debates*, New York and London: Routledge.

Cleary, S., 1997. *The Role of NGOs Under Authoritarian Political Systems*, New York: St. Martin's Press.

Cogswell, E., 2002. 'Private Philanthropy in Multiethnic Malaysia.' *Macalester International*, Volume 12, pp. 15–121.

Deguchi, M., 2001. 'The Distinction between Institutionalized and Noninstitutionalized NPOs. New Policy Initiatives and Non-profit Organizations in Japan,' in J. Kendall and H, Anheier (eds.), *Third Sector Policy at the Crossroads. An International Nonprofit Analysis*, London: Routledge, pp. 153–167.

Diamond, L., 1994. 'Toward Democratic Consolidation.' *Journal of Democracy*, Volume 5 (3), pp. 4–17.

Doreenspleet, R. and Nijzink, L. (eds.), 2013. *One-party Dominance in African Democracies*, Boulder, CO: Lynne Rienner.

Economist, 1998. 'The Other Government in Bangladesh.' July 28, p. 30.

Edwards, M., 2004. *Civil Society*, London: Polity Press.

Elbayar, K., 2005. 'NGO Laws in Selected Arab States.' *International Journal of Not-for-Profit Law*, Volume 7 (4), pp. 3–27.

Englebert, P., 1997. 'The Contemporary African State: Neither African nor State.' *Third World Quarterly*, Volume 18 (4), pp. 767–775.

Farrington, J. (ed.), 1993. *NGOs and the State in Asia: Rethinking Roles in Sustainable Agricultural Development*, London: Routledge.

Fernando, J., 2011. *The Political Economy of NGOs: State Formation in Sri Lanka and Bangladesh*, London: Polity Press.

Fisher, J., 1998. *Non-governments: NGOs and the Political Development of the Third World*, Bloomfield, CT: Kumarian Press.

Fruttero, A. and Gauri, V., 2005. 'The Strategic Choices of NGOs: Location Decisions in Rural Bangladesh.' *Journal of Development Studies*, Volume 41 (5), pp. 759–787.

Geithner, P., Johnson, P. and Chen, L. (eds.), 2004. *Diaspora Philanthropy and Equitable Development in China and India*, Cambridge, MA: Harvard University Press.

Gerard, K., 2014. *ASEAN's Engagement of Civil Society: Regulating Dissent*, New York and London: Palgrave Macmillan.

Howell, J. and Pearce, J., 2001. *Civil Society and Development: A Critical Exploration*, Boulder, CO: Lynne Rienner.

Hsiao, H. M., 2003. 'NGOs and democratization in Taiwan: their interactive roles in building a viable civil society,' in D. Schak and W. Hudson (eds.), *Civil Society in Asia: In Search of Democracy and Development in Bangladesh*, Aldershot: Ashgate, pp. 180–191.

Civil society and the rise of NGOs

Hudson, W., 2003. 'Problematizing European theories of civil society', in D. Schak and W. Hudson (eds.), *Civil Society in Asia: In Search of Democracy and Development in Bangladesh*, Aldershot: Ashgate, pp. 9–19.

Hudson Institute, 2015. *Index of Philanthropic Freedom*, Washington, DC: Hudson Institute.

Institute of Development Studies, 2015. 'Realising the Potential of Civil Society-led South–South Development Cooperation,' Policy Briefing 84, January. Available at: www.ids.ac.uk/publication/realising-the-potential-of-civil-society-led-south-south-development-cooperation [Accessed 9 October 2017].

Jafar, A., 2011. *Women's NGOs in Pakistan*, New York: Palgrave.

Kandil, A., 1997. 'Egypt,' in L. Salamon and H. Anheier (eds.), *Defining the Nonprofit Sector*, Manchester and New York: Manchester University Press, pp. 350–368.

Kaneko, Y., 2002. 'Malaysia: dual structure in the state–NGO relationship,' in S. Shigetomi (ed.), *The State and NGOs: Perspectives from Asia*, Singapore: Institute of Southeast Asian Studies, pp. 178–199.

Kilby, P., 2010. *NGOs in India: The Challenges of Women's Empowerment and Accountability*, New York and London: Routledge.

Koch, D., 2009. *Aid from International NGOs: Blind Spots on the Aid Allocation Map*, London and New York: Routledge.

Kunz, F., 1995. 'Civil Society in Africa.' *Journal of Modern Africa Studies*, Volume 33 (1), pp. 181–187.

Lee, H. G. (ed.), 2004. *Civil Society in Southeast Asia*. Singapore: Institute of Southeast Asian Studies.

Lele, J. and Quadir, F. (eds.), 2004. *Democracy and Civil Society in Asia*, Volume 2, Houndmills and New York: Palgrave MacMillan.

Mamattah, T., 2014. 'Building civil society in West Africa: notes from the field,' in E. Obudare (ed.), *The Handbook of Civil Society in Africa*, New York, Heidelberg, Dordrecht, and London: Springer, pp. 143–156.

Manji, F. and O'Coill, C., 2002. 'The Missionary Position: NGOs and Development in Africa,' *International Affairs*, Volume 78 (3), pp. 567–583.

Mann, G., 2015. *From Empires to NGOs in the West African Sahel: The Road to Nongovernmentality.* New York: Cambridge University Press.

Michael, S., 2005. *Undermining Development: The Absence of Power among Local NGOs in Africa*, Bloomington, IN: Indiana University Press.

Mmanda, O., 2008. *NGOs Working in Tanzania*. Helsinki: KEPA Working Paper 25, pp. 4–2. Available at: www.kepa.fi/tiedostot/julkaisut/ngo-work-in-tanzania-2012-update.pdf [Accessed 10 May 2016].

Monga, C., 1995. 'Civil Society and Democratisation in Francophone Africa.' *Journal of Modern African Studies*, Volume 33 (3), pp. 359–379.

Morfit, N. S., 2010. '"AIDS is Money": How Donor Preferences Reconfigure Local Realities.' *World Development*, Volume 39 (1), pp. 64–76.

Mw Makumbe, J., 1998. 'Is there a Civil Society in Africa?' *International Affairs*, Volume 74 (2), pp. 305–317.

Najam, A., 2006. *Portrait of a Giving Community: Philanthropy by the Pakistani-American Diaspora*, Cambridge, MA: Harvard University Press.

Najita, T., 2004. 'Civil society in Japan's modernity: an interpretive overview,' in G. Steunebrink and E. van der Zweerde (eds.), *Civil Society, Religion, and the Nation*, Amsterdam and New York: Rodopi, pp. 101–115.

Nathan, A., 2015. 'China's Challenge.' *Journal of Democracy*, Volume 2 (1), pp. 156–170.

Nega, B. and Schneider, G., 2014. 'NGOs, the State, and Development in Africa.' *Review of Social Economy*, Volume 72 (4), pp. 485–503.

Nejima, S., 2002. 'Pakistan: regulation and potentiality in a fragmented society,' in S. Shigetomi (ed.), *NGOs and the State: Perspectives from Asia*, Singapore: Institute of Southeast Asian Studies, pp. 94–109.

Nobusue, K., 2002. 'Bangladesh: A large NGO sector supported by foreign donors,' in S. Shigetomi (ed.), *NGOs and the State: Perspectives from Asia*, Singapore: Institute of Southeast Asian Studies, pp. 34–56.

Obiyan, A. S., 2005. 'A Critical Examination of the State Versus Non-governmental Organizations (NGOs) in the Policy Sphere in the Global South: Will the State Die as the NGOs Thrive in Sub-Saharan Africa and Asia?' *African and Asian Studies*, Volume 4 (3), pp. 301–325.

Obudare, E. (ed.), 2014. *The Handbook of Civil Society in Africa*, New York, Heidelberg, Dordrecht, and London: Springer.

Opoku-Mensah, P., 2008. 'The state of civil society in sub-Saharan Africa,' in V. F. Heinrich and L. Fioramonti (eds.), *CIVICUS Global Survey of the State of Civil Society*, Volume. 2, Bloomfield, CT: Kumarian Press, pp. 75–90.

Pekkanen, R., 2006. *Japan's Dual Civil Society: Members without Advocates*, Stanford: Stanford University Press.

Pinckney, R., 2009. *NGOs, Africa, and the Global Order*, New York and Houndmills, Basingstoke: Palgrave Macmillan.

Pongsapich, A., 1997. 'Thailand,' in L. Salamon and H. Anheier (eds.), *Defining the Nonprofit Sector*, Manchester and New York: Manchester University Press, pp. 446–468.

Potter, D. and Khondaker, M. R., 2015. 'The Charitable Sector in Islamic Asia.' *Nanzan Management Review*, Volume 30 (2), pp. 105–119.

Potter, D. and Potter S., 2016. 'Aid by Other Means: A Comparison of Three NGO Subsidies in Japan.' *Academia Social Sciences*, Volume 10, pp. 79–92.

Reid, A., 2010. *Imperial Alchemy: Nationalism and Political Identity in Southeast Asia*, Cambridge: Cambridge University Press.

Raposo, P. A., 2014. *Japan's Foreign Aid Policy in Africa: Evaluating the TICAD Process*, New York and Abingdon: Routledge.

Salamon, L. and Anheier, H. (eds.), 1997. *Defining the Nonprofit Sector: A Cross-national Analysis*, Manchester: Manchester University Press.

Salamon, L. and Anheier, H. (eds.), 1998. *The Nonprofit Sector in the Developing World: A Comparative Analysis*, Manchester: Manchester University Press.

Salamon, L. and Sokolowski, S. (eds.), 2004. *Global Civil Society*, Volume 2, Bloomfield, CT: Kumarian Press.

Salamon, L., Sokolowski, S. and List, R., 2004. 'Global civil society: an overview,' in L. Salamon et al. (eds.), *Global Civil Society*, Volume 2, Bloomfield, CT: Kumarian Press, pp. 3–60.

Schak, D. and Hudson, W., (eds.), *Civil Society in Asia: In Search of Democracy and Development in Bangladesh*, Aldershot: Ashgate.

Sen, S., 1997. 'India,' in L. Salamon and H. Anheier (eds.), *Defining the Nonprofit Sector: A Cross-national Analysis*, Manchester: Manchester University Press, pp. 401–445.

Sen, S., 1998. 'The nonprofit sector in India,' in L. Salamon and H. Anheier (eds.), *The Nonprofit Sector in the Developing World: A Comparative Analysis*, Manchester: Manchester University Press, pp. 198–294.

Shigetomi, S. (ed.), 2002. *The State and NGOs: Perspectives from Asia*. Singapore: Institute of Southeast Asian Studies.

Shivji, I., 2007. *Silences in NGO Discourse: The Role and Future of NGOs in Africa*, Nairobi: Fahamu.

Sidel, M. 2010. 'Maintaining Firm Control: Recent Developments in Nonprofit Law and Regulations in Vietnam.' *International Journal for Not-for-Profit Law*, Volume 2(3). Available at: www.icnl.org/research/journal/vol12iss3/art_1.htm [Accessed 4 July 2017].

Silk, T. (ed.), 1999. *Philanthropy and Law in Asia*, San Francsico: Jossey-Bass.

Smillie, I., 2008. *Freedom from Want: The Remarkable Success Story of BRAC, the Global Grassroots Organization That's Winning the Fight against Poverty*, Sterling, VA: Kumarian Press.

Srivastava, S. S. et al., 2004. 'India,' in L. Salamon and S. Sokolowski (eds.), *Global Civil Society*, Volume 2, *Dimensions of the Nonprofit Sector*, Bloomfield, CT: Kumarian Press, pp. 157–169.

Stiles, K., 2002. *Civil Society by Design: NGOs, and the Intermestic Development Circle in Bangladesh: Donors, NGOs and the Intermestic Development Circle in Bangladesh*, London and Westport, CT: Praeger.

Tandon, R. and Kak, M., 2008. 'The effects of rapid socioeconomic growth on civic activism in emerging democracies: an analysis of civil society in the Asia-Pacific region,' in V. F. Heinrich and L. Fioramonti (eds.), *CIVICUS: Global Survey of the State of Civil Society*, Volume 2, Bloomfield, CT: Kumarian Press, pp. 91–109.

Tar, A. U., 2014. 'Civil society and neoliberalism,' in E. Obudare (ed.), *The Handbook of Civil Society in Africa*, New York, Heidelberg, Dordrecht, and London: Springer, pp. 253–272.

Tarrow, S., 1998. *Power in Movement: Social Movements and Contentious Politics*, 2nd ed., Cambridge, MA: Cambridge University Press.

The Economist, 1998. 'The Other Government in Bangladesh.' 28 July, 30.

Wiktorowicz, Q., 2002. 'The Political Limits of Nongovernmental Organisations in Jordan,' *World Development*, Volume 30 (1), pp. 77–93.

Woo-Cummings, M. (ed.), 1999. *The Developmental State*. Ithaca, NY: Cornell University Press.

Yamamoto, T. (ed.), 1998. *The Nonprofit Sector in Japan*, Manchester and New York: Manchester University Press.

Yamauchi, N., Shimizu, H., Sokolowski, S. W. and Salamon, L. M., 1999. 'Japan,' in L. Salamon, H. K. Anheier, R. List and S. Toepler (eds.), *Global Civil Society: Dimensions of the Nonprofit Sector*, Baltimore, MD: Johns Hopkins Center for Civil Society Studies, pp. 243–259.

18
EDUCATION AND GENDER IN THE GLOBAL SOUTH

Inadequate policy environment at the confluence in sub-Saharan Africa

Emefa Juliet Takyi-Amoako

Introduction

The Millennium Development Goals (MDGs) adopted in 2000, the third goal of which (Promote gender equality and empower women) shaped Education for All (EFA), sought to eliminate gender disparities in primary and secondary education by 2005, and attain gender equality in education by 2015, with an emphasis on guaranteeing girls' complete and equal access to, and achievement in, basic education of good quality. The approach for attaining this goal was to implement combined strategies for gender equality in education that acknowledged the necessity of transforming attitudes, values and practices. Responsible for this implementation were partnerships contextualised by MDG 8 (Developing a partnership for development), which evolved post-2015 as Sustainable Development Goal (SDG) 17 (Revitalise the global partnership for sustainable development), and aimed to reinforce the implementation processes and invigorate the global partnership for sustainable development (SDSN, 2015a). Efforts to attain MDG 3 and EFA Goal 5 occurred largely within an MDG 8 partnership environment. Unfortunately, in sub-Saharan Africa (SSA), this partnership failed to accomplish this MDG/EFA goal – a goal not even comprehensive enough, owing to its exclusion of higher levels of education (UNESCO, 2015a).

The problem

According to a recent gender report compiled by UNESCO's Education for All (EFA) Global Monitoring Report (GMR) team, and released jointly with the United Nations Girls' Education Initiative (UNGEI) on 12 October 2015 to mark International Day of the Girl Child, despite some progress in recent years, attainment of gender parity, let alone gender equality, in education has been intransigent. Less than half of countries globally had achieved the goal of gender parity at both primary and secondary levels of education by 2015. While in a few contexts boys were disadvantaged, essentially, girls continued to suffer severe disadvantage and exclusion in education systems throughout their lives. An estimated 31 million girls of primary school age and 32 million girls of lower secondary school age were out of school in 2013

(UNESCO, 2015a, 2015b; Thomson Reuters Foundation, 2015). In the Global South, SSA had the lowest proportion of countries with gender parity, only 2 out of 35 countries achieving it, while no country in the region achieved parity at both primary and secondary levels by the deadline. The story was worse at the upper secondary and tertiary levels. More women than men were enrolled in tertiary education globally except in SSA (ibid.). The report indicates that immense difficulties persist, with gender gaps increasing at each educational level with under-privileged girls continually disadvantaged in the region. Nearly 70 per cent of the poorest girls had never participated in formal education compared with fewer than 20 per cent of the wealth-iest boys in Guinea and Niger, for instance. While gender gaps in youth literacy were reducing elsewhere, fewer than seven out of every ten young women in SSA were expected to have basic literacy skills by 2015. While two-thirds of adults needing basic literacy skills were women, a fraction unaltered from 2000, half of adult women in SSA could neither read nor write (see UNESCO, 2015a, 2015b for comprehensive information). Why this bleak picture in SSA?

Despite the argument that institutional constraints and deep-rooted unfair social practices undermine gender parity and equality in education in SSA, there is a more sophisticated view which extends this perspective to encapsulate the inadequacy of global development policy ecology. Drawing on the notions of *undoing gender, the confluence* and Gore's 'Faustian bargain', this reflective chapter conceptualises education and gender policy processes and poor outcomes in the Global South, particularly within the context of SSA, as the consequences of the rejection of the long-standing notion of fostering growth in SSA state economies (Takyi-Amoako, 2015; Gore, 2010, 2015; Amoako, 2009; Butler, 2004; Deutsch, 2007). While the MDGs engendered a fresh global progress accord, this consensus essentially failed to alleviate poverty as it was based on what is called a 'Faustian bargain' (Gore, 2010: 70). In other words, the advantages of this accord were realised at the expense of a significant loss. International obligation to endorse economic progress and address income inequalities globally has disappeared, while national and international policies have concentrated on advancing 'global integration rather than production and employment' in SSA countries, an indication of the power imbalance in North–South partnerships (ibid.). This represents a significant reason why attempts to address gender disparities and inequalities even at the basic level of education and attainment MDGs have not yielded the desired outcomes in SSA. Employing the MDG (now the SDG) informed global development partnership framework including recent China–Africa and India–Africa partnerships, this chapter examines North–South and South–South partnerships and their effect on education and gender outcomes in SSA.

The analysis is divided into four main sections. While Section One states the problem and its background including the study's rationale and its objectives, Section Two defines its question and outlines its conceptual/methodological framework. Section Three then demonstrates how a flawed global policy ecology hinders the attainment of gender equality in education in SSA, and discusses possible steps to address it. Section Four concludes the analysis with recommendations.

Gender and education processes and outcomes have occurred largely within the policy settings of official development assistance (ODA) delivered through North–South partnerships (represented by aid donor–recipient relations between SSA and multilateral/international finan-cial institutions (e.g. Bretton Woods institutions, United Nations, etc.) and bilateral entities from countries in the Global North), and to a lesser degree, South–South partnerships (trade relations between SSA and other countries or institutions of the Global South, in this case, China and India). These form components of the global partnership for development and create a complex confluence on the cusp of the global and local. Gore (2010) argued that it was crucial for this global partnership to create a fresh agreement that would contextualise global sustain-able development and a different policy discourse established on the generation of industrious

Rationale and objectives

The negative picture of poor education and gender outcomes demands a deeper understanding of how education and gender policies interact in the Global South through these partnerships, specifically, in SSA, the worst performing region, while suggesting how the challenges may be addressed. The chapter argues that this analysis offers a unique opportunity to examine the development partnership processes for an indepth appreciation of the merits and pitfalls. The prospect of exploring how these partnerships could be characterised and strengthened to enable them to help transform the depressing gender and education profile in the region is crucial, since a prerequisite for attaining gender equality in schooling is educational quality and vice versa (Aikman & Unterhalter, 2005).

Moreover, the urgent need to analyse gender and education in the Global South is due to the unequal North–South drift in notions of gender in the field, and the manner in which development programmes initiated in the North impact implementation of gender programmes in Africa (Manuh, 2007; Abdullah, 2007).

Additionally, although it has been acknowledged that gender represents one of the most dynamic areas in scholarship, and has gained widespread currency in Africa (Miescher et al., 2007), paradoxically, depending on where one is positioned, gender remains a subject that has on occasion been non-existent or at best marginalised instead of mainstreamed in scholarly analysis of issues. This gap is more noticeable after a quick glance at the daily schedule and programme overview of the inaugural conference *Asian Studies in Africa: Challenges and Prospects of a New Axis of Intellectual Interactions*, held in Accra, Ghana from 24th to 26th September 2015. It was obvious that gender was not on the menu despite its centrality to 'intellectual interactions' (Conference Programme, 2015).

This chapter aspires to demonstrate the connection between gender and education from two different vantage points: a policy phenomenon occurring within the context of partnerships riddled with global integration (embedding power and income inequalities) that undermines the growth of state economies and generation of productive capacities in SSA; and a process of un/doing gender at the confluence (Takyi-Amoako, 2015; Gore, 2010, 2015; Amoako, 2009; Butler, 2004; Deutsch, 2007).

Certainly, the link between education and gender complicates oversimplifications. The former as both a requirement and a right with the latter intricately overlaps with a multitude of social indicators for example class, race, age, geography, the rural-urban rift, intra-urban inequalities, citizenship, ethnicity etc. (Dhar, 2014). Kabeer observed that,

> [w]hile 'gender is never absent', it is never present in pure form. It is always interwoven with other social inequalities, such as class and race, and has to be analyzed through a holistic framework if the concrete conditions of life for different groups of women and men are to be understood.
>
> *(Kabeer, 1994: 65)*

These connections have a resultant influence on the link between gender and education. Recognising the intersectionality of gender – the manner in which gender coalesces with other inherent traits and social indicators generating hindrances and benefits in certain instances – commands a thorough inspection of gendered forms and their likely associations (or their absence) with interrelated battles and tensions (Stromquist & Fischman, 2009). This chapter explores the way forward for strengthening the connection between gender and education in SSA for educational, socioeconomic, cultural and developmental benefit. It intends to take stock and look ahead. Meanwhile, a brief statement on the concept and methodology is relevant.

Conceptual and methodological framework

Perspectives and assumptions

Gender and education 'as a field owes its very existence to feminist activism and struggle' (Weaver-Hightower & Skelton, 2013: x). Indeed, feminism critiques male dominant ways of knowing and queries precisely the power hierarchies that shape viewpoints and research results. However, the aim of non-Western feminism is broader: to dismantle male hegemonic discourses, while deconstructing the monopoly of Western knowledge paradigms over gender discourses, through archaeology and reconstruction of history and philosophy (Channa, 2013).

A personal experience on a graduate Gender/Women's Studies programme, which was Western oriented (in its discussions of feminist theories) albeit very fulfilling, made me realise that knowledge was political and hegemonic even in spaces where it was meant to liberate. Whose voice or knowledge gains mainstream recognition? Who has the right to legitimise knowledge? Who has the power to name knowledge and render it credible? It has been argued that since colonial/postcolonial periods, knowledge has been dominated and channelled through the West in a manner that 'even knowledge about non-Western people has been legitimised and made available by Western scholars both to the world and to the people who are the subjects of this knowledge' (ibid.: 2).

The above assumptions and perspectives continue to plague my thoughts and deepen my sensitivity to the differential power dynamics in knowledge creation and legitimisation. The task of writing a chapter on gender and education in the Global South is a mammoth one, and dovetails with these questions. Despite focusing on SSA, the challenge is reflected not least in the word limitation imposed on such a broad topic, but also, the near impossibility of comprehensively examining how gender and education interact within a huge region with vast diversities in population, culture, history and so forth. While arguing that this chapter represents a situated knowledge and is therefore partial, indicating just a version of the story of gender and education in the Global South (Haraway, 1988), I am conscious of the view that criticises urban (African) scholars who generate discourses and scholarships that oppress and render African women and men from alternative locations (e.g. urban/rural, etc.), classes, histories and cultures as 'Other' (Mohanty, 1988; Nnaemeka, 1996).

The Global South

For that matter, I argue that the Global South is not a monolithic entity, hence the focus on a selected component, Africa, which is neither a monolith, hence the chapter's emphasis on SSA, nor a region that is inherently heterogeneous. The concept 'South' or 'Global South' implies so-called developing or least developed countries (LDCs) situated predominantly in the Southern Hemisphere. The North–South divide is largely regarded as a socioeconomic and political divide. Mostly, characterisations of the Global South include Africa, Latin America and developing Asia, including the Middle East. The Global South, with three-quarters of the world's population, and access to one-fifth of the world's income, is usually considered poorer. 'It lacks appropriate technology, it has no political stability, the economies are disarticulated, and their foreign exchange earnings depend on primary product exports' (Mimiko, 2012: 47; Wikipedia, n.d.).

Gender interacting with education in the Global South encapsulates issues regarding both boys/men and girls/women, and is seen as local/national/regional, international/global, inter-disciplinary, multidisciplinary and trans-disciplinary (Unterhalter, 2014). Exploring the link between education and gender within this region/continent, and across its regional/continental associations, benefits from a novel emerging framework referred to as the confluence, a context/field that enables un/doing gender in education. Hence, the argument to examine the relationship between education and gender in the context of SSA at this confluence and through the lens of undoing gender, since it reveals a number of ways which education and gender interact and must interact in the Global South, as well as the means by which these can be characterised.

Defining the question

Acknowledging the gaps in existing gender and education scholarship and the obdurate gender disparities and inequalities in education in SSA, this chapter argues for undoing gender in education at the confluence (UNESCO, 2015a). Assuming a 'proactive mode' that shifts from detecting problems to persistent efforts at advancing enhancements and discovering answers – after decades of attempts to understand the working and outcomes of prejudice based on sexual and gender differences and inequalities – is important (Stromquist & Fischman, 2009). Consequently, attempts to characterise and study effective ways of influencing fresh gender routines, and to comprehend how they develop and the effects they might engender, become central. The aim is to move from a language of criticism to one that, with no loss of critical view, acknowledges transformations and trials, and engender brand-new experiences (ibid.). In this regard, this chapter's question is both theoretical and practical: How can we undo the effects of external and internalised domination in the global policy environment in a manner that would reduce income and power inequities between and within nations/regions and several masculinities and femininities within education?

Analytical method

In addressing this question, this chapter adopts a reflective, interpretative approach built on documentary analysis and conceptual enunciation, with some realistic exemplifications to examine education and gender in SSA. Using existing studies on gender in international and comparative education and extant development paradigms, this chapter provides an analysis of gender and education in SSA from the perspective of undoing gender at the confluence, entrenched with global integration that repudiates economic growth and creation of productive capacities in SSA, and fails to address global income inequalities. This perspective does not only entail addressing power and gender inequities between males and females in education, but also between education and gender policy actors that populate global (e.g. North–South, South–South) partnerships within the development paradigm under scrutiny, while consolidating the gender and education component of South–South partnerships in SSA (Deutsch, 2007; Takyi-Amoako, 2015; Gore, 2010; Amoako, 2009). In this context, it proposes the relevance of the concept of the confluence explained in the next section, and the usefulness of the notion of undoing gender defined later in this chapter.

The notion of the confluence

The notion of education and gender policy choices, processes and practices at the point where partners and agents meet is referred to as the confluence. This confluence represents the meeting point of different actors and ideas (national/regional and international) within the context of MDGs (and now, SDGs) development paradigms, whose aim is not to grow but to integrate the economies of SSA countries globally, while repudiating their productive capacities. It is located on the cusp of the global and local, the international and national/regional where North–South/South–South partnerships occur (Takyi-Amoako, 2015; Amoako, 2009).

While portrayals of policy and its processes, as constituting state-centred control and different contexts and stages of a cycle, are copious (Ball, 1994; Bowe et al.,1992; Ozga, 1990; Apple, 1989; Dale, 1989; Vidovich, 2001; Taylor, 1997; Ranson, 1995; Troyna, 1994; Lingard, 1993), what is not well known is the depiction of policy processes as the confluence of interactions between global/international and local/national/regional actors and agents (e.g. foreign aid donors, recipients, non-governmental organisations, both public and private sector entities, etc.), whose actions and decisions are subject to the forces of globalisation, partnership, funding/ foreign aid, policy and power processes. In other words, policy is understood in terms of stages and contexts in a cycle. However, we have little understanding of the notion of policy processes in a space/field, which this chapter identifies as the confluence, the cusp of the global and local. See Table 18.1, for further explanation.

Table 18.1 The confluence defined further

Relevant to the confluence is Bourdieu's positing of social arrangements as comprising numerous social fields, each with its individual rationalities of praxis entirely subsumed by a field of power (Hilgers & Mangez, 2015). His concept of field is an organised scheme of precise and general social linkages, inherently structured with respect to power relations that determine access to the particular goods or capital at stake (Thompson, 1991; Jenkins,1992; Calhoun, 1993).	This field represents 'the analytical space defined by the interdependence of the entities that compose a structure of positions among which there are power relations' (Hilgers & Mangez, 2015: 5). By this I mean that the structuring of education and gender policy processes in different countries in general and those in SSA in particular is clothed within a complex web of both endogenous (local/national/regional) and exogenous (global/ international) influences and differential power dynamics at this confluence (Amoako, 2009; Takyi-Amoako, 2012). This social reality is considered essentially relational (Hilgers & Mangez, 2015).	The growing intersection of the global and local in policy processes is culminating in fresh modes of network and polycentric governance. In other words, policy processes occurring on the cusp of the local and global, namely the confluence, are creating spaces, fields or systems with numerous centres of decision-making and heightened influences (Thompson et al., 2015). This confluence could also be perceived as global policy convergence of national/regional and international, as well as policy assemblages and networks shaping relationships of exchange and interaction (Ball & Exley, 2010; Thompson & Cook, 2014). A strong grasp of this confluence can generate sensitivity to culture and context, which subsequently can empower education and gender policy actors and agents who/which operate at this meeting point to collaborate efficiently to mitigate some of the educational challenges and gender disparities and inequalities.

Source: Author.

In this respect, education processes with their gender dynamics as comparative and international are significant. This chapter highlights the global and local dimensions of the confluence with their implications, and suggests ways that education and gender policy processes (while being local/national) as comparative and international, can promote this confluence as a democratic policy space for sharing and learning, as well as encouraging the growth of state economies and cultivation of productive capacities in order to formulate and implement relevant, comprehensive, resource-rich and effective education and gender policies, closely aligned with local/national/regional needs for mutual benefit.

Overall, the confluence is an essential construct worth engaging within the context of development processes, in general, and in regards to education and (un/doing) gender processes that occur in contexts where countries in SSA interact with the world, in particular. How, therefore, is un/doing gender in education perceived at this confluence? First, understanding gender is crucial.

Un/doing gender in education

Gender, a mixture of social, cultural and historical formations, is perceived as an indispensable and compelling lens through which the function of education in society, and the manner in which it influences social transformation, can be viewed – a powerful means with which to grasp the dynamics of power at the level of society and at the level of the most private male and female existences (Arnot & Mac an Ghaill, 2006). Conventionally, the term gender has been defined linguistically as masculine, feminine and neuter, but since the 1950s, its meaning has been complicated by academics who assign it extra notions. While the term differentiates manliness from womanliness, its essence has also been a derivative of feminist thought, and with contention and complexities, it is frequently utilised in social science discourses (Money, 1955; Oakley, 1997; Stromquist & Fischman, 2009).

It is therefore unsurprising that despite scholarship and numerous publications on the connection between gender and education, what the term gender means continues to perplex and remains equivocal. It is regularly used synonymously with the word 'sex' or an indication of interest in 'women's' issues or matters of sexuality: femininity and masculinity. While the term sex is used to biologically differentiate between women and men, gender is employed to explain the social and cultural dimensions of the biological grouping of sex. Gender provides the opportunity to research not only women but men too and encourages interpersonal examination between the sexes. Gender stresses the distinction between biological sex in one sense and enacted selves of masculinity and femininity on the other (Miescher et al., 2007).

Nevertheless, gender issues are often perceived exclusively as women's issues (Channa, 2013; Manuh, 2007). Some have argued that because women have been subordinated and unvoiced in a masculine world, a gendered strategy often narrowly focuses on them (de Beauvoir, 1949; Channa, 2013). Whatever the origin of gender, it has been appropriated, indigenised and institutionalised in non-Western worlds (Channa, 2013; Manuh, 2007). Nonetheless, it is worth stating, paradoxically, that gender notions and practices have always occurred in Africa from time immemorial, and as a field of study, gender is seen as dynamic. African gender perspectives pre-date and transcend the preserve of Western perspectives and paradigms, as well as the realm of academics, and embrace varying histories, cultures and general populations.

It has been argued that the reality of African women fighting for equality in different areas of life has been part of their heritage even before the advent of feminism (Nfah-Abbenyi, 1997; Aidoo, 1998; Kolawole, 2002). Numerous studies indicate that although precolonial Africa was not sexism-free, there were flexible gender relations between men and women. African women

Table 18.2 Effect of colonialism on gender in sub-Saharan Africa elaborated

Indeed, colonial legacy, hardly rendered any women prepared and armed to assume roles in the formal economy and institutions (e.g. universities, etc.) across Africa (Mama, 2003: 106). Thus, there were only a handful of female employees in the colonial public service in Africa, who often had to abandon their professions as soon as they entered marriage. Colonial influence and Western values deepened a gendered education and shaped professional configuration to the disadvantage of the female population in Africa (Assié-Lumumba, 2015; Mama, 2003: Denzer, 1989).	Consequently, during the 1940s, 1950s and later periods, some progressive newly independent African nationalist governments attempted to redress the imbalance by promoting gender equality in national policies, which re-catapulted women into active participation in various public sectors (Soothill, 2007; Mama, 2003). Simultaneously, the Western academies being modelled by these African nationalists were themselves excluding their own intellectually accomplished Western women (Mama, 2003; Dyhouse, 2001).	Studies have shown that the public/private domain contrast does not exactly portray the African reality and demonstrates the unique fashions in which women employed agency in precolonial/colonial/ postcolonial eras in challenging notions of correct gender interactions (Ampofo, Beoku-Betts, Njambi & Osirim, 2004; Denzer 1995; Johnson-Odim & Mba, 1997; Mbilinyi 1989; Mukurasi, 1991; Shawulu, 1990; Tsikata, 1989).

participated both in the private and public spheres of life just like their male counterparts. However, the advent of colonialism rigidified these relations through its colonial machinery which institutionalised gender inequality through its gender biased policies (Akyeampong & Fofack, 2012; Assié-Lumumba, 2015; Nfah-Abbenyi, 1997; Nnaemeka, 1997; Manuh, 2007; Ogundipe-Leslie, 1994). See Table 18.2 for elaboration.

In spite of the effort to clarify, 'gender' remains a complex term. The term continually engenders discords, and this signifies the problems faced when tackling gender gaps. It is therefore argued that the debates on 'gender' must be appreciated in the context of the disciplines that shape them, which are neither history-free nor disconnected from philosophical tensions and social linkages (Stromquist & Fischman, 2009). The signification of gender or its concern is not a simple manifestation of the social, racial, religious, political, ethnic and economic undercurrents shaping the educational encounters of the fe/male in human society. Rather, gender is formed in the crucible of these circumstances (ibid.). Gender identities are integral to social formation (Arnot, 2002). Gender habits, dialogues, principles and conventions occur within contexts of power associations or history. Grasping the interdependence of gender intricacies is vital to discovering instances where the shaping of novel social outlooks and praxes may be nurtured (Stromquist & Fischman, 2009).

The framework of 'doing gender' was first proposed for exploring gender as the outcome of social relationships (West & Zimmerman, 1987). It offered a foundation for numerous studies, and knowledge of gender as an interactive, situational and location-specific routine that is capable of shedding light on human gendered experiences in educational systems within societies, such as those in the Global South (Bajaj, 2009). However, a call for a re-visioning of this viewpoint by feminists led to the undoing of the gender approach, which not only records the phenomenon of inequities, but also aims to deconstruct structures of inequalities in order to transform and engender gender balance (Butler, 2004; Deutsch, 2007).

Gender viewpoints in comparative and international education have complicated our grasp of education and society by examining linkages between gender, power and the state (Stromquist, 1995), and by querying causal relationships within development theory and praxis, like those concerning education and socioeconomic well-being (Vavrus, 2003, 2005). Studies on gender in international and comparative education have moved from fundamentally tackling female access to formal education (Prather & Tietjen, 1991; Stromquist et al., 2000) to embracing a wider variety of subjects, comprising shaping of masculinity and femininity within and outside formal educational spaces (Mirembe & Davies, 2001; Naseem, 2004); female notions of real gendered experiences in teaching and learning (Adely, 2004; Kirk, 2004; Stambach, 2000); and the function of organisations in formal and non-formal education worldwide (Stromquist, 2004; Vavrus, 2005). Existing scholarship has also offered knowledge regarding gendered routines within formal education and evaluated new gender and education models that have been external to schools and implemented by non-governmental organisations (NGOs) and other entities (Anderson & Mendoza, 2000). Also, the centrality of gender to human capabilities, and the loss to a nation's socioeconomic achievement when repudiated, has been acknowledged (Sen, 1999; Nussbaum, 2000; Assié-Lumumba, 2007). Voices from Africa and Asia express concern that when the term 'gender' is employed it diminishes and depoliticises female rights as well as repudiates serious issues and confuses feminist assertions, rendering women's petitions more favourable to the patriarchal and male-dominated governance that pervades international aid, development institutions and governments (Spivak, 1999; Staudt, 2002; Kolawole, 2004; Lazreg, 2005; Stromquist & Fischman, 2009). At this point, it is worth tracing briefly the role of the international community in addressing gender and education issues in SSA.

International commitment to gender equality in education: treatises and promises

The international community has been seen as devoted to removing gender disparities in primary and secondary education. This commitment is contextualised within a human rights paradigm that reinforces education and recognises the personal, social and economic advantages of educating the female population of every society. Two kinds of instrument indicate international commitment to gender equality in education. They are 'International treatises' and 'Political promises'. The former is meant to be ratified by each nation thus bestowing on them legal credence, while the latter are designed by means of international accord to be an added inducement to advance action,

Towards gender equality in education in sub-Saharan Africa: identifying and addressing inadequate global policy environment and partnerships at the confluence

The international commitment outlined in Figure 18.1 and MDGs development consensus represented through North–South cooperation in SSA, in theory, impressively depict a strong commitment to gender equality in education. In practice, however, the process was plagued by a Faustian bargain and power differentials which led to poor education and gender policy outcomes (Gore, 2010). Additionally, South–South partnerships exemplified in this study by China–Africa and India–Africa cooperation appear to thrive on equality and win-win relations but are relatively weak on the connection between education and gender. While in SSA, foreign aid mostly drives North–South partnerships, South–South partnership is driven to a

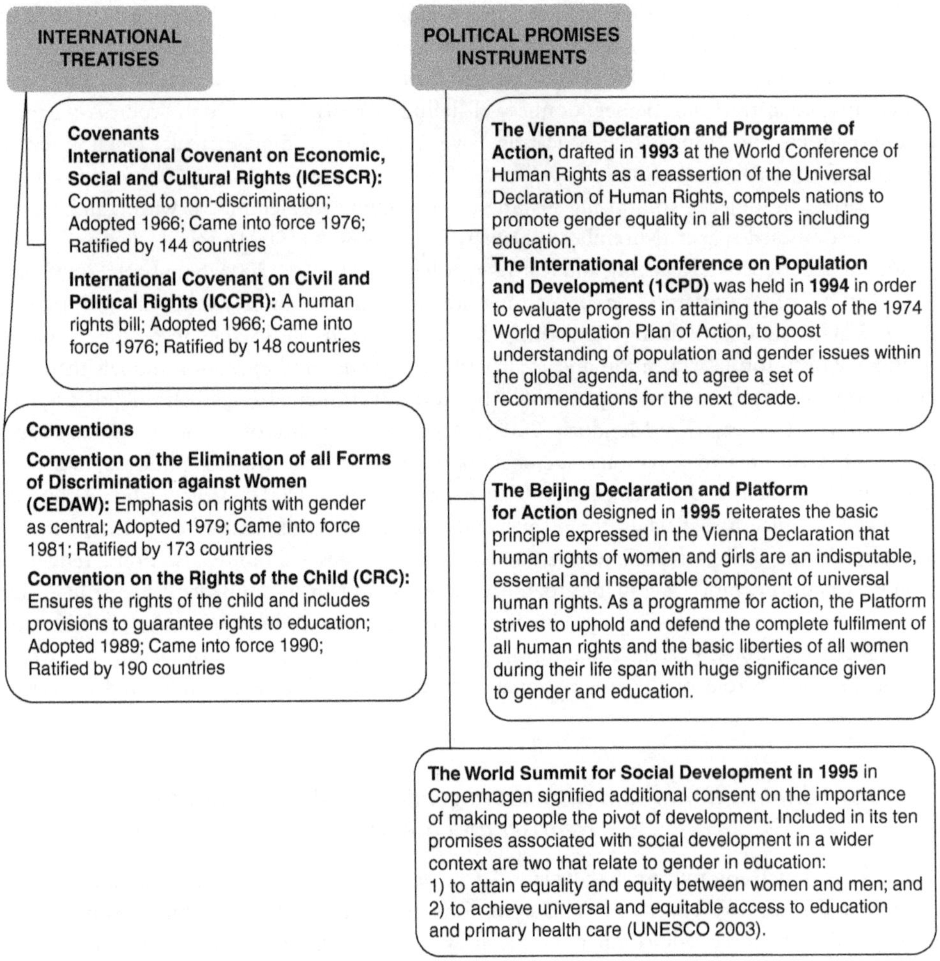

INTERNATIONAL TREATISES

Covenants
International Covenant on Economic, Social and Cultural Rights (ICESCR): Committed to non-discrimination; Adopted 1966; Came into force 1976; Ratified by 144 countries

International Covenant on Civil and Political Rights (ICCPR): A human rights bill; Adopted 1966; Came into force 1976; Ratified by 148 countries

Conventions
Convention on the Elimination of all Forms of Discrimination against Women (CEDAW): Emphasis on rights with gender as central; Adopted 1979; Came into force 1981; Ratified by 173 countries

Convention on the Rights of the Child (CRC): Ensures the rights of the child and includes provisions to guarantee rights to education; Adopted 1989; Came into force 1990; Ratified by 190 countries

POLITICAL PROMISES INSTRUMENTS

The Vienna Declaration and Programme of Action, drafted in **1993** at the World Conference of Human Rights as a reassertion of the Universal Declaration of Human Rights, compels nations to promote gender equality in all sectors including education.

The International Conference on Population and Development (1CPD) was held in **1994** in order to evaluate progress in attaining the goals of the 1974 World Population Plan of Action, to boost understanding of population and gender issues within the global agenda, and to agree a set of recommendations for the next decade.

The Beijing Declaration and Platform for Action designed in **1995** reiterates the basic principle expressed in the Vienna Declaration that human rights of women and girls are an indisputable, essential and inseparable component of universal human rights. As a programme for action, the Platform strives to uphold and defend the complete fulfilment of all human rights and the basic liberties of all women during their life span with huge significance given to gender and education.

The World Summit for Social Development in 1995 in Copenhagen signified additional consent on the importance of making people the pivot of development. Included in its ten promises associated with social development in a wider context are two that relate to gender in education: 1) to attain equality and equity between women and men; and 2) to achieve universal and equitable access to education and primary health care (UNESCO 2003).

Figure 18.1 International commitment: treatises and promises

Source: UNESCO EFA-GMR (2003).

large extent by trade/investments and to a lesser degree by aid. Anyway, despite tremendous goodwill and efforts by both global and local agents to undo gender disparity in education, gender parity let alone equality remains unattained as an MDG in SSA.

North–South partnership

Educational and gender ideologies are transported into the policy spaces of SSA countries, theoretically, through economic or cultural globalisation, and more tangibly through foreign aid by donors from the Global North. They are not, for apparent reasons, named ideologies, but the perspectives assumed in relation to gender and educational progress are entrenched in the diplomacy of aid contracts. Certainly, to disguise any implication of an ideology, the concept of 'partnership' is employed to obtain a consensus of ideas. This concept is disputed, and critics of the notion of partnership in aid frequently stress the asymmetric nature of donor–recipient relationships, conjuring up the idea of unequal power (see Amoako, 2009).

The pre-2015 MDG framework was the basis for the specific development and poverty alleviation strategy shaping North–South partnerships. It comprised an international development cooperation plan and a rational and policy discourse regarding ways to advance state progress and alleviate poverty respectively. Both represented the new global development agreement. The MDGs as global integration with a human face constituted an extended form of the Washington Consensus which is often declared defunct but has remained active. This meant that the social values which MDGs exemplify should both emerge from, and enable, the course of global integration. Yet, more credibly, the MDGs have been perceived as the lowest social level that policy agents should aim for as they enact policies whose fundamental purpose is liberalisation and global integration (Gore, 2010).

South–South/Africa–Asia partnerships

On the other hand, while South–South partnerships represented, in this case, by China–Africa and India–Africa cooperation thrive on principles of equality, win-win cooperation, friendship, mutual benefit and solidarity, hence, more equality in the dynamics of power between the partners, there remains the need for the parties to consciously and comprehensively integrate the undoing gender paradigm within the education and skills development policies and programmes that characterise both partnerships.

Recent China–Africa relations date back to the 1950s. However, for the past decade and half, China has intensified its relations with Africa through the triennial summits of the Forum on China–Africa Cooperation (FOCAC). The recent 2015 FOCAC was the sixth forum at which China tripled its pledges to Africa to the tune of $60 billion US dollars (Jinping, 2015). Although power equality in China–Africa cooperation seems more credible, and showcases a generous support package for education, it lacks a comprehensive gender mainstreaming component despite the mention, in passing, of a poverty reduction plan aimed at women and children (ibid.). For instance, a study discovered that with regards to gender, the population of African students studying in China as a consequence of this partnership is skewed in favour of males. Findings suggest that gender imbalance pervades the African student population in universities in Chongqing and all over China and the need to tackle this gender inequality should be discussed in subsequent FOCAC meetings (Bodomo, 2014).

The Third India–Africa Forum Summit in 2015 built on two previous summits held in 2011 and 2008 and proposed capacity building in nearly all the general areas of cooperation, including education. This India–Africa partnership seems to lay more emphasis on gender equality than the China–Africa plan does. It aims to deepen cooperation through not only knowledge sharing and capacity building but also gender-specific training programmes (India–Africa Summit Website, n.d.). Yet still, like the China–Africa partnership, this partnership equally needs a more comprehensive approach to addressing gender inequality in its education and human resource development strategies.

Addressing global inequalities, promoting growth and generating productive capacities for gender equality in education

Since the MDG development paradigm in SSA is to integrate the region globally and not to nurture and facilitate its economic growth and productive capacities, the ODA dependent national governments in the region lack the financial capabilities needed to confidently assume full control of their education systems and ensure the attainment of the gender equality in education goal. Indeed, the bleak picture of poor gender and education policy outcomes in SSA unfolds within the context of mainly North–South partnerships, notwithstanding the recent emergence of South–South partnerships, leading to the promotion of what is called a triangular cooperation.

Recommendations to strengthen efforts to achieve gender parity at all education levels from pre-primary through to tertiary have been given. They include:

- the need for SSA national/regional governments to provide education absolutely free to their populations, especially those disadvantaged;
- develop and implement policies that address challenges confronting both boys and girls in accessing and completing school;
- provide alternative forms of schooling for those who, for whatever reasons, cannot access formal schooling.

Simultaneously, to attain gender equality in education, governments must:

- mainstream gender in all policy and planning processes, not only in education but also in all sectors;
- initiate a detailed strategy of statutory transformation, advocacy and community mobilisation for female education;
- collaborate with global institutions and education providers to address school-related gender based violence in all its configurations;
- reinforce and coordinate research and monitoring on the issue.

The participation of all stakeholders including school managers, teachers, parents, communities and government executives is key to finding efficient answers.

Governments must also:

- display dedication and guidance on the issue by integrating it into national policies and action plans;
- form societies and associations to embolden girls and urge them to confront inequalities and various shapes of gender prejudice;
- employ, coach and assist teachers efficiently to tackle gender inequalities in school;
- enhance the payment and training of teachers and safeguard impartial equilibrium of female to male teachers at all levels of education, including in school management;
- offer all teachers good quality pre- or in-service training in gender-sensitive practices so they can dispute social customs and their own gender outlooks;
- provide locally pertinent training to teachers and back them with pedagogical resources that challenge gender typecasts and encourage unbiased conduct.

(UNESCO, 2015b)

Nevertheless, these recommendations have huge resource implications and the way to achieve them in SSA is to promote economic growth, generate productive capacities, and look beyond foreign aid, which for over fifty years has failed to yield the desired development outcomes. Foreign aid represents a very restrictive mechanism for the attainment of any development goals, including education and gender goals in SSA. Moreover, the benefits of the aid effectiveness principles encapsulated by the confluence have not been deployed comprehensively, rendering it less democratic. The power inequalities that riddled North–South partnerships led to the Paris Declaration of the aid effectiveness agenda, which foregrounded the fact that it was not only the amount of aid delivered but also how it was delivered that guaranteed its success in realising its objectives (HLF, 2005; Takyi-Amoako, 2010). Thirteen targets were set, to be reached in 2010. However, the monitoring survey results indicated that only one had been attained. Overall, there is a huge discrepancy between objectives and outcomes (Addison & Scott, 2011; Killen, 2011; Kharas, 2014).

Using Gore's work, I argue that global integration, as a national approach was incapable of tackling the main institutional limitations of SSA nations, and that existing state policies are inadequate in tackling the development difficulties facing SSA nations (Gore, 2010). I further argue that the partnership strategy for development cooperation is equally problematic. This strategy inherently suggests that true and equal partnership engenders aid effectiveness. However, the logical question is what constitutes the rubrics of development partnerships between donor and recipient nations when substantial inequities regarding resources, capacities and power characterise the relationship. Findings suggest that the undercutting of national ownership persists in these countries. This is not merely caused by not aligning assistance with country plans, though this counts nonetheless. It also exposes fragile technical competences besides compelling inducements for recipients to expect and adopt donor concerns in policy design as well as prioritising donor programmes in policy execution using the functioning of policy conditionality, organisational leadership through monitoring indicators and discrimination in donor funding preferences. At worst, SSA nations are placed in a Catch-22 situation in which they are obligated to attain international development goals by adopting national development processes which render their accomplishment unfeasible (Gore, 2010

The achievement of gender equality in education remains a challenge for social justice at the confluence. Gender equality as a more comprehensive concept than gender parity is more difficult to assess. It transcends the boundaries of counting the numbers of female and male pupils/students in education institutions and encompasses the quality of their experiences in the overall school environment, their accomplishments in educational spaces and their career ambitions (UNESCO, 2015b). The international frameworks associated with gender equality in education, which are formulated and implemented within the context of North–South partnerships, are difficult to fulfil due to conflicting methodologies within the applicable international frameworks, comprising those which apply a very limited concept of gender equality and education, and those that use a broader understanding (Unterhalter, 2012).

Hence, the calls for a new global development paradigm for the post-2015 SDGs since the previous framework of the MDGs failed to deliver and drew sharp criticisms including its lack of universality (ibid.). Now, the post-2015 agenda includes: ensuring inclusive and equitable quality education; promoting lifelong learning opportunities for all; achieving gender equality and empowering all women and girls globally (SDSN, 2015b). While it seems the SDGs appear to have overcome this challenge of universality, the SDG text is still accused of failing to encapsulate the essence of global partnership for development and usurping the policy space for developing countries (Gore, 2015; Muchhala & Sengupta, 2014). Moreover, analysis of the World Bank's World Development Indicators data set shows that the colonial legacy represents a formidable source of global inequalities (Böröcz, 2016). Therefore, there are concerns that the SDGs, which are supposed to rectify the above issues, remain inadequate.

While there is significantly enhanced donor rhetoric, it fails to translate into donor routines. The fundamental tenets of keeping promises, executing as well as pronouncing, and harmonising to support national development approaches, are the essence of successful development cooperation (Kharas, 2014). SSA countries assuming leadership and ownership of the agenda in the North–South partnerships are crucial. The first review of the inaugural UN Economic and Social Council (ECOSOC) Forum on Financing for Development (FfD) failed to deliver meaningful outcomes in the area of capacity development, which is integral to the achievement of the 2030 SDGs (Sengupta & Muchhala, 2016). Consequently, SSA countries must avoid too much reliance on North–South cooperation while consciously assuming control and taking the 'driving seat' in their policy affairs in order to reassess their options, and identify alternative sources of funding from within their national/regional spaces, and prospects in South–South partnerships, a confluence of win-win relations where they have scope for negotiation. Indeed, North–South and South–South partnerships can complement each other's efforts, hence the call for triangular partnerships. However, SSA actors must assume leadership at the confluence since they are indigenously qualified to explore cultural prospects and knowledge to determine relevant solutions to the poor education and gender outcomes, while preventing North–South partnerships from shaping South–South partnerships and transforming them into processes of power inequalities currently undermining the effectiveness of the former. It is therefore obligatory for national, regional and continental governments in SSA to offer the necessary leadership for indigenous and other Africans who possess a stronger experiential, cultural, historical and native grasp of their gender processes and education systems, and are more capable of deeply defining the predicament that afflicts most of SSA's education and gender systems, and delineating suitable solutions (Nsamenang & Tchombe, 2011; Nnaemeka, 1996).

Conclusion

In theory, the policy processes of North–South partnerships in SSA depict a strong link between education and gender, but are plagued by this Faustian bargain, along with its power differentials and the ineffectiveness of foreign aid in practice, hence the poor education and gender policy outcomes in SSA. The South–South partnerships exemplified in this study by China–Africa and India–Africa cooperation appear to repudiate this Faustian bargain and thrive on equality and win-win relations in practice, but they can do more as far as gender equality in education is concerned.

Foreign aid or ODA within the context of North–South partnership represents an inadequate approach to attaining the development goals of SSA. In this vein, efforts are required to generate a global development consensus to promote partnerships that would not only engender more comprehensive gender sensitive processes to improve education and gender outcomes, but also commit to effectively alleviating poverty through elevating economic growth, reducing global income inequalities and focusing national and international policies on generating productive capacities and employment in SSA instead of global integration. SSA nations would then have more national resources to invest in their gender and education policies, which would enable them to assume full control and accountability of the policy processes and outcomes. This would equally accelerate the achievement of the aid effectiveness goals for national policy processes to become genuinely country-led in SSA. In other words, SSA governments must assume leadership of the education and gender policy and partnership processes at the confluence, creatively identify and secure alternative sources of funding, while bringing relevant cultural and indigenous knowledge and practices to bear on these processes for the improvement of education and gender policy outcomes in the region.

Bibliography

Abdullah, H. J., 2007. 'Women as emergent actors: A survey of new women's organizations in Nigeria since the 1990s', in C. M. Cole, T. Manuh and S. F. Miescher (eds.), *Africa after Gender?* Bloomington: Indiana University, pp. 150–170.

Adely, F., 2004. 'The Mixed Effects of Schooling for High School Girls in Jordan: The Case of Tel Yahya', *Comparative Education Review*, Volume 48 (4), pp. 353–373.

Addison, T. and Scott, L., 2011. 'Linking Aid Effectiveness to Development Outcomes: A Priority for Busan'. Briefing Paper. Helsinki: UN–Wider.

Aidoo, A. A., 1998. 'The African woman today', in O. Nnaemeka (ed.), *Sisterhood Feminisms & Power: From Africa to the Diaspora*, Trenton, New Jersey: Africa Wide Press, pp. 39–50.

Aikman, S. and Unterhalter, E., 2005. *Beyond Access: Transforming Policy and Practice for Gender Equality in Education*, Oxford: Oxfam GB.

Akyeampong, E. and Fofack, H., 2012. 'The Contribution of African Women to Economic Growth and Development: Historical Perspectives and Policy Implications Part I: The Pre-Colonial and Colonial Periods', *Policy Research Working Papers* (April). doi: 10.1596/1813-9450-6051. Available at: https://dash.harvard.edu/bitstream/handle/1/23955422/24933671.pdf?sequence=1 [Accessed 26 May 2016].

Amoako, E. J. A., 2009. Shaping policy at the confluence of the global and national: Ghana's Education Strategic Plan. DPhil thesis, University of Oxford.

Ampofo, A. A., Beoku-Betts, J., Njambi, W. N. and Osirim, M., 2004. 'Women's and Gender Studies in English-Speaking Sub-Saharan Africa: A Review of Research in the Social Sciences', *Gender & Society*, Volume 18 (6), pp. 685–714.

Anderson, J. and Mendoza, R., 2000. 'Educating about gender', in R. Cortina and N. Stromquist (eds.), *Distant Alliances: Promoting Education for Girls and Women in Latin America*, New York: Routledge, pp. 119–150.

Apple, M., 1989. 'Critical introduction: Ideology and the state in educational policy', in R. Dale (ed.), *The State and Education Policy*, Milton Keynes: Open University Press, pp. 1–20.

Arnot, M., 2002. *Reproducing Gender: Critical Essays on Educational Theory and Feminist Politics*, London: Routledge Falmer.

Arnot, M. and Mac an Ghaill, M., 2006. '(Re)contextualising gender studies in education schooling in late modernity', in M. Arnot and M. Mac an Ghaill (eds.), *The RoutledgeFalmer Reader in Gender and Education*, Abingdon & New York: Routledge, pp. 1–14.

Assié-Lumumba, N. T., 2007. 'Human capital, human capabilities, and gender equality: Harnessing the development of human potential as a human right and the foundation for social progress', in N. Assié-Lumumba (ed.), *Women and Higher Education in Africa: Reconceptualizing Gender-Based Human Capabilities and Upgrading Human Rights to Knowledge*, Abidjan: CEPARRED, pp. 15–37.

Assié-Lumumba, N. T., 2015. 'Ivory Coast: Evolving gender representation in higher education from peace to the era of political instability and post-conflict reconstruction', in E. J. Takyi-Amoako (ed.), *Education in West Africa*, London: Bloomsbury, pp. 247–263.

Bajaj, M., 2009. 'Un/doing gender? A case study of school policy and practice in Zambia', *International Review of Education*, Volume 55, pp. 483–502.

Ball, S. J., 1994. *Education Reform: A Critical and Post-Structural Approach*, Buckingham: Open University Press.

Ball, S. J. and Sonia Exley, S., 2010. 'Making Policy with "Good Ideas": Policy Networks and the "Intellectuals" of New Labour', *Journal of Education Policy*, Volume 25 (2), pp. 151–169.

Bodomo, A., 2014. 'Africans in China: The Experiences from Education and Training'. A paper presented at the Christian Michelsen and CASS conference in Beijing on the theme: Africa and China: Media, Communications, and Public Diplomacy, Grand Concordia Hotel, 26 Xiaoyun Road, Beijing 10 and 11 September 2014.

Böröcz, J., 2016. 'Global Inequality in Redistribution: For a World Historical-Sociology of (not) Caring', *Intersections: East European Journal of Society and Politics*, Volume 2 (2), pp. 57–83.

Bowe, R., Ball, S. J. and Gold, A., 1992. *Reforming Education and Changing Schools: Case Studies in Policy Sociology*, London: Routledge.

Butler, J., 2004. *Undoing Gender*, New York: Routledge.

Calhoun, C., 1993. 'Habitus, field, and capital: The question of historical specificity', in C. Calhoun, E. Lipuma and M. Postone (eds.), *Bourdieu: Critical Perspectives*, Cambridge: Polity Press, pp. 61–88.

Channa, S. M., 2013. *Gender in South Asia: Social Imaginations and Constructed Realities*, New York: Cambridge University Press.

Conference Programme, 2015. Africa-Asia: A New Axis of Knowledge, Accra, Ghana 24–26 September 2015 Daily Panel Schedule.

Dale, R., 1989. *The State and Education Policy*, Milton Keynes: Open University Press.

de Beauvoir, S., 1949. *Le deuxième sexe*, Paris: Gallimard.

Denzer, L., 1995. *Constance Cummings-John: Memoirs of a Krio Leader*, Ibadan, Nigeria: Humanities Research Center.

Denzer, L., 1989. *Women in Government Service in Colonial Nigeria, 1862–1945*, Boston University African Studies Center, Working Paper 136.

Deutsch, F., 2007. 'Undoing Gender', *Gender and Society*, Volume 21 (1), pp. 106–127.

Dhar, D., 2014. *Education and Gender (Education and Gender as a Humanitarian Response)*, London: Bloomsbury Publishing.

Dyhouse, C., 2001. 'Family Patterns of Social Mobility through Higher Education in England in the 1930s', *Journal of Social History*, Volume 34 (4), pp. 817–842.

Gore, C., 2010. 'The MDG Paradigm, Productive Capacities and the Future of Poverty Reduction', *IDS Bulletin*, Volume 41 (1), pp. 70–79.

Gore, C., 2015. 'The Post-2015 Moment: Towards Sustainable Development Goals and a New Global Development Paradigm', *Journal of International Development*, Volume 27, pp. 717–732.

Haraway, D., 1988. 'Situated Knowledges: The Science Question in Feminism and the Privilege of Partial Perspective', *Feminist Studies*, Volume 14 (3), pp. 575–599.

High Level Forum, 2005. Paris declaration on aid effectiveness. HLF, Paris, 28 February–2 March, 2005.

Hilgers, M. and Mangez, E., 2015. *Bourdieu's Theory of Social Fields: Concepts and Applications*, Abingdon and New York: Routledge.

India–Africa Forum Summit Website. Available at: http://www.iafs.in/documents-detail.php?archive_id=323 [Accessed 25 May 2016].

Jenkins, R., 1992. *Pierre Bourdieu*, London: Routledge.

Johnson-Odim, C. and Mba, N., 1997. *For Women and Nation: Funmilayo Ransome-Kuti of Nigeria*, Champaign: University of Illinois Press.

Jinping, X., 2015. 'Open a new era of China–Africa win-win cooperation and common development'. Speech delivered by President Xi Jinping, the 2015 Summit of the Forum on China–Africa Cooperation (FOCAC), Johannesburg, South Africa. Available at: http://english.cri.cn/12394/2015/12/05/4083s906994.htm.

Kabeer, N., 1994. *Reversed Realities: Gender Hierarchies in Development Thought*, London and New York: Verso.

Kharas, H., 2014. 'Development Assistance,' in B. Currie-Alder, R. Kanbur, D. M. Malone and R. Medhora (eds.), *International Development: Ideas, Experience, and Prospects*, Oxford: Oxford University Press, pp. 847–865.

Killen, B., 2011. 'How Much Does Aid Effectiveness Improve Development Outcomes? Lessons from Recent Practice', *Busan Background Papers*. 29 November–1 December, Busan, Korea. Available at: www.oecd.org/development/effectiveness/48458806.pdf [Accessed 1 July 2016].

Kirk, J., 2004. 'Impossible Fictions: The Lived Experiences of Women Teachers in Karachi', *Comparative Education Review*, Volume 48 (4), pp. 374–396.

Kolawole, M., 2002. 'The Dynamism of African Feminism: Defining and Classifying African Feminist Literatures', in S. Arndt (ed.), *The Dynamism of African Feminism: Defining and Classifying African Feminist Literatures*, Trenton, New Jersey: Africa World Press Inc., p. 31.

Kolawole, M., 2004. 'Re-conceptualising African gender theory: Feminism, womanism and the arere metaphor', in S. Arnfred (ed.), *Re-thinking Sexualities in Africa*, Uppsala: The Nordic Africa Institute.

Lazreg, M., 2005. 'Decolonizing feminism', in Oyeronke Oyěwùmí (ed.), *African Gender Studies: A Reader*, New York: Palgrave Macmillan.

Leach, F., 1998. 'Gender, Education and Training: An International Perspective', *Gender & Development*, Volume 6 (2), pp. 9–18, Doi: 10.1080/741922727 [Accessed 20 February 2016].

Lingard, B., 1993. 'The Changing State of Policy Production in Education: Some Australian Reflections on the State of Policy Sociology', *International Studies in Sociology of Education*, Volume 3 (1), pp. 25–47.

Mama, A., 2003. 'Restore, Reform but do not Transform: The Gender Politics of Higher Education in Africa', *JHEA/RESA*, Volume 1 (1), pp. 101–125.

Manuh, T., 2007. 'Doing gender work in Ghana', in C. M. Cole, T. Manuh and S. F. Miescher (eds.), *Africa after Gender?* Bloomington: Indiana University Press, pp. 125–149.

Mbilinyi, M., 1989. 'Women's Resistance In "Customary Marriage": Tanzania's Runaway Wives', in A. Zegeye and S. Ishemo (eds.), *Forced Labour and Migration*, London: Hans Zell, pp. 211–254.

Miescher, S. F., Manuh, T. and Cole, C. M., 2007. 'Introduction: When was Gender?', in C. M. Cole, T. Manuh and S. F. Miescher (eds.), *Africa after Gender?* Bloomington: Indiana University Press, pp. 1–14.

Mimiko, O., 2012. *Globalisation: The Politics of Global Economic Relations and International Business*, Durham, North Carolina: Carolina Academic.

Mirembe, R. and Davies, L., 2001. 'Is Schooling a Risk? Gender, Power Relations, and School Culture in Uganda', *Gender and Education*, Volume 13 (4), pp. 401–416.

Mohanty, C., 1988. 'Under Western Eyes: Feminist Scholarship and Colonial Discourses', *Feminist Review*, Volume 30, pp. 61–88.

Money, J., 1955. 'Hermaphroditism, Gender and Precocity in Hyper-adrenocorticism: Psychologic Findings', *Bulletin of the Johns Hopkins Hospital*, Volume 96, pp. 253–254.

Muchhala, B. and Sengupta, M., 2014. 'A Déjà Vu Agenda or a Development Agenda? A Critique of the Post-2015 Development Agenda from the Perspective of Developing Countries, *Economic and Political Weekly*, Volume 49 (46), pp. 28–30.

Mukurasi, L., 1991. *Post Abolished: One Woman's Struggle for Employment Rights*, London: Women's Press.

Naseem, M. A., 2004. 'State, Education and Citizenship Discourses, and the Construction of Gendered Identities in Pakistan', in N. Peter and M. Sonia (eds.), *Re-Imagining Comparative Education: Postfoundational Ideas and Applications for Critical Times*, New York & London: Routledge, pp. 85–106.

Nfah-Abbenyi, J. M., 1997. *Gender in African Women's Writing: Identity, Sexuality, and Difference*, Bloomington and Indianapolis: Indiana University Press.

Nnaemeka, O., 1996. 'Development, Cultural Forces, and Women's Achievements in Africa', *Law and Policy*, Volume 18 (3–4), pp. 251–279.

Nnaemeka, O., 1997. *The Politics of (M)Othering: Womanhood, Identity, and Resistance in African Literature*, London and New York: Routledge.

Nsamenang, B. A. and Tchombe, T. M. S., 2011. *Handbook of African Educational Theories and Practices: A Generative Teacher Education Curriculum*, Bamenda: Human Development Resource Centre (HDRC).

Nussbaum, M., 2000. *Women and Human Development*, Cambridge: Cambridge University Press.

Oakley, A., 1997. 'A brief history of gender', in A. Oakley and J. Mitchell (eds.), *Who's Afraid of Feminism? Seeing through the Backlash*, London: Hamish Hamilton, pp. 29–55.

Ogundipe-Leslie, M., 1994. *Re-Creating Ourselves: African Women and Critical Transformations*, Trenton, New Jersey: Africa World Press, Inc.

Ozga, J., 1990. 'Policy Research and Policy Theory: A Comment on Fitz and Halpin', *Journal of Education Policy*, Volume 5 (4), pp. 359–362.

Prather, C. and Tietjen, K., 1991. *Educating Girls: Strategies to Increase Access, Persistence, and Achievement*, Washington, DC: USAID.

Ranson, S., 1995. 'Theorizing Education Policy', *Journal of Education Policy*, Volume 10 (4), pp. 427–448.

Sen, A., 1999. *Development as Freedom*, Oxford: Oxford University Press.

Sengupta, M. and Muchhala, B., 2016. First FfD Review forum fails to deliver meaningful outcomes (TWN). New Delhi and New York, 29 April. https://csoforffd.org/2016/05/02/first-ffd-review-forum-fails-to-deliver-meaningful-outcomes-twn/ (Accessed 30 June, 2016)

Shawulu, R., 1990. *The Story of Gambo Sawaba*, Jos: Echo Communications Ltd.

Soothill, J. E., 2007. *Gender, Social Change and Spiritual Power: Charismatic Christianity in Ghana*, Leiden and Boston: Koninklijke Brill NV.

Spivak, G., 1999. *A Critique of Postcolonial Reason*, London: Harvard University Press.

Stambach, A., 2000. *Lessons from Mount Kilimanjaro: Schooling, Community, and Gender in East Africa*, New York: Routledge.

Staudt, K., 2002. 'Dismantling the master's house with the master's tools: Gender work in and with powerful bureaucracies', in K. Saunders (ed.), *Feminist Post-development Thought: Rethinking Modernity, Postcolonialism and Representation*, London: Zed Books, pp. 57–68.

Stromquist, N., 1995. 'Romancing the State: Gender and Power in Education', *Comparative Education Review*, Volume 39 (4), pp. 423–454.

Stromquist, N., 2004. 'Preface to Special Issue on Gender and Comparative Education', *Comparative Education Review* Volume 48 (4), pp. iii–v.

Stromquist, N. P. and Fischman, G. E., 2009. 'From Denouncing Gender Inequities to Undoing Gender in Education: Practices Programmes Toward Change in the Social Relations of Gender', *International Review of Education*, Volume 55, pp. 463–482.

Stromquist, N., Klees, S. and Miske, S., 2000. 'USAID efforts to expand and improve girls' primary education in Guatemala', in R. Cortina and N. Stromquist (ed.), *Distant Alliances*, New York: Routledge Falmer, pp. 239–260.

Sustainable Development Solution Network Secretariat, 2015a. *Getting Started with the Sustainable Development Goals: A Guide for Stakeholders*, SDSN. Available at: http://unsdsn.org/wp-content/uploads/2015/12/151211-getting-started-guide-FINAL-PDF-.pdf (Accessed 20 May 2015).

Sustainable Development Solution Network Secretariat, 2015b. *Indicators and a Monitoring Framework for the Sustainable Development Goals: Launching a Data Revolution for the SDGs.* A report to the Secretary-General of the United Nations by the Leadership Council of the Sustainable Development Solutions Network. Paris and New York: SDSN.

Takyi-Amoako, E., 2008. 'Poverty reduction and gender parity in education: An alternative approach', in S. Fennell and M. Arnot (eds.), *Gender Education and Equality in a Global Context: Conceptual Frameworks and Policy Perspectives*, London and New York: Routledge, Taylor and Francis Group, pp. 196–210.

Takyi-Amoako, E., 2010. 'Examining the Current Aid Effectiveness Paradigm Through Education Policy Making in an Aid Dependent Country', *International Journal of Educational and Psychological Assessment*, Volume 5, pp. 4–18.

Takyi-Amoako, E., 2012. 'Globalisation in Comparative and International Education: Towards a Theory of the Confluence', *Journal of International and Comparative Education*, Volume 1 (1), pp. 61–70.

Takyi-Amoako, E., 2015. *Education in West Africa*, London: Bloomsbury Publishing.

Taylor, S., 1997. 'Critical Policy Analysis: Exploring Contexts, Texts and Consequences', *Discourse*, Volume 23 (13), pp. 23–5.

Thompson, G., Savage, G. C. and Lingard, B., 2015. 'Think Tanks, Edu-Businesses and Education Policy: Issues of Evidence, Expertise and Influence', *Australian Educational Researcher*, Volume 43 (1), pp. 1–13. doi:10.1007/s13384-015-0195-y

Thompson, G. and Cook, I., 2014. 'Education Policy-making and Time', *Journal of Education Policy*, Volume 29 (5), pp. 700–715.

Thompson, J. B., 1991. 'Editor's introduction', in J. B Thompson and P. Bourdieu (ed.), *Language and Symbolic Power*, Oxford: Polity Press, pp. 1–31.

Thomson Reuters Foundation, 2015. 'Sub-Saharan Africa rates poorly in equal education for boys and girls: UN' *Reuters/World*, 11 October. Available at: http://www.reuters.com/article/2015/10/12/us-gender-schooling-un-idUSKCN0S600M20151012 [Accessed 12 October 2015].

Troyna, B., 1994. 'Reforms, research and being reflexive about being reflective', in D. Halpin and B. Troyna (eds.), *Researching Education Policy: Ethical and Methodological Issues*, London: The Falmer Press, pp. 1–14.

Tsikata, D., 1989. 'Women's political organizations 1951–1987', in E. Hansen and K. Ninsin (eds.), *The State, Development and Politics in Ghana*, Dakar, Senegal: CODESRIA, pp. 73–94.

UNCTAD, 2002. *The Least Developed Countries Report 2002: Escaping the Poverty Trap*, Geneva and New York: United Nations.

UNESCO, 2003. *Education for All Global Monitoring Report 2003/4: Gender and Education for All–The Leap to Equality*, Paris: UNESCO Publishing.

UNESCO, 2015a. *Gender and EFA 2000–2015: Achievements and Challenges (Gender Summary)*, Paris: UNESCO Publishing.

UNESCO, 2015b. *Education for All 2000–2015: Achievements and Challenges*, Paris: UNESCO Publishing.

Unterhalter, E., 2012. 'Mutable Meanings: Gender Equality in Education and International Rights Frameworks', *The Equal Rights Review*, Volume 8, pp. 67–84.

Unterhalter, E., 2014. 'Thinking About Gender in Comparative Education', *Comparative Education*, Volume 50 (1), pp. 112–126. Available at: http://dx.doi.org/10.1080/03050068.2013.872321 [Accessed 7 September 2015].

Vavrus, F., 2003. *Desire and Decline: Schooling Amid Crisis in Tanzania*, New York: Peter Lang.

Vavrus, F., 2005. 'Adjusting Inequality: Education and Structural Adjustment Policies in Tanzania', *Harvard Educational Review*, Volume 75 (2), pp.174–244.

Vidovich, L., 2001. 'A Conceptual Framework for Analysis of Education Policy and Practices', Paper proposed for presentation at the Australian Association for Research in Education, Fremantle, December 2001.

Weaver-Hightower, M. B. and Skelton, C., 2013. *Leaders in Gender and Education: Intellectual Self-Portraits*, Rotterdam and Boston/Taipei: Sense Publishers.

West, C. and Zimmerman, D., 1987. 'Doing Gender', *Gender & Society*, Volume 1 (2), pp. 125–151.

Wikipedia, (n.d.). 'North–South Divide', Available at: https://en.wikipedia.org/wiki/North%E2%80%93South_divide (Accessed 28 June 2016).

PART III

Africa–Asia contemporary relations

Economic and development cooperation

19

BRICS IN AFRICA AND HUMAN RIGHTS

Ian Taylor

Introduction

Emerging economies have been acknowledged as playing an important role in diversifying Africa's international relations and thus granting Africa new and exciting possibilities. This has often been associated with the idea that the emerging powers are proffering an alternative vision of the world, one more amenable to the interests of the Global South. Emblemised by the BRICS (Brazil, Russia, India, China and South Africa), a great deal of interest has been generated to suggest that not only is Africa on the up, but that this is taking place within a global context where we are on the cusp of radically changing the global order. The BRICS have been cast as playing leading roles in such processes and Africa's place in the world is thus said to be 'rising'.

This chapter looks at such claims through the prism of human rights, arguing that the nature of the engagement of the BRICS in Africa is based squarely on capitalism and thus, the agenda of human rights inevitably falls below that of capital accumulation and profit. The findings of the research are that the BRICS do not in any meaningful way promote human rights in Africa; rather, they are in the continent for their own economic and political reasons and human rights is far down the list of priorities. As Tetah Mentan notes:

> To understand Africa in global capitalism we may view it from two perspectives. That is, there are two ways of picturing Africa in the context of global capitalism. One is from the point of view of the people living and hoping to improve their lot in Africa's fifty-four nation states with a considerable variety of kinds of 'insertion' into the global capitalist economy, and a corresponding range of experiences of development (or lack of it). The other is from the point of view of capital, for which Africa is not so much a system of states, still less a continent of people in need of a better life, as simply a geographic—or geological—terrain, offering this or that opportunity for global capital to make money.
>
> *(Mentan, 2010: xi)*

From the point of view of capital, human rights are a distraction and, in the wider context of the type of capitalism pursued by the BRICS (particularly by China and Russia), an irrelevance.

294

Despite all the rhetoric, the BRICS are in Africa for one main reason—commerce. Africa is in fact a region where the BRICS might accomplish much of their self-proclaimed 'national interests' and with significant returns on investments. As the Chinese Ministry of Commerce puts it, Africa is 'one of the most important regions for carrying out our "go outward" strategy' (quoted in Gu, 2005). The BRICS are acutely aware that Africa is indispensable to satisfy various growing requirements for minerals and energy, as well as providing important and emergent markets for their exports. To achieve a position of strength and influence in Africa, the elites within the BRICS have been rather adept at using the rhetoric of cooperation and Southern solidarity, mixed with a populist message that encourages African elites to reject Western prescriptions.

It has to be said that from one perspective, BRICS activity in Africa *has* benefited the continent, particularly with regard to the fixed investments, infrastructure construction and the upsurge in commodity price receipts owing to their unremitting needs. What Africa does with this increased engagement really is the key to any discussion of BRICS–African engagement. Much of the perceived negative downsides associated with BRICS–African engagement can be located in two concrete areas: the failure thus far by African leadership to craft a coherent and serious relationship with the BRICS, and secondly, the nature of the vast majority of trade between the BRICS and Africa which serves to reify Africa's dependent position within the global political economy.

This chapter however concerns itself with the rise of interest in Africa by the BRICS and the concomitant escalation in expressions of concern about the issue of human rights in public discourse, primarily from Western sources, but increasingly from African. At this point it should be pointed out that with the exception of China, the rest of the BRICS have been given a free pass by 'world opinion' (i.e. Western pundits) when it comes to the human rights angle. It is only Beijing that has been singled out for criticism and opprobrium. It does need to be pointed out there are *some* genuine causes for concern that China's expansion into Africa may threaten to undermine attempts to advance new norms relating to constitutional rights and privileges, as well as more broader governance issues. These are not simply promoted by the liberal West but have been embraced by selected African leaders and are expressed in New Partnership for Africa's Development (NEPAD). However, the concerns are rather speculative and often based on fear of a rising China, rather than on any objective evaluation. Hardly surprisingly, given that the vast majority of critiques emanate from the capitalist West, there is virtually no condemnation from the angle of the intrinsic problems associated with capitalism.

Capitalism and human rights

The idea of 'human rights' as they are formulated today stems from the Enlightenment and the era of modernity, ushered in by capitalism. As capitalist social relations became entrenched, the philosophical formulations of intellectuals such as John Locke and Immanuel Kant reflected the realisations formed as a part of the process of industrialisation. Such formulations, historically specific to time and place, have become universalised and generalised, indeed fetishised. The context within which they were drawn up has been forgotten, in fact is deemed irrelevant. Human rights are global and apply everywhere and anywhere and any societies or regimes that reject or question this totalising discourse are deemed pariahs to be educated and/or democratised to the realisation of capitalist normality.

One such example of this universalistic claim under the rubric of human rights was captured in the *Declaration of Human and Civic Rights of France*, which asserted the 'natural, unalienable and sacred rights of man . . . born and remain free and equal in rights' (Conseil Constitutionnel,

2002). This was re-echoed in the, by now famous, claim that 'We hold these truths to be self-evident, that all men are created equal, that they are endowed by their Creator with certain unalienable Rights' (National Archives, 1776). Though clearly originating at a time of great flux, when the bourgeoisie in the emerging core struggled for supremacy with the landed classes, their motif has progressively been accepted as common sense—most graphically seen in the Universal Declaration of Human Rights of the United Nations which acknowledges the 'recognition of the inherent dignity and of the equal and inalienable rights of all members of the human family' (United Nations, 1948). This statement of rights most definitely forms the foundation of contemporary human rights law and membership of the UN is, at least theoretically, contingent on the acceptance of these norms.

For many (most?) observers, these rights are unproblematic and indeed, it is difficult to argue against many of the individual privileges enunciated by the Declaration. However, if one adopts a more structural approach to the question of rights and its linkage to capitalism, a number of issues arise. Through locating individual human rights as 'natural', human rights are postulated as ahistorical things separate from social relations. Secondly, because of this genesis in emergent capitalism, exploitative social structures and relations are normalised. Thirdly, by asserting an equality of access to these rights (with Man, 'born and remain free and equal in rights'), exploitation is obfuscated if not denied outright. A fictional level playing field is assumed. Finally, given that these rights were formulated by intellectuals from the bourgeoisie, class interests are hidden and, at the same time, alternative rights agendas that might prioritise the interest of the exploited majority are effectively cut off.

This is somewhat remarkable given that it is surely obvious that ideas cannot be detached from the material actions and interests contingent in social relations. All state institutions and the intellectual project that underpins state–society relations (exemplified and exercised through morality and laws) are products of material dealings. The material conditions through which these ideas are produced and reproduced define the ideas themselves. As Marx & Engels (1991) wrote, '[l]ife is not determined by consciousness, but consciousness by life'. The agents who generate ideas and institutions are themselves creations of the society and its social relations within which they live, which the current human rights regime actively denies. In current dominant readings, human rights are considered almost mystical in content, separated from any social interface necessary to produce them (Kolakowski, 1983).

The class interests behind such mystification are clear: property rights and individualism are sacrosanct. Contemporary human rights discourse hides the reality that property generates the mode through which capitalist exploitation takes place. Rather than facilitating freedom, property rights create other people as obstacles to the full realisation of the individual. The working class must sell their labour to fabricate commodities for the capitalist, who through property rights possesses the land and the factories, to trade at a profit. The workers, in exchange for their labour, are allotted a fraction of this profit so as to enable them to access the basic necessities to live. The assumed right to own private property is protected through laws and institutions and, as a human right, is deemed incontrovertible. Yet within capitalist societies, no explanation is given for the inequality in social reality that emerges from such relations of production. The worker is transformed into a commodity, whose only value is measured by his or her ability to sell their labour. In this way, the right to private property is placed central to 'human rights' and the human rights discourse is essentially an elaborate defence for capitalist elites to uphold an unequal distribution of material. After all, 'The ruling ideas are nothing more than the ideal expression of the dominant material relationships, the dominant material relationships grasped as ideas; hence of the relationships which make the one class the ruling one, therefore, the ideas of their dominance' (Marx & Engels, 1991).

Why is this detour necessary? Two reasons. Firstly, 'African economies are integrated into the very structure of the developed capitalist economies; and they are integrated in a manner that is unfavourable to Africa and insures that Africa is dependent . . . [S]tructural dependence is one of the characteristics of underdevelopment' (Rodney, 2012: 25). In other words, Africa's very existence within the world system is predicated upon capitalism and the social relations that this engenders and thus necessarily informs what constitutes 'human rights'. Secondly (and for the purpose of this chapter, perhaps more importantly), because the BRICS practise capitalism in Africa and thus are no different from the 'traditional' historic exploiters of the continent.

The BRICS as capitalist exploiters

All of the BRICS have experienced ruptures from previous models of accumulation, particularly with internally based paths being abandoned and national development strategies being set aside. As this has occurred, class forces deriving from such reorganisation have progressively developed an outlook and material interests beyond the national. Transnational class formation has followed. The growth of the emerging economies has meant that corporations from these countries have surplus capital to invest overseas. This is not something which is particularly new or dramatic:

> Capital is being exported . . . into the developing countries . . . with the express purpose of deriving the highest possible profit. This does not mean that we should blame the exporters of capital for any particular wickedness: the laws of international capitalist economy exert an unrelenting pressure, and if investment of capital in the developing countries did not result in an outflow from them, capitalism would not be capitalism.
>
> *(Goncharov, 1977: 176)*

This appraisal of the dynamics of global capital should be sufficient to take out some of the bitter moralising about whether Chinese or Indian capitalist engagement with Africa is better or worse than other sources and actors. The underlying logic and driving force of capitalism and capital is the accumulation of profits; in the words of Marx, the 'boundless drive for enrichment' and the 'passionate chase after value' (Marx, 1867/1976: 254). It is this 'dynamic of endless accumulation' and quest for 'accumulation for its own sake' (Bremmer, 2006: 80) that makes it such a pioneering and productive economic system, albeit intrinsically and pitilessly exploitative. Capitalists pursue profit through the exploitation of the worker. The degree of exploitation is not dependent on the inclinations—good or bad—of the singular capitalist: 'Under free competition, the immanent laws of capitalist production confront the individual capitalist as a coercive force external to him' (ibid.: 381). This makes the recent 'Declaration of the Second BRICS Trade Union Forum' that the BRICS 'do not exploit unequal conditions between countries, driving down wages and eroding workers' rights by playing workers against one another', rather naïve (COSATU, 2013).

In some emerging economies, the domestic market is saturated or too competitive, meaning a declining rate of profit, so new markets have been sought after. Market is crucial and explains the worldwide nature of capital: the 'need of a constantly expanding market for its products chase the bourgeoisie over the whole surface of the globe. It must nestle everywhere, settle everywhere, establish connections everywhere' (Marx & Engels, 1888/2004: 37). Some of the emerging economies produce products that are compatible with the types of consumer markets in Africa, which are generally underdeveloped and towards the lower price index. The market-seeking impulse has been strong in propelling the outward engagement of commerce from the BRICS into Africa. Equally, the demand for commodities from Africa as inputs into the growing economies—particularly oil and minerals—has played a strong role in further propelling them to engage in the continent.

The interests of the emergent dominant social forces and their reproduction within the BRICS lie in capitalist economies locked into the global economy on the terms that transnational fractions and transnational capital favour. Vishwas Satgar (2008: 65) has identified in South Africa the social forces that that have come together to advance this project. These are, inter alia, transnationalised corporations, private and parastatals; global transnational corporations operating within global production, financial and trade structures; technocrats within the state bureaucracy, particularly those staffing the ministries and departments at the meeting points with the global political economy, as well as managers in provincial and local government wanting to 'globalise'; the new capitalist classes both in the private sector and public sector that restructuring has engendered; a faction within the ruling party, including various intellectuals that hover around the party giving 'advice', and other elements adhering to an agenda to promote global capitalism; and most mainstream corporate-owned media, in particular financial journalists. This set of social actors may be readily identified in all of the BRICS countries. Indeed, reflecting on Zambia, Pádraig Carmody (2009: 1,203) notes that 'there would appear to be a "quadruple alliance" between the Chinese and Zambian states, TNCs, and fractions of local capital in favour of dependent development . . . a kind of transnational contract of extroversion'.

The BRICS elites have equally sought after such an outcome. In China, for instance, 'both the Chinese and the US governments have responded to the current world crisis with strategies designed to maintain the status quo' (Hart-Landsberg, 2010: 14). Acting out 'middlepowermanship' roles (Cox, 1989), the elites of these select emerging economies support the process of global governance as it stands because they, and the social actors from whom they draw most support. have an intrinsic interest in a stable and orderly environment in which to accumulate. Background noise about South–South solidarity aside, none of the BRICS have any serious agenda to change the world. The New Development Bank (NDB, often referred to as the BRICS Development Bank), founded in 2014, is emblematic of this reality.

Historically, development banks have been tools of state capitalist development and the NDB follows in this tradition. The rationale behind the NDB is to offer capital in the context of funding needed for capital-intensive infrastructure projects. The most that can be expected from the NDB is that it may serve better the interests of the ruling classes in the South and their pursuit of capitalist development. The difference with the existing multilateral banks is that the NDB will be dominated by and serve as an instrument of the ruling classes in the South, whereas the international financial institutions (IFIs) such as the World Bank and International Monetary Fund are obviously led by—and dominated by—Northern interests. But whether this superficial difference will result in a radical break depends on various factors. The first is the reality that the NDB is based on capitalism and any discussion of its 'difference' from the IFIs needs to be squarely set within this limiting framework. Secondly, whether the NDB challenges the extant global financial architecture and thus opens up space for a more inclusive development financing regime will depend upon the normative behaviour of the state–society complexes that underpin the bank. Given that China is the dominant actor in this regard, this is unlikely. Thirdly, whether the NDB will be different from the lending practices of the IFIs is crucial. Given that the NDB is grounded in standard banking lending practices, this is also unlikely. Finally, whether the NDB acts as a tool of state-led development by regimes pursuing capitalism (in some cases, naked neoliberalism) and whether this can bring in a more sustainable development trajectory, one that centre human rights onto the agenda, will be of interest, although again, unlikely.

In short, there is no preconceived ideal world order that the BRICS wish to promote and initiatives such as the NDB fit very easily into the extant system. Increasing the bargaining power of their respective states vis-à-vis the core is the sum total of the 'vision' of the ruling classes in the BRICS. Indeed:

> BRIC states, while officially denouncing US-originated neo-liberalism, are implementing neo-liberal economic policies to boost their own economic growth . . . The rise of the BRIC states will not bring the new economic world-order the redistribution of economic power through the existing system, since the BRIC states have in general accepted (not all of them in the same degree) the neo-liberal economic ideology and applied neo-liberal economic policies or some of its aspects.
>
> *(Kurečić & Bandov, 2011: 30)*

This reality is utterly essential to grasp when anything is discussed about the BRICS.

Human rights in theory and practice

Currently, some of the BRICS' expansion into Africa is provoking a flurry of concerns about the impact on Africa's human security situation. Human Rights Watch, for instance, alleged that 'China's policies [in Africa] have not only propped up some of the continent's worst human rights abusers, but also weakened the leverage of others trying to promote greater respect for human rights' (Human Rights Watch, 2006). Similarly, Amnesty International argued that,

> China is having an adverse effect on human rights in other countries because by dealing with repressive regimes, such as in Sudan, and putting its economic and trading interests ahead of concern for human rights it's allowing these regimes to be provided with resources that they would not otherwise get so easily
>
> *(Sariah Rees-Roberts, a press officer for London-based Amnesty International, quoted in UN Integrated Regional Information Networks (Dakar) June 27, 2006)*

One British newspaper in 2006 went so far as to state that 'A year on from Live 8, China has trounced all hope of change in Africa by doing deals with its kleptocrats,' adding cynically that 'China will deal with anyone, and pariah states are a gap in the market' (*The Times* (London) July 4, 2006). This is deemed to have important implications for foreign policy towards Africa as:

> [T]he Department for International Development is now trying to encourage good governance, by cutting back aid to countries that persecute opposition leaders and supporters. The latest approach makes sense. But, sadly, the game is up: China makes it irrelevant.
>
> *(The Times (London) July 4, 2006)*

It should be pointed out however that it is only sporadically that there has been any real interest in human rights. Usually this happens when the material interests of the core capitalist countries are at stake. For instance, in the post-Mao period and as China more and more opened itself up to the global economy and international capital,

> Beijing was throughout the 1980s given favourable treatment by the Western media who saw/hoped that China was being remade as a Chinese imitation of the West's self-image. Western policy-makers replicated this wishful aspiration, and ... complaints over China's *laogai* (forced labour) system, public executions and lack of democracy were eerily absent
>
> *(Taylor, 1998: 446)*

Certainly, the West appeared quite happy that Beijing's contribution to any human rights regime was more rhetorical than anything else. Chinese praise for the Universal Declaration of Human Rights as 'the first international instrument that systematically sets forth the specific contents regarding respect for and protection of fundamental human rights', in spite of transgressions, underscores this point (quoted in Zhang, 1998: 188).

The same goes for the other BRICS countries. There has been very little talk of any notional human rights abuses from these states. In fact, the opposite: an active and well-documented encouragement of these emerging economies to ditch their former economic models and fully embrace neoliberal capitalism. The originator of the whole concept of the BRICS (Jim O'Neill) framed it thus: 'many signs suggest that US policymakers are coping admirably with the emergence of the BRICS, allowing the economic forces of globalisation to benefit their globally minded companies and thereby supporting an environment in which the BRICs can emerge' (O'Neill, 2001: 158). In an interview with the *Financial Times* (January 15, 2010), O'Neill was more explicit about the need to socialise the Growth Markets into the extant neoliberal world order, saying that 'In order for globalisation to advance, it had to be accepted by more people.' What was interesting about O'Neill's comments was that he stated that incorporating the BRICS into the present world order would not be 'by imposing the dominant American social and philosophical beliefs and structures' (ibid.). But here O'Neill misses the point. Dominance by a state is not particularly central to the notion of hegemony: it is the promotion of a particular dominant ideology and the construction of an international institutionalisation that underpins the system that is important:

> hegemony is understood to involve not dominance of one state by another, but rather the institution and maintenance of a world order which serves the interests of the dominant class of the dominant state while at the same time it serves the interests of the dominant classes of other states as well.
>
> *(Neufeld, 1995: 13)*

What O'Neill depicted as important properties of the BRICS' elites ('governments that appeared willing to embrace global markets and some elements of globalisation') more than fits within the liberal world order. The goal is to manage their rapid future growth, but within the dominant neoliberal capitalist paradigm, one that will not threaten the economic status quo of close market integration and the freedom of finance capital. 'The strategy of the Atlantic ruling class, which continues to occupy the commanding heights of the global political economy . . . has been to open up the contender state–society complexes', resulting in 'a governing class submitting to liberal global governance and "open for business" (van der Pijl, 2012: 504). Given the discussion of the link between 'human rights' and capitalism, the implication for the rights of the working classes in the BRICS countries is quite clear.

Interestingly, it appears that O'Neill and Goldman Sachs are more than aware of the cultural dimension and need to acculturate, with a complex 'process of consensus formation' socialising non-Western elites into the dominant paradigm. In a report on Goldman Sachs' operations in the BRICS countries, the bank's expansion:

> is going hand in hand with a complex process of cultural engineering. As the bank acquires more non-Western staff, it is devising programmes to rotate its locally hired employees through headquarters, to ensure that they learn 'Goldman values' . . . says one top executive. 'That is our goal across the world. The idea is to get embedded, to show that we are there for the long term . . . but also to ensure that our Goldman values are everywhere in the world.'
>
> *(Financial Times, January 15 2010)*

Indeed, Goldman Sachs' construction of the BRICS concept was not just a matter of selling the BRICS as a portfolio category to investors but also of recruiting local talent or, as the *Financial Times* put it, 'Goldman is trying to raise a new generation of local leaders' (ibid.).

The China/BRICS model?

That said, there has been a body of opinion that has argued that the BRICS countries are somehow different from the West and are not pursuing capitalism but rather are involved in the construction of some sort of counter-hegemonic project. According to Naidu & Davies (2006: 80) for instance, China is seen as 'A refreshing alternative to the traditional engagement models of the West . . . African government see China's engagement as a point of departure from Western neocolonialism and political conditions.' As Radhika Desai has framed it, 'Not since the days of the Non-Aligned Movement and its demand for a New International Economic Order in the 1970s has the world seen such a coordinated challenge to western supremacy in the world economy from developing countries' (quoted in *Hindustan Times* (New Delhi), April 2, 2013).

Within this broad narrative, alternative economic and political models are said to be advancing, bringing a foreclosure to neoliberalism and its various manifestations, with the BRICS specifically 'banding together and promulgating policies that challenge the hegemony of the United States and the institutions that have been produced by the European and Asian core powers' (Chase-Dunn, 2013: 2). The emerging powers are, in short, bringing about the end of influence for the capitalist core (Cohen & DeLong, 2010).

Such a narrative has been particularly popular post-2008, with some claiming that:

> the crisis has now opened up space for rising powers of the global South to play an increasingly active role in the reform of global economic and political governance, to the extent that a 'regime change' in global governance is now at least a distinct possibility.
>
> *(Gray & Murphy, 2013: 184)*

Although this phenomenon will be discussed later, it would be fair to say that various manifestations regarding concerns about the capitalist core's resilience and supremacy have flowed out from assorted quarters, all proclaiming the basic message that we are (or are about to be) living in a post-American world (Zakaria, 2009), where the so-called American Century is over (Nye, 2015). Linked inextricably to the 'rise of the rest' (the subtitle of Zakaria's book, but see also Amsden, 2001 for an earlier statement of this theme), a supposed disturbance in the global order has occurred that will see the West losing control, with concomitant 'emerging threats to

Western prosperity' (King, 2010). In this scenario, countries such as Brazil, China and India have fashioned economic links and systems that threaten the dominant patterns that underpin Western dominance. This will see, according to the global chief economist at HSBC, both a retreat from 'market values' and an abandonment of the neoliberal project and also the dilution of broad Western values. Such developments will have a revolutionary effect on the global political economy and world order (ibid.).

In countering the Western promotion of neoliberal reforms in Africa, Chinese sources have argued that this imposition of an essentially Western ideology on African states is a form of neoimperialism. In what has been termed the post-Washington Consensus era, the search for a new developmental path is understandable (Fine, Lapavitsas & Pincus, 2001) and China's 'model' of development has been implicitly promoted as providing an appealing alternative. Ramo (2004) has cast this as the 'Beijing Consensus', consisting of three key parts: a commitment to innovation and constant experimentation, instead of a one-size-fits-all neoliberal project; a rejection of per capita GDP as the be-all and end-all, i.e. sustainability and equality must be equally part of policy; and self-determination and opposition to any hierarchy of nations. It is a 'model' within the neoliberal paradigm, but with idiosyncratic facets. Although Chinese diplomats deny that they seek to export any model to Africa or elsewhere, it is a fact that Ramo's ideas have been promoted within China and approvingly cited by *Xinhua* and elsewhere, and Chinese academics see soft power as intrinsic to building Sino-African ties.

However, Africa's intellectuals must approach with caution the notion that China or the other BRICS offer up an alternative model of development. Firstly, conceptions of Chinese 'soft power' built on 'the appeal of China as an economic model' (Kurlantzick, 2006: 5) overstate the ability of China to project and promote an alternative economic type. It is true that economically liberalising whilst preserving an authoritarian political system might be appealing to some African autocrats, but this surely has its limits, not least to the Chinese themselves in promoting such a message, given that supporting authoritarian elites in Harare and Khartoum has already stimulated anti-Chinese feelings amongst African civil society leaders. Furthermore, China's sustained growth has taken place not only with no reference to democracy or transparency and with serious consequences for the issue of the rights of workers, but has also generally shunned policy reforms promoted from outside. This must seem attractive for those African leaders who have no real legitimacy or who are tired of having to fend off criticisms from the IFIs and the wider donor community.

Yet, the irony is that those who applaud alternatives to Western-dominated IFIs often—sometimes perhaps without realising so—end up in a position where they not only support the authoritarian status quo in some African states, but also the emerging leadership of China. Opposition to neoliberalism—something that has considerable appeal—can result in the promotion not of social democracy, nor even Keynesian liberalism, but of illiberal authoritarianism. And, as Zha Daojiong (2005) notes, within China itself there is a debate as to whether or not the Latin American fate of social polarisation, international dependency and economic stagnation is China's future fate unless appropriate policies are implemented. These debates often question the capitalist direction of Beijing's current course, again destabilising the notion of a 'model' (see Fewsmith, 2001).

Besides, as Hart-Landsberg and Burkett (2005) show, market reforms in China have led inevitably toward a capitalist and foreign-dominated developmental path, with massive social and political implications, which have yet to be fully played out (see also Hinton, 1991). Even though a key criterion of capitalism, i.e. private ownership of the means of production, is not wholly present in China, profit motivation, capital accumulation, free wage labour, marketisation and most of the general features of profit-making, competition and the rule of capital are increasingly dominant as the determinant driving forces of societal development. This has generated dislocations across the country, as well as acute uneven development. The speedy growth figures that have staked out post-Mao China have arguably not been because of improvements in efficiency, but have gone hand in hand with a systematic dismantling of the social benefits that facilitated a significant level of equality during the socialist construction period (Hart-Landsberg & Burkett, 2005). Today, the transition to a liberal market system in China has been conceivably predicated on intensified exploitation, which has attracted a mass incursion by foreign corporations (Chossudovsky, 1986). Ironically, given the Chinese economy's arguably excessive dependence on exports and FDI (around three-fifths of its exports and nearly all of its high technology exports are manufactured by non-Chinese firms), foreign companies are routinely denounced within Africa as 'neocolonialists'. How such realities fit into a Chinese model for Africa is unclear.

This process is taking place 'at a time when as a rising power India is integrating with the US-led neoliberal economic system, both as a producer and consumer of commodity capitalism' (Thussu, 2012: 441). The stability of this development model for India in the long-term is itself open to question. As Chandrasekhar notes:

> [F]or much of India's population growth seems to make little difference to their standard of living. That is a severe indictment of the strategy of growth, especially when the growth rate figures are remarkably high, as was true in India for a period after 2003, and those figures are used to argue that India is a successful nation en route to great power status. However, such reasoning serves two purposes. First, it provides the propaganda to make India an attractive site for speculative global capital, the entry of which triggers the speculative run that delivers expected profits for a period of time. Second, it helps divert attention from the predatory nature of the regime of accumulation that has come to prevail in the age of finance. However, the economic success involved here is necessarily transient. That is the realisation that slowly dawns as evidence of a crisis even of neoliberal growth surfaces in India.
>
> *(Chandrasekhar, 2012: 28)*

Whilst in no way suggesting a 'coming collapse of India' thesis, the above *does* raise some questions and undermines the argument that India, as one of the BRICS, poses an alternative path of development which Africa may somehow copy. In fact, the 'hegemonic bloc that rules Indian society is well integrated into the rationale of dominant capitalist globalisation and so far none of the various political forces through which it is expressed challenges it' (Amin, 2005: 12). This points to a fundamental reality about the BRICS in Africa that has already been noted: they are *not* proposing any particular qualitative alternative (or even adjustment) to the dominant economic paradigm. The implications for human rights are obvious.

In the process of 'burying Mao' in China (Baum, 1994), a waning health system, high levels of unemployment, rocketing state debt, regional inequality and serious social dislocations across the country have followed (Weil, 1996). Furthermore, when people speak of the 'Chinese model' it is actually only one part of China they are interested in—the economies of coastal and southern China. The other parts, 'the central rural belt of poor peasant farmers, the underinvested western regions of Xinjiang, Ningxia and Tibet, and the ailing industrial areas of northeastern China around Jilin and Heilongjiang provinces', are overlooked (French, 2007: 105).

At the same time, China's economic revolution has deepened the contradictions of capitalist development in other countries, particularly in China's neighbourhood but also elsewhere, and the pathologies associated with the post-Mao reforms are regularly played out wherever Chinese actors operate (again, ironically, something which has started to attract anti-Chinese sentiment within Africa). Furthermore, significant social change in China, generated by deepening liberalisation, provoked 74,000 protests and riots involving more than 3.7 million people *in 2004 alone*, according to China's own Security Minister, Zhou Yongkang (Keidel, 2006). Meanwhile, 0.1 per cent of the total number of households in China possess 41.4 per cent of the country's total wealth (*People's Daily*, October 31, 2007). Is this a 'model' that any African society wishes to follow?

Arguably, the most we can say about China as a 'model' is that an overarching ideology, with a strong state and an elite dedicated to development but prepared to indulge in policy experimentation utilising sub-national officials and social institutions, can stimulate growth and development. But that is not specific to China—it is a generic developmental state model and one that Africa has long needed (Taylor, 2005). As Peerenboom (2005) points out, China is plainly following the patterns of its East Asian neighbours. Perhaps the idea of a strong state, which might serve as a shield for authoritarian leaders to maintain control over policy and, in the African context, continue their patronage networks, accounts for some of the receptivity in various African countries to the notion of a 'Chinese model'. But the key difference between China and Africa is that the state in Beijing has promoted rapid (albeit uneven) development—this is something largely absent from most African experiences, with a few exceptions.

Conclusion

The BRICS—at least rhetorically—have sought independence from Western political influence and on the other hand have sought to 'catch up' with the West and modernise the economy through ever-deeper integration with the capitalist world market. This contradiction is often played out around human rights issues and in fact, taking the analysis further, it might be argued that infringing some human rights within the BRICS itself, as when BRICS corporations invest overseas, is a *precondition* for Beijing's reintegration into the global political economy, something which is actively encouraged by the West and its profit-seeking corporations. Indeed, it is a fact that human rights abuses under the banner of 'preserving order' are aimed at maintaining the position of the ruling elements in China. But it is also undeniable that the state sees the need to maintain long-term stability of the system in order to attract foreign investment and technology. In this light, critiquing the BRICS' human rights stance when it is played out in Africa, whilst selectively overlooking the abuses that underpin much of the consumer boom in the developed world, driven in part by cheap imports from places such as China and India, lacks coherence, as does ignoring continued Western support for assorted dictators and corrupt regimes across Africa.

Beyond the desire to promote a neoliberal world order and open up opportunities for externally oriented capitalist fractions in each country, other subsidiary motivations for membership of the BRICS can be identified. For Brazil, the BRICS present an opportunity to promote its emerging status and solidify its self-proclaimed status as the voice of Latin America. Russia eagerly joined as a means to recover some prestige lost in the aftermath of the collapse of the Soviet Union and to balance China's rise. India has used its BRICS membership to demand the international respect its elites believe they are due, whilst China sees the BRICS as a useful tool to promote a stable international environment through a reformist agenda. For South Africa, membership of the BRICS feeds into Pretoria's long-held exceptionalism, the belief that South Africa is (or should be) the default African nation and to compensate for the decline in interest in South Africa internationally post-Mandela and after the debacle of Mbeki's tenure.

The idea of human rights—however defined—is not high on the agenda of the BRICS countries and, indeed, given the explicitly capitalist path that they have chosen, the negation of human rights is in fact part and parcel of their rise (and thus intrinsic to their relationships) with Africa. As has been noted, the NDB is a good example of this reality. Expecting otherwise of

BRICS in Africa and human rights

the BRICS, some of which are authoritarian, corrupt and famed for disregarding rights of most kinds, is somewhat unrealistic. Setting aside the rhetoric of 'mutual benefit', 'win-win situations', etc, defenders of human rights in Africa need to take a strong stance in their engagement with these 'new' actors on the continent.

References

Amin, S., 2005. 'India, a Great Power?', *Monthly Review*, Volume 56 (9), pp. 1–13.

Amsden, A., 2001. *The Rise of "The Rest": Challenges to the West from Late-Industrialising Economies*, Oxford: Oxford University Press.

Baum, R., 1994. *Burying Mao: Chinese Politics in the Age of Deng Xiaoping*, Princeton: Princeton University Press.

Bremmer, I., 2006. 'Taking a Brick out of BRIC', *Fortune*, February 20, pp. 8–9.

Carmody, P., 2009. 'An Asian-Driven Economic Recovery in Africa? The Zambian Case', *World Development*, Volume 37 (7), pp. 1197–1207.

Chandrasekhar, C., 2012. 'India's Economy: The End of Neoliberal Triumphalism', *The Marxist*, Volume 28 (2), pp. 1–28.

Chase-Dunn, C., 2013. 'BRICS and the Potentially Progressive Semi-periphery', *Pambazuka News*, March 19, pp. 2–3.

Chossudovsky, M., 1986. *Towards Capitalist Restoration? Chinese Socialism after Mao*, New York: St. Martin's Press.

Cohen, S. & DeLong, J. (2010). *The End of Influence: What Happens When Other Countries Have the Money?*, New York: Basic Books.

Conseil Constitutionnel, 2002. Declaration of Human and Civic Rights of 26 August 1789 [online]. Available at: http://www.conseil-constitutionnel.fr/conseil-constitutionnel/root/bank_mm/anglais/cst2.pdf.

COSATU, 2013. 'Declaration of the Second BRICS Trade Union Forum', press release, March 26.

Cox, R., 1989. 'Middlepowermanship, Japan, and the Future World Order', *International Journal*, Volume 44 (3), pp. 823–862.

Fewsmith, J., 2001. *China Since Tiananmen: The Politics of Transition*, Cambridge: Cambridge University Press.

Fine, B., Lapavitsas, C. and Pincus, J. (eds.), 2001. *Development Policy in the Twenty-First Century: Beyond the Post-Washington Consensus*, London: Routledge.

French, P., 2007. *North Korea: The Paranoid Peninsula—A Modern History*, London: Zed Books.

Goncharov, L., 1977. 'On the Drain of Capital from African Countries', in P. Gutkind and P. Waterman (eds.), *African Social Studies: A Radical Reader*, London: Heinemann.

Gray, K. and Murphy, C., 2013. 'Introduction: Rising Powers and the Future of Global Governance', *Third World Quarterly*, Volume 34 (2), pp. 183–193.

Gu, X., 2005. 'China Returns to Africa', *Trends East Asia*, Volume 9 (8), pp. 6–10.

Hart-Landsberg, M., 2010. 'The US Economy and China: Capitalism, Class, and Crisis', *Monthly Review*, Volume 61 (9), pp. 14–31.

Hart-Landsberg, M. and Burkett, P., 2005. *China and Socialism: Market Reforms and Class Struggle*, Delhi: Aakar.

Hindustan Times (New Delhi), April 2, 2013

Hinton, W., 1991. *The Privatization of China: The Great Reversal*, London: Earthscan.

Human Rights Watch, 2006. *China–Africa Summit: Focus on Human Rights, Not Just Trade: Chinese Leadership Should Pressure Sudan, Zimbabwe on Human Rights*, New York: Human Rights Watch.

Keidel, A., 2006. 'China's Social Unrest: The Story Behind the Stories', in Carnegie Endowment for International Peace Policy Brief no. 48, September 1–2.

King, S., 2010. *Losing Control: The Emerging Threats to Western Prosperity*, New Haven: Yale University Press.

Kolakowski, L., 1983. 'Marxism and Human Rights', *Human Rights*, Volume 112 (4), pp. 81–92.

Kurečić, P. and Bandov, G., 2011. 'The Contemporary Role and Perspectives of the BRICS States in the World-Order', *Elektronik Siyaset Bilimi Araştırmaları Dergisi*, Volume 2 (2), pp. 13–32.

Kurlantzick, J., 2006. 'China's Charm: Implications of Chinese Soft Power', Carnegie Endowment Policy Brief, no 47.

Marx, K., 1867/1976. *Capital*, Volume I, Harmondsworth: Penguin.

Marx, K. and Engels, F., 1888/2004. *Manifesto of the Communist Party*, Beijing: Foreign Languages Press.

Marx, K. and Engels, F., 1991. *The German Ideology*, New York: International Publishers.

Mentan, T., 2010. *The State in Africa: An Analysis of Impacts of Historical Trajectories of Global Capitalist Expansion and Domination in the Continent*, Bamenda: Langaa.

Naidu, S. and Davies, M., 2006. 'China Fuels its Future with Africa's Riches', *South African Journal of International Affairs*, Volume 13 (2), pp. 69–83.

National Archives, 1776. Declaration of Independence [online]. Available at: www.archives.gov/exhibits/charters/declaration_transcript.html.

Neufeld, M., 1995. 'Hegemony and Foreign Policy Analysis: The Case of Canada as a Middle Power', *Studies in Political Economy*, Volume 48, pp. 7–29.

Nye, J., 2015. *Is the American Century Over?* Cambridge: Polity Press.

O'Neill, J., 2001. *Building Better Global Economic BRICs*, Global Economics Paper no. 66. London: Goldman Sachs.

Peerenboom, R., 2005. 'Assessing Human Rights in China: Why the Double Standard?' *Cornell International Law Journal*, Volume 38 (1), pp. 71–172.

People's Daily, October 31, 2007.

Ramo, J., 2004. *The Beijing Consensus*, London: The Foreign Policy Centre.

Rodney, W., 2012. *How Europe Underdeveloped Africa*, Oxford: Pambazuka Press.

Taylor, I., 1998. 'China's Foreign Policy Towards Africa in the 1990s', *Journal of Modern African Studies*, Volume 36 (3), pp. 443–460.

Taylor, I., 2005. *NEPAD: Towards Africa's Development or Another False Start?*, Boulder, CO: Lynne Rienner.

Thussu, D., 2012. 'A Million Media Now! The Rise of India on the Global Scene', *Round Table*, Volume 101 (5), pp. 435–446.

The Times (London) July 4, 2006.

van der Pijl, K., 2012. 'Is the East Still Red? The Contender State and Class Struggles in China', *Globalisations*, Volume 9 (4), pp. 503–516.

Weil, R., 1996. '*Red Cat, White Cat: China and the Contradictions of "Market Socialism"*', New York: Monthly Review Press.

Zakaria, F., 2009. *The Post-American World and the Rise of the Rest*, London: Penguin.

Zha Daojiong, 2005. 'Comment: Can China Rise?', *Review of International Studies*, Volume 31 (4), pp. 775–785.

Zhang, Y., 1998. *China in International Society Since 1949*, Oxford: St. Antony's Series.

20

CONTEMPORARY SINO-AFRICA RELATIONS

Zhang Chun

Introduction

The rapid development of the China–Africa relationship has been attracting much global attention. However, various misreadings and misunderstandings exist in much of the literature including for example that, 'China is a newcomer in Africa'; 'China only cares about trade or economic interests in Africa'; 'China supports rogue states in Africa'; 'China does not respect labor, environmental, and other social standards in Africa'; and so on (Cargill, 2008; Michel and Beuret, 2009; Southall and Melber, 2009).To be frank, all these misreadings and misunderstandings are partly correct and partly wrong. There is a lack of comprehensive and objective description of China–Africa relations due to their complexity as well as to the different perspectives and concerns that observers may have. The core goal of this chapter is to give a concise and comprehensive view of China–Africa relations, with a fresh explanation of their evolution and a more detailed exploration of their complexity and portrayal by third-party observers. Finally, some thoughts are offered about the future development of these ties.

Is China a newcomer in Africa?

China is both a newcomer and an old-timer in Africa. When comparing China's economic engagement in Africa with that of traditional powers, especially in terms of investment, trade, energy imports, etc., China is quite new; however, if looking back at earlier historical periods, China–Africa relations can be traced back to the fourteenth century or even earlier (Rotberg, 2008; Zhang, 2006; Li & Xu, 1982). If we limited discussion to the contemporary era, China has been developing relations with Africa for more than six decades since the establishment of diplomatic relations between China and Egypt in 1956.

Why do most scholars and observers, especially foreign ones, only stress the newer dimension/s of this bilateral relationship? The key lies in the lack of full understanding of its historical evolution. For example, most Chinese scholars describe the development of China–Africa relations based on calendar years (Li, 2006; Liu & Luo, 2011).[1] However, such an approach is weak at grasping the momentum changes of this relationship.

We argue for a new approach that describes the development of China–Africa relations based on the state of its different pillars, which would be political, economic, peace and security, and societal relations. Using this approach we can identify three development stages in the China–Africa relationship.

The first stage can be called the 'unicycle period'. From the early 1950s to mid 1990s, the political pillar of China–Africa relations overshadowed the other three pillars, a typical unicycle approach can be observed. Before China's adoption of the Reform and Opening-up Policy in the late 1970s, both China and Africa focused on their political relationship because as newly emerged post-colonial/post-revolutionary states, the core of their bilateral relationship was mutual political support. This built emotional intimacy, with anti-colonialism and anti-imperialism as the core political relationship. Beyond political and military support, China's most enduring contribution in this period was the construction of Tazara, the railway linking Zambia to Tanzania, which at the time served to free Zambia from its dependence on trade routes to the sea via white-minority ruled Rhodesia.

The adoption of the Reform and Opening-up Policy did not inject energy into China–Africa economic relations; such effects happened around two decades later. In fact, the adoption of the Reform and Opening-up Policy turned China toward the industrialized developed West for its abundant capital and development experience. Only after this strategy achieved notable results almost ten years later, along with political pressures from the West from the end of cold war, did China gradually shift its strategic attention back to Africa, followed by economic interests a little later – after China initiated the 'Going Global' strategy.

The second stage can be framed as a 'bicycle period'. The launching of 'Going Global' in the late 1990s highlighted the economic dimension or pillar of China–Africa relations. Shifting its eyes back to Africa after the end of the cold war, along with the new search for external support of domestic development, China added, or at least strengthened, the economic dimension of this relationship; or to use Ian Taylor's (1998) term, China began to re-engage actively with the continent in the 1990s, 'now on different terms'. Indeed, Sino-Africa trade gained dynamism since this period. Thus, the China–Africa relationship has had two strong pillars since then: the stable development of political exchanges and fast growing economic relations, which upgraded this relationship from a unicycle to a bicycle.

The third stage can be called a 'four-wheel car period'. Entering into the 2010s, a series of new challenges and issues emerged along with the fast development of China–Africa economic linkages, including, for example, how to protect China's overseas interests and nationals in Africa; how to make the West and Africa better understand the China–Africa relationship; how to improve the corporate social responsibility (CSR) performance of Chinese companies in Africa; how to enhance China's engagement in African peace and security; among others. To deal with these new challenges and emerging issues, China now tries hard to engage Africa by strengthening additional pillars, especially peace and security cooperation, and social exchange. The most important developments are the 'Initiative on China–Africa Cooperative Partnership for Peace and Security' in 2012, and the establishment of the China–Africa People's Forum in 2011. Such developments imply that China–Africa relations now rest on four pillars – political; economic; peace and security; and social exchanges – which together have transformed this relationship further into a 'four-wheel car'.

From 'unicycle' to 'bicycle' and then 'four-wheel car', the China–Africa relationship has been developing a broader and more balanced basis, though there is still a very long way to go. From such a perspective, we can understand why there are the misreadings and misunderstandings of China–Africa relations among different observers, and even how bias is created when observers only focus on the economic dimension of this relationship.

Do economic concerns dominate the China–Africa relationship?

China–Africa economic ties are usually the focus of academic research and news reports. However, any economic engagement must be based on good and stable political relations and perhaps with some minimum conditions in terms of bilateral peace and security and mutual socio-cultural understanding. Thus, when emphasizing the highlights of China–Africa relations in the past 15 years, one must bear in mind that such progress is the natural result of strong political solidarity between China and Africa.

Historical review helps us to understand better the development path of economic ties. Sino-African trade volume was a mere US$ 12 million in 1950, growing to US$ 34.74 million in 1955, and reaching US$ 100 million and US$ 250 million in 1960 and 1965 respectively. Since carrying out the Opening-up and Reform policy in the late 1970s, China has attached great importance to friendly cooperation with African countries, and since then Sino-African trade has seen annual growth of 3.6 percent on average. Bilateral total export and import volume kept growing throughout the 1980s and 1990s, and in some years it was not unusual to see increases of over 40 percent. For example, the figure in 1980 was US$ 1 billion, then in 1999 it reached US$ 6.484 billion.

Entering into the twenty-first century, there has been fast growth of bilateral trade. In 2000, bilateral trade volume for the first time exceeded US$ 10 billion, and in 2008 it reached a record US$ 106.84 billion. While set back in 2009 by the global financial crisis, Sino-Africa trade gained momentum once again in 2010, with US$ 126.9 billion in 2010; US$ 200 billion in 2012; reaching US$ 220 billion in 2014. In 2015, due to various reasons, especially the 'new normal' of China's economy, trade volume dropped by 19 percent compared with the previous year.

The number of African countries with which China had more than US$ 1 billion in engagement is broad, and extensive, and reaches across the whole continent.

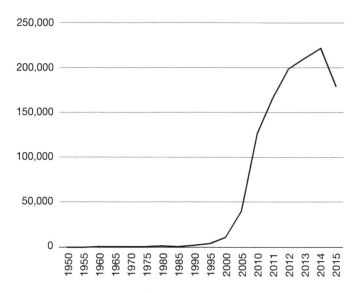

Figure 20.1 China–Africa trade relations, 1950–2015 (US$ millions)

Resource: National Data, National Bureau of Statistics of China, http://data.stats.gov.cn/easyquery.htm?cn=C01.

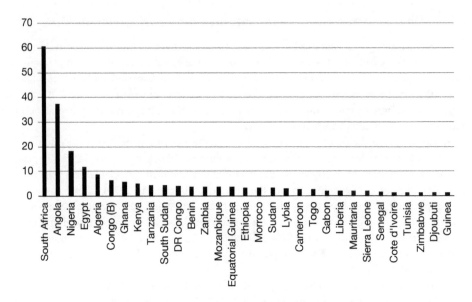

Figure 20.2 African countries with bilateral trade volume over US$ 1 billion, 2014
Resource: National Data, National Bureau of Statistics of China, http://data.stats.gov.cn/easyquery.htm?cn=C01.

China's investment in Africa experienced a similar development. In the early days when China began to invest in Africa in the 1980s, Chinese businesses relied heavily on government-sponsored assistance projects to gain a presence in local markets. Due to the limited strength of Chinese enterprises, most of their investment projects were small. Between 1979 and 1990, China invested US$ 51.19 million in 102 projects in Africa, equivalent to US$ 500,000 per project. In 1990s, China's investment in Africa witnessed a steady expansion against the background of Africa's improved investment environment and Chinese businesses' 'going global'. Since 2000, China's investment in Africa entered into a fast track facilitated by both governmental policies as well as market drivers.

Added together, over the past 30 years, China has made sizeable investments in Africa. According to the Chinese Ministry of Commerce, in 2010 China invested $2.1 billion in Africa or 3.1 percent more than in 2009; however, since 2014, China's investment in Africa has been slowing down, though the number is still growing slowly (see Figure 20.3). In 2015, flows to the Africa region reached to $2.98 billion, with a year-on-year decrease of 7 percent and accounting for 2 percent of China's total outward foreign direct investment flows. Chinese investment in Africa mainly went to countries such as Ghana, Kenya, South Africa, Tanzania, Democratic Republic of the Congo, Algeria, Uganda, etc. (MOFCOM & National Bureau of Statistics, 2016:98).

Africa now has become a major investment destination for Chinese enterprises, where over 3,000 Chinese companies have invested in various sectors ranging from electronics, telecommunications to transport. China's accumulated investment in Africa reached $34.69 billion by the end of 2015, accounting for 3.2 percent of the total Chinese investment abroad. The stock was mainly concentrated in South Africa, Congo (DRC), Algeria, Nigeria, Zambia, Sudan, Zimbabwe, Ghana, Angola, Tanzania, Ethiopia, Kenya, Congo (Brazzaville), Mauritius, etc. (MOFCOM & National Bureau of Statistics, 2016:103).

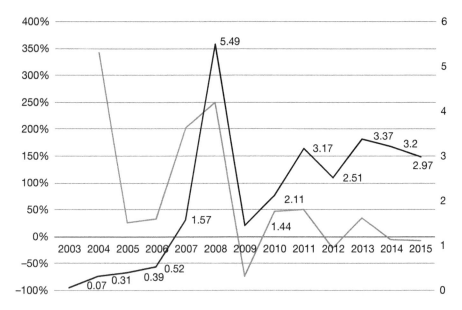

Figure 20.3 China's investment in Africa and its growth rate, 2003–2014 (US$ billions)

Source: MOFCOM 2003–2015 (online) available at http://fec.mofcom.gov.cn/article/tjsj/tjgb/

As to development assistance to Africa, as implied by the *China's Foreign Aid (2014)* White Paper, from 2010 to 2012, China appropriated in total 89.34 billion yuan (US$ 14.41 billion) for foreign assistance of three types: grant (aid gratis), interest-free loans and concessional loans (SCIO, 2014). The share of Africa in China's foreign assistance is about 30 per cent, thus the number is about US$ 1.5 billion per year.

In sum, while the growth rate of economic linkages between China and Africa is remarkable, its share in China's engagement with the world is still quite small. And it is important to note that good and stable political relations are the fundamental basis for this development. Of the continent's 54 countries, 52 have established diplomatic ties with China so far, with Gambia the newest one in 2016. China and Africa have shared a comprehensive consensus on major international issues, common interests, and a willingness to further enhance and deepen their cooperation. Frequent high-level reciprocal visits (called by some in Africa the 'frequent flyer' form of diplomacy) have promoted mutual understanding and trust, and have effectively boosted the healthy development of bilateral ties. Now, China has a nice tradition that every year, the first visit destination of the Chinese Foreign Minister is always Africa.[2] China–Africa relations contribute to both sides' struggle for higher international status as well.

How does China behave in African peace and social domains?

The fast growth of bilateral economic exchange is a double-edged sword that can consolidate its political foundations, but also bring up new issues for bilateral cooperation that may include rising security challenges and societal misunderstandings. For those elements in the international community that are suspicious of the nature and development of China–Africa relations, these new issues and challenges become excuses for criticism of China and Africa. However, the new challenges are stimulating China to update and perfect this relationship.

After entering into the twenty-first century, a series of developments highlighted the importance for China of engaging in African peace and security affairs: the Sudan Darfur Crisis from 2004; the separation of South Sudan in 2011; and South Sudan's civil war from 2013. There were also the 2011 Syrian Crisis, the Somalian piracy problem, and numerous terrorist attacks, as well as other incidents. While China has been working with Africa in peace and security affairs since the very beginning of contemporary China–Africa relations, peace and security cooperation as a pillar of this relationship is a new development that was kicked off by the launch of the 'Initiative on China–Africa Cooperative Partnership for Peace and Security' (ICACPPS) at the 5th Ministerial Conference of the Forum on China–Africa Cooperation (FOCAC) in July 2012 (FOCAC, 2012).

China has always attached great importance to China–Africa peace and security cooperation, which has been a topic in each and every FOCAC Ministerial Conference. The 2006 *China's African Policy* White Paper lists the four dimensions of China–Africa peace and security cooperation, including military cooperation, conflict settlement and peacekeeping operations, judicial and police cooperation, and non-traditional security cooperation (MOFA-PRC, 2006). In 2012 then Chinese President Hu Jintao proposed the ICACPPS for upgrading this cooperation further. The second *China's African Policy* paper, published in December 2015, states that China will support Africa in realizing peace and security, deepen military cooperation, and support Africa in confronting non-traditional security threats (Xinhua News Agency, 2015).

Currently, China–Africa peace and security cooperation is proceeding on bilateral, sub-regional, continental, and international levels simultaneously. Bilaterally, China has close cooperation with African countries that have diplomatic relations with China, including high-level military exchanges, military-related technological exchanges and cooperation, judicial and law enforcement, etc. Continentally and sub-regionally, China has cooperated with the African Union (AU), East Africa Community (EAC), Economic Community of West African States (ECOWAS), Southern African Development Community (SADC), and so on. At the FOCAC Johannesburg Summit in December 2015, China strengthened its commitments by:

> providing the AU with US$60 million of free military assistance over the next three years, [to] support the operationalization of the African Peace and Security Architecture, including the operationalization of the African Capacity for the Immediate Response to Crisis and the African Standby Force.
>
> *(FOCAC, 2015)*

Multilaterally, China participates in various international efforts for improving African peace and security. Chinese President Xi Jinping announced at the UN Peacekeeping Summit in September 2015 that:

> In the next five years, China will train 2,000 peacekeepers for all countries and launch 10 mine-sweeping assistance programs. In the following five years, China will provide free military aid worth 100 million USD in total to the African Union . . .
>
> *(Jiniping, 2015)*

Another example is that China has been participating in UN peacekeeping operations in Africa proactively since the 1990s. Currently, China has contributed more than 2,200 peacekeepers to 7 UN peacekeeping operations in Africa (see Table 20.1).

In addition to peace and security cooperation, social and cultural exchange has gained momentum in the second decade of the twenty-first century. For the past six decades, there has

Contemporary Sino-Africa relations

Table 20.1 Peacekeeping operations, China participating, August 2016

Mission	Troops	Police	Experts on Mission	Total
MINURSO			10	10
MINUSMA	397			397
MONUSCO	219		12	231
UNOCI			2	2
UNAMID	230			230
UNMIL	127	155	1	283
UNMISS	1,051	12	3	1,066
Total	2,024	167	28	2,219

Source: UN Peacekeeping Department, *UN Mission's Summary Detailed by Country*, August 31, 2016, http://www.un.org/en/peacekeeping/contributors/2016/aug16_3.pdf.

been vigorous development of China–Africa cultural exchanges, which have played a unique role in promoting cooperation and friendship between the two sides. Up to the end of 2005, China had entered into 62 inter-governmental agreements on cultural exchanges and cooperation with 45 African countries, under which the two sides have organized over 200 cultural exchange delegations and hosted hundreds of cultural or art exchange events (FOCAC, 2006).

However, the fast growing economic linkages to some extent make the traditional social and cultural exchanges less relevant today. There is now excessive focus on economic questions that trigger lots of misunderstandings and even blame, for example, blaming China for a 'textile tsunami' in South Africa, Nigeria, and some other African countries. To build a better social and cultural environment for bilateral cooperation, the first *China's African Policy* paper published in 2006 proposed, 'China and Africa will learn from and draw upon each other's experience in governance and development, strengthen exchange and cooperation in education, science, culture and health' (MOFA-RPC, 2006). In 2015, the second *China's African Policy* paper goes further by stressing 'Deepening and expanding cultural and people-to-people exchanges', including:

1   expanding exchanges and cooperation in culture and sports;
2   expanding tourism cooperation;
3   broadening cooperation on press, radio, film and television;
4   encouraging exchanges between academia and think tanks;
5   enhancing people-to-people exchanges.

(Xinhua News Agency, 2015)

Under this policy framework, social and cultural exchanges have been growing very fast. Taking Chinese government-sponsored scholarships as an example, the number in 2006 was 2,000 scholars per year, then moving to 4,000 per year by 2009, then to 5,500 by 2012, then to 10,000 by 2015. Another example is the development of the China–Africa People's Forum that was created in 2011 with the four round meeting held in 2015, with lots of NGOs and civil society groups participating and contributing to the FOCAC process.

While still weak compared with the political and economic pillars of bilateral relations, the two pillars of peace and security cooperation and social and cultural exchange are today being added to China–Africa relations, where they will contribute to a more stable and balanced bilateral relationship. If one overlooks such important ongoing developments today, then one will be 'surprised' when in the coming years great forward strides are achieved in this relationship.

Table 20.2 The six FOCAC ministerial conferences to date

Year	Place	Results
2000	Beijing	Beijing Declaration of FOCAC
		Program for China–Africa Cooperation in Economic and Social Development
2003	Addis Ababa	Addis Ababa Action Plan (2004–2006)
2006	Beijing Summit	Beijing Declaration
		Beijing Action Plan (2007–2009)
2009	Sharm El Sheikh	Declaration of Sharm El Sheikh
		Sharm El Sheikh Action Plan (2010–2012)
2012	Beijing	Beijing Declaration
		Beijing Action Plan (2013–2015)
2015	Johannesburg Summit	Johannesburg Declaration
		Johannesburg Action Plan (2016–2018)

The role of FOCAC

The rapid development of China–Africa relations benefited from the establishment of the Forum on China–Africa Cooperation (FOCAC) in 2000. Echoing the calls from several African countries, the Chinese government proposed to create a collective platform for facilitating the development of bilateral relations, and most African countries warmly welcomed it (Li, 2012). Since then, the China–Africa relationship has been injected with fresh momentum and has drawn huge international attention.

Established in 2000, FOCAC has held six ministerial conferences and two summits (by the end of 2015).

FOCAC is designed as follows. Its objectives include: equal consultation, enhanced understanding, expanded consensus, strengthened friendship and fuller cooperation. As prescribed in the Programme for China–Africa Cooperation in Economic and Social Development, China and Africa have agreed to set up follow-up mechanisms to conduct regular evaluations of FOCAC actions and initiatives. The FOCAC dialogue and consultation mechanism is three-leveled: the Ministerial Conference, which is held every three years; the Senior Official Follow-up Meeting and Senior Official Preparatory Meeting which are held in the previous year and a few days before the Ministerial Conference respectively; and meetings of African diplomats in China with the Chinese Follow-up Committee, which are held at least twice a year. The Ministerial Conference and Senior Official Meeting are held in China and Africa alternately. China and the organizing African state of the meeting jointly preside over the meeting and take the lead in implementing the outcomes of the meeting. The Ministerial Conference is attended by FOCAC members' foreign ministers and ministers in charge of international economic cooperation. The Senior Official Meeting is attended by director-general level officials of the competent departments (FOCAC ABC, 2013).

In addition, due to the ever-expanding and deepening China–Africa cooperation under the FOCAC framework, various sub-forums spanning the fields of agriculture, science and technology, law, finance, culture, think tanks, youth, NGOs, women, media, and local governments have been created, with some becoming regularized, further enriching the content of FOCAC (see Table 20.3). Currently, FOCAC has around 16 sub-forums and another three will be created in the next few years (FOCAC, 2015).

The establishment of FOCAC has significantly contributed to the development of China–Africa relations. Today, FOCAC, which assembles all 51 states[3] that have diplomatic relations

Table 20.3 Sub-forums of FOCAC

Established	To Be Created
Investing in Africa Forum	Forum on Energy and Natural Resources
Forum on China–Africa Media Cooperation	
Forum on China–Africa Health Cooperation	Ministerial Forum on Marine Economy
Forum on China–Africa Financial Cooperation	
FOCAC-Women Forum	Forum on China–Africa Publishing Cooperation
FOCAC-Think Tank Forum	
FOCAC-Legal Forum	
FOCAC Think Tanks Forum	
FOCAC Science and Technology Forum	
FOCAC Cultural Ministers' Forum	
China–Africa Young Leaders' Forum	
China–Africa Radio and Television Cooperation Forum	
China–Africa Poverty Eradication and Development Conference	
China–Africa People's Forum	
China–Africa Forum on Cultural Heritage Protection	
China–Africa Forum on Cooperation between Local Governments	

Source: author compiled.

with China, can be regarded as best practice in Africa's external bilateral relations, and it has arguably provided the political platform for launching a boom in bilateral relations (Grimm, 2012).[4] Since its establishment, FOCAC has been steadily institutionalized and has become the main platform for collective dialogue and an effective mechanism for enhancing practical cooperation between China and African countries.

It is important to note that China–Africa relations have taken a great leap forward since the establishment of FOCAC. At its beginning in 2000, the two sides proposed to establish 'a new-type of long-term and stable partnership based on equality and mutual benefit'; then in 2003, the two advocated 'a new-type of partnership featuring long-term stability, equality and mutual benefit and all-round cooperation'; and in 2006, the two were committed to 'a new type of strategic partnership between China and Africa featuring political equality and mutual trust, mutually beneficial economic cooperation, and cultural exchanges'. More recently in December 2015 at the FOCAC Johannesburg Summit, Chinese President Xi Jinping proposed to upgrade further the China–Africa relationship from 'a new type of strategic partnership' to 'comprehensive strategic and cooperative partnership', which was agreed unanimously by all 51 African members and the African Union. Besides pushing forward FOCAC, the Chinese government has issued two Africa Policy papers in 2006 and 2015 respectively. All these landmark developments, together with the above discussed progress in political, economic, security, and social domains, prove that FOCAC is a catalyst of China–Africa relations, and as discussed in the next section, it has become an example for the international community to develop relations with Africa.

International and African perceptions of China

In 2006 during the run up to the FOCAC Beijing Summit, the West suddenly discovered that China had 'crept' into Africa while it was preoccupied with the War on Terrorism and the Iraq War. It then lost its temper and attacked China's 'rogue' behavior in Africa with various accusations mentioned earlier. Since then, the international image of China–Africa relations has not improved significantly, which has caused most Chinese specialists on Africa to react defensively and seek to justify China's actions (Li, 2008; Zhang, 2013). However, the real question is how much better or worse this relationship has become.

For those outside the China–Africa relationship, views about China–Africa relations have experienced three stages of development since 2000. The first stage was from 2000 to 2005, which can be called 'ignorance' because after September 11, 2001, no one in the West was paying attention to FOCAC or to China–Africa relations more generally. The size and success of the 2006 FOCAC Beijing Summit drew global attention and shocked the West which, when faced with this unanticipated development, responded with various attacks. From 2008, with the opening of the Beijing Olympic Games, the subsidence of the Sudan Darfur Crisis, and the global financial crisis, the West calmed down but more academic research and official naming and shaming efforts emerged.

In Africa, views about China–Africa relations have followed a similar trajectory, but the content has been a little bit different. For example, while the West stressed the problem of low-quality Chinese goods, such as food, clothing, textiles, and electrical goods, many Africans realized that the pocketbook decides the quality of the goods that are bought and sold. Indeed, many African consumers complain about the quality of Chinese goods while local businesspeople complain about being pushed out of business. However, African academic researchers and observers have also pointed out that, while problematic, the majority of African consumers can afford only Chinese-made products; and it is worth noting that some of these low-quality Chinese goods do not come directly from China but from neighbouring countries (Pigato & Tang, 2015; Geerts et al., 2014). Most importantly, the price that consumers are willing to pay determines the quality of goods on the market. China can produce goods for all markets (Ruzvidzo, 2014). On almost every issue, African observers maybe have similar concerns but the understanding of problematic situations is always more sophisticated. Meanwhile, it is very important to note that, while China's image is more negative in academic discussions and newspaper reporting, the views of ordinary Africans on China–Africa relations have remained positive. For example, the Pew Center has been doing its global attitudes survey since the start of this millennium, and it has gathered data on 'opinion of China'. Given the African data of this survey from 2007 until 2015, one has to conclude that China has always been welcomed by Africans (PewResearchCenter, online). Among 11 countries surveyed, Ghana has highest favorable views (80%), while even the lowest (South Africa) has a positive majority view (52%) in 2015. The most positive finding was in the Ivory Coast and Mali in 2007 when as many as 92% of respondents indicated a favorable view, while during this survey period South Africa had the least positive score in 2008 (37%) (ibid.).

The Gallup poll echoes Pew's findings. According to its survey on global leadership, in all surveyed countries in Africa, majorities approved China's leadership with the highest figure in Mali (82%) in 2015; even in South Africa, China's approval rate reached 59%, with 11 points gained in 2015 (Clifton, 2015). Another survey from Gallup that surveys the rate of 'African Approval of China's Leadership, 2014–2015' (Rheault & McCarthy, 2015) shows how China is welcomed in Africa (Eastern, Western, and Southern Africa as well as the Sahel region). President Obama is quite popular in Africa due to his black ethnic background. However,

Kenyans' approval of American leadership from 2009 to 2014 went steadily down in all the above regions, while China's score kept stable (ibid.).

In October 2016, the African polling organization Afrobarometer published its first polling report on China–African relations. Findings from Afrobarometer's 2014/2015 surveys in 36 African countries, which included a special series of questions on China, suggest that the public holds generally favorable views of China's economic and assistance activities. Africans rank the United States and China No. 1 and 2, respectively, as development models for their own countries (Lekorwe et al., 2016:3). Remarkably, in three of five African regions, China either matches or surpasses the United States in popularity as a development model. In terms of their current influence, the two countries are outpaced only by Africa's former colonial powers. African public perceptions not only confirm China's important economic and political role in Africa, but also generally indicate that China's influence is beneficial. China's infrastructure/development and business investments contribute to China's positive image in Africa, but that image is tainted by perceptions of poor-quality Chinese products (Lekorwe et al., 2016). Thus, with respect to China's relationship with Africa, a comparison of Western commentary with African public polling data shows that Western observers tend to focus on certain negative parts of the whole story, or provide only a partial analysis of the whole relationship for readers.

Conclusion: future prospects

Taking account of today's growing popular backlash against globalization, notably Britain's vote for Brexit and Donald Trump's stunning victory in the US presidential election, both of which occurred in 2016, we must make an assessment of the future prospects of China–Africa relations. Before dealing with this question, we have to dig further into the changing nature of this relationship. Aside from a broader foundation for bilateral relations based on the four pillars discussed in this chapter, today there are three trends or transitions impacting its future development.

The first important trend in bilateral relations is a transition from ideological/emotional considerations to calculations of economic interest. Looking back to the China–Africa relationship during the period from the 1950s to the early 1990s, intimate emotional and/or ideological ideas and human exchanges, to a very great extent, supported this bilateral relationship and made it one of China's closest foreign relationships. Meanwhile, because of geographical distance and the weak economic situations of both parties, the trade and investment dimension of the China–Africa relationship was quite weak. However, fast growing economic linkages since the late 1990s, along with a generational change of national leaders across the whole African continent, have been eroding the emotional foundations of this bilateral relationship (Li et al., 2010:8). That is one of the reasons why more and more Africans are persuaded by the arguments of Western critics of China.

The second transition in bilateral relations is a shift of emphasis from economic interest promotion toward the protection of existing economic interests. In the late 1990s, China initiated a 'Going Global' policy to advance Chinese economic interests worldwide. The establishment of the FOCAC in 2000 strengthened this effort in Africa greatly (Brown & Chun, 2009:5–6). Since then, we witnessed the fast growth of China's trade and investment interests across the African continent. However, at the same time, there has been concern for the security of China's economic interests in Africa in the midst of rising global and African uncertainties, affecting mainly energy security, civilian protection, investment security, and others. Based on the principle of 'People First', the protection of overseas Chinese and economic interests is becoming one of China's global foreign policy priorities and a high priority in China's Africa policy.

The third transition is a shift from asymmetrical interdependence toward symmetrical interdependence. The current Sino-African relationship is asymmetrical because China depends more on African natural resources, while Africa depends more on China's rise and growing interest in Africa. However, the 'new normal' of slower growth in China's economy, Africa's own rise, and growing interest on the part of many other nations in developing relations with Africa, together will jointly change the current configuration of relations between China and Africa in the mid- to long term.

The success of these transitions, together with the developments mentioned above, will determine whether China and Africa will advance their relations into a new 'high-speed train' era. Two things are required to make this a reality.

On the one hand, the relationship needs more balanced support from the existing four pillars. That is to say, China–Africa political relations, economic ties, peace and security cooperation, and socio-cultural exchange must all advance on a broad front together.

In order to strengthen Chinese contributions to African peace and security, China now has a general blueprint for peace and security cooperation but deeper involvement may risk violating China's traditional principle of non-interference. Thus, China needs a comprehensive strategic plan for peace and security cooperation using multilateral institutions as the main platform.

To deal with growing socio-cultural frictions, China will have to shift its development assistance from 'hard' infrastructure assistance to 'soft' forms of aid. Because NGOs still lack capacity, current people-to-people exchange may aggravate rather than reduce frictions. China should nurture NGOs and civil society groups to create better platforms for public diplomacy.

As more symmetrical interdependence develops between China and Africa, both sides will have to consider how to build real friendship between a soon-to-be 'developed' country (China) and a still 'developing' continent (Africa). Both sides will have to consolidate a Global South network that includes cooperative relations with other developing countries, etc.

Finally, in order to inaugurate a 'high-speed train' era in China–Africa relations, priority should be given to two new areas of cooperation.

One new priority is local engagement between both sides. Besides central governmental ministries and agencies, there are still many other actors involved in bilateral relations that are governmental or non-governmental, such as state-owned companies, provincial agencies, province-owned companies, private companies, and even individuals. For example, national companies no longer dominate China's investment in Africa. Both African and Chinese small and medium-sized enterprises (SMEs) are growing in importance, and more and more Chinese SMEs are investing in Africa. Now, SMEs account for more than 85% of the 2,000 Chinese companies that currently operate in Africa. To keep pace with this diversification of actors, both China and Africa should restructure bilateral relations to build a more inclusive and multi-layered partnership.

The other new priority is to include relevant third parties into this bilateral relationship based on comparative advantages. The international community largely ignored Africa during the decade after the collapse of the Soviet Union. However, after the 'shock' of the successful 2006 Beijing FOCAC summit, both traditional powers and emerging powers redoubled efforts to build relations with Africa and establish or strengthen cooperation platforms, including for example, the EU–Africa Summit, India–Africa Summit, America–Africa Summit, Tokyo International Conference for African Development (TICAD), Turkey–Africa Summit, among others. It is important to note that different platforms have different comparative advantages, and coordination among them to build a division of labor to promote sustainable development in Africa is both logical and feasible. China has advocated three principles for guiding trilateral or triangular development cooperation in Africa, namely, any proposal must be 'Africa-proposed, Africa-agreed, and Africa-led' (Xinhua News Agency, 2015).

As explained in this chapter, the China–Africa relationship has progressed from a unicycle era to the current four-wheeled car era. There are today real prospects for a further advance into a 'high-speed train' era. However, at the same time, the quickly deepening bilateral relationship faces growing challenges on several fronts that may lead to misunderstandings and frictions. How well these are managed will depend on the confidence and commitment that both China and Africa feel toward the continuing success of this relationship.

Notes

1 Most identify one decade as one phase of development.
2 While 2011 was an exception because of the Sino-America summit held in mid January, if counting the lunar New Year, the first trip of the Chinese Foreign Minister in 2011 was still to Africa.
3 Gambia re-established diplomatic relations in 2016 and has not benefited from the FOCAC; thus it should not be included.
4 It is interesting to note that foreign observers—and many Africans—rather emphasize the more than 50 states of the continent and thus understand FOCAC rather as a multilateral platform.

References

Brown, K. and Chun, Z., 2009. 'China in Africa – Preparing for the Next Forum for China Africa Cooperation', *Chatham House Briefing Note*, June, pp. 5–6.

Cargill, T., 2008. 'China and Africa: A Literature Review', Unpublished Chatham House Review.

Clifton, J., 2015. 'Rating World Leaders: US, China, Russia, EU and Germany', *Gallup*, April 22 Available at: www.gallup.com/opinion/gallup/182801/rating-world-leaders-china-russia-germany.aspx [Accessed 3 April 2017].

FOCAC, 2006. 'Cultural Exchanges and Cooperation', FOCAC Beijing Summit, September 21, Available at: http://english.focacsummit.org/2006-09/21/content_899.htm.

FOCAC, 2012. 'President Hu Jintao, Open Up New Prospects for A New Type of China–Africa Strategic Partnership', Speech at the Opening Ceremony of the Fifth Ministerial Conference of The Forum on China–Africa Cooperation, Beijing, July 19, Available at: http://www.focac.org/eng/dwjbzjjhys/hyqk/t953115.htm.

FOCAC, 2013. 'FOCAC ABC', FOCAC Website, April 9, Available at: http://www.focac.org/eng/ltda/ltjj/t933522.htm.

FOCAC, 2015. *The Forum on China–Africa Cooperation Johannesburg Action Plan (2016–2018)*, FOCAC Website, December 25, Available at: www.focac.org/eng/ltda/dwjbzjjhys_1/hywj/t1327961.htm.

Geerts, S., Xinwa, N. and Rossouw, D., 2014. *African's Perception of Chinese Business in Africa: A Survey*, Pretoria: Ethics Institute of South Africa, August, pp. 1–62.

Grimm, S., 2012. 'The Forum on China–Africa Cooperation – Political Rational and Functioning', *CCS Policy Briefing*, May, Centre for Chinese Studies, Stellenbosch, pp. 1–4.

Jiniping, X., 2015. 'Xi Jiniping Attends and Addresses UN Leaders' Summit on Peacekeeping', Ministry of Foreign Affairs of the People's Republic of China, September 29, Available at: http://www.fmprc.gov.cn/mfa_eng/topics_665678/xjpdmgjxgsfwbcxlhgcl70znxlfh/t1304147.shtml.

Lekorwe, M., Chingwete, A., Okuru, M. and Samson, R., 2016. 'China's Growing Presence in Africa Wins Largely Positive Popular Reviews', *Afrobarometer Dispatch*, Volume 122, October 24, pp. 1–29.

Li A., 2006. 'On Adjustment and Transformation of China's African Policy', *West Asian and African Studies*, Volume 8, pp. 11–20.

Li A., 2008. 'In Defense of China: China's African Strategy and State Image', *World Economics and Politics*, Volume 4, pp. 6–15.

Li A., 2012. 'Why the Forum on China–Africa Cooperation? Analyzing China's Strategy in Africa', *Foreign Affairs Review* (Chinese), Volume. 29 (3), pp. 165–187.

Li Q. and Xu, Y., 1982. 'Ancient China and Africa', *History Teaching*, Volume 9, pp. 16–23.

Li Weijian, Zhang Zhongxian, Zhang Chun, and Zhu Min, 2010. 'Towards a New Decade: A Study on the Sustainability of FOCAC', *West Asia and Africa*, Volume 209, September, pp. 5–10.

Liu, H. and Luo, J., 2011. *Sino-African Development Cooperation: Studies on the Theories, Strategies and Policies*, Beijing: China Social Science Press, pp. 171–195.

Michel, S. and Beuret, M., 2009. *China's Africa Safari: On the Trail of Beijing's Expansion in Africa*, New York: Nation Books.

MOFA-PRC (Ministry of Foreign Affairs of the People's Republic of China), 2006. *China's African Policy*, Beijing, January 12, Available at: http://www.focac.org/eng/zt/zgdfzzcwj/t230479.htm.

MOFCOM and National Bureau of Statistics, 2016. *2015 Statistical Bulletin of China's Outward Foreign Direct Investment*, Beijing, p. 98.

PewResearchCenter, *Global Attitudes & Trends* 'Opinion of China: Do you have a favorable or unfavorable view of China?' [online]. Available at: www.pewglobal.org/database/indicator/24/group/5/ (Accessed 3 April 2017).

Pigato, M. and Tang, W., 2015. 'China and Africa: Expanding Economic Ties in an Evolving Global Context', Investing in Africa Forum, World Bank, March 1, pp. 1–40.

Rheault, M. and McCarthy, J., 2015. 'US Still Leads China in Leadership Approval in Africa', August 6, Available at: www.gallup.com/poll/184481/still-leads-china-leadership-approval-africa.aspx (Accessed 3 April 2017).

Rotberg, R. I. (ed.), 2008. *China into Africa: Trade, Aid, and Influences*, Washington, DC: Brookings Institution.

Ruzvidzo, V., 2014. 'There's room for improvement on Chinese products', *The Herald Business* (Zimbabwe), May 22. Authors' interview with Prof. Charity Manyeruke, University of Zimbabwe, Harare.

SCIO, 2014. Information Office of the State Council, *China's Foreign Aid (2014)*, July, Beijing, Available at: www.scio.gov.cn/zfbps/wjbps/Document/1435360/1435360.htm.

Southall, G. and Melber, H. (eds.), 2009. *A New Scramble for Africa? Imperialism, Investment and Development*, Pietermaritzburg: University of KwaZula-Natal Press.

Taylor, I., 1998. 'China's Foreign Policy Toward Africa in the 1990s', *Journal of Modern African Studies*, Volume 36 (3), pp. 443–460.

Xinhua News Agency, 2015. *China's Second Africa Policy Paper*, December 5, Available at: http://news.xinhuanet.com/english/2015-12/04/c_134886545.htm.

Zhang, C., 2013. *On International Contributions of China–Africa Relationship*, Shanghai: Shanghai People's Publishing House.

Zhang, X., 2006. 'New Inspirations of Longstanding and Well-established Sino-Africa Relations', *West Asian and African Studies*, Volume 6, pp. 53–58.

21

ASIA IN LUSOPHONE AFRICA

Carmen Amado Mendes

Introduction

This chapter seeks to provide a broader perspective on several aspects of the main Asian powers in Lusophone Africa, adding some value to the on-going discussion of Asia and Africa. Despite growing interest in African and Asian studies, this is an under-researched topic, due mainly to the absence of scholars interested in Asian studies who are also fluent in Portuguese and interested in focusing on Lusophone Africa. Research is also limited by a lack of incentives in Portuguese-speaking countries to study Asia. The main body of literature focuses on China's relations with the African continent in general, not Lusophone Africa specifically.

The first generation of China–Africa literature, which broadly speaking emerged during the first decade of the twenty-first century, resulted in several think tank reports and a few academic articles and books – from authors such as Alden (2009), Ian Taylor (2009), Deborah Brautigam (2009), and Shinn & Eisenman (2012). The novelty of the growing dimension of Asian presence in the region brought a great deal of attention to this relationship and many narratives emerged on different modus operandi. China in particular received a great deal of attention for pursuing resources, bringing its own workers to key projects, building alliances with authoritarian governments such as that in Angola, turning a blind eye to corruption and, perhaps, even encouraging corruption. Although many of those assumptions were proved inaccurate over time, they did hold elements of truth, including the existence of turnkey projects, problems with environmental and labour relations, huge groups of Chinese labourers that exclusively worked on projects, and the Chinese engaging in self-serving activities. However, a more sophisticated understanding tells us that there is much more to the story than those initial images.

These narratives have been combined with a view of Asia as a head-to-head rival in the continent, spreading throughout Africa trying to secure, in a kind of mercantilist fashion, exclusive rights and control over territory, government relations, and energy markets while entering the world stage as a competitor for oil, gas, and mineral resources. Western literature also conjures images of Asia as a competitor that does not consider local needs, anxious to export manufactured goods and import natural resources in the short-term; or as a neo-colonizer with a long-term strategy to replace the West, presenting itself as a partner for development, willing to share its experience and successful economic model (Brautigam & Tang, 2011:28; Lagerkvist & Jonsson, 2011:9; Ilhéu, 2011:49). The nature of this trade balance is considered damaging for the region in the long term because Asians buy raw materials instead of manufactured goods, delaying the development of local industries and leading to unemployment. Thus emerges a common argument in the literature: tensions in political relationships and in interactions with locals increase when industrialization processes evolve (see, for example, the arguments presented in the East Asia Special Issue, Mendes, 2013b).

Lusophone Africa refers to the five African countries where Portuguese is an official language: Angola, Cape Verde, Guinea-Bissau, Mozambique, and Sao Tome and Principe. The Asian powers with the most visible presence in Lusophone Africa are Japan, India, South Korea, and especially the People's Republic of China, except in Sao Tome and Principe, which maintains diplomatic relations with Taiwan. This chapter analyses Asian countries' policy goals and the kinds of relations they have established with each Lusophone country. The first section provides an overview of Asia's cooperation mechanisms in Africa, at both bilateral and multilateral levels. The second section looks at the presence of and the different approaches adopted by China, Japan, India, and South Korea towards each of the Portuguese-speaking African countries. The question raised is are they genuinely building a new relationship of collaboration, or one of competition, helping Lusophone Africa or helping themselves? In other words, it analyses if development cooperation – aid, trade, and foreign direct investment – is an instrument to secure access to natural resources and if economic links are used for political leverage.

Asian powers allocate different types of aid to Lusophone Africa, as the nature of their bilateral relations varies. Two of them, Japan and Korea, are OECD/DAC donors, i.e., they follow the Western development concept, which is more altruistic and directed towards 'soft aid' or social sectors. China's model differs from the West's in that it not only imposes conditions on providing aid, it also provides policy advice (Eggen & Roland, 2014:94–95). It adopts a very pragmatic approach, leaving each country to find its own path out of poverty, although its aid model is also changing towards increased poverty reduction. India's aid is somewhere in between the two models. This chapter sheds some light on the discussion over which Asian donors provide Africans with the right instruments and conditions.

Asia–Africa cooperation mechanisms

Despite sharing some goals and principles, Asian powers do not take a homogeneous approach towards the Portuguese-speaking countries; they prioritize different interests and follow specific models of cooperation to achieve them. However, they share similar interests in importing natural resources and exporting manufactured products, and concentrate aid on infrastructure projects, health, and human development sectors. The Chinese are better known for the resources-for-infrastructure deals and the no-strings-attached approach. The only political condition that Beijing imposes on its formal external relations is respect for the 'One China' policy, which holds that there is but one China and that Taiwan is part of China. Non-interference in domestic affairs, one of China's Five Principles of Peaceful Coexistence,[1] is also acknowledged by Japan's Development Cooperation Charter of 2015. Japan considers human security as one of its basic policies (Atanassova-Cornelis & Mendes, 2010:409), along with economic development and consolidation of peace (Raposo, 2011:336). The Indian cooperation model is very much focused on human development and is more service-oriented, inspiring other countries to bypass industrialization and go straight from agriculture to the modern service sector (Mendes, 2013a:75).

Japan and South Korea strike a balance between Asian and Western values, following OECD-DAC norms but positioning themselves as stakeholders able to make connections with G-77 countries. This underpinned South Korea's offer to host Busan and Japan's sympathy with the south–south cooperation ideal of transferring Asian experience to Africa (Raposo & Potter, 2010:190). In political terms, Seoul carefully monitors North Korea's gradual strengthening of its African links, namely in Angola (Darracq & Neville 2014:8). The Japanese presence in Africa can either be understood as an independent strategy concentrated on national interests (Lagerkvist & Jonsson 2011:11), such as attracting votes for a permanent seat at the UN Security Council (Raposo & Potter, 2010:183); or as a reaction to China's use of aid to attain great power status, which in turn seems to encourage Tokyo to raise its own diplomatic profile (Atanassova-Cornelis & Mendes 2010:405). In any case, Japan's substantial presence in the continent, not only regarding aid but also trade and investment, does not have the media coverage or the visibility of China's, whose competition thus fosters Japan's 'hidden agenda' in Africa (Lehman, 2013).

Asian development cooperation institutions are all structured differently, and decision-making is more centralized at the capital level in China and India (Castillejo & Hackenesch, 2014:4) than it is in Japan, where aid decision-making within the Japan International Cooperation Agency (JICA) is an administrative decision, not a political one (Raposo & Potter, 2010:181). The government of South Korea provides financial aid to developing nations worldwide through the Korea International Cooperation Agency (KOICA, 2008). After decades of sustained economic development and becoming a member of the DAC in 2010, South Korea holds the title of first official aid-recipient-turned-donor (Roehrig, 2013).

Despite favouring bilateral relations, Asian countries have shown some multilateral activism in Africa: the Forum on China–Africa Cooperation (FOCAC) was created in 2000; the first Tokyo International Conference on African Development (TICAD) was organized in 1993; the first edition of the India–Africa Forum Summit (IAFS) took place in New Delhi in 2008; and the Korea–Africa Forum, first held in 2006, had its fourth edition in 2015. These regional initiatives state very similar goals, which include serving as multilateral platforms for cooperation with African countries in different dimensions and providing alternatives to the Washington Consensus[2] cooperation framework in Africa. It does seem, however, that FOCAC stands out. Over the past 15 years, it has consolidated a comprehensive structure and operating mechanisms, which include multi-level interactions, reaching a considerable level of institutionalization, both in China and in Africa, beyond regular high-level meetings (Li Anshan et al., 2012:15–22).

The TICAD, initially conceived as a consultative forum for extensive discussions on development with African leaders, was used to increase Japan's international influence in Africa, especially after the failure of Japan's attempt to be elected a permanent member of the United Nations Security Council in 2005. Its primary focus has shifted from development assistance to the promotion of private sector trade and investment. The 2013 TICAD 5 included the participation of heads of state and governments of 51 African countries, UN Secretary-General Ban Ki-moon, representatives from Asian nations, international organizations, and private sector organizations. TICAD differs from the forums promoted by China and India in endorsing neither non-interference nor the reform of existing international institutions; it rather relies on them, as TICAD 5 was jointly organized by the Government of Japan, the African Union Commission, the United Nations Office of the Special Advisor on Africa, the United Nations Development Programme, and the World Bank (UN, 2008:6; Japan, 2014; Japan, 2013a, 2013b:22–23).

The IAFS reflects the evolution of India–Africa relations, with the third summit being announced as India's largest-ever outreach event towards Africa, reflecting a clear intent to increase participation after the limited numbers present at the first two editions – 14 countries in 2008 and 15 countries in 2011. The first official declaration of the IAFS focused on the issue of climate change and emphasized principles of non-interference, echoing the rhetoric of the BRICS (Brazil, Russia, India, China, South Africa) official documents, while also arguing for reform of the 'international financial architecture, especially the international financial institutions, to reflect the changing global situation' (Africa & India, 2008:3), as well as improving south–south cooperation. In the second summit, the need to reform the United Nations and the political weight India and Africa ought to secure in it are specifically mentioned (Africa & India, 2011a), reflecting the Ezulwini Consensus[3] and reviews of the 2010 Africa–India Framework for Enhanced Cooperation.[4]

Just like its Asian counterparts, South Korea has come to promote a cooperation mechanism to help boost its influence and increase cooperation with the African continent: the Korea–Africa Forum, which has moved from a dialogue on trade and investment to encompassing socio-economic issues. Between the first and second editions, the number of African countries represented more than doubled, increasing from 15 to 35 (Kim, 2012). The 2009 Seoul Declaration recognizes the complementary structures of both economies and a commitment to promote 'enlarged cooperation in such fields as railways, ports, roads, electricity, communication systems and natural resources'. Furthermore, the Framework for Korea–Africa Development Cooperation 2009–2012 and the Korea–Africa Green Growth Initiative 2009–2012 act as important roadmaps for bilateral policies (South Korea, 2009:5, 7).

Asian interests in Lusophone Africa

Lusophone Africa achieved independence from Portugal after the 1974 Carnation Revolution and created, with its former colonizer and Brazil, the Community of Portuguese-Speaking Countries (CPLP) in 1996, in which Japan gained observer status in 2014 (CPLP, 2015). However, despite sharing a common identity and traditions, Lusophone Africa is not monolithic. In sub-Saharan Africa, Angola is a large country, very rich in oil and other natural resources and capable of defending its own interests; it has caught China's attention, particularly over the past decade. Mozambique, with the discovery of off-shore gas deposits and prospects for extensive coal mining, is also starting to attract growing investment. None of the other Portuguese-speaking African countries holds a similar bargaining position. The archipelago of Cape Verde is a small country made up of different types of islands with an important geopolitical location, in the middle of the Atlantic Ocean, at the crossroads of three continents. It does not have resources besides sun, scenery, and sandy beaches; however, it has a parliamentary democracy, low corruption levels, and good human development, which translates into economic and political stability and a staff well suited to participate in advanced training. Sao Tome and Principe is apparently trying to evolve in this direction. It is one of the smallest countries in Africa, with two volcanic islands and located in the oil-rich waters of the Gulf of Guinea. Petroleum discoveries in the Joint Development Zone with Nigeria, along with the potential for improving the tourist industry, may contribute to reducing this heavily-indebted, poor nation's dependency on cocoa. The West African country of Guinea-Bissau, considered a narco-state (a country whose economy is dependent on the trade in illegal drugs), suffers from great instability and its resources are limited to wood and fishery; its offshore waters are among the world's richest in fish stocks.

China currently enjoys the most visible presence in Lusophone Africa. At the multilateral level, the Forum on China–Africa Cooperation, which targets the whole continent, does not pay special attention to Lusophone Africa as suggested by the sixth Ministerial Conference held in Johannesburg in 2015. However, Beijing hosts the Forum for Economic and Trade Cooperation between China and the Portuguese-speaking Countries, also known as the 'Macau Forum', as its permanent secretariat is headquartered in this Chinese Special Administrative Region. The Forum includes all Lusophone countries except Sao Tome and Principe, which has the status of observer because it established diplomatic relations with Taiwan in 1997 (Mendes, 2014:231–232).

Taiwan is one of Sao Tome and Principe's main partners along with the EU, the UNDP, and Portugal. Taiwanese development aid focuses on agriculture, food security, and public health – including medical assistance and malaria eradication, education and human resources, infrastructures and rural development, energy and information, and communications technology (Lopes, 2013:99–100; Macauhub, 2014a; STP & EU, 2014:12, 22). In exchange, Sao Tome helps Taipei promote its bid to participate in international organizations (*The China Post*, 2013). Despite these ties to Taiwan, the Chinese Communist Party maintains connections in the country, due to its support during the colonial war, to the political party that proclaimed independence – which is now the main opposition party. Moreover, the Chinese state-owned enterprise (SOE) Sinopec has an indirect presence in Block 2 of the Nigeria–Sao Tome and Principe Joint Development Zone (CGD, 2014:29–30). In November 2013, a few days before the fourth ministerial conference of the Macau Forum, the Foreign Minister of Sao Tome visited Beijing, and China decided to reengage economically with the island state. A Chinese trade representative office was set up in Sao Tome and Principe, which became the first of Taiwan's four diplomatic allies in Africa to have a Chinese trade mission (Shih, 2013:1, 2014:3). Besides building roads, commercial facilities, sewage disposal plants, and upgrading the main airport, Beijing announced the construction of a deep-water port to facilitate oil exportation and sea-borne commerce (Rotberg, 2013).

Guinea-Bissau also maintained diplomatic relations with Taiwan, from 1990 to 1998. Before declaring the end of the relationship in 1990, China constantly renewed its agreement on economic and technological cooperation with Guinea and built several infrastructures. From 1998 onwards, besides the rehabilitation of public housing, schools, and health facilities, Beijing announced funding for the construction of a massive dam, a deep-water port, a bridge, and the rehabilitation of two main highways. In terms of symbolic buildings, China constructed the justice palace and the national parliament building, and rehabilitated the presidential palace. Besides infrastructure, they have focused on power-generating equipment, agro-technology, and fishery cooperation (PRC, 2006); the 2006 deep-water fisheries agreement opened the door for Chinese fishing vessels to operate in Guinea's Exclusive Economic Zone. China provides local assistance in those areas, training for public servants and military officers, and scholarships to Chinese universities. Budget and humanitarian assistance is also provided, along with shipments of rice and the exemption of selected local products from Chinese tariffs (Horta, 2010, 2012:35; Macauhub, 2014b; Nguema & Doland, 2007; ANGOP, 2013).

The Chinese government also constructed public buildings in Cape Verde, such as the National Assembly and the government palaces, as well as a dam; it also provides health, education, military, and information and communications technology cooperation. For China, Cape Verde is a bridge to Africa and an attractive market for its manufactured products. Small-scale Chinese traders established shops throughout the archipelago, especially from the mid 1990s onwards, contributing to the development of a market economy and creating a few jobs, despite also being blamed for promoting competition (Macauhub, 2013a; Horta, 2008).

China's relations with the other two Portuguese-speaking African countries are very different, being mainly focused on energy security concerns and natural resources. In Mozambique, considering the value of the loans, infrastructure projects, and assistance provided through FOCAC, China is by far its most important Asian partner, although India, Japan, and South Korea have also increased their engagement in recent years (Castillejo & Hackenesch, 2014:5). Besides gas and coal, the Chinese are interested in fishery, agriculture, and timber, while building public infrastructures and exporting manufactured products. With Luanda, Beijing developed its strongest and most opaque relationship in Africa, framed by the credit line negotiated with a post-war Angola in desperate need of reconstruction. Chinese SOE investments favour infrastructure, transport, and the oil and diamond sectors, while funds from the credit line have been channelled to technical and social cooperation, including the construction of schools and medical facilities, utility services such as water and sanitation, and training programmes for human resource development (Kiala & Ngwenya, 2011:16–17).

China's multi-tier strategy has reached a level of sophistication that enables the country to draw on its experience in creating Special Economic Zones (SEZ),[5] formally sponsored by the Chinese government through its Ministry of Commerce (Hendler, 2014). Exporting the concept to developing countries to facilitate foreign direct investment and technology transfer, Beijing vowed that Africa would receive Chinese overseas SEZ (FOCAC, 2009). Among Lusophone countries, Angola's SEZ in Luanda-Bengo, established in 2009, has proved to be a successful enterprise and is regarded as a reference (Angola, 2015). Mozambique established a SEZ in 2012 in Manga-Mungassa, under the management of China's Dingsheng International Investment Company (Sogecoa Group), and in 2014 announced the creation of a new SEZ, in Mocuba (Macauhub, 2015a). Cape Verde has also shown great interest in creating an SEZ in Sao Vicente, which would be initially linked to fishing activities (Panapress, 2007).

Japan's presence in Africa tends to be discussed in terms of aid, but there is also considerable amounts of private companies, investment, and trade involved (Japan, 2013b:20–21). As in the case of China, Japanese private investment in Africa, despite growing interest in manufacturing and services, targets resources and infrastructure. In Angola and Mozambique, Japanese firms such as Mitsubishi, Nippon Steel, and Sumitomo Mitsui Banking Corp. obtain contracts to process resources and to build or rehabilitate roads, railways, and ports to create logistics corridors for resources, linking Africa's interior to Indian Ocean trade routes and Japan.

With Angola, one of Japan's major oil suppliers, technical assistance focuses on mineral resources, rice cultivation, and development of human resources, and a Japanese–Angolan bilateral investment agreement is currently being negotiated (Japan, 2011, 2013c). In Mozambique, besides natural gas, coal, and rare earths, Tokyo is interested in creating a more reliable energy source in Maputo, in part due to Mitsubishi's presence in aluminium smelting, and has announced funding for the construction of an electrical substation (Stratfor Global Intelligence, 2014; Macauhub, 2015b). Prompted by the lack of food in Mozambique, agriculture is another sector of growing cooperation; in conjunction with Brazil, Japan is developing an agricultural development zone, the so-called ProSAVANA – it is highly controversial, however, as small farmers fear land-grabbing (Chichava, et al., 2013:5, 12–14, 22; see also Classen, 2013; Classen et al., 2014). Along with Mozambique, Cape Verde has received a much greater share of Japanese aid in the past years, including construction of desalination plants (Stratfor Global Intelligence, 2014; JICA, 2013). In Sao Tome and Principe, Japan decided to extend food aid, namely by donating rice, and develop fishery cooperation. It is one of Sao Tome's main partners in fisheries, along with the European Union, and announced it was going to fund the construction of a fishing port in 2015 (Japan, 2010; STP & EU, 2014:12, 22; Macauhub, 2014c).

Sao Tome and Principe also receives support from India in the agricultural, educational, and health sectors (STP & EU, 2014:14). In exchange, it offered support for India's non-permanent seat on the UN Security Council for the 2011–2012 term and for eventually becoming a permanent member. However, high-level contacts have been limited to side-line talks at multilateral meetings and bilateral trade is almost negligible, mainly due to shipping time and high costs. The lines of credit offered by India in 2009 remained unused as the government of Sao Tome and Principe did not prepare the groundwork for specific infrastructure projects (India, 2014a). In Guinea-Bissau, India grants scholarships, training, and assistance programmes, although bilateral cooperation is far more recent than trade ties in the cashew nut sector, making India the first destination of the country's exports (India, 2013a; AfDB et al., 2011:3).

With Maputo, the Indian government maintains regular high-level exchanges and scholarship offers for Mozambican nationals, as well as training for government officials. The first of the five Indian credit lines granted in 2003, which cover several projects from sanitation to transmission lines, became operational one year later through an agreement between India's EXIM Bank and the Mozambican government (India, 2014b). Mozambique is the third largest recipient of Indian credit lines in Africa (Castillejo & Hackenesch, 2014:5) and India is one of its biggest investors, attracted by the large reserves of natural gas – much needed to feed its power stations – exploring coal through the International Coal Ventures Ltd consortium (India, 2013b:4–5; Macauhub, 2014d). This is framed by the 2009 Bilateral Investment Promotion and Protection Agreement and the 2014 memorandum of understanding on oil and gas cooperation (India & Mozambique, 2009; Lusa, 2014). Bilateral trade also increased in recent years: Mozambique mainly exports coal coke to India, along with raw cashew, coconut, metal ores, and scrap metal; it imports Indian pharmaceuticals, rice, wheat, machinery, and manufactured products (India, 2014c). The Indian Ocean is perceived as 'a route for travel and cooperation' and not a 'barrier' (UN, 2008:6), with exchanges starting during the pre-colonial period. The Lusophone connection is highlighted by the fact that many Indians holding Mozambican nationality originally came from Goa, Daman, and Diu, all former Portuguese colonies (India, 2013b:1, 6).

In Angola, India is surpassed by China, being the second largest trading partner, granting lines of credit for railway rehabilitation and agricultural equipment, including tractors. Indian exports also include leather, paper and wood products, pharmaceuticals and cosmetics, and food and drinks. Fast-growing bilateral trade reveals the importance of Angola as a source of crude oil for India, which is also interested in Liquefied Natural Gas (LNG) and in the diamond sector. India frames participation in infrastructure programmes within a south–south cooperation logic aiding Angolan national reconstruction (India, 2013c).

South Korea has been another important partner for Angola, following the same pattern of other Asian powers by providing loans in exchange for natural resources (Darracq & Neville 2014:5). Bilateral cooperation focuses on industry, public transportation, education (ANGOP, 2012), reconstruction and construction of infrastructures, and Seoul is also interested in LNG. In the oil sector, Angola's state-owned oil producer (Sonangol) cooperates with Daewoo, and deals with Angola's national electricity producer (Empresa Nacional de Electricidade – ENE) reveal South Korean business interests in hydroelectric, solar, and alternative energy.

In Mozambique, Seoul also has interests in the energy sector, offering courses on the natural gas industry, including risk management, and regional development policy (Macauhub, 2014e). The Trade-Investment Promotion Agency opened a Korea Business Centre in Maputo, soon after the establishment of the Korean Embassy in 2013 (Macauhub, 2013b), and South Korean companies increased their investments in infrastructure and mining. Seoul has only recently begun providing aid to Mozambique (Castillejo & Hackenesch, 2014:5), supporting socio-economic development efforts through priority areas of the Action Plan for Poverty Reduction: education, health, public infrastructures, roads and bridges, and environment (Jackson, 2012; Panapress, 2014).

Conclusion: Asia as an alternative donor?

This chapter focused on the bilateral relationships between major Asian countries and each of the Portuguese-speaking African countries individually, instead of focusing on the region in general.

The first section explained the cooperation mechanisms supporting Asian policies towards Lusophone Africa while the second section discussed the typology of Asian goals and actions and the different types of cooperation established in Lusophone Africa, including political cooperation, trade, and development aid. The chapter raised the question of whether development cooperation is used to obtain natural resources and facilitate trade and foreign direct investment. It highlighted that Asian governments are driven by foreign policy strategies, defined in terms of national interest, including looking for new markets and securing natural resources to feed their own economies. Therefore, analysis of the priority goals of Asian countries, including access to raw materials to guarantee economic growth, suggests that their presence is more visible in countries that are richer in natural resources, following a pattern of resource diplomacy.

These goals are arguably implemented in Lusophone Africa through south–south cooperation rhetoric, disguising a paternalistic relationship with a win-win partnership discourse, employed to obscure goals of political power and wealth. Asians position themselves as development partners, rather than donors in the Western sense. Relations are framed by a south–south cooperation approach of two types. On the one hand, Japan and Korea share Western and DAC norms and accept dialogue within the OECD. Despite sharing Asian values[6] with their neighbours, they are closer to norms such as democracy and human rights. On the other hand, China and India promote the principle of non-interference and stand for a business-approach to south–south cooperation, showing a lack of interest in initiatives to better coordinate development, noticeable within the G-77 and the UN.

Thus, norms that are obligatory for Japan and Korea are arbitrary for China (although to a lesser extent) and India, who do not show interest in defining international rules that may limit their external action. As a result, African Lusophone countries, which have transitioned to multiparty systems but are suspicious of discussing issues regarding human rights and good governance in the near future, compromise with the 'conditions' of Japan and South Korea, compared with China's and India's 'emptiness', or absence of them. This chapter highlighted the similarities and differences between the models followed by these four Asian donors and their impact on Asia–Lusophone Africa relations. One of the major findings is that Lusophone Africa is increasingly becoming an economic and diplomatic battleground between Asian countries, and it is not clear if this competition will evolve to collaboration and coordination in the field. China is now the lead trading partner, considering both its bilateral relationships and its role as a central strategic player on the continent.

The perception of Asia as an alternative donor to traditional aid donors within the north–south dichotomy was also analysed, considering the criticism that is often levelled regarding involvement in Portuguese-speaking Africa. The south–south cooperation strategies have contributed towards strengthening Asia's relations with Lusophone countries, arguably challenging Western interests. However, the West cannot stop Asian donors from becoming more powerful in global relations. They are important politically, diplomatically, in peacekeeping, and, first and foremost, economically, including in investment and trading, with an increasing presence of Asian traders as actors in local markets. There is currently a natural readjustment occurring in the hierarchy of power that reflects Asia's position as an important actor.

A wide range of factors determines power in international relations, including economic power and political power. Some of those factors are resources and size: countries with more financial and economic resources are naturally more important players in the global economy and in global politics. In the case of Asian countries, there was a discrepancy between their economic size and role in the international system: a focus on domestic development and isolation from the outside world resulted in a low-profile foreign policy lasting decades. In the past years, Asian governments have developed external relations through economic diplomacy: economic ties with Africa, including African exports to Asian countries and Asian foreign direct investment in Africa, grew rapidly. However, the future of Asia in Lusophone Africa should be made compatible with the interests of developing countries, in terms of economic development, well-being, and good governance.

Asian donors' south–south cooperation model is also affecting the balance of power between Lusophone nations. Lusophone Africa must overcome this divide, finding its comparative advantages and attracting Asian powers to a dialogue focused on common interests, guaranteeing long-lasting collaborations. The question is whether Africa can develop and take this partnership as an opportunity for trading more and better, beyond an aid-recipient mentality.

Notes

1 The Five Principles of Peaceful Coexistence, articulated by Premier Zhou Enlai in 1955, include: mutual respect for sovereignty and territorial integrity, mutual non-aggression, non-interference in each other's internal affairs, equality and mutual benefit, and peaceful coexistence.
2 The Washington consensus, a broader set of understandings of the Bretton Woods institutions rooted in Anglo-American views, over time has come to mean macroeconomic stabilization, broader economic liberalization, democracy and democratization, and governance reforms.
3 The Ezulwini Consensus refers to a common African position on the United Nations reform, adopted by the Executive Council of the African Union in March 2005, advocating for a stronger representation of Africa in the Security Council (AU, 2005).
4 Regarding the Africa–India Framework for Enhanced Cooperation, it was agreed to continue building on cooperation on economic and political issues, science, technology, research and development, social development and capacity building, health, culture and sports, tourism, infrastructure, energy and environment, and media and communications (Africa & India, 2011b).
5 Special Economic Zones are regions/cities with special economic policies and flexible governmental measures that provide tax incentives for foreign enterprises, to attract investments.
6 'Asian values have been defined as putting emphasis on a consensual approach, communitarianism rather than individualism, social order and harmony, respect for elders, discipline, a paternalistic State and the primary role of government in economic development. This would, in theory, contrast with "Western values", associated with transparency, accountability, global competitiveness, a universalistic outlook and universal practices, and an emphasis on private initiatives and the independence of the private sector' (Pföstl, 2008:8).

Bibliography

Adebajo, A. and Whiteman, K. (eds.), 2012. *The EU and Africa: From EURAFRQQUE to Afro-Europa*, London: Hurst & Company.
AfDB, OECD, UNDP and UNECA 2011. 'Guinea-Bissau 2011', *African Economic Outlook*, African Development Bank, Organization for Economic Co-operation and Development, United Nations Development Programme and United Nations Economic Commission for Africa, Available at: www.africaneconomicoutlook.org/fileadmin/uploads/aeo/Country_Notes/2011/Full/Guinea-Bissau.pdf.
Africa and India, 2008. 'Delhi Declaration India–Africa Forum Summit 2008', New Delhi, 9 April, Available at: www.idsa.in/resources/documents/India–AfricaForumSummit2008.
Africa and India, 2011a. 'Addis Ababa Declaration', Second Africa–India Forum Summit 2011, Addis Ababa, Ethiopia, 25 May, Available at: http://mea.gov.in/bilateral-documents.htm?dtl/35/Second+AfricaIndia+Forum+Summit+2011+Addis+Ababa+Declaration.
Africa and India, 2011b. 'Africa–India Framework for Enhanced Cooperation', Second Africa–India Forum Summit 2011, Addis Ababa, Ethiopia, 25 May, Available at: http://summits.au.int/en/sites/default/files/Frameworkenhancedcoop%2021%20May%202011%20-%20clean-2_0.pdf.
Alden, C., 2009. *China in Africa*, London: Zed Books.
Alves, A. 2008. 'China's Lusophone Connection', *The South African Institute of International Affairs*, Volume 2, pp. 1–33.
Angola, 2015. ' Zona Económica Especial é referência', Embaixada da República de Angola em Portugal, Available at: www.embaixadadeangola.pt/zona-economica-especial-e-referencia/.

ANGOP (Agency Angola Press), 2012. 'Ambassador to South Korea satisfied with bilateral relations', 21 May, Available at: www.portalangop.co.ao/angola/en_us/noticias/politica/2012/4/21/Ambassador-South-Korea-satisfied-with-bilateral-relations,cf62db54-949a-45bc-b723-50fa0c36fd53.html.

ANGOP (Agency Angola Press), 2013. 'Palácio presidencial reconstruído e entregue pela China', 6 July, Available at: www.portalangop.co.ao/angola/pt_pt/noticias/africa/2013/6/27/Palacio-presidencial-reconstruido-entregue-pela-China,83b966b0-c062-4b49-89bb-439977c2eb9a.html.

Atanassova-Cornelis, E. and Mendes, C. A., 2010. 'Dynamics of Japanese and Chinese Security Policies in East Asia and Implications for Regional Stability', *Asian Politics & Policy*, Volume 2 (3), pp. 395–414.

AU (African Union), 2005. 'The Common African Position on the proposed reform of the United Nations: The Ezulwini Consensus', Executive Council – 7th Extraordinary Session, Addis Ababa, Ethiopia, 7–8 March, Available at: www.centerforunreform.org/sites/default/files/Ezulwini%20Consensus.pdf.

Brautigam, D., 2009. *The Dragon's Gift: The Real Story of China in Africa*, Oxford: Oxford University Press.

Brautigam, D., 2011. 'Aid "With Chinese Characteristics": Chinese Foreign Aid and Development Finance Meet the OECD-DAC Aid Regime', *Journal of International Development*, Volume 23 (5), pp. 1–13.

Brautigam, D. and Tang X., 2011. 'African Shenzhen: China's Special Economic Zones in Africa', *Journal of Modern African Studies*, Volume 49 (1), pp. 27–54.

Carmody, P., 2013. *The Rise of the BRICS in Africa: The Geopolitics of South–South Relations*, London: Zed Books.

Castillejo, C. and Hackenesch, C., 2014. 'The EU and its Partners on Development: How Strategic on the Ground?' *Policy Brief* 13, European Strategic Partnerships Observatory (ESPO), FRIDE, Available at: http://fride.org/download/PB13_The_EU_and_its_partners_on_development.pdf.

CGD (Caixa Geral de Depósitos), 2014. 'São Tomé e Príncipe: oportunidades e potencial de desenvolvimento', Internacionalização das Economias, Lisbon, 3 and 4 June, Available at: https://www.cgd.pt/Empresas/Negocio-Internacional/Apoios-Caixa-Empresas-no-Mundo/Sao-Tome-Principe/Documents/Estudo-CGD.PDF.

Chatuverdi, S., Fues, T. and Sidiropoulos, S. (eds.), 2012. *Development Cooperation and Emerging Powers*, London: Zed Books.

Cheru, F. and Obi, C. (eds.), 2010. *The Rise of China & India in Africa*, London: Zed Books.

Chichava, S. et al., 2013. 'Chinese and Brazilian Cooperation with African Agriculture: The Case of Mozambique', Working Paper 49, China and Brazil in African Agriculture Project Working Paper Series, Futures Agricultures Consortium, Available at: www.future-agricultures.org/publications/research-and-analysis/working-papers/1637-chinese-and-brazilian-cooperation-with-african-agriculture-the-case-of-mozambique/file.

Classen, S. F., 2013. 'Analysis of the Discourse and Background of the ProSAVANA Programme in Mozambique – Focusing on Japan's Role', Tokyo, January 20, Available at: www.open.ac.uk/technology/mozambique/sites/www.open.ac.uk.technology.mozambique/files/files/ProSavana%20Analysis%20based%20on%20Japanese%20source%20(FUNADA2013).pdf.

Classen, S.F., Watanabe, N. and Akimoto Y., 2014. 'ProSAVANA Civil Society Report 2013: Findings and Recommendations – English Summary', 10 April, Available at: www.ajf.gr.jp/lang_ja/ProSAVANA/9kai_shiryo/ref7.pdf.

CPLP (Comunidade dos Países de Língua Portuguesa), 2015. 'Observadores Associados', Available at: www.cplp.org/id-2765.aspx.

Darracq, V. and Neville, D., 2014. 'South Korea's Engagement in Sub-Saharan Africa: Fortune, Fuel and Frontier Markets', Research Paper, Africa Programme, Chatham House, The Royal Institute of International Affairs, October, Available at: www.chathamhouse.org/sites/files/chathamhouse/field/field_document/20141021DarracqNeville.pdf.

Eggen, O. and Roland, K., 2014. *Western Aid at a Crossroads: The End of Paternalism*, New York: Palgrave Pivot.

FOCAC, 2009. Forum on China–Africa Cooperation, 'Sharm El Sheikh Action Plan (2010–2012)', Available at: www.focac.org/eng/dsjbzjhy/hywj/t626387.htm.

Gabriel, J. and Lagerkvist, J., 2011. *Foreign Aid, Trade and Development: The Strategic Presence of China, Japan, and Korea in sub-Saharan Africa*, Stockholm: Utrikespolitiska Institutet.

Hendler, B., 2014. 'Zonas Econômicas Especiais Made in China: Do modelo de exportações à exportação do modelo, por Bruno Hendler', *Boletim Mundorama*, 9 January, Available at: http://mundorama.net/2014/01/09/zonas-economicas-especiais-made-in-china-do-modelo-de-exportacoes-a-exportacao-do-modelo-por-bruno-hendler/.

Horta, M. L., 2008. 'China in Cape Verde: The Dragon's African Paradise', Center for Strategic and International Studies, 2 January, Available at: http://csis.org/publication/china-cape-verde-dragons-african-paradise.

Horta, M. L., 2010. 'Guinea-Bissau: China sees a risk worth taking', Center for Strategic and International Studies, Available at: http://csis.org/print/13863.

Horta, M. L., 2012. 'China's relations with the Portuguese-speaking countries: a growing but unnoticed relation', Master Thesis, Naval Postgraduate School, Monterey, California, September, Available at: http://calhoun.nps.edu/bitstream/handle/10945/17351/12Sep_Da_Silva_Horta_Maubere.pdf?sequence=1.

IDSA (Institute for Defence Studies and Analyses), 2008. 'Delhi Declaration India–Africa Forum Summit', New Delhi, India, 9 April, Available at: www.idsa.in/resources/documents/India–AfricaForum-Summit 2008.html.

Ilhéu, F., 2011. 'The Role of China in the Portuguese Speaking African Countries: The Case of Mozambique (Part II)', *Economia Global e Gestão*, Volume 16 (1), pp. 41–59.

India, 2013a. 'India–Guinea Bissau Relations', Ministry of External Affairs, July, Available at: www.mea.gov.in/Portal/ForeignRelation/Guinea_Bissau_July_2014.pdf.

India, 2013b. 'India–Mozambique Relations', Ministry of External Affairs, December, Available at: www.mea.gov.in/Portal/ForeignRelation/Mozambique.pdf.

India, 2013c. 'India–Angola Relations', Ministry of External Affairs, July, Available at: http://mea.gov.in/Portal/ForeignRelation/India-Angola_Relations.pdf.

India, 2014a. 'India–Sao Tome & Principe Relations', Ministry of External Affairs, August, Available at: www.mea.gov.in/Portal/ForeignRelation/Sao_Tome___Principe_Aug_2014_.pdf.

India, 2014b. 'Aid/Assistance/Cooperation', High Comission of India in Maputo, Available at: http://www.hicomind-maputo.org/maputo.php?id=Aid%20Assistance%20Cooperation.

India, 2014c. 'Bilateral trade relations', High Comission of India in Maputo, Available at: http://www.hicomind-maputo.org/maputo.php?id=Bilateral%20trade%20relations.

India and Mozambique, 2009. 'Agreement between the Government of the Republic of India and the Republic of Mozambique for the Reciprocal Promotion and Protection of Investments', New Delhi, India, 19 February, Available at: http://www.hicomind-maputo.org/docs/BIPA%20 FINAL.pdf.

Jackson, T., 2012. 'Mozambique Accelerates Cooperation with South Korea', *Ventures*, 12 July, Available at: www.ventures-africa.com/2012/07/mozambique-accelerates-cooperation-with-south-korea/.

Japan, 2010. 'Exchange of Notes for Grant Aid (Food Aid) for the Democratic Republic of Sao Tome and Principe', Ministry of Foreign Affairs, 15 January, Available at: www.mofa.go.jp/announce/announce/2010/1/0115_01.html.

Japan, 2011. 'Agreement in Principle on the Investment Agreement between Japan and the Republic of Angola', Ministry of Foreign Affairs, 21 February, Available at: http://www.mofa.go.jp/announce/announce/2011/2/0221_01.html.

Japan, 2013a. 'The Fifth Tokyo International Conference on African Development: Hand in Hand with a More Dynamic Africa', Embassy of Japan in the Republic of Rwanda, Available at: www.rw.emb-japan.go.jp/TICAD%20pub.pdf.

Japan, 2013b. 'Sub-Saharan Africa is the Hot Investment Region Now!', *METI Journal*, Ministry of Economy, Trade and Industry, September, Available at: www.meti.go.jp/english/publications/pdf/journal2013_08c.pdf.

Japan, 2013c. 'Meeting between Japanese Foreign Minister and Minister of External Relations of the Republic of Angola', Ministry of Foreign Affairs, 2 June, Available at: www.mofa.go.jp/region/page6e_000041.html.

Japan, 2014. 'What is TICAD?', Ministry of Foreign Affairs, Available at: www.mofa.go.jp/region/africa/ticad/what.html.

JICA (Japan International Cooperation Agency), 2013. 'Signing of Japanese ODA Loan Agreement with the Republic of Cape Verde – Using Japanese Technology to Improve Access to Safe Drinking Water', 24 December, Available at: www.jica.go.jp/english/news/press/2013/20131224_02.html.

Kiala, C. and Ngwenya, N., 2011. 'Angola's Strategic Co-operation with the BRIC Countries', occasional paper no. 85, South African Foreign Policy and African Drivers Programme, South African Institute of International Affairs, May, Available at: www.saiia.org.za/images/stories/pubs/occasional_papers/saia_sop_85_kiala_ngwenya_20110531.pdf.

Kim, Y., 2012. 'Korea's Approach for Africa's Inclusive Growth: KOAFEC', Centre for Chinese Studies, Stellenbosch University, 10 December. Available at: www.ccs.org.za/wp-content/uploads/2012/12/YK-Korea-Africa.pdf.

KOICA (Korea International Cooperation Agency), 2008. Government of South Korea, Available at: www.koica.go.kr/english/koica/mission_vision/index.html.

Lagerkvist, J. and Jonsson, G., 2011. "Foreign Aid, Trade and Development – The Strategic Presence of China, Japan and Korea in sub-Saharan Africa", Occasional Paper, 5, The Swedish Institute of International Affairs, Available at: www.diva-portal.org/smash/get/diva2:482353/FULLTEXT01.pdf.

Lehman, H., 2005. 'Japan's Foreign Aid Policy to Africa since the Tokyo International Conference on African Development', *Pacific Affairs*, Volume 78(3), pp. 423–442.

Lehman, H., 2013. 'Trade not Aid behind Japan's Policy to Africa', *East Asia Forum*, 27 July, Available at: www.eastasiaforum.org/2013/07/27/trade-not-aid-behind-japans-policy-to-africa/.

Li Anshan et al., 2012. 'FOCAC Twelve Years Later: Achievements, Challenges and the Way Forward', Discussion Paper 74, School of International Studies, Peking University, Available at: http://www.safpi.org/sites/default/files/publications/FOCAC74.pdf.

Lingebiel, S., 2014. *Development Cooperation: Challenges of the New Aid Architecture*, New York: Palgrave Macmillan.

Lopes, H., 2013. 'Sucessos e incertezas: o papel da ajuda médica nas relações entre Taiwan e São Tomé e Príncipe', *Relações Internacionais*, Volume 37, pp. 99–113.

Lusa (Portugal News Agency), 2014. 'Moçambique e Índia assinam acordo petrolífero', *Público*, 28 November.

Macauhub, 2013a. 'Building on Ambition – China Helps Build Cape Verde after Independence', 13 December, Available at: www.macauhub.com.mo/en/2013/12/13/building-on-ambition-china-helps-build-cape-verde-after-independence/.

Macauhub, 2013b. 'Coreia do Sul abre escritório de promoção comercial na capital de Moçambique', 25 November, Available at: http://www.macauhub.com.mo/pt/2013/11/25/coreia-do-sul-abre-escritorio-de-promocao-comercial-na-capital-de-mocambique/.

Macauhub, 2014a. 'Taiwan's aid to São Tome and Principe totals US$ 15 million in 2014', 8 April, Available at: http://www.macauhub.com.mo/en/2014/04/08/taiwan%E2%80%99s-aid-to-sao-tome-and-principe-totals-us15-million-in-2014/.

Macauhub, 2014b. 'China Builds Main Courthouse in Guinea-Bissau', 31 October, Available at: www.macauhub.com.mo/en/2014/10/31/china-builds-main-courthouse-in-guinea-bissau/.

Macauhub, 2014c. 'Japão financia construção de porto de pesca em São Tomé e Príncipe', 3 March, Available at: http://www.macauhub.com.mo/pt/2014/03/03/japao-financia-construcao-de-porto-de-pesca-em-sao-tome-e-principe/.

Macauhub, 2014d. 'Indian Consortium Receives First Shipment of Coal from Mozambique', 19 November, Available at: www.macauhub.com.mo/en/2014/11/19/indian-consortium-receives-first-shipment-of-coal-from-mozambique/.

Macauhub, 2014e. 'South Korea Funds Training in Natural Gas for Staff from Mozambique', 14 October, Available at: www.macauhub.com.mo/en/2014/10/14/south-korea-funds-training-in-natural-gas-for-staff-from-mozambique/.

Macauhub, 2015a. 'Moçambique com condições para adoptar modelo chinês das Zonas Económicas Especiais', 9 February, Available at: www.macauhub.com.mo/pt/2015/02/09/mocambique-com-condicoes-para-adoptar-modelo-chines-das-zonas-economicas-especiais/.

Macauhub, 2015b. 'Japan Funds Construction of Electrical Substation in Mozambique', 21 January, Available at: www.macauhub.com.mo/pt/2015/01/21/japao-paga-construcao-de-subestacao-electrica-em-mocambique/.

Mangala, J. (ed.), 2010. *Africa and the New World Era: From Humanitarianism to a Strategic View*, New York: Palgrave Macmillan.

Mendes, C. A., 2013a. 'Portuguese-Speaking Countries: A Niche for Indian Foreign Policy', *Extraordinary and Plenipotentiary Diplomatist*, special supplement, June, 74–75, Available at: http://www.diplomatist.com/specialreport/Portugal.htm.

Mendes, C. A. (coord.), 2013b. 'Special Number on "China in South America: Argentina, Brazil and Venezuela"', *East Asia – An International Quarterly*, Volume 30 (1), pp. 1–65.

Mendes, C. A., 2014. 'Macau in China's Relations with the Lusophone World', *Revista Brasileira de Política Internacional*, special issue on China, September, Volume 57, pp. 225–242, Available at: www.scielo.br/scielo.php?script=sci_arttext&pid=S0034-73292014000300225&lng=en&nrm=iso.

Nguema, R. and Doland, A., 2007. 'China Pays for Parliament, Promises Military Hospital', *saukvalley*, Available at: www.saukvalley.com/articles/2007/01/05/news/national/81157467603168.txt.

Osei-Hwedie, Bertha Z., 2015. "China–Japan Rivalry in Africa", in E. Shiza and L. Diallo (eds.), *Africa in the Age of Globalization: Perceptions, Misperceptions and Realities*, London: Ashgate.

Panapress, 2007. 'China anuncia zona económica especial em Cabo Verde', 21 October, Available at: www.panapress.com/China-anuncia-zona-economica-especial-em-Cabo-Verde--3-423324-45-lang4-index.html.

Panapress, 2014. 'Coreia do Sul constrói aterros sanitários em Moçambique', 26 May, Available at: www.panapress.com/Coreia-do-Sul-constroi-aterros-sanitarios-em-Mocambique--3-912619-41-lang4-index.html.

Pföstl, E. (ed.), 2008. *Human Rights and Asian Values*, Rome: Editrice Apes.

PRC – People's Republic of China (2006) 'FOCAC Beijing Summit – African Member States: Guinea-Bissau', *China Internet Information Center,* Chinese Foreign Ministry, 10 October, Available at: www.china.org.cn/english/features/focac/183519.htm.

Raposo, P. A. and Potter, D. M., 2010. 'Chinese and Japanese Development Co-operation: South–South, North–South, or What?' *Journal of Contemporary African Studies*, Volume 28 (2), pp. 177–202.

Raposo, P. A., 2011. 'Japan's Foreign Aid Policy to Angola and Mozambique', *Politikon*, Volume 38 (2), pp. 315–342.

Raposo, P. A., 2014a. *Japan's Foreign Aid to Africa: Angola and Mozambique Within the TICAD Process*, London: Routledge.

Raposo, P. A., 2014b. *Japan's Foreign Aid Policy in Africa: Evaluating the TICAD Process*, New York: Palgrave Macmillan.

Raposo, P. A., 2015. 'China's and Japan's Foreign Aid Policies vis-à-vis Lusophone Africa', *Africa Spectrum*, Volume 50 (3), pp. 49–79.

Roehrig, T., 2013. 'South Korean foreign aid: contributing to international security', *The Strategist: The Australian Strategic Policy Institute Blog*, 24 October, Available at: www.aspistrategist.org.au/south-korean-foreign-aid-contributing-to-international-security/.

Rotberg, R. I., 2013. 'China and São Tomé', *China US Focus*, 20 November, Available at: www.chinausfocus.com/foreign-policy/china-and-sao-tome/.

Sampaio, M., 2014. 'Guiné-Bissau e União Europeia normalizam as relações', *Deutsche Welle*, 16 July, Available at: www.dw.de/guin%C3%A9-bissau-e-uni%C3%A3o-europeia-normalizam-as-rela%C3%A7%C3%B5es/a-17790732.

Seabra, P., 2011. 'Japan and Lusophone Africa: Tepid Outcomes, Greater Opportunities', *Portuguese Journal of International Affairs (IPRIS)*, Available at: http://www.ipris.org/?menu=6&page=38.

Shih H., 2013. 'China Opens Trade Office in Sao Tome', *Taipei Times*, 15 November, Available at: www.taipeitimes.com/News/front/print/2013/11/15/2003576896.

Shih, H., 2014. 'São Tome Leader's China Visit not Political: MOFA', *Taipei Times*, 8 June, Available at: www.taipeitimes.com/News/taiwan/print/2014/06/08/2003592266.

Shimomura, Y. and Hideo, O. (eds.), 2013. *A Study of China's Foreign Aid: An Asian Perspective*, New York: Palgrave Macmillan.

Shinn, D. and Eisenman, J., 2012. *China and Africa: A Century of Engagement*, Philadelphia: University of Pennsylvania Press.

South Korea, 2009. 'Seoul Declaration of the Second Korea–Africa Forum', 24 November, Available at: http://forum.mofa.go.kr/koafec_uploads/2nd/Seoul%20Declaration%20of%20the%20Second%20Korea-Africa%20Forum%20(2009)(final).pdf.

STP and EU (Sao Tome and Principe and European Union), 2014. 'Programme indicatif national pour la période 2014–2020', Nairobi, 19 June, Available at: http://eeas.europa.eu/development-cooperation/docs/national-indicative-programme_2014-2020/2014-2020_national-indicative-programme_saotome-et-principe_fr.pdf.

Stratfor Global Intelligence, 2014. 'Japan Increases Its Investments in Africa', 17 February, Available at: https://www.stratfor.com/sample/analysis/japan-increases-its-investments-africa.

Taylor, I., 2009. *China's New Role in Africa*, Boulder: Lynne Rienner.

Taylor, I., 2011. *The Forum on China–Africa Cooperation (FOCAC)*, London: Routledge.

Taylor, I. and Williams, P. (eds.), 2004. *Africa in International Politics: External Involvement on the Continent*, London: Routledge.

The China Post, 2013. 'Premier Jiang Hails Staunch Taiwan–São Tome relations', 19 November, Available at: www.chinapost.com.tw/taiwan/foreign-affairs/2013/11/19/394006/Premier-Jiang.htm.

TICAD (Tokyo International Conference on African Development), 2011. 'Africa–Japan (TICAD) Process', African Union, Available at: http://pages.au.int/ticad.

UN (United Nations), 2008. 'Japan Summit Promotes "Vibrant Africa"', *Africa Renewal*, United Nations Department of Public Information, July, Available at: http://www.un.org/africarenewal/magazine/july-2008/japan-summit-promotes-%E2%80%98vibrant-africa%E2%80%99#sthash.jZVa5tjW.dpuf.

UNCTAD, 2010. *Economic Development in Africa Report 2010: South–South Cooperation: Africa and New Forms of Development Partnership*, Available at: http://unctad.org/en/Docs/aldcafrica2010_en.pdf.

Working Paper, 2009. Working Papers on South–South Cooperation, Argentina: Ministry of Foreign Affairs, International Trade and Worship, Available at: http://cooperacionarg.gob.ar/userfiles/1_w.p._working_papers_on_south_south_cooperation.pdf.

22
AFRICA–ASIA REGIONAL PARTNERSHIPS AND SOUTH–SOUTH DEVELOPMENT COOPERATION

Annette Skovsted Hansen

Introduction

Interactions between the African and Asian continents from the 1990s have increasingly taken place without the intermediation of Europe and North America. Although still partly defined by or framed as a reaction to European and North American interactions with African and Asian countries, the current linkages between Africa and Asia such as those related to development cooperation form an alternative to development cooperation efforts initiated by European or North American countries. Furthermore, the African and Asian stakeholders have defined South–South cooperation to encompass many other aspects of cooperation than development.

In an attempt to answer the question of how Africa–Asia regional partnerships and South–South development cooperation (SSDC) have influenced each other in shaping South–South cooperation (SSC) since the turn of the millennium, this chapter identifies two shifts. Firstly, the New Partnership for African Development (NEPAD) from 2001 outlined an explicitly common African development agenda, in which African countries take more responsibility for their own development and, thereby, ensure their own ability to manage external partners. In 2005, the first Summit of the New Asia–Africa Strategic Partnership (NAASP) explicitly referred to the NEPAD framework. The second shift came ten years later at the second NAASP Summit in 2015, when a general climate of reconsidering the aid paradigm contributed to a move away from a development to a public–private partnership focus.

The trend favoring private sector involvement and responsibility in, for example, the aid-to-trade modality adopted by the UN system is similar to Japan's aid scheme since its inception in the 1950s. Asian partners have long officially involved private sector stakeholders in their partnerships with various African partners. In February 2015, the Japanese government explicitly emphasized the role of Japanese companies in its New Development Cooperation Charter. Many other Northern partners have followed suit, for example the Netherlands, the United Kingdom, Sweden, and Denmark (Japan's Ministry of Foreign Affairs, 2015: 13; Danish Ministry of Foreign Affairs, 2016). By analyzing the documents of NEPAD and NAASP in their contemporary historical context, this chapter illustrates how they signal attempts at, and the limitations of, cooperation in a climate of competition among partners from the same and different regions.

Defining Africa and Asia requires an eye to the pluralism within these continents that are both composed of many countries or areas, with different histories and geographic and political conditions. Defining Africa and Asia as the continents by these names also obfuscates the region they share between them, the Middle East. The 'South' includes many African and Asian countries; however, the connotations or implications of this term are very diverse depending on the criteria applied. 'South' could be a geographic and relative term as south of some countries, but of what countries? Or as the southern hemisphere, which would be clearer, but would leave out a number of countries that would fit in the category, if we used other criteria. South could be continents such as South America, Africa, and Asia, but in the context of development, economic and social criteria would seem more relevant than geography. There also seems to be quite a lot of overlap between the Cold War terms, Third World and the South.

If applying dissemination or distribution of foreign aid as criteria, the question of whether receipt or distribution is more significant arises, because many countries still receive aid after embarking on their own distribution of aid schemes. For example, Japan until 1964 was the largest recipient of World Bank loans (Fujikura & Nakayama, 2016:44) and provided aid to South Korea until 1995, to China till 2008, and increased aid to India after 2007 (Jain, 2016: 64–66). Should we include the countries that still receive some aid even if they also 'give' aid or countries that at some point in time received foreign aid? Depending on how we answer these questions, South–South cooperation carries different meanings. In this chapter, which deals specifically with development cooperation, South includes all current recipients of development aid including official development assistance (ODA).

The main findings of this chapter are that:

1   The new millennium has already brought significant changes in South–South cooperation, as seen in new intra- and interregional partnerships and agreements.
2   The New Asia–Africa Strategic Partnership (NAASP) as an overarching interregional organization has by 2015 largely left South–South development cooperation to bilateral partnerships.
3   The future will most likely see an increase in cross-regional economic, social, and technical cooperation defined not as North–South or even South–South development cooperation partnerships, but based on identification of specific mutual interests at a particular time.

For the time being, private sector involvement and responsibilities in, for example, public–private partnerships (PPP) appear to be a strong mutual interest inspired by competition and requiring alliances for cooperation (Bandung Message, 2015:7)

Literature review

South–South cooperation (SSC) and South–South development cooperation (SSDC) have attracted the attention of practitioners as well as researchers within the field of development. The research literature focuses on how South–South development cooperation differs from the principles of the Development Assistance Committee (DAC) under the Organization for Economic Cooperation and Development (OECD) and reflects the interests of so-called emerging donors (Kragelund, 2011). Much of the literature on emerging donors is not regional, but rather on the heterogeneity of the Asian donors – China, India, and Japan (Hyo-sook & Potter, 2012). Many describe Chinese aid to Africa as overwhelming and detached from local communities (Aguilar & Goldstein, 2009). The work on India in Africa focuses on capacity development – exemplified also by India's full membership in the Africa Capacity Building Foundation (ACBF) in 2005 – and India's needs, and describes Indians as newcomers to Africa (Fuchs & Vadlamannati, 2013; Taylor, 2012:786; Tilak, 2014). Paradoxically, the Indian presence has been the most dominant Asian presence in East Africa with legacies of several thousand years of Indian Ocean interactions apparent in the current countries of Kenya and Tanzania, for example. Japan's Official Development Assistance has a 60-year-long history, which has been the topic of many books and articles (Orr, 1990; Islam, 1991; Arase, 1995, 2005). A few recent works also cover Japanese foreign aid to African countries, specifically Raposo (2014).

The larger emerging Asian partners are typically referred to as 'donors,' whereas the South–South development cooperation nomenclature emphasizes the equality, solidarity, support, and mutual benefit of all partners involved and avoids labeling different actors and countries as either 'donor' or 'recipient' (Mawdsley, 2012). Recent research articles on South–South development cooperation include studies on Latin America and, specifically, on Brazilian cooperation in Lusophone Africa and Turkey in Sub-Saharan Africa (Apaydin, 2012; Bry, 2016; Roblelo, 2015). Many of the overarching themes are relevant also for Africa–Asia development cooperation and researchers have dealt with them in broader comparisons (for example, Kragelund, 2011). Even in comparative work, however, focus is often on the larger Asian stakeholders such as Japan, China, and India, but countries such as Indonesia, Malaysia, Singapore, South Korea, Thailand, and Vietnam have also entered into various development cooperation relations with African countries (DFC Republic of Korea, 2015).

In the 1980s, political scientists, anthropologists, and economists analyzed the development of South–South relations. The interest among development researchers in the 1970s of analyzing the increased South–South cooperation was limited. However, the PhD thesis by political scientist Jørgen Dige Pedersen compared Brazilian and Indian relations with those of other countries in the South, specifically in terms of questioning international relations and development theories of the time. In his statistics, the Sub-Saharan focus was negligible compared with North Africa, the Middle East, and Asia. However, Brazilian engineering and consultancy projects abroad, besides Mozambique, also went to Nigeria and Algeria (Pedersen, 1988:407). The geographic distribution of building and construction contracts, established by Indian companies abroad until 1982, was highest in Iraq with 53 per cent of the total, followed by about half that amount to Libya. Only two other African countries appeared on the list: Algeria and Tanzania (Pedersen, 1988:227). The limited number of African countries receiving aid in the form of capital flows and/or technical assistance from Brazil and India in the 1980s reflected Brazil's and India's limited surplus to engage overseas at the time. More significantly, even as late as the 1980s the persistent and exclusive dominance of the former colonizers in Anglophone and Francophone Africa, respectively, contributed to the coining of the term neo-colonialism.

Language and culture have played a role in the sense that old colonial or slave trade and other trade relations dating back millennia mattered, or coincided with the choices of partner countries in Sub-Saharan Africa. Peter Kragelund's analysis from 2011, for example, still identifies colonial languages and culture as determinants for what South–South relations are established. Therefore, patterns of relations within Anglophone, Francophone, and Lusophone Africa, respectively, dominate, even though exceptions occur. I would also add that familiarity with colonial languages and culture, as well as the personal connections and administrative institutions and structures built on similar principles, have facilitated the preferences for partners from the same colonial empire.

Many of the reports and articles written during the first ten years of the new millennium on non-DAC stakeholders in development cooperation seemed to be based on an assumption that competition from non-members of the OECD/DAC would compromise aid objectives as defined by DAC since its inception in 1961 (Davies, 2008; Mawdsley. 2014). The focus on different national interests among the Southern partners outside of Africa reflects the competitive rather than cooperative dimension of South–South cooperation. This is indicative of the important fact that the South is not a coherent or monolithic entity, just as neither Africa nor Asia is.

What is new in the new millennium?

The new intra- and interregional organizations and partnerships show different degrees of competition and cooperation in Africa and Asia, respectively. The New African Initiative outlined an African attempt at defining the common interests of the continent in integrating foreign aid relationships into a complex picture of priorities. Thereby, African countries took the lead in the first part of the millennium with representatives of the South taking responsibility and ownership in defining, not only South–South as well as North–South development cooperation, but also broader South–South cooperation.

South–South cooperation (SSC) has long been on the agenda of multilateral organizations such as the UN and the Development Assistance Committee under the Organization for Economic Cooperation and Development (OECD/DAC). For decades, OECD/DAC members have encouraged South–South development cooperation, but have increasingly criticized the form it has taken. Often, they have directed their critique at Chinese aid. The timing of the critique coincided with the increased volume and popularity of non-DAC partners in development cooperation from 2000. South–South cooperation gained more attention in the new millennium with the first ever Summit of the South in Havana (Cuba), in April 2000 within the G77 (now G77 plus China), to discuss the challenges related to globalization and development (G77, 2000). The third High-Level Forum on Aid Effectiveness (HLF) in 2008, in Accra, Ghana, presented an explicit call to (all donors) to accept South–South cooperation as a suitable approach to development (World Bank, 2008). In April 2013, the Conference of Southern Providers met in New Delhi to discuss 'South–South Cooperation: Issues and Emerging Challenges.' The conference participants emphasized how this was the first self-supported dialogue on development in decades.

The issue of self-reliance was central to the understanding of South–South cooperation at the conference in New Delhi, where participants defined it as a policy of self-reliance that 'rests on strengthening autonomous capacity for goal-setting, decision-making and national implementation.' They argued that North–South cooperation 'is seen as a historical responsibility,' whereas South–South cooperation 'should be viewed as a voluntary partnership' (Conference of Southern Providers, 2014: 2). The reference to historical responsibility diminishes African responsibility, whereas they combine voluntary partnerships with the idea of self-reliance. This understanding has brought them to the following definition of modalities for South–South cooperation (SSC):

> The modalities for SSC have taken different and evolving forms, which include capacity building, training, technology transfer and financial assistance. SSC has evolved in such a way that it is multifaceted engagement covering different areas, such as trade, investment, S&T cooperation, SMEs, trade facilitation, etc., with the potential to foster regional integration, which is a steppingstone for global integration.
>
> *(Conference of Southern Providers, 2014: 3)*

The goal is the global integration of the diversity of the South and the way is demand-driven capacity building within the entrepreneurial and private sector.

The United Nations system – including the Economic and Social Council, one of the six main organs of the UN, and United Nations Development Program (UNDP), the UN program for development cooperation established in 1966, with the largest budget of any UN program – is involved in the definitions and practices of South–South cooperation. In 2014, the Economic and Social Council sponsored a report by the Secretary-General titled *Trends and Progress in International Development Cooperation*. In the report, one suggestion, among many, was the need for more exchanging of information on best practices of development in different countries in the South (Economic and Social Council, 2014: 13). On a practical level, UNDP was involved when, in September 2014, Techonet Asia contacted Sarath Buddhadasa from Sri Lanka, an external consultant in Singapore. UNDP asked him to conduct a three-week, and subsequent two-week, follow-up training workshop for 300 trainers of entrepreneurs in five African countries: Cameroon, Ghana, Mozambique, South Africa, and Tanzania, under the South–South cooperation scheme of the UNDP office based in Johannesburg, South Africa. This is just one concrete example of the various multilateral organizations involved in engaging individuals in South–South development cooperation (Esteves & Assunção, 2016; Buddhadasa, 2014, 2015).

In the report from the Conference of Southern Providers, reference was made to multilateral organizations as knowledge brokers – rather than knowledge providers – and regional institutions as places for creating a multi-level approach for coordinating the views of all countries within the region (Conference of Southern Providers, 2013:5–6). In spite of much divergence on the African continent, the Organization of African Unity (OAU) provided a platform for negotiating common interests in African cooperation: integrated infrastructure; common export standards; and more local food processing. The conference participants also saw cooperation as a way to manage donors and other external partners, and to get them to respond to the African agenda and not simply drive through their own agendas. Increased African coordination and cooperation has inspired more South–South cooperation, because it has shown the benefits of cooperation rather than the divergence and competition seen among Asian countries – not least the largest economies: China, India, and Japan. The competition between those three countries is a legacy of thousands of years of competition over leadership in Asia, where both India and Japan have consistently objected to subordinating themselves to the Chinese world order.

The interregional cooperation as exemplified in the New Asian–African Strategic Partnership (NAASP) of 2005, to follow up on the Bandung conference of 1955, is based on agreed common threats to African and Asian countries and a common interest in countering these threats. The Bandung conference in 1955, the Organization of the Petroleum Exporting Countries (OPEC) from 1960, the non-aligned movement from 1961, the Group of 77 from 1964, and many other institutions and initiatives of South–South cooperation were already in place, but building on these networks, experiences and new initiatives took shape within the first five years of the new millennium.

Regional organizations work to coordinate interests within a region, and as such, are responses to competition between nations within a region. Some perceive this competition as undesired and unproductive, where cooperation might ensure better outcomes for members. The new millennium is seeing an increase in South–South cooperation; however, earlier attempts can be seen in the Group of 77 established in 1964 at a meeting of United Nations Conference on Trade and Development (UNCTAD) with the stated aim:

> The Group of 77 is the largest intergovernmental organization of developing countries in the United Nations, which provides the means for the countries of the South to articulate and promote their collective economic interests and enhance their joint

negotiating capacity on all major international economic issues within the United Nations system, and promote South–South cooperation for development.

(Group of 77, 1964)

The G77 had many of the same members as the non-aligned movement founded in Belgrade in 1961, as a bloc of countries not formally aligned with or against either the USA or the Soviet Union during the Cold War. Other member states of the United Nations saw the G77 group as an example of South–South political cooperation that had misunderstood the intentions for how South–South cooperation could benefit the South and the North, because the cooperation at times benefited the South to the detriment of the North.

Asian countries have approached development cooperation in different ways. In 1964, Japan joined the Development Assistance Committee under the Organization for Economic Cooperation and Development (OECD/DAC). In 1993, Japan was the first Asian country to organize a conference to define an Africa strategy, the first so-called Tokyo International Conference on African Development (TICAD) under the auspices of the United Nations. More TICAD conferences have followed. Both China and India, as two other strong economies and players in Asia, have chosen not to become DAC members and have launched their own Africa initiatives. Forum on China–Africa Cooperation (FOCAC) held its first summit in Beijing in 2000 and the first India–Africa Forum Summit took place in New Delhi in 2008. Countries such as South Korea, a DAC member since 2009, Malaysia, Indonesia, Singapore, Thailand, and Vietnam have established bilateral activities in various African countries. These conferences and forums are examples of inter-Asian competition, each wanting their share of influence on the African continent.

An African perspective allows for the impression of increasing intra-Africa cooperation in countering or welcoming the approaches from individual countries and regional organizations in other parts of the South. Many stakeholders in African countries can see an advantage in the lack of cooperation in the other regions and the approaches from individual partners, which gives them more room for 'donor management' as defined in *Aid Relationships in Asia* (Jerve et al., 2008:5–16). At times, some of the 'outsiders' appear overwhelming and here a concerted African front can be seen by individual African countries as beneficial even though they also compete over the most generous and lucrative offers.

Recently, African countries seem more adept than the Asian countries at coordinating their agendas in spite of significant differences. The African Union (AU), the Organization of African States (OAS), and the African Development Bank (AfDB) define their common interest in order to guide the involvement of partners from outside the African continent. African countries reach out to Asian cooperation partners in various spheres of economic, cultural, and social exchange. The new millennium offers new options in aid modalities including aid-to-trade and new strong development partners such as Thailand, Malaysia, Vietnam, South Korea, and Singapore. A matrix of cooperation and competition within and between the two regions, Africa and Asia, shows a new and concerted effort of the African countries to cooperate across the continent. The Organization of African Unity approved *A New African Initiative: Merger of the Millennium Partnership for the African Recovery Programme (MAP) and Omega Plan* on July 11, 2001, which encouraged intra-regional cooperation. This New African Initiative (NAI) mirrored acknowledgement of the potential and mutual need for intra-African cooperation.

The opening statement of the approved initiative reads:

This new African initiative is a pledge by African leaders, based on a common vision and a firm and shared conviction, that they have a pressing duty to eradicate poverty and to place their countries, both individually and collectively, on a path of sustainable growth and development, and at the same time to participate actively in the world economy and body politic. The Programme is anchored on the determination of Africans to extricate themselves and the continent from the malaise of underdevelopment and exclusion in a globalizing world.

(A New African Initiative, 2001:3)

The driving force of this argument is the ownership of the African continent and the willingness of Africa to take responsibility to change the role assigned to African countries in the global economy.

The causes of African countries suffering from 'the malaise of underdevelopment' and other countries generally excluding them from reaping the benefits of globalization are mentioned in articles 18–20 of the initiative:

18. The impoverishment of the African continent was accentuated primarily by the legacy of colonialism, the Cold War, the workings of the international economic system and the inadequacies of and shortcomings in the policies pursued by many countries in the post-independence era.

(A New African Initiative, 2001:5)

Here, the selection of post-independence policies highlights African agency, but the emphasis is on the history of African victimhood. The subsequent article further substantiates the argument:

19. For centuries, Africa has been integrated into the world economy mainly as a supplier of cheap labour and raw materials. Of necessity, this has meant the draining of Africa's resources rather than their use for the continent's development. The drive in that period to use the minerals and raw materials to develop manufacturing industries and a highly skilled human base to sustain growth and development was lost. Thus, Africa remains the poorest continent despite being one of the most richly endowed regions of the world.

(A New African Initiative 2001:5)

Essentially, the article presents a story of exploitation as the reason for the present predicament of the African continent.

Then follows an article on the possible solution to all the problems – the way other continents gained more influence and generated more wealth, historically, than Africa:

20. In other countries and on other continents, the direct opposite happened. There was an infusion of wealth in the form of investments, which created larger volumes of wealth through the export of value-added products. It is time that African resources are harnessed to expand wealth creation on the continent for the well-being of her peoples

(A New African Initiative 2001:5)

They identified the infusion of wealth with an industry of 'value-added' products for export which had come from foreign direct investments (FDI) as well as local affluent communities. The characteristics of many Asian partnerships that focus on FDI – and foreign aid of various kinds – seem particularly appropriate, because they typically prepare economic and social infrastructures that allow for securing investments. The section on priority sectors mentions infrastructure followed by information and communications technology, human development: health and education, culture, agriculture, diversification of production and exports, and market access (A New African Initiative, 2001:10–13).

Section 5 of the agreement is the Programme of Action, which lists objectives and actions under a long list of topics. Actions include training facilities, technology transfer, and agreements on standards for easy access and cooperation across borders within Africa, but also specifics on market access for African products beyond the African continent. For example, under the Infrastructure Initiative two of the actions are:

> With the assistance of sector-specialised agencies, put in place policy and legislative frameworks to encourage competition. At the same time, introduce new regulatory frameworks as well as build capacity for regulators, so as to promote policy and regulatory harmonization in order to facilitate cross-border connectivity and market enlargement; . . .
>
> Initiate the development of training institutions and networks, which can develop and produce high-skill technicians and engineers in all infrastructure sectors.
>
> *(A New African Initiative 2001:18)*

Here, the stakeholders emphasize the key importance of both common standards and human resource development.

The next section is titled 'Diversification of production and exports,' where 'Actions' are divided into 'On the African level' and 'On the international level,' which includes both African actors as well as stakeholders outside Africa. Among the international actions are research development and encouragement of 'access for African food and agricultural products, particularly processed products so as to meet the standards required by international markets,' and assistance 'in strengthening African training institutions for industrial development, particularly through the promotion of networking with international partners' (A New African Initiative, 2001:21, 23). The document identified overarching needs for collaboration and input from external partners as easily applied technology and capacity development for infrastructure integration and maintenance and for food processing to meet international standards.

Based on A New African Initiative (NAI) cited above, the 37th session of the Organization of African Unity (OAU) Assembly of African Heads of state and government adopted New Partnership for African Development (NEPAD), in July 2001 in Lusaka, Zambia. In 2002, the OAU became the African Union (AU) and, at its inaugural Summit, it endorsed the adoption of NEPAD as a program of the AU with a secretariat as implementation agency. In February 2010, the NEPAD secretariat became the NEPAD agency and the AU integrated it into the AU structures and processes. The NEPAD agency has four investment programs: skills and employment for youth; industrialization, science, technology, and innovation; regional integration, infrastructure, and trade; and natural resources governance and food security.

The NEPAD goals of regional integration, infrastructure, and trade program are 'The harmonization of regional and national policies on infrastructure, market development and trade, as well as improve regional infrastructure in ICT, transport, water and energy' (African Union homepage, 2016). The homepage of the AU opens with the introductory sentence on the entry page reading 'Towards a Peaceful, Prosperous & Integrated Africa,' followed by an icon-based menu with the first heading on top left 'Agenda 2063.' The guiding vision for Agenda 2063 is '[a]n integrated, prosperous and peaceful Africa, driven by its own citizens and representing a dynamic force in international arena' (Agenda 2063, 2016). The text recognizes the people of African countries as the drivers of change and establishes African countries as dynamic forces in international affairs.

Immediate reactions to NEPAD included an article by the economist Ravi Kanbur who focused on the poverty reduction dimension, yet almost left out aid partnerships, arguing that aid would be better dealt with by the African Development Bank (Kanbur, 2001:8, 10). However, the NEPAD secretariat can ensure a degree of contextualization and the implications of the shared and combined African agenda came to affect the African–Asian partnerships including those involving foreign aid. The mutual opposition to previous and continued dominance and practices of European and North American stakeholders in the two regions reflects a certain degree of anti-North sentiments of distrust based on experiences of colonization, neo-colonization, and failures such as the World Bank structural adjustment policies. Besides, African stakeholders often emphasize practical and concrete applicability and suitability of technology, circumstances, and contexts of Asian versus European and North American partners as reasons for choosing Asian partners. In the case of Japan, many African and Asian countries perceived it as a country that successfully stood up to, competed with, and matched the standards of European and North American countries since the late 1800s. Compared with European or US aid, countries in the South also focused on the ability of Japan to preserve and not compromise their cultural heritage in pursuit of the modern, the way Europeans were perceived to have abandoned their 'traditions.'

The new millennium has witnessed an intensification of African intra-regional cooperation within the African Union and representatives of the South increasingly define South–South cooperation through national, intra-regional, and interregional organizations and institutions.

New Asia–Africa Strategic Partnerships (NAASP)

Even though Asian countries seemed unable to reach an agreement on a common agenda, common interests and threats of all kinds requiring cooperation between Africa and Asia became the main drivers behind the increased coordination of African and Asian interests. One example of a common interregional agenda was the African and Asian under-representation in multilateral organizations and their various organs such as the Development Assistance Committee (DAC) of the Organization of Economic Cooperation and Development (OECD) and the Security Council of the United Nations. However, the African intra-regional cooperation may also have intrigued the Asian countries. The competition between the Asian countries became increasingly prominent and led to the shift in 2015, when the NAASP documents deleted South–South development as an interregional instrument.

In April 2005 at the commemoration of the Bandung conference of 1955, suggestions for interregional approaches to addressing diplomatic, environmental, economic, and other challenges formed the basis for the establishment of the New Asian–African Strategic Partnership (NAASP). A mutual interest in circumventing previous colonizers in colonial and neo-colonial terms as well as applicability of technology and ideas in local contexts inspired a wish for cooperation without European or North American mediation. Some countries perceive previous or continuous foreign aid recipient partners to be better models, because they have similar histories of dependence and offer technologies and solutions that are more appropriate and directly applicable to their own situation.

African leaders attempted intra-regional cooperation in the New Partnership for African Development (NEPAD) and the African Union and welcomed the alternatives to European and North American partnerships offered by Asian countries, not least because they enabled

African countries to manage partners rather than be managed by donors (Jerve et al., 2008). However, the Asian Development Bank (ADB) and the NAASP are two of the few examples of coordinating Asian efforts in the context of Asian–African partnerships. The NAASP declaration from the Asia–Africa Summit held in Jakarta April 22–23, 2005, stated that their leaders commit to align different initiatives to achieve coherence and avoid duplication. The NAASP is based on a ministerial statement of 2005, where 106 country members, 54 Asian and 52 African countries, identified three areas of cooperation: 1) political solidarity, for example in combatting racism, 2) economic cooperation, and 3) socio-cultural relations. Capacity development and training courses of various kinds constitute many of the core activities.

The declaration included several references to historical ties and cultural heritage. The historical ties may be trade and/or religious networks, political movements, or cultural exchanges. The link to the past appeared in the first paragraph of the *Declaration on the New Asian–African Strategic Partnership* signed on April 24, 2005:

> We, the Leaders of Asian and African countries, have gathered in Jakarta, Indonesia on 22–23 April 2005 for the Asian–African Summit to reinvigorate the Spirit of Bandung . . . and to chart the future cooperation between our two continents towards a New Asian–African Strategic Partnership.
>
> *(NAASP, Declaration on the New Asian–African Strategic Partnership, 2005:1)*

At the same time, the opening sentence pointed to the future.

Evidence of previous accomplishments support the conviction that the cooperation would achieve its objectives:

> We note with satisfaction that since the 1955 Conference, Asian and African countries have attained significant political advances. We have all successfully combated the scourge of colonialism and consistently fought racism. In particular, the abolishment of apartheid represents a milestone in Asian–African cooperation and we reaffirm our continued determination to eradicate racism and all forms of discrimination. As a result of our efforts over the last fifty years, we are all independent, sovereign and equal nations striving for the promotion of human rights, democracy, and the rule of law. However, having made these political gains, we are concerned that we have not yet attained commensurate progress in the social and economic spheres.
>
> *(Declaration on the New Asian–African Strategic Partnership, 2005:1)*

The *New African Initiative* (NAI) in many ways reflected the future focus on further or more significant progress in social and economic spheres.

The South–South development cooperation potential emphasizes the construction of stable and effective transport and information infrastructure, international standards as well as sustainable agricultural production as prerequisites for more foreign direct investments and export market shares.

> We acknowledge the New Partnership for Africa's Development (NEPAD) as the African Union's programme for poverty eradication, socio-economic development and growth and accept it as the framework for engagement with Africa. . . . We visualize an affluent Asian–African region characterized by equitable growth, sustainable development as well as a common determination to enhance the quality of life and well-being of our people.
>
> *(Declaration on the New Asian–African Strategic Partnership 2005:2)*

NEPAD is, explicitly, mentioned as giving the 'framework for engagement with Africa' to be respected by all external partners.

By 2015, Indonesia had offered and set up the Asian–African Center that ensured an institutional support base for the New Asia–Africa Strategic Partnership (NAASP) (Bandung Message, 2015:8). International changes and debates had inspired the two main conference documents, *Message of Bandung* and the *Declaration on Strengthening New Asian–African Strategic Partnership*. Asian partners working individually on the African continent and individual Asian countries approaching individual African countries saw a challenge in the coordination of African interests. The lack of coordination among Asian countries appears to be a potential weakness when they try to influence developments in Africa in competition with the European Union (EU) and with countries in North and South America. However, the documents that came out of the second NAASP Summit in 2015 held to commemorate the 60th anniversary of the Bandung Conference in 1955 no longer explicitly mentioned the New Partnership for African Development (NEPAD).

The *Bandung Message* refers to the principles of the UN Charter in connection with various topics and the *Declaration on Reinvigorating the New Asian–African Strategic Partnership* includes the following paragraph, number 4 out of 32.

> 4. Reiterating the principle and benefits of multilateralism, we resolve to further strengthen and support the United Nations and other multilateral and regional forums so they work more effectively towards strengthening peace and prosperity in Asia and Africa as well as other regions. We call for continued efforts to reform the United Nations, including the revitalization of the General Assembly and a comprehensive reform of the Security Council, which corresponds to the collective interests of developing countries. A reformed Security Council will significantly increase representation of Asia and Africa.
>
> (*Declaration on Reinvigorating, 2015:2*)

Here the participants at the NAASP Summit state their position on multilateralism as embodied by the UN system – a system they applaud, but also see as in need of reform in order to represent Asian and African voices, specifically in the Security Council, to ensure peace. Both documents distance themselves from the Development Assistance Committee under the Organization for Economic Cooperation and Development (OECD/DAC) and emphasize the role of the UN system in defining South–South development cooperation, increasingly, as South–South cooperation is not framed as 'development' or 'progress.' African and Asian stakeholders in NAASP saw the South–South cooperation agenda as better represented in the multilateral setting of the United Nations system, than by the excluding OECD/DAC arena, where the voices of the North dominate. At the UN, each member country has one vote in the General Assembly and they take turns representing their region according to geographical distribution in the Economic and Social Council – both organs are directly relevant for South–South cooperation. The countries of the South represented in the Group of 77 have a coordinated voice and a voting bloc that can compete with and challenge the voices of the North as opposed to at the OECD/DAC, where only providers of aid are members. The only main organ of the UN where Africa and Asia have continuously felt underrepresented is the Security Council, and they here reiterate their demand for reform to reflect their influence on, and their role and interests in, the world. Besides, they mention the opportunity for organizing biennial ministerial consultations 'to provide strategic direction for Asian–African partnership,' when their ministers are attending the UN General Assembly in New York every year in the autumn. This is a further understanding of the practical benefits of the multilateralism of the United Nations (Declaration on Reinvigorating, 2015:5).

Paragraph 10 of the *Declaration on Reinvigorating the New Asian–African Strategic Partnership* from April 24, 2015, includes an indirect critique of OECD/DAC:

> 10. *While reaffirming that South–South Cooperation and its agenda have to be set by countries of the South, we call for the active involvement of development partners and other related stakeholders in various mechanisms within South–South Cooperation and triangular cooperation to inter alia, mobilize their support, share, and exchange best practices, as well as promote transfer and development of technology, to further enhance South–South cooperation initiatives based on the principles of mutual benefit, non-conditionality, equality, national ownership, respect for national sovereignty, as well as non-interference in domestic affairs. We also recognize that South–South Cooperation continues to serve as a complement to, and not a substitute for, North–South development cooperation.*
>
> *(Declaration on Reinvigorating, 2015:2)*

The specific references to non-conditionality and non-interference in domestic affairs are comments on the practice of conditionalities and budget or basket funding in aid from many DAC members.

Critical voices that see the New Partnership for African Development (NEPAD) development ideology as too close to the neo-liberal philosophy of the Washington Consensus have partly discredited the strong contribution of Africa through NEPAD that was recognized in the 2005 revival of the Bandung spirit as mentioned in the first NAASP Summit Declaration (Murithi, 2010:199–200). However, perhaps more importantly, the Asian agenda to discredit NEPAD or other common African agendas by referring to a North-driven neo-liberal foundation strengthens a diverse Asia that is not able to cooperate – and enables Asia to divide and conquer. By 2015, individual Asian and African donors defined and executed their versions of South–South development cooperation. Examples include Japan at the Tokyo International Conference on African Development (TICAD), China in Forum on China–Africa Cooperation (FOCAC), India in India–Africa Forum (IAF), and South Korea in Korea–Africa Forum (KAF). The declaration, further, lists the Indonesia–Brunei Darussalam sponsored Non-Alignment Movement Center for South–South Cooperation, Iran–Africa Forum, Arab–Africa Forum, South African Development Partnership Agency, Malaysia Technical Cooperation Program, Africa–Turkey Partnership, Pakistan's Special Technical Assistance Program (STAP), Egyptian Agency of Partnership for Development, and the Thai–Africa Initiative (Declaration on Reinvigorating, 2015:4). The bilateral arrangements allow for less coordination around common African interests and reflect the high degree of competing Asian interests on the African continent.

Even though the bilateral forums and partnerships still all include an aspect of aid relationships, it is worth noting that many do not explicitly mention aid, development, or the older terms technical assistance and technical cooperation in their titles, which leave them ready for a non-development, non-progress paradigm. This contradicts Klingebiel's (2014:19) argument that a horizontal and equal relationship is the basis for South–South cooperation, because all aid relationships are asymmetrical (Klingebiel, 2014:19). Many non-national initiatives have grown over the past couple of decades to replace some of the East/West competition driven investments and expressions of loyalty during the Cold War. In this context, the reference to the 'supportive role' of the private sector as key to both peace and prosperity in the Bandung declaration is important. The Co-Chairs' statement from the Asia–Africa Sub-Regional Organization

Conference (AASROC) in 2003 tied the word 'progress' to an idea of development in the context of NAASP. However, 'progress' was not in the title of the 2015 Summit: 'Strengthening South–South Cooperation to Promote World Peace and Prosperity.' However, the section titled 'A Strategic Partnership of the Future' lists Public Private Partnerships (PPPs), which underscores a certain interpretation of the idea of prosperity.

The declaration emphasizes the role of the private sector in the context of 'quality growth' – originally a Japanese concept (e.g. Japan's Ministry of Foreign Affairs, 2015:5–6):

> 19. We reiterate the importance of 'Quality Growth' which values inclusiveness, sustainability, and resilience for poverty reduction. In order to realize 'Quality Growth' in all Asian–African countries, we share the intention to promote public–private partnership, especially for quality infrastructure development, advance capacity building among local people and share our knowledge and experiences for enhancing resilience to climate change, natural disaster and for the attainment of both the millennium and Sustainable Development Goals.
>
> ...
>
> 21. We recognize the importance of pursuing more conducive and enhanced trade and investment policies that would push forward better flow of goods and services. We underscore the importance of promoting inter-regional economic cooperation in the two continents, inter alia through the promotion and facilitation of direct trade and investment and in this regard, we applaud the WTO's decision to hold its Ministerial Conference in Nairobi, Kenya in December 2015, for the first time in Africa.
>
> *(Declaration on Reinvigorating, 2015:3–4)*

The mention of the World Trade Organization (WTO) meeting in Kenya is significant, because it is an acknowledgement of its potential for the South after the initial G77 protests against the creation of WTO as an alternative to the United Nations Conference on Trade and Development (UNCTAD), which is a UN program with broad representation of African and African countries. WTO and UNCTAD also cooperate today (WTO, website).

The 'aid-to-trade' scheme recognizes the role of the private sector in achieving national prosperity and poverty reduction. Years of experience have inspired the recognition of the potential role of the private sector. Not least in NAASP's focus on the private sector, the new partnership builds on many years of dispersed and smaller scale experiences of cooperation between the two continents. One example is the World Network of Friends. In 1992, a group of alumni from private sector technical and management courses held in Japan, and financed partly by Japanese foreign aid, suggested the establishment of a South–South network to facilitate South–South communication and activities, which would be more or less independent from their common host country, Japan. In 1997, the Association of Overseas Technical Scholarships under the Ministry of Economy, Trade, and Industry officially established the World Network of Friends (WNF) (HIDA, website). The World Network of Friends has chapters in many countries and draws on connections to an alumni network that has chapters in more than 40 countries. One main use of the World Network of Friends has been to offer courses in specific fields not least in different Indian cities for professionals from various African countries and from Nepal, Bangladesh, and Sri Lanka. These courses predate the Asia–Africa Sub-Regional Organization Conference (AASROC) in 2003 and the New Asia–Africa Strategic Partnership (NAASP) of 2005 which called for the strengthening of South–South cooperation through training and capacity building programs.

Today, the World Network of Friends has members in many countries, but the alumni societies in India and Thailand offer the majority of courses. In Pune in India, the World Network of Friends has established a partnership with Larsen and Toubro, a large Indian engineering company, where the World Network of Friends can send up to 20 professionals from African countries on a two-week intensive course taught by Indian electrical engineers. Over the past ten years, students selected by the alumni societies in Ghana and Sudan formed by alumni who have previously attended courses in Japan have attended courses at Larsen and Toubro (Larsen & Toubro, 2016; Electric Company Ghana, 2017). Other courses are offered for example to Tanzanian and Sudanese participants by the Mumbai chapter of the alumni society, tied to overseas courses in Japan funded by Japanese foreign aid ('Report . . . ,' 2009: 14). Whether at grass roots, governmental, or multilateral level, what appears to be the objective of competition or cooperation is profit. Most stakeholders seem to understand, however, that their own profit relies on mutual profit for all stakeholders involved and requires investments that depend on a reliable and effective social and economic infrastructure.

Conclusion

Tensions between cooperation and competition have constituted the driving force in Africa–Asia regional partnerships and South–South development cooperation. Intra- and interregional partnerships and alliances work where they are useful. Initially, what framed and motivated cooperation within and between regions in South–South cooperation were common challenges in overcoming the legacies of colonialism and exploitation led by European and North American actors. The importance of cooperation among African countries in order to focus and manage external partners became evident to enough African leaders in 2001 for them to prioritize the African Union and New Partnership for African Development (NEPAD), whereas some Asian countries with agendas of competition over leadership still overrule most attempts at cooperation within Asia. The European Union (EU) and the African Union (AU) have cooperated in the interest of meeting common challenges, but this has not been possible in Asia, yet. The question remains whether Africa–Asia regional partnerships and South–South development cooperation, in order to circumvent the North, will be relevant in the future. Is this a real or perceived danger – and if so for whom? Can the North manage marginalization or is that exactly why the Development Assistance Committee (DAC) members so heavily criticize the emerging donors and their foreign aid schemes for not harmonizing with DAC standards? Thereby, they offer what DAC members see as flows of capital that undermine the DAC endorsed conditionalities.

The concrete content or measures of South–South development cooperation focused on appropriate, applicable, and transferable experiences of development, technology, and skills. Therefore, the South repeatedly mention and practice the transfer and application of technology and infrastructure coupled with training and human resource development schemes as part of South–South development cooperation. The sources show this to be the case regardless of what level or sector is involved in South–South development cooperation, whether governments, the New Asian–African Strategic Partnership (NAASP), private sector stakeholders, or grass roots, such as the World Network of Friends. However, more and more South–South cooperation takes the form of peace diplomacy, trade negotiations, and private sector investments and works to ensure international production standards in favor of African and Asian products, rather than South–South development cooperation. The shift in agendas of the interregional organization, NAASP, in 2015, reflects the decrease in perceived relevance of foreign aid and increase in alternative partnership models.

Competition rather than cooperation, evident in the multitude of options, may determine forms and outcomes of future South–South cooperation and regional and interregional partnerships, when the common challenge of North–South interdependency becomes less pronounced, therefore, not a mutual focus of competition or opposition for the South. On the other hand, as Africa as a region strengthens its position to direct and manage more powerful external partners in the North and among Asian or South American countries, the African–Asian common challenges posed by the North, or related to geographic proximity or shared space such as the Indian ocean, invite cooperation to develop. Alternative flows of ideas, material goods, and capital may facilitate new solutions rather than official development assistance (ODA) and other forms of aid. Based on the recent developments it seems likely that the people involved will define new understandings of development and partnerships and the trend of parallel multiple paradigms and approaches may continue and expand beyond any current definitions of North, South, Asia – or Africa.

Bibliography

African Union (AU), 2016. Available at homepage: http://au.int/ (Accessed 29 May 2016).

Agenda 2063, 2016. Available at: http://au.int/en/agenda2063/about#sthash.B4BJFklv.dpuf (Accessed 29 May 2016).

Aguilar, R. and Goldstein, A., 2009. 'The Chinisation of Africa: The Case of Angola', *The World Economy*, Volume 32 (11), pp. 1543–1562.

A New African Initiative: Merger of the Millennium Partnership for the African Recovery Programme (MAP) and Omega Plan, 2001. Approved by OAU Summit July 11. www.afbis.com/analysis/new_african_initiative.htm (Accessed 19 February 2016)

Apaydin, F., 2012. 'Overseas Development Aid across the Global South: Lessons from the Turkish Experience in Sub-Saharan Africa and Central Asia', *European Journal of Development Research*, Volume 24 (2), pp. 261–282.

Arase, D., 1995. *Buying Power: The Political Economy of Japan's Foreign Aid*. New York: Lynne Rienner.

Arase, D. (ed.), 2005. *Japan's Foreign Aid: Old Continuities and New Directions*. New York: Routledge.

Asia–Africa Sub-Regional Organization Conference (AASROC), 2003. *Co-Chairs Statement*. Bandung, Indonesia, July 29–30.

Association of Overseas Technical Scholarships (AOTS), 2009. 'Report on WNF Activities in FY2008', *Kensh*, Volume 189, pp. 14–15.

Bandung Message, 2015. *Strengthening South–South Cooperation to Promote World Peace and Prosperity*. http://en.mirajnews.com/2015/04/bandung-message-2015-strengthening-southsouth-cooperation-promote-world-peace-prosperity.html (Accessed 7 August 2017).

Bry, S. H., 2016. 'The Evolution of South–South Development Cooperation: Guiding Principles and Approaches', *European Journal of Development Research*, Volume 28 (1), pp. 1–16.

Buddhadasa, S., 2014. Interview in Tokyo, October 31.

Buddhadasa, S., 2015. E-mail Communication, May 20.

Calais, M. and Cheru, F., 2010. 'Countering "new imperialisms": What role for the New Partnership for Africa's development?', in Fantu Cheru and Cyril Obi (eds.), *The Rise of China & India in Africa*, London: Zed Books, pp. 221–237.

Conference of Southern Providers, 2013. *South–South Cooperation: Issues and Emerging Challenges*. www.un.org/en/ecosoc/newfunct/dcfdelhi.shtml (Accessed 10 June 2016).

Danish Ministry of Foreign Affairs, 2016. *Verden 2030. #voresDKaid Udkast Danmarks udviklingspolitiske og humanitære strategi.* [The World 2030. #voresDKaid: Draft of Denmark's development political and humanitarian strategy] file:///C:/Users/AU123398/AppData/Local/Microsoft/Windows/INetCache/IE/Z75NZWMD/Udkast%20til%20udviklingspolitisk%20og%20humanitr%20strategi%20-%20med%20forside.pdf (Accessed 22 August 2016).

Davies, M. J. (2008). 'Special Economic Zones: China's Developmental Model Comes to Africa', in Robert I. Rotberg (ed.), *China into Africa: Trade, Aid and Influence*, Washington, DC: Brookings Institution Press, pp. 137–154.

Declaration on the New Asian–African Strategic Partnership, 2005. April 24. Available at: <http://mea.gov.in/bilateral-documents.htm?dtl/6608/Declaration+on+the+New+Asian+African+Strategic+Pertnership> (Accessed 19 February 2016).

349

Declaration on Reinvigorating the New Asian–African Strategic Partnership, 2015. April 24, Available at: www.mirajnews.com/declaration-reinvigorating-asianafrican-strategic-partnership/60519 (Accessed 12 August 2016).

DFC Republic of Korea High-level Symposium, 2015. ' Workshop in preparation for the Third International Conference on Financing for Development: The role of catalytic aid in financing sustainable development', Incheon, Republic of Korea.

Economic and Social Council (ESC), 2014. 'Trends and Progress in International Development Cooperation', Report of the Secretary-General. UN document number: E/2014/77.

Electric Company Ghana, 2017. Group Interview, Accra, Ghana, January 30.

Esteves, P. and Assunção, M., 2016. 'South–South Cooperation and the International Development Field: Between the OECD and the UN', *Third World Quarterly*, Volume 35 (10), pp. 1775–1790.

Fuchs, A. and Vadlamannati, K. C., 2013. 'The needy donor: An Empirical Analysis of India's aid motives', *World Development*, Volume 44, pp. 110–128.

Fujikura, R. and Nakayama, M., 2016. 'Origins of Japanese aid policy – Post-war reconstruction, reparations, and World Bank projects', in H. Kato, J. Page and Y. Shimomura (eds.), *Japan's Development Assistance: Foreign Aid and the Post-2015 Agenda*. New York: Palgrave Macmillan, pp. 39–56.

Group of 77 (G77), 1964. Joint Declaration of the Seventy-Seven Developing Countries made at the conclusion of the United Nations Conference on Trade and Development, 15 June. Available at: www.g77.org/doc/Joint%20Declaration.html (Accessed 11 October 2016).

Group of 77 (G77), 2000. 'Declaration of the South Summit', April 10–14, 2000, Available from: www.g77.org/summit/Declaration_G77Summit.htm> (Accessed 28 June 2016).

HIDA Website, 2016. www.hidajapan.or.jp/en/network/alumni/wnf.html (Accessed 11 August 2016).

Hyo-sook K. and Potter, D. M. (eds.), 2012. *Foreign Aid Competition in Northeast Asia*. Boulder, CO: Lynne Rienner.

Islam, S. (ed.), 1991. *Yen for Development: Japanese Foreign Aid and the Politics of Burden-Sharing*. New York: Council on Foreign Relations.

Jain, P., 2016. 'Japan's foreign aid: Institutional change and shifting policy directions', in H. Kato, J. Page and Y. Shimomura (eds.), *Japan's Development Assistance: Foreign Aid and the Post-2015 Agenda*. New York: Palgrave Macmillan, pp. 56–68.

Japan's Ministry of Foreign Affairs (MOFA), 2015. *Development Cooperation Charter: For Peace, Prosperity and a Better Future for Everyone*. Available at: www.mofa.go.jp/files/000067701.pdf (Accessed 22 August 2016).

Jerve, A. M., Shimomura, Y. and Hansen, A. S. (eds.), 2008. *Aid Relationships in Asia: Exploring Ownership in Japanese and Nordic Aid*. New York: Palgrave Macmillan.

Kanbur, R., 2001. 'The New Partnership for Africa's Development (NEPAD) An Initial Commentary.' Available at: www.arts.cornell.edu/poverty/kanbur/POVNEPAD.pdf (Accessed 27 May 2016).

Klingebiel, S., 2014. *Development Cooperation: Challenges of the New Aid Architecture*. New York: Palgrave Macmillan.

Kragelund, P., 2011. 'Back to BASICs? The Rejuvenation of Non-traditional Donors' Development Cooperation with Africa', *Development and Change*, Volume 42 (2), pp. 585–607.

Mawdsley, E., 2012. *From Recipients to Donors: Emerging Powers and the Changing Development Landscape*. London: Zed Books.

Mawdsley, E., 2014. 'Human Rights and South–South Development Cooperation: Reflections on the "Rising Powers" as International Development Actors', *Human Rights Quarterly*, Volume 36 (3), pp. 630–652.

Murithi, T., 2010. 'The African Union as an international actor', in J. Mangala (ed.), *Africa and the New World Era: From Humanitarianism to a Strategic View*. New York: Palgrave, pp. 193–205.

Orr, R. M, Jr., 1990. *Japan's Foreign Aid Power*. New York: Columbia University Press.

Pedersen, J. D., 1988. 'Syd-Syd-relationer: En analyse af Indiens og Brasiliens relationer til den tredje verden siden 1970 – med særligt henblik på at belyse staternes rolle i internationaliseringsprocessen', unpublished thesis, Institut for Statskundskab, Aarhus Universitet.

Rampa, F., Bilal, S. and Sidiripoulos, E., 2012. 'Leveraging South–South Cooperaton for Africa's Development', *South African Journal of International Affairs*, Volume 19 (2), pp. 247–269.

Raposo, P. A., 2014. *Japan's Foreign Aid to Africa: Angola and Mozambique within the TICAD Process*. London: Routledge Contemporary Japan Series.

Roblelo, C., 2015. 'New Donors, Same Old Practices? South–South Cooperation of Latin American Emerging Donors', *Bandung: Journal of the Global South*, Volume 2 (3), pp. 1–9.

Secretary-General (SG), 2014. 'United Nations Counts on Development Cooperation Forum to Steer Efforts to Meet Needs of World's People, Says Secretary-General', Press release July 10. UN document number: SG/SM/16014-ECOSOC/6641-DEV/3105.

Taylor, I., 2012. 'India's Rise in Africa', *International Affairs*, Volume 88 (4), pp. 779–798.

The Group of 77 at the United Nations, 2016. Available at: www.g77.org/doc/ (Accessed 6 June 2016)

Tilak, J., 2014. 'South–South Cooperation: India's Programme of Development Assistance – Nature, Size and Functioning', *Asian Education and Development Studies*, Volume 3 (1), pp. 58–75.

Toubro and Larsen, 2016. Visit, Pune, India, January 6.

World Bank (WB), 2008. 'Accra Agenda for Action', 3rd High Level Forum on Aid Effectiveness, September 2–4, 2008, Accra, Ghana. Available at: http://siteresources.worldbank.org/ACCRAEXT/Resources/4700790-1217425866038/AAA-4-SEPTEMBER-FINAL-16h00.pdf (Accessed 28 June 2016).

World Trade Organization (WTO), 2016. Website. Available at: www.wto.org/english/thewto_e/coher_e/wto_unctad_e.htm (Accessed 12 August 2016).

23

ASIA AND AFRICA AND POST-2015 DEVELOPMENT AGENDA

Shalini Chawla

Introduction

The post-Cold War period has witnessed major power shifts with the fulcrum of economic development beginning to move towards the South. The immediate aftermath of the Cold War left the political and economic power concentrated in the West. The dominance of the Western institutions, the World Bank and the International Monetary Fund, indicated that the West was generally writing the rules of global governance. The Millennium Development Goals (MDGs), written after the Cold War, were crafted by the Western countries for the developing world, which included large parts of Asia and Africa. The MDGs that were set to be achieved by 2015 did serve the purpose of providing a framework of thinking and actions with the objectives of reducing poverty and driving social development. Taking the framework forward, the United Nations adopted Sustainable Development Goals (SDGs) on September 25, 2015 (United Nations, 2015: A/RES/70/1) covering economic and social development, as well as environment protection, with the overarching goal of poverty eradication. These goals were far more ambitious and their fulfillment would demand a more coordinated approach between the North and the South and also South–South cooperation.

The populous states of Asia are either already major economic powers (e.g. China) or are aspiring economic powers and are seeking to play larger roles on the global platform. While emerging economies have significant long term growth potential, these economies are also plagued with major challenges of governance, security and climate change. The post-development agenda would require an integrated approach from the emerging economies, adequately supported by the West, to be able to pursue the development agenda. The continents of Asia and Africa might be thousands of miles apart but they are closely linked by the common experience of colonialism and a scrimmage for development. The announcements of the MDGs and then the SDGs have been efforts from the West which aim towards more balanced global development.

This chapter analyzes the inexorable global power shift towards the South, the emerging powers of Asia and their engagement with Africa, which is home to as many as seven countries that are projected to be among the ten fastest growing economies of the world. The role of the G20 as a global platform to facilitate the attainment of the Sustainable Development Goals is crucial. This chapter argues that there is tremendous scope for Asia and Africa to meaningfully engage with each other for furthering development: bilaterally, multilaterally and through a globally representative forum like the G20. There is greater possibility of this cooperation due to the global power shift and the growing economic potential of the South. China as a major growing power, and to some extent India, can also play a crucial role in implementing the development agenda in Asia and Africa.

This chapter is divided into three parts: the first part analyzes the global power shift, the transition of G7 to G8, the evolution of G20 and the announcement of the MDGs followed by the transition to the SDGs. The second part discusses the emerging powers and the cooperation between the emerging economies of Asia (China and India) and Africa. The third section discusses the challenges related to the growth of Asia–Africa cooperation and the potential role of the G20 in the implementation of the SDGs.

Global power shift

The political and economic power dynamics have completely altered as compared with the Cold War era, with new meanings attached to power and the rise of significant regional powers: Asia (specifically, China) and Africa. The post-Cold War period brought changes in two phases: one immediately after the collapse of the Berlin Wall and the fall of the Soviet Union, leaving the United States' hegemony unchallenged. The second, after the September 11, 2001 attacks on the World Trade Center, saw the emergence of distinctly threatening security challenges to the US (and the West), including the rise of anti-American sentiments in the developing world, diminishing willingness to accept the West's dictates as well as significant rise of regional powers. There are gradual, rather obdurate and fundamental changes taking place leading to a shifting of power towards Asia and Africa. There have been consistent economic headwinds in the United States and Europe. Simultaneously, there has been a rise of the developing economies, particularly China, India and, somewhat more inconsistently, those of Brazil and Russia. There is also growing acknowledgement of the potential of Africa which not only offers natural resources but also a market for the expanding Asian economies.

The post-Cold War era witnessed remarkable shifts in the international system, struggle for distribution of power and international actors redefining their roles and priorities. The period immediately after the disintegration of the Soviet Union led to a scenario where the US was left completely unchallenged and was in a position to take decisions prioritizing its own objectives and strategic interests. The other aspect of the end of the Cold War era was the struggle to arrest Europe's decline.

There was a unipolar moment after the end of Cold War where the US was seen asserting itself in most of the important global situations and decisions. The disintegration of the USSR also allowed Washington to extend its security umbrella to eastern and central Europe and to extend its influence in Europe. However, the balance of power was altering with the emergence of regional actors with new strengths, which was also changing the meaning of 'power'. Thus, what eventually emerged was not a unipolar world (defined as a system with one super power and no other significant power). The United States was certainly the indispensable decisive power but other states which had started asserting themselves were certainly not dispensable. These included Russia, China, Japan, India, Germany, France and South Africa. Hence, the 1990s was a defining decade and witnessed major shifts in the international system, as follows. Japan's economy stagnated after its stock market and property bubble burst; China's economic boom was very distinctly visible; the United States entered into a badly calculated war in Iraq which lasted over a decade and finally ended with multiple unresolved challenges; and the structure of the European Union was outlined.

The G7, G8 and G20

The transition of the G7 to the G8 and then the evolution of the G20 do represent the emerging issues of the developing countries and also the influence and power wielded by the emerging economies.

The G7 originated in the mid 1970s out of the need for a better coordination of financial policies following the collapse of the Bretton Woods system and the oil crisis in 1973–74. In the 1990s, the G7, and then the G8 continued to dominate world affairs and decide on major issues. The US had the support of the most industrially advanced nations (the United Kingdom, France, Germany, Japan, Italy and Canada) and was in a strong position to control global macroeconomic policies. In the 1990s, the aggregate GDP of the G8 countries represented nearly 68% of the world's GDP. In 1996, former US President George Bush, in an article in *The New York Times*, talked about the G7 opening up to the four other major countries qualifying as emerging: Brazil, China, India and Russia (Postel-Vinay, 2014:3).

Although Russia became a part of the G7 and the G7 became the G8, the working of the organization continued to be dominated by the seven major economies which shared military alliance with the United States (Smith, 2011:4). Over the years, the agenda of the G8 remained focused on financial and economic issues. Eventually, its agenda expanded to incorporate security and other developmental issues which concerned and appeased the G7/G8 member nations and their political audience (ibid.).

The G8 was not without criticism. It was accused of representing the interests of elite groups and not addressing global problems of third world debt, global warming, HIV/AIDS, etc. One critic, political analyst Titus Alexander, described the G7 as a 'cabinet' of global minority rule with a coordinating role in world affairs (Alexander, 1996:212). The G8 was criticized for imposing a neo-liberal economic model charaterized by privatization, deregulation and trade liberalization that served the interests of the rich and the powerful. Arguably, the world's poorest economies have not gained much from trade liberalization. A United Nations study by S. M. Shafaeddin found that liberalization benefited the industries, which were near maturity, mainly in developed countries as their competitive edge made them more efficient. On the contrary, the industries at early infancy stage, mainly in developing countries, or the ones which were inefficient, could not survive the reform (Shafaeddin, 2005). The Washington consensus in the 1990s laid down universal and uniform trade liberalization which implied that all developing countries were to follow a similar trade policy regime as well as trade liberalization and would be subject to similar tariff rates, irrespective of their level of development and industrial capacity (ibid.). The United Nations Conference on Trade and Development reported that the majority of the people in countries that opened their markets for free trade continue to survive on less than US$1 a day (Hubbard & Miller, 2005:3).

According to one observer:

> By virtue of its combined economic, military and diplomatic power and influence the G7/G8 can exercise tremendous influence over the multinational institutions of global governance. This power gives the G7/G8 great influence on the policies, programs, and decisions of the UN Security Council, World Trade Organization (WTO), International Monetary Fund (IMF), World Bank, and Organization for Economic Cooperation and Development (OECD) . . . For those negatively impacted by the policy agendas advanced by the G7/G8's influential role in global governance is highly resented and frequently criticized.
>
> (Barry, 2002)

Criticism of the G8 was voiced from Asia and Africa for ignoring the development of Africa and also for the lack of regional participation in decision making in the forum. Even when the G8 released its action plan for Africa, the action plan could not address the main issues in Africa. A study on the G8's role in Africa concluded that while the G8 did emphasize investment as the development tool for Africa, the concentration on the interests of the investors led to added troubles for the population of the African countries (Miller, 2005:96).

Six of the largest African NGOs and the National Network issued a statement on the G8 delivery on Africa in 2003:

> The outcome of the 2003 G8 Summit has been stunning on its failure to make progress on the debt, health, trade and agricultural issues.
>
> *(Pambuzka News, 2003)*

In 1997, Jeffery E. Garten, a former Under Secretary of Commerce in the Clinton administration, identified 10 'big emerging markets' (BEMs), including China, India and Brazil as the leading three along with Mexico, Indonesia, South Korea, South Africa, Argentina, Turkey and Poland. Garten saw the big emerging markets as:

> *The key swing factor in the future of world trade, global financial stability, and the transition to free market economies in Asia, Central Europe and Latin America. They are also crucial to nuclear nonproliferation, the improvement of human rights, environmental cooperation, and the avoidance of war in several critical hotspots.*
>
> *(Garten, 1997:3)*

In particular Garten did predict China's growth as a major power in the world economy:

> *China is by far the biggest of the BEMs . . . it is likely to be one of the three largest economies within the next decade . . . No market holds more long-term potential for America, and China has become a key element in the global strategy of hundreds of America's top firms . . . It is likely that our relationship with China will emerge in the next decade as the most important focus of our foreign policy.*
>
> *(Garten, 1997:10)*

A series of financial crises erupted in the 1990s, and the G7/G8 was increasingly seen as incapable of handling the situation. The influence of the emerging economies went up. In 1997, the global financial crisis, which erupted from Thailand, did concern the G8, and the need to strengthen the global financial system was seriously felt. President Clinton, at the meeting of Asia-Pacific Economic Cooperation (APEC) leaders in Vancouver in 1997, announced a short-lived official level Group of 22 (G22) to discuss the Asian financial crisis (Kirton, 2013:55). The G22 was followed by the announcement of the G33 and finally in 1999, the G20 was endorsed by the G7 in the Cologne summit of June 18–20 (ibid.).

The creation of the G20 did recognize countries including China, India, Russia and Brazil as powerful drivers of the world economy. The G20 started on a sound note and the idea was to have more representative decision making, engaging emerging economies, which could help in tackling the financial crisis. Although the finance ministers of the G20 met periodically, the first formal meeting of the G20 with the heads of states took place in 2008. The White House called together the leaders of the G20 countries to, *review progress being made to address the current financial crisis, advance a common understanding of the causes and, in order to avoid a repetition, agree on a common set of principles for reform of the regulatory and institutional regimes for the world's financial sectors.*

(Financial Times, 2008)

The creation of the G20 was an acknowledgement of the fact that the global economic crisis could not be managed by the developed countries alone and that the G7 countries should have a say in the management of the global economic and financial system. The G20 has a diverse representation and can play a crucial role in stabilizing the world as the membership is beyond the Western powers and is focused on addressing a wide range of non-economic issues as well. The G20, in a way, also represented the new trend which emphasized cohesive functioning by the developed and the developing economies to address the economic crisis. The nature of the G20 does give it potential to incorporate diverse subjects for development.

Redefining goals: transition from Millennium Development Goals to the Sustainable Development Goals

The MDGs, announced following the UN Millennium summit in 2000, expressed a public concern about poverty, hunger, disease, gender inequality and access to water and sanitation. The MDGs did bring global attention to these issues and provided a narrative for the direction of aid in the post-Cold War period. However, the discussion of the MDGs, while they were being crafted, was reportedly casual. The high level panel, appointed by Ban Ki-moon, crafted the MDGs in the basement of the UN office in New York and the members missed out on including environment development on the agenda (Tran, 2012: online).

The MDGs, as Ban Ki-moon described:

were an expression of solidarity with the world's poorest and most vulnerable. They translated noble principles and great aspirations into a set of time-bound, shared targets. The Goals mobilized the world to tackle poverty's many dimensions, forming a framework for a global partnership that ushered in a new era of development cooperation.

(World Bank Group, 2016: Online)

While it is difficult to calculate the impact of the MDGs on actual development outcomes, they certainly did bring global attention, awareness and accountability towards these issues. The idea was to continue with the existing efforts and take 'awareness and efforts' beyond 2015. There have been widespread, growing concerns regarding the challenges of climate change and the impact it would have in the future (especially in Asia and Africa, even though these nations are largely not responsible for environmental degradation). The idea of the SDGs came into being to encourage synergy towards the efforts to fight poverty while spurring sustainable development across the globe. The challenge of climate change obviously needs concerted attention and efforts along with economic development and social inclusion. The concept of the SDGs surfaced at the United Nations Conference on Sustainable Development, or Rio+20, in 2012. On January 1, 2016 the Sustainable Development Goals for 2030 agenda for Sustainable Development came into force. The SDGs, although not legally binding, do provide a global consensus on 17 goals and 169 targets of sustainable development. The SDGs include new priority areas like Innovation, Economic Inequality, Peace and Justice and Responsible Consumption, which are interconnected and the member states need to work in the spirit of partnership and pragmatism.

The SDGs are universally applicable and include all three dimensions of sustainable development: environment, social and economic. The three aspects of sustainable development are not just confined at the local level and they have a spiraling impact due to enhanced globalization. The growth of China and its impact on Africa and other poor nations is significantly visible. The post-Cold War period has witnessed the rise of emerging economies, and there is a strong need for these nations to balance their economic growth along with social issues (gender inequality, illiteracy and health) and growing environmental challenges to be able to sustain growth and development.

The MDGs were aimed mainly at the poor nations where the rich and developed were to provide 'aid and assistance' to the poor to help towards achieving the goals. The SDGs, on the other hand, are more comprehensive and global goals for the entire planet, where the rich and the poor need to work together for the well-being of future generations (Sacha, 2012: online). The growing economies – China, India, Africa – while driving growth, are facing significant social and environmental challenges and would be the key partners in the SDGs. The membership of the Open Working Group on Sustainable Development (which worked for a period of 17 months) did have a significant representation of the emerging economies, i.e. Africa (Algeria, Tunisia, Tanzania, Ghana, Kenya, Congo, Zimbabwe) and Asia (India, China, Bangladesh, Pakistan, Bhutan).

Ban Ki-moon defined the SDGs as:

> *The 2030 Agenda for Sustainable Development now sets the vision for the next 15 years of global action. It encompasses the unfinished business of the MDGs but goes well beyond poverty eradication, breaking significant new ground. It is a universal, integrated and human rights-based agenda for sustainable development. It balances economic growth, social justice and environmental stewardship and underlines the links between peace, development and human rights.*
>
> *(World Bank Group, 2016: online)*

Emerging power equations and cooperation

The first decade of the twenty-first century saw important developments. While the financial crisis in the West was already gaining momentum, strategic developments were a significant factor in leading to the shift of power towards the South. The role of the US and its influence had started to slowly diminish with the series of crises (financial and security) that emerged in the 1990s. By any measure, the September 11 terrorist strike on the US was an extraordinary event and the most severe blow to American supremacy and its position as a super power. On the other hand, in Asia what was seen was a rise of regional powers and of China in particular. India's growth has also been remarkable, and being home to one sixth of the world's population, India has a large stake in how the world order would develop. Also, Africa's role and potential in global rebalancing was starting to be acknowledged.

China's rise

China has invested aggressively in building all the attributes of power and has managed to develop a political culture which reinforces the legitimacy of its policies in economy, society and politics. Beijing has been cautious to distinguish its rise from the colonial or the imperial states. It adopted the policy of 'peaceful rise' (*Zhonggou heping jueqi*) under the leadership of Hu Jintao, which carried the assurance of its development not being a threat to the established world order. The policy of peaceful rise did project China as a responsible nation which relied on soft power and was focused on the welfare of its own people. The Chinese claim has been that its economic efforts are to build up South–South cooperation.

China's free market economic policies are seen as responsible for its economic growth. It managed to sustain an average growth rate of 10% for nearly three decades since it started market reforms in 1979. A contributing factor of Chinese economic growth has been the slow-down of the American economy, which may have allowed the market for Chinese products to flourish. China adopted a focused approach on outward foreign direct investment (OFDI) as a complementary strategy to inviting investments. While Asia is the main destination of Chinese OFDIs, Africa has emerged as a significant region in the Chinese investment agenda. China trades with about 53 African nations and provides zero-tariff treatment for the poorest African countries since 2005 (Guerrero, online).

Chinese investments have not only created market space for its products but have also helped to develop enabling processes and technology. Its economic growth is indeed remark-able and is now the engine for regional growth. Although there has been significant debate on the sustainability of Chinese economic growth, Beijing is confident of overcoming obstacles and maintaining its growth. According to the Chinese Finance Minister (2015):

> major reforms will be accomplished by 2020, including the structural reforms . . . China is building a new open economy by removing institutional shackles . . . is accelerating the trans-formation of growth model and adjusting economic structure . . . It is predicted that China will continue to maintain around 7% growth in the coming few years with solid economic foundation, sound growth conditions and sufficient driving power at disposal.
>
> *(Jiwei, 2015)*

China's economic growth has enabled it to spend more on defense. After the Taiwan Strait Crisis of 1996, its investment in defense capabilities went up. Defense expenditure has gone up by 11% per year since then. China is the second biggest military spender in the world and the new budget for the People's Liberation Army (PLA) is more than three times that of the other big spenders – Japan, France and the United Kingdom (Bitzinger, 2015: online). The focus of the defense modernization has been a build-up of air and naval capabilities, conventional and ballistic missiles and space and cyber capabilities (see Ghosh, 2012).

China's diplomacy has grown more confident and it has coupled these developments with its claim of 'peaceful rise'. Its expanding influence is derived not only from its hard power (military and economic growth) but also its soft power. David Shambaugh, in his book *Power Shift*, talks about two areas where Beijing has managed to exert influence. The first is through China's assertion of 'New Security Concept' and 'Strategic Partnerships', and other initiatives to fashion different norms to govern interstate relations, which have been received positively by the South Asian nations. Second, Beijing's soft power lies in the realm of higher education. Its efforts to educate and train the younger generation help to expand its influence among the young (Shambaugh, 2005:25–29).

China's enhanced economic and military power and its diplomatic posture, which has invariably directed national efforts in strengthening soft power, has managed to build alliances rather successfully and, in fact, has created significant dependencies in the Asian neighborhood.

China's engagement in Africa

Over the past decade, Beijing has emerged as an active and influential player in Africa, driven by its quest for energy, desire to explore the African market for its products and fulfillment of the geopolitical objectives. Beijing sees Africa as an active global player and seeks political legitimacy for its proclaimed principles of 'non-interference' and 'South–South solidarity' through active engagement and investment in Africa.

For Africa, the engagement with China serves the purpose of attracting investment in Africa, expansion of trade, elevation of its political stature and human development. Africa's strategic options and its development pattern is being redefined with the change in the international environment and the global power shift post-Cold War. Africa's energy resources, young population and its economic potential present an opportunity to the continent to alter its position on the global platform. Africa's growth and its potential (with rich natural resources and human capital) place it as a new frontier for growth and development. China's interest and engagement in Africa has provided wider options to the African nations without the political interference of the West.

The creation of the Forum on China–Africa Cooperation (FOCAC) in 2000 formalized the bilateral relationship between the two. The entity was created by China's Ministry of Foreign Affairs (MFA) to coordinate China's activities in Africa, and it manages China's relationship with Africa across the range of political, technical and economic activities through the FOCAC (Hanauer & Morris, 2014: online).

In January 2006, *China's African Policy*, the White Paper promulgated by the Chinese government, outlined the general principles and objectives of China's African policy based on: Sincerity, Friendship and Equality; Mutual Benefit, Reciprocity and Common Prosperity; Mutual Support and Close Coordination; Learning from Each Other and Seeking Common Development. The White Paper outlined a comprehensive plan for China's engagement in Africa and stressed the One China principle as the principal foundation for the establishment of China's relations with African countries (*People's Daily*, 2006).

China's Second African Policy Paper (Xinhua, 2015b) outlined that in 2006 the Chinese government proposed a different approach towards the China–Africa strategic partnership, featuring political equality and mutual trust, economic win-win cooperation and cultural exchange. In the past decade, the trust between the two has been strengthened and since 2009, China has emerged as Africa's largest trading partner. According to the Fourth China–Africa Industrial Forum, China's trade with African states has grown about ten times in the past decade. China's trade with African countries, which was US$10 billion in 2000, grew to $220 billion in 2014. China aims to take the trade to $400 billion in 2020 (Xinhua, 2015a). China is leveraging the fact that most of the African countries are in the early stages of industralization, while China is already in an advanced stage of industalization and has technology and funds to offer (ibid.).

Chinese foreign direct investments have also shown an increase in Africa. The White Paper on China–Africa Trade and Economic Cooperation noted that between 2009 and 2012, China's direct investment in Africa grew at an annual rate of 20.5%. Although there have been widespread speculations regarding China's real motives in Africa and there are views that point out challenges related to Chinese investment in Africa, including the adverse impact on local manufacturing, the benefits of Chinese investment in Africa for the continent cannot be denied. Large scale investments in infrastructure and trade have played a role in economic growth and assisted poverty alleviation, better education and enhanced political engagement within the countries (Kuo, 2015). While the negative aspects need resolution, Africa has had much to gain from Chinese investment and aid.

India's growth and engagement with Africa

India is among the top ten economies today in terms of GDP. With China's continuing growth, as well as the other populous Asian countries' growth, it will make Asia the world's economic hub. The US Department of Agriculture said that India was the fastest growing economy since 2000. It is estimated that, in real terms, the Indian economy will become one of the largest economies in 2030 (United States Department of Agriculture Economic Research Service, online). India has been focused on economic growth and the GDP growth has been an average of about 7% in the past decade or so. It has one of the fastest growing service sectors, contributing around 57% of GDP. A liberalized economy, fast expanding service sector, vast population of educated youth, enhanced investor confidence and now the decline in oil prices have been instrumental in India's growth and expanding economic network. India will benefit in the near future from its demographic dividends, as it will be the world's youngest country by 2020. According to a UNFPA report, *State of World Population 2014*, India has the world's highest number of 10 to 24 year olds (UNFPA, 2014). The decline in oil prices is likely to reduce inflation which would invariably assist in bringing down interest rates and also cutting down of state subsidies, giving a further boost to the economy.

New Delhi has been active in building strategic partnerships which serve its political and economic interests. The past decade has seen strategic engagement with more than 12 nations. The partnerships aim to serve its core national interests: defense modernization, development of nuclear energy, cooperation in science and technology, support in critical diplomatic areas, trade and investment, banking, as well as multiple other sectors. Each partnership has a distinct character fulfilling different interests (Kumar et al., 2011). Its strategic partnership with the major powers, United States, Russia, France and Japan, is serving it well on the global front, strengthening its image and position, enabling New Delhi to assert itself in economic and political affairs.

One of the key features of India's foreign policy in the post-Cold War period has been its ambition to emerge as a global player and its relationship with Africa can be seen in this context. India's relationship with Africa in the past had been restricted and Africa was seen more as a colonial brother. India's relationship with Africa has been stepped up in the past two decades both bilaterally and with regional economic communities. India has adopted the pragmatic approach of attracting investment and expanding trade. Its vision of becoming a global player, its economic growth and enhanced connectivity have contributed to its fresh, engaged approach towards Africa. New Delhi is aiming to build sustainable partnerships through capacity building in industry, agriculture and infrastructure. India was the first Asian country to become a full member of the African Capacity Building Foundation (ACBF) and committed US$1 million to sustainable development and poverty alleviation (Cheru & Obi, 2010:69).

Under the Heavy Indebted Poor Countries (HIPC) Paris Initiative, India wrote off debt owed by the African nations and restructured commercial debts (ibid.). Structured engagement with Africa took shape in 2008 following the first India Africa Summit Forum (IASF) in New Delhi. The second IAFS was held in Addis Ababa in 2011. Both these events were limited to engagement with a few African leaders under the AU's Banjul format. The third IASF was hosted by New Delhi in 2015 and was a landmark event with the vast participation of African countries. The 2015 IASF witnessed the participation of 54 African nations and the *Delhi Declaration 2015*, and the *India–Africa Framework for Strategic Cooperation* outlined a multi-faceted strategy bringing together the India growth story with *Africa Agenda 2063* (Ministry of External Affairs, New Delhi, online).

The 2015 summit was held in a landmark year which marked the 70th anniversary of the UN, the adoption by the African Union (AU) of Agenda 2063 and the adoption of 2030

Agenda of Sustainable Development by the UNGA in September 2015. The 2015 summit called for mutual cooperation:

Call it the power of 55. Home to over two billion people, India and the 54-nation African continent are scripting a new chapter of renewal and resurgence. It's a winning combination of mutual empowerment, blending of rich resources and energy of Africa with technical expertise and capacity of India, one of the world's fastest growing economies and an emerging knowledge power.

(Ministry of External Affairs, New Delhi, online)

Indian leadership clearly foresees immense potential in the India–Africa relationship and intends to take it forward for mutual growth. The Indian Prime Minister during interaction with African journalists (2015) said that, 'India and Africa have a significant part of the global youth population in this century. Their future will shape the course of this world to a great extent' (Modi, 2015).

India's intentions and optimism towards sustainable development through this bilateral relationship were highlighted rather graphically in the message of the Indian Prime Minister during the latest India Africa Forum Summit (IAFS) in 2015:

India and Africa are now the bright spots of hope for the global economy. India is the fastest growing major economy today. Africa is experiencing rapid growth, too. While India and Africa will both do much on their own to advance prosperity and peace for their people, our partnership can be a source of great strength for each other, both to reinforce and accelerate each other's economic development and to build a more just, inclusive, equitable and sustainable world. We have complementary resources and markets; and the power of our human capital. We have shared global vision.

(Text of Prime Minister's Interaction, 2015: online)

The span of India's engagement with Africa is vast and Indian investment has been funneled in multiple directions. India has offered US$9 billion concessional credit in the past decade since IAFS-I in 2008. The approved projects include diversified sectors such as power generation and distribution, agriculture, renewable energy, water supply and irrigation, construction of infrastructure, etc. Capability building has been an area of focus for India in Africa and New Delhi has offered about 100 training programs at different institutions encompassing a variety of areas, including food processing, vocational training, agriculture, English language, etc. (Chand, 2015: online). India is Africa's fourth largest trading partner and the exports as well as imports from Africa have been growing significantly, catering to mutual needs and deficiencies.

India's relations with Africa centered, for a long time, around the struggle against colonialism, apartheid, poverty, hunger and disease. The areas of cooperation between the two regions have grown significantly and also the approach towards policy and implementation. Not only trade, economic and capacity building, but the two regions need mutual support to address multilateral and global issues such as terrorism, UN Security Council membership, security issues, climate change and the international trading regime. This was reflected very vividly in the two documents signed during the third summit: *Delhi Declaration 2015* and *India–Africa Framework for Strategic Cooperation*. The documents identify issues of bilateral, regional and international interests and the priorities of India and Africa, and also agree to establish a formal monitoring mechanism to review implementation of the agenda.

The recent developments in India–Africa relations do reflect the intentions and optimism from both sides to move together towards a global agenda of sustainable development. The implementation of the program would require sustained efforts from both sides.

Challenges to Asia–Africa cooperation and the role of the G20 in achieving the Sustainable Development Goals

Asia–Africa relations have been on the rise, complementing each other's economic and strategic requirements. China's rise in the past two decades has been distinct and India looks committed towards a sustained growth path. Africa has emerged as a new hub of growth and according to a report by Federation of Indian Chambers of Commerce and Industry (FICCI), 'Nowhere in the world is the impact of economic growth and development as visible as in Africa.' According to the FICCI report, Africa's real GDP (5.2% per annum in Africa and 5.7% in Sub-Saharan Africa) in the past decade has grown at more than twice the rate of the 1980s and 1990s. This growth is expected to continue through to 2020 (FICCI, online).

China and India have been actively engaged in Africa and writing themselves in the Africa growth story. China is the largest trading partner of Africa and India is the fifth largest trading partner. It is estimated that in the coming years Africa's growth in imports from India and China will surpass the rest of the world (FICCI, online). Gains for Asia (China and India) and Africa are not restricted to the economic development from this relationship but also extend to the strategic and political arena. Both China and India have not only provided extended development assistance to Africa but have given its countries the status of equal power without any prescriptions on democracy and good governance. Africa, on the other hand, is a partner with whom Beijing seeks political legitimacy on the international forum. India is keen for partnership with the African countries on the issues of human rights, terrorism and its bid for a permanent membership at the United Nations Security Council (UNSC).

However, China's role in Africa has sparked debates at the regional and international level and there are pessimisms attached to China's deepening engagement in Africa. Concerns have been raised regarding violations of human rights and investments with low local content. The West accuses China of 'neo-colonialism' and has not reacted positively to China's expanding role in Africa, and there are views which see China as a 'neo-colonist' and a 'resource-hungry' power. Hillary Clinton, during her tour to Africa in 2011, in an interview said:

> *We saw that during colonial times – it is easy to come in, take out natural resources, pay off leaders, and leave. And when you leave, you don't leave much behind for the people who are there. You don't improve standard of living. You don't create a ladder of opportunity . . . We don't want to see a new colonialism in Africa.*
>
> *(Clinton, 2011: online)*

Chinese have invested aggressively in Africa and acquired substantial goodwill, according to the Afrobarometer's findings released in 2016, including surveys in 36 African countries (Lekorwe et al., 2016: online). Although Beijing has expanded its presence as an active investor, it still faces concerns which cannot be ignored if it wishes to maintain its momentum of investment and presence. According to Wang and Elliot, Beijing struggles to win hearts and minds in Africa, mainly due to the 'opportunistic and extractive nature' of its business activities and its inability to offer a value-based system (Wang & Elliot, 2014: online). There are differing opinions about China in different areas and aspects of society in Africa. While there is indeed a large section of Africans who trust China as a reliable business partner, there is a section which is concerned about the negative aspects of the Chinese presence. One of the concerns raised is Chinese overemphasis on economic development over civil and political rights. China's failure to promote and encourage human rights in Africa is being discussed repeatedly in the Western and African media.

A critical aspect of human rights concerns can be traced to continued Chinese engagement with authoritarian regimes in Africa, which, in the long term, are likely to hinder the development of democratic practices and liberty, and may encourage human rights abuses. One of the examples quoted by Sisheng Zhao has been a multibillion dollar deal struck by China International Fund for oil and mineral extraction under the military junta, right after the September 28, 2009 massacre in Guinea (Zhao, 2014). Another example is China's sale of significant quantities of arms, including military aircraft and helicopters, to Sudan, which assisted the civil war in the south and Darfur (Shinn, 2006: online). In 2006, Amnesty International released a report on China's irresponsible export of arms to authoritarian regimes and nations with a gross record of human rights violations. The report provided the details of the delivery of large quantities of arms to Liberia from China, in violation of the UN arms embargo on Liberia (Amnesty International, 2006: 13–15).

The Africans are currently enjoying the immediate and direct effects of Chinese investment, but Chinese disregard for labor laws and the environment is something to watch out for. The lack of Chinese concerns for the African environment has been debated specifically in the case of the timber industry. A report by the International Institute for Environment Development, UK (2014) stated: 'Amongst the range of African and international stakeholders, there appears to be a perception that the environment performance of Chinese companies is poor and that many Chinese companies are only interested in Africa's natural resources' (Sun et al., 2014:50).

There are concerns from Africa regarding the blow to the local industries in Africa due to Chinese products. Also, the Chinese have been accused of poor labor and environmental practices. Some African politicians are taking or have taken a stance against China. As an example, Michael Sata, while contesting the 2006 Zambia elections, played the China card and attacked Chinese investors relentlessly. Sata, in fact, promised to recognize Taiwan as an independent country if he won the 2006 elections (China Africa Research Initiative, 2011: online).

Despite massive Chinese investment in Africa, Beijing does not enjoy soft power dominance in Africa. Experts differ in their views on the non-economic influence China exercises there (Shih, 2013: online). There is little enthusiasm for Chinese culture and their way of governance, although Africans do admire the economic rise of China.

Despite the challenges, Africans welcome Chinese investment and do see the gains for the African economy (Kuo, 2015: online). Beijing has managed to construct its relationship with Africa with an 'exceptionalist approach', a current feature of China's continental and bilateral engagement as discussed in a study by Alden and Large. Beijing's exceptionalism is understood as a normative modality of engagement where, although there is economic asymmetry, there is a clear recognition of equality in economic gains and also political standing (Alden & Large, 2011:21–22).

Africa's engagement with India has a positive growth trajectory and the current Indian leadership looks committed to continuing and growing the cooperation between the two. The initiatives pronounced in the 2015 India–Africa summit need sustained efforts from both sides and thus the challenge would be to continue the efforts with the same energy which has been pronounced by the current government of India, even if there is regime change in the future. The recent initiatives by New Delhi are driven by its economic and strategic goals and its vision for India to be recognized as a global player.

Asia and Africa are seen as engines of future growth but these regions also confront significant global security challenges which could restrict their future growth trajectory and their progress towards achieving sustainable development goals. There is a complex interplay of intra-state tensions, inter-state tensions, regime legitimacy, terrorism, security challenges posed by non-state actors, violent conflicts and changing power equations in the region. Although Asia and Africa have the most youthful population, which is regarded as an asset, rampant population growth also poses the challenges of national integration, social stability and rural-to-urban migration.

Role of the G20 in achieving Sustainable Development Goals

The potential and challenges in Asia–Africa cooperation bring to bear the significance and responsibility of the G20, which includes more emerging economies than any other global grouping. Although the likely challenges don't appear to be affecting cooperation at present, they need to be addressed under a broader umbrella, with an integrated approach for a sustained growth of cooperation between the two regions.

The membership of the G20 is much more inclusive than any other world body. The G20 could be expected to form a critical forum in facilitating sustained development in Asia and Africa and to help enhance the cooperation between the two regions.

The G20 has been engaged in crisis management and building a new financial architecture which caters to the interests of the emerging economies (Ito, 2010:8–10). However, global financial issues and sustainable development cannot be seen in isolation. The SDGs are broad goals which are applicable universally and would require integrated efforts: nationally and internationally, financially and non-financially and politically and technically. A world body such as the G20 with adequately broad representation is required to deal with the global economic issues impacting development. The G20 has the potential to assist economic growth, create job opportunities, improve infrastructure and help build institutions.

The Communiqué of the G20 London summit in 2009 reaffirmed commitment of the G20 in meeting the MDGs, to 'lay the foundation for a fair and sustainable world order', recognized 'that the current crisis has a disproportionate impact on the vulnerable in the poorest countries', and its 'collective responsibility to mitigate the social impact of the crisis to minimize long-lasting damage to global potential' (G20 Communiqué, online). The G20 summits have gradually started endorsing development in their agenda but perhaps the seminal moment came under the Korean Presidency. The Seoul Summit in 2010 placed development as a prominent issue on its agenda by adopting the Seoul Development Consensus for Shared Growth which affirmed the commitment of the G20 'to work in partnership with other developing countries, and LICs in particular, to help them build the capacity to achieve and maximize their growth potential, thereby contributing to global rebalancing' (G20 Communiqué, online). Following the Seoul Summit each G20 summit has chosen priority pillars with the objectives of addressing different areas: poverty, food security, green growth, infrastructure and refugees. For example, the Cannes Summit discussed issues relating to infrastructure, food security and innovative financing. The Los Cabos Summit announced commitment towards gender equality and 'inclusive green growth'. The Petersburg Summit discussed the post-2015 Development Agenda and endorsed the St Petersburg Development Outlook to focus on five areas: improve food security, financial inclusion, infrastructure, human resource development and domestic resource mobilization (G20 Communiqué, online). The Brisbane Summit in 2014 included the development agenda as an extension of the G20's broader growth agenda. The Antalya Summit (2015) supported 'Buttressing Sustainability' and identified key areas of sustainable development. The foundation of the G20 agenda in 2016 was 'Towards an Innovative, Invigorated, Interconnected and Inclusive World Economy'

(G20 Communiqué, online) The G20 Action Plan on the 2030 Agenda for Sustainable Development ensures the G20's commitment 'to further aligning its work with the 2030 Agenda for Sustainable Development' (G20: online).

The G20 is not a permanent institution with its own secretariat and its legitimacy is often contested. It has no distinct legal base and thus, its ability to lay down rules and enforcement mechanisms for the non-G20 members and for that matter even the G20 members is limited. The implementation of the development agenda (announced in the G20 summits) depends on the ability of the member countries to promote respective goals in their own countries and under the bilateral cooperation agreements. Promotion of sustained growth would require the member states to back their commitments with carefully calibrated macroeconomic policies. Also, the member states need to coordinate their polices and activities with the United Nations system and also the Bretton Woods institutions. The legitimacy and effectiveness of the G20 depend on its ability to motivate the member states to accept the endorsed ideas and also how it is able to rally support through regional organizations (Hawke, 2010:21).

The achievement of the SDGs demands sustained efforts from the developed and developing/emerging economies. The G20 provides an opportunity to Asian countries to voice their economic and development challenges which require global decision making. The strengths of the G20 which could be leveraged in achieving the SDGs can be highlighted as follows.

Firstly, it provides a common forum to the leaders of the member states to share experiences and learning (Hawke, 2010:21). It provides an opportunity to engage bilaterally and multilaterally on issues of common interest and also to address common challenges. The growing nations have much to learn from the experiences of the developed economies. On the other hand, the developed nations need to be more aware of the challenges of the emerging/growing/developing economies. This exchange certainly assists in aligning the national and international policies for sustainable development. It provides an option to identify and act on the problems which demand collective actions. G20 can potentially act as a forum where the nations come together not owing to historical alliances but on the basis of commonality of challenges they confront. This is helpful as implementation of the SDGs demands collective actions.

Secondly, the G20 members represent 85% of the world's GDP and two-thirds of its population. They includes the wealthiest nations, major rising powers as well as the less developed economies. The implementation of the SDGs can only be achieved with the sustained support of the developed nations towards the emerging economies. The G20 has more experience, more resources and offers options for growth and development through various modalities: South–South cooperation, North–South cooperation, North–North cooperation.

Thirdly, a forum like the G20 is an opportunity for the leadership of the member states to take a much broader view of their domestic issues which might have spillover effects on other states. It is often debated that the growing economies today are facing challenges which are actually an outcome of the policies pursued by the developed states in the past. Challenges like climate change and cyber security are some of examples where developed countries share major responsibility.

Fourthly, there is synergy between the G20 development agenda and the SDGs. The development agenda endorsed in the G20 links well with the SDGs. The London Summit in 2009 was moderate in pronouncing its commitment to the MDGs and was focused on building a financial architecture to deal with the economic crisis. But successive summits have endorsed the development agenda quite lucidly. The priorities of the 2017 G20 summit under the German Presidency include the G20's commitment to 'ensure, both through individual and collective action, the rapid and comprehensive implementation of the 2030 Agenda, with its global goals for sustainable development, and of the Addis Ababa Action Agenda' (G20: online).

Asia is well represented in the G20, but currently, South Africa is the only member state from Africa. There have been few efforts in the G20 to relate to Africa in a structured way. For example, in the Seoul Summit, a suggestion was made that the G20 would invite five non-member states, out of which two would be African states. The G20 under the Chinese leadership in 2016 pronounced its willingness for a greater role for Africa. The Communiqué at the Hangzhou Summit endorsed China's goal 'to initiate cooperation to support industrialization of Africa and least developing countries (LDCs)'. Major Asian countries in the G20 (China and India) have individual African policies which include the objective of achieving the SDGs through bilateral cooperation. There is certainly a need for the G20 to have an African strategy and also a somewhat larger representation of Africa. Integration of national polices of the states at the global level, targeting a global agenda and expanded international cooperation for emerging/developing economies, is indispensable for sustainable development. Adolf Kloke-Lesch (2015) argues that it is time to 'embark on a new and comprehensive narrative of International Cooperation for Sustainable Development (ICSD)' (Kloke-Lesch, 2015: online). The narrative would involve all forms of cooperation (North–South, South–South and North–North) to work towards sustainable development. Kloke-Lesch argues that with its unique composition the G20 is 'well placed to contribute significantly to the new world of ICSD' (Kloke-Lesch, 2015: online).

The G20 could potentially play a crucial role in achieving the SDGs by acting as a forum for discussion, mediation and policy formulation between Asia and Africa, which are seen as major drivers of future growth and development. Asia–Africa cooperation has gained momentum and its sustenance would be important in order to implement decisions facilitating the achievement of the SDGs.

Conclusion

The global power shift has led to a notable shift of economic and political influence towards the South, and the creation of the G20 as a body to address the global financial crisis with active engagement of the emerging economies. The G20 has gradually embraced a much broader agenda which includes various aspects of development, e.g. climate change, poverty, refugees and human rights. China's growth has been remarkable along with a few others, including India and Africa which have been on an upward growth trajectory. Alterations in the post-Cold War power dynamics have brought in new power equations and cooperation models. China has invested heavily in Africa and looks towards Africa to fulfil its energy requirements and as a growing market for its products. India shares a historic legacy of colonialism with Africa and has shown an increasing interest in enhancing its development cooperation with Africa. The engagement models of the emerging/developing economies do incorporate the objective of achieving the SDGs through bilateral and multilateral cooperation. China is an active player with a phenomenal growth record, and can potentially play the most important role, along with a supporting role from India, in the implementation of the SDGs. Sustained development in Asia and Africa would require support from the major economies, and thus the role of the G20 becomes critical to addressing economic as well as social and political concerns at the global level. At the bilateral level, Asia–Africa cooperation does face a few challenges which include: China being accused of neo-colonialism, Beijing's disregard for human rights and environment laws, existing security challenges in Asia and Africa with a rise of extremism and the rebellious role of non-state actors, inter-state conflicts, etc. These problems do have the potential to restrict the future growth of bilateral cooperation (China–Africa, India–Africa) and subsequently the implementation of the SDGs. The G20 is a platform with global representation which brings in the experience, learning and initiatives of the developed and developing economies. It could play a critical role in policy formulation and implementation to support the achievement of the SDGs. The SDGs, which are broad universal goals, would require initiatives at the national, regional and international levels.

Bibliography

Africa Desk, 2016. *The Rising Africa*, Report on economic trends, trade, investments and economic projections in Africa, FICCI. Available at: http://ficci.in/spdocument/20566/The-Rising-Africa.pdf [Accessed 5 December 2016].

Alden C. and Large D., 2011. 'China's Exceptionalism and the Challenge of Delivering Difference in Africa', *Journal of Contemporary China*, Volume 20 (68), pp. 21–38.

Alexander, T., 1996. *Unravelling Global Apartheid: An Overview of World Politics*, Cambridge: Polity Press.

Amnesty International, 2006. 'People's Republic of China: Sustaining conflict and human rights abuses: The flow of arms accelerates', June. Available at: www.amnesty.org/download/Documents/72000/asa170302006en.pdf [Accessed 25 January 25, 2017].

Barry, T., 2002. 'G8: Falling Model of Global Governance', *Foreign Policy in Focus*, Volume 7, p. 9. Cited in Shah, A., 2008. 'G8 Summits: Empty Promises Each Year', *Global Issues*, August 25, 2008. Available at: www.globalissues.org/article/720/g8-summits-empty-promises-each-year [Accessed 10 December 2015].

Bitzinger, R. A. 2015. 'China's Double-digit Defense Growth: What it Means for a Peaceful Rise', *Foreign Affairs*, March 19, 2015. Available at: www.foreignaffairs.com/articles/china/2015-03-19/chinas-double-digit-defense-growth [Accessed 30 November 2015].

Chand, M., 2015. 'India and Africa: Sharing Interlinked Dreams', Ministry of External Affairs, New Delhi, India. Available at: www.mea.gov.in/in-focus-article.htm?24742/India+and+Africa+Sharing+interlinked+dreams [Accessed 2 December 2016].

Cheru, F. and Obi, C. (eds.), 2010. *The Rise of China and India in Africa*, London: Zed Books.

China Africa Research Initiative Blog, 2011. 'Micheal Sata and China in Zambia', China in Africa the Real Story, *Johns Hopkins School of Advanced International Studies*, Available at: www.chinaafricarealstory. com/2011/10/michael-sata-and-china-in-zambia.html [Accessed 2 December 2016].

China Energy Outlook (2015-2016), CASS Innovation Program World Energy China Outlook 2015–2016, Interim Report. Available at: http://docplayer.net/24830050-China-energy-outlook. html [Accessed 10 December 2016].

Clinton, H., 2011. Secretary of State, Interview on Africa 360. Lusaka, Zambia, June 11, 2011, US Department of State. Available at: https://2009-2017.state.gov/secretary/20092013clinton/rm/2011/06/165941.htm [Accessed 9 July 2017].

Dollar, D., 2016. 'China's Engagement with Africa: From Natural Resources to Human Resources', The John L. Thornton China Center, Brookings. Available at: www.brookings.edu/wp-content/uploads/2016/07/Chinas-Engagement-with-Africa-David-Dollar-July-2016.pdf [Accessed 21 November 2016].

Financial Times, 2008. 'Bush to Call G20 Summit on Crisis', October 23. Available at: www.ft.com/cms/s/0/34a9c294-a09b-11dd-80a0-000077b07658.html?ft_site=falcon&desktop=true#axzz4Qq0HYt4B [Accessed 14 October 2016].

G20 Action Plan on the 2030 Agenda for Sustainable Development, 2016. G 20 2016, China. Available at: www.g20.org/Content/DE/_Anlagen/G7_G20/2016-09-08-g20-agenda-action-plan.pdf?__blob=publicationFile&v=4 [Accessed 20 November, 2016].

G20 Communiqué: London Summit, 2009. *The Global Plan for Recovery and Reform*. Available at: www.g20.org/Content/DE/StatischeSeiten/Breg/G7G20/Anlagen/G20-erklaerung-london-en.pdf?__blob=publicationFile&v=3 [Accessed 12 December 2016].

G20 Germany 2017, Hamburg, 2016, 'Priorities of the 2017 G20 Summit'. Available at: www.g20.org/Content/DE/_Anlagen/G7_G20/2016-g20-praesidentschaftspapier-en.pdf?__blob=publicationFile&v=2 [Accessed 14 December 2016].

G20 Leaders' Communiqué Hangzhou Summit, September 4–5 2016. Available at: www.g20.org/Content/DE/_Anlagen/G7_G20/2016-09-04-g20-kommunique-en.pdf?__blob=publicationFile&v=6 [Accessed 1 December 2016].

G20 Leaders' Declaration, September 6, 2013, St Petersburg, G20 Information Centre, University of Toronto. Available at: www.g20.utoronto.ca/2013/2013-0906-declaration.html [Accessed 11 December 2016].

G20 Seoul Summit Leaders' Declaration, 2010. November 11–12. Available at: online.wsj.com [Accessed 2 December 2016].

Garten, J. E., 1997. *The Big Ten: The Big Emerging Markets and How They Will Change Our Lives*, New York: Basic Books.

Ghosh, P., 2012. 'Chinese People's Liberation Army architecture and its approach to modernisation', in J. T. Singh (ed.), *Essays on China*, New Delhi: Knowledge World, pp. 61–102.

Guerrero, D. G., 2016. 'China Rising: A New World Order or an Order Renewal?' *TNI* Paper, Transnational Institute. Available at: www.tni.org/sites/www.tni.org/files/download/shifting_power-china_0.pdf [Accessed 10 November 2016].

Hanauer, L. and Morris, L. J., 2014. 'Chinese Engagement in Africa: Drivers, Reactions, and Implications for US Policy', *RAND*, Santa Monica, CA: RAND. Available at: www.rand.org/content/dam/rand/pubs/research_reports/RR500/RR521/RAND_RR521.pdf [Accessed 21 November 2015].

Hawke, G., 2010. 'Consensus, Compliance and the Limits of Legitimacy', *East Asia Forum Quarterly*, Volume 2 (4), p. 21.

Hubbard, G. and Miller, D., 2005. 'Introduction: Barbarism Inc.', in Hubbard, G. & Miller, D. (eds.), *Arguments Against G8*, London: Pluto Press.

International Energy Agency, 2014. *World Energy Outlook 2014*, France. Available at: http://www.iea.org/publications/freepublications/publication/WEO2014.pdf [Accessed 28 November 2016].

Ito, T. I, 2010. 'Towards a New World Financial Architecture', *East Asia Forum Quarterly*, Volume 2 (4), pp. 8–10.

Jiwei, L., 2015. Statement, Ministry of Finance, The People's Republic of China. Annual Meetings of the Boards of Governors of the World Bank Group and the International Monetary Fund, LIMA Annual Meetings, October 9, Lima, Peru. Available at: https://www.imf.org/external/am/2015/speeches/pr29e.pdf [Accessed 10 December 2015].

Kirton, John G., 2013. *G20 Governance for a Globalised World*, Burlington, VT: Ashgate Publishing.

Kloke-Lesch, A., 2015. 'The G20 and the Sustainable Development Goals (SDGs): Reflections on Future Roles and Tasks', Third Annual G20 Think Tank Summit 'Global Governance and Open Economy', July 30–August 1, 2015, Chinyang Institute for Financial Studies, Renin University, Beijing (online). Available at: www.die-gdi.de/uploads/media/Kloke-Lesch_The_G20_and_the_Sustainable_Development_Goals.pdf [Accessed 10 November 2016].

Kumar, S., Pradhan, S.D., Sibal, K., Bedi, R. and Ganguly, B., 2011. *India's Strategic Partners: A Comparative Assessment*, FNSR Group of Experts Foundation for National Security Research, New Delhi. Available at: http://fnsr.org/files/Indias_Strategic.pdf [Accessed 13 October 2015].

Kuo, S., 2015. 'China's Investment in Africa: The African Perspective', *Forbes*, Available at: www.forbes.com/sites/riskmap/2015/07/08/chinas-investment-in-africa-the-african-perspective/#3465e51016e2 [Accessed 20 October 2016].

Lekorwe, M., Chingwete, A., Okuru, M. and Samson, R. 2016. 'AD122: China's growing presence in Africa wins large positive popular views', *Afrobarometer*, Round 6. Dispatch No. 122. Available at: http://afrobarometer.org/publications/ad122-chinas-growing-presence-africa-wins-largely-positive-popular-reviews [Accessed 16 January 2017].

Miller, E., 2005. 'The Gang of 8: The good governance roadshow', in Hubbard, G. L and Miller, D. (ed.), *Arguments Against G8*, London: Pluto.

Ministry of External Affairs, 2015. New Delhi, India, India–Africa Forum Summit III: New Hopes, New Horizons. Available at: http://mea.gov.in/india-africa-forum-summit-2015/index.html. [Accessed 1 November 2016].

Modi, N., 2015. Text of Prime Minister's interaction with African journalists at the Editor's Forum for the 3rd India–Africa Forum Summit, 2015. October 23. Available at: http://www.narendramodi.in/prime-minister-s-interaction-with-african-journalists-at-the-editors-forum-for-3rd-india-africa-forum-summit-365531 [Accessed 9 July 2017].

Pambazuka News, 2003. Joint Statement from African NGOs and Trade Unions, 'G8 Summits 2002 to 2003: From a Trickle to a Drop', June 5, Available at: https://www.pambazuka.org/governance/g8-summits-2002-2003-trickle-drop [Accessed 9 July 2017].

People's Daily Online, 2006. 'China's African Policy'. Available at: http://en.people.cn/200601/12/eng20060112_234894.html [Accessed 10 November 2016].

Postel-Vinay, K., 2014, *The G-20: A New Geopolitical Order*, Basingstoke: Palgrave Macmillan.

Sacha, J. D., 2012. 'From Millennium Development Goals to Sustainable Development Goals', *Lancet*, 379, pp. 2206–2211. Available at: http://www.grips.ac.jp/forum/IzumiOhno/lectures/2015_Lecture_texts/S16_From-MDGs-to-SDGs-Lancet-June-2012.pdf.

Shafaeddin, S. M., 2005. 'Trade Liberalistaion and Economic Reform in Developing Countries: Structural Change or De-industralization?' UNCTAD, Discussion Papers, No. 179, April 2005. Available at: http://unctad.org/en/docs/osgdp20053_en.pdf [Accessed January 15 2017].

Shambaugh, D., 2005. 'The Rise of China and Asia's New Dynamics', in Shambaugh, D. (ed.) *Power Shift: China and Asia's New Dynamics*, London: University of California Press, pp. 25–29.

Shih, T. H., 2013. 'Experts differ on China's 'soft power' in Africa', *South China Monitoring Post*, 22 July. Available at: www.scmp.com/news/china/article/1287767/experts-differ-chinas-soft-power-africa [Accessed 17 January 2017].

Shinn, David, 2006. 'The China Factor in African Ethics', *Policy Innovations*, December 21. Available at: www.policyinnovations.org/ideas/commentary/data/ChinaAfricaEthics [Accessed 21 January 2017].

Smith, G., 2011. 'G7 to G8 to G20: Evolution in Global Governance', *CIGI G20 Papers*, Volume 6, p. 4.

Sun, X., Ren, P. and Van Epp, M., 2014. 'Chinese Views of African Forests: Evidence and Perception of China–Africa Links that Impact the Governance of Forests and Livelihoods', IIED Natural Resource Issues, International Institute for Environment Development, UK.

Tran, M., 2012. 'Mark Malloch-Brown: Developing the MDGs was a Bit Like Nuclear Fusion', *The Guardian*, November 16, Available at: www.theguardian.com/global-development/2012/nov/16/mark-malloch-brown-mdgs-nuclear [Accessed 3 January 2015].

UNFPA, 2014. State of World Population 2014, *The Power of 1.8 Billion: Adolescents, Youth and the Transformation of the Future*, p. 5. Available at: http://eeca.unfpa.org/sites/default/files/pub-pdf/EN-SWOP14-FINAL-web.pdf [Accessed 11 December 2015].

United Nations General Assembly, 2015. 'Transforming Our World: The 2030 Agenda for Sustainable Development', A/RES/70/1. Available at: www.un.org/ga/search/view_doc.asp?symbol=A/RES/70/1&Lang=E [Accessed 15 May 2016].

United States Department of Agriculture Economic Research Service, 2016. Available at: www.ers.usda.gov/data-products/international-macroeconomic-data-set.aspx [Accessed 3 December 2015].

Wang, F. and Elliot, E. A., 2014. 'China in Africa: Presence, Perceptions and Prospects', *Journal of Contemporary China*, Volume 23 (90), pp. 1012–1032.

World Bank Group, 2016. *Transitioning from the MDGs to the SDGs*, New York: UNDP.

Xinhua, 2015a. 'China–Africa Trade Approaches $300 Billion in 2015', *China Daily*. Available at: www.chinadaily.com.cn/business/2015-11/10/content_22417707.htm [Accessed 1 December 2016].

Xinhua, 2015b. China's Second African Policy Paper. Available at: www.china.org.cn/world/2015-12/05/content_37241677.htm [Accessed 12 December 2016].

Zhao, S., 2014. 'A Neo-Colonialist Predator or Development Partner? China's Engagement and Rebalance on Africa', *Journal of Contemporary China*, Volume 23 (90). Available at: www.tandfonline.com/doi/full/10.1080/10670564.2014.898893?scroll=top&needAccess=true [Accessed 10 October 2016].

Security and governance

24

RELIGIONS, (IN)SECURITY AND CONFLICT IN AFRICA AND ASIA

Jeffrey Haynes

In recent years, religion has made a remarkable return to prominence in international politics. Confounding the expectations of secularists, today religion has a strong – perhaps growing – significance as a strong source of identity for millions of people, especially in the developing world. In many countries, religious individuals and organisations are important carriers of ideas, norms and values. They often play important roles both as a source of conflict and as a tool for conflict resolution and peace building via early warnings of conflict, as good offices once conflict has erupted, as well as in advocacy, mediation and reconciliation. As a result, religions are strongly associated with issues of security versus insecurity, as their hatreds and differences are central to many recent and current conflicts in the developing world.

This chapter will explain and account for religions' involvement in issues of security and conflict in Africa and Asia. Religion is often an ambivalent dimension to conflict, conflict resolution and peace building. How religion behaves in this regard will depend upon a number of factors, analysed in this chapter. There is no single, elegant theoretical model enabling us to deal with all relevant cases of religious involvement in security and conflict issues in Africa and Asia. Nonetheless, the influence of religion is said to be increasing in relation to 'good governance' issues in the developing world, an issue often affected by the multiple impacts of globalisation; and sometimes issues linked to governance can also be seen to influence the trajectory of conflict in Africa and Asia. Recent and current globalisation – characterised in the developing world by its often destabilising economic, political, cultural and technological effects – can also affect religions by undermining associated traditional value systems. A consequence is that, in many developing countries, including in Africa and Asia, large numbers of people are said to feel both disorientated and troubled and in response (re)turn to religion to try to deal with associated existential angst. Such people may find in religion a source of comfort, serenity, stability and spiritual uplifting. Some may experience new or renewed feelings of identity that not only help provide believers' lives with meaning and purpose but can also, in some cases, contribute to inter-religious competition and conflict (Norris & Inglehart, 2004).

Globalisation leads to greatly increased interaction between people and communities. Such interactions are not always harmonious, leading in some cases to what Kurtz labels 'culture wars' (Kurtz, 1995:168). Kurtz argues that culture wars can occur when religious or secular worldviews encourage different allegiances and standards in relation to various areas, including the family, law, education and politics. 'Culture war' conflicts can 'take on "larger-than-life" proportions as the struggle of good against evil' (Kurtz, 1995:170). Such conflicts can seriously affect a country's chances of development, necessary to increase security and undermine chances of conflict. As we shall in this chapter, some of the conflicts in African and Asian countries can be seen as being characterised by culture war concerns, which can make their resolution very difficult. In sum, many recent and current conflicts in the developing world, including in Africa and Asia, are associated with religious differences, which drive accompanying hatred and violence.

A key implication of the involvement of religion in conflicts is that religion can either be assessed as an 'angel of peace' or be regarded as a 'warmonger'. As Appleby notes, and Kurtz seems to underline, religion's *ambivalence* is characterised by the fact that the relationship of the world religions (that is, Buddhism, Christianity, Hinduism, Islam and Judaism) to violence is always uncertain and evidence can be referred to which depicts religion in a good or less favourable light (Appleby, 2000).

> All great God-narratives are familiar with traditions that legitimise force in certain cir-
> cumstances, claim victims in the battle for their own beliefs and demonise people of
> other religions. However, at the same time there are sources that proclaim the incom-
> patibility of violence with religion, demand sacrifices for peace and insist on respect
> for people of other religions.
>
> *(Holenstein, 2005:10)*

Ambivalence becomes clear when we focus upon current religious involvement in large-scale conflicts, key causes of insecurity for large numbers of people. For example, large-scale violence in Africa, Asia and other parts of the developing world is increasingly associated with serious social conflicts, some of which involve religious tensions. Barringer (2006:2) notes that religious tensions are very often linked to other issues, including 'ethnicity, culture, class, power and wealth, played out' in many African and Asian countries, such as Nigeria, Sri Lanka, India and Pakistan.

A key to eventual peace, implying enhanced security and declining conflict, may well be the achievement of significant collaborative efforts among different religious entities, which, along with external religious and secular organisations, for example, the European Union or the United Nations, may, through collaborative efforts, eventually work to develop a new model of peace and cooperation to enable many regional countries to escape from what often seems an endless cycle of religion- and culture-based conflict. It is important to note that the role of religion in both African and Asian conflicts is twofold: religion can play a significant, even a fundamental, role in contributing to conflicts in various ways, including how they are intensified, channelled or reconciled; but it can also play an important role in seeking to resolve conflicts and build peace.

These introductory comments point to the fact that religion is by no means invariably associated with conflict, as it can play a significant role in attempts to resolve inter- and intra-group clashes and help build peace. Bartoli (2005:5–6) notes that 'all religious trad-itions contain references in the form of didactical stories, teaching or even direct recom-mendation as to how the faithful should act in order to achieve harmony and peace within him/herself in the first place'. In recent years, numerous books and journal articles have appeared, collectively focusing on how religious actors can play a role in ending conflicts and building peace. It is this recent literature that stresses religion's ambivalence when it comes to conflict, conflict resolution and peace building. Summarising an initial set of findings regarding religious peace building and faith-based diplomacy, Appleby (2006) notes the following:

- Religious leaders are uniquely positioned to foster nonviolent conflict transformation through the building of constructive, collaborative relationships within and across ethnic and religious groups for the common good of the entire population of a country or region.
- In many conflict settings around the world, the social location and cultural power of religious leaders make them potentially critical players in any effort to build a sustainable peace.
- The multigenerational local or regional communities they oversee are repositories of local knowledge and wisdom, custodians of culture, and privileged sites of moral, psychological and spiritual formation.
- Symbolically charged sources of personal as well as collective identity, these communities typically establish and maintain essential educational and welfare institutions, some of which serve people who are not members of the religious community.

(Appleby, 2006:1)

The structure of this chapter is as follows. Following the introductory section, we turn to the issue of religions' involvement in conflict and conflict resolution, in order to highlight the ambivalence of religions in relation to this issue. After that, we focus on relevant African and Asian case studies, particularly Sudan and Sri Lanka, in religious identity, (in)security and conflict, in order to highlight and examine religion's ambivalence to conflict, conflict resolution and peace building. Before concluding, we assess the transnational and inter-regional jihadist groups which affect the two regions and significantly influence conflicts and their outcome. This enables us to highlight more generally the impact of globalisation and the associated impact of values, norms and beliefs in the context of religion-linked conflict, conflict resolution and peace building.

Religions, conflict and conflict resolution

Although many religious believers would regard their chosen religious expressions as both benevolent and inspiring, sometimes religious faiths are linked to violence and conflict – both between and within religious groups (or at least entities with a religious veneer). We can note the ramifications of September 11, 2001, in this regard. In the 16 years since then, a mass of literature has appeared on religious contributions to conflict and violence (see Marsden, 2012, and Seiple et al., 2012). In addition, various armed groups, such as al Qaeda, claim religious justifications for their terrorist activities in both Africa and Asia.

It is not that surprising that religion is implicated in both domestic and international conflicts. This is because religious conviction contains within it various sources of related danger:

- *Religion is focused on the absolute and unconditional and as a result can adopt totalitarian characteristics.* The monotheistic religions – Christianity, Islam and Judaism – may have especial difficulty trying to distinguish between, on the one hand, claims of the absolutely divine and, on the other, the traditions and history of human existence.
- *When claiming both absolute and exclusive validity, religious conviction can lead to intolerance, over-zealous proselytisation and religious fragmentation.* Religious exclusiveness is also typically hostile to both pluralism and liberal democracy.
- *Religion can increase aggressiveness and the willingness to use violence.* Added symbolic value can be an aspect of religious conviction, deriving from profane motivation and aims that become 'holy' objectives.

- *Leaders within faith-based organisations may seek to legitimise abuses of power and violation of human rights in the name of religious zeal.* Because such leaders are nearly always men, there can also be specific gender issues and women's human rights concerns.

According to Holenstein (2005:11), religious power interests may try to make use of the following susceptibilities:

- Domination strategies of identity politics may seek to harness real or perceived 'ethnic-cultural' and 'cultural-religious' differences.
- Misused religious motivation informs some recent and current terrorist activities.
- Leaders of religious fundamentalist movements 'lay claim to a single and absolutist religious interpretation at the cost of all others, and they link their interpretation to political power objectives'.

Holenstein's last point relates to what Kurtz (1995:238) calls 'exclusive accounts of the nature of reality', that is, followers only accept religious beliefs that they regard as *true*. Examples include the 'religions of the book' – Judaism, Christianity and Islam – because each faith claims an authority that emanates principally from exclusive sacred texts. On the one hand, such exclusivist truth claims can be a serious challenge to religious toleration and diversity, essential to our co-existence in a globalised world, and make conflict more likely. On the other hand, many religious traditions have within them beliefs that can help develop a peaceful, multicultural world. For example, from within Christianity comes the idea of non-violence, a key attribute of Jesus, the religion's founder, who insisted that all people are children of God, and that the test of one's relationship with God is whether one loves one's enemies and brings good news to the poor. As St Paul said, 'There is no Jew or Greek, servant or free, male or female: because you are all one in Jesus Christ' (Galatians 3:28).

In terms of contemporary conflicts, two forms involving religion, security and conflict are common in both Africa and Asia: (1) religious fundamentalism, and (2) 'religious terrorism' which thrives in 'failed' and 'failing' states, of which there are many in Africa and Asia (Appleby, 2000; Juergensmeyer, 2016).

First, some religious 'fundamentalisms' are associated with religious and political conflicts in both Africa and Asia (Ozzano, 2016). Although often individually distinctive, many religious fundamentalists share a common characteristic: believing themselves to be under threat, followers adopt a

> 'set of strategies, by which [these] beleaguered believers attempt to preserve their distinctive identity as a people or group' in response to real or imagined attacks from non-believers who, they believe, are trying to draw them into a 'syncretistic, areligious, or irreligious cultural milieu'.
>
> *(Marty & Appleby, 1993:3)*

In such a context, fundamentalists' 'defence of religion' can develop into social or political offensives with domestic and/or international ramifications.

Second, 'failed' and 'failing' states, as we shall see, may provide ideal circumstances encouraging conflicts linked to religious terrorism (Juergensmeyer, 2016). Examples of recent and current failed states in Africa and Asia include Somalia, Iraq and Afghanistan (Haynes, 2005:224–243). Such states are very unstable environments lacking effective central government, circumstances that are often conducive to the development of secular or religious terrorism. Circumstances prevailing in failed states may encourage people to turn to religion as a result of a feeling that their existential security is threatened. In addition, absence of effective central government provides circumstances that allow international religious terrorist groups, such as al Qaeda, to thrive; in some cases, failed states – including Afghanistan, Iraq and Somalia – have recently become 'safe havens' for al Qaeda and other similar jihadist groups, launching pads for attacks. For example, Gunaratna (2004) claims that al Qaeda has cells in up to 60 countries worldwide, dispensing money and logistical support and training to radical Islamist groups in numerous countries, many of which are geographically distant, including the Philippines and Indonesia.

Conflict resolution and peace building

I am not arguing that religions in Africa and Asia are *necessarily* associated with conflict and violence. However, conflict in these regions, as elsewhere in the developing world, is rarely if ever one-sided. This is because the world religions contain various voices with different views, reflecting the concerns of many people who share a faith but who nevertheless may see the world differently and as a result act differently too. Religious leaders may play a pivotal role in helping to resolve inter- and intra-group clashes and conflicts and help build peace. They may draw on key teachings of their religious faith, serving to emphasise that 'all religious traditions contain references in the form of didactical stories, teaching or even direct recommendation as to how the faithful should act in order to achieve harmony and peace within him/herself in the first place' (Bartoli, 2005:5–6). Nonetheless, there are today many examples of religion's involvement in *both* conflict *and* cooperation. Summarising an initial set of findings regarding religious peace building and faith-based diplomacy, Appleby (2006:1) notes that:

- Religious leaders are uniquely positioned to foster nonviolent conflict transformation through the building of constructive, collaborative relationships within and across ethnic and religious groups for the common good of the entire population of a country or region.
- In many conflict settings around the world, the social location and cultural power of religious leaders make them potentially critical players in any effort to build a sustainable peace.
- The multigenerational local or regional communities they oversee are repositories of local knowledge and wisdom, custodians of culture, and privileged sites of moral, psychological and spiritual formation.
- Symbolically charged sources of personal as well as collective identity, these communities typically establish and maintain essential educational and welfare institutions, some of which also serve people who are not members of their religious community.

While in recent years the role of religious leaders in the these respects has been highlighted, it is not an entirely new phenomenon. Religious individuals and/or representatives of various faith-based organisations have, for decades, carried out such mediations, with variable success. Examples include: mediation undertaken by a Christian sect, the Quakers, and financed by the US Ford Foundation in the Nigerian Civil War, 1967–1970; the work of the World Council of Churches and the All Africa Conference of Churches in mediating a (temporary) cessation to the Sudan conflict in 1972; efforts made by a professor of international peace building at the University of Notre Dame, John Paul Lederach, in Nicaragua in the 1980s; and, in the 1990s and early 2000s, work by the Muslim Imam of Timbuktu in helping to mediate various West African conflicts (Ilo, 2016). Thus to focus exclusively and single-mindedly on *conflicts* within and between religions not only oversimplifies causal interconnections between religion and the absence of peace, in particular by disregarding important alternative variables, but also leads to a potential underestimation of attempts emerging from various religious traditions to help resolve conflicts and build peace. When successful, religion's role in helping resolve conflicts and build peace is a crucial component in helping achieve both peace and human development.

Success depends on the activities of the 'religious peacemakers', religious leaders, often representatives of religious organisations, who attempt to help resolve inter-group conflicts and build peace. Appleby (2006:1) suggests that religious peacemakers are most likely to be successful when they: (1) have an international or transnational reach, (2) consistently emphasise peace and avoidance of the use of force in resolving conflict, and (3) encourage good relations between different religions in a conflict situation. The three 'religions of the book' – Christianity, Islam, and Judaism – share a broadly similar set of theological and spiritual values and this can potentially underpin the ability to provide positive inter-faith contributions to conflict resolution, peace building and, more generally, inter-faith cooperation. Such efforts are increasing, with growing numbers and types of religious peacemakers working to try to build peaceful coexistence in multi-faith societies, while advocating reconciliation and fairness in a world increasingly characterised by economic polarisation, a key cause of both social and political strife (Bartoli, 2005). These observations lead to the following summary points regarding religious individuals/ organisations and their contributions to conflict resolution and peace building:

- Religious leaders and their organisations are active in attempts at peace building.
- Religious leaders have a special role to play in zones of religious conflict, yet related peace building programmes do not need to be confined to addressing religious conflict only.
- Although in some cases religious peace building projects resemble very closely peace building by secular peace builders, the religious orientation of religious leaders and organisations helps shape their peace building attempts.
- Religious peace building agendas are diverse, ranging from high-level mediation to training and peace building-through-development at the grassroots.
- Peace can be often promoted by building peace initiatives into wider relief and development activities, which do not necessarily have a religious component at all.

Overall, religious-focused efforts can contribute positively to peace building in four main ways. They can: (1) offer 'emotional and spiritual support to war-affected communities', (2) provide effective mobilisation for 'their communities and others for peace', (3) supply mediation 'between conflicting parties', and (4) serve as a conduit in pursuit of 'reconciliation, dialogue, and disarmament, demobilization and reintegration' (Bouta et al., 2005:ix). On the other hand, religious ambivalence can surface in two main ways: (1) some religious leaders fail to 'understand and/or enact their potential peace-building roles within the local community', and/or (2) lack the ability to 'exploit their strategic capacity as transnational actors' (Appleby, 2006:2).

Sudan: religious identity, security and conflict

Some African countries, including Sudan, Mauritania, Mali, Niger, Nigeria, Somalia, Chad and Eritrea, share a controversy: the relative religious, social and political positions of Muslims and non-Muslims. These African countries are all located on the 'periphery' of Arab centres of political and commercial power, historically experiencing long periods of Arab political and commercial dominance. They straddle an African geographical and cultural Arab/non-Arab division, located approximately 15–20 degrees north of the Equator. In this section, we look at the issue of religious identity in one of those countries, Sudan, and its role in the country's long-running civil war.

The question of national identity and the socio-political role of Islam has long been a key focus of political competition and conflict in Sudan. Sudan is unique among African countries south of the Sahara, because it is only there that, until recently, Islam had the status of state ideology. Sudan has long been associated with a poor human rights regime, with certain non-Arab, partially Christian, ethnic groups – such as the Dinka, Nuer and Nuba – victimised by successive regimes whose policy appeared to be both the Arabicisation and the Islamicisation of the entry country (Haynes, 1996:157).

Sudan achieved independence in 1956. Its population is about 40 per cent Arab, living mostly in the north. The remaining Sudanese are black Africans, living mostly in the south. Sunni Muslims overall comprise about 70 per cent of the population, Christians about 5 per cent, and the remainder (about 25 per cent) comprising followers of various local traditional religions. Until 2005, the National Islamic Front (NIF) government was in power, a northern- and Arab-based regime. Founded by Muslim Brotherhood leaders (particularly Hassan al-Turabi, who, as the late President Numeiry's attorney general in the 1980s, played a key role in introducing *sharia* law), the NIF was the main political force behind the 1989 military coup that brought the NIF government to power. The National Congress, created in early 1999 by President Al-Bashir, served as a front for the NIF and NIF members dominated the government until a change of regime in 2005.

Following the accession to power of the NIF regime, an Islamist government took over. Its stated ambition was to bring about a radical transformation of public life throughout north-eastern Africa, a notoriously unstable region long riven with multiple civil conflicts and traditional rivalries. During the 1990s, the Islamist regime helped create community associations, many of which were able to deliver much-needed welfare and social services. Yet the regime also had fatal ideological flaws: it was too rigid and one-dimensional, lacking sufficient constructive direction to form an appropriate basis to rule a modern nation-state (de Waal, 2004). Instead, the lure of apparently permanent *jihad* was strong – leading the Sudanese government into a tragically pointless civil war with various ethnic groups, mainly in the south of the country, as well as destructive relations with its neighbours, including Uganda.

Sudan's civil war began in the early 1970s, and over the next three decades more than two million people died, and over four million were displaced from their homes. The background to the long-running conflict was that at the time of Sudan's independence, the country's nationalist leaders did not regard Islamic ideas as progressive. They were primarily motivated by the fervour of anti-colonial success, looking to modernist, temporal ideologies, especially socialism, to express and convey national unity even in Sudan, a predominantly Muslim country. In other words, the preferred developmental model was not indigenously derived but drew on European models, whereby secularisation was an integral part of developmental strategy. As a result, Islam remained culturally, socially and historically important, but not judged to be significantly progressive to form a basis for the ideological, political and developmental advancement of post-colonial Sudan.

Things began to change in the early 1980s, following the failure of the country's post-colonial development programme. From then until recently, successive governments attempted to emphasise their power by underlining what they saw as Sudan's 'Arab-Muslim' identity, involving a concentrated process of attempted Arabicisation. The then state president, Ja'far al-Numeri, adopted Arab-Islamic dress in public, with the *jellabiya* (robe) and *anima* (turban) worn for many public appearances. This served to jettison the military uniform that Numeri had previously preferred to wear in public. Numeri also supervised the issue of new currency at this time, with bank notes depicting him as resplendent in his new persona. In addition, *sharia* law was adopted as the country's national law from 1983 (although it was never made to stick in the largely non-Arab, partially non-Muslim, south). Such acts, Bernal notes, served to bolster 'Sudan's Muslim and Arab identity while associating Islam with power and nationalism' (Bernal, 1994:48). Underlying the move towards Arabicisation and Islamicisation were both foreign and domestic pressures. In terms of the former, Sudan's then chief aid provider was the government of Saudi Arabia.[1] The Saudi government joined forces with the country's most important domestic Islamic movement, the Muslim Brotherhood, to demand more dynamic manifestations of Islam in public life. The result was that political discourse in Sudan became increasingly phrased in Islamic terminology, while Numeri's political opposition also adopted the language of Islam to press their case. Following Numeri's overthrow, the military-Islamic regime of Omar Hassan al-Bashir, which achieved power following a military *coup d'état* in June 1989, sought to juxtapose a form of Islamic social control by use of the military's organisational skills. It attempted to use the *sharia* in a way reminiscent of communist states' use of Marxist-Leninist dogma to justify policy.

The attempt at domination by mainly northern Arab-Muslims in Sudan, striving for control of the non-Arabs of the south, was often portrayed as a rare phenomenon in Africa: a religious war. However, it is more appropriate to see the conflict as primarily informed by the attempts of northern Arabs to dominate southern non-Arabs, not as a conflict about religion as such, but with ethnic and cultural competition as the key focal point. In other words, the conflict was *de facto* a struggle for Sudan's national identity – should it be one based in Arab-Islamic domination or should it be secular and multi-ethnic pluralism? We can see this issue coming to the fore in the case of Sudan's Nuba people, non-Arab but mostly Muslim. The Nuba live in the area of the Nuba Mountains in the north of the country, and have been consistently victimised by the Arab north for not being 'real' Muslims. However, the most significant issue is that the Nuba are not Arabs, but black Africans.

These factors – involving northern attempts to Arabicise the south, including attempted countrywide imposition of *sharia* law; non-representative, authoritarian governments, backed by the military; and significant cultural differences between the Arab north and the predominantly non-Arab south – form the backdrop to Sudan's three-decade civil war. For 30 years, armed resistance to the state in the south was focused in the two wings of the Sudan People's Liberation Army (SPLA), led respectively by the late Colonel John Garang de Mabior and Riek Machar Teny-Dhurgon. The civil war dragged on for so long because while both sides could avoid defeat, neither was strong enough to impose its preferred outcome. The SPLA could prevent the victory of the Arab-dominated Sudanese army – but it could not defeat it. Similarly, the army could keep the SPLA confined to its strongholds but not beat it through force of arms. The result was stalemate, until January 2004 when both the government and the SPLA signed a peace deal following foreign, especially US, pressure.

There was extensive foreign involvement in negotiations to end the conflict. Earlier, in the late 1990s and early 2000s, the civil war, once confined to the south, had spread to Sudan's north-east border with Eritrea. Sudan government forces encountered not only several thousand soldiers of the SPLA but also six other opposition armies, which had recently organised themselves to fight together under a single command. This threat of a wider regional conflict prompted peace initiatives from Libya and Egypt as well as from Africa's intergovernmental Authority for Development. Later, in November 2002, a peace envoy from the US government, John Danforth, visited Sudan and met leaders of both the government and the SPLA. Danforth not only proposed a series of confidence-building measures to bring the warring parties together but also managed to broker a ceasefire allowing aid agencies to airlift supplies to the beleaguered Nuba Mountains. On the other hand, as Danforth admitted, years of mutual distrust between the warring parties made reconciliation especially difficult.

It took 15 months of extensive negotiations, until January 2004, before Sudan's government and rebel leaders signed a peace deal that appeared to mark the end to one of Africa's longest civil wars of modern times. It was expected that the south would henceforward enjoy considerable political autonomy, with an administration to be called the 'government of southern Sudan'. The late SPLA leader John Garang was not only to lead the southern government but also to become a national vice president. Garang was, however, killed in a suspicious air crash in August 2005. Immediately following his death, 36 people died in riots in Sudan's capital, Khartoum. Most southerners had hoped that he would be able to lead them in the future, putting into effect policies to change their lives and end discrimination in favour of Arabs. Following Garang's death, Sudan's president, Omar al-Bashir, said he was determined to continue the peace process in which John Garang had played such a central role, ending more than 20 years of civil war.

Sri Lanka, religious identity, security and conflict

Like Sudan, Sri Lanka endured a long-running civil war between two religious and cultural groups. In this section, we examine, first, the extent to which Sri Lanka's civil war, which ended in 2009, was informed by religious factors. Second, we look at reasons for India's frequent interventions in the civil war. Did India intervene for religious and ethnic reasons, to support the claim of Sri Lanka's Hindu Tamil minority for a separate state, carved out of the existing political territory of Sri Lanka? We shall see that Sri Lanka's civil war attracted the attention of successive Indian governments, for two main reasons: the conflict (1) was regionally destabilising, and (2) centrally involved Tamils, millions of whom live in India.

The forerunner to Sri Lanka, Ceylon, became independent in 1948. The country changed its name to Sri Lanka (in Sinhalese: 'resplendent land') in 1972. In 1978, the country's legislative and judicial capital was moved from Colombo to nearby Sri Jayewardenepura Kotte, and the national flag was also changed: orange and green vertical bars were added, representing the Hindu Tamil and Muslim minority populations. Despite this attempt to indicate that Sri Lanka was not solely a Buddhist nation, it remained the case that what Young identifies as 'Buddhist nationalism' has played a consistently significant political role in Sri Lanka, aiming to serve as a unifying force among the Sinhalese majority (Young, 2000). Buddhist Sinhalese comprise three-quarters of the population, while Hindu Tamils make up around 18 per cent of the population. The remaining Sri Lankans – fewer than 10 per cent – are mainly Muslims and Christians.

The civil war in Sri Lanka set Sinhalese Buddhists against Tamil Hindus. It was a conflict about identity, an issue that includes both ethnicity and religion. As Young (2000:1) notes, 'religion plays a role in the conflict, [although] most Sri Lankans view its origins more in ethnic rather than religious terms'. There was also a pronounced developmental dimension to the war. Sri Lanka was once hailed for its impressive developmental indicators, including 'a high literacy rate and life expectancy, and low rates of infant and maternal mortality'. As a consequence, however, of the civil war – which erupted in 1983 – these indicators deteriorated sharply. Overall, the civil war had a 'devastating impact ... on demography, health, education, and housing', while highlighting 'wide disparities within ethnic and regional groups'. Believing that they would never get a fair deal because of demographic reasons, many Tamils fought for their own independent state, a demand which diminished after the civil war ended.

It is often observed that Sri Lanka's civil war had its roots in the British colonial period, with inherited political and economic grievances following independence not adequately addressed by successive governments. Following the end of British rule, Sinhalese majority governments in Ceylon/Sri Lanka sought to overturn what they regarded as British colonial favouritism towards the Tamil minority, especially in relation both to education and distribution of government jobs. As a result, successive Sinhalese-majority governments introduced policies that favoured the Sinhalese over the Tamils, including giving the Buddhist religion a privileged position constitutionally. Over time, Tamil grievances grew, escalating to the point that civil war broke out in 1983 following the killing in the city of Jaffna of 13, mostly Tamil, soldiers. Over the next quarter century the conflict was often extremely violent, a wide-ranging struggle between the two ethnic/religious groups over political, developmental, religious and ethnic concerns. The civil war resulted in over 65,000 deaths on both sides (Young, 2000:1).

During the 1980s and 1990s, successive governments officially did away with some of the policies discriminating against Tamils and, in addition, recognised Tamil as one of the country's official languages. But for many Tamils this was inadequate and fighting continued between Sri Lanka's armed forces and those of the Liberation Tigers of Tamil Eelam (LTTE). After 9/11, the Tamil Tigers found their international support diminishing. Various influential governments – including those of India, the USA, Britain, Canada and Australia – declared the LTTE to be a terrorist organisation. This meant that henceforward the Tigers found it very difficult to find international support for their struggle.

A ceasefire was declared in 2001 although this did not lead immediately to the end of the conflict, despite attempts led by the government of Norway to resolve the parties' concerns. Several major obstacles to peace remained, notably:

- Intense rivalry between the two main (secular) Sinhalese political parties, the People's Assembly (PA) and the United National Party (UNP).
- Fierce opposition from sections of the Buddhist clergy, opposed to any accommodation of the Tamils and their grievances, concessions which they viewed as threatening to the dominant position of Buddhism in Sri Lanka.
- Governmental reluctance to accept the mediation of external parties.
- Apparent unwillingness of the LTTE to entertain any settlement short of a separate state.

(Young, 2000)

To this list of barriers to a settlement to the conflict, we can also add both secular nationalist and religious concerns. This combination of factors made the situation impossible to resolve without severe bloodshed. As a result, the period from the time of the signing of the ceasefire in 2001 built to a climax when in 2008 the government's forces finally crushed the Tamil Tigers with pronounced ferocity. In May 2009 the Tamil Tigers had to accept defeat in the three decades-long conflict.

We noted that the Sri Lankan civil war was a conflict that drew the attention of successive Indian governments, and which at times led to India's overt involvement in the war. India's government was keen to resolve the conflict, for three main reasons:

1. To underline India's credentials as South Asia's leading regional power.
2. To try to undermine the claims of India's own Tamils for autonomy or independence, through denial of the demands of Sri Lanka's Tamil separatists.
3. To emphasise the Indian government's stated belief that Sri Lanka's Tamils were unacceptably discriminated against by the Sinhalese majority.

(Pal, 2006)

The major point to emphasise, however, is that there was no knee jerk support of the Sri Lankan Tamils simply because they were, in the main, Hindus, in common with over 800 million Indians. In fact, Indian involvement in the civil war was mainly linked to secular national interests and concerns, because of India's close geographical position to Sri Lanka. This point can be illustrated by reference to the 1970s and early 1980s, a period when India was often controlled by secular Congress governments led by Indira Gandhi. At this time, India's key foreign policy goal in relation to Sri Lanka was to prevent its government building closer ties not only with various Western countries, including Britain and the USA, but with neighbouring countries, including Pakistan and China (Pal, 2006). For the Indian government this posed an unacceptable challenge to India's position as South Asia's chief regional power. According to Krishna (2001), on various questions, including 'the Soviet invasion of Afghanistan [1979], declaring the Indian ocean a zone of peace, the issue of broadcast facilities to the Voice of America, the use of Trincomalee harbour, [and] membership in ASEAN [Association of South East Asian Nations]', the prime minister, Indira Gandhi, believed that, in relation to India, Sri Lanka's government was acting too independently and provocatively. Seeking an issue to help her focus India's concerns and as a result to deal with Sri Lanka, she focused upon the situation of the Tamil minority in Sri Lanka. She declared that the Tamils' fate was a crucial issue for India's national security. In sum, at this time, India's foreign policy under Mrs Gandhi was pursued 'for reasons having to do with assertion of India's hegemony over Sri Lanka' (Pararajasingham, 2004). India trained and armed Tamil militants, not in order to achieve a Tamil state (Tamil Eelam), but to complement diplomatic pressures already being exerted on Sri Lanka's government to compel it to toe the line and bend to India's will.

In the late 1980s, following unsuccessful attempts to get Sri Lanka to bend to India's will, India's government negotiated an agreement with the government of Sri Lanka on the Tamils' behalf – but without consulting the Liberation Tigers of Tamil Eelam. India promised Sri Lanka's government military support if needed to enforce Tamil compliance with a deal that gave the Tamils a few political concessions – including constitutional changes to grant them more local power – but certainly not the independence being demanded. Perhaps unsurprisingly, the initiative did not resolve the conflict – although it did achieve India's foreign policy aim of bringing Sri Lanka's government firmly under its influence if not control. Later, in 1991, when a government led by Indira Gandhi's son, Rajiv, tried to flex India's muscles by intervening in Sri Lanka militarily – both to exercise India's new-found influence and to overturn the earlier policy to arm the LTTE – he was assassinated by a Tamil extremist. This suggests that India seriously underestimated the depth of feeling underpinning Tamil nationalism in Sri Lanka, which by this time had grown to be a major force of such potency that even applied Indian firepower could not obliterate it. Indeed, India's physical intervention appears to have achieved the opposite effect to that intended: it served significantly to help consolidate Tamil nationalism in Sri Lanka. Overall, however, the situation was made more complex by a lack of agreement among Indian governments over the direction and thrust of India's policy. Under Congress Party rule the issue was viewed in secular nationalist and national interest terms. The government consistently supported Sri Lanka's (Sinhalese) government – as it was seen as the best means to curtail regional instability because of the war. BJP administrations, on the other hand, saw the conflict more through a *Hindutva* (seeking to establish the hegemony of Hindus and the Hindu way of life) focus. This led them to make statements supporting the Tamils on religious grounds, a stance that also gained the backing of the regional government of Tamil Nadu, which had long backed the LTTE on ethnic grounds.

The case studies in this section indicate historical and ideological similarities between Sudan and Sri Lanka which similarly help to explain the incidence of long-running civil wars in both countries. Both countries experienced colonial rule, based on the principle of divide and rule which, after independence, encouraged separate religio-cultural groups to vie for supremacy in an environment of material shortages. More generally, it indicates that these African and Asian states had similar founding experiences after colonial rule which were focused into conflicts which lasted for decades and which were played out in heightened religious and cultural divisions. In sum, Sudan and Sri Lanka both experienced similar post-colonial periods of serious conflict based on comparable cultural and religious divisions.

Transnational jihadist groups in Africa and Asia: ideational networks of congruity

Islamist-nationalist groups, such as Sudan's National Islamic Front, and Buddhist-nationalist groups among the Sinhalese in Sri Lanka see their struggles for domination as national conflicts. Transnational jihadist groups, such as al Qaeda and Lashkar-e-Taiba, on the other hand, regard national conflicts, such as ongoing insurgencies in various African and Asian countries – including Afghanistan, Pakistan, Yemen, Somalia and Nigeria – as individual components of wider regional and global wars. The overall aim is to establish a borderless Islamic state (*khalifah*) which could include swathes of territory from different regions, including Africa and Asia, without recourse to individual states and accompanying frontiers. For example, al Qaeda, Lashkar-e-Taiba and al Shabaab are jihadi organisations active in Africa and/or Asia which explicitly seek to redraw the international map. International relations has long been dominated by a small group of Western states, especially the United States, and Western-led international organisations, including the United Nations, the World Bank, the International Monetary Fund and the World Trade Organisation (Haynes et al., 2011). Jihadi transnational organisations pursue a competing logic to the Western- and sovereignty-dominated international system, working to replace (Sunni) Muslims' allegiances to their nation-state and national government in Africa and Asia by adherence to a border-less (Sunni) nation, the *ummah* ('community' or 'nation') (Haynes, 2012).

The key way they seek to fulfil their goals is via violence and conflict with the goal of destabilising the current international order. This was made explicit in recent *Human Security Reports* which noted that international terrorism – including importantly that perpetuated by transnational jihadi organisations – was, at the time,

> the only form of political violence that appears to be getting worse. Some datasets have shown an overall decline in international terrorist incidents of all types since the early 1980s, but in the mid-2000s there was a dramatic increase in the number of high-casualty attacks since the September 11 attacks on the US.
>
> *(Human Security Report Project, 2005)*

The 2010 *Human Security Report* highlighted the continued destabilising effect of transnational jihadi organisations. They had a major role in destabilising four of the world's most fragile states – Iraq, Afghanistan, Pakistan and Somalia – and were centrally involved in more than 25 per cent of serious conflicts which began during 2004–2008 (Human Security Report Project, 2010).

However, even the most high profile jihadi transnational organisation – al Qaeda – has not been able to control territory for long. Territory is a very important resource in international relations because every state bases its significance ultimately on the territory it controls. One of the characteristics of religious transnational actors such as al Qaeda is that their importance does not come from territory but from ability to encourage followers to act in certain ways. Al Qaeda was able to control territory in Afghanistan between 1996 and 2001 due to the complicity of the theocratic Taliban government, although lack of territory has not been a barrier to al Qaeda managing to win hearts and minds, because of the attractiveness of its militant ideas to some.

'Failed' states, such as Somalia, and 'failing' states, such as Pakistan, are often safe havens for jihadi transnational groups. This is because the state is just too weak to prevent their activities, allowing by default much freedom of action. The overall point is that jihadi transnational actors exploit the circumstances of failed and failing states in order to try to achieve their objective: to overthrow the existing international order and replace the current configuration of nation-states with the borderless *ummah*. The success or failure of jihadi transnational groups is not linked to their ability to command significant military resources or territory. Instead, progress towards achieving their goals is dependent on the capacity to convince Muslims of the appropriateness and desirability of their goals. In other words, jihadi transnational groups need to have sufficient soft power – the ability to persuade, cajole or encourage – to achieve success. What the activities of jihadi transnational actors have in common with the Roman Catholic Church's championing of democracy or the Anglican Church's defence of co-religionists in Zimbabwe is that, to achieve their objectives, they must convince key decision makers to act in certain ways and not others. Put another way, the Roman Catholic and Anglican churches, jihadi transnational actors and other religious transnational actors all have one thing in common: the objective of shaping the norms and values of the international system, by the only means they have at their disposal: soft power (Haynes, 2012).

Conclusion

This chapter has sought to explain and account for religions' involvement in (in)security and conflict in Africa and Asia. We looked at religions' involvement in conflict and conflict resolution in both regions, highlighting the ambivalence of religious actors in this regard. The reason for this ambivalence is that religious teachings can be interpreted in various ways – both for good and ill – and the involvement of religious actors who claim to be followers of the same faith can be quite different in different circumstances. This is especially the case in the conditions associated with conflict where the stakes are high and positions often polarised.

The chapter then examined African and Asian case studies (Sudan and Sri Lanka), stressing the importance in both of the ambivalence of religion in conflict. The case studies also highlighted and briefly examined and contested competing religious identities and the impact on security and conflict issues in both countries. Both case studies also stressed that religion in both conflicts can be seen as ambivalent in the way that 'religious' actors in both Sudan and Sri Lanka see religious identity as a component of a wider competition between groups. In Sri Lanka this involves the mainly-Buddhist Sinhalese and majority-Hindu Tamils and in Sudan the competition is between the majority-Muslim Arab north of the country and the mixed animist/Christian/Muslim south. This highlights religion's ambivalence in these conflicts by underlining that it can be used by often cynical political actors to help polarise communities in pursuit of their own ambitions to rule and dominate. It is not clear, however, the extent to which the conflicts in both countries should be characterised as primarily religious or mainly about material issues (land, jobs, welfare) in situations of scarcity, with religion providing a 'handy' focal point of difference between competing groups.

The final section focused on transnational and inter-regional jihadist groups affecting the two regions, and stressed the importance of ideational congruity, which encourages such groups to work transnationally, transcending international frontiers. What unites them is their shared worldviews and beliefs. This is not to assert however that transnational jihadi groups all have the same beliefs - because in all such cases their ideologies and associated actions are but one component of a larger sense of alienation and frustration that impels such groups to engage in violence and conflict, often in the name of a religious objective, such as jihad or the domination of one religious group over another.

Note

1 Following the rupture of Sudan's relations with Saudi Arabia during the Gulf war of 1991, Iran became Sudan's most important patron and aid provider.

References

Appleby, R. S., 2000. *The Ambivalence of the Sacred: Religion, Violence and Reconciliation*, Lanham, MD: Rowman and Littlefield.

Appleby, R. S., 2006. 'Building sustainable peace: The roles of local and transnational religious actors', Conference paper prepared for the Conference on New Religious Pluralism in World Politics, Georgetown University, 17 March.

Barringer, T., 2006. 'Taking faith seriously in International Relations and Development Studies'. Paper presented at the conference, 'Governance in the Commonwealth: Civic Engagement and Democratic Accountability', the Institute of Commonwealth Studies, London, 11–13 March.

Bartoli, A., 2005. 'Conflict prevention: The role of religion is the role of its actors', *New Routes*, Volume 10 (3), pp. 3–7.

Bernal, V., 1994. 'Gender, culture and capitalism', *Comparative Studies in Society and History*, Volume 36 (1), pp. 36–67.

Bouta, T., Ayse Kadayifci-Orellana, S. and Abu-Nimer, M., 2005. *Faith-Based Peace-Building: Mapping and Analysis of Christian, Muslim and Multi-faith Actors*, The Hague: Netherlands Institute of International Relations.

de Waal, A. (ed.), 2004. *Islamism and Its Enemies in the Horn of Africa*, Bloomington, IN: Indiana University Press.

Gunaratna, R., 2004. 'Defeating Al Qaeda – The pioneering vanguard of the Islamic movements', in R. Howard and R. Sawyer (eds.), *Defeating Terrorism. Shaping the New Security Environment*, Guilford, CT: McGraw-Hill/Dushkin, pp. 1–28.

Haynes, J., 1996. *Religion and Politics in Africa*, London: Zed.

Haynes, J., 2005. *Comparative Politics in a Globalizing World*, Cambridge: Polity.

Haynes, J., 2012. *Religious Transnational Actors and Soft Power*, Aldershot, UK: Ashgate.

Haynes, J., Hough, P., Malik, S. & Pettiford, L. 2011. *World Politics*, London: Pearson.

Holenstein, A.-M., 2005. 'Role and significance of religion and spirituality in development co-operation. A reflection and working paper'. (Translated from German by Wendy Tyndale.) Bern: Swiss Agency for Development and Co-operation, March.

Human Security Report, 2005. Oxford: Oxford University Press.

Human Security Report Project, 2010. Vancouver, Canada, Simon Fraser University Available at: www. hsrgroup.org/human-security-reports/20092010/overview.aspx [Accessed 1 May 2012].

Ilo, P., 2016. 'The rise of religious peacebuilding', in J. Haynes (ed.), *The Routledge Handbook of Religion and Politics*, 2nd ed., London: Routledge.

Juergensmeyer, M., 2016. 'Religious terrorism', in J. Haynes (ed.), *The Routledge Handbook of Religion and Politics*, 2nd ed., London, Routledge.

Krishna, S., 2001. *India's Role in Sri Lanka's Ethnic Conflict*, Colombo: Marga Institute.

Kurtz, L., 1995. *Gods in the Global Village*, Thousand Oaks, CA: Pine Forge Press.

Marsden, L. (ed.), 2012. *Ashgate Research Companion on Religion and Conflict Resolution*, Farnham: Ashgate.

Marty, M. E. and Scott Appleby, R. (eds.), 1993. *Fundamentalisms and the State*, Chicago: The University of Chicago Press.

Norris, P. and Inglehart, R., 2004. *Sacred and Secular. Religion and Politics Worldwide*, Cambridge: Cambridge University Press.

Ozzano, L., 2016. 'Religious fundamentalisms', in J. Haynes (ed.), *The Routledge Handbook of Religion and Politics*, 2nd ed., London: Routledge.

Pal, A. 2006, 'Sri Lanka on verge of civil war – again', *The Progressive*, May, p. 1.

Pararajasingham, A. 2004, 'India's Sri Lanka policy: Need for a review', South Asia Analysis Group, Paper no. 1187, 13 December.

Seiple, C., Hoover, D. and Otis, P. (eds.), 2012. *The Routledge Handbook of Religion and Security*, London: Routledge.

Young, M., 2000. 'Sri Lanka's long war', *Foreign Policy in Focus*, Volume 5 (35) (October), pp. 1–3.

25

THE LAND–WATER–FOOD–ENERGY NEXUS

Green and blue water dynamics in contemporary Africa–Asia relations

Larry A. Swatuk

Introduction

As many of the previous chapters in this collection have made clear, there is a long history of conflict and collaboration in relations between specific parts of Asia and Africa, much of it elite-driven and self-initiated, but a good portion of it resulting from Occidental imperial and colonial practices over time. From the Portuguese–Spanish division of the world at the Treaty of Tordesillas in 1494, to the post-1945 Cold War era, to neoliberal globalization today, Africa and Asia have long been a battleground for competing alien interests. Metaphorically, they have often found themselves together 'in the soup', in a pot not of their own making. A shared predicament, generally combined with elite-defined national interests, has led to various forms of collaboration, much of it symbolic – such as membership in the Group of 77 (G-77) – but some of it concrete – such as the Tazara Railway built between Zambia and Tanzania by the Chinese in support of southern African states' struggle for liberation from colonial and racial oppression. This is not to say that all contact has been peaceful. The Asian diaspora reaches into all parts of the African continent, primarily in the form of small trading communities. At best, these groups have been tolerated by their host communities. During moments of political unrest, these groups have often been the target of xenophobic attacks: South Korean shopkeepers in Lesotho; their Chinese counterparts in South Africa; and, perhaps the best known extreme case, Indians of all social classes in Idi Amin's Uganda.

This up and down history forms the foundation of present-day Asia–Africa relations whose symbolic emphasis is on the 'up', i.e. mutual social benefits through collaborative economic development. The concrete side of collaboration is more varied, as one would expect. In this chapter, the focus is on an assessment of emerging and existing practices of Asian–African cooperation in the Land–Water–Food–Energy Nexus. There have been numerous nexi trotted out for public consumption over the past ten years or so, most also involving 'climate change' and 'security' either explicitly or implicitly. So, the recent 'land rush' across large swaths of Latin America, Africa and Asia has been in part a response to emerging global concerns regarding economic vulnerabilities attached to carbon-based energy dependence. This land rush toward biofuels production had the knock-on effect of driving up both land prices, through speculation, and food prices, through crop-switching (Ghosh, 2010; Kaufman, 2010). One of the consequences of these actions was the negative impact on economically powerful, but food-insecure countries across the Middle East and Asia, such as Saudi Arabia, Japan and South Korea. These global dynamics have driven Asia and Africa together once again in a situation not necessarily of their own choosing. Some scholars regard this as a 'new scramble for Africa' (see Southall & Melber, 2009, for an overview) with positive and/or benign (Naidu, 2010) or almost entirely negative (Bracking & Harrison, 2003) outcomes for Africa.

In this chapter, I review African–Asian relations in relation to the land–water–food–energy nexus. As an overview, the chapter can only touch on key issues, highlighting certain actors, forces and factors in contemporary Africa–Asian relations. The chapter argues that elite interests, responding to local, national and global political economic challenges and opportunities, are driving the character and content of activity. Given Africa's difficult history of underdevelopment, a significant portion of these activities serves to exacerbate African state pathologies rather than alleviate them (see Bayart, 2000; Bayart et al., 1999; Callaghy, 1987; Clapham, 1996; and Mamdani, 1995 for background on the African state). In particular, Africa's smallholder farmers and rural poor seem to be most harmed by all of this activity. If Africa–Asia economic interactions are to have widespread benefits for all, investors must abide by emerging progressive regulations; they therefore must be held to account for their actions, if not by host states then by social movements and donor states and organizations within and beyond the continent. Given current trends, the simultaneous occurrence of conflict and collaboration will continue to mark Asia–Africa relations across the nexus.

Far from a unique or innovative approach, the so-called 'nexus' is rather a new way of seeing very old resource access, use and management challenges, practices and interests. Indeed, after presenting a short history of warfare, John Keegan poses the question:

> Is it true, then, that the zone of organised warfare coincides, inside seasonal variables, with that which geographers call 'the lands of first choice', those easiest to clear of forest and yielding the richest crops when brought under cultivation? Does warfare, in short, appear cartographically as nothing more than a quarrel between farmers?
>
> *(Keegan, 1994:73)*

I am not suggesting that all questions of land, water and food lead ultimately to warfare (though, the historical record suggests this to be a reasonable conclusion). I am suggesting that civilisation is a direct consequence of food surplus, itself emerging from humanity's ability to harness water and land through the deployment of energy (human labour, technological development and application, etc.), and it was this capacity that not only created the capacity for organized warfare but also the object of desire, 'lands of first choice', over which we have been fighting ever since (Ponting, 2007; Crosby, 2004). It is these 'lands of first choice' across the African continent over which powerful national and international actors are now 'scrambling'.

What is driving the so-called 'new scramble for Africa'? In short: land for speculative investment, biofuels, food, cash crops, conservation and tourism enterprises; commoditizable resources of almost every conceivable type – from timber and traditional non-timber forest products to oil, minerals, fish and gene pools; cheap labour; and access to markets, in Africa and beyond. In Thompson's (2009:299) words: 'What is new about the twenty-first century scramble is its all-embracing reach.'

A nexus approach helps us see the interrelatedness of decisions and actions, so we will not lose sight of this as the chapter proceeds. However, in this chapter I have chosen to organize the discussion along two lines: a green water pathway and a blue water pathway to conflict and cooperation. Stated simply, blue water comprises standing and flowing surface water and easily accessible groundwater; green water is that which enters the soil through rainfall and either evaporates directly back to the atmosphere or is transpired through plants, thereby creating biomass (Falkenmark & Rockstrom, 2004). This distinction is important. The vast majority of agricultural production, in particular food production for intra-continental consumption, in Africa is rain fed, i.e. green water. At the same time, the vast majority of Africa's cash crop and export crop production is irrigated, i.e. blue water. Given Africa's history, the distinction between green water and blue water further divides along class and, in some settler societies such as Kenya, South Africa and Zimbabwe, race lines. As technologies have improved, commercial agriculture has expanded into rain fed zones by bringing blue water via supplemental or extensive irrigation. This tension, between high value crops farmed intensively by the few and low value crops farmed extensively by the many, sets the proper context for current global interests in acquiring African land for agriculture. The World Bank (2009) argues that there is a 'yield gap' in many parts of Africa. This may well be true, but – aside from ecosystem limits – the gap is the result of deeply embedded class/race and state/civil society inequalities (Mamdani, 1995).

It is no accident that civilization emerged along the banks and floodplains of great rivers: the Yellow and Yangtze in China; the Tigris-Euphrates in the so-called 'fertile crescent'; the Indus and Ganges/Brahmaputra/Megna in south Asia; the Nile in Africa, among many others. It is also no accident that great civilizations disappeared when rains failed, rivers changed course, and hydrological cycles were fundamentally altered (Solomon, 2010 for a well wrought overview). The greatest and most enduring of these societies were those best able to harness blue water for human use. Wittfogel (1981) labelled these 'hydraulic societies', highlighting their authoritarian characteristics, in his particular case 'Oriental Despotism' – the bulkiness of water requiring organized mass labour. According to Solomon,

> For millennia authoritarian irrigation societies produced the most advanced civilizations in the world. Although the hydraulic model would be supplemented, and eventually superseded, by new social formations, it produced a recognizable prototype that has endured through history. Whatever the era, huge water projects requiring vast mobilization of resources tended to go hand in hand with large, centralized state activity. Vestiges of this hydraulic tendency were evident in the giant dams built in the twentieth century by centralizing liberal democratic, communist, and totalitarian states, often in the early stages of restoration periods.
>
> *(Solomon, 2010)*

In the context of the nexus, Asian technical, financial and human capital have come together and aligned with a clearly articulated political will to form an almost irresistible force for change across the African hydraulic landscape. If this force for change is to have a predominantly positive impact across all social classes, it will have to consider the peculiarities of African state forms (Bayart, 2000). This, however, requires a degree of reflexivity among dominant actors that to date is not demonstrated in their actions.

Green water scramble: 'lands of first choice'

Neither all land nor all water was created equal. At least not in relation to human needs and desires. Europeans undertook the first 'scramble for Africa' in a haphazard fashion, based largely on avarice and jealousy. 'Is the Zambezi River navigable all the way to the Indian Ocean?' asked Queen Victoria of her cousin Kaiser Wilhelm II. Not knowing the answer, he nevertheless agreed to exchange a piece of German West Africa for a slice of Bechuanaland, so creating what is today the Caprivi Strip. More than one hundred years later, this strip remains hotly contested between those indigenous to the space and those perceived as colonizers from the Namibian capital, Windhoek: first the Germans, then the South Africans, and now Namibians themselves. The strip also entitles Namibia to a portion of the waters flowing through the Okavango River Basin, and presents the government with visions of both potable water transported by pipeline to the people of the capital, and irrigation water for sugar cane as an export crop. So, the impact of that initial deal made many years ago has continued to ripple across water–land–food policy and practice landscape to this day.

In the context of contemporary Asia–Africa relations, this offers an important lesson: current land/water access, use and management profiles reflect deep inequalities first created under empire and later cemented in the independence era. Moreover, most of these land/water disputes remain unresolved. All across Africa, as colonists became more rooted in and knowledgeable about their adopted landscapes, they came to understand the vast differences in soil productivity between and around the tropics. Hence, using the power of the state, often in concert with (willing or coerced) African elites, the lands of first choice were given over to the settlers and indigenous people were pushed into the margins. Over time, technological innovation allowed settlers to expand further into the landscape, bringing formerly marginal lands under cultivation, sometimes profitably, thereby further marginalizing Africans in their homelands. Homer-Dixon (1999) has usefully articulated this process as 'resource capture' by the few and 'ecological marginalization' of the many. Most of the continent's hydraulic works – from dams and canals to complex systems of irrigation dependent on surface and groundwater, to the layout of cities and the extent of piped delivery – reflect this history of aggression and alienation. This is a festering socio-economic and socio-political issue across the continent, and the little acknowledged basis for chronic underdevelopment.

Fast forward to the first decade of the twenty-first century, and you find the second scramble taking place in a context of near-ubiquitous underdevelopment. Most of Africa's states are to be found at the lower end of the UNDP's Human Development Index, so signalling the very difficult context within which the current scramble is taking place. While Asian–African cooperation forums such as the Forum on China–Africa Cooperation (FOCAC), the India–Africa Business Forum (IABF) and the Tokyo International Conference on African Development (TICAD) announce their good intentions (Thakur, 2015), it is, in my view, doubtful that land/water/food/energy deals on-going in the continent can resolve Africa's abiding developmental challenges. Put differently, more of the same is likely to make matters worse, not better.

In the context of contemporary Asian–African relations, the scramble for green water should be interpreted in two ways. First, much of Africa's 'unutilized' land stays that way due to the limits placed on it by nature: high evaporative demand; rainfall regimes and soils unsuitable for the growing of food crops except, perhaps, under shifting cultivation. Legal systems and land tenure regimes across Africa have hemmed in smallholders so that traditional practices such as slash-and-burn are less and less viable. As larger chunks of arable land end up in private/state hands, those on communal lands have had to make their living on less and less desirable lands. The green water grab, in this instance, reflects the fact that lands most suitable for cultivation under both irrigated and rain fed processes have already been captured by elites, be they private sector or public or a combination of both. This leaves peasants crowded on to lands insufficient for their needs. Second, smallholders are being further hemmed in as large scale, commercial enterprises bring blue water into areas previously thought unsuitable for anything but smallholder production. Sugar cane plantations along the Senegal River and the Okavango/ Chobe/Linyati river system are good examples of lands where the application of technology (canals, pumps, fertilizers, pesticides) has resulted in the undesirable suddenly becoming highly desirable.[1] With nowhere to go, villages and communities are promised benefits from PPCP (public–private–community–partnership) style arrangements. These lands may be regarded as 'the last of the green water', and constitute the current intellectual and practical battlefield over 'land grabbing' in Africa (see Anseeuw et al., 2012; Kachika, 2010).

Vulnerabilities and insecurities

In the context of land–water–food, much of the discussion is framed in terms of data aggregated at country, region and global levels. Generally stated, high (Chinese, Sub-Saharan African, world) populations with increasing incomes and changing/Westernizing diets drive up demand for food and put pressure on current abilities to produce, suggesting that more land must come under cultivation, especially irrigation which, in turn, increases pressure on water resources and energy demands (e.g. World Bank, 2009:7). The vast majority of policy makers have taken this alarmist narrative at face value, leading them to make pronouncements regarding the need to take 'the necessary steps to ensure national food security'. The Food and Agriculture Organization (FAO)of the United Nations has compiled food security and vulnerability data at country level (see www.fao.org/economic/ess/ess-fs/ess-fadata/en/#.Vzd-RYSDGko). Among other things, that data shows that economically wealthy Asian states such as Japan and Korea are net importers of basic foodstuffs, including key dietary staples such as rice, wheat and soy. Today, Japan produces about 39% of the food it consumes, down from a level of 79% in 1960 (Feldhoff, 2014:79). In the FAO's terms, they show high cereal import dependency and low food self-sufficiency rates. For Feldhoff (2014), the threat isn't shortage of supply; rather, it is the cost of imported food. As long as the price remains low or at least stable and therefore predictable, then Japan's food security can be assured. However, as the rush toward biofuels production showed in the mid 2000s, sudden sharp spikes in food prices, due to a combination of farmers' changing crop choice and institutional investment in land speculation, wreaked havoc across much of the world, particularly in urban areas.

Japan has committed to achieving a food self-sufficiency rate of 50% by 2020. This includes improvements in production at home, where the country faces a complex set of challenges largely related to an ageing and urbanizing population, but also 'supporting agricultural development in current and potential supplier countries' (Feldhoff, 2014:82). In other words, if Japan can grow the food it needs, then it will be able to guarantee both price and supply. Africa as a whole faces many of the same vulnerabilities, but is involved in the food security narrative in a different way. Unlike Asia, with diminished land/water availability, either due to limited natural endowments (e.g. Japan, Korea) or degradation through industrial and agro-industrial practices (e.g. China; see Varis et al., 2014), Africa south of the Sahara is portrayed as resource-rich but poor in human/technical/financial capital. Where the narrative justifying the first scramble for Africa centred on 'empty spaces', the second scramble narrative centres on the claim that much of Africa's arable land is at best underutilized. Indeed, the title of a World Bank 2009 study reveals all: *Awakening Africa's Sleeping Giant*. Among other things, the Bank shows that farm level inputs are competitively priced with comparative regions in Latin America and Southeast Asia; however, yields on African farms are generally much lower. The message, therefore, should be clear: markets, incentives, commercialization, infrastructure, inputs. Just as the robber barons of the nineteenth century never bothered to interrogate the assumption that African lands really were empty, few of those interested in commercialization and 'scaling up' of agriculture have bothered to question the observation that African arable land is not only underutilized but, in many instances, unutilized (Ong'wen Okuro, 2015: 106).

Ferguson (1994), in *The Anti-Politics Machine*, suggests that deep inquiry is not needed because the World Bank and similar organizations build the answer into the initiative: a project fails because the people who are the objects of the intervention lack the capacity/drive/initiative/knowledge to make it a success. The goal here is not to demonstrate the veracity of this claim, but to highlight one potentially important sticking point as Asian investors and entrepreneurs pursue their interests in Africa: just as the land was never empty, the land not un/underutilized (Ong'weng Okuro, 2015).

Never one to be deterred by the natural limits to human expansion that are set by ecosystems, the World Bank frames Africa as an opportunity for great agricultural expansion. According to the Bank, while 42% of agricultural production in South Asia is dependent upon irrigation, only 4% of the total cropped area in Africa is irrigated, with the balance being rain fed. The Bank argues that, under climate change, dependence upon rain fed agriculture is likely to become more problematic given increasing rainfall variability; hence, the need for increased storage capacity and irrigation. In Africa, states the World Bank, there are 'large un-tapped water resources for agriculture' (http://wdi.worldbank.org/table/3.2#). In its data tables, the World Bank highlights large swaths of West Africa (e.g. Niger, Ghana, Togo, Benin), East Africa (Ethiopia, Uganda, South Sudan, Sudan), and Southern Africa (South Africa, Lesotho, Swaziland, Botswana) as having a mismatch between actual and potential food production due to the underutilization of available blue water resources. For example, while 80% of South African land is arable, only 1.7% is under irrigation. This is similar to Ethiopia (36% arable; 0.5% irrigated), Sudan (46% arable; 1.4% irrigated), Niger (35% arable; 0.2% irrigated), and Uganda (72% arable; 0.1% irrigated). Given that countries such as Uganda (71.9%) and Ethiopia (72.7%), among many others, have large percentages of their populations engaged in agriculture, there seems to be a gap between abundant input availability (land and water) and poor output (production of food and cash crops for household security and national wealth creation). As the 2009 report suggests, the problem seems to be that Africans are 'sleeping' rather than working.

Such an analysis looks painfully similar to the 'vicious cycle of poverty' articulated by 1950s development economists: suspicious and uneducated peasants simply needed incentives to change, these incentives coming most often in the form of an injection of capital. With capital, investments could be made which would improve production; this in turn would create surplus for sale in the market; profit would lead to reinvestment and so on until a virtuous cycle displaced the vicious one. But where are we some 60 years later? Across the continent, poverty has grown, incomes have contracted, and vulnerabilities have increased. Clearly, it is not for a lack of effort on the part of smallholder farmers, but due to a complex matrix of factors, two important ones being access to lands difficult to farm, and weak state–civil society relations (Alexander et al., 2000).

This casts light on the stark differences in vulnerabilities faced by Africans across the continent and across the social spectrum. Poverty is endemic but most acutely felt in rural areas. Those in support of land grabbing – 'agricultural investment' in World Bank-speak – argue that the potential exists to lift Africans out of poverty and increase their food security while also doing the same for their Asian counterparts, and making economic profit along the way. Ong'wen Okuro (2015: 108) lists the potential benefits of these investments:

- Increased farm employment
- Increased off-farm employment
- Development of rural infrastructure

- Access to new agricultural techniques and practices
- Global price stability for food
- Increased food production at local to global scales
- Development of anti-poverty measures such as health and education facilities.

He lists the potential threats from these projects as follows (Ong'wen Okruo, 2015: 109):

- Destruction of smallholder livelihoods
- Environmental destruction
- Highly unequal outcomes, tending in some cases toward zero-sum
- Radical change in agriculture negatively impacting social organization.

Feldhoff (2014:81) points out that this action, by 'protecting the wealthy at the expense of the vulnerable and poor developing countries poses a serious ethical issue'. But I would argue that, unlike the first scramble where Africa's leaders either played along or were shot dead, this second scramble sees those most powerful indigenous actors across Africa as willing accomplices. Even 'vulnerable and poor developing countries' have well-protected and wealthy elites. Those most critical of 'land grabbing' often make this point: the character and conduct of these deals and their deal-makers reflect not the potential for fundamental, progressive change across Africa, but the persistence and reinforcement of predatory states overseen by pernicious and oppressive (at worst) or indifferent (at best) elites (Pearce, 2012 for many detailed case studies).

In any event, and irrespective of my claims staked out in this chapter, is it possible that the land grabs could in fact yield more benefits than costs, and share the wealth rather than facilitate yet another 'trickle-up' effect? We turn now to look at Asia's involvement in African agriculture in slightly more detail.

Asia in African agriculture

The forms of cooperation and investment are many and varied, involving state-owned enterprises (SOEs), private companies, national and international financial institutions of all kinds, and direct state supports. Most prominent has been China – according to CIA data, the leading trade partner with most African states – but Japan, India, South Korea, Malaysia and Singapore also have a presence. The interest in agricultural investment is straightforward: people require food, clothing and energy on a daily basis. According to a World Bank report, 'For the poorest people, GDP increase originating in agriculture is about four times more effective in raising incomes of extremely poor people than GDP growth originating outside the sector' (Webber & Labaste, 2010). The implication for the World Bank, then, is that profit, poverty alleviation and food/energy security may go hand in hand.

Asian FDI in agriculture as a percentage of total FDI is small. For example, China's State Council reported at the end of 2011 that 2.5% of the stock in FDI in Africa was devoted to agriculture (Brautigam & Zhang, 2013). Nevertheless, a small percentage of a very large number is also a large number. *Africa Renewal* reports, for example, that Japanese FDI has increased from $758 million in 2000, to $10.5 billion in 2014 (www.un.org/africarenewal/magazine/special-edition-agriculture-2014/africa%E2%80%99s-land-grabs). Brautigam & Zhang (2013:1680) compiled data from China's Ministry of Commerce showing there to be 2,372 Chinese companies registered across 27 African countries, with only 212 of them engaged in some form of agriculture. Most of these activities were on a scale much smaller than reported by Anseeuw and colleagues (2012) and across the popular media. Clearly, interest in FDI in agriculture is there. In 2002, Chinese Vice-Minister Wei Jianguo announced that 'Chinese–African agricultural cooperation in the new century must be conducted by enterprises and should be market-oriented' (quoted in Brautigam & Zhang, 2013:1681). India has taken a similar stance, choosing state-based incentives to encourage Indian private enterprise investments in the agricultural sector in Africa. Naidu (2010) reports there to be more than 80 Indian companies active in the agricultural sector in Ethiopia, Madagascar, Kenya, Senegal, Sierra Leone, Cameroon and Mozambique (see, also, Nnabuko & Uche, 2015). Indian entrepreneur Vashisht (as quoted by Pearce, 2012) cites the relative inexpensiveness of land in Africa which is of similar quality to land in India as a motivator for private enterprise, with the amount of money needed to purchase one acre in India fetching up to 60 acres in select countries in Africa. Chen et al. (2013) label this enterprise-based approach 'firing from the bottom'. De Haan (2011), Liang (2012) and Brautigam and Xiaoyang (2011) describe China state support for private sector activity in Africa as the exercise of 'soft power'.

Soft power, i.e. the need to be seen to be proactive in African 'development', is necessary to offset China's image as the new imperial power in the continent, sucking raw materials out and siphoning finished goods in. This classic dependency pattern of trade is actually quite accurate. According to Thakur (2015), whereas African trade with India is in the order of $70 billion, the total with China exceeds $220 billion, more than doubling since 2000. India's approach is deliberately private-sector led, which is somewhat different from China's state-centric approach (especially in relation to infrastructure development; see below). Yet, Indian entrepreurs' shared belief that Africa is suffering 'China fatigue', and ready for a change, seems to be overstated, particularly based on trade data.

Once again, according to CIA data, while China is the dominant trade partner in terms of both exports and imports across most of Africa, India is an increasingly significant player. Africa has gone from a net exporter of food crops to a net importer. For example, FAO data for 2015 shows 22 African countries to be net importers of rice, with Nigeria being at the high end (2.5 million tonnes; second largest importer in the world behind only China) and Togo at the low end (100,000 tonnes). China is a net importer of rice, exporting 350,000 tonnes while also importing 4 million tonnes. India is the world's largest exporter of rice, alongside Thailand, each exporting approximately 10 million tonnes. The rice trade, therefore, accounts for a significant amount of Indian trade in Africa. Overall, Asian exports of agricultural commodities to Africa total roughly $25 billion and constitute 6.2% of Asia's world agricultural trade. At the same time, Africa's exports of agricultural commodities to Asia total roughly $14 billion, consti-tuting 22.2% of Africa's world agricultural trade.

Another way of thinking of this trade in agricultural commodities is as the exchange of what Tony Allan (2011) describes as 'virtual water' – the amount of water used in growing, produc-ing, packaging and shipping a commodity. It is important to note that while a piece of fruit, such as a mango, may contain up to 80% of its mass as water, virtual water should not be mistaken for this direct transportation of water as food. That is only part – an important part to be sure – of the story. However, the most important part of the story involves the opportunity cost of producing one type of crop for a particular purpose with water that might otherwise be used for another purpose. In the context of seasonal rainfall regimes, water that arrives only once a year and is used to grow cotton for export, means that there is no water left to grow food for the domestic market.

Hoekstra and Mekonnen (2012) show that 76% of all virtual water is devoted to crops and 'derived crop products', 12% to animals and 12% to industry. China (143 Gm^3/yr) and India (125 Gm^3/yr) rank numbers two and three in the world, behind the United States, in virtual water export. At the same time, China (121 Gm^3/yr) and Japan (127 Gm^3/yr) are the world's largest importers of virtual water. Japan and South Korea are the largest net virtual water importers in the world. For Japan, oil crops account for 43% of their virtual water imports (cotton, soy, oil, sunflower, rape), with cotton (more than 50%) and soy (more than 20%) accounting for the bulk of their imports. A significant amount of this trade in virtual water is green water, i.e. water that is taken up by the plant directly following rainfall. Given all the talk regarding water scarcity and its impact across different sectors (WEF, 2011; Ozturk, 2015), it will be important to disaggregate agricultural production and trade data in order to better understand the types of water being used for what, and for whom, clearly a task beyond the scope of an overview chapter such as this. What is well known (Falkenmark & Rockstrom, 2004) is that smallholder agriculture is heavily dependent upon green water and that across Africa some 60 million smallholder farmers produce more than 80% of the continent's food crops. Asian and African actors interested in food security should focus on what Falkenmark and Rockstrom call 'vapour shift' – encouraging more transpiration and less evaporation – based on 'where the rainfall hits the soil', as opposed to the massive expansion of land under agriculture and the capture of blue water through big infrastructure (see Swatuk et al., 2015 for an elaboration of this point).

Should and will are very different things, especially given the incentives available. African Union member states, through CAADP (Comprehensive Africa Agriculture Development Programme), have committed to increase government spending in agriculture. According to Jonathan Brooks, an agricultural economist at the OECD, African governments have regularly committed less than 10% of their budgets to agriculture – this despite the fact that the vast majority of their populations live in rural areas. As a result, African agriculture, in Brooks' view, has been 'starved for investment for decades', so roughly $80 billion a year of investment is needed if improvements in production and poverty alleviation are to be realized (see the interview at: www.youtube.com/watch?v=GxFTGq94dXs, accessed 18 May 2016).

China, for one, has committed to support through a variety of mechanisms, all falling under its 'going global' campaign. Brautigam and Zhang (2013) ably chronicle these developments, some of the highlights of which are as follows. In 2006, the Ministry of Agriculture and the Chinese Development Bank signed an agreement to use overseas water and land in agricultural development. Following this, the Chinese government promised to create more than 24 agro-tech demonstration centres in Africa, and requested tenders from the private sector to operationalize them. In 2008, the EximBank and the Ministry of Agriculture agreed to supports for overseas investment. In 2010, a joint venture, the China–Africa Agricultural Investment Co. Ltd, was created by the Chinese National Agricultural Development Corporation Group and the China–Africa Development Fund. Initial capital investment amounted to $161 million to help promote Chinese agriculture in Africa. Lastly, the 2011–15 twelfth Five Year Plan committed to involving SOEs in agricultural investment in Africa; in 2012, private companies were encouraged to participate as well.

Although Brautigam and Zhang (2013) convincingly contest the accuracy of the data in Anseeuw et al. (2012), particularly in terms of numbers and scale of land grabs, the analysis of the latter is revealing when one considers the types of land being reported as 'up for grabs'. Anseeuw and colleagues divide the land being contested into four types: T1 – arable land available/high yield gap; T2 – little arable land available/high yield gap; T3 – little arable land/low yield gap; T4 – arable land available/low yield gap. What they find is that of the reported 'land grabs', 58% fall within T1, with an emphasis on East Africa, while 13% of the cases fall within T2, mostly in West Africa. Interestingly, T4 land, which constitutes 12% of reported cases, is predominantly found in Laos and China. In addition, 43% of all reported cases occur in land that is classified as cropland, 24% as forest (so suggesting possible trade-offs for environmental services), 28% as shrubland/grassland, and 5% as a variety of other land types, including wetlands and peri-urban areas. Reliable evidence supports these findings, with a number of high profile cases most often in the media:

- Karuturi Global (based in Bangalore) active in Ethiopia
- Siva Group (based in Chennai) active in Liberia, the DRC and Cameroon
- ProSavana (a consortium of Brazilian, Japanese and Mozambican interests) active in Mozambique.

Each of these is a large-scale mechanized agriculture scheme in various states of completion designed to grow a mix of food crops and biofuels primarily for export. Pearce (2012), Von Braun & Meinzen-Dick (2009), and Wertz-Kanounnikoff et al. (2013) also discuss a number of large scale endeavours. Brautigam and Zhang (2013) list a number of much smaller Chinese agricultural enterprises, some supported by the host government, some by the home state, some with private finance available to them. A partial list is as follows:

- Sinochem (an SOE) with 51% stake in Singapore-based GMG Global (active in rubber plantations in Cameroon and Cote d'Ivoire)
- Segori Sugar in Mali
- Magbass Sugar in Sierra Leone
- Koba Farm in Guinea
- Mbole Farm in Mauritania
- China State Farm Agriculture Group (2 sisal farms in Tanzania).

Behind every one of these endeavours is the claim of 'mutual benefits'. Assessing the outcomes is difficult, however, partly because many of these enterprises are relatively new, and often suffering start-up problems (Nnabuko & Uche, 2015; Brautigam & Zhang, 2013; Brautigam & Xiaoyang, 2011). They are also mired in the hyperbole of 'land grabbing', be it overly negative (Anseeuw et al., 2012) or overly positive (World Bank, 2009). What one can say, based on the empirical evidence, is the following:

- Multiple stakeholder (including community groups) enterprises on a relatively small scale (e.g. 5,000–10,000 ha) seem to reap a more diverse range of benefits than do massive projects
- Takeovers of existing and/or historical but moribund projects are less controversial than greenfield developments
- The larger the project the greater the chance of failure on a number of fronts: political, social, economic and ecological
- Evidence from the Karuturi project in Ethiopia suggests that extensive projects involving contested land and water rights exacerbate existing rifts between state and civil society so project 'success' requires the use of state power, including deadly force.

If future conflicts are to be avoided, or remediated favourably for all parties, regulation matters. Part of the problem across Africa is that actors claim to be acting 'within the rule of law', forgetting that the law as presently shaped favours the haves against the have-nots. We will return to the question of regulation.

Blue water pathways to cooperation (and conflict)

Facilitating green water capture is blue water development, at the heart of which lies the new era of dam building. Conca (2006), in *Governing Water*, reflected on the place of water in development through four lenses: damming, draining, diverting and dumping. These four activities stand at the centre of modern civilization and mark out the continuities between antiquity and our twenty-first-century world. For example, the 1,776 km long Grand Canal in China pre-dates the industrial era by more than 1,000 years, and connects the high-flowing Yangtze River in the south with the lower-flowing Yellow River in the north. Today it is still considered one of the great symbols of the 'hydraulic society', where political will combined with perceived need and authoritarian rule makes just about anything possible. Its present day complement is without doubt the Three Gorges Dam – politically, economically and environmentally controversial but most certainly emblematic of the continuing importance of water to both the demonstration and preservation of state power.

Dam building is a direct consequence of settled society. The earliest dams were constructed for flood control and to provide water for irrigation. While dams continue to be built, they remain highly controversial. The main arguments in support of dam building are tied to the expressed need for dependable flows of water for agricultural and industrial production and maintaining a steady supply of water for cities: thus, single and multipurpose dams are regularly constructed in the name of irrigation, recreation, flood control, flow regulation, improved navigation, hydropower and drinking water.

At the same time, there are many valid criticisms of dams, particularly large dams, defined as those more than 15 metres in height and/or with a capacity greater than 3 million cubic metres. These criticisms focus on negative impacts such as habitat degradation, loss of biodiversity, fisheries destruction, de-oxygenation of waters behind the reservoir and in downstream flow, destruction of cultural and social spaces, to name several. Many environmental organizations, such as International Rivers (see www.internationalrivers.org/), partner with marginalized social groups in order to raise public consciousness regarding the high social and environmental costs of dam building. Perhaps the most damning criticism of all, however, is that 'dams displace democracy' – a rather clever way of pointing out that the decision to impound water and to flood farms, forests, and even cities and villages is rarely if ever taken outside the main halls of political power.

Indian scholar and social activist Vandana Shiva is a well-known anti-dam advocate who has tirelessly worked to make the world aware of the social and environmental costs of, among other things, the Narmada Water Project in India. She has also worked very hard to mobilize citizens groups at local, national and global levels in order to stand up to the powerful set of interests that drive dam development. To paraphrase Ms Shiva, the argument in support of large dams is invariably 'improved agricultural production', but rarely is the question ever asked 'to what end?' This is an important point, particularly as we enter an era of 'land-grabbing' – which invariably entails water rights grabbing as well – where irrigated industrial cash-crop agriculture is displacing smallholder production of food crops for the household and for local markets. In Steven Solomon's words (2010), this transfer of water from one group of users to another is zero-sum economics, that is, 'my absolute gain in water and land is your absolute loss in water and land'. History is replete with these examples, from the Tonga of present-day Zimbabwe, flooded out by Lake Kariba, to the millions of Chinese citizens forced to move or suffer the consequences of rising waters trapped behind the Three Gorges Dam – the same outcome separated by 50 years of history.

Post war economic reconstruction in Europe was complemented by show-piece project developments across the decolonizing world, Japan, China and the newly emergent Soviet

The land–water–food–energy nexus

Union. By the mid 1950s, multi-purpose dams were 'development'. Some four decades later, large dam building projects had slowed to a trickle, mostly because social and environmental movements were better organized and more effective in challenging the claims made in support of these mega projects. In 1997 the World Bank and the IUCN helped convene the World Commission on Dams. According to their final report (WCD, 2000),

> Dams have made an important and significant contribution to human development, and the benefits derived from them have been considerable. In too many cases an unacceptable and often unnecessary price has been paid to secure those benefits, especially in social and environmental terms, by people displaced, by communities downstream, by taxpayers and by the natural environment.
>
> *(WCD, 2000)*

The Commission's final report, *Dams and Development*, provided a blueprint for dam building that would ensure the wrongs of the past would not be repeated. As shown with dams and dam building projects such as the Lesotho Highlands Water Project, the Three Gorges Dam in China, the Grand Renaissance Dam in Ethiopia and the Xayaburi Dam in Laos, the lessons of the past have not been learned.

Today, it is really only China and India that exhibit any such predilection toward a sustained, state-directed 'hydraulic mission', that is directing the full power of the state toward the harnessing of water resources for 'the national interest'. No matter what the other states say that they are interested in, early twenty-first-century democracies everywhere are having a very difficult time generating either the social consensus or financial capital necessary for infrastructure maintenance, let alone new development.

According to the International Rivers Network (IRN), China is currently undertaking roughly 330 dam building projects in 74 countries. Table 25.1 shows that 80 dams are either under construction, being negotiated or have been completed in 30 countries across Africa. This includes eight in Ethiopia (two completed; three under construction; three proposed), eight in Zambia (four under construction; three proposed; one completed), and five in various stages of completion in each of Algeria, Democratic Republic of Congo, Nigeria, Republic of Congo and Sudan.

Financial support for these projects comes from a wide variety of sources. For example, in Angola, finance is supplied by the Government of Angola and the China Exim Bank. In Kenya, the Japan Bank for International Cooperation is active, while in Madagascar, the Arab Bank for Economic Development in Africa and the Chinese company Gezhouba provided the necessary capital. In Niger, the Islamic Development Bank and OPEC have provided the finance for a dam being built by Sinohydro. In fact, in all of these cases, the state-owned Sinohydro was the builder. While Sinohydro is most active in these dam building projects, a number of other Chinese companies are also in the mix: e.g. China International, China Geoengineering Corporation, China National Heavy Machinery Corporation, Gezhouba, Chinese International Water and Electricity Corporation (CIWEC), and China National Electric Engineering Company (CNEEC).

Dams are not discrete entities. They require radical modifications of the surrounding landscape, including the displacement of tens of thousands of the rural poor. Dams also require access roads, and evidence shows that where roads are built, there is the significant knock-on effect of environmental change. Beyond the direct alteration of the natural environment – e.g. deforestation – roads often lead to the small-scale destruction of forests through the infiltration of people in search of land and other livelihood-supporting resources such as timber (fuelwood, building material) and

Larry A. Swatuk

Table 25.1 Selected dam projects in Africa

Country	Number of dams	Main builders	Main sources of finance	Comments
Angola	1	Sinohydro	China Exim Bank	Completed
Ethiopia	8	Sinohydro Gezhouba Enka (Turkey) Salini (Italy)	African Development Bank China Exim Bank Ethiopia Electric Power Corporation	2 completed; 3 under construction; 3 proposed
Kenya	3	Sinohydro	Japan Bank for International Cooperation Government of Kenya	1 under construction; 2 proposed
Madagascar	1	Sinohydro	Arab Bank for Economic Development in Africa Gezhouba	Completed
Mali	1	Sinohydro	World Bank European Investment Bank SOGEM	Completed
Sierra Leone	2	Gezhouba	Government of China UNIDO	1 under construction; 1 proposed
Sudan	5	Gezhouba	Arab Fund for Economic Development Kuwaiti Fund	1 completed; 1 under construction; 3 proposed
Uganda	3	Gezhouba/ Sinohydro CIWEC	China Exim Bank	1 under construction; 2 proposed
Zambia	8	Sinohydro	India Exim Bank Development Bank of Southern Africa (DBSA)	1 completed; 4 under construction; 3 proposed

Source: Excel file downloaded from www.internationalrivers.org/campaigns/china-s-global-role-in-dam-building.

non-timber forest products (honey, wildlife, bush meat). In most cases, then, the lands in and around dam building exercises in Africa reflect a sort of anarchistic 'Wild West'. Companies active in these spaces employ private security firms to 'manage' security (Gumedze, 2007).

As with dams, so with mines. According to a recent report,

> In less than 10 years since Chinese authorities called for mineral resources diversification globally, the number of major mining/mineral processing assets in Africa with China-headquartered companies' interest, increased from only a handful in 2006 to more than one hundred and twenty in 2015. And those are only assets in advanced stages of their development, i.e. the figures exclude early exploration and other greenfield projects.
>
> *(www.mining.com/feature-chinas-scramble-for-africa/ accessed 21/5/2016)*

In 2006, China was active only in South Africa, Zambia and the DRC. By 2015, it was active in Mali, Liberia, Sierra Leone, Ghana, Chad, Ethiopia, Eritrea and 14 other countries in

Central/Southern/Eastern Africa – from the Central African Republic to Madagascar. Driving this interest in African resources is Chinese concern for secure supply chains of resources to fuel its on-going economic development. According to the same report, while the West has been reluctant to expand in many of these countries, Chinese companies (state-owned and state-supported) seem to be much more tolerant of risk. India, too, has extensive interests in African mining enterprises, but mostly further along the supply chain (Naidu, 2010), in keeping with former Indian Prime Minister Singh's claim that 'the commerce between India and Africa will be of ideas and services, not manufactured goods against raw materials after the fashion of Western exploiters' (also attributed to Mahatma Gandhi in Mathews, 1997 and Naidu, 2010:111).

The implications for the nexus are readily apparent. Mining requires land, water and energy, often in vast quantities. So while the environmental footprint of a mine may be geographically limited, the social, ecological, political and economic knock-on effects can be significant. Land and water 'grabbing' in weak states – what Callaghy (1987) labels 'Lame Leviathans' – too often sets up zero-sum outcomes at the local level, although wealth creation holds the possibility of enhanced food security and livelihood security (through primary, secondary and tertiary job creation and increased state revenues) for people directly and indirectly involved in all aspects of the creation, operation and maintenance of the mining enterprise, including ancillary services from telecommunications to teeth cleaning. China, Japan and more recently India, particularly through the private sector, are extensively involved across the entire range of production (primary, secondary, tertiary) processes and within and across often lengthy commodity/value chains (Brautigam & Xiaoyang, 2011).

Assessing Asia's scramble for African land, water, food and energy

What are we to make of all this activity? If we juxtapose the claims made with the observed outcomes, we see a disjuncture, sometimes extreme, between the proposed spread of benefits and the facts of highly uneven outcomes that disproportionately favour Asian states and companies and their African counterparts at the expense of local communities. The World Bank argues that there is great potential for enhanced agricultural production across significant swaths of Africa. As shown above, countries and companies from China, India, Japan, South Korea, Singapore and Malaysia are actively engaged in this proposition. Data compiled by Anseeuw et al. (2012) shows the extent of this activity, not only by Asians for Asians but by other powerful actors in the Global South (e.g. Brazil) and North (e.g. USA, Great Britain, The Netherlands) in pursuit of their own national and corporate interests. The playing field is diverse and complex, leading Strauss & Saavedra (2009:551) to encourage those interested to 'disaggregate "China" and "Africa"' in order to better see, and be able to assess, the actions of 'a multiplicity of actors'. No doubt many are in fact benefiting from all of this activity, but rarely are the beneficiaries the rural people whose land it was before it was grabbed.

Kachika (2010) reflects critically on the Continental Framework and Guidelines on Land Policy in Africa, adopted in July 2009 by the African Union Heads of State and Government. The guidelines are reasonable and suggest a nuanced understanding of just what is at stake and for whom in the rush to new agricultural investment.

* Land policies must be comprehensive and must anchor policies for related sectors
* Land policies should recognize the role of local and community land based administration and management institutions and structures along with those of the state
* Land policies should strengthen the rights of women
* Land policies must balance pro-poor priorities with market orientation

- Land policies should protect pastoral ecosystems
- Land policy reforms should impact on reducing tensions between the tourism industry and other social and economic uses
- Land policy reforms should guarantee net gains for African populations for use of land for functions like energy development
- Land policies should clarify systems of property under which land for agriculture is held and used
- Land policy processes should meaningfully engage civil society.

According to the United National Economic Commission for Africa (UNECA), the

> Framework and Guidelines is much more than simply another document on land. It reflects a consensus on land issues; and serves as a basis for commitment of African governments in land policy formulation and implementation and a foundation for popular participation in improved land governance.
>
> *(www.uneca.org/publications/framework-and-guidelines-landpolicy-africa)*

In reflecting on the potential of the Framework and Guidelines to achieve its goals, Kachika (2010:11) states that it 'is a critical tool that provides possibilities for African governments to reshape the direction of foreign agricultural investments, and neutralize the land grabbing related risks that are threatening marginalized groups of African rural communities'.

Shortly following the AU declaration, the World Bank, in 2010, initiated a consultation process regarding establishment of the Principles for Responsible Agricultural Investment (PRAI). According to the UNCTAD website (www.unctad.org/en/Pages/DIAE/G-20/PRAI.aspx) devoted to it, ultimately these principles were 'jointly developed' by UNCTAD, FAO, IFAD and the World Bank and designed to 'respect rights, livelihoods and resources'. The seven principles are as follows:

- Principle 1: Existing rights to land and associated natural resources are recognized and respected.
- Principle 2: Investments do not jeopardize food security but rather strengthen it.
- Principle 3: Processes relating to investment in agriculture are transparent, monitored, and ensure accountability by all stakeholders, within a proper business, legal and regulatory environment.
- Principle 4: All those materially affected are consulted, and agreements from consultations are recorded and enforced.
- Principle 5: Investors ensure that projects respect the rule of law, reflect industry best practice, are viable economically, and result in durable shared value.
- Principle 6: Investments generate desirable social and distributional impacts and do not increase vulnerability.
- Principle 7: Environmental impacts of a project are quantified and measures taken to encourage sustainable resource use, while minimizing the risk/magnitude of negative impacts and mitigating them.

Leaders of G20 member states – which include China, India, Indonesia, Japan, South Korea and South Africa – reaffirmed their support for PRAI at their November 2011 and June 2012 summits.

Given this seeming consensus, why are these various investments in green and blue water so contentious across the continent? Part of the problem, it seems to me, is the way in which these activities are ahistorically inserted into global narratives regarding food and energy security. So, World Bank analysts feel no shame in claiming that while several African states show great potential for dramatically increased agricultural production, they are hobbled by a 'lack of social cohesion, political stability, bureaucratic capacity', therefore requiring 'policy reforms, scaled up investments, strengthened institutions'. This raises an important question: Where is the proof that attention to the latter is sufficient to address the former? Put differently, how can institutions be strengthened such that they do not reinforce the existing social relations of production, commonly understood as 'underdevelopment'? In my view, the answer is simple: they cannot. Recent research by Brautigam and Zhang (2013), described above, suggests that Chinese investors are well aware of the risks involved in agricultural expansion across much of Africa. Where projects were extensive they were undertaken on already existing plantations in Cameroon, Mali and Sierra Leone. Other projects, in places such as Mozambique, Nigeria, Sudan, Zimbabwe and Zambia, were much smaller; several intended for scaling up had not come to fruition due to a perception that the (political, social, economic) risks were too high (Brautigam & Zhang, 2013). This suggests that while China is 'going global', it is going global slowly in many parts of Africa.

In my view, neither China's involvement in Africa in particular, nor Asia's in general, is a problem because it is 'Chinese' or 'Asian'. Rather, it is an aspect of a greater problem facing rural communities everywhere. As suggested by Akram-Lodhi (2012:130), among others, the second scramble looks very much like a final enclosure, whereby the modernizers will have gotten their wish and the peasantry may finally be 'captured' by the forces of neoliberal globalization, not through cooptation but rather through coercion: what Akram-Lodhi (2012:135) calls 'dispossession by displacement'. Strauss & Saavedra (2009:556) ask, somewhat rhetorically, does this not 'simply reflect a global logic of capital accumulation'? Perhaps, but only if one understands this 'logic' to be grounded in 'might makes right'. State-centric narratives of 'developing' and 'developed', of 'sleeping' and 'awake', combine with concepts such as 'sovereignty', 'national interest', 'security' and 'mutual respect', to enable and legitimize highly questionable practices undertaken by influential actors within Africa and across Asia, with unsavoury social, economic and environmental effects (Anseeuw et al., 2012; Akram-Lodhi, 2012). In the words of Strauss & Saavedra (2009:556), who reflect on the finding of Esteban (2009) in Guinea-Bissau: 'The lack of effective civil society and regulation allows China's principles of non-interference and respect for absolute state sovereignty to be translated into nearly unconditional and open support for a repressive and authoritarian regime.' There has been a great deal of criticism in the West of China's 'not my business' approach to bad governance in its African partner countries. While a valid criticism, it nevertheless distracts observers from the more pernicious process of dispossession by displacement. Following World Bank logic of the need for the 'extensification of intensification' across Africa (and Asia and Latin America), and abandonment of the belief in the potential of small-scale farming to satisfy market demands for food, the door has been opened wide through the pseudo-scientific logic of the 'yield gap'. African small-scale farmers are under-producing; the answer, therefore, is to bring in commercial agriculture with its knowledge of markets, mechanization and economies of scale.

At best, smallholders can participate as out-growers, a sort of reframing of feudalism with the 'Lords' being faceless corporations such as the Hong Kong based Vicwood Group which, according to Pearce (2012:265), 'has a total of 17 million acres of forest awaiting its chainsaws', across Cameroon, Congo-Brazzaville and the Central African Republic. Pearce (2012) presents a rogue's gallery of late modern carpet-baggers who claim that their goal is to lift the peasantry out of the dark ages. One of the problems, of course, is that where food is being grown it is grown largely for export and, if by peasants, then through their cheap labour on lands formerly farmed by them (Borras & Franco, 2012; Vermeulen & Cotula 2009). In many places, lands used by peasants for subsistence agriculture have been handed over to groups such as the Singapore based Wilmar and Olam, or the Malaysian based Atama Plantation for palm oil production (Pearce, 2012:88). Anseeuw et al. (2012) illustrate the largely negative impacts felt by local people, with displacement and death being the most egregious.

Whereas 75% of all reliably reported land grabs across the Global South are for agricultural projects, significant amounts of land have been given over by African states to Asian state-owned enterprises (SOEs) or private companies engaged in mining, livestock farming, tourism, industry and forestry/carbon sequestration (Anseeuw et al., 2012:26). Brautigam and Zhang (2013) and Strauss & Saavedra (2009:556) encourage us to search for 'African voices, perceptions and agency' in all of this activity. They are there and readily apparent, reflecting not the 'yield gap' but the more significant gap between elites talking up the benefits at endless global forums and the masses, heard only and less often through international non-governmental and advocacy organizations, and the too-little-read publications of progressive academics. So, while I agree wholeheartedly with the observations of De Schutter (2011:250) that 'the most pressing issue regarding investment in agriculture is not how much, but how', and that 'what we need is not to regulate land-grabbing as if this were inevitable, but to put forward an alternative programme for agricultural investment', the analysis put forward here suggests that those who are least food secure, long living on the lands now up for grabs, actually matter almost not at all in global food/energy security equations. Akram-Lodhi (2012:136) quotes De Schutter:

> [L]and investments implying an important shift in land rights should represent the last and least desirable option, acceptable only if no other investment model can achieve a similar contribution to local development and improve the livelihoods within the local communities concerned.
>
> *(De Schutter, 2010:20)*

Chen et al. (2013:13) counsel that land productivity improvement (i.e. vapour shift), not cultivated land expansion (through damming and diverting blue water), should be at the heart of African agricultural research and practice. This is a perspective wholeheartedly supported by the multi-year, multi-intergovernmental and non-governmental organization (IGO and INGO) supported Comprehensive Assessment of Water Management in Agriculture (Molden, 2007). However, in my view, the extraverted, predatory African state is neither capable of, nor interested in, improving smallholder agriculture beyond its 1 tonne/ha/yr average. Unfortunately, such state forms constitute the bulk of Africa's sovereign states (Bayart, 2000; Clapham, 1996). Even in a few scattered cases where smallholders do seem to matter, the impetus for assistance comes less from home governments and more from donors (like China), research institutes (such as the International Water Management Institute, IWMI, and the Consultancy Group on International Agricultural Research, CGIAR) and NGOs (like GRAIN, the Oakland Institute and Global Witness). Typical of these state forms, it is far easier to work directly with an external actor, cut a deal, extract a rent and repeat the process (Bayart, 2000; Bayart et al., 1999). This seems to fit the interests not only of Asian actors engaged in the second scramble for Africa, but others from the Global South and North as well. Such an arrangement works particularly well in relation to blue water infrastructure, e.g. dams, canals, pipelines; less so in relation to green water, as it runs head long into activists and increasingly mobilized local communities. Asian states and companies active in Africa have chosen to work with counterparts who have the poorest governance records, the weakest land tenure regimes, and the highest proportion of people active in agriculture, which itself symbolizes low GDP/capita (Anseeuw et al., 2012).

The likelihood, therefore, of the PRIA or of the AU Framework and Guidelines being implemented in future Asia–Africa relations is in my view slim to none.

Similar dynamics are operative in South Asia, Southeast Asia, China and Latin America as well. If there is to be positive engagement, it must come from an organised transnational civil society, meaning Asian and African organizations interested in seeing the stated myths of Asian–African partnership for food/energy/water security become not only a reality but a reality that serves the majority, not only the world's 1 percent. There must also be creative coalitions constructed out of differently placed and empowered groups, organizations and individuals. It is difficult to see a way forward that might be satisfactory to all, particularly when so many powerful interests are in alignment behind ideas as compelling as 'the yield gap' and 'awakening a sleeping giant'.

To be honest, food security for the rural poor is a green water issue (Molden, 2007): how to encourage rainfall to infiltrate the soil rather than to evaporate? How to achieve more crop per drop? How to create supplemental blue water out of rainfall through small-scale dams and irrigation systems? How to practise better land management on land that is already difficult to manage? But in Africa, as elsewhere in the Global South, the poor constitute a problem and an obstacle, not a potential solution and an ally. Abandoning these challenges in pursuit of a new 'blue water revolution' merely exposes the true yield gap, where the exercise of 'governance' in Africa consistently yields benefits for the few, not the many. Asian investors in Africa's green and blue water scramble know this; as shown in this chapter, some are willing to chance the risk, so great are the perceived benefits; others choose to 'go global' but also to 'go slow'.

Note

1   This is similar to the land rush in terms of mineral exploitation, where lands long regarded as 'useless' to elites, and so made available to people such as the Masaai in East Africa and the San in the Kalahari, are now regarded as highly desirable because of extensive mineral or oil and gas deposits beneath the ground.

References

Akram-Lodhi, H., 2012. 'Contextualizing Land Grabbing: Contemporary Land Deals, the Global Subsistence Crisis and the World Food System', *Canadian Journal of Development Studies*, Volume 33 (2), pp. 119–142.

Alexander, J., J. McGregor and T. Ranger, 2000. *Violence and Memory. One Hundred Years in the 'Dark Forests' of Matabeleland*, Oxford: James Currey.

Allan, T., 2011. *Virtual Water*, New York: I.B. Taurus.

Anseeuw, W., M. Boche, T. Breu, M. Giger, J. Lay, P. Messerli and K. Nolte, 2012. 'Transnational Land Deals for Agriculture in the Global South', Analytical Report based on the Land Matrix Database. Bern/Montpellier/Hamburg: CDE/CIRAD/GIGA.

Bayart, J-F., 2000. 'Africa in the World: A History of Extraversion', *African Affairs*, Volume 99, pp. 217–267.

Bayart, J-F., S. Ellis and B. Hibou, 1999. *The Criminalization of the State in Africa*, London: James Currey.

Borras, S. M. and J. C. Franco, 2012. 'Global Land Grabbing and Trajectories of Agrarian Change: A Preliminary Analysis', *Journal of Agrarian Change*, Volume 12 (1), pp. 34–59.

Bracking, S. and G. Harrison, 2003. 'Africa, Imperialism and New Forms of Accumulation', *Review of African Political Economy*, Volume 30 (95), pp. 5–10.

Brautigam, D. and H. Xiaoyang, 2011. 'African Shenzhen: China's Special Economic Zones in Africa', *Journal of Modern African Studies*, Volume 49 (1), pp. 27–54.

Brautigam and Zhang, 2013. 'Green Dreams: Myth and Reality in China's Agricultural Investment in Africa', *Third World Quarterly*, Volume 34 (9), pp. 1676–1696.

Bracking, S. and G. Harrison, 2003. 'Africa, imperialism and new forms of accumulation', *Review of African Political Economy*, Volume 30 (95), pp. 5–10.

Callaghy, T., 1987. 'The State as Lame Leviathan: The Patrimonial Administrative State in Africa', in Z. Ergas (ed.), *The African State in Transition*, Palgrave: Macmillan.

Chen, K. Z., C. Hsu and S. Fan, 2013. 'Steadying the Ladder: China's Agricultural and Rural Development Engagement in Africa', *China Agricultural Economic Review*, Volume 6 (1), pp. 2–20.

Clapham, C., 1996. *Africa and the International System*, Cambridge: Cambridge University Press.

Conca, K., 2006. *Governing Water*, Cambridge, Mass.: MIT Press.

Cotula, L., Vermeulen, S., Leonard, R. and Keely, J., 2009. *Land Grab or Development Opportunity? Agricultural Investment and International Land Deals in Africa*, London: IIED/FAO/IFAD.

Crosby, A. W., 2004. *Ecological Imperialism*, 2nd ed., Cambridge: Cambridge University Press.

De Haan, A., 2011. 'Will China Change International Development as We Know It?' *Journal of International Development*, Volume 23, pp. 881–908.

De Schutter, O., 2010. *Report of the Special Rapporteur on the Right to Food*. Available at: https://docs.escr-net.org/usr_doc/SRFood_access-to-land-report_en.pdf [Accessed 23 May 2016].

De Schutter, O., 2011. 'How Not To Think of Land-Grabbing: Three Critiques of Large-Scale Investments in Farmland', *Journal of Peasant Studies*, Volume 38 (2), pp. 249–279.

Esteban, M., 2009. 'The Chinese *Amigo:* Implications for the Development of Equatorial Guinea', *China Quarterly*, 199, pp. 667–685.

Falkenmark, M. and J. Rockstrom, 2004. *Water for Humans and Nature*, London: Earthscan.

Feldhoff, T., 2014. 'Japan's Food Security Issues: A Geopolitical Challenge for Africa and East Asia?' *Journal of Global Initiatives*, Volume 9 (1), pp. 75–96.

Ferguson, J., 1994. *The Anti-Politics Machine*, Minneapolis, MN: University of Minnesota Press.

Ghosh, J., 2010. 'The Unnatural Coupling: Food and Finance', *Journal of Agrarian Change*, Volume 10 (1), pp. 72–86.

Gumedze, S. (ed.), 2007. *Private Security in Africa: Manifestation, Challenges and Regulation*, ISS Monograph Series No 139 (November), London: Institute for Security Studies.

Hoekstra, A. Y. and Mekonnen, M. M., 2012. 'The Water Footprint of Humanity', *Proceedings of the National Academy of Sciences*, Volume 109 (9), pp. 3232–3237.

Homer-Dixon, T., 1999. *The Environment, Scarcity and Violence*, Princeton: Princeton University Press.

Kachika, T., 2010. *Land Grabbing in Africa: A Review of the Impacts and the Possible Policy Responses*, Oxford, UK: Oxfam International.

Kaufman, F., 2010. 'The Food Bubble: How Wall Street Starved Millions and Got Away With It', *Harper's Magazine* (July), pp. 27–34.

Keegan, J., 1994. *A History of Warfare*, Toronto: Vintage Books.

Liang, W., 2012. 'China's Soft Power in Africa: Is Economic Power Sufficient?' *Asian Perspective* 36, pp. 667–692.

Mamdani, M., 1995. *Citizen and Subject: Contemporary Africa and the Legacy of Late Colonialism*, Princeton: Princeton University Press.

Mathews, K., 1997. 'A Multi-Faceted Relationship: A Synoptic View', *Africa Quarterly*, Volume 37, pp. 1–26.

Molden, D. (ed.), 2007. *Water for Food, Water for Life: A Comprehensive Assessment of Water Management in Agriculture*, London: Earthscan.

Naidu, S., 2010. 'India's Engagements in Africa: Self-Interest or Mutual Partnership?' in R. Southall and H. Melber (eds.), *A New Scramble for Africa? Imperialism, Investment and Development*, Scottsville, South Africa: University of KwaZulu Natal Press.

Nnabuko, J. O. and C. U. Uche, 2015. 'Land Grab and the Viability of Foreign Investments in Sub-Saharan Africa: The Nigerian Experience', in E. Y. Vubo (ed.), *Environment, Agriculture and Cross-border Migrations*, Dakar: CODESRIA. Available at: www.codesria.org/spip.php?article2533.

Ong'weng Okuro, S., 2015. 'Land Grab in Kenya: Risks and Opportunties', in E. Y. Vubo (ed.), *Environment, Agriculture and Cross-border Migrations*, Dakar: CODESRIA. Available at: www.codesria.org/spip.php?article2533.

Ozturk, I., 2015. 'Sustainability in the Food–Energy–Water Nexus: Evidence from BRICS (Brazil, the Russian Federation, India, China and South Africa) Countries', *Energy*, Volume 93, pp. 999–1010.

Pearce, F., 2012. *The Land Grabbers*, Boston: Beacon Press.

Ponting, C., 2007. *A New Green History of the World*, Toronto: Vintage.

Solomon, S., 2010. *Water, the Epic Struggle for Wealth, Power and Civilization*, New York: HarperCollins.

Southall, R. and H. Melber (eds.), 2009. *A New Scramble for Africa? Imperialism, Investment and Development*, Scottsville, South Africa: University of KwaZulu Natal Press.

Strauss, J. C. and M. Saavendra, 2009. 'Introduction: China, Africa and Internationalization', *The China Quarterly*, 199, pp. 551–562.

Swatuk, L. A., M. McMorris, C. Leung and Y. Zu, 2015. 'Seeing "Invisible Water": Challenging Conceptions of Water for Food, Agriculture and Human Security', *Canadian Journal of Development Studies*, Volume 36 (1), pp. 24–37.

Thakur, R., 2015. 'India's Drive to Increase Involvement in Africa', *The Japan Times* (4 November). Available at: www.japantimes.co.jp/opinion/2015/11/04/commentary/world-commentary/indias-drive-increase-involvement-africa/#.Vzdk34QrJdh.

Thompson, C., 2009. 'The Scramble for Genetic Resources', in R. Southall and H. Melber (eds.), *A New Scramble for Africa? Imperialism, Investment and Development*, Scottsville, South Africa: University of KwaZulu Natal Press.

Varis, O., M. Kummu, C. Lehr and D. Shen, 2014. 'China's Stressed Waters: Societal and Environmental Vulnerability in China's Internal and Transboundary River Systems', *Applied Geography*, Volume 53, pp. 105–116.

Von Braun, J. and R. Meinzen-Dick, 2009. '"Land Grabbing" by Foreign Investors in Developing Countries: Risks and Opportunities'. *IFPRI Policy Brief* 13 (April). Washington, DC: International Food Policy Research Institute.

Webber, C. M. and P. Labaste, 2010. *Building Competitiveness in Africa's Agriculture: A Guide to Value Chain Concepts and Applications*, Washington, DC: The World Bank.

Wertz-Kanounnikoff, S., M.P. Falcao and L. Putzel, 2013. 'Facing China's Demand for Timber: An Analysis of Mozambique's Forest Concession System with Insights from Cabo Delgado Province', *International Forestry Review*, Volume 15 (3), pp. 387–397.

Wittfogel, K., 1981. *Oriental Despotism: A Comparative Study of Total Power*, New York: Vintage.

World Bank, 2009. *Awakening Africa's Sleeping Giant: Prospects for Commercial Agriculture in the Guinea Savannah Zone and Beyond*, Washington, DC: World Bank.

World Commission on Dams (WCD), 2000. *Dams and Development – A New Framework for Decision Making*. The Report of the World Commission on Dams, London: Earthscan.

World Economic Forum (WEF), 2011. *Water Security: The Water, Energy, Food and Climate Security Nexus*, Washington, DC: Island Press.

26

DEVELOPMENTS IN EUROPEAN UNION–AFRICA RELATIONS AND THEIR IMPLICATIONS FOR ASIA

Laura C. Ferreira-Pereira and Alena Vieira

Introduction

The European Union's (EU) international relations have been subject to the force of both regional and global pressures which have been testing its resilience. The former's response to several dramatic international developments, notably, the conflicts in Lebanon and Libya, the global financial crisis and the resulting strains in the Eurozone, the international air strikes interventions in Syria, the massive flow of irregular migrants and refugees, and the terrorists attacks in many countries, notably in France and Belgium during 2015 and 2016 – all have put the EU's mixed bag of rhetorical claims, strategies and institutional structures, related to its external role, to the test. At the same time, the continual extension of the objectives, instruments and activities associated with the Common Foreign and Security Policy (CFSP) has enabled the EU to strive in the international arena as an autonomous, albeit limited, security provider, besides being a unique political actor with a sizeable leverage. The gradual consolidation of a partnership policy (Ferreira-Pereira & Vieira, 2016) founded mainly on the establishment of more or less institutionalized bilateral strategic partnerships with pivotal global and regional powers, such as China, Brazil and Russia, has contributed to this expansion, which unfolded significantly in the post-9/11 landscape.[1]

Most, if not all, of these aspects have impacted on the quality of the EU's interactions with two regions of the world, namely Africa and Asia, during the past decade or so. That said, in the case of Africa, the original ties binding what is now the EU[2] to this continent date back to the early days of the European integration process, more concretely the 1960s, when the 'Six' founding members of the then European Communities decided to establish a post-colonial contractual arrangement designed to promote sustainable economic and social development. This arrangement originally took the form of the Yaoundé Agreement[3] and afterwards of the Lomé Conventions, which have governed the relationship between the EU and associated states from Africa, the Caribbean and the Pacific (ACP) over 25 years, on the basis of a development-oriented focus.[4] The replacement of the Lomé Conventions by the Cotonou Partnership Agreement in 2000 brought about favourable conditions for breeding deeper political dialogue with political stability, democracy, security and peace within ACP states in view. Equally important, before the advent of the twenty-first century, the EU launched the Euro-Mediterranean Partnership, also known as the Barcelona Process, by means of which it has framed its relations with some North African states.[5] In 2008, the Barcelona Process received renewed vigour as it expanded and evolved into the Union for the Mediterranean.[6]

During the past decade, the EU came to give unprecedented attention and salience to African security actors and policies. This is largely because since 2003 the traditional development cooperation, based on a diverse range of trade and aid instruments, came to be complemented by active security cooperation as a result of the EU's engagement in both military crisis management and capacity building on the African ground. The gradual implementation of the European Security and Defence Policy (ESDP) against the backdrop of the European Security Strategy (ESS) approved in 2003 has contributed to this. At that time, the ESDP, which had been formally established in 1999, had strategically targeted Africa as a regional testing ground for securing the credibility and respectability of the EU's role on the global stage. Symptomatic of this was the fact that the first European autonomous military operation, called Artemis, was launched in the Democratic Republic of Congo (DRC), a state which then became the base for various EU-led police and military missions, notably EUPOL Kinshasa, EUSEC RD Congo, EUFOR RD Congo and EUPOL RD Congo. By 2003, several external stimuli had led to the adoption of a more salient African agenda in the framework of CFSP and ESDP activities. On the one hand, there was the growing strategic interest exhibited by the United States (US) vis-à-vis Africa alongside the significant economic Chinese presence in the region. On the other hand, there was the necessity to engage African countries in multilateral efforts needed to address complex challenges with high security resonance related to issues ranging from illegal migration and illicit traffic of small arms and light weapons (SALW) to terrorism and climate change. Furthermore, the creation of the African Union (AU) in 2002 reinforced the conviction that conditions existed for the EU, despite its commitment to African ownership, to become involved in conflict management in Africa with its own capabilities.[7] Operation Artemis launched in 2003, and the setting up by the EU of a financing scheme to strengthen the AU's peace support operations capabilities, known as African Peace Facility (APF),[8] in the following year, pointed in that direction. Equally important was the approval of a European Strategy for Africa, in December 2005, which, combined with the launching of the operations EUSEC RD Congo and EUPOL Kinshasa during that same year, has clearly lent the still fledgling ESDP a more defined African élan. As this chapter will demonstrate, in the post-Lisbon Treaty context, the EU's security engagement in Africa grew even stronger considering the number of both civilian and military operations conducted under the aegis of the now designated Common Security and Defence Policy (CSDP).

The principal aim of this chapter is to explore and discuss the evolving relationship between the EU and Africa.[9] It argues that the EU's cooperation with Africa has incorporated a deeper security dimension and this change has enabled the EU to foster stronger security interactions with Asia. This will be made through the prism of the European engagement in the African security dynamics in the realm of CFSP and CSDP, between 2003 and 2016, a period during which these common policies have developed under the umbrella of both the ESS and the *Report on the Implementation of the European Security Strategy*, approved in 2008.[10] Such an analytical exercise shall allow one to outline the resulting implications of the experience accumulated by the EU in African crisis management for its own developing security rapport with Asia; and to capture, in a comparative light, the differences underlying the EU's political and security role in the two continents. A focus on the EU's security profile in Africa and its bearing upon EU–Asia relations constitutes a somewhat intriguing analytical angle since the EU is a relative 'newcomer' in the global security arena. Here, the EU cannot look back at decades of solid experience as is the case with trade and development aid. But it is rather confronted with unchartered territory, having to build many approaches and tools designed to carve out its relations with both African and Asian counterparts on a distinctive basis from scratch. Moreover, by taking the assessment of the evolving EU involvement with major African security actors and processes as a basis for understanding its resonance in changing and stronger EU–Asia security interactions, the present work makes a tangible contribution to the scholarship given the very limited existing literature which addresses this trilateral perspective while consolidating knowledge on the growing European role in the provision of security in the world.

This chapter starts by casting light on how endeavours undertaken by the EU to reach out to the world and assert itself as a global security actor have been feeding back into its relationship with both Africa and Asia. It then provides a broad thematic and historical overview of the EU–Africa relationship. At this point of the analysis, it will be outlined that the incorporation of Africa into the EU's CFSP agenda has largely taken the form of engagement in African crisis management, with security cooperation with the AU becoming of critical importance. In this regard, this chapter claims that the African experience was not without consequence for the EU's developing role in Asia, where the manifestations of a more active political and security role could be seen in both the expansion of strategic partnerships and emergent cooperation in the fight against piracy and transnational terrorism.

The European Union in the world: reaching out to Africa and Asia

The assumption that Africa and Asia have been assigned a different place in the EU's foreign and security policy agenda seems uncontroversial. Given the colonial relations prevailing between the founding members of the European Communities and some African countries, Africa has been part of the European project since its inception, with the development of the African continent featuring in the Schuman Declaration as one of the essential tasks of the economically recovered and united post-1945 Europe.[11] Such a historical legacy would acquire great significance in, and impact upon, the quality of the EU–Africa relations throughout the decades until present times. For example, the persistence of the design of the European Development Fund, which was established by the Treaty of Rome in 1957 and targeted the former European colonies (i.e. the British, Dutch, Belgian and French), presents itself as a reflection of the influence of the colonial history on the longstanding EU–Africa relationship. Hence, relations with Africa can be said to be a key substantive area within the EC/EU's foreign policy from its early days.

In its turn, as a consequence of its geography and a history less marked by the shadow of European colonialism, Asia has traditionally remained more 'distant' from the European ambitions and achievements. Despite these differences, important commonalities – old and new – can be identified in the evolution of the EU's relationship with Africa and Asia. Traditionally speaking, these two regions of the world have been more or less associated with the EU's external assistance, especially with humanitarian and development aid-related issues. After the UK's accession to the European Communities in 1973, the organization has evolved into the second largest development provider to the Pacific area. Thus, both Africa and Asia have become important beneficiaries of the EU's development policy. Nevertheless, while Africa came to be perceived as a domain of EU 'special responsibility' and, for that reason, a foreign policy priority – something widely supported by the public opinion of its member states (Special Eurobarometer, 2010:10) – the EU's cooperation with Asia has developed in the so-called 'African shadow', that is, in the shadow of the longstanding cooperation between the EU and

Africa (Holland & Kelly, 2012:249). Furthermore, in Asia, the EU, in its condition of development aid actor, has been able to rely on cooperation with key regional players like Australia, with the 2011 Australia–EU delegated cooperation agreement for aid delivery being illustrative of this (Murray, 2016).[12]

Significantly, in recent times, these two regions have presented themselves as privileged spaces for the EU's external policy actions in the field of security, a concept understood here in broader terms. In the case of Asia, this can be readily associated with the international 'turn to Asia' promoted especially by Barack Obama's US administration. Yet, the challenges and opportunities posed over the past decade or so by China's rise were not without resonance for the political calculus made by the EU. At the same time, as anticipated in this chapter's introduction and further elaborated in the following section, European engagement in Africa's security dynamics has been a consequence of the growing number of complex threats and risks originating from the African continent.

In practical terms, all of these developments in both Africa and Asia have shown the EU the need to find creative responses in the framework of its distinctive multilateral cooperative strategy, founded on an inclusive approach to crisis management which comprised diplomatic, military, civilian, developmental and humanitarian tools. This strategy enables a differentiation between the EU and other international organizations engaged in security and peace promotion programmes, thereby giving it a comparative advantage or competitive edge. The EU's distinctiveness should be further linked to the setting up of the Framework Participation Agreement (FPA), on the basis of which a third state is allowed to participate in its crisis management operations conducted under the umbrella of the CSDP. Among the African countries which have participated in the European operations, those which stand out include Angola (EUPOL Kinshasa, EUPOL RD Congo), Mali (EUPOL Kinshasa), Morocco (EUFOR Althea) and South Africa (Artemis). As for the Asian states, participants in the CSDP missions include Brunei, Malaysia, Philippines, Singapore and Thailand (all of them, AMM Aceh), and New Zealand (EUFOR Althea and EUPOL Afghanistan). It is interesting to note that there is no FPA with any African country, while Australia, New Zealand and South Korea all have signed an FPA with the EU.

Such relatively recent evolution in EU–Africa and EU–Asia relations, linked to a more ambitious role in the provision of stability and security, has called for an adaptation of the EU's institutions and actors traditionally involved in cooperation with these two regions. It has also brought with it a more intense urge to get to grips with the emerging CSDP setback derived from defence cuts made by member states, particularly those affected by the crisis in the Eurozone, namely Greece, Italy, Spain and Portugal (SIPRI, 2016).[13]

Against the backdrop of the EU's efforts to increase its force and weight as a foreign policy player on the global stage, both Africa and Asia became test cases for the organization to play a more active and respected role in the domains of crisis management and conflict prevention. To be sure, Africa has been a special case in point if one considers the number of European missions conducted in this continent, in the first years of ESDP, more concretely, between 2003 and 2009: 9 out of 24. This trend has remained to date as over the past five years or so, 10 out of 11 new operations were undertaken in African countries. These were the following: EUNAVFOR MED (2015), EUBAM Libya (2013), EUMAM RCA (2015), EU CAP Sahel Mali (2014), EUFOR RCA (completed, 2014–2015), EUTM Mali (2013), EU AVSEC South Sudan (completed, 2012–2014), EUCAP Sahel Niger (2012), EUCAP Nestor (2012) and EUTM Somalia (2010).

Besides the peace-support activities carried out under the aegis of CSDP, relations with Africa and Asia have been further defined by the establishment of the so-called Strategic partnerships (SPs), a foreign policy instrument which tends to impact not only upon the growing role and influence of the EU as a global political and security player, but also upon the behaviour of third states that eventually engage in such a privileged rapport. The SPs were officially acknowledged in the framework of the 2003 ESS that has enumerated a limited number of countries with which the EU intended to strengthen a strategic relationship. Among these states are Canada, China, India, Japan, Russia and the US. In a proactive endeavour to engage further countries, the EU signed an SP with South Africa, Brazil and Mexico in 2006, 2007 and 2008, respectively. The formal existence of these partnerships was recognized in the *Report on the Implementation of the European Security Strategy* approved in 2008. Finally, in 2010, South Korea was added to this exclusive list, which eventually came to gather ten strategic partners. The significance of the EU's strategic partnership-based policy, whose consolidation has been receiving the political impetus of the successive High Representatives of the EU for the Foreign Affairs and Security Policy and Presidents of the European Council, was made plain in the Conclusions of the European Council of September 2010 which equated the strategic partnerships with instruments at the disposal of the EU for the pursuit of its own objectives and interests (European Council, 2010:2).

Along with the signing of strategic partnerships with both established and emerging countries in Africa and Asia, the EU sealed in 2007 a strategic partnership with the African Union (AU) which stands out as a milestone in the evolutionary process of cooperation between the EU and Africa. Its major contours shall be outlined in the next section.

European Union–Africa relations: from trade and aid cooperation to synergy towards fostering security and stability

Throughout successive decades, the collaboration between the EU and African states was largely characterized by economic and trade interests and objectives while being inextricably informed by historic and cultural links connecting former European colonial powers, particularly France, to their former colonies. After the Yaoundé Conventions were signed, with the strong support of France, the first Lomé Convention was set up in 1975 under the impetus of British membership. Throughout more than two decades (1975–2000), the Lomé Conventions (i.e. Lomé I, II, III and IV) came to be at the centre of the EU's development policy designed to promote cooperation in trade as well as financial and technical assistance. Consequently, a growing number of associated African countries came to benefit from privileged access to the European market(s) and annual STABEX *(Système de Stabilisation des Recettes d'Exportation*, a European Commission compensatory finance scheme to stabilize export earnings of the ACP countries) payments – albeit this did not take place without disadvantages; exceptions which were linked to agrarian products as well as to insufficient loans and grants.

The Lomé IV, which was negotiated in 1988/1989 against the backdrop of momentous changes sweeping the European continent, introduced an important innovation, namely an explicit political conditionality provision (Article 5) which would be expanded in 1995 to encompass respect for democratic principles, the rule of law and good governance. The tone and major principles[14] guiding a more holistic thinking on African developmental issues, combining economic development, democratization and peace, were laid out by the European Commission in its *Communication to the Council on Conflicts in Africa* produced in 1996. The latter was preceded by the 1995 EU General Affairs Council document titled *Preventive Diplomacy, Conflict Resolution and Peacekeeping in Africa*, whose conception was as a result of the Rwanda genocide that "strengthened the willingness of EU policy-makers to increase European capabilities in the field of conflict prevention and management" (Sicurelli, 2013:39).

Eventually, the *Communication to the Council on Conflicts in Africa* became the basis of the Commission's approach to the issue of violent crisis and conflict in the continent and would contribute to the shaping of the EU's role in the prevention, management and resolution of conflicts in African countries.[15]

Cooperation between the EU and African partners continued under the auspices of the Cotonou Partnership Agreement signed in June 2000, in the aftermath of the historic first EU–Africa Summit held in Cairo (April 2000) where the Organization of African Unity (OAU) stood out as the "African focal point" (Sheriff & Kotsopoulos, 2013:306). The Cairo declaration has managed to improve the political and security dimensions of the EU–Africa relationship, not only in inaugurating a more structured political dialogue based on regular meetings of senior officials and ministers, but also in renewing the commitment of both European and African states towards cooperation in the areas of peace building and conflict management.

As it is acknowledged, the Cotonou Agreement, concluded for a 20-year period (i.e. 2000 to 2020), has opened up a new chapter in the EU–ACP rapport (Pape, 2013:738; Carbone, 2012; Bretherton & Vogler, 2006: 122–123). This chapter was marked by a quantitative increase in development aid and the conclusion of the so-called regional Economic Partnership Agreements (EPAs) between the EU and ACP partners founded on the principle of reciprocity in trade concessions and aimed at encouraging regional economic integration. It was further characterized by a comprehensive political dialogue around initiatives and strategies conceived to address conflict prevention and conflict resolution and, ultimately, to promote security and peace across African countries (Marsh & Mackenstein, 2005:231–232; Holland, 2004:277–288). Novel references to peace building and conflict prevention in the Cotonou text substantiated a natural consequence of the incorporation of development goals within the realm of CFSP, something that has bestowed the European development policy a political character as well (Holland, 2004:288). The Cotonou political *acquis* has signalled a move away from the classical exclusive focus on development assistance to an increased concern with political and security matters, notably with the promotion of democratic governance and dialogue on peace building and conflict prevention among African states (Bretherton & Vogler, 2006: 124, 126). Equally important was that as of 2003, it came to inform the EU's commitment to military and civilian action in troubled spots of Africa. The Cotonou revisions in 2005 and 2010 have only strengthened the prioritization ascribed by the EU to cooperation in areas of peace and security, something that has received negative feedback from African representatives more preoccupied with economic issues, notably with better aid arrangements and trade deals (Carbone, 2012).

In the first years of the new millennium, the gradual prioritization of security and political cooperation vis-à-vis Africa should be understood in the light of a number of geopolitical changes which ascribed African international prominence, thereby contributing to the shift in its perception from 'a charity case' to 'an opportunity' in the eyes of the EU (Sheriff & Kotsopoulos, 2013:307). The creation of New Partnership for Africa's Development (NEPAD) at the OAU Summit in the summer of 2001 stands out as illustrative of this new role of Africa – one related to a more dominant role in promoting its own growth and development, whilst working against its marginalization in globalized world politics and economics. Moreover, the perceived failure of development policies and the mounting number of violent conflicts in this continent,[16] with a disruptive impact on the EU in such areas as migration, organized crime and terrorist activities, called for a proactive security approach on the part of the European states. Finally, the transformation of the OAU into the AU in 2002 represented a new turning point in EU–Africa relations in political and security terms. It imparted important signals as to the

Africans' resolve to address their own security problems through conflict prevention and crisis management mechanisms and peace-support programmes.

Yet, again, the chronic lack of financial resources and the weak operational capabilities experienced by the African states became a source of unexplored opportunities for an EU resolved to foster a respectable credible and effective role as a political and security actor on the global stage. Such determination was clearly affirmed in the ESS that has pinpointed transnational terrorism, proliferation of weapons of mass destruction, regional conflicts, state failure and organized crime as the key threats to European security. In this way, the framework document has inherently identified Africa as one of the most eligible regions for the EU's undertakings towards a more 'secure Europe' and a 'better world' under the evolving realm of ESDP. This window of opportunity to help African states, but also regional and sub-regional organizations, to carry their own burden in terms of peacekeeping and crisis management emerged when the EU had defined its security role in terms of the so-called Petersberg tasks and missions, and thus was focused on the process of building up its own military capabilities in support of "humanitarian and rescue tasks, peacekeeping tasks and tasks of combat forces in crisis management, including peace-making", as identified in the Treaty of the European Union.[17]

The EU's engagement in African crisis management was given a concrete start with an operation codenamed Artemis, initiated in June 2003 in Bunia, in the Eastern part of DRC, upon the political impetus of the UN's Secretary-General, to prepare the ground for the subsequent launch of a reinforced MONUC mission. Despite being *de facto* almost exclusively based on French military personnel and capabilities, Artemis was *de jure* the EU's first fully autonomous military crisis management operation carried out outside Europe. Interestingly enough, while inaugurating the EU's military role in Africa, the pioneering Artemis would pave the way for other examples of innovative operations on the African soil. Operation Atalanta was the first EU's naval operation. It was launched in 2008 in the Gulf of Aden and in the Indian Ocean, and aimed to deter piracy and support the vessels of the World Food Programme. This has led some to consider, rightly, this continent a field for the experimentation or a 'test-bed' of the CSDP (Whitman & Haastrup, 2013:58).[18]

Overall, the CSDP missions in Africa have been launched in response to requests from the UN and deployed until the latter's contingents could take over. Their mandates have been specific in character and their tangible impact on African conflict management limited (Rye, 2013:36, 39; Gegout, 2007). Most European operations have been civilian in nature and some have been conducted in cooperation with the AU. In the case of military operations, the leading roles were played by France, and to a lesser extent by the UK and Germany, and whenever they were based on short-term mandates, circumscribed in geographical terms, with low risk of casualties, and judged as critical to signal the EU's capacity to act independently from the US, principally on the African ground (Gegout, 2007). In sum, CSDP missions have clearly demonstrated the shortcomings of European capabilities and revealed major difficulties for the European multinational forces, not only in going beyond low-level peacekeeping and civilian crisis management, but also in transcending the function of bridging operations to facilitate UN interventions (Griffin, 2007:42) as well as the task of assisting the AU with the management of on-going conflicts. Incidentally, these shortcomings and difficulties have raised criticism among AU leaders, with the CFSP outcomes being criticized for their limited effectiveness and inconsistency (Sicurelli, 2009:186–189). Nevertheless, the expeditionary operations have helped the EU to enhance its role in African security affairs, notably vis-à-vis the US, while retaining its image as a "model of achieving and maintaining peace" (ibid.: 186) in the eyes of African leaders, and to strengthen its external perception as a global political actor capable of making a concrete contribution to international peace and security.

The EU–AU cooperation in the domain of crisis management became particularly noticeable in the establishment of the APF in April 2004. The latter was launched at the request of the AU, conveying €300 million from the European Development Fund to support African peacekeeping operations.[19] The EU's financial support has facilitated two AU operations (AMIS I and AMIS II) in Darfur (Sudan), as well as missions in Burundi, the Central African Republic and the Comoros. More generally, the EU–AU relationship has been based upon a "clear division of labour: the African Union deploys troops and the EU supplies economic resources and advice in support of the troops, disarmament and general elections" (Rye, 2013:49). The EU has, thus, emerged as the sponsor of or "funder" in the EU–AU relationship (ibid.). And this has been subject to criticism for engendering a kind of "outsourcing" of the EU's security (Gowan & Witney, 2014:1) and for its subsequent negative impact upon both the reinforcement of the AU and the international standing of the EU itself (Gowan & Witney, 2014; Mackinda et al., 2016:122).

At the same time, the EU's collaboration with the AU has been increasingly oriented towards local military and civilian capacity building (Tardy, 2015:3). To this end, support has been provided in terms of training, technical assistance and funding of the AU's personnel. The General Secretariat of the Council of the EU has been contributing to the development of concepts for police, rule of law and civilian administration, along with the contribution to the doctrine and standing operating procedures of the African Standby Force (Boin et al., 2013:71). To foster local security capabilities has been indeed an integral part of all recent CSDP operations in Africa. Examples of this can be seen in the training of Somalian recruits on behalf of AMISOM (African Union Mission in Somalia) in the framework of EUTM Somalia, the strengthening of maritime capabilities in the Horn of Africa under the umbrella of EUCAP Nestor, and the reform and strengthening of the Malian national army in the context of EUTM Mali. This growing tendency reflects the idea of the African states' ownership and leadership of their own security policies. It also resonates with the EU's comprehensive approach to crisis management as well as with its security–development nexus narrative, according to which, underdevelopment leads to violence and insecurity precludes development (Franke, 2009:69).

Despite this, the European approach to capacity building in Africa has been exhibiting both contextual and material limitations, as testified by the post-2008 landscape. Indicative of this is the focus on smaller and cheaper capacity building which has sprung from a certain CSDP "missions fatigue" (Mattelaer & Marijnen, 2014:58), and was aggravated by the economic difficulties afflicting the EU and, particularly, the Eurozone. Further limitations are also related to the narrow scope of some of the associated EU financing instruments (Tardy, 2015:2).[20] Moreover, the EU has been stipulating specific restrictions such as the non-provision of lethal equipment, based on the assumption that newly developed capabilities may not be used as originally planned, as demonstrated by the Guinea-Bissau coup d'état[21] (2012) following the security sector reform mission (EUSSR Guinea-Bissau) launched in 2008 (Tardy, 2015:2). Be that as it may, as asserted by some like Mattelaer & Marijnen (2014:67), the EU's indirect engagement in African capacity building has been the only one both "within the material reach of European states" and "within political reach in terms of finding consensus". Moreover, it has been allowing the EU to maintain an "affordable influence" in Africa while pursuing its aspiration to shape the broad dynamics in the African strategic environment (Mattelaer & Marijnen, 2014:67).

While acknowledging that, as some put it aptly, none of the EU's military missions have solved the African conflicts (Gegout, 2007:131), it can be said that the evolution of the security dimension underlying the EU–Africa relationship has been more or less commensurate with African requests and expectations of cooperation with the EU. It has also been in line with the EU's manifest ambition to enhance its visibility and political leverage under the umbrella of both the CFSP and CSDP by means of a growing role and presence in international peacekeeping and crisis management, alongside other key international organizations like the UN and NATO. The provision of security in Africa has been of particular relevance to the EU in retaining its influence in view of mounting competition of interests arising not only from US increased geo-strategic and military interests in the region, as revealed by the creation of a new US military command for Africa (i.e. the US Africa Command or AFRICOM),[22] but also from the remarkable Chinese economic and trade presence in various African countries, within which it came to challenge the EU's external role, also in the security sphere.[23]

In view of Africa's rising strategic importance, which became particularly evident with the continent's international momentum in 2005 – designated the 'Year of Africa'[24] – the EU–Africa dialogue has intensified. This was demonstrated by the establishment of a strategic partnership with Africa in the framework of the second EU–Africa Summit which took place in Lisbon, on 8–9 December 2007. By then, 80 African statesmen and European leaders formally endorsed the Africa–EU Strategic Partnership, which included a Joint Africa–EU Strategy and an Action Plan for its implementation. While signalling the purpose, on the part of the EU, to foster a more coherent foreign policy for the African continent (Carbone, 2012), the Africa–EU Strategic Partnership conveyed a paradigm shift in the relationship between the two actors: the previous joint strategy for Africa was due to be replaced by a European strategy with Africa based on a "partnership between equals". The principal aspiration was that a "joint responsibility" and "joint ownership" became the cornerstone of this rapport while moving it beyond the immediate postcolonial focus on aid and trade (Sheriff & Kotsopoulos, 2013:305). In more concrete terms, under the Joint Africa–EU Strategy, a renewed and more intensive political dialogue was initiated. Symptomatic of this were the circumstances in which EU–Africa relations came to include triennial heads of government summits and a reinforced parliamentary dimension, with both the European Parliament and the Pan-African Parliament getting involved in the creation of a joint progress report on the implementation of the Strategy and its Action Plans, in their condition of actors expected to play 'crucial roles' in the EU–Africa dialogue and summitry (Kingah & Cofelice, 2015:149).

Significantly, the Africa–EU Strategic Partnership corresponded to the follow up of the EU's Strategy for Africa, adopted in December 2005, which was originally enshrined in the *Communication from the Commission to the Council, the European Parliament and the European Economic and Social Committee of 12 October 2005, EU Strategy for Africa: Towards a Euro-African Pact to Accelerate Africa's Development*. This strategy delineated the steps which the EU intended to undertake, until 2015, to support African efforts towards democratic stability, sustainable development and security. Under its umbrella, EU–Africa cooperation came to target new areas, notably cooperation in the fight against terrorism, proliferation of weapons of mass destruction and mercenary activities (Sicurelli, 2013). All this indicates the extension of the EU's foreign policy profile, which becomes further noticeable when casting a comparative light upon the operation of the EU in the Asian continent.

The operation of the European Union in Africa and Asia: a comparative perspective

As we have already discussed, Africa and Asia have become more important in the security sphere during the past decade or so, as reflected in the incremental expansion and institutionalization of the EU's relations with these regions. That said, it seems clear that each poses different constraints and challenges, thereby putting to the test the EU's ability to assert itself as a respected international foreign policy and security player.

During recent years, the EU's capacity to provide security in Africa, as well as the coherence of its external role, has been under enormous strain. This is so not only because the EU has been grappling with a volatile political and military environment still imbued with legacies of the past, but also the necessity in dealing with multidimensional security threats, such as those emanating from the refugee crisis, conflicts in Central Africa, civil war and jihadist-dominated rebellions in Mali, and the activities of groups like Boko Haram and ISIS. Thus, it does not come as a surprise to see Africa as the geographical focus of CDSP missions, despite the fact that their scope is widely referred to as "spanning the Western Balkans, the Caucasus, the Middle East, Asia and Africa" (Bremberg, 2015:68).

As far as EU–Asia relations are concerned, the increasing emphasis placed upon the security sphere is due to the EU's apprehension regarding the growing international relevance of the region. As a result, there was also the necessity to find a response to the widespread criticism regarding its lack of strategic vision for Asia (Bersik, 2014:285). Such criticism, which gained further salience in the context of the 'Asian turn', coincided with the crisis in the Eurozone and, in more general terms, with the EU's perceived international "delivery deficit" (Smith, 2013:115). Eventually, the recognition by the EU of the region's critical importance, not only in political, economic, trade, but also in security terms, was revealed in the formulation and implementation of the *Guidelines on the EU's Foreign and Security Policy in East Asia* as well as in the incremental expansion of its strategic partnership policy.[25] The EU has acknowledged the existence of five individual strategic partners in Asia, namely China, Russia, India, Japan and South Korea, something which stands in marked contrast with the recognition of only one in Africa, which is South Africa (Ferreira-Pereira & Vieira, 2016).

Equally important, the security dynamics underlying the EU–Asia relationship came to encompass the conduct of, albeit few, CSDP missions, notably the Aceh Monitoring Mission (AMM) in Indonesia, launched in 2005, and the EU Police Mission in Afghanistan (EUPOL Afghanistan), undertaken two years later. What is more, it came to be marked by cooperation in the domains of anti-terrorism and anti-piracy. Incidentally, the EU's concerns with the maritime security within the CSDP purview have led to unprecedented collaboration with Asian countries. In the framework of Operation Atalanta, joint naval anti-piracy training has been conducted with the Chinese, Japanese and South Korean naval forces in the Indian Ocean. After the launching of that operation, the EU has become more actively involved in maritime security in the Western Indian Ocean. An illustrative example of this can be seen in the launching of the Critical Maritime Routes Programme (CMR) established in 2009, which aims to improve maritime governance by enhancing information sharing and the training of maritime law enforcement, with special emphasis being placed on coastal guards. Further instances of the EU's engagement in the region comprise a €37 million investment into the Regional Maritime Security Programme (MASE) which started in 2013, and the Critical Maritime Routes in the Indian Ocean (CRIMARIO), launched in 2015 to support the maritime situation awareness.[26] In that sense, one can say that the evolution of the naval component of the CSDP, which was inaugurated in Africa with Operation Atalanta, has created a space for a greater European role in the provision of maritime security in the Indian Ocean. By taking stock of its various experiences, the EU can also develop, henceforth, into a motor for cooperative security governance dynamics within this crucial area which links Africa to Asia.

Despite many shortcomings and drawbacks prevailing at the level of CFSP/CSDP, the EU has been emerging in the African continent as an increasingly committed security provider by taking the lead in diverse crisis management missions and supporting the AU's capacity-building efforts, particularly through the funding of its conflict prevention, management and resolution activities. Along these lines, the evolution of the EU's security and military role in Africa enables the EU to present itself as a more credible political and strategic actor on the Asian continent, where it has been attempting to meet some countries' concerns with maritime security governance. In that sense, there are conditions for a stronger EU–Asia collaboration in the domain of maritime security.

Be that as it may, in the eyes of the Asian elites, the intensification of the security cooperation underpinning the relationship between the EU and Asia does not outweigh what is considered to be the EU major weakness, which is the "non-existent military capabilities in the region and an underdeveloped CFSP" (Bersik, 2014:119).[27] Moreover, particularly in East Asia, the EU has been depicted as being among the "free-riders that rely on the US military posture in Asia-Pacific" (ibid.: 122). The fact that the EU has been framing its strategy vis-à-vis Asia in cooperation and coordination with the US gave rise to the perception that in East Asia the EU seconds the US path in terms of its general conduct and major specific interests in the area. This was exemplified by the joint statement on developments in Asia-Pacific set forth by the High Representative of the Union for Foreign and Security Policy, Catherine Ashton, and the US Secretary of State, Hillary Clinton, on the occasion of the 2012 ASEAN Regional Forum forum (Bersik, 2014:162). The perceived free-rider image of the EU has been mitigated by its emphasis on the importance of international law as the most appropriate guide for and response to a more assertive and aggressive China, when it comes to its sovereignty claims in the South China Sea and to the ensuing territorial and maritime disputes against other Southeast Asian states.[28] In this regard, it is worth noting that the EU's defence of international law has reinforced conditions for some ASEAN countries like Vietnam to develop a hedging-oriented foreign policy (Tran et al., 2013) informed by a 'third way'-type politico-diplomatic stance enabling the country not only to safeguard its own strategic interests, but also to feel free from the necessity of choosing between 'balancing' (i.e. supporting the US strategy) and 'bandwagoning' (i.e. giving in to China's interests).[29]

As already advanced above, both in Africa and Asia, the EU has been facing fierce competition from other extra-regional powers. In the case of Asia, it is worth noting that apart from the US, the influence of Russia, and also of Brazil, has become an even greater challenge. As for the African continent, the weight of China in economic, trade and security spheres has been steadily growing, thereby challenging clearly the traditional predominant role of the EU as the main extra-regional actor. The lack of a systematic US African policy tends to make the Chinese presence and leverage in Africa even more pronounced. Although China has been standing out as *primus inter pares* among external actors operating in Africa, the engagement of Brazil in the region should be borne in mind. This was particularly noticeable during the Lula da Silva administration and continues to produce its effects (Ferreira-Pereira, 2016).

A common basis governing the EU's relationship with these two regions of the world is linked to the key role of intraregional and interregional organizations, which has been seen as a precondition for the stability of both the regional and international order. This is especially the case with EU–Asia relations, in the context of which the regional integration builds upon strong institutional structures like the Association of Southeast Asian Nations (ASEAN), the ASEAN Regional Forum (ARF), and the South Asian Association for Regional Cooperation (SAARC). The EU supports the regional integration process in Asia by acting as a major development partner of ASEAN and the biggest donor of the ASEAN Secretariat. Here, again, given the growing number of common security concerns "ranging from border management and transnational crime to radicalisation, illegal migration, and climate change and cyber security" (Pejsova, 2016:2), EU–ASEAN cooperation has been reinforced in 2012, after the EU's accession to the *Treaty of Amity and Cooperation in Southeast Asia*. In 2015, the EU appointed its first Ambassador to ASEAN, Francisco Fontan Pardo, and established a mission in Jakarta to enhance the bilateral relationship (ibid.:1).

Overall, the EU welcomes the furtherance of its collaborative action interregionally and multilaterally fora in both regions. Such significance ascribed by the EU to the interregional dialogue is underpinned by the putative assumption that the European integration experience can inspire the region-building processes in Africa and Asia, like those substantiated by the African Union and ASEAN. One can say, nonetheless, that the perception of the EU as a 'model' for regional integration has been seriously eroded by a state of continued political, economic and social crisis it finds itself in since the beginning of the global financial crisis of 2008 – a scenario which was particularly difficult under the recent refugee emergency crisis and terrorist attacks at the very heart of Europe.

Conclusion

This chapter has sought to provide a critical analysis of the evolving nature of the EU–Africa relationship, while addressing some of its major implications for developing European relations with Asia. In this regard, the emphasis has been placed upon the EU's changing role in the provision of security in African and Asian continents under the aegis of CFSP activities, which include the CSDP missions.

The evolution of EU–Africa relations outlined by this chapter has demonstrated the extension of the EU's external role from limited trade- and aid-based programmes mainly targeting the ACP group of countries to the current position, whereby the EU has the ability to advance a political and security agenda at both bilateral and multilateral level, as part of its CFSP and CSDP objectives. Representative of the progress is the expressive number of CSDP police and military missions carried out since 2003 to date, which shows that the African continent has been consigned the category of a regional laboratory for the EU's endeavours in building its political and security influence on the international stage, in general, and its status as a security provider in Africa, in particular.

As we have argued here, the African crisis management experience was not without resonance for the EU's developing security role in Asia. This is so to the extent that the EU has attempted to capitalize on the dividends gained on the African ground to improve its political and security visibility and leverage in Asia. Although in this continent the EU continues to be seen as a security 'free rider' and a weak military power, there have been positive developments in EU–Asia security interactions. These encompass the extension of the EU's partnership policy. Furthermore, the participation of ASEAN countries in the first CDSP missions in Asia, namely AMM Aceh and EUPOL Afghanistan, the joint naval training in the framework of the first European naval mission, Operation Atalanta, and the establishment of framework FPAs with key Asian actors, all point in that direction. Such recent developments have helped the EU to present itself as a more credible security actor in Asia, where it has been seizing opportunities linked to Asian states' concerns with maritime security. The unprecedented committed and active role of the EU in the security management and governance of the Indian Ocean is a particular case in point, which may well create/favour conditions for the EU to evolve into a security bridge builder between Africa and Asia.

Overall, the examination of the principal political dynamics and security manifestations underpinning the EU's interactions with the two regions provided by this chapter has also shown how this organization has been tackling complex security challenges and seizing a variety of opportunities to promote itself as a capable international actor in world affairs while competing for political and strategic influence vis-à-vis other powers interested in Africa and Asia, such as China, the US and Russia.

Ferreira-Pereira and Vieira

Considering that many issues and developments brought into the scope of this chapter are recent and still unfolding, the trilateral perspective adopted here to scrutinize EU–Africa and EU–Asia security relations calls for further academic enquiry. This opens up new avenues for future research that should further unravel, substantiate and appraise the extent to which, and the ways in which, a more assertive EU security role in Africa is leveraging more visible, active and stronger EU–Asia security interactions, and the consequences of this 'trilateralization' dynamics in the (re)definition of the EU's political, security and strategic interests in Africa and Asia.

Notes

1 For a detailed account of the EU's partnership policy towards Brazil and Russia, see Vieira (2016) and Laura C. Ferreira-Pereira (2016).
2 In the early 1970s the organization, which was originally referred to as the European Communities or the European Economic Community (EEC), came to be known as the European Community (EC). When the Maastricht Treaty came into force on 1 November 1993, the latter was transformed into the European Union (EU). Although throughout this chapter the terminology will shift, depending on the time period at issue, when referring to the integration process, more generally, it will be described as the EU.
3 The two Yaoundé Conventions were signed in 1964 and 1971 with 18 associated African states and Madagascar.
4 The first Lomé Convention, set up in 1975 between the then 9 member states of the EEC and 46 ACP countries, is generally considered as marking the beginning of the *de facto* EEC's Development Policy. After Lomé I being in force between 1976 and 1980, Lomé II became operational between 1981 and 1985. Lomé III governed the relations between 1985 and 1990, and Lomé IV, which came to comprise 70 ACP partners, was in force between 1990 and 1999.
5 This contribution does not bring the EU's relations with North Africa into the analysis. This is because North Africa has been ascribed a differentiated treatment by the EU, not only as part of the latter's Mediterranean approach (substantiated in both the Union for Mediterranean, launched in July 2008, and the Euro-Mediterranean Partnership established in 1995), but also in the context of the European Neighbourhood Policy. Thus, treating both regions separately has become "academic convention" (Hurt, 2004:155).
6 The Barcelona Process was launched in November 1995 by 15 EU member states and 12 partners, namely Algeria, Cyprus, Egypt, Israel, Jordan, Lebanon, Malta, Morocco, Palestine, Syria, Tunisia and Turkey. The EU enlargement, as well as the accession of Albania and Mauritania to the Barcelona Process in 2007, resulted in a larger membership (27+10). The Union for the Mediterranean is composed of 28 EU member states, the European Commission, the Arab League and 15 countries, notably Albania, Algeria, Bosnia and Herzegovina, Egypt, Israel, Jordan, Lebanon, Mauritania, Monaco, Montenegro, Morocco, Palestine, Syria (suspended), Tunisia and Turkey.
7 This was clearly put forward in the Common Position on conflict prevention, management and resolution in Africa adopted in January 2004. See Council Common Position 2004/85/CFSP of 26 January 2004 concerning conflict prevention, management and resolution in Africa and repealing Common Position 2001/374/CFSP, Official Journal of the European Union, 28.1.2004, available at http://eur-lex.europa.eu/legal-content/EN/TXT/PDF/?uri=CELEX:32004E0085&from=EN
8 The money allocated to the PFA comes from the European Development Fund under the Cotonou Agreement.
9 This chapter does not aim to analyse individual foreign policies of the major EU member states vis-à-vis Africa and Asia. Nor does it intend to examine their national perspectives or national inputs into both EU–Africa and EU–Asia relations. For an analysis of the individual member states' approaches and initiatives, see contributions by Julia Gallagher, Ian Taylor and Ulf Engel (Gallagher, 2009; Taylor, 2012; Engel, 2000).
10 The High Representative Federica Mogherini presented a new strategic framework document titled 'EU Global Strategy on Foreign and Security Policy' at the EU summit held in Brussels on 28 June 2016. This occurred five days after the EU referendum in the United Kingdom. When the writing of this chapter was concluded all these developments had not taken place as yet. Hence they fall outside the remit of the analysis presented herein.
11 According to the Schuman Declaration of 9 May 1950: "The solidarity in [coal and steel] production thus established will make it plain that any war between France and Germany becomes not merely

unthinkable, but materially impossible. This production will be offered to the world as a whole without distinction or exception, with the aim of contributing to raising living standards and to promoting peaceful achievements. With increased resources *Europe will be able to pursue the achievement of one of its essential tasks, namely, the development of the African continent"* (Authors' emphasis).

12 The agreement allowed for the delivery of food security assistance by the EU on Australia's behalf to South Sudan, as well as for the delivery of a component of the EU's assistance by Australia to Fiji.

13 For details, see Hensel (2016).

14 The four major principles were the following: principle of ownership, principle of prevention, principle of early warning and principle of coherence.

15 The European policy towards conflict prevention in Africa was somewhat streamlined in the framework of the *Commission Communication of 2001 on Conflict Prevention and the EU Programme on the Prevention of Violent Conflicts*, adopted at the Gothenburg Council of June 2001.

16 Among these, the conflicts in Somalia, Rwanda, Liberia, Sierra Leone, Guinea-Bissau, Guinea and Côte d'Ivoire stand out.

17 The Petersberg tasks were originally integrated in the Treaty of Amsterdam which entered into force on 1 May 1999; they were then replicated in the subsequent (revised) European Treaties to date.

18 For more details, see Bagoyoko & Gilbert (2009).

19 Eventually, the EU established a more visible presence in Addis Ababa, the location of the African Union headquarters, through the nomination of the EU SR to the AU and a larger diplomatic team. The AU also has an embassy in Brussels and an ambassador accredited to the EU.

20 For instance, the legal basis for the Development Cooperation Instrument explicitly rules out the procurement of arms or ammunition, as well as support of military operations in more general terms. The APF, which is financed from the European Development Fund, has been used to fund AU-led military operations, but such critical items as ammunition, arms, military equipment, salaries for soldiers and military training for soldiers are non-eligible for the funding under the APF. An overview of EU instruments, legal provisions and their implications is presented by Tardy (2015:2).

21 The coup d'état was materialized in April 2012 by elements of the armed forces before the second round of a presidential election between Carlos Gomes Júnior and Kumba Ialá.

22 This new regionally focused headquarters was formally established in October 2007.

23 Among these are the following: Angola, Sudan, Chad, Kenya, Rwanda, Uganda, South Africa and Zimbabwe.

24 Symptomatic of this international momentum was also the establishment of the UN Office of the Special Advisor on Africa in 2003 and the creation of the Commission for Africa to provide impetus for the development of the continent, an objective which was subsequently taken up by the G8 in Gleneagles. See www.commissionforafrica.info [Accessed 04 April 2016].

25 These were preceded by the *EU East Asia Policy Guidelines*, established in 2007, whose revision by the European Council in 2012 paved the way for the adoption of *Guidelines on the EU's Foreign and Security Policy in East Asia* (Council of the European Union, 2012).

26 A summary of the EU efforts to support regional maritime capabilities is available at http://eeas.europa.eu/piracy/regional_maritime_capacities_en.htm [Accessed 7 April 2016]. See also Pejsova (2016).

27 For more on this matter, see also Stumbaum (2015: 138). Drawing on the results of analysis of 210 interviews of Asian elites in 20 Asia-Pacific locations (corresponding to six countries, namely India, China, Malaysia, Singapore, Thailand and the Philippines), Chaban et al. (2015:238) demonstrate that the EU is generally perceived as an economic power, with the military dimension playing a limited role. Only three countries (Singapore, Thailand and Philippines) attributed some importance to the EU as an international military power, while India was the most critical of the EU's military capabilities.

28 This is not to say that, to date, the EU has been able to produce a well-defined collective response to China's more aggressive posture.

29 In contrast to the US, the EU is a party to the United Nation Convention of the Law of the Sea (UNCLOS).

References

Bagoyoko, N. and Gilbert, M., 2009. 'The Linkage Between Security, Governance and Development: The European Union in Africa', *Journal of Development Studies*, Volume 54 (5), pp. 789–814.

Bersik, S., 2014. 'Europe's role in Asia: Distant but involved', in M. Yahuda and D. Shambaugh (eds.), *International Relations of Asia*, Lanham: Rowman and Littlefield, pp. 115–146.

Boin, E. R., Ekengren, M. and Rhinard, M., 2013. *The European Union as Crisis Manager: Patterns and Prospects*, Cambridge: Cambridge University Press.

Bremberg, N., 2015. *Diplomacy and Security Community-Building: EU Crisis Management in the Western Mediterranean*, London: Routledge.

Bretherton, C. and Vogler, J., 2006. *The European Union as a Global Actor*. London, New York: Routledge.

Carbone, M., 2012. 'The European Union in Africa: In search of a strategy', in Federiga Bindi and Irina Angelescu (eds.), *The European Union Foreign Policy: Assessing Europe's Role in the World*, Washington, DC: Brookings Institution Press, pp. 256–269.

Chaban, N., Holland, M. and Lai, S.Y., 2015. 'Dysfunctional relations? Asian stakeholders' views on the European Union', in N. Witzleb, A. Martinez Arranz and P. Winand (eds.), *The European Union and Global Engagement: Institutions, Policies and Challenges*, Cheltenham and Northampton: Edward Elgar Publishing, pp. 237–255.

Council of the European Union (CEU), 2012. *Guidelines on the EU's Foreign and Security Policy in East Asia*. Brussels, 15 June 2012, Available at: http://eeas.europa.eu/asia/docs/guidelines_eu_foreign_sec_pol_east_asia_en.pdf [Accessed 02 April 2016].

Engel, U., 2000. *Die Afrikapolitik der Bundesrepublik Deutschland 1949–1999: Rollen und Identitäten*, Hamburg: LitVerlag.

European Council, 2010. European Council Conclusions. EUCO 21/1/10 REV 1, CO EUR16. (Brussels, 16 September). Available at: www.consilium.europa.eu/uedocs/cms_data/docs/pressdata/en/ec/116547.pdf [Accessed 6 April 2016].

Ferreira-Pereira, L. C., 2016. 'The European Union's Partnership Policy Towards Brazil: More Than Meets the Eye', Special Issue 'The Strategic Partnerships of the European Union: Conceptual Insights, Cases and Lessons', *Cambridge Review of International Affairs*, Volume (29) 1, pp. 55–77.

Ferreira-Pereira, L. C. and Vieira, A., 2016. 'Introduction: The European Union's Strategic Partnerships: Conceptual Approaches, Debates and Experiences', Special Issue 'The Strategic Partnerships of the European Union: Conceptual Insights, Cases and Lessons', *Cambridge Review of International Affairs*, Volume 29 (1), pp. 3–17.

Franke, B., 2009. 'EU–AU Cooperation in Capacity Building', *Studia Diplomatica* LXII, Volume 3, pp. 69–74.

Gallagher, J., 2009. 'Healing the Scar? Idealizing Britain and Africa, 1997–2007', *African Affairs*, Volume 108 (432), pp. 435–51.

Gegout, C., 2007. 'EU conflict management in Africa: The limits of an international actor', in Nathalie Tocci (ed.), *The EU and Conflict Resolution: Promoting Peace in the Backyard*, London and New York: Routledge, pp. 126–137.

Gowan, R. and Witney, N., 2014. *Why the EU Must Stop Outsourcing Its Security*, European Council on Foreign Relations Policy Brief 121, Available at: www.ecfr.eu/page/-/ECFR121_WHY_EUROPE_MUST_STOP_OUTSOURCING.pdf [Accessed 02 April 2016].

Griffin, C., 2007. 'France, the United Kingdom, and European Union Capacities for Military Action in Africa', *Paper Prepared for the Sixth Annual Pan-European Conference on International Relations*, 12–15 *September* 2007, Turin (Italy).

Hensel, N., 2016. *The Defense Industrial Base: Strategies for a Changing World*, London and New York: Routledge.

Holland, K., and Kelly, S. 2012. 'A payer or player? EU developmental action in the Pacific', in S. Gaenzle, S. Grimm and D. Makhan (eds.), *The European Union and Global Development: An 'Enlightened Superpower' in the making?* Basingstoke: Palgrave Macmillan, pp. 245–260.

Holland, M., 2004. 'Development policy: paradigm shifts and the "normalization" of a privileged partnership?', in M. Green Cowles and D. Dinan (eds.), *Developments in the European Union*, Basingstoke: Palgrave Macmillan, pp. 275–295.

Hurt, S., 2004. 'The European Union's external relations with Africa after the Cold War. Aspects of continuity and change', in I. Talyor and P. Williams (eds.), *Africa in International Politics: External Involvement on the Continent*, London: Routledge.

Kingah, S. and Cofelice, A., 2015. 'The European Parliament and the engagement with African regional parliaments', in S. Stavridis and D. Iterra (eds.), *The European Parliament and its International Relations*, London: Routledge, pp. 145–160.

Mackinda, S., Okumu, W. and Mickler, D., 2016. *The African Union: Assessing the Challenges of Peace Security, and Governance*, Abingdon: Routledge.

Marsh, S. and Mackenstein, H., 2005. *The International Relations of the European Union*, Harlow: Pearson Longman, pp. 226–233.

Mattelaer, A. and Marijnen, E., 2014. 'EU peacekeeping in Africa: Towards an indirect approach', in M. Wyss and T. Tardy (eds.), *Peacekeeping in Africa: The Evolving Security Architecture*, Abington: Routledge.

Murray, P., 2016. 'EU–Australia Relations: A Strategic Partnership in All but Name?' *Cambridge Review of International Affairs*, Volume 29 (1), pp. 171–191.

Pape, E., 2013. 'An Old Partnership in a New Setting: ACP–EU Relations from a European Perspective', *Journal of International Development*, Volume 25, pp. 727–741.

Pejsova, E., 2016. *Scrambling for the Indian Ocean*, ISS Issue Brief, Available at: www.iss.europa.eu/publications/detail/article/scrambling-for-the-indian-ocean/ [Accessed 04 April 2016].

Rye, O. G., 2013. 'The EU's Africa policy between the US and China: Interests, altruism and cooperation', in M. Carbone (ed.), *European Union in Africa: Incoherent Policies, Asymmetrical Partnership, Declining Relevance?* Manchester: Manchester University Press, pp. 43–56.

Sheriff, A. and Kotsopoulos, J., 2013. 'Africa and the European Union: An assessment of the EU–Africa joint strategy', in T. Murithi (ed.), *Handbook of Africa's International Relations*, Abingdon: Routledge, pp. 305–315.

Sicurelli, D., 2009. 'Regional partners: Perceptions and criticism at the African Union', in Sonia Lucarelli and Lorenzo Fioramonti (eds.), *External Perceptions of the European Union as a Global Actor*, London: Routledge, pp. 180–194.

Sicurelli, D., 2013. *The European Union's Africa Policies: Norms, Interests and Impact*, Farnham: Ashgate.

SIPRI, 2016. SIPRI Military Expenditures Database (1988–2015). Available at: www.sipri.org/research/armaments/milex/milex_database [Accessed 04 April 2016].

Smith, K., 2013. 'Can the European Union be a Pole in a Multipolar World?', *International Spectator*, Volume 48 (2), pp. 114–126.

Special Eurobarometer (SE), 2010. Available at: http://ec.europa.eu/public_opinion/archives/ebs/ebs_353_en.pdf [Accessed 04 April 2016].

Stumbaum, M.-B., 2015. 'Drivers and barriers to security integration in traditional security fields: Europe and Asia-Pacific and the role of great powers', in L. Brennan and P. Murray (eds.), *Drivers of Integration and Regionalism in Europe and Asia: Comparative Perspectives*, Abingdon: Routledge, pp. 127–147.

Tardy, T., 2015. Enabling Partners to Manage Crises. From 'Train and Equip' to Capacity-building, European Union Institute for Security Studies Briefing Paper 18 (June 18), Available at: www.iss.europa.eu/uploads/media/Brief_18_Train_and_Equip.pdf [Accessed 02 April 2016].

Tran, T. P., Vieira, A. and Ferreira-Pereira, L. C., 2013. 'Vietnam's Strategic Hedging Vis-à-vis China: The Roles of the European Union and Russia', *Revista Brasileira da Política Internacional*, Volume 56 (1), pp. 163–182.

Taylor, I., 2012. 'Spinderella on Safari: British Policies Toward Africa Under New Labour', *Global Governance: A Review of Multilateralism and International Organizations*, Volume 18 (4), pp. 449–460.

Vieira, A., 2016. 'Ukraine, Russia and the Strategic Partnership Dynamics in the EU's Eastern Neighbourhood: Recalibrating EU's 'Self', 'We' and 'Other', Special Issue The Strategic Partnerships of the European Union: Conceptual Insights, Cases and Lessons', *Cambridge Review of International Affairs*, Vol. 29 (1), pp. 128–150.

Whitman, R. and Haastrup, T., 2013. 'Locating EU strategic behaviour in sub-Saharan Africa: An emerging strategic culture?', in M. Carbone (ed.), *The European Union in Africa: Incoherent Policies, Asymmetrical Partnership, Declining Relevance?* Manchester: Manchester University Press, pp. 57–76.

Migration, environment and politics

27

MIGRATION AND GLOBAL POLITICS IN AFRICA AND ASIA

Patterns and drivers of change throughout time

Pedro Miguel Amakasu Raposo de Medeiros Carvalho

Introduction

Most studies of migration focus either on the Americas or Asia or Africa but few focus on both Africa and Asia and the impact of migration on these two continents. This chapter explores migration flows – the movement of a person or a group of persons from one place to another – in Africa and Asia from pre-modern to contemporary times. In terms of territory Asia is the largest region in the world with 50 countries. It is also the most populous, with more than 4.4 billion people, which to a great extent explains why, in 2015, nearly half of all international migrants worldwide (104 million of 244 million) were born in Asia (IOM, 2015). In contrast, in Africa in 2015 only 34 million international migrants were born in the continent, despite a population of 1.2 billion people spread over 54 countries. These numbers complement recent studies which show that in the post-colonial period African migration has been overwhelmingly intra-continental (Flahaux & De Haas, 2016; Fernandez, 2014; Castles & Miller, 2003). The porous borders and geography help to explain the high incidence of inter-state migration in sub-Saharan Africa, while people in the North are more prone to migrate due to their proximity to Europe (Lucas, 2013:12). Strangely (or not), according to Shimeles (2010:5) and Zeleza (2010:4), those of African descent living outside of the continent number 140–160 million people. Past African mass migrations explain this trend. To a certain extent, migrants have always been 'forced' to leave home as migration has always implied some kind of grievance, with several studies showing that migrants tend to be less happy than the indigenous host population (Collier, 2013:172). Given the scope of migration the focus of this chapter is on international migration not internal, though according to Castles & Miller (2003) the process of mobility begins with this latter type. Since ancient times (before the fifteenth century) sub-Saharan Africans experienced forced migration (Zeleza, 2010:12; Collins, 2008:7–8). This chapter argues that earlier, modern and even contemporary forms of human mobility share some of the causes of human displacement across and within borders, as kingdoms and great powers victimized thousands or millions of people in both continents to attain their geostrategic, economic, development and trade interests. Enslaved Islam, the transatlantic slave trade, and the mass movement of Asian labour under colonialism and European contemporary interactions after decolonization are all disguised forms of 'forced' migration that intentionally or not connected these two continents and led to the establishment, expansion and rupture of global empires and the formation of modern states in Africa and Asia. Though in a strict sense the above migrants do not fit into the category of forced migration, which includes refugees and internally displaced persons, also studied in this Handbook (see Bose, Chapter 29), Gold & Nawyn (2013a:97) observe that scholarship has aptly criticized the dichotomy between forced and economic migrants and, as this chapter will show, most of them did not have a choice but to move. To understand how the actions of nation-states are associated with global migrations, here seen as transcontinental connections, one must see them through the lens of changes in world politics with an emphasis on geopolitical and economic factors. Further, how has migration changed in Africa and Asia throughout time? What are the underlying causes and the effects of these migrant connections from and within continents? These questions provide an overview of the mobility trends, geographical patterns and recent forms of international migration from a global, historical and contemporary perspective beyond the disciplinary and methodological limitations that often hinder migration studies.

The literature on migration is vast both empirically and theoretically. Most of the studies are focused on specific statistics, timely trends and theories. Castles & Miller (2003) provide a comprehensive assessment of the nature, extent and dimensions of human migration and of their consequences. They note how European colonialism, first in Africa and Asia, then in the Americas and Oceania, gave rise to many kinds of migration (ibid.:51). Until then, labour migration through enslavement and deportation of conquered people was the most frequent form of migration. Zeleza (2010:8–9) criticizes the overemphasis among scholars of the Afro-Atlantic model by seeing Africans' movements primarily in terms of slavery and sub-Saharan Africans. He argues for the need to de-Atlanticize and de-Americanize the histories of African migrations, thus reflecting the dominance in the European American academy of the Atlantic model and of race in the fields of African studies (ibid.: 5, 7). The problem arises perhaps from the lack of awareness of Asian activity within Africa as, according to Horton (n.d.), historical sources are more slender and difficult to read. Amrith (2011:3) argues that though the Asia-Pacific region is home to considerable international movement, until the middle of twentieth century the distinction between internal and international migration was marginal in the Asian context, as most of it happened within and across empires. Batistela (2014:11) explains this rigidity as due to the preponderance of the role of the state within the migration system, particularly regarding labour. This began to change with the decolonization process, in particular after the mid 1970s. However, Zeleza (2010:11) notes that Afro-Asian interactions go back to Pharaonic Egypt and Western Asia and ancient Ethiopian connections with the Arabian Peninsula. Interactions continued under the Greek and Roman empires and in the Islamic era. Long before the global European hegemony in the sixteenth and seventeenth centuries, Asia had already experienced the mobility of merchants, itinerant pilgrims, soldiers and sailors throughout the Red Sea and the Indian Ocean to Asia (Collins, 2008:58). One begins to understand that the causes of international migration in Asia, despite its accounting for 60 per cent of the world's population, are not demographic (though they have demographic characteristics), being rather politically, socially and economically driven. This is also the argument of Massey & Taylor (2007) to explain contemporary North–South tensions over migration. In this quest Hugo (2007:77) argues that given the ethnic, religious, cultural, political institutions and social diversity of the Asian population, migration from and within Asia is no longer limited to defined social groups as in the past, but has diversified in terms of its scale, gender and types. Adepoju (2013), Bilger & Kraler (2005) and Jonsson (2009) agree that African history, like Asian migration, is deeply rooted in migration associated with the slave trade, colonialism, state formation and capitalist development.

In a hyper-globalized world with continuous political, economic, social and climate changes, it is clear from the aforementioned that the study of migration is beyond core types, such as labour migration (here studied), settler migrants and refugees. Other driving forces for migration also include lack of development, poverty, poor governance and human rights, environmental issues, rapid urbanization (internal rural–urban migration is linked to economic growth, but also to food shortages), and highly developed migration that generates important remittances (Koser, 2007; ADB, 2012:13–16). According to King (2012:11, 25) migration is so diverse and multifaceted that one single theory is not enough to understand the whole phenomenon, in part because the increasing globalization of the world makes it almost impossible to explain all the new challenges and trends that respond to the changed nature of migration, and in part because, as he says, migration is a transnational process that includes economic, political, cultural and religious activities. As with Betts (2009:11) and Gold & Nawyn (2013b: 5), this chapter also finds that the actions of nation-states within global politics have influenced the direction of migration flows.

In this light, the chapter divides in four sections. After the introduction, section two reviews the historical patterns of migration from pre-modern to the early modern and modern era to address its causes. Section three links European expansion and imperialism to and in Asia with two major types of migration – indentured and contract labour. Section four reviews contemporary patterns of migration in Asia and African migrations, before concluding.

Historical patterns of migration in Africa and Asia: from pre-modern to the modern era

One can affirm that we are all Africans as originally humans developed there around 200,000 years ago when *Homo sapiens* emerged near the coastal areas between the borders of present Namibia and Angola, eventually spreading to Eurasia, Australasia and the Americas with geography having a role in migration (Manning, 2005:16–17; Lucas, 2013:7; Adepoju, 2013:59). In Africa the desertification of the Saharan region between 3000 and 1000 BC separated sub-Saharan Africa migrations from North Africa, which saw people migrate southwards to Central and West Africa (Du Bois, 2007b:106). Meanwhile, the so-called Bantu people began a slow movement from what is now Cameroon and Nigeria, to the east and south – they settled on the Indian Ocean coast 100 years before the common era (BCE) where they began to interact with Arab traders – and also to South Africa, Northern Natal around 250 CE (common era) (Held et al., 2000:287–88; Du Bois, 2007b:107). Swahilis from Persia and the Gulf established a complex network of migrant communities with trading stations along the East African coast from the twelfth to the fifteenth century. The Islamic Hausa people migrated from Western Sudan to what is now Northern Nigeria between the thirteenth and eighteenth centuries, establishing new states and sultanates in the region.

In Asia initial migrations to the Americas ranged from 12,000 to 25,000 people before the common era (BCE) (McKeown 2014:76). Around the third millennium BCE, Central Eurasian horse cultures dominated human mobility, as did Austronesian seafaring cultures in much of maritime Asia. At the time mobility was mostly prevalent in agricultural states which differed from nomads and the communal relocation that was common in the hills, steppes and littoral areas. The beginning of urbanization, with the concentration of wealth in the cities, and growing military power facilitated migration in Central Asia. Yet, the sea was still a geographical barrier. The emergence of the silk roads increased interactions between states and people within inner and peripheral Asia, and helped to create a common Eurasian space, which was unmatched in size and scope in the rest of the world (ibid.: 77). Patterns of trade and labour, peasant, elite and coerced migration were forged in Eurasia and helped to shape migration till this day. By the beginning of the common era these trading routes across China reached India and the Mediterranean, both overland and via the oceans. Chinese reached Africa through the sea during the

Migration and global politics

eighth to the twelfth centuries, which supports the argument that Asian and African trade connections have always been close. Ethnologists believe that Africa had a strong influence on the colonization of Southeast Asia, India and the Easter Islands, as it was in Asia before 200 BCE that the first mass migration of almost two million people took place, encouraged by the imperial armies of the Chinese Han dynasty who aimed to consolidate the empire (Held et al., 2000:287; Cotterell, 2011:91). This migration is only comparable to the great migrations in the eighteenth and nineteenth centuries. But there is a difference between them as the first migrations were regional rather than global, though Islam's African, European and South east Asian outposts suggest processes of global migration (Held et al., 2000:289).

Trade, slavery and colonialism

Portuguese discoveries between 1415 and 1543, together with the voyage of Columbus in 1492, conferred a new dynamic on European migration, which eventually brought the world under European domination. At first trade, not slaves, was the major motive behind Portuguese discoveries in Africa (Guinea), Asia (India and Japan) and the Americas (Brazil). With the trade in gold, the importation of labour to Portugal and Europe also began. At first the slave trade did not compete with legitimate commerce but by 1540 the export of slaves across the Sahara, the Red Sea and the Indian Ocean reached 10,000 a year (Du Bois, 2007a:30; Collins, 2008:62). With the establishment of the colonial influence along the coastline of the continent the pre-existing African routes of trade changed their internal orientation to the coastline (Fernandez, 2014:135). In addition, the migration of the Limbas and Bantu from Central Africa to the West Coast meant cheap labour was now available to be exported. Portugal began supplying the European market for house slaves. With this slave trade conflicts arose between the Portuguese De Sousas and the natives, and also between African groups whose involvement in slave trading increased (Du Bois, 2007a:20; Fernandez, 2014:135).

After 1530, the French began competing for dominance of Guinea with Portugal, who in turn, were also competing with Britain over the direct traffic with Africa from 1561 onwards. Portuguese dominance on the coast of Africa ended in 1581 when Philip II of Spain encompassed Portugal. Thereafter, from 1580 until 1640 the two countries became united under the Hapsburgs (Cotterell, 2011:204). Eventually, in the eighteenth century Portugal was overtaken by Great Britain, which was fighting with the Netherlands to dominate the Atlantic slave trade.

Beginning in the seventeenth century the African slave trade to America expanded and continued until the mid nineteenth century. The arrival of Columbus in the Caribbean inevitably increased the colonial interest of Europeans as land was plentiful and labour scarce. Europeans from all economic backgrounds in search of a better economic life crossed the Atlantic, which prompted major changes in the economic structures and cultures in both European society and American colonies. The presence of Europeans was a catastrophe for the natives of the Americas and the Caribbean. According to Allen (2011:66) the population dropped from 57 million in 1500 to perhaps 5 million in 1750, mostly due to the introduction of diseases that together with warfare, enslavement and ill treatment of settlers discouraged Europeans from migrating to the New World.

Slaves became the ultimate export commodity in the 'triangular trade' between Europe, Africa and the Americas, which developed into a routine circuit of commodity exchange of manufactured goods, labour and agricultural production (Castles & Miller, 2003:53; Held et al., 2000:293). While the transatlantic slave trade from 1501 to 1866 is estimated to have involved around 11.3–15 million Africans, the Asian trade totalled 12.5 million African slaves from 800 to 1900 CE (Jayasuriya, 2016:18; Collins, 2008:58; Castles & Miller, 2003:53). According to Collins

427

(2008:59) the important difference between the exportation of slaves to the Americas and to Asia relates first to the time span: almost four centuries for the first and eleven centuries for the second. Then, the millions of slaves, captured and transported across the Atlantic, suffered traumatic social consequences, with all the implications this had on the colonial system, such as the decrease of the African population, and the global political economy, as a world market emerged (Collins, 2008:59). If, as we think, the population of Africa stood at 50 million in the seventeenth century and around half of this number were traded as merchandise to the Americas, Indian Ocean islands and Asia, one can understand why this loss of population became so destructive, especially as the slave trade and slavery were very much part of African life until the 1930s (Osborne & Kent 2015:37; Collins, 2008:75).

Different forms of servitude and slavery have always existed in many pre-capitalist societies; however, the colonial system not only vastly increased the size of the slave trade, it also contributed to the emergence of global empires and a new capitalism. The slave mode of production was a determinant of the colonies' prosperity as their labour supplied Europe with goods for processing or to export to Africa to buy more slaves (Castles & Miller, 2003:55; Klein, 1993:3, 10).

The abolition of the slave trade and slavery: consequences

The problem was that in the seventeenth and eighteenth centuries the 'triangular trade' was profitable to all mercantile powers – in particular to Great Britain as the slave trade from West Africa provided the capital (or part of it) for the industrial revolution that began in the 1760s. However, by the end of the eighteenth century the British West Indies slave plantations had declined in profits and in their importance to Great Britain (Williams, 1944).

The independence of America destroyed the British mercantile system which was built around the triangular trade and its monopoly of the West African slave trade whereby slaves were shipped to the Caribbean and the West Indies in return for sugar and similar tropical products. The West Indian situation was aggravated by competition in the sugar industry from the French colonies and Brazil, also heavily dependent on the slave trade for its labour force (ibid.: 152). Once a promoter of slavery and the slave trade, with its Royal African Company, Britain suddenly became the main defender of its abolition. Now all British society agreed on the inhumanity and cruelty of the slave system. Finally, the rise to power of the colonial state was the fundamental reason for the end of the institution of slavery (Reid, 1993).

Britain abolished the slave trade in 1807 and imposed a similar ban at the Congress of Vienna in 1815. With the end of the slave trade, the abolitionists turned to slavery itself, which ended in 1833. However, the Act of 1833 did not apply to India and Ceylon, which were controlled by the East India Company (Klein, 1993:16). In the 1830s, slavers, some British, but mostly French, Spanish and Portuguese, still exported 20,000 Africans from the Gulf of Guinea. This trade continued in the 1840s, but dropped to 10,000 and then to 3,000 in the 1850s (Osborne & Kent, 2015:26). Although the Netherlands banned the slave trade in 1818, the possession of slaves was not forbidden in the Dutch East Indies until 1860, as to free the slaves would have astronomic economic costs. Elsewhere in Southeast Asia, abolition came later. In Cambodia it was only in 1844 and 1877 that antislavery legislation was produced. In British-ruled Malaya, the abolition of slavery and the bondage system (a system of obligation to labour for a patron without direct recompense) was not completed until 1915 (Reid, 1993:65).

In Africa, *de facto* abolition was not introduced until the period from the late 1870s to the early 1900s. The legal status of slavery was abolished on the Gold Coast only in 1874. Although Portugal decreed the abolition of slavery in 1875 throughout its empire, freed slaves were then obliged to sign contracts with the 'redeemer' such that at the end of the five-year contract they were automatically re-contracted (Clarence-Smith, 1993:155–56). With this scheme, Portugal continued importing slaves from Dahomey and Gabon until 1877, and until much later from Angola and São Tomé and Principe, which was one of the world's four largest producers of cocoa until the early 1900s. It took an international boycott from Britain and Germany on the cocoa from São Tomé and Principe, and a republican revolution in the Portuguese constitutional monarchy in 1910, to end slavery. However, the situation was short lived as the republicans soon replaced slavery with a system of forced labour, which also existed in other Portuguese colonies (ibid.: 159, 165).

The abolition of the slave trade required a new system of slavery, as the 'triangular trade' no longer could support the old colonial system (Du Bois, 2007a:40; Reid, 1993:77). The appearance of Germany in Africa and the United States across the Atlantic reinforced international rivalries between European powers. European expansion into Africa and Asia prompted a 'new imperialism' in terms of colonial acquisition, with the redrawing of the political map on both continents (Osborne & Kent, 2015). Economics also played a role in Europe's 'new imperialism' since colonial governments were supposed to finance their expenditure with their own revenues (Allen, 2011:102–03). The second industrial revolution after the 1860s created enormous demand for raw materials and new markets that could not be found in Europe. It also changed the scale of migration made possible by a revolution in transportation, as the railway and the steamship made long distance travel easier, faster and cheaper than before (Amrith, 2011). In sum, prior to colonialism, the rise and fall of empires, trade and the slave trade were an external impulse that influenced patterns of migration from and within Africa but also to and from Asia. As the next section will show, warfare, which was the major instrument in acquiring colonies and the European empires' expansion in Asia, also depended on slavery and other forms of coerced migration (Gabaccia, 2013).

European expansion and Asian 'forced' migrations

This section links European imperialism with the Asian mass migration needed to develop the colonies and expand capitalism. It also explains why this migration replaced existing labour flows, eventually ending with slavery.

The first European power to arrive in Asia was the Portuguese in 1498, when Vasco da Gama sailed to Calicut in southwestern India via the Cape of Good Hope. Chartered trading companies used slaves to construct their fortresses and to work in the households of their officials. By then Portugal had a chain of fortresses to sustain the authority of the Estado da India (State of India), the name by which the Portuguese knew their Asian empire. Portugal's headquarters was Goa, conquered in 1510 by the second viceroy, Afonso de Albuquerque. Portugal expanded across the Bay of Bengal, capturing the great Malay entrepôt of Malacca in 1511, but it was lost to the Dutch in 1641 (Cotterell, 2011). Gradually, Portugal lost the monopoly of commerce, first to the Dutch East India Company that established its trade base in Batavia (Jakarta) in 1619 on the island of western Java, and then to the English, who in 1757 gave the English East India Company control over Bengal from where it expanded across the Indian subcontinent (Amrith, 2011:21). By late eighteenth century, the European demand for Southeast Asian products to trade in exchange for Chinese tea stimulated further slave-raiding in Borneo, the southern Philippine archipelago and the outer islands of Indonesia.

Political shifts and modern migration in Asia

Within Asia, migration underwent a dramatic change after 1850. The spread of technology and capitalist investment, backed by the force of empires, coincided with significant political shifts across Asia. British imperialism into Southeast Asia resulted in two great conflicts. The first was the First Opium War (1839–42) which saw China powerless to ban the trade in opium which opened up China for Western enterprises. The second was the Indian rebellion (1857), which began with a mutiny in the Indian army after an accumulation of social tensions among peasantry, artisans and deposed aristocracies following over a century of British expansion which led to the creation of new economic connections and economic, social and demographic transformations. Further, the defeat of both rebellions consolidated British control over India and China, and led directly to an increase in migration caused by the millions of refugees in flight from conflict. Britain also gained control of Malaya, including Singapore and Burma, while the French acquired Indochina after 1862. The Dutch consolidated their control over the East Indies (Indonesia), while the Philippines, previously under Spanish rule, were annexed by the United States in 1898. In 1885, British expansion in Burma was completed. Japan also began to learn the 'spirit of capitalism and imperialism' and took control of Taiwan in 1895, defeated China in a war (1894–95) over Korea, later annexed (1910), and also took control over Taiwan (1895) (McNeill & Iriye 1971:144).

From the standpoint of the larger labour history, European expansion and globalizing capitalism, in search for new resources, new plantations and new markets for both domestic consumption and export, required the development of a permanent wage labour force in Southeast Asia (Kaur, 2014:166). The problem was that Southeast Asian states had much lower population density than China and India. Britain's imperial presence in Burma, Ceylon and Malaya, and the defeat of China in the First and Second Opium Wars (1839–42 and 1856–60), not only allowed European powers to trade freely, but also to recruit workers for their colonies without legal restraints.

Indentured and contract labour

With European imperialism and the spread of capitalism, China and India became directly linked with Southeast Asia and transformed older schemes for labour recruitment. As noted European industrialization also facilitated the integration of labour markets and created a single economy on a global scale driven by world prices. The main mechanism for recruiting Chinese and Indian immigrant labour was the indenture contract that became institutionalized in Asia after the suppression of the slave trade and slavery. Hence, the switch in the form of labour involved a switch from the labour supply from Africa to Asia as the main source of plantation labour (Cohen 2008:64). The system provided labour for sugar plantations in the West Indies and the Indian Ocean, for tea plantations in Ceylon, for rubber plantations in Malaya, for railway construction in Malaya, East Africa and Fiji, and for gold mining in South Africa.

Indenture, also known as the 'coolie system', involved recruitment, transportation and placement of workers in colonial states, whereby employers used sanctions to enforce wage labour agreements (Castles & Miller, 2003:55; Kaur, 2014:168). The British also recruited Chinese 'coolies' for Malaya and other colonies. The Dutch East India Company, the largest slave owner in the archipelago in the seventeenth and eighteenth centuries, also used Chinese labour in its construction projects. However, there were some differences between the Chinese coolie and the Indian indenture system. While the Chinese trade involved people purchased and sold, the Indian system was essentially a free migration. As for the French indenture system, it remained a disguised slave trade until 1862, whereas the Dutch applied mostly the indenture system for the mining and plantation sectors, covering both Chinese and Javanese workers (Klein, 1993:20–21; Kaur, 2014:173). However, for public works the Dutch also used *corvée* labour (unpaid labour required by states or local rulers), while indentured labour was mostly for private purposes. Here, contract labour differed from slavery in that it was voluntary and temporary. However, the coercion used to employ indenture workers was such that the system was harsher than traditional forms of slavery as there was no physical means of escape (Reid, 1993:77; Kaur, 2014:167).

The 'up' and 'down' of Asia labour migration, 1850–1940

Between the 1850s and the 1940s two main strands of migration, with similar patterns, characterized the 'boom' and the decline of migration in Asia. Circular migration, or sojourning, was the dominant feature of migration until the 1930s, underpinned by a more permanent process of peasant colonization in frontier regions. In the beginning of the twentieth century these patterns began to shift as women joined the process of long-distance migration. There were also other factors that caused the downturn in Asian mass migration. The agricultural over-production in rubber, sugar and other commodities after the economic depression in the US in the late 1920s was followed by the Second World War which transformed Asian migration from one of mass labour opportunities to one of mass migration of refugees and segregation caused by warfare, which brought to an end Southeast Asia's colonial economic expansion (Brown, 2014:161; Amrith, 2011:91).

Still, at its peak this labour migration assumed such proportions that the impact was felt in and beyond Asia. It comprised indentured labourers, later replaced by the *kangary* (intermediary) method, which in turn gave way to free movement under contractual agreements (Kaur 2014:171). The system of indentured labour was gradually abolished in the early twentieth century, but persisted in the Dutch East Indies until 1941.

The need for a plentiful and cheap supply of labour for rubber, sugar and tobacco plantations, rice fields, and the tin mining industry of colonial powers explains this mass migration. Heavy immigration of labourers, moneylenders, traders and merchants secured the colonial expansion in production and trade; Southeast Asia saw the rapid growth of major port-cities, the commercial, financial and administrative capitals of booming economies in British-ruled Burma, Cochinchina brought under French rule and the Netherlands East Indies (Brown, 2014:156).

From the 1850/70s to the 1930s, 30 million Indians and 20 million Chinese workers migrated from southern India and southern China to Southeast Asia. The bulk of Indians, around 28 million, were confined to the British Empire, arriving in the plantations of Burma (15 million), Ceylon (8 million) and Malaya (4 million). But 24 million returned, giving a net migration number of 6 million. As for Chinese migrants, a total of 11 million migrated to Singapore and Malaysia, 3 million were shipped to Indonesia, 4 million to Thailand, and another 3–4 million to Indochina, the Philippines and other parts of the Pacific. Indians also migrated to Tanzania, Kenya, Malawi, Zambia, South Africa and Uganda (Held et al., 2000:294). The Malay Peninsula was the place where these two migrations met. Malaya received more Chinese emigrants than any other single destination and a large flow of Indian migrants. This migration grew simultaneously with the transatlantic migrations, but at slightly lower rates. It did not peak until the 1920s, averaging over one million per year. In Northeast Asia Japanese migration, some of which involved indentured labour, began in the 1860s with the Meiji restoration and continued throughout the 1870s to Hawaii and other South Pacific islands. Between 1900 and 1942, 620,000 Japanese also left for Brazil and around 130,000 emigrants left for North America, Hawaii and Peru (Held et al., 2000:294; McKeown, 2014:83). The Japanese not only migrated but also 'forced' migration as a result of the annexation of Korea in 1910 from where it recruited 40,000 workers between 1921 and 1941 (Castles & Miller, 2003:155). In 1931, Japan also annexed Manchuria in China, which led to full-scale war in 1937.

Development of contemporary migration in Asia and Africa

Between 1937 and 1945 the war produced around 95 million refugees and millions more were conscripted to work on Japanese construction projects in Manchuria, North China, Mongolia and Tibet (Amrith, 2011:100–01). The years of the depression and war were a turning point in Asian mobility as millions of refugees and forced labourers changed the patterns of migration that had moved millions since the 1870s.

Development of contemporary migration in Asia and Africa

This section reviews the contemporary migration patterns of Asia and Africa within the broader context of induced political and demographic shift from the post-colonial era to this day.

There is no denying that post-war decolonization undermined Western imperial rule in Southeast Asia, with the exception of that of Britain, which reoccupied Malaya – the Dutch and the French failed to do so in their territories. Hence, the contemporary era of migration begins with the end of the Second World War, which induced massive population displacements across Southeast Asia, but also migrations to Europe connected with decolonizing European powers, such as the Netherlands, France, Britain and Portugal (Castles & Miller, 2003:157).

The process of state formation had important implications for millions of people who had to choose between settlement and return. The problem was that most states had imposed upon them an internal administrative division as to what constituted post-colonial borders. That between two sovereign states, India and Pakistan, was the most important case, but also East Pakistan and Burma, which were formerly part of the British Empire (Amrith, 2011:118–19).

For the first time, passports and visas were now governing the mobility of Asians across borders. International (labour) migration within Asia declined as new states were defining their post-colonial boundaries. India and China, which in the nineteenth century were responsible for one of the biggest mass migrations ever, were now encouraging internal migrations in support of national development projects. The Philippines and Indonesia, too, pursued projects of state-directed migration.

The post-war decade also saw an acceleration of Asia's urban growth connected with the idea of development in post-colonial Asia. The movement from rural to urban areas became the most common form of mobility in Asia as people were forced to leave the countryside in search of better conditions in the growing cities. In 1950, 230 million of the population in Asia and the Pacific were in urban areas (17 per cent); this reached 1.5 billion (39 per cent) in 2005 and it is expected to reach 50 per cent by 2025 (ADB, 2012:14). A particular feature of Asian urbanization has been the emergence of mega-cities with densely populated tenement slums, sometimes with a cultural and ethnic diversity, with all the social constraints that minorities face in them. Another new trend, from the post-war period and until the 1970s, was the decline in international migration within Asia.

During the 1950s, only 11 million Chinese could be found outside China and 4.5 million Indians outside India. The circular migrations that had connected Southeast Asia with both India and China became difficult. However, the legacy of those earlier mass migrations across Southeast Asia became significant. According to Amrith (2011:122), in the Federation of Malaya the Chinese minority of 2.95 million and 600,000 Indians were as numerous as the territories' Malay majority. In the 1960s Chinese migrants also faced the conflicting pressures of assimilation and exclusion in Indonesia. At the same time, Cold War politics within Asia also affected migration flows, as migrants in Asia's post-colonial cities were refugees from the conflicts in India, Pakistan and Indochina and later Cambodia, Laos and Vietnam.

In the 1970s and 1980s Asia and the Pacific recovered its past trend of large-scale migration driven by a wide array of factors, including labour market segmentation, pushed by the economic rise of East (Japan, Hong Kong, South Korea and Taiwan) and Southeast Asia

(Singapore, Malaysia, Thailand, Philippines, Indonesia), and the growing power of the oil-producing nations of the Middle East. This latter became the primary destination of labour migration, followed by North America and Australia (ADB, 2012:13; Koser, 2007:110). In addition, the market-led transformation of China has strengthened the weight of East Asia in the global economy. The new inter-regional economic inequalities, together with technological transformations and the expansion of global trade and investments from America and within Asia (particularly from Japan), led to a booming labour migration, including women, into the new industrialized countries in East and Southeast Asia. The tendency towards increasing conditions of flexible mass production brought about by globalization, particularly in the garment and shoe-manufacturing industries, further increased the feminization of the work-force and its migration (Amrith, 2011:171; ADB, 2012).

Volume

Despite the Asian financial crisis in 1997–98 migration for employment within Asia grew at around 6 per cent with Singapore, Malaysia and Thailand the first destinations for millions of migrants from South Asia, Indonesia, the Philippines, Burma and Vietnam (Koser, 2007: 110). In the new millennium between 2000 and 2015 Asia added more international migrants than any other major area (IOM, 2015). Demographic and development inequalities, which involve primarily low-skilled workers, though with a small portion of highly skilled and professional people, spurred by regional integration explain why Asia is currently the most dynamic and diverse migrant region. Another important factor inducing migration in Asia and the Pacific is environmental changes, as the region is the most affected by disasters, already affecting millions of people every year.

In the future, this trend will be further reinforced by both climate change and population growth. About 80 million of the estimated 244 million international migrants worldwide live in Asia and the Pacific (ADB, 2012). Asia is also the primary source of migrants to the world with 62 million persons (60 per cent), followed by Europe with 40 million (66 per cent) and Africa with 18 million or 52 per cent (IOM, 2015: 16). By country China, India and the Philippines are the top three migrant-sending countries, with the PRC diaspora estimated at 40 million, India's at 20 million, and the Philippines' at 7 million (ADB, 2012:2).

Migration in Africa: from colonial to contemporary times

The legacy of European maritime imperialism and colonialism from the fifteenth century, initially with the slave trade and later through the partition of Africa in the Conference of Berlin (1885), seems to suggest that African migration flows were more affected than those in Asia, as the coercion and time span in which European imperialism took place lasted for a longer time. The slave trade forced the mass-displacement of millions of Africans to the Americas with profound demographic, economic and political consequences (Fernandez, 2014:135).

If, in 1500, Africa was the poorest region in the world, and it remains so, the slave trade de-populated whole parts of Africa and constrained, even more, its development. Some authors say that the slave trade was repugnant, as it was both a stimulus and a trigger for the destruction of the West Coast, as by the time of the Portuguese arrival gold mines were already exploited and exhausted (Chamberlain, 2013:14). Because state revenue came only from trans-Saharan trade and gold production (not agriculture, as agrarian states could not support themselves due to the land extension), slavery became profitable to all parties involved (Allen, 2011:97). The slave period assisted the rise of Benin, Dahomey and the Ashanti Confederation. Yet, in

Asia the rise of maritime mobility and European expansion came hand in hand with the proliferation of port-cities in East Africa, around the South Asian peninsula and across Southeast Asia. In contrast to Africa, European competition in Asia often meant the encouragement of massive frontier settlement, as well as increased urbanization and growing labour markets (McKeown, 2013:80).

The Berlin conference had important consequences for African migratory patterns as the establishment of borders divided ethnic groups within the countries concerned and cut across migratory and nomadic routes. To a certain extent, the colonial partition facilitated cross-border migrations as most African countries shared ethnic, religious and linguistic ties along their vast borders (Shimeles, 2010:11). Despite their adoption by colonial powers to restrict contacts between populations, including rotating pasture or cultivation habits, they soon realized that imperial boundaries had limitations (Bach, 2016:53). Colonial powers did not have the economic and military resources to control cross-border trade and migration, sometimes of entire villages. Hence, in Eastern and Southern as well as West Africa, migrations were common and continued until the Second World War (ibid.).

After decolonization African migration became as complex and diverse as in the previous periods. Independence did not bring political stability, as the post-colonial state could not manage its most important legacy: the state was now viewed as an alien institution imposed by colonial powers (Getahun, 2013:87). As in Asia, in the wake of decolonization, there was an imposition of barriers to free movement that, with the rise of nationalism in Africa and related inter-state and intra-state violence and conflicts in West, Southern and the Horn of Africa, severely affected migration flows and made millions of refugees. Migration seemed to be easier when countries were under the same colonial authority. As a result, in 1973, Algeria unilaterally suspended further emigration of its citizens for employment in France (Castles & Miller, 2003:123). Egypt, and Côte d'Ivoire and Portugal had already in the 1930s taken similar measures to control emigration or out of the fear of a 'brain drain' of doctors, engineers, nurses and other professionals, who were represented in terms of the loss of state investment (Fernandez, 2014:137; Flahaux & De Haas, 2016:6; Castelo, 2012:111).

The 1970s and the 1980s were no better, with civil wars, rising oil prices and IMF-driven economic adjustment policies that resulted in socio-economic and political dislocation which created an enormous refugee population (Getahun, 2013:89). In 2015 (UNHCR, 2015:3), 54 per cent of refugees worldwide came from Somalia (1.1 million), Afghanistan (2.7 million) and Syria (4.9 million). Hence, it becomes easy to understand how conflict induces migration as development is impossible without political stability and security is not sustainable without peace in which to live and prosper. If in the early 1990s Central, Southern and the Horn of Africa assisted in a large-scale repatriation of refuges and resettlement of internal displaced persons, after 1995 improved political and economic stability has allowed growing intra-migration. From the late 1980s to the 2000s, despite an increasing migration from Africa to the rest of the world – beyond colonial ties to the Gulf countries, the Americas as well as Europe – to this day the bulk of African migrants move within the continent (Flahaux & De Haas, 2016:8–10; Kane & Leedy, 2013:3, 13).

Volume

In recent years, African migration has shifted away from post-colonial patterns in contradiction of current thinking that sees African migration as mostly illegal – or irregular with a larger share of migrants that are legal (Jonsson, 2009; Flahaux & De Haas, 2016:2). This suggests that Africans migrate to reunite with family, to study or to work abroad. The number of tertiary educated migrants originating from Africa increased to reach 2.9 million in 2010–11 (OECD, 2013).

Further analysis of migration trends from Africa indicates that African migration to developed countries is marginal.

In the early 2000s, OECD countries officially received 1.2 million West Africans. Despite the geographic proximity of Africa to Europe, North America is the main destination for West African nationals. In 2004 there were only 7.4 million officially identified African migrants in OECD countries (Bossard, 2009:4–6). According to the World Migration Report (WMR) (2013:77) China is growing as an attractive destination for African migrants due to its rapid economic growth and demographic changes. Malaysia is another new destination that hosted over 70,000 African migrants in 2012. Working, studying or the dream of a better life remain strong reasons to migrate to Asia. In the coming years, the WMR (2013) reveals that workers from the North are heading to new Southern destinations such as the BRICS countries and emerging African economies.

Conclusion

As argued in this chapter it is clear that the relationship between migration and global politics has several dimensions. The causal link between the actions of states as agents and international human mobility seems now obvious as migration, since early times, became a global phenomenon driven by power politics, colonial and imperialist interests, conflict and exploitation, economic and commerce relations within and between states, in particular European powers, with economic, social and demographic consequences. What can we learn from the history of international migration in Africa and Asia? And what does the future hold for African and Asian international migration? In light of the facts demonstrated one can affirm that mass migrations and migrants contributed to the transition from empires to the rise of modern nation-state, but also to economic prosperity and suffering. If in the modern era economic factors were the primary movers of migratory flows, in the contemporary era geopolitical reasons induced massive population displacements, particularly after the Second World War. This chapter has also shown that Asia and Africa have similar patterns of migration in modern and contemporary eras as colonial powers and independent states thereafter developed new forms of labour, instituted policies to prevent migration or 'forced' thousands if not millions of persons to migrate in the name of economic and political goals.

Then, as today, geostrategic relations, economic, demographic and environmental causes in Africa and Asia will continue to impact migration worldwide. Its many factors will determine the geography of the international migration of Africa, Asia and the world in the coming decades with higher intensity than preceding eras. Within today's context of major uncertainties, it seems that some trends will continue. The first trend concerns the increase in international labour migration, the consequences of economic globalization and trade development, state interests and actions. Unless exceptional circumstances arise, the growth recorded over the past five decades should continue. The United Nations suggests that the number of international migrants to developed countries should reach 2.2 million per year over the 2005–50 period. Still, this figure represents only a 4 per cent increase in the population of developing countries over the same period.

Bibliography

ADB (Asian Development Bank), 2012. *Addressing Climate Change and Migration in Asia and the Pacific*, Final Report, Philippines: Asian Development Bank. Available at: www.adb.org/publications/addressing-climate-change-and-migration-asia-and-pacific [Accessed 9 August 2016].

Adepoju, A., 2013. 'Trends in International Migration in and from Africa', in D. S. Massey and J. E. Taylor (eds.), *International Migration: Prospects and Policies in a Global Market*, Oxford and New York: Oxford University Press, pp. 59–76.

Allen, R. C., 2011. *Global Economic History: A Very Short Introduction*, Oxford: Oxford University Press.

Amrith, S. S., 2011. *Migration and Diaspora in Modern Asia*, Cambridge: Cambridge University Press.

Bach, D. C., 2016. *Regionalism in Africa: Genealogies, Institutions and Trans-state Networks*, London and New York: Routledge.

Bakwesegha, C. J., 1994. 'Forced Migration in Africa and the OAU Convention', in H. Adelman and J. Sorenson (eds.), *African Refugees: Development Aid and Repatriation*, Boulder: Westview Press, pp. 3–18.

Batistela, G., 2014. *Global and Asian Perspectives on International Migration*, Quezon City: Springer.

Betts, A., 2009. *Forced Migration and Global Politics*, Chichester: Wiley-Blackwell.

Bilger, V. and Kraler, A., 2005. 'Introduction: African Migrations, Historical Perspective and Contemporary Dynamics', *Stichproben: Wiener Zeitschrift für kritische Afrikastudien*, Volume (5), pp. 1–21. Available at https://stichproben.univie.ac.at/fileadmin/user_upload/p_stichproben/Artikel/Nummer08/03_Introduction.pdf [Accessed 9 August 2016].

Bossard, L., 2009. *The Future of International Migration to OECD Countries Regional Note West Africa*, Paris: OECD, pp. 1–15. Available at: www.oecd.org/futures/43484256.pdf [Accessed 1 September 2016].

Brown, I., 2014. 'Colonial Capitalism and Economic Transformation', in N. G. Owen (ed.), *Routledge Handbook of Southeast Asian History*, London and New York: Routledge, pp. 155–164.

Castelo, C., 2012. 'Colonial Migration to Angola and Mozambique', in E. M. Genoud and M. Cahen (eds.), *Imperial Migrations: Colonial Communities and Diaspora in the Portuguese World*, New York and London: Palgrave Macmillan, pp. 107–128.

Castles, S. and Miller, M. J. (eds.), 2003. *The Age of Migration: International Population Movements in the Modern World*, 3rd ed., New York and London: The Guilford Press.

Chamberlain, M. E., 2013. *Scramble for Africa*, 3rd ed., London and New York: Routledge.

Clarence-Smith, W. G., 1993. 'Cocoa Plantations and Coerced Labor in the Gulf of Guinea, 1870–1914', in M. A. Klein (ed.), *Breaking the Chains: Slavery, Bondage, and Emancipation in Modern Africa and Asia*, Madison, Wisconsin: The University of Wisconsin Press, pp. 150–170.

Cohen, R., 2008. *Global Diasporas: An Introduction*, London: Routledge.

Collier, P., 2013. *Exodus: How Migration Is Changing Our World*, Oxford and New York: Oxford University Press.

Collins, R. O., 2008. 'The African Slave Trade to Asia and the Indian Ocean Islands', in S. de S. Jayasuriya and J. P. Angenot (eds), *Uncovering the History of Africans in Asia*, Leiden and Boston: Brill, pp. 57–79.

Cotterell, A., 2011. *Asia: A Concise History*, Singapore: John Wiley & Sons (Asia).

Du Bois, W. E. B., 2007a. 'The Rape of Africa', in H. L. Gates (ed.), *The World and Africa: Color and Democracy*, Oxford and New York: Oxford University Press.

Du Bois, W. E. B., 2007b. 'Central Africa and the March of Bantu', in H. L. Gates (ed.), *The World and Africa: Color and Democracy*, Oxford and New York: Oxford University Press.

Fernandez, B., 2014. 'Borders and Boundaries: Containing African International Migration', in T. Murith (ed.), *Handbook of Africa's International Relations*, London and New York: Routledge, pp. 134–144.

Flahaux, M. L. and De Haas, H., 2016. 'African Migration: Trends, Patterns, Drivers', *Comparative Migration Studies*, Volume 4 (1), pp. 2–25.

Gabaccia, D. R., 2013. 'Migration History in the Americas', in S. J. Gold and S. J. Nawyn (eds.), *The Routledge International Handbook of Migration*, London and New York: Routledge, pp. 64–74.

Getahun, S., 2013. 'Charting Refugee and Migration Routes in Africa', in S. J. Gold and S. J. Nawyn (eds.), *The Routledge International Handbook of Migration Studies*, London and New York: Routledge, pp. 87–95.

Gold, S. J. and Nawyn, S. J., 2013a. 'Refugees and Forced Migrants', in S. J. Gold and S. J. Nawyn (eds.), *The Routledge International Handbook of Migration Studies*, London and New York: Routledge, pp. 1–8.

Gold, S. J. and Nawyn, S. J., 2013b. 'Introduction', in S. J. Gold and S. J. Nawyn (eds.), *The Routledge International Handbook of Migration Studies*, London and New York: Routledge, pp. 97–98.

Held, D., McGrew, A., Golblatt, D. and Perraton, J., 2000. 'People on the Move', in Held et al., *Global Transformations: Politics, Economics and Culture*, 2nd ed., Cambridge: Polity Press, pp. 282–326.

Horton, M., n.d. 'Did Asia Underdevelop Africa? An Archaeological Perspective on African Poverty', University of Bristol. Available at: Did Asia Underdevelop Africa – iBrarian [Accessed 4 September 2016].

Hugo, G., 2007. 'International Migration in the Asia-Pacific Region: Emerging Trends and Issues', in D. S. Massey and J. E. Taylor (eds.), *International Migration: Prospects and Policies in a Global Market*, Oxford and New York: Oxford University Press, pp. 77–103.

IOM (International Organization for Migration), 2011. *Key Migration Terms*, Glossary on Migration, International Migration Law Series No. 25. Available at: www.iom.int/key-migration-terms [Accessed 6 August 2016].

IOM, 2015. 'Migration and Cities: New Partnerships to Manage Mobility', *World Migration Report 2015*, Switzerland: Geneva. Available at: http://publications.iom.int/system/files/wmr2015_en.pdf [Accessed 4 August 2017].

Jayasuriya, S. de S., 2016. 'Indian Ocean African Migrants: Recognition and Development', in K. Kitagawa (ed.), *African and Asia Entanglements in Past and Present: Bridging History and Development Studies, Conference Proceedings*, Osaka: Faculty of Economics, Asian and African Studies Group, Kansai University, pp. 17–20.

Jonsson, G., 2009. *Comparative Report: African Migration Trends*, 'International Migration Institute, James Martin 21st Century School University of Oxford'. Available at: www.imi.ox.ac.uk/completed-projects/aphm/case-studies/comparative-report.pdf [Accessed 9 August 2016].

Kane, A. and Leedy, T. H., 2013. 'African Patterns of Migration in a Global Era: New Perspectives', in A. Kane and T. H. Leedy (eds.), *African Migration: Patterns and Perspectives*, Bloomington, Indiana: Indiana University Press, pp. 1–19.

Kaur, A., 2014. 'Migrant Labour and Welfare in Southeast Asia', in N. G. Owen (ed.), *Routledge Handbook of Southeast Asian History*, London and New York: Routledge, pp. 165–176.

King, R., 2012. *Theories and Typologies of Migration: An Overview and a Primer*, Willy Brandt Series of Working Papers, 3, pp. 3–43. Available at: www.researchgate.net/publication/260096281_Theories_and_Typologies_of_Migration_An_Overview_and_A_Primer [Accessed 9 August 2016].

Klein, M. A., 1993. 'Introduction: Modern European Expansion and Traditional Servitude in Africa and Asia', in M. A. Klein (ed.), *Breaking the Chains: Slavery, Bondage, and Emancipation in Modern Africa and Asia*, Madison, Wisconsin: The University of Wisconsin Press, pp. 3–36.

Koser, K., 2007. *International Migration: A Very Short Introduction*, Oxford and New York: Oxford University Press.

Lucas, R. E. B., 2013. 'Africa Migration', in B. R. Chiswick and P. W. Miller (eds.), *The Handbook on the Economics of International Migration*, Volume 1B, Amsterdam: Elsevier. Available at: www.bu.edu/econ/files/2012/11/African-Migration_Lucas.pdf [Accessed 9 August 2016].

Manning, P., 2005. *Migration in World History*, New York and London: Routledge.

Massey, D. S. and Taylor, J. E. (eds.), 2007. *International Migration: Prospects and Policies in a Global Market*, 2nd ed. Oxford and New York: Oxford University Press, pp. 1–14.

McKeown, A., 2014; 2nd edn 2013. 'Asian migration in the longue durée', in S. J. Gold and S. J. Nawyn (eds.), *The Routledge International Handbook of Migration*, London and New York: Routledge, pp. 75–86.

McNeill, W. H. and Iriye, M. 1971. 'Japan's Struggle for Modernisation', in W. H. McNeill and M. Iriye (eds.), *Modern Asia & Africa, Readings in World History*, Volume 9, London and Toronto: Oxford University Press, pp. 144–146.

OECD, 2013. *World Migration in Figures*, New York: United Nations, Department of Economic and Social Affairs, Population Division. Available at: www.oecd.org/els/mig/World-Migration-in-Figures.pdf [Accessed 6 August 2016].

Osborne, M. and Kent, S. K. (eds.), 2015. *Africans and Britons in the Age of Empires, 1660–1980*, London and New York: Routledge.

Peycam, P., 2016. 'Towards an Autonomous Academic Africa–Asia Framework', International Institute for Asian Studies (IIAS), *The Newsletter Encouraging Knowledge and Enhancing the Study of Asia*, Volume 73 (Spring), p. 48 [online] Available at: http://www.iias.asia/sites/default/files/IIAS_NL73_FULL.pdf [Accessed 6 August 2017].

Reid, A. 1993. 'The Decline of Slavery in Nineteenth-Century Indonesia', in M. E. Klein (ed.), *Breaking the Chains: Slavery, Bondage, and Emancipation in Modern Africa and Asia*, Madison, Wisconsin: The University of Wisconsin Press, pp. 64–82.

Shimeles, A., 2010. *Migration Patterns, Trends and Policy Issues in Africa*, Working Paper Series African Development Bank Group, 119. Available at: www.afdb.org/fileadmin/uploads/afdb/Documents/Procurement/Project-related-Procurement/WORKING%20119%20word%20document%20AA.PDF [Accessed 31 August 2016].

UNHCR, 2015. 'Trends at a Glance: 2015 in Review', *Global Trends Forced Displacement 2015*, pp. 1–68. Available at: http://www.unhcr.org/576408cd7.pdf [Accessed 1 October 2017].

Williams, E., 1944. *Capitalism & Slavery*, Richmond, Virginia: The University of North Carolina Press.

World Migration Report (WMR), 2013. *Migrant Well-Being and Development*, Geneva: International Organization for Migration. Available at: http://publications.iom.int/system/files/pdf/wmr2013_en.pdf [Accessed 2 September 2016].

Zeleza, P. T., 2010. 'African Diasporas: Toward a Global History', *African Studies Review*, Volume 53 (1), pp. 1–21.

28

ASIAN STAKES IN AFRICA'S NATURAL RESOURCES INDUSTRIES AND PROSPECTS FOR SUSTAINABLE DEVELOPMENT

Thomas Feldhoff

Introduction

In the new millennium, perceptions of the African continent changed dramatically as new powerful Asian actors, such as China and India, emerged to alter Africa's international position. In May 2000, the front page of *The Economist* ran its famous "hopeless continent" headline, while more than a decade later, in December 2011, it maintained that Africa was the "rising continent". Findings indicate that African nations have achieved remarkable economic growth. This has been attributed to administrative reforms and institutional development, an improved revenue allocation structure, particularly in favour of infrastructure investments, and economic reforms improving productivity and the business climate. In addition, the reforms have paved the way for a revival of foreign direct investment in Africa's natural resources industries, with China leading the way. This is now part of a broader economic trend of accelerating investment and trade between African nations and emerging countries, including India, Brazil and the Middle East, profoundly re-ordering global trade and investment patterns (CII-WTO, 2013; UNECA, 2011:1–3).

Despite the fact that foreign direct investment and trade with mineral commodities have enhanced economic growth in many mineral-rich African countries, it remains unclear what the true potential of natural resources is and how this sector could effectively contribute to broader social and economic development goals (ADF-VIII, 2012). Progress and opportunities for development are regularly assessed by international organisations, including the United Nations (AfDB et al., 2011, 2013, 2015). The UN Millennium Development Goals have now expired, and the Post-2015 Development Agenda "Transforming our world" has been adopted by the General Assembly only recently. It reaffirms the international community's commitment "to create conditions for sustainable, inclusive and sustained economic growth, shared prosperity and decent work for all, taking into account different levels of national development and capacities" (UN, 2015). Determined action is indeed required as tens of millions of people across Africa are still suffering from poverty – and Africa will account for the bulk of world population growth expected this century, further constraining efforts to address poverty issues. This performance below potential is despite the stronger integration of African countries into the global economy, and one obvious reason is that this integration is largely based on the natural comparative advantage. As Broadman (2007:140) notes with regard to Chinese and Indian investment in Africa, this "reflects complementarities . . . based on factor endowment of natural resources in Africa versus skilled labour in China and India".

The "Africa Mining Vision", adopted by the African Heads of State and Government in 2009, addressed this issue, and called for action to integrate the mining sector into the wider development agenda (African Union, 2009). This chapter argues that Asian countries, which have emerged as important stakeholders in Africa's natural resources industries, will have to play a major role in supporting this endeavour. Rashly denouncing their engagement as "neo-colonisation" is a widespread misconception, one that is kept alive, deliberately, by competing powers. Asian involvement in Africa rather reflects globalising processes, which continuously alter the nature and the degree of interconnection between different parts of the world (Dicken, 2015:8), and a global trend of increasing South–South cooperation among emerging markets. Taking into account the imaginaries used by Western stakeholders to blame China for 'neo-colonialism', is a challenge for critical geopolitics, which offers an additional perspective to the analysis here. Negative Western imaginaries of Chinese businesses have a long history (Barclay & Smith, 2013:133–134), and the extractive industries have become a widely recognised symbol of China's alleged exploitation of Africa. Critical geopolitics interrogates "the implicit and explicit meanings" that are given to certain places in order to influence and to determine international political and military policy (Flint & Taylor, 2007:69). The approach sees power as mediated by ways of talking about and seeing the world, and understands international conflict in terms of competing narratives each side tells about itself and the "other" (Agnew et al., 2008:4). As Africa's long-term structural socio-economic transformation is the challenge, however, Africa dealing with these power struggles in ways that enable African ownership of the development process is a key factor to success.

The aim of this chapter is to study how, especially, China and India have been shaping Africa's international position in recent years. In the first section, the chapter reviews Africa–Asia relations with a focus on natural resources. Then, it identifies the patterns of foreign direct investment and trade, followed by the analysis of how African–Asian state–state relations have changed established global economic and geopolitical power relations. The fourth section looks at the resource curse issue, and finally, prospects for the development of a sustainable resource-based economy will be considered. This includes an assessment of the proliferation of transnational regulatory activities, which are going beyond traditional state-to-state interactions to foster greater entanglement, and also issues of regional integration and cooperation in order to understand how transregional partnership agreements are promoting both Asian and African interests. The conclusion sums up the overall arguments and offers some thoughts for further consideration.

African development and the new Africa–Asia relations in the literature

The renewed focus on Africa's potential for development has been largely linked to three closely interrelated aspects: firstly, the relative abundance of sought-after natural resources, including mineral, metal and land resources, in many developing countries of the region; secondly, the increasing economic strength of China, India and other emerging countries from the Global South, requiring secure access to natural resources for their growth; thirdly, the changing balance of power between nation states, which is highly dynamic and contingent, as new constellations of geopolitical world orders arise. The natural resources sector has been widely discussed as a strategic option for economic development in Africa (ADF-VIII, 2012; AfdB et al., 2013, 2015; Africa Progress Panel, 2013; African Union, 2009; UNCTAD, 2007; UNECA, 2011). Concurrently, some major shortcomings with a single-sector approach have been identified, and various adverse experiences have revived the notion of the natural resource curse (AfDB et al., 2015; Alao, 2007; Ndikumana & Abderrahim 2010; Runge & Shikwati, 2011), i.e. underdevelopment being further compounded by narrowly defined sectoral approaches due to Dutch Disease effects. Dutch Disease refers to the link between increasing raw materials exports, appreciation in currency, and competitive disadvantages for other sectors of the economy (Sala-i Martin & Subramanian, 2003). Furthermore, policy coherence has been lacking to ensure that this sector can contribute to sustainable development in the long-term as extractive industries cause negative externalities. This includes the depletion of valuable natural resources, ecosystem degradation and the loss of biodiversity, the displacement of local communities, labour conflicts and eroding government credibility with the population (Emuedo et al., 2014; ICMM, 2014:7; UNCTAD, 2007:129). Many African leaders welcomed China as a strategic partner leading a way forward by investing in mining and vital infrastructure developments, providing "unconditional" aid and investment based on its practice of non-interference (Alden & Large, 2011; Besada et al., 2011; Hodzi et al., 2012). Plus, China presents a model for development that many African countries are hoping to replicate in order to sustain their development process (Hirono & Suzuki, 2014; Williamson, 2012).

The rapid growth of Sino-Africa partnerships has also aroused wide academic interest (Alden & Large 2011; Ampiah & Naidu, 2008; Brautigam, 2009; Cheru & Obi, 2010; Dietz et al., 2011; Harneit-Sievers et al., 2010; Manji & Marks, 2007; Pal, 2010; Taylor, 2009). Given the strategic importance of the extractive industries for all developed nations, these industries are characterised by interstate rivalry and competition. For states and firms seeking to exploit natural resources, because of their territorial embeddedness, access is available only through the nation state in which they are located (Dicken, 2015:408–413). Therefore, the role of the state as the primary agent for the exploitation of natural resources is a crucial factor. Nationalisation in the extractive industries was a strong trend in African countries in the aftermath of decolonisation. However, according to UNCTAD (2007), many of the nationalisations turned out to be failures, and from the mid 1980s, laws were liberalised in order to attract foreign investment from private companies. With growing resource demands and constraints due to the long-term depletion of non-renewable resources, the territorial control, exploitation and mobilisation of natural resources has emerged as a major geopolitical issue in Africa–Asia relations (AfDB et al., 2013; Alao, 2007; Alden, 2007; Ampiah & Naidu, 2008; Andrews-Speed et al., 2012; Barclay & Smith, 2013; BMI, 2013; Dubey, 2016; ICMM, 2014; Nguepjouo & Runge, 2014; Obi, 2010; Runge & Shikwati, 2011; Schofield, 2011; Whalley, 2011).

As a key driver of recent African economic growth, increased Chinese investment in the extractive industries and beyond has been identified. Alden (2007) showed that in many African countries, Chinese state-owned enterprises and large private companies have become major investors in capital-intensive mining projects. In its language policy in international relations, China has successfully promoted itself as a reliable cooperation partner in "mutually beneficial relations" with its African partners (Chidaushe, 2007; Large, 2007). The "Beijing Consensus" (Ramo, 2004; Williamson, 2012) became indicative of China's authoritarian capitalism approach to investment, trade and development aid, but critics warned of the disadvantages for inviting countries (Barclay & Smith, 2013; Hirono & Suzuki, 2014). Framing the issue mostly in moral terms, China was blamed as a "neo-colonial power" grabbing Africa's resources and prioritising infrastructure investments for natural resource exploitation; supporting unsustainable trade patterns of Chinese nationals and private firms; establishing unjust labour practices; ignoring the existence of illegitimate regimes, corruption, human rights abuse and environmental destruction; eroding standards of good governance (Chan-Fishel, 2007; Obiorah, 2007; Sachikonye, 2008; Vittorini & Harris, 2011; Zhao, 2014). Dubosse (2010) found that in the case of Zambia, though Chinese companies invested heavily in copper and other extractive industries, there was no evidence of technology transfer. Gill & Reilly (2007) identified Chinese corporate behaviour in the mining sector as a force crowding out African businesses, because of poor working conditions, low wages and reduced safety standards.

Challenging the widespread perception that China's heavy investment to the region is solely driven by short-term economic interests, Brautigam (2009) emphasised that Chinese motivations were much broader and more long-term orientated. Practically speaking, the Chinese approach to facilitating development in Africa builds on hard infrastructure investments as a prerequisite to mobilise the factors of production (Alden & Large, 2011; Hodzi et al., 2012), and on the promotion of softer ties and relationship-building measures in the context of South–South cooperation (Pal, 2010; Grimm, 2014). China's contribution to Africa's infrastructure construction was assessed in detail in a World Bank research report "Building Bridges" (Foster et al., 2009). Broadman (2013) notes, "China and Africa has nothing to do with colonization, and everything to do with economics and diplomacy." Similarly, rapidly growing India is now also seeking a "functional economic partnership" with African countries, and energy sources are the most prominent area (Broadman, 2007; CII–WTO, 2013; Dubey, 2016).

Alao (2007) draws attention to the fact that within studies on Africa's natural resources only little attention has been paid to land and water resources. With a look at Africa's relative abundance of land, agricultural raw materials and low-cost labour, evidence for economic growth potential came from the World Bank (2009). Based on an analysis of the factors that contributed to the successes in the development of commercial agriculture in Brazil and Thailand, the authors argued that opportunities abound for farmers in Africa to gain international competitiveness. Indeed, large-scale land investments made by foreign agro-energy corporations, states and private equity funds have increased remarkably since the 2007–2008 global food and energy crises (AfDB et al., 2013; Clements & Fernandes, 2012; Cuffaro & Hallam, 2011; Land Research Action Network, 2011; Von Braun & Meinzen-Dick, 2009). Sage (2013) criticised these investments as dominated by powerful financial interests, largely ignoring sustainable forms of smallholder agriculture, neglecting the interests of existing land users and dispossessing the rural poor of their land and resource rights.

African resource wealth: patterns of foreign direct investment and trade

Africa's rich natural resources were a major incentive for the colonial conquering of the continent in the nineteenth century, and this continues to this day as transnational corporations are controlling much of the exploration, exploitation and exportation of these resources and related products. Based on a broad-brush look at the territorial embeddedness of resources in African countries, leading regions and key commodities can be identified as follows:

- The rapidly expanding "energy regions" in North (Algeria, Libya), West (Nigeria), Central (Gabon) and Southern Africa (Angola) with oil and natural gas, some in the West with offshore exploration and production, as well as South Africa providing coal and uranium;
- The "precious metal regions" in Southern Africa (with gold and platinum in Zambia, Zimbabwe, Botswana and South Africa) and in West Africa (gold in Sierra Leone, Liberia and Cameroon);

- The "diamond regions" in Central, West and Southern Africa, including Botswana as the world's largest diamond producer by value, but also South Africa, Namibia and Angola;
- The "metal regions" of Southern Africa (uranium from Namibia, copper from Zambia, copper and cobalt from the DR Congo, aluminium from Mozambique) and Central-Western Africa (Guinea, Liberia, Sierra Leone).

East Africa has been less dependent on mineral exports than most other parts of the continent, but the region is rich in agricultural products, such as coffee, tea, grains and livestock. The trend has changed only recently since the discovery of natural gas off the coast of Mozambique (Africa Progress Panel, 2013:48). At a more disaggregated spatial level, however, densely populated regions with important mining, industrial and service sectors only appear as circumscribed, nucleated sites because of the lack of a broader spread of economic activities in many African countries. Obviously, this is not a consequence of China actually exploiting Africa's energy and other natural resources, but mostly Western colonial legacy.

Foreign direct investment

With regard to foreign direct investments (FDI), in fact, Western multinational companies have been playing the decisive role in Africa for decades. Given the history of colonial and post-colonial Africa, not surprisingly, firms from advanced Western countries still account for about 90 per cent of the stock of FDI in Africa. Recent FDI flows reveal some slowly changing patterns though. UNCTAD (2015) statistics show that FDI inflows to Africa remained flat at US$54 billion in 2014, decreasing in unrest-stricken North Africa and rising in Sub-Saharan Africa. Whereas multinationals from developed countries, France and the United Kingdom in particular, continued to divest from Africa, demand from emerging-market investors for these divested assets was significant. Moreover, announced green-field FDI projects for the 2013–2014 period indicate that the investment from developing countries, China, India and the United Arab Emirates, is on the rise.

Sectoral investment trends reflect the continued importance of services and manufacturing and indicate continuing diversification across many sectors, a trend already referred to by

Table 28.1 Announced green-field FDI projects by region/country (US$ millions, 2013–2014)

Partner region/country	Africa as destination	
	2013	2014
World	**55,124**	**88,295**
Developed economies	**28,010**	**63,024**
European Union	16,939	46,957
United States	2,559	8,014
Developing economies	**27,013**	**25,180**
Africa	13,082	10,209
Asia	13,735	14,886
China	289	6,132
India	5,311	1,122
Transition economies	**101**	**90**

Source: Compiled based on UNCTAD (2015).

Table 28.2 Announced green-field FDI projects by industry (US$ millions, 2013–2014)

Sector/industry	Africa as destination	
	2013	2014
Total	**55,124**	**88,295**
Primary	**6,114**	**21,974**
Mining, quarrying and petroleum	3,750	21,974
Manufacturing	**14,722**	**28,787**
Food, beverages and tobacco	1,347	2,099
Textiles, clothing and leather	1,744	2,091
Non-metallic mineral products	3,921	2,213
Services	**34,287**	**37,534**
Electricity, gas and water	11,537	10,648
Construction	3,536	9,229
Transport, storage and communications	7,774	5,909
Business services	7,099	6,323

Source: Compiled based on UNCTAD (2015).

Broadman (2007:2, 304). Services FDI amounted to 48 per cent of Africa's total stock in 2014 and are heavily concentrated in North Africa (Morocco), manufacturing to just 21 per cent and the primary sector to 31 per cent (UNCTAD, 2015:35). In 2014, the services sector accounted for the majority of announced green-field investment data (see Table 28.2).

Despite falling global commodity prices, nearly 25 per cent of planned capital expenditure related to green-field FDI projects in Africa was still in mining, quarrying and petroleum, mainly in Sub–Saharan Africa. This percentage has remained fairly stable since the mid 2000s. China's expectation of growing natural resource import dependency was a key motivation to acquire interests particularly in oil projects in many African countries, including fragile states with high political risks. Part of the reason is, of course, that most resources in politically stable African countries have already been taken up by Western oil companies. State-owned enterprises have been playing a critical role as developers of China's African energy strategy (Gill & Reilly, 2007).

While China has led the way, FDI flows from India are also rising. India's African engagement was historically driven by small and medium-size enterprises and traders (Dubey, 2016; UNECA, 2011:40). After nearly a decade of economic liberalisation reforms, however, from the late 1990s, Indian multinationals strategically enhanced their outward orientation and economic cooperation with African countries. Most of the Indian FDI has gone into extractive industries and infrastructure development, and it is mostly from private sector multinational enterprises. With India's rapid industrialisation and urbanisation, similarly to China, the quest for energy security is one of the major driving forces for persistently investing in Africa (UNECA, 2011:40). Dubey (2016:37) stresses India's traditional goodwill, multidimensional relations and the large Indian disapora as unique features in its African engagement.

Despite their fast growth in recent years, however, non-traditional investors from emerging markets in Asia still do not match what Western partners have at stake in the African continent. Compared with the investment of Western or Chinese companies in Africa's mining sector, industrialising India is still far behind, but expected to expand as its consumption of key minerals continues to increase (BMI, 2013). Overshadowed by China, the Japanese government announced support to encourage stronger private investment in Africa in 2013 (Lehman, 2013). Generally speaking, while there are differences with regard to players and strategies, the scope and the breadth of investments, Asian investors have much in common in their African operations and share similar interests with their Western counterparts.

Merchandise trade

Africa's rich endowments are also reflected in merchandise trade. Oil, gas, minerals and other natural resources are the most important export goods in terms of value in many African countries. WTO statistics indicate that, overall, the mining and quarrying of some 60 mineral products represents around 20 per cent of Africa's economic activity. Minerals are the continent's second-largest export category. Africa's share in the world export for crude petroleum oils and oils obtained from bituminous minerals was 46.8 per cent and 13.7 per cent for liquefied natural gas in 2013. The economies of Angola, Chad, Congo, Gabon, Libya, Nigeria and South Sudan show the highest dependencies on oil exports. Overall, Africa's international trade patterns reveal both change and continuity. While China's position in Africa has been growing steadily over the past decade, it is worth emphasising that Western countries still remain the largest consumers of Africa's natural resources. The European Union is Africa's largest trading partner despite the fact that Africa's trade with Asia rose by 22 per cent between 2012 and 2013, which highlights changes in trade dynamics

Fuels make up the highest share in Africa's merchandise exports to Asia, which now surpass both the EU and the US in this exported product group. Chinese trade and investment, in particular, is still concentrated in a comparatively small number of resource-rich states, but the character of trade flows is very similar to Africa's relations with Western countries.

Within the "Asian" region, the rapid growth of India's merchandise trade with Africa is notable. India's increasing demand for fuels and mining products, which accounted for about half of its total imports in 2013, has been the major driving force, and Africa now supplies about a fifth of India's total crude oil imports. Overall, the value of India–Africa trade increased from US$5.3 billion in 2001 to US$63 billion in 2011, and was projected to reach US$176 billion by 2015 (CII-WTO, 2013:15). Some other Asian countries, such as Japan and South Korea, have also seen their trade with Africa surge over recent years, but total volumes are still comparatively small.

In summing up, AfDB et al. (2015) point to the fact that African trade is dominated by oil exports and South Africa, indicating the need for greater industrialisation, value addition

Table 28.3 Africa's merchandise exports by region

Exports by destination	Value, mn $ 2013	Share	
		2005	2013
Europe	215,621	43	36
Asia	160,200	15	27
Africa	97,349	10	16
North America	53,827	21	9
South and Central America	29,579	3	5
Middle East	18,302	2	3
Commonwealth of Independent States	1,877	0	0
World	602,496		

Note: Unspecified destinations are excluded.
Source: Compiled based on World Trade Organization World and Regional Export Profiles 2013.

and diversification. Also, stronger global economy integration comes with major risks. The WTO (2014) identified four key trends since the start of the millennium which have altered the way that trade affects development outcomes: the accelerated economic growth in developing countries, spurred by demand for commodities; the expansion of global value chains as indicated by the increasing share in total trade of intermediate goods, services and components between developing countries; the surge in agricultural and natural resource prices and the growing importance of commodity exports; the increasingly global nature of macroeconomic shocks. African countries are affected by all of these trends, both in positive and negative ways. Those developing countries that are in a position to export goods have gained significantly, also from increasing intra-African trade. But because of the impact of shocks to the global economy and price volatility, one-export sector or even one-export good dependence puts those countries into a highly vulnerable position (African Union, 2009: 8; Dicken, 2015:35). Therefore, Asian partners' commitment irrespective of turmoil in international markets has become an increasingly important factor of economic and political stability.

Questioning notions of Asian "neo-colonialism" in Africa

The enhanced fluidity, dynamism and complexity in state–state relations has altered established economic and geopolitical power relations. So far, African nations have gained substantially from the new patterns of multi-directional interconnections and the diversification of economic, political and geostrategic interests (Olsen, 2011; Hirono & Suzuki, 2014). Most African countries now deal with Western as well as with Chinese or Indian interests, and, "unsurprisingly, African ministers are very reluctant to praise or court one outside party over another when benefits can be derived across the board" (Vittorini & Harris, 2011:291). Nevertheless, China remains at the centre of a strategically motivated construction of antagonistic tensions with Western powers (including Japan) on the African continent. Therefore, exaggerating the darkness of China is a sustained, deliberate misconception which may well be interpreted as a symptom of Western fear of loss of power and control. Though China's usual practice of non-interference in African nations marks a difference from the West, they also have shared interests: in economic development, stability and predictability for their investment, alongside the liberalisation of markets (Gamora & Mathews, 2010; Olsen, 2011). Reasons for providing aid are also similar to those of Western donors: "strategic diplomacy, commercial benefit, and as a reflection of society's ideologies and values" (Brautigam, 2009:15). What is more, China's pragmatic approach to its engagement with Africa is characterised by flexibility and adaptability, encompassing shifts in positions without abandonment of underlying principles. Zhao (2014:1045) points out, for example, that China has now taken actions to adjust its practices, moving beyond resource grab to address local needs and sensitivities and being more cautious with repressive regimes.

It should also be noted that the one-sided interest in China's economic and political activities in Africa tends to ignore the fact that China itself is equally involved in other parts of the world (Ampiah & Naidu, 2008; Harneit-Sievers et al., 2010). In particular, China has been placing a greater strategic value on Central Asia, including resource-rich countries such as Kazakhstan, and South Asia, where it has further strengthened its close relationship with Pakistan (Small, 2015). Currently, China's ambitious transport infrastructure building programmes of the "New Silk Roads Strategy" promise increased stability in its influence sphere through economic growth. So, for the Chinese, Africa is only part of a broader and well-integrated geopolitical strategy.

BMI (2013) highlights that Indian mineral investment has generally not followed the same pattern as that of China. Chinese investment in the African mining sector has typically been accompanied by high-level government-to-government agreements as well as substantial infrastructure development projects. Indian investment has followed a more Western approach with little political involvement or high profile developments in infrastructure or the construction of public prestige projects. Private companies have provided the lion's share of the investment. It is within this context that India has frequently been postulated as the "better and more democratic" development model alternative to China (Habib, 2008; Dietz et al., 2011). Without carrying out an assessment here, at least, there are a whole range of choices available for African nations today because of the diversity of partners. African policy-makers are now facing the great opportunity "to genuinely participate – and most importantly, benefit from – the new patterns of international commerce" (Broadman, 2007:3).

Revisiting the resource curse issue

The debate on how African countries can build on their low value-added, natural resources industries to achieve sustainable development based on higher value-added activities, is ongoing and pressing (Africa Progress Panel, 2013:84). Theoretically, the potential of a properly managed natural resources sector to contribute to economic development is well understood (AfDB et al., 2013, 2015; ICMM, 2014). Most investments are capital-intensive and risky, and tend to have long gestation periods, so transnational corporations' activities in extractive industries were most welcomed by African developing countries in the course of their liberalisation policies (UNCTAD, 2007:130).

Figure 28.1 is adapted from the third edition of the ICMM (2016:33) report and represents the macro-level contributions of mining in low- and middle-income countries. The percentages indicate the range of stand-alone contributions in each area. However, the contribution of mining to the generation of government revenue is limited in many mineral-rich African countries. Ndikumana & Abderrahim (2010) found that African resource-rich countries have performed rather poorly in terms of tax revenue generation relative to their potential, when compared with their resource-scarce counterparts and the oil-rich Middle Eastern economies. This is due to several factors, mainly brought about by poor policy decisions (AfDB et al., 2013, 2015; African Union, 2009; Ndikumana & Abderrahim, 2010; Nguepjouo & Runge, 2014; Runge & Shikwati, 2011):

- A lack of capacity to design and negotiate exploration and exploitation concessions and licences with international businesses properly;
- The failure to increase tax revenues by effectively taxing transnational corporations operating in the natural resources industries and abandoning profit shifting practices;
- The lack of investment of resource export revenues in human capital development and diversification of the economic basis through the development of non-resource economic activities;
- Carelessness towards the need to further strengthen the rule of law and principles of good governance, including combating corruption and patronage, the clarification of the rules governing ownership and the establishment of mechanisms for accountability.

Revealingly, small-scale artisanal mining is widespread in many resource-rich countries as a result of regulatory enforcement failures, especially the lack of efficient land management systems and the impoverishment of the people (Bomba, 2011). At the same time, for the

Foreign Direct Investment (FDI)	
Mining FDI often dominates the total flow of FDI in low-income economies that have only limited other attractions for international capital	**60–90 %** of total FDI

Exports	
Mineral exports can rapidly rise to be a major share of total exports in low-income agrarian economies even when starting from a low base	**30–60 %** of total exports

Government Revenue	
Mineral taxation has become a very significant source of total tax revenues in many low-income economies with limited tax-raising capacity	**3–25 %** of government revenues

National Income (GDP and GNI)	
Modern-day mineral processing technology is sophisticated and highly capital intensive; locations are centralized as a result and most upstream value addition takes place outside the mine-host country	**3–10 %** of total national income

Employment	
Mine employment on its own is usually small relative to the total national labour force	**1–2 %** of total employment

Figure 28.1 Macro-level contributions of mining in low- and middle-income countries

Source: Adapted from ICMM (2016:33).

political-military-economic elites, resources have been a major source of enormous individual wealth, much of which has been gained through illegal activities and ignorance towards negative externalities (Alao, 2007). Furthermore, overreliance on non-renewable resource extraction has short-term risks, when economic downturns cause falling commodity prices, and it could have significant negative ramifications over the long term because increasing pressures on Africa's resources and environmental problems will become greater issues.

Nevertheless, in February 2004, 30 African mining ministers launched the African Mining Partnership (AMP), which aimed to coordinate mining and mineral-related initiatives across the continent (African Union, 2009:41; ADF-VIII, 2012). AfDB et al. (2013) argue reasonably that since natural resources (energy, minerals and agriculture) will remain the continent's comparative advantage for the foreseeable future, the priority should be to build on this comparative advantage to develop a strong, diversified resource-based economy. A four-layer policy approach to successful implementation has been developed (see Figure 28.2). Asian countries will have to play the role as supporters in this because they are important stakeholders in Africa's natural resources industry. More precisely, Asian countries have a social and moral responsibility to promote a mineral sector that contributes to sustainable socio-economic development in Africa by addressing social issues and adverse environmental problems – if they are interested in strong and stable long-term relationships. A resource-based development concept, transforming the abundance of raw materials into a source of common wealth for all the people, also requires some strategic policy considerations. The final part of this chapter is devoted to some selected key policy issues in natural resource rich economies across the continent.

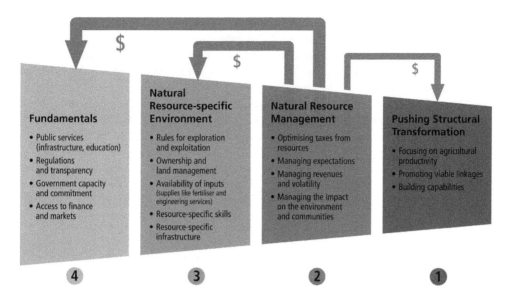

Figure 28.2 A four-layer approach to the implementation of a natural resource-based economy
Source: Adopted from AfDB et al. (2013:44).

Prospects for the development of a sustainable resource-based economy

One important lesson from previous development experience is that universal formulas should not be overestimated, but country-specific and context-sensitive assessment should be provided for the diverse realities of African nations (AfDB et al., 2013:21–22). In any case, governments must be careful to retain their credibility as functioning entities that are not eroded by the sole economic interests of businesses or foreign agents; contractor licensing, in particular, must be improved to enhance inter-enterprise competition and realise better value for Africa. Long-term goals require a more strategic approach towards sustainable development policies, building capabilities that enable African policy actors to play the decisive role in setting goals, developing plans and implementing programmes. Because of the transnational entanglements, diversity, fragmentation and rather loose institutional binding are major challenges for cross-country approaches to development (Acharya, 2008; Mbaye, 2010).

Regulatory frameworks

The lack of regulatory, contract and revenue transparency and the lack of accountability have been widely recognised as major issues in Africa's natural resource industries (Land Research Action Network, 2011). Schnell & Großmann (2011) discussed new forms of intersectional, transnational governance, such as the Extractive Industries Transparency Initiative (EITI) and the Kimberly Process Certification Scheme, and a more active role for non-governmental organisations as an attempt to create regulatory capacity where it does not exist. The "Africa Mining Vision" calls for a transparent and inclusive mining sector that is environmentally and socially responsible, and there has also been a proliferation of international and regional initiatives tackling human rights abuses (Africa Progress Panel, 2013:85–87). Civil society's transparency movement "Publish What You Pay" (PWYP) supports citizens in holding their respective governments accountable for the management of the resources sector. Corporate Social

Responsibility is also a key component of mining businesses, requiring a broad and transparent policy debate on government efforts and the industry's obligations regarding social development objectives (UNECA, 2011:81–89). In addition, multinational agreements provide helpful guidance for internationally operating private businesses to meet certain economic, social and environmental standards, e.g. the Global Reporting Initiative guidelines for mining (2004), the Natural Resource Charter (2010), the United Nations Global Compact agreement (2010), the OECD Guidelines for Multinational Enterprises (2000), the UNCTAD/FAO/IFAD/World Bank Principles for Responsible Agricultural Investment (2010), the FAO Voluntary Guidelines on the Responsible Governance of Tenure of Land, Fisheries and Forests (2012). Most initiatives are voluntary and enforcement mechanisms are rather weak, but governmental organisations and big businesses should get involved for ethical reasons alone. In order to ensure African leadership in extractive industry governance, the Africa Progress Panel (2013) has endorsed the implementation of the African Peer Review Mechanism's codes and standards.

Spatial inclusion and small-scale mining

With regard to regional development within African countries, AfDB et al. (2015) advance the idea of "spatial inclusion", defined as the objective of connecting people to assets and public goods regardless of where they live or work and overcoming narrowly defined sectoral approaches that overlook local knowledge, aspirations, resources and dynamics. In this sense, Fofack (2014) argued for a greater need for self-reliance by African countries in charting their course to development, and the African Union committed its members to structural transformation building on each economy's unique assets (AfDB et al., 2015). Linkage development between mining projects and other sectors of the local and regional economy ("up-, down and side-stream linkages") is central to overcoming the enclave nature of mining industries and realising value addition (UNECA, 2011). Additionally, the tradition of indigenous artisanal and small-scale mining (ASM), which retains strong continuities with precolonial practices across Africa, could support development because it is labour-intensive and provides more employment than large-scale mining (African Union, 2009:26–29; UNECA, 2011:11). The Yaounde Vision on ASM adopted in Cameroon in November 2002 was a notable attempt to show how to mitigate the negative consequences of ASM as a key poverty-driven and poverty-alleviating activity for many African rural economies by integrating it into local and regional economic development and land-use plans and strategies (African Union, 2009:28–29; Africa Progress Panel, 2013:88–90). Among others, active participation of the small-scale miners in policy development, the provision of specialised training and the empowerment of community leaders as agents of the change process are identified as major challenges in developing this sector to improve rural livelihoods.

Resource corridors

From a supra-national trans-African perspective, one approach to overcome infrastructure constraints and more closely integrate countries is the idea of natural resource-based corridors, based on the Spatial Development Initiative model originally conceived by the South African government in 1995. The goal has been to attract private investment through the identification of investment opportunities, providing infrastructure and the removal of a range of policy, legislative and institutional bottlenecks (Mtegha et al., 2012). It was later expanded under the 2001 New Partnership for Africa's Development (NEPAD), which was termed the NEPAD Spatial Development Programme (SDP). NEPAD was a milestone outlining a common vision for Africa's economic cooperation and its integration in the world economy (Hodzi et al., 2012:80–81). So far, Mtegha et al. (2012) note that resource corridors have had varied experiences and that certain ingredients for success are required, including: the identification of the inherent economic and infrastructure potential; participation of all relevant government organisations; effectiveness of the project management; attractive packages for investors, promotion and marketing of the corridor; binding bilateral or multilateral agreements. They conclude that the case for resource corridors has been dramatically strengthened due to the "Asian Boom", the surge in mineral exploration and new project development across the continent (Mtegha et al., 2012:51).

Regional integration and transregional partnership agreements

Japan and African countries designated trans-African infrastructure development as a key activity to increase regional trade along so-called Cross Border Transport Infrastructure (CBTI) corridors during the fourth Tokyo International Conference on African Development (TICAD IV), held in Tokyo in May 2008 (Matsushita, 2013:233). It is important to emphasise the role of transregional partnership agreements, such as TICAD, as important vehicles shaping Asian–African relations today; cooperation in fields such as trade, investment, finance and tourism has been expanded gradually. Initially, TICAD was set up by the Japanese government as early as 1993, well before China's advent on the continent, to strengthen Japan's relations with African nations. It has recently been reinforced in reaction to China's growing presence on the African continent (Ampiah, 2010; Yamada, 2011) and changed its focus from government aid for development towards the promotion of stronger private business ties through trade and investment (Lehman, 2013). In 2013, the African Union officially became one of the TICAD co-organisers, and also an official member of the Forum on China–Africa Cooperation (FOCAC) in 2012. FOCAC was established in 2000 as a strategic mechanism for strengthening Sino-African relations, based on: win-win economic ties; political mutual trust; cultural interaction; security cooperation; and close coordination in international affairs (Obi, 2010:183). Major plans to further boost cooperation were accounted at FOCAC VI in Johannesburg in December 2015 (Xinhuanet, 2015). Similarly, the India–Africa Forum Summit (IAFS) shapes India's relations with African nations, which are based on an "equitable partnership model" (Dubey, 2016:35). This is the trans-African and transnational dimension of the extractive resources industries, and there is still plenty of room to further African interests through these mechanisms. Toigo (2015) stresses the need for regulatory harmonisation and common standards while maintaining flexibility to capture country and project level differences; the use of regional integration as an enabler for natural resources to develop capacities needed for a broader industrialisation; the promotion of common interests as a means to strengthen the collective bargaining power of African countries in the global context of regulatory frameworks and their negotiations (also see AfDB et al., 2011; UNECA, 2011).

Conclusion and outlook

Natural resource development is an important part of the fabric of Africa's economy and a determinant of its strategic position in the global economy and geopolitics. The territorial control, exploitation and mobilisation of natural resources has been identified as a major economic and (geo)political issue in Africa–Asia relations. Thus, Asia's interest in trade and investment with Africa has created opportunities for integration into the global economy and development-oriented partnerships, but certainly also new dependencies.

China, India, other Asian and Western countries have similar, but competing interests in Africa and follow different approaches to their African engagement – a diversity that has opened up opportunities for African ownership of the process. In order to make the natural resources sector fit for substantial contributions to the broader social and economic development agenda, some primary strategic orientations must be met by African countries. Embedded in a comprehensive development framework that takes into consideration economic, foreign trade and investment policies as well as institutional and human capacity building strategies, the allocation of mineral revenues should be designed to develop the basis for stronger economic diversification, job creation and investments in poverty reduction, education, health and social protection. This should help to transform natural resources into a source of common wealth for all the people, and not only for small power elite groups. Certainly, the long-term goal is to master the shift from resource-dependence to more advanced industrial structures and value addition, also by creating common interests within the continent. Strong regional cooperation with key African as well as international partners is another important element to achieve synergies and to strengthen Africa's voice and position globally as transnational entanglements are becoming ever more complex. The analysis of regulatory frameworks has shown that government accountability and joint responsibility with businesses in new standard setting regimes are equally important factors. Apart from economic and political issues, bilateral and multilateral platforms should also be the place to discuss some of the most significant challenges of the twenty-first century, such as food security, climate change and environmental degradation. Such platforms also offer opportunities to provide non-governmental and civil society groups a forum for engagement with state actors. Their voices should be heard and their capabilities should be valorised by state actors domestically and internationally in order to achieve long-term sustainable development goals. Because of the increasing scope of the transnational mobility of people, capital, goods, knowledge, technologies and ideas, and the spread of trans-local connections, Smith (2002:221) invited academia "to think of the intertwining of locals by stretching relations over space". This also includes multi-level, multi-disciplinary approaches to further our understanding of Africa's widening and deepening interdependencies. Therefore, while the perspective here has been mainly on the "upstairs" dimension of official ties, i.e. on the level of economic and (geo)political connections, it should be stressed that the "downstairs" relations, or the interpersonal contacts between ordinary Africans and Asians, are becoming increasingly important in studies on African–Asian interactions (Alden & Park, 2013; Alden & Large, 2011).

References

Acharya, A., 2008. 'China and Southeast Asia: Some Lessons for Africa?', in K. Ampiah and S. Naidu (eds.), *Crouching Tiger, Hidden Dragon? Africa and China*, Scottsville: KwaZulu-Natal Press.

ADF-VIII (Eighth African Development Forum), 2012. *Governing and Harnessing Natural Resources for Africa's Development*, ECA/ADF/8/2, 18 October 2012.

AfDB et al., 2011. *African Economic Outlook 2011: Africa and its Emerging Partners*, Paris: OECD Publishing.

AfDB et al., 2013. *African Economic Outlook 2013: Structural Transformation and Natural Resources*, Paris: OECD Publishing.

AfDB et al., 2015. *African Economic Outlook 2015: Regional Development and Spatial Inclusion*, Paris: OECD Publishing.

Africa Progress Panel (APP), 2013. *Equity in Extractives: Stewarding Africa's Natural Resources for All*, Africa Progress Report 2013. Available at: www.africaprogresspanel.org/wp-content/uploads/2013/08/2013_APR_Equity_in_Extractives_25062013_ENG_HR.pdf [Accessed 20 January 2016].

African Union (AU), 2009. *Africa Mining Vision*, Report February 2009. Available at: www.africaminingvision.org/amv_resources/AMV/Africa_Mining_Vision_English.pdf [Accessed 20 January 2016].

Agnew, J., Mitchell, K. and Toal, G., 2008. 'Introduction', in J. Agnew, K. Mitchell and G. Toal (eds.), *A Companion to Political Geography*, Malden, MA: Blackwell Publishing.

Alao, A., 2007. *Natural Resources and Conflict in Africa: The Tragedy of Endowment*, Rochester: University of Rochester Press.

Alden, C., 2007. *China in Africa*, London: Zed Books.

Alden, C. and Large, D., 2011. 'China's Exceptionalism and the Challenges of Delivering Difference in Africa', *Journal of Contemporary China*, Volume 20 (68), pp. 21–38.

Alden, C. and Park, Y. J., 2013. 'Upstairs and downstairs dimensions of China and the Chinese in South Africa', in U. Pillay, J.P. Jansen, F. Nyamnjoh and G. Hagg (eds.), *State of the Nation: South Africa 2012–2013*, Pretoria: HSRC Press.

Ampiah, K., 2010. 'Japan and Commonwealth Africa', *The Round Table*, Volume 99 (409), pp. 413–428.

Ampiah, K. and Naidu, S. (eds.), 2008. *Crouching Tiger, Hidden Dragon? Africa and China*, Scottsville: KwaZulu-Natal Press.

Andrews-Speed, P., Herberg, M. E., Hosoe, T., Mitchell, J. V. and Daojiong, Z. (eds.), 2012. *Oil and Gas for Asia: Geopolitical Implications of Asia's Rising Demand*, Seattle: The National Bureau of Asian Research Special Report #41.

Barclay, K. and Smith, G., 2013. 'Introduction: The International Politics of Resources', *Asian Studies Review*, Volume 37 (2), pp. 125–140.

Besada, H., Wang, Y. and Whalley, J., 2011. 'China's growing economic activity in Africa', in J. Whalley (ed.), *China's Integration into the World Economy*, Singapore: World Scientific Publishing.

BMI, 2013. 'The Coming Boon in India–Africa Mineral Investment', Research Report, 1 January 2013. Available at: www.bmiresearch.com/news-and-views/the-coming-boom-in-india-africa-mineral-investment [Accessed 20 January 2016].

Bomba, F. A., 2011. 'Artisanal mining activity: A benefit or a burden for sustainable development in Central Africa?', in J. Runge and J. Shikwati (eds.), *Geological Resources and Good Governance in Sub-Saharan Africa*, Leiden: CRC Press.

Brautigam, D., 2009. *The Dragon's Gift: The Real Story of China in Africa*, Oxford: Oxford University Press.

Broadman, H. G., 2007. *Africa's Silk Road: China and India's New Economic Frontier*, Washington, DC: The World Bank.

Broadman, H. G., 2013. 'Separating fact from fiction in the China–Africa relationship', PwC Gridlines, Summer 2013. Available at: www.pwc.com/gx/en/psrc/pdf/pwc-gridlines-separating-fact-from-fiction-in-the-china-africa-relationship.pdf [Accessed 20 January 2016].

Chan-Fishel, M., 2007. 'Environmental impact: More of the same?' in F. Manji and S. Marks (eds.), *African Perspectives on China in Africa*, Cape Town: Fahamu Books, Pambazuka Press.

Cheru, F. and Obi, C. (eds.), 2010. *The Rise of China and India in Africa: Challenges, Opportunities and Critical Interventions*, London and New York: Zed Books.

Chidaushe, M., 2007. 'China's grand re-entrance into Africa: Mirage or oasis?', in F. Manji and S. Marks (eds.), *African Perspectives on China in Africa*, Cape Town: Fahamu Books, Pambazuka Press.

CII-WTO, 2013. 'India–Africa: South–South Trade and Investment for Development', Available at: www.wto.org/english/tratop_e/devel_e/a4t_e/global_review13prog_e/india_africa_report.pdf [Accessed 20 January 2016].

Clements, E. A. and Fernandes, B. M., 2012. 'Land Grabbing, Agribusiness and the Peasanty in Brazil and Mozambique', Paper Presented at the International Conference on Global Land Grabbing II, 17–19 October 2012.

Cuffaro, N. and Hallam, D., 2011. 'Land Grabbing in Developing Countries: Foreign Investors, Regulation and Codes of Conduct', Paper Presented at the International Conference on Global Land Grabbing, 6–8 April 2011.

Dicken, P., 2015. *Global Shift: Mapping the Changing Contours of the World Economy*, 7th edn, New York, London: The Guilford Press.

Dietz, T., Havenik, K., Kaag, M. and Oestigaad, T. (eds.), 2011. *African Engagements: Africa Negotiating an Emerging Multipolar World*, Leiden: Brill.

Dubey, A. K., 2016. 'India–Africa relations: Historical goodwill and a vision for the future', in A. K. Dubey and A. Biswas (eds.), *India and Africa's Partnership: A Vision for a New Future*, Berlin: Springer.

Dubosse, N., 2010. 'Chinese development assistance to Africa: Aid, trade and debt', in A. Harneit-Sievers, S. Marks and S. Naidu (eds.), *Chinese and African Perspectives on China in Africa*, Kampala: Pambazuka Press.

Emuedo, O. A., Anoliefo, G. O. and Emuedo, C. O., 2014. 'Oil Pollution and Water Quality in the Niger Delta: Implications for the Sustainability of the Mangrove Ecoystem', *Global Journal of Human-Social Science (B)*, Volume 14 (6), pp. 9–16.

Flint, C. and Taylor, P., 2007. *Political Geography: World-Economy, Nation-State and Locality*, Harlow: Pearson Education.

Fofack, H., 2014. *The Idea of Economic Development: Views from Africa*, WIDER Working Paper 2014/093, Helsinki: World Institute for Development Economics Research.

Foster, V., Butterfield, W., Chen, C. and Pushak, N., 2009. *Building Bridges: China's Growing Role as Infrasnucture Financier for Sub-Saharan Africa*, Washington, DC: The World Bank.

Gamora, G. and Mathews, K., 2010. 'Ethio-China relations: Challenges and prospects', in A. Harneit-Sievers, S. Marks and S. Naidu (eds.), *Chinese and African Perspectives on China in Africa*, Kampala: Pambazuka Press.

Gill, B. and Reilly, J., 2007. 'The Tenuous Hold of China Inc. in Africa', *Washington Quarterly*, Volume 30 (3), pp. 37–52.

Grimm, S., 2014. 'China–Africa Cooperation: Promises, Practice and Prospects', *Journal of Contemporary China*, Volume 23 (90), pp. 993–1011.

Habib, A., 2008. 'Western hegemony, Asian ascendancy and the new scramble for Africa', in K. Ampiah and S. Naidu (eds.), *Crouching Tiger, Hidden Dragon? Africa and China*, Scottsville: KwaZulu-Natal Press.

Harneit-Sievers, A., Marks, S. and Naidu, S. (eds.), 2010. *Chinese and African Perspectives on China in Africa*, Kampala: Pambazuka Press.

Hirono, M. and Suzuki, S., 2014. 'Why Do We Need "Myth-Busting" in the Study of Sino-African Relations?', *Journal of Contemporary China*, Volume 23 (87), pp. 443–461.

Hodzi, O., Hartwell, L. and de Jager, N., 2012. '"Unconditional Aid"': Assessing the Impact of China's Development Assistance to Zimbabwe', *South African Journal of International Affairs*, Volume 19 (1), pp. 79–103.

ICMM (International Council on Mining & Metals), 2014. 'The Role of Mining in National Economies (2nd edn)', Report October 2014. Available at: https://www.icmm.com/website/publications/pdfs/society-and-the-economy/romine_2nd-edition [Accessed 4 August 2017].

ICMM (International Council on Mining & Metals), 2016. 'The Role of Mining in National Economies (3rd edn)', Report October 2016. Available at: www.icmm.com/website/publications/pdfs/society-and-the-economy/161026_icmm_romine_3rd-edition.pdf [Accessed 5 April 2017].

Land Research Action Network, 2011. 'Introduction: Global Land Grabs: Investments, Risks and Dangerous Legacies', *Development*, Volume 54 (1), pp. 5–11.

Large, D., 2007. 'As the beginning ends: China's return to Africa', in F. Manji and S. Marks (eds.), *African Perspectives on China in Africa*, Cape Town: Fahamu Books, Pambazuka Press.

Lehman, H. P., 2013. 'Trade not aid behind Japan's policy to Africa', East Asia Forum, 27 July 2013. Available at: www.eastasiaforum.org/2013/07/27/trade-not-aid-behind-japans-policy-to-africa/ [Accessed 20 January 2016].

Manji, F. and Marks, S. (eds.), 2007. *African Perspectives on China in Africa*, Cape Town: Fahamu Books, Pambazuka Press.

Matsushita, K., 2013. 'Cross Border Transport Infrastructure (CBTI)', in JICA-RI (Japan International Cooperation Agency Research Institute), *For Inclusive and Dynamic Development in Sub-Saharan Africa*. Available at: https://www.jica.go.jp/jica-ri/publication/booksandreports/jrft3q00000029aw-att/For_Inclusive_and_Dynamic_Development_in_Sub-Saharan_Africa_JICA-RI.pdf [Accessed 20 January 2016].

Mbaye, S., 2010. 'Matching China's Activities with Africa's needs', in A. Harneit-Sievers, S. Marks and S. Naidu (eds.), *Chinese and African Perspectives on China in Africa*, Kampala: Pambazuka Press.

Mtegha, H. et al., 2012. 'Resources Corridors: Experiences, Economics and Engagement. A Typology of Sub-Saharan African Corridors', EI Source Book. Available at: www.eisourcebook.org/cms/files/EISB%20Resources%20Corridors.pdf [Accessed 20 January 2016].

Ndikumana, L. and Abderrahim, K., 2010. 'Revenue Mobilization in African Countries: Does Natural Resource Endowment Matter?', *African Development Review*, Volume 22 (3), pp. 351–65.

Nguepjouo, D. and Runge, J., 2014. 'Geological Resources, Nature of Mining and Interest of Asian Companies to Invest in Cameroon and Central African Republic (CAR)', *Zentralblatt für Geologie und Paläontologie*, Volume 1 (1), pp. 195–213.

Obi, C., 2010. 'African Oil in the Energy Security Calculations of China and India', in F. Cheru and C. Obi (eds.), *The Rise of China and India in Africa: Challenges, Opportunities and Critical Interventions*, London and New York: Zed Books.

Obiorah, N., 2007. 'Who's afraid of China in Africa? Towards an African civil society perspective on China–Africa-relations', in F. Manji and S. Marks (eds.), *African Perspectives on China in Africa*, Cape Town: Fahamu Books, Pambazuka Press.

Olsen, G. R., 2011. 'China into Africa: Conflict or the triumph of Western order?' in T. Dietz, K. Havenik, M. Kaag and T. Oestigaad (eds.), *African Engagements: Africa Negotiating an Emerging Multipolar World*, Leiden: Brill.

Pal, P., 2010. 'The surge in Indian outbound foreign dirct investment to Africa: A new form of South–South cooperation?', in K. P. Sauvant and J. P. Pradhan (eds.), *The Rise of Indian Multinationals: Perspectives on Indian Outward Foreign Direct Investment*, New York: Palgrave Macmillan.

Ramo, J. C., 2004. 'The Beijing consensus: Notes on the new physics of Chinese power', London: The Foreign Policy Centre. Available at: http://fpc.org.uk/fsblob/244.pdf [Accessed 30 October 2015].

Runge, J. and Shikwati, J. (eds.), 2011. *Geological Resources and Good Governance in Sub-Saharan Africa: Holistic Approaches to Transparency and Sustainable Development in the Extractive Sector*, Leiden: CRC Press.

Sachikonye, L., 2008. 'Crouching tiger, hidden agenda?', in K. Ampiah and S. Naidu (eds.), *Crouching Tiger, Hidden Dragon? Africa and China*, Scottsville: KwaZulu-Natal Press.

Sage, C., 2013. 'The Interconnected Challenges for Food Security from a Food Regimes Perspective: Energy, Climate and Malconsumption', *Journal of Rural Studies*, Volume 29: 71–80.

Sala-i Martin, X. and Subramanian, A., 2003. *Addressing the Natural Resource Curse: An Illustration from Nigeria*, Technical Report, Cambridge, MA: National Bureau of Economic Research.

Schnell, M. and Großmann, M., 2011. 'International approaches to improve resource governance in Africa', in J. Runge and J. Shikwati (eds.), *Geological Resources and Good Governance in Sub-Saharan Africa*, Leiden: CRC Press.

Schofield, C. (ed.), 2011. *Maritime Energy Resources in Asia: Energy and Geopolitics*, The National Bureau of Asian Research Special Report #35, Seattle: The National Bureau of Asian Research.

Small, A., 2015. *The China–Pakistan Axis: Asia's New Geopolitics*, New York: Oxford University Press.

Smith, A., 2002. 'Trans-locals, Critical Area Studies and Geography's Others, or why Development should not be Geography's Organizing Framework: A Response to Potter', *Area*, Volume 34 (2), pp. 210–213.

Taylor, I., 2009. *China's New Role in Africa*, Boulder, CO: Lynne Rienner.

Toigo, P., 2015. Can extractive resources help integrate Africa? African Development Bank Group blog entry, 7 Dec 2015. Available at: www.afdb.org/en/blogs/integrating-africa/post/can-extractive-resources-help-integrate-africa-15156/ [Accessed 20 January 2016].

UN (United Nations), 2015. 'Transforming our world: The 2030 Agenda for Sustainable Development. Resolution adopted by the General Assembly on 25 September 2015', Available at: www.un.org/ga/search/view_doc.asp?symbol=A/RES/70/1&Lang=E [Accessed 24 October 2015].

UNCTAD, 2007. *World Investment Report 2007: Transnational Corporations, Extractive Industries and Development*, New York: United Nations.

UNCTAD, 2015. *World Investment Report 2015: Reforming International Investment Governance*, New York: United Nations.

UNECA (UN Economic Commission for Africa), 2011. *Minerals and Africa's Development: The International Study Group Report on Africa's Mineral Regimes*, Addis Ababa: Economic Commission for Africa.

Vittorini, S. and Harris, D., 2011. 'New topographies of power? Africa negotiating an emerging multipolar world', in T. Dietz, K. Havenik, M. Kaag and T. Oestigaad (eds.), *African Engagements: Africa Negotiating an Emerging Multipolar World*, Leiden: Brill.

Von Braun, J. and Meinzen-Dick, R., 2009. '"Land grabbing" by foreign investors in developing countries: risks and opportunities', IFPRI Policy Brief 13, Washington, DC: International Food Policy Research Institute.

Whalley, J. (ed.), 2011. *China's Integration into the World Economy*, Singapore: World Scientific Publishing.

Williamson, J., 2012. 'Is the "Beijing Consensus" Now Dominant?', *Asia Policy*, Volume 13, pp. 1–16.

World Bank, 2009. 'Awakening Africa's Sleeping Giant: Prospects for Commercial Agriculture in the Guinea Savannah Zone and Beyond', Available at: http:// elibrary.worldbank.org/doi/pdf/10.1596/978-0-8213-7941-7 [Accessed 15 May 2014].

WTO (World Trade Organization), 2014. 'World Trade Report 2014', Available at: www.wto.org/english/res_e/reser_e/wtr14_brochure_e.pdf [Accessed 15 October 2015].

Xinhuanet, 2015. 'Spotlight: Xi charts course for upgrading China–Africa ties at landmark summit', 5 December 2015, Available at: http://news.xinhuanet.com/english/2015-12/05/c_134886595.htm [Accessed 20 January 2016].

Yamada, S., 2011. 'The Discourse on Japanese Commitment to Africa: The Planning Process of the Fourth Tokyo International Conference on African Development (TICAD IV)', *Journal of Contemporary African Studies*, Volume 29 (3), pp. 315–330.

Zhao, S., 2014. 'A Neo-Colonialist Predator or Development Partner? China's Engagement and Rebalance in Africa', *Journal of Contemporary China*, Volume 23 (90), pp. 1033–1052.

29

REFUGEES AND INTERNALLY DISPLACED PERSONS IN AFRICA AND ASIA

Pablo Shiladitya Bose

Introduction

In recent years, the world has witnessed a surge in the forced migration of diverse peoples to levels unseen in decades. In 2016 nearly 60 million people were displaced from homes, livelihoods, and lands by conflict alone, often forced across borders or into exile within their own country (UNHCR, 2016a). Millions more have been displaced by economic deprivation, by development projects and policies, and by degraded or dangerous environmental conditions (Bose et al., 2016). While the total proportion of the world's people who can be accurately described as migrants remains small – less than 5 percent of the overall global population (UNFPA, 2016) – their departures and arrivals have caused increased anxieties and tensions among national governments, international organizations, human rights groups, local citizens, and many others besides. Variously described as 'migrant crises', the movements of populations both forced and voluntary are one of the pre-eminent social, political, economic, and cultural challenges of our time. Issues of justice, fairness, equity, democracy, integration, acculturation, alienation, and economic vitality are but a few of the questions confronting migrants and host communities alike. How we understand and address the causes of forced migration is a complex problem, as is the attempt to find both short term and durable solutions to these issues. One of the key challenges is a definitional one – who is deemed a 'legitimate' refugee and thereby entitled to protection or possible resettlement? The global refugee regime as it is currently constituted is based on assisting those forced to flee their homes and homelands due to war, conflict, and various forms of persecution based on identity. Yet as this chapter explores in greater detail, there are a great many overlapping, complex, and sometimes contradictory motivations that drive displacement. The international systems of protection remained firmly rooted in a post-Second World War structure of addressing forced migration, with concepts of borders, repatriation, temporary refuge, and occasional resettlement guiding many of the responses to various conflict-related crises (Loescher et al., 2008). It was indeed many decades until the international community began to recognize the existence of internally displaced persons (IDPs), those who had been forced out of homes but not across an international border. In recent years, there have been attempts to extend the definition of refugee to those affected not only by conflict and political and identity-based persecution, but also those displaced by other factors such as various forms of development and a range of environmental causes

457

(White, 2011). Such efforts have not been successful for many reasons. Some argue that it has been difficult enough to provide protection for conflict-related refugees and that trying to also address other kinds of forced migration would simply dilute the existing protections and stretch thin already scarce resources (UNHCR, 2012). Others see the causes for displacement as being qualitatively different – conflicts and persecution often have a goal of displacing specific populations whereas such dislocation is often an unintended consequence of development projects and environmental degradation. Intentionality, not outcome, is key from such perspectives (Warner, 2010).

In this chapter I suggest that while understandable, such a narrow view of refugees and forced migration fails to fully comprehend the interconnected and complicated nature of the problem and thereby results in both practical and moral dilemmas for the global community. Not only does conflict often arise as a direct result of developmental and environmental factors, the various traumas suffered by the victims are often quite similar whether one has been displaced by war, a development project, or a degraded environment (Vandergeest et al., 2006). Regardless of the cause, refugees are the result of such processes and from an ethical standpoint should be seen as equally deserving of protection and redress. Therefore, as a way of illustrating the complex nature of contemporary displacements, I explore several specific examples that are distinct yet interrelated. I draw, in particular, on examples from two of the main sources of forced migration at the present time: several countries in Africa and Asia. While displacements are certainly not uncommon in other areas – Colombia, for example, remains one of the largest sources of IDPs globally and Central American countries have witnessed a mass exodus in recent years due to rising crime and environmental degradation – African and Asian countries are presently the major sources of refugee flows across the world. Of the top ten refugee producing countries in 2016, six are in Africa (Somalia, South Sudan, Sudan, Democratic Republic of Congo, Central African Republic, and Eritrea), while three are in South or West Asia (Syria, Afghanistan and Myanmar), and one is in the Americas (Colombia) (UNHCR, 2016a). It should also be recognized that the vast majority of refugees are housed in neighbouring countries; thus, the challenge is as much a regional as it is an international one.

I begin this chapter by reviewing the most commonly understood form of population displacement – conflict. This may take many forms – a more traditional war between nations, a secessionist movement within a state, the oppression of a particular minority group or identity, or another form – and remains the most widely recognized driver of forced migration. The second example I consider in this chapter is development-induced displacement, which, like conflict, has been creating conditions of forced migration for generations and yet receives far less attention – and its victims receive little to no protection or recognition under international law. In this section I look specifically at hydroelectric projects and petroleum extraction as representative cases. For the final section of the chapter, rather than reviewing existing experiences of forced migration, I consider an emerging and potential form – that of 'environmentally-induced' displacements, which may include conservation, resource extraction, or climate change among their causes. The particular cases I focus on through each of these various forms of displacement demonstrate once again the importance of countries in Africa and Asia when considering these phenomena, linked as many of them are to many of the most significant examples of forced migration in the world today. While there are clearly distinctions between these forms of displacement in terms of the immediacy and severity of the harms faced by those affected, I argue that we must look at displacement in its totality if we are to create effective, sustainable, and just solutions to these cases of forced migration.

Conflict

The sheer number and range of conflicts that have roiled the world over the past decades and embroiled the African and Asian continents in particular are depressingly overwhelming. The hope and potential presented by decolonization especially following the Second World War soon gave way to the rise of dictatorships, often brutal regimes, failed political and economic experiments, and entrenched poverty and inequality. From wars over political power and legitimacy to struggles for self-determination and secession, from ethnic clashes, transnational terrorism, and racial tensions to fights over resources, environmental goods, and economic opportunities, vast numbers of people – soldiers and civilians alike – have found themselves killed, wounded, raped, tortured, imprisoned, and/or displaced by these many and multifaceted conflicts. There are many exceptions to this narrative, with a significant number of countries – especially in parts of East Asia – making considerable gains in standard of living and economic prosperity. Indeed, one could argue that both Africa and Asia today are largely much more peaceful than they were two decades ago and that the conflict that exists – as horrific as its effects are – is much more localized than it was in previous eras. Yet by and large there still remain far too many unresolved and protracted conflicts throughout Africa and Asia which are significant drivers of forced migration. In this first section of this chapter I examine three specific examples of conflict-induced displacement – 1) interstate warfare and cross-border conflict in the Congo region since the mid 1990s, 2) the civil war in Syria that began in 2011, and 3) ethnic cleansing in the case of the expulsion of the Lhotshampa minority in Bhutan in the 1990s.

Inter-state war – Lake Victoria region

When one imagines conflict-induced displacement there are several elements that are commonly expected – a conflict across a border, national interests, identifiable combatants, a peace process, and treaties, for example. The turmoil in Africa in recent years displays many of these characteristics. Since the early 1990s and stretching over the past two decades, the First and Second Congo Wars (sometimes known as the Great African Wars) have gripped much of the continental region, eventually involving nine African countries and at least two dozen armed forces (paramilitaries, rebel groups, and transnational organizations among them). Often described as the deadliest war in modern African history, between three and eight million people are estimated to have died due to violence, disease, and starvation, while a further two million have been forced to flee to neighbouring countries and another three million are thought to be internally displaced in the Democratic Republic of Congo alone (Spagat et al., 2009; IDMC, 2013).

The roots of the tensions that have repeatedly flared up date back to at least the colonial era and the independence period of the 1960s, though the immediate catalyst for the conflict was the Rwandan genocide of 1994 which sent hundreds of thousands of refugees across the border into Zaire (now known as the Democratic Republic of Congo). Some of those who fled included members of Hutu militias who had taken part in the killings and many of whom were actively engaged in plotting against the Tutsi-dominated government that ruled Rwanda in the aftermath of the genocide. By 1996 the Rwandan government had begun to confront these Hutu groups across the border; at the same time a domestic uprising known as the Banyamulenge Rebellion against Zaire's leader Mobutu Sese Seko had spread across and destabilized much of the country. Over the next few years Rwanda, Uganda, Angola, Burundi, Zimbabwe, Zambia, Eritrea, Ethiopia, and Sudan all became embroiled – either militarily, diplomatically, or financially – in the conflict (Kisangani, 2012). This conflict officially ended in 1997, approximately a year after it had started, but within another year, the so-called Second Congo War began and lasted until 2003. The closeness in time and the overlapping sets of reasons why the conflict began anew have led many scholars to describe the two together as simply the Great Congo War or Great African War. Once again the echoes of the Rwandan genocide and both the domestic and regional interests of various states were to play significant roles. Finally, in 2002, under South African leadership a comprehensive peace agreement was signed between the different factions – yet peace continues to elude the daily lives of most of the local populations who, in the more than a decade since that signing, still find their lives deeply disrupted by conflict. Killings, abductions, rapes, mutilations, and forced recruitment of child soldiers are some of the ongoing consequences of these conflicts, atrocities carried out by national armies, militia groups, ethnic communities, and security forces alike (Daley, 2013).

The conflicts in the Congo and its neighbouring countries demonstrate the difficulties in categorizing types of forced migration as one thing or another. This is the clearest example of a cross-border conflict yet it also involves internal and domestic tensions, rebellions, political infighting, and struggles over not only politics, but religion, ethnicity, and ecology. Some scholars and politicians have argued that a key driver of the conflict in the Congo is the desire for access to natural resources and in particular mineral wealth including precious gems and components used in electronics manufacturing. Such dynamics demonstrate the complex nature of these conflicts.

Civil war – Syria

The Syrian Civil War emerged in the shadow of the Arab Spring protests of 2011, initially as a protest against the abuses and excesses of the Assad government in Syria. These protests spread across the country and as the security forces cracked down brutally on the opposition, eventually morphed into an armed rebellion. Large parts of the country came under the control of rebel groups and the conflict began to reformulate along sectarian lines, with the Assad-backed Alawites and other minorities on one side and a number of different primarily Sunni forces on the other. The rebel groups included secularist, moderate, and also more radical Islamist forces including branches of the Al-Qaeda movement and eventually the Sunni Arab Islamic State in Iraq and Syria (ISIS) movement. The conflict is fractured along many lines – sectarian (Sunni, Shia, other religious groups and denominations), ethnic (Kurd, Arab, Alawite), regional, economic, political – and has drawn on numerous actors from outside of Syria as well. Some rebel groups have received arms and air support from Western nations including the US, Canada, the UK, Australia, Belgium, and France, while the Assad government has been backed with military and financial aid from Iran and Russia (Carpenter, 2013). Other actors in this increasingly international struggle have included Saudi Arabia, Jordan, Iraq, Turkey, the Lebanese militia Hezbollah, and transnational jihadi elements from across the Middle East, Asia, North Africa, and Europe fighting against the Syrian army and often against one another as well. The involvement of regional Sunni and Shia governments in the conflict has led some analysts to describe the situation as a de facto proxy war between Iran and Saudi Arabia amongst others (part of similar struggles in other countries such as Yemen) (Hokayem, 2014).

The war in Syria has ebbed and flowed, with the first years seeing the serious diminishment of the Assad regime's control over territory – by 2015 less than a third of the country's territory and roughly two thirds of the country's population was said to be under control of the Syrian Army. Since October 2015, the direct intervention by the Russian military as well as more coordination between the US-led coalition and local proxies, including the Kurds, have led to serious reversals for groups such as ISIS as well as the more 'moderate' rebel groups (Lucas et al., 2016). Significant amounts of territory – held by ISIS and other Islamist forces as well as the Kurds and other rebel groups – have been regained by the Syrian government and in August 2016 one of the main battlegrounds to emerge was the city of Aleppo, long a stronghold of anti-Assad forces but now encircled by government forces (Bakke & Kuypers, 2016). A peace process initiated in February 2016 by the international community has had limited effect.

As with the Congolese wars, the impact of this conflict on both the country of Syria and its surrounding neighbours has been significant. Many cities have been left in ruins as a result of the war, notably Homs, Raqqa, Palmyra, and large sections of Aleppo and the capital Damascus. The economic and civil infrastructure of the country is badly damaged, including the crucial oil industry as well as agriculture, electricity, and roads. Casualty estimates of the dead, including rebel and army combatants as well as civilians, range from 150,000 to over 400,000 since 2011 (Barnard, 2016). The UN has listed some 13.5 million Syrians as in need of assistance including 6.6 million who are internally displaced and a further 4.8 million who are refugees or asylum seekers abroad (UNHCR, 2016b). The mass exodus of Syrians has had a profound effect on the global refugee regime, with Europe, and Turkey in particular, straining under the burden of what they see as an overwhelming migrant flow. Despite increasingly draconian measures to prevent the crossing of borders, the civil war in Syria continues to send migrants across dangerous land and sea routes to try and reach safety elsewhere. Many have not been successful, as drownings at sea and deaths on land can attest to. Others yet find themselves detained in camps and temporary shelters along the way. A rise in terrorist attacks across Europe, in particular during 2015 and 2016, and the explicit links drawn by ISIS and others between the struggle in Syria and attacks worldwide by jihadist returnees from the civil war as well as others inspired by them, have made the situation for refugees ever more fraught.

Ethnic conflict – Bhutan

Unlike the previous two examples, forced migration from Bhutan is not a result of war across or within borders but rather is a result of the oppression and expulsion of an ethnic, linguistic, and religious minority through a process of what some would call ethnic cleansing. Bhutan is a small landlocked Himalayan mountain state which until 2008 functioned as an absolute monarchy, with only recent transitions to slightly more representative forms of parliamentary democracy. Its majority population is Buddhist while prior to the 1990s it had a significant Nepali-speaking minority known as the Lhotshampa (a large number of whom are also Hindu). Both groups share significant ethno-racial origins, though they possess significant linguistic, religious, and cultural differences. The Lhotshampa in Bhutan trace their arrival to at least the seventeenth century, though migration through the various Himalayan mountain states was especially fluid during the British imperial era in the Indian subcontinent and immigrants from Nepal to Bhutan continued to grow throughout the twentieth century, especially following the British departure from South Asia. By the 1950s the Bhutanese government had begun to introduce legislation limiting further immigration, especially of Indian and Nepali workers working on construction and development projects throughout the country (Hutt, 2005). In the 1980s, long-simmering tensions between the Bhutanese majority and Lhotshampa minority led to further retrenchment by the government in the form of legislation meant to emphasize the cultural identity of Bhutan through a 'One Nation, One People' policy, with the culture in question being that of the majority. This meant that Dzongkha (the language of the majority) would be adopted as the sole national language (with the concomitant discontinuation of Nepali in schools) and the requirement of citizens to wear traditional Bhutanese national dress favoured by the majority in public places, as a way of increasing integration of minorities into the larger community (Evans, 2010). These issues were further exacerbated during Bhutan's first census in 1988 when much of its population was arbitrarily deemed to be either 'genuine' or 'non-national', often by poorly trained census takers (Rizal, 2004). For the Bhutanese majority the demands placed on the Lhotshampa were necessary and justifiable in light of Nepali secessionist movements in neighbouring states including India. For the Lhotshampa however these actions were perceived as discrimination and antigovernment protests involving thousands of participants became increasingly common. As the government in turn became increasingly repressive in its treatment of dissidents – with human rights groups asserting that torture and restrictions on freedom of speech were becoming commonplace – southern Nepal where most Lhotshampa were located became increasingly volatile and home to significant militant activity. Bombings and clashes between protestors and both police and the army began to escalate by 1990, and an insurgency in the south of Bhutan became increasingly strong (Hutt, 2005). By 1992 tensions and violence led to the departure of over 100,000 Lhotshampa from Bhutan, some of their own volition but many who claimed to have been forcibly evicted by the military and forced to sign 'Voluntary Migration Forms' (Rizal, 2004).

The majority of these individuals settled in camps in Nepal, while some were placed in camps in India. Some of those who were in camps in Nepal were claimed to have been Nepalese individuals attracted by the possibility of migration overseas rather than refugees from Bhutan. In either event, the situation became a protracted one – Nepal saw the refugees as Bhutanese in origin regardless of their language, ethnicity, or religion while Bhutan was not prepared to accede to the repatriation solution urged by both Nepal and the international community. While living in the camps in Nepal the Lhotshampa refugees lived under severe restrictions on movement, ability to work, and general rights. In the end the situation was resolved through significant third-party resettlement – since 2008 nearly all of the camp population has been resettled in a number of Western countries, with the vast majority (over 75,000) placed in the US and smaller numbers in Canada, Australia, Denmark, New Zealand, and Norway (Dhungana, 2010). Bhutanese refugees thus represent a significant forced migration population being addressed by the global refugee regime today, though their circumstances and experience are markedly different from those of other groups – including their potentially successful resettlement elsewhere, a 'solution' that seems lacking for others.

Development

When one thinks of population displacement, conflict-related causes such as those described above are primarily what come to mind. And yet while such involuntary or forced migration is indeed an urgent problem facing the world, some scholars argue that at least as many people – and perhaps even more – have been displaced by processes of global development through what has been described as 'development-induced displacement' (DID). Development itself is of course a hotly contested term – what it means, how it is deployed, how and what it affects. DID may thus constitute a particular project such as a dam, it might represent a political or economic policy such as land reform, or it might be a seemingly unrelated phenomenon such as conservation (Penz et al., 2011). In any of these cases it is the effect on which our focus remains – the forcing of communities and individuals out of their homes – often also their homelands – for the purposes of development. Such geographic displacement can be within a city or district, from one village or neighbourhood to another; it can also involve displacement across long distances and borders, sometimes to economically, socially, and culturally quite different settings. A broader conception of displacement is also possible;

this includes displacement from economic activities and cultural practices without geographic moves. When the latter do occur, they often result in the former. DID thus involves a fundamental dilemma: development to improve people's living conditions, aspirations, or opportunities may be desirable, yet how those gains are realized and to whom they accrue remains at the heart of any meaningful discussion of global improvements (Vandergeest et al., 2006).

The estimates of how many people across the world are affected by DID vary considerably with some suggesting that as many as 100 million have been dislocated as a result of processes of economic development alone since the end of the Second World War (Satiroglu & Choi, 2015). Many scholars also note that the effects of DID are felt especially strongly amongst socially and economically vulnerable (and often politically marginalized) groups and indigenous communities worldwide (Neef & Singer, 2015; Oliver-Smith, 2010; De Wet, 2006). There has been a particular intensification of DID in recent years as a result of increasing globalization and what some have termed 'land-grabs'. In effect, economic liberalization policies, structural adjustment, and stabilization programmes have made the problem of development-induced displacement all the more urgent. While examples like hydropower and resource extraction explored later in this section are seemingly more obvious sources of development-induced displacement, so-called mega-events – often meant to catalyse regional and urban growth strategies (Pillay & Bass, 2008) – have similarly been criticized for the various deleterious impacts they have had on local populations. Examples include large-scale festivals, international conferences, trade shows, political conventions, and sporting events. Mega-events have been embraced for a multitude of reasons by governments and others as a way of strengthening both the ideological and material foundations of various cities and countries. Yet they have also come under increasing criticism not only for their financial and ecological cost, but also because of their potential for causing displacement. How many people are forcibly evicted by mega-events, whether through the building of stadiums on their homes, the disruption of their livelihoods by new commercial agreements, or by their physical removal because their very bodies are an undesirable presence on a carefully managed stage? The Olympic spectacle in Beijing was criticized for just such forced displacements of poor inhabitants so as not to 'clutter' the scene (Hopkins, 2006), while the Olympics in Rio were harshly criticized for the disinvestment in improving slum conditions of favelas at the same time that scarce public resources were directed towards schooling (Richmond, 2016). The Commonwealth Games in Delhi in 2010 were likewise critiqued for the destruction of informal housing for the purpose of stadium construction (Rao, 2016). The critique of mega-events therefore is that they intensify rather than alleviate inequality and do little to address underlying developmental issues. Their promised benefits are often nothing like those that are used to promote them in the first place.

Unlike conflict-induced displacement, those forced to move by development are generally unlikely to be recognized as official refugees and afforded the protections that can accompany such categorization. They are also less likely to have been displaced across a border and instead swell the numbers of the so-called 'internally displaced persons'. The crisis of 'development refugees' is becoming increasingly recognized world-wide, as multilateral agencies and world governments struggle to deal with the problem. Yet the focus of such organizations (and of the existing academic literature on development-induced displacement) has been on projects such as the building of dams and railways or on resource extraction operations such as logging and mining. To address displacement as a broader and more multi-layered phenomenon, in this second section of this chapter I examine two specific examples of development-induced displacement – 1) dam building and the Narmada Valley Development Projects (NVDP) in India, and 2) oil extraction in Nigeria.

Dam development in India

The Narmada controversy has been ongoing for over half a century – plans to build a series of dams on the fifth largest river in India were first proposed in 1947. Construction began in the early 1960s; however, disputes over project costs and benefits between various riparian states resulted in delays of over a decade as a federally appointed Water Disputes Tribunal sorted things out, announcing its award in 1978 after ten years of deliberation. The final outcome of the project envisions the construction of 30 major dams, 135 medium dams, 3,000 minor dams, and over 30,000 micro-harvesting (conservation) schemes throughout the valley: 250,000 people will be directly displaced, while over a million will see their livelihoods disrupted or erased (Bose, 2006). This project is paralleled in size and scope by the Three Gorges Dam Projects in China.

Supporters of the dam argue for the benefits it will bring – primarily increases in available drinking water to hundreds of villages in four states, irrigation of thousands of hectares, and the provision of hydroelectric power for expansion of numerous industries and to improve rural electrification. Critics of the project point, on the other hand, to massive social and ecological (as well as financial) costs. These include the flooding of 245 villages in order to create the dam's reservoir as well as the lands of another 140,000 farmers to make way for irrigation canals. Thousands more may be affected by the project, including farmers and fisher folk downstream from the dam whose livelihoods will be disrupted. It is also worth noting that a majority of those destined to be affected by the plans are from indigenous groups. The full cost of the project is estimated at more than $5 billion and its completion date is 2040 (Khagram, 2004). Given these considerable social, financial, and environmental costs, it is unsurprising that there has been a long and sustained opposition to the dam project within the Narmada Valley – as early as the 1960s. Opponents of the NVDP have criticized the plans on multiple grounds, decrying the lack of transparency and accountability in planning, implementation, and the sharing of costs and benefits (Mehta, 2001). A vigorous social movement known as the Narmada Bachoa Andolan (Save Narmada Society) has since the 1980s drawn international attention to the situation and through mass protests and a series of alliances with international non-governmental organizations delayed and at times stopped construction (Baviskar, 2005). They have convinced the World Bank and other international funders to pull out of the project and launched several successful court challenges to the plans. Part of their objection has been on environmental grounds – that there is much rich farm- and forestland that will be inundated by the full scope of the project – but the central point of contention is with regard to displacement. What will happen to those whose lands and livelihoods will be lost due to the rising waters? Decades of inadequate resettlement efforts in those parts of the project already completed have left those affected by the dams unconvinced that a better (or at least equal) life awaits them in their new homes. Instead the opponents of the dams and their advocates have asked why their lives and opportunities should be sacrificed in order that others might receive the fruits of development – whether new agricultural productivity, cheaper hydroelectricity, or even drinking water for drought-parched regions. Despite the successes of the Narmada Bachao Andolan in raising the issue and getting the courts and occasionally central governments to listen to their criticisms, the dams continue to be built – if slowly and at much cost to the state and communities alike (*Times of India*, 2016). The current national government is led by Narendra Modi, formerly the chief minister of Gujarat – the Indian state that is the main beneficiary of the proposed dams. Momentum for building the dams has regained much force. Yet still the opposition continues, for the displaced have little choice but to protest. In their struggle they have become an inspiration for social movements and civil disobedience not only in India but all across the world.

Oil development in Nigeria

Petroleum extraction is one of the largest parts of Nigeria's economy – for several decades since it became an independent nation, oil production has slowly emerged as a crucial part of its national programme. While many Nigerians have benefited from this trade – especially wealthy urbanites who are connected to the industry in different ways – for those living in the Niger Delta region (over 30 million people), its major oil-producing region, the picture has not been so rosy. The area is densely populated, rapidly urbanizing, and has significant levels of poverty (Idemudia, 2012). A particular controversy that has become associated with oil development in the area has been the impact on minority ethnic groups such as the Ogoni. Numbering nearly half a million people, the Ogoni have accused the central government of forcibly displacing them since the 1950s (when oil was discovered) from their lands or offering them negligible compensation to move. Later constitutional amendments allowed the Nigerian government to essentially appropriate land for oil development and offer the previous owners only partial value in return (Ikelegbe, 2005). During the 1970s and 1980s local protest movements gathered steam in the Niger Delta, much as they had in the Narmada Valley during a similar period of time, and a series of non-violent actions became increasingly intensified. Both the Ogoni and the oil companies escalated the conflicts to the point of violence. While the Ogoni threatened to disrupt oil production entirely, the national government (on behalf of the oil companies) began to repress the local population both through the courts and the military. In 1994 both military and private security forces hired by the oil companies undertook a campaign of terror and intimidation that left over 2,000 dead and displaced a further 100,000. The Ogoni opposition leader Ken Saro-Wiwa and several other activists were accused of the killing of several Ogoni elders and were executed in what was widely condemned internationally as a travesty of justice. While the situation in the area (known as Ogoniland) has improved with the transition to democratic rule in Nigeria in 1999, tensions over oil development continue in the country (Idemudia, 2012).

In 1998, for example, another Niger Delta-based indigenous community known as the Ijaw raised the issue of control over petroleum extraction in their lands. Like the Ogoni, they complained that their lives and livelihoods were endangered through oil spills, uneven and unhealthy development, and corruption associated with the oil industry (Ukiwo, 2007). They asked the oil companies to withdraw from their lands. In response, the Nigerian government deployed thousands of troops and several warships to the area and subjected local residents to beatings, detention, rape, and death – hundreds were killed in the months that followed. In 2000, the government established the Niger Delta Development Commission with the primary goal of developing the region in a more sustainable and just fashion (Ukiwo, 2007). Yet for many of the ethnic groups in the Niger Delta its work has been incomplete and deeply unsatisfying. As a result, a number of armed militias have emerged since the late 1990s, drawing their membership primarily from poor, disaffected, and underemployed young men in the region. Such groups have attacked petroleum infrastructure – in particular pipelines – not so much to disrupt production as to actually steal and resell the oil (Ikelegbe, 2005). The resulting violence between the militias, security forces, and other local residents, as well as the widespread environmental degradation and not-uncommon fires and explosions caused by leaking pipelines, have all led to further displacements from the region and severely disrupted agriculture and housing (Idemudia, 2012). While the violence between government forces and militias has become much more muted and a national amnesty programme has curtailed the theft of oil, the underlying problems of uneven development, chronic poverty, and significant environmental pollution due to spills remain acute.

Environment

The third and final example of forced migration I will explore is that of environmentally induced displacement. In many ways environmentally induced displacement has emerged as a sub-set of development-induced displacement – certainly in the scholarly view – in recent years. Disappearing coastlines, fields and homes flooded by rising waters, lands left cracked and barren by desertification, a snowpack shrinking in circumpolar regions year by year – these are only a few of the iconic images of climate change that have evoked discussion, debate, and consternation within communities both global and local. Equally alarming has been the threat of what such degraded and destroyed landscapes might mean for those who depend upon them for their livelihoods – as their homes, as their means of sustenance, and as an integral part of their cultural and social lives. A mass of humanity on the move – some suggest 50 million, 150 million, perhaps even a billion people – the spectre of those forced to flee not due to war or conflict but rather a changed environment, haunts the imaginaries of national governments, international institutions, and public discourse alike (Black et al, 2011; Warner, 2010). Are these environmental refugees? Should they be granted the same protections and support as those who can prove their fear of and flight from persecution? Do the sheer numbers contemplated by the scale of the events and factors threaten to overwhelm the international refugee system? In this final section of this chapter I look at such groups, albeit not in the same detail as in the previous two cases – in part because the notion of 'environmental refugees' is itself a contested term, and consists of a population that is both difficult to quantify and represents a group that may *potentially* be displaced as opposed to those who have already been forced to move because of conflicts and development projects. Moreover, the effect of an altered climate is but one of the drivers of what might be termed 'environmentally induced displacement' (EID). Extractive industries – oil, gas, minerals, and lumber among them – have left scarred and despoiled lands in their wake. Collapsing fisheries and livestock herds bring their own forms of environmental disruption to the lives of those who depend upon them. Conservation initiatives meant to protect such resources and biodiversity alike have often resulted in the displacement of those already living in such zones or in restrictions on their ability to access or use their lands. Added to these human-made processes are the effects of so-called 'natural disasters' including hurricanes, earthquakes, floods, and tornadoes that have swept people from their homes in a series of well-publicized events in recent years (White, 2011; UNHCR, 2012).

These processes disproportionately affect marginalized groups within their respective contexts – indigenous communities, poor, and women. Many of the most affected groups are often vulnerable to begin with, lacking secure rights and access to resources and to formal recourse once these are jeopardized. Despite this apparent lack of power, the subjects of EID have consistently organized to contest their dislocation – often in highly visible ways, as global protests against dams, oil development, and parks creation can attest (Bose et al., 2016). Yet even with such notoriety, EID has not abated in recent years; if anything the scale of extraction, the expansion of conservation zones, and the threat of climate change and what to do about it have only served to intensify processes of environmental displacement (Zoomers, 2010).

Since at least the 1980s, the topic of environmental refugees more generally, and of climate-induced migration more specifically, has been a controversial one amongst international organizations, nation states, and local movements alike. Among the debates are definitional questions – how many people might be displaced and by what specific events/processes? Is the term 'refugee', with all that it connotes and implies and the systems of protection it might suggest, an appropriate one to use? To some extent these controversies extend far beyond the use of the label 'refugee' to the contestation of climate science and global environmental politics.

Amongst those who do agree that climate change – no matter what its cause – exists, there remains a great deal of disagreement as to what it portends (Myers, 1999; Brown, 2008; McNamara & Gibson, 2009; Stavropoulou, 2008). When contrasting the experience of displacement due to the other factors considered earlier in this chapter versus the potential of EID to displace many millions more, we must also consider the inadequacies of a global refugee regime that recognizes the legitimacy primarily of those whose lives have been disrupted by a conflict or persecution on the basis of race, religion, nationality, ethnicity, or political ideology. The constraints of such a narrow definition have been tested in recent decades by new instances of conflict that are distinct from the post-Second World War context in which the structures of global refugee protection are based – as the earlier section of this chapter demonstrates. The preponderance of forced migration within, rather than across, borders has given rise to the category of Internally Displaced Persons (IDPs), while protracted situations, the role of non-state actors, and the context of global geopolitics have meant a radical re-examination of ideas such as repatriation and non-refoulement (Loescher et al., 2008).

The UNHCR's *Guiding Principles on Internal Displacement* do explicitly include the effects of development projects and natural or human-made disasters as amongst the drivers of forced migration within borders; however, the principles remain dominated primarily by a focus on conflict (UNHCR, 2004). Increasing attention over the past half century has also been paid to the fact that forced migration is and has been caused by many factors beyond armed conflict – in some cases the drivers may be overlapping, as with so-called 'resource wars' or resistance movements against particular forms of large scale development. But whatever the reasons for dislocation the outcomes are often quite similar: homelessness, landlessness, the loss of livelihoods and connection to important cultural and/or religious spaces, and in many cases physical and mental harm. Why then does the apparatus for global refugee protection not recognize other factors in forced migration?

Some might suggest that to address all the forms of displacement in the world would be to overwhelm the current system given the sheer numbers involved and the complexities involved in determining causality. Yet this remains an unsatisfactory answer – if forced migration constitutes a violation of human rights then logistical difficulties are an insufficient reason for not pursuing adequate protections for the affected. As the previous section of this chapter demonstrated, those displaced by development are not any less worthy of protection than those affected by war and ethnic strife. A similar set of issues thus emerges when one considers environmentally induced displacement. The landscape may be irrevocably altered by a number of different environmental factors, rendering it uninhabitable – as farmlands parched by desertification or islands swallowed by rising waters attest. The populations of such regions have little to no chance of returning – yet they experience scant luck in being deemed a legitimate refugee. Perhaps more so than with development, the issue of causality becomes even more complicated and challenging in environmental displacement – who is to blame for the hazard posed to the Maldives, Tuvalu, or the deltas of Bangladesh? The nascent climate justice movement would certainly point to the overly-consumptive and waste-producing economies and lifestyles of the industrial world as a culprit and one might similarly point a finger at extractive industries and conservation initiatives for intensifying other forms of environmental displacement. However, these are all difficult to hold accountable for the impacts on a wide range of local communities.

Some critics – and certainly much of the political and public discourse – regarding environmental refugees have characterized them as little more than economic (or other) migrants who seek to use the trendy topic of climate change as a justification for making a move. While volition is often considered a key part of any definition of displacement – a coercive rather than a voluntary migration – the complicated manner in which environmental displacement occurs calls into question an easy distinction between the 'choices' made to move. Displacement due to a 'natural disaster' and its destruction of a landscape may seem straightforward, but what of those much longer-term processes (such as those engendered by certain types of climate change) that degrade an environment? How do the inhabitants of such lands – who may not be forced to flee by a cataclysmic and spectacular event, but by a slow and inexorable weakening of their socio-economic capacities – justify their need for sanctuary? How do communities who have adapted to certain forms of cyclical environmental hazard – seasonal flooding, for example – by migrating to nearby regions temporarily make the argument that their risk has grown beyond their capability to manage it due to a changing climate? The question of voluntariness in migration is seen as key in such situations as to whether nation states, international agencies, and the general public believe relief or refugee status should be accorded to the person in flight. The question of volition and coercion also reminds us that the distinctions between environmentally induced, conflict-induced, and development-induced displacement are rarely discrete; rather they describe processes (and often justifications) that overlap, reinforce, and often stimulate one another.

How are Africa and Asia in particular affected by EID? Certainly some of the most iconic areas under threat by these environmental factors lie within these continents. Bangladesh, for example, is an often paradigmatic case of the potential effects of climate change – a low-lying deltaic country prone to flooding and under constant threat from rising waters. Yet as I have argued elsewhere (Bose, 2016), the vulnerabilities of Bangladesh have as much to do with economic, social, political, and seasonal phenomena and context as they do with longer-term climate change. Similarly, while desertification and lands made increasingly inhospitable due to rising temperatures are driving populations out of traditional homes in many parts of Africa, resource extraction – as shown in the case of Congo – and conservation efforts across the continent (but especially in Sub-Saharan Africa) are equally culpable for forced migration (Massé & Lunstrum, 2016).

Conclusion

As the preceding sections of this chapter have shown, the displacement of people across the world remains one of the key challenges of the contemporary world. Forced migration is an issue that concerns economic progress and inequality, national security and development, and above all human rights and dignity. All across the world – but as this chapter has suggested in particular in a number of countries in Africa and Asia – populations are being forced out of their homes, subjected to rape, torture, and death, displaced from traditional and culturally important lands, and denied opportunities in work, education, and social advancement due to a variety of reasons. Conflict, as seen in cross-border conflicts such as in the Congo, in civil wars such as we witness today in Syria, and in cases of internal ethnic strife as in Bhutan in the 1980s and 1990s, has displaced tens of millions both within and across borders. While those made homeless through such processes are granted legitimate (if often partial or insufficient) protections and occasionally the chance to rebuild their lives in new countries, many others are denied such opportunities. In the case of those displaced by development – such as populations forcibly evicted to make room for dams or for the extraction of resources like oil – the ousted are rarely recognized. Finally, there are emerging threats related to a variety of environmental factors that are already displacing populations but have the potential to affect many millions in the future, as climate change, resource extraction, and conservation efforts continue to transform the world.

How do we address such multifaceted and complex challenges as an international community, as local residents, as citizens of the world, or as national governments? What is our collective obligation to those who have been displaced or is there one? The solution to such difficult questions lies not in categorizing some forms of forced migration as more deserving of 'solving' than others or in ranking the degree to which harm has been caused, but rather by focusing on the root causes – the various drivers of forced migration – that are creating these circumstances in the first place. As I have tried to show in this chapter, the circumstances of forced migration are all too often linked by cause, as often as by outcome. Yes, it is challenging to think how we might aid environmental or developmental refugees when we seem to be barely able to cope with refugees caused by conflict and persecution. But it is morally and ethically irresponsible to abdicate our responsibilities to those many others who have been uprooted simply because it is difficult to imagine how we might provide such protection. We must focus, therefore, on the justifications we provide and the motivations that move us to wage war, to pursue particular development strategies and projects, or conversely to abandon sustainable practices and connect these with the consequences of such action and inaction – and prominent amongst such outcomes, the forced migration of people who have not chosen to migrate.

Bibliography

Bakke, P. C. and Kuypers, J. A., 2016. 'The Syrian Civil War, International Outreach, and a Clash of Worldviews', *KB Journal*, Volume 11 (2), pp. 1–3.

Barnard, A., 2016. 'Death Toll from War in Syria now 470,000, Group Finds'. Available at: www.nytimes.com/2016/02/12/world/middleeast/death-toll-from-war-in-syria-now-470000-group-finds.html [Accessed 9 October 2016].

Baviskar, A., 2005. *In the Belly of the River: Tribal Conflicts over Development in the Narmada Valley*, Oxford: Oxford University Press.

Black, R., 2001. *Environmental Refugees: Myth or Reality?* New Issues in Refugee Research Working Paper No. 34, University of Sussex, Geneva: UNHCR Evaluation and Policy Unit.

Black, R., Adger, N., Arnell, N., Dercon, S., Geddes, A. and Thomas, D., 2011. 'The Effect of Environmental Change on Human Migration', *Global Environmental Change*, Volume 21, pp. S3–S11.

Bose, P., 2006. 'Dams, development and displacement', in P. Vandergeest, P. Idahosa and P. Bose (eds.), *Development's Displacements: Ecologies, Economies and Cultures at Risk*, Vancouver: University of British Columbia Press, pp. 316–345.

Bose, P. 2016. 'Vulnerabilities and Displacements: Adaptation and Mitigation to Climate Change as a New Development Mantra', *Area*, Volume 48 (2), pp. 168–175.

Bose, P., Lunstrum, E. and Zalik, A. 2016. 'Environmental Displacement: The Common Ground of Climate Change, Extraction and Conservation', *Area*, Volume 48 (2), pp. 130–133.

Brown, O. 2008. *Migration and Climate Change*, Geneva: International Organization for Migration.

Carpenter, T. G., 2013. 'Tangled Web: The Syrian Civil War and Its Implications', *Mediterranean Quarterly*, Volume 24 (1), pp. 1–11.

Daley, P., 2013. 'Refugees, IDPs and Citizenship Rights: The Perils of Humanitarianism in the African Great Lakes Region', *Third World Quarterly*, Volume 34 (5), pp. 893–912.

De Wet, C., 2006. *Development-Induced Displacement: Problems, Policies and People*, New York: Berghahn Books.

Dhungana, S. K., 2010. 'Third Country Resettlement and the Bhutanese Refugee Crisis: A Critical Reflection', *Refugee Watch*, Volume 35, pp. 14–36.

Evans, R., 2010. 'The Perils of Being a Borderland People: On the Lhotshampas of Bhutan', *Contemporary South Asia*, Volume 18 (1), pp. 25–42.

Hokayem, E., 2014. 'Iran, the Gulf States and the Syrian Civil War', *Adelphi Papers*, Volume 54 (447–448), pp. 39–70.

Hopkins, M. M., 2006. 'Olympic Ideal Demolished: How Forced Evictions in China Related to the 2008 Olympic Games Are Violating International Law', *Housing Journal of International Law*, Volume 29 (2006), pp. 156–189.

Hutt, M., 2005. 'The Bhutanese Refugees: Between Verification, Repatriation and Royal Realpolitik', *Peace and Democracy in South Asia*, Volume 1 (1), pp. 44–56.

Idemudia, U., 2012. 'The Resource Curse and the Decentralization of Oil Revenue: The Case of Nigeria', *Journal of Cleaner Production*, Volume 35 (2012), pp. 183–193.

IDMC, 2013. Internal Displacement Monitoring Centre: Democratic Republic of Congo: internal displacement in brief. Available at: www.internal-displacement.org/sub-saharan-africa/democratic-republic-of-the-congo/summary [Accessed 13 July 2016].

Ikelegbe, A., 2005. 'The Economy of Conflict in the Oil Rich Niger Delta Region of Nigeria', *Nordic Journal of African Studies*, Volume 14 (2), pp. 208–234.

Khagram, S., 2004. *Dams and Development: Transnational Struggles for Water and Power*, Ithaca: Cornell University Press.

Kisangani, E. F., 2012. *Civil Wars in the Democratic Republic of Congo, 1960–2010*, Boulder: Lynne Rienner Publishers.

Klingensmith, D., 2007. *One Valley and a Thousand: Dams, Nationalism, and Development*, New York: Oxford University Press.

Leckie, S., Simperingham, E. and Bakker, J. (eds.), 2012. *Climate Change and Displacement Reader*, New York: Earthscan.

Loescher, G., Betts, A. and Milner, J., 2008. *The United Nations High Commissioner for Refugees (UNHCR): The Politics and Practice of Refugee Protection into the 21st Century*, London: Routledge.

Lucas, S., Yakinthou, C. and Wolff, S., 2016. 'Syria: Laying the Foundations for a Credible and Sustainable Transition', *RUSI Journal*, Volume 161 (3), pp. 22–32.

Massé, F. and Lunstrum, E., 2016. 'Accumulation by Securitization: Commercial Poaching, Neoliberal Conservation, and the Creation of New Wildlife Frontiers', *Geoforum*, Volume 69, pp. 227–237.

McNamara, K. and Gibson, C., 2009. '"We Do Not Want to Leave Our Land": Pacific Ambassadors at the United Nations Resist the Category of "Climate Refugees"', *Geoforum*, Volume 40 (3), pp. 475–483.

Mehta, L., 2001. 'The Manufacture of Popular Perceptions of Scarcity: Dams and Water-Related Narratives in Gujarat, India', *World Development*, Volume 29 (12), pp. 2025–2041.

Myers, N., 1999. 'Environmental Refugees'. *Population and Environment: A Journal of Interdisciplinary Studies*, Volume 19 (2), pp. 609–613.

Neef, A. and Singer, J., 2015. 'Development-Induced Displacement in Asia: Conflicts, Risks and Resilience', *Development in Practice*, Volume 25 (5), pp. 601–611.

Oliver-Smith, A., 2010. *Defying Displacement: Grassroots Resistance and the Critique of Development*, Austin: University of Texas Press.

Penz, P., Drydyk, J. and Bose, P., 2011. *Displaced by Development: Ethics, Rights and Responsibilities*, Cambridge: Cambridge University Press.

Pillay, U. and Bass, O., 2008. 'Mega-Events as a Response to Poverty Reduction: The 2010 FIFA World Cup and Its Urban Development Implications', *Urban Forum*, Volume 19 (3), pp. 329–346.

Rao, U., 2016. 'Urban negotiations and small-scale gentrification in a Delhi resettlement colony', in S. Charavorty and R. Negi (eds.), *Space, Planning and Everyday Contestations in Delhi*, Delhi: Springer India, pp. 77–89.

Richmond, M., 2016. 'The urban impacts of Rio's mega-events: The view from two "unspectacular" favelas', in G. Poynter and V. Vierhoff (eds.), *Mega-Event Cities: Urban Legacies of Global Sports Events*, London: Routledge, pp. 249–260.

Rizal, D., 2004. 'The Unknown Refugee Crisis: Expulsion of the Ethnic Lhotsampa from Bhutan', *Asian Ethnicity*, Volume 5 (2), pp. 151–177.

Satiroglu, I. and Choi, N. (eds.) 2015. *Development-Induced Displacement and Resettlement: New Perspectives on Persisting Problems*, New York: Routledge.

Spagat, M., Mack, A., Cooper, T. and Kreutz, J. 2009. 'Estimating War Deaths: An Arena of Contestation', *Journal of Conflict Resolution*, Volume 53 (6), pp. 934–950.

Stavropoulou, M., 2008. 'Drowned in Definitions', *Forced Migration Review*, Volume 31, pp. 11–12.

Terminski, B., 2013. 'Development-Induced Displacement and Resettlement: Theoretical Frameworks and Current Challenges', *Development*, Volume 10, p. 101.

Times of India, 2016. 'We will complete Narmada dam by December 2016'. Available at: http://timesofindia.indiatimes.com/city/ahmedabad/We-will-complete-Narmada-dam-by-December-2016-Gujarat-CM/articleshow/52383109.cms [Accessed 9 October 2016].

Ukiwo, U., 2007. 'From "Pirates" to "Militants": A Historical Perspective on Anti-State and Anti-Oil Company Mobilization Among the Ijaw of Warri, Western Niger Delta', *African Affairs*, Volume 106 (425), pp. 587–610.

UNFPA, 2016. United Nations Population Fund—Migration. Available at: http://www.unfpa.org/migration [Accessed 13 July 2016].

UNHCR, 2004. *Guiding Principles on Internal Displacement*, New York: United Nations.

UNHCR, 2012. 'Climate change, natural disasters and human displacement: A UNHCR Perspective,' in S. Leckie, E. Simperingham and J. Bakker (eds.), *Climate Change and Displacement Reader*, 149. New York: Earthscan.

UNHCR. 2016a. United Nations High Commissioner for Refugees – Global Trends 2015. Available at: www.unhcr.org/en-us/statistics/unhcrstats/576408cd7/unhcr-global-trends-2015.html [Accessed 13 July 2016].

UNHCR. 2016b. Syria Emergency. Available at: www.unhcr.org/en-us/syria-emergency.html [Accessed 9 October 2016].

Vandergeest, P., Idahosa, P. and Bose, P., 2006. *Development's Displacements: Ecologies, Economies and Cultures at Risk*, Vancouver: University of British Columbia Press.

Warner, K., 2010. 'Global Environmental Change and Migration: Governance Challenges', *Global Environmental Change*, Volume 20 (3), pp. 402–413.

White, G., 2011. *Climate Change and Migration*, Oxford: Oxford University Press.

Zoomers, A., 2010. 'Globalisation and the Foreignisation of Space: Seven Processes Driving the Current Global Land Grab', *Journal of Peasant Studies*, Volume 37 (2), pp. 429–447.

CONCLUSION

Pedro Miguel Amakasu Raposo de Medeiros Carvalho

While returning to the theme concerning an Afro-Asian worldview and of research perceptions, this conclusion also highlights some of the most important claims on the subject based on the contributing authors' findings. Overall, the Handbook reveals that a geopolitical reconceptualization of knowledge production is in fact occurring. This manifests in terms of the following dimensions: political, security, economic, development, environment, cultural, religious, societal, intellectual and academic interconnectedness between Africa and Asia. However, there are challenges that certainly can hinder the production of a common Afro-Asia worldview. According to Ali A. Mazrui (2013: xii), some of these challenges (religious, technological, economic and empire/political) are not new as they were at work in Africa long before the trans-Atlantic slave trade. The difference is that today these challenges, or forces as he calls them, are major engines of globalization and they are not weakening, they are just changing "hands", from the West to the East in the reverse direction of Orientalism as Africa and Asia have been seeking to penetrate Western institutions to exert counterinfluence (ibid.: xxi). The problem as Mazrui points out is that though China and India are contributing towards further globalization in Africa, they also help to stem the tide of Westernization and Eurocentrism in African societies (ibid.). It seems that globalization is not contributing to balance African and Asian aspirations of a shared worldview.

Having said that, this, the Handbook asked the extent to which the growth of this interconnectedness in the above dimensions is symmetrical or asymmetrical as there is a *de facto* imbalance in the knowledge agenda between the two continents in favor of Asia. According to Peycam (2016: 48), this imbalance is characterized by an overdependence on macro rather than micro forms of knowledge with an overreliance on colonial and post-independence Western categories. Hence, the previous chapters attempted to minimize this overdependence in Afro–Asian studies beginning in the pre-modern period through to modern and contemporary times. In the first period, Oloruntuba and Ndlovu-Gatsheni found (see Chapter 1) that Africa–Asia *interactions have been ignored in diaspora studies*, in part because as they say "it seems the future world is a Sino-centric one in which increased interactions between Africa and Asia is assuming a new and high level of importance". They suggest that a new avenue of research seems to be a "de-westernization that has a potential of contributing immensely to the re-crystallization of Africa–Asia relations and consolidation of Afro-Asian Diasporas hold for the future of Afro-Asian relations." Thus, the crisis of African and Asian studies suffers from its postcolonial condition that is its lack of recognition

Conclusion

and understanding of the other as the West still looks at Africa (and Asia as well) in terms of a one-way North–South relationship of domination and power-over (Abrahamsen, 2003: 207). However, the opposite also occurs. As Kwame Nimako (see Chapter 3) pointed out "the re-orientation of the world economy to the Orient is not a result of any innate quality of Asians; rather it is challenging the false Eurocentric historical narrative that has been forced through as a result of European colonial enterprise." In other words, it seems South–North interactions are not a product of a real concern for mutual understanding, rather as Abrahamsen (2003: 195) notes the "post" in postcolonial studies should not be understood as a temporal end here, "post", but rather as an indication of continuity. In fact, the pattern of continuity is present throughout time in Africa–Asia relations. Patterns of racial, ethnic and religious discrimination in the Indian Ocean still prevail as a result of centuries of forced migration and economic exploitation as Daniel Domingues da Silva found (see Chapter 2; and also Pedro A. R. Carvalho, Chapter 27). However, overall "East African Asian communities have helped to bolster the presence of Muslim communities in public discourse even in a hostile political environment where Islam is increasingly equated with extremism" (see Iqbal S. Akhtar, Chapter 4).

Part II of this volume also identified "continuities and changes" in the modern interactions between Africa and Asia. As Peycam (2016: 48) notes it "seems to only exist as a research-field for its contemporary relevance, primarily in geopolitical and economic terms, with often little reference or knowledge of their deeper historical, cultural or even religious significance." In this context, Jörg Haustein and Emma Tomalin (see Chapter 5) observed that the "emergence of the 'development'/'underdevelopment' rhetoric after the Second World War is a continuation of the colonial vision of the world." Accordingly, the authors found that given the low knowledge production linking religion and development studies, the relationship with ideas about religion still needs to be deconstructed, for example through researching the benefits or dangers of religion in fostering development (ibid.). In a similar vein, Mayke Kaag (see Chapter 16) also found "how religious humanitarianism has increasingly entered into difficulties, especially after 9/11, because of accusations of contributing to Islamic extremism and the funding of terrorism." Jeffrey Haynes (see Chapter 24) reached a similar conclusion in terms of the ambivalent association of religion with both security and insecurity issues. Accordingly, religious actors can be both a source of conflict and a tool for conflict resolution and peace-building on the one hand, but they can also be manipulated by political leaders in pursuit of their own ambitions to rule and dominate local communities. The implications of the use of religion for political power and wealth prevent those countries from producing knowledge as religion has the capacity to bring nations together against joblessness, pain and starvation or to disunite them in the name of the same religion whether Islamic or Christian (Falola, 2013: 331).

On the diplomatic and political front, Kweku Ampiah (see Chapter 7) explained why Japan's past (*Datsu-A ron* or the departure from Asia during the Meiji Restoration in terms of de-Asianization to catch up with the West) still hinders its relations with Asia. It also affects (though less) its relations with Africa too, despite the launch in 1993 of the Tokyo International Conference on African Development (TICAD), which has "constructively contributed to the discourse about Africa's economic development by endeavouring to find ways to deal with some of the region's structural economic problems" (see Chapter 7). One can even say that with TICAD, Japan's African policy has gone through a *process of Africanization* because it has recognized African knowledge in terms of ownership and partnership to make whatever reforms are needed based on their visions, values and individual socio-economic background (Carvalho, 2016: 9). Therefore, in the aftermath of the Cold War, Japan has inaugurated a new development discourse between Asia and Africa, and without realizing, it also created some *tensions* (see Annette S. Hansen, Chapter 22) as other southern countries followed it and launched their development partnerships (Carmen A. Mendes, Chapter 21). According to Annette S. Hansen (see Chapter 22), these *tensions between the global South constitute the driving force in Africa—Asia regional partnerships and South—South development cooperation*. Ultimately, these tensions might compromise an Afro-Asian homogeneous view of the world. According to Christopher J. Lee (see Chapter 6), although the Bandung Conference in 1955 initiated a new kind of Afro-Asia diplomacy *essential to postcolonial nationalisms in* both continents, the fact is that the political and ideological divisions within the "Third World" *must be understood as more limited and complex than public diplomatic rhetoric might suggest*. As Sanjukta B. Bhattacharya's chapter (in this volume) makes clear, although "today's world is a different one from the 1970s to the 1990s, the very factors that created the tensions in the above decades also created areas of convergence among developing countries." However, as Part III of this volume shows, several challenges persist, for instance in the field of human rights as their disregard, in the case of BRICS, "is in fact part and parcel of their rise (and thus intrinsic to their relationships) with Africa," particularly in the case of China (see Ian Taylor, Chapter 19). Other challenges that prevent South—South production of knowledge arise in education in terms of gender equity or lack thereof, as the prevalent inequality in schools and African universities goes beyond the institutional level and extends to politics both at national and international level (Aina, 2010: 29, 35). Accordingly Aina (2010) notes that although gender equity is recognized in international forums, she doubts the politics of neoliberal reforms, as the material interests of Bretton Woods institutions have not been in confluence with African interests, as Emefa Juliet Takyi-Amoako (see Chapter 18, this volume) also sees. Thus, the problems are just too many to be discussed in one chapter as Takyi-Amoako found out, thus needing further research. However, Takyi-Amoako called our attention to the problem that the achievement of gender equality in education remains a challenge for social justice at the confluence. Paradoxically, another obstacle to knowledge production in terms of building a common policy view of the world between Africa and Asia relates to China's economic, development and trade expansion into Africa which helped to fuel trade with commodity exporters (see Alicia Garcia-Herrero and Carlos Casanova, Chapter 11). The problem is that Africa's dependence on commodity (mineral) exports to China (ibid.) and to the rest of the world is increasing instead of decreasing, which ultimately undermines its sustainable development (UNCTAD, 2015: 15). In addition, China's influence in Africa is also political, offsetting and isolating Taiwan from previous privileged partners, such as South Africa (see Yejoo Kim and Ross Anthony, Chapter 13). This has raised concerns of neocolonialism because of its linkage with exploitative capitalism and human rights violations as a driving force of "blind" economic growth (see Ian Taylor, Chapter 19). The question is whether China is different from Japan, Malaysia or any other Western country with similar commercial objectives in exports and strategic value (natural resources) for imports (Akyeampong & Xu, 2015: 778; Carvalho, 2015: 21). It seems it is not. This is also the conclusion of Chun Zhang (see Chapter 20), and Thomas Feldhoff as well (see Chapter 28). While Zhang defends the China—Africa relationship as one of symmetrical interdependence based on what China buys and Africa sells, he also found that it needs four different pillars (political, economic, peace and security, and socio-cultural) to understand China—Africa relations in its totality, otherwise it will always be a biased perspective. As Feldhoff mentioned, if it were not for Asia's interest in trade and investment and Africa's mineral resources the continent would not be as integrated in the global economy; however, it also created new dependencies. Regardless of one's perspective on the advantages and disadvantages of China's policy for Africa economic growth and development, strong regional cooperation with Africa as well as with international partners through Free Trade Agreements (FTA) is advanced as one of the many solutions to strengthen Africa's voice and position as a response to the reorganization of global trade through Global Value Chains (GVC) (see Feldhoff, Chapter 28; Bach 2016: 126–27).

Conclusion

In this context, it is important to mention that although African countries are benefiting from Chinese investment flows that in 2015 reached \$2.98 billion compared with \$2.1 in 2010 (see Zhang, Chapter 20), beyond official development assistance to cover South–South development cooperation, the biggest Asian investor in Africa is not China but Malaysia (see Evelyn S. Devadason and VGR Chandran Govindaraju, Chapter 12). Africa–Asia relations do not end in China; on the contrary. According to Devadason and Govindaraju, Malaysia is an example of sectoral and geographical diversification in the continent, reflecting the growing interest of the private sector to explore markets beyond ASEAN.

In the contemporary period (Part III of this volume) Africa and Asia interactions present many forms, such as South–South cooperation (SSC), South–South development cooperation, South–South labour migrations – now seen as new diasporas, but as seen in this Handbook, they are not entirely "new" types of cooperation relations, but have adjusted themselves to the post-Cold War challenges. Thus, aside from traditional donors, among which the European Union stands out as the biggest player in global development, Laura C. Ferreira-Pereira and Alena Vieira (see Chapter 26) have demonstrated that the EU has developed an ability to advance a political and security agenda beyond the aid and trade role with Africa, Caribbean and Pacific (ACP). Nevertheless, the authors noted that *EU–Africa and EU–Asia security relations call for further academic research that should further unravel, substantiate and appraise the extent to which and the ways in which a more assertive EU security role in Africa is leveraging more visible, active and stronger EU–Asia security interactions* (ibid.). Although economic relations between Africa and its old partners like the EU remain substantial (Stegmann & Cheru 2014: 399), new alliances through multilateral arrangements have emerged, such as the G20 as Shalini Chawla found (see Chapter 23). Accordingly, the G20 offers options for growth and development through the above modalities of SSC, or similar, i.e. North–South cooperation and North–North cooperation. Yet, these kinds of strategic cooperation or multilateral arrangements have risks associated. As many authors advanced in this Handbook, political, economic, development, religious, social and capitalist relations add tensions and issues to Africa–Asian interconnections given the diversity and complexity of human relations. Understanding the constraints for a common worldview between Africa and Asia is a research necessity. Although in this late period Africa and Asia relations have been fruitful, serious demographic challenges, land-grabbing, harsh climate variations, terrorism activity, migration and refugee crises persist. The causes are just too many to enumerate here, but range from weak economic institutions and lack of good governance to heavy dependence on natural resources, deprived human capital, and persistence of conflict that did not end with decolonization. On the contrary, as Pablo Shiladitya Bose (see Chapter 29) found, the displacement of people as a product of conflicts across the world remains one of the key challenges due to the economic and development inequality, political and security instability, but also human rights violations.

As pointed out here, part of the solution requires the renewing of the "Bandung Spirit" which started with the first Asian–African Sub-Regional Organizations Conference (AASROC) in 2003 in Bandung, Indonesia, followed by the 2nd AASROC in Durban, South Africa, in 2004 (Bandungspirit.org). However, as Seifudein Adem and Darryl Thomas (see Chapter 10) have shown, in practical terms it needs a friendly relationship between China and Japan rather than an unfriendly cooperative relationship. Hyo-sook Kim (see Chapter 8 in this volume) also recognizes the need for a variety of research approaches from several policy areas to diminish competition between Asian (including South Korea) countries in Africa. In other words, political and societal actions are needed to contribute effectively to the "Spirit of Bandung" based on the values of solidarity and mutual respect between humans in harmony with nature (Bandungspirit.org). Here, the activities of non-government organizations (NGOs), e.g. capacity building, advocacy and service delivery, have been extremely important to African empowerment as they do what governments are not able or willing to do (Elbers & Gunning, 2015: 639). In addition, as David M. Potter (see Chapter 17) found, they also have the potential to foster institutional linkages between African and Asian civil society organizations. The problem, according to Potter, is that much of this kind of interaction has not been systematically documented and analyzed (ibid.). One thing is certain: Western civilization no longer is accepted as the sole pole of knowledge. Yoichi Mine (see Chapter 15) suggests a different route to the Africa–Asia production of knowledge in terms of countering Westernization of Africa and Asian societies. Accordingly, "the key to an Afrasian revival is to realize political stability in the joint point of Afrasia, the Middle East and North Africa" (ibid.). Yet, the construction of an Africa–Asia worldview, as this Handbook foresees, faces considerable challenges, which need to be solved all together rather than separately. This is also the opinion of Larry Swatuk (see Chapter 25) who among other things found that the land–water–food–energy nexus *is not a Chinese nor an Asian problem but is more a structural problem facing rural communities everywhere*. According to him, African small-scale farmers are underproducing and so they need to bring in commercial agriculture with its knowledge of markets, mechanization and economies of scale (Swatuk, Chapter 25). As for the land grabbing, rather than regulating it Swatuk suggests an alternative program for agricultural investment, which he thinks would be a much better solution. Ultimately, he doubts the willingness of African states to improve smallholder agriculture beyond its 1 tonne/ha/yr average. Water and energy problems suffer from similar problems; paradoxically, this unwillingness of African governments fits the interests of Asian investors in relation to Africa's green and blue water scramble for construction, e.g. dams, canals or pipelines (ibid.). In sum, as seen throughout this volume, an Afro-Asian view of the world in terms of knowledge production depends on Africans' ability to solve their own problems that are political, economic, religious, societal, educational, developmental and environmental. Finally, as Takuo Iwata suggested (see Chapter 14), if Asia also keeps developing economic, political, social, cultural and academic networking with Africa as it has been doing in recent years, without any "*nostalgia of egalitarian Third World solidarity, but in a more realistic framework of global competition,*" the Africa–Asia/Asia–Africa network formation already created and under construction within the Bandung Spirit Network, for instance the Asia–Africa–Latin America (ASAFLA) (Bandungspirit.org), and in the same spirit the Association for Asian Studies (A-ASIA) in Africa, the Africa–Asia worldview will broaden and strengthen, with the production of knowledge being the natural result.

Bibliography

Abrahamsen, R., 2003. 'African Studies and the Postcolonial Challenge', *African Affairs*, Volume 102, pp. 189–210.

Aina, T. A., 2010. 'Beyond Reforms: The Politics of Higher Education Transformation in Africa', *African Studies Review*, Volume 53 (1), p. 40.

Akyeampong, E. and Xu, L., 2015. 'The Three Phases/Faces of China in Independent Africa: Reconceptualizing China–Africa Engagement', in C. Monga and J. Y. Lin (eds.), *The Oxford Handbook of Africa and Economics*, Volume 2, *Policies and Practices*, Oxford: Oxford University Press, pp. 762–779.

Bandungspirit.org., 2017. [online] Available at: http://www.bandungspirit.org/spip.php?rubrique44 (Accessed 16 February 2017).

Bach, D., 2016. *Regionalism in Africa: Genealogies, Institutions and Trans-State Networks*, London and New York: Routledge.

Carvalho, P.M.A.R.M., 2015. 'China's and Japan's Foreign Aid Policies vis-à-vis Lusophone Africa', *Africa Spectrum*, Volume 50 (3), pp. 49–79.

Carvalho, P.M.A.R.M., 2016. 'The Evolution of Japan's Role in "Lusophone" Africa: From Inertia to Action', *South African Journal of International Affairs*, Volume 23 (3), pp. 257–277.

Conclusion

Elbers, C. and Gunning, J. W., 2015. 'What do Development NGOs Achieve?', in C. Monga and J. Y. Lin (eds.), *The Oxford Handbook of Africa and Economics*, Volume 2, *Policies and Practices*, Oxford: Oxford University Press, pp. 629–640.

Falola, T., 2013. *The African Diaspora: Slavery, Modernity, and Globalization*, New York: University of Rochester Press.

Mazrui, A. A., 2013. 'Introduction: Toward Afro-Asian Strategies for Containing Globalization', in A. A. Mazrui and S. Adem (eds.), *AFRASIA: A Tale of Two Continents*, New York: University Press of America, pp. xi–xxv.

Peycam, P., 2016. 'Towards an Autonomous Academic Africa–Asia Framework', International Institute for Asian Studies (IIAS), *The Newsletter Encouraging Knowledge and Enhancing the Study of Asia*, Volume 73 (Spring), p. 48 [online] Available at: http://www.iias.asia/sites/default/files/IIAS_NL73_FULL.pdf [Accessed 6 August 2017].

Stegmann, G. and Cheru, F., 2014. 'Repositioning Africa in the World', in T. Ahlers, H. Kato, H. S. Kholi, C. Madavo, and A. Sood (eds.), *Africa 2050: Realizing the Continent's Full Potential*, Oxford: Oxford University Press, pp. 399–425.

UNCTAD, 2015. *State of Commodity Dependence 2014*, New York and Geneva: United Nations [online] Available at: http://unctad.org/en/PublicationsLibrary/suc2014d7_en.pdf [Accessed 6 August 2017].

INDEX

9/11 attacks 254–5, 353, 357, 374

Acharya, Amitav 233
Aden 37
Afghanistan 143, 157, 238, 375, 383, 434
"Afrasia" (word origin) 239–41
'Africa Mining Vision' 440
Africa–Asia Development University Network
   (AADUN) 227
Africa–Europe Group for Interdisciplinary Studies
   (AEGIS) 225, 226, 228, 230
Africa–India Framework for Enhanced
   Cooperation 324, 329
Africa's Asian Options (AFRASO) project 227, 231
African Affairs (journal) 140
African Development Bank (AfDB) 340, 445
African diaspora 26–8, 29–30
African Mining Partnership (AMP) 448
African Muslims Agency 250
African National Congress (ANC) 145, 206
African studies 223–9
African Studies Association of India 222
African Union (AU) 55, 57, 140, 243, 315, 340
Afro-Asian 1–4, 9–10
Afro-Asian Peoples' Solidarity Organization 103, 146
Afrobarometer 317
Aga Khan 63
Aga Khan Development Network 268
agency as social and political action 10, 16, 55, 95,
   97–8, 104, 240, 242, 280, 341–402
agriculture 392–5
Ahmadiyya movement 64–5, 69, 252, 256, 257
al-Bashir, Omar Hassan 379
al-Numeri, Ja'far 85, 378–9
al-Qaeda 254, 376, 460
al-Samman 249
Alagappa, Muthiah 261

Alexander, Titus 354
Algeria 146, 157, 173
Algerian War of Independence 100, 157
Allan, Tony 393
Allman, Jean 97
Ambedkar, B. R. 100
Amnesty International 299
Anderson, Benedict 96
Anglo-Chinese Wars (Opium Wars) 50, 428
Angola 126, 147, 148, 173, 177, 322, 324, 326,
   327, 397
Ansei treaties 116
antislavery movement 78
Apartheid system 51, 55, 119
Arab League 102
Arndt, H.W. 246
Arrighi, Giovanni 241
ASEAN (Association of the Southeast Asian
   Nations) 192, 243
Ashanti kingdom 116
Ashton, Catherine 416
Asian diaspora 28–30; *see also* South Asian Muslims
Asian financial crisis (1997) 190, 204, 433
Asian People's Conference (1947, New Delhi) 55
Asian–African Conference (1955): *see* Bandung
   Conference
Asian–African Conference (2005, Jakarta) 344
Asian–African Legal Consultative
   Organization 146
Asian studies 1, 7–11, 22, 124, 140–1, 216, 225–8,
   275, 321, 472, 476
Atlantic Charter 94
Atlantic slave trade 39, 47, 427–8

Babu, Mohamed Abdulrahman 100
Balochi Muslims 62
Ban Ki-Moon 356, 357

Index

Bandung Asian–African Conference (1955) 5, 101, 102–3, 144, 156–8, 239
Bangladesh 53, 83, 143, 262, 266
Bangladesh Rural Advancement Committee 268
Bantu people 426
Barcelona Process (Euro-Mediterranean Partnership) 407, 418
Barre, Siad 85
Battle of Dien Bien Phu 54, 157
'Beijing Consensus' 302, 441
Beijing Foreign Studies Institute 220
Belgrade Conference of Non-Aligned States (1961) 103
Ben Bella, Ahmed 101
Berlin Conference (1884–5) 51, 156–7, 433, 434
Bhutan 458–9
Biko, Steve 240
Bohra Muslims 63–4, 65, 70
borders 51, 149, 342, 424, 426, 432, 434, 457, 461–2, 467
Boserup, Ester 243
Bratton, Michael 264
Brazil 38, 304, 324, 326, 337, 416; *see also* BRICS countries
Brexit 317
BRICS countries 30, 154, 294–5, 297–305
Brooks, Jonathan 394
Brown vs. Board of Education of Topeka 157
Buddhadasa, Sarath 339
Burkina Faso 170, 202, 212
Burma 430, 431
Burton, Antoinette 141
Bush, George W. 86
Bush, Roderick 155
Busia, K.A. 56
Buxton, Thomas Fowell 78
Buzan, Barry 233
Byung-se Yun 133

Calicut 35
Cameroon 126, 339, 450
Cape Verde 322, 324, 325
Carmody, Pádraig 298
Césaire, Aimé 99, 100, 239
Chad 251–2, 252
Chang Yongkyu 223
Charter Act (Britain 1813) 79
Chilembwe, John 99
China 50, 53, 55, 120–2, 146–7, 158–60, 168–83, 219–21, 301–3, 307–19, 357–9, 438–9; *see also* BRICS countries, People's Republic of China, Taiwan
China–Africa relations 307–19
Christian missions 77–80
Chun Doo-hwan 132
citizenship 47
CIVICUS Global Civil Society Index 264

civil society 6, 11, 209, 219, 259
civil society organizations (CSOs) 265
Clemenceau, Georges 117
Clinton, Bill 355
Clinton, Hillary 362, 416
Cochinchina 431
Cogswell, Elizabeth 263
Cold War 154–6
Colombo Conference (1954) 144
Columbus, Christopher 2, 34, 39, 48, 425
colonialism 341, 343, 348, 361
Community of Portuguese-Speaking Countries (CPLP) 324
Confucian institutes 220
Congo 51, 148; *see also* Democratic Republic of Congo, Republic of Congo
Congress of Vienna 50, 426
connections 1, 5, 11, 33, 39, 62, 67, 104, 136, 155, 185–6, 188–90, 250, 275, 297, 322, 325, 337, 347, 376, 425, 427, 430, 446, 452, 475; Muslim connections 250–1
coolie system: *see* indentured laborer
Cooper, Frederick 98
Cotonou Partnership Agreement 411
Crowther, Samuel Ajayi 78
Cultural Revolution 220, 221

da Cunha, Tristão 36
da Gama, Vasco 35, 48, 429
da Silva, Lula 416
Damas, Léon-Gontran 99
dams 396–8, 464
Danforth, John 379
Darfur crisis (2004) 312
Dark Princess (W.E.B. Du Bois) 4
Datsu-a-ron movement 113–15, 122
Davidson, Basil 218
de Albuquerque, Afonso 36, 429
de Albuquerque, Francisco 36
de Almeida, Francisco 36
de Mabior, John Garang 379, 380
Declaration of Human and Civic Rights of France 295
defensive imperialism 53
Democratic Republic of Congo (DRC) 126, 170, 177, 178, 407, 459–60
Deng Xiaoping 159, 170
Deobandi movement 80–1
Desai, Radhika 301
development-induced displacement (DID) 462–65
development model 134–5, 303, 317, 447
Diamond, Jared 241
Diange, Blaise 118
Dias, Bartolomeu 34
diaspora studies 23–6; *see also* African diaspora, Asian diaspora

479

Index

Du Bois, W.E.B. 4, 118, 155, 239
Duara, Prasenjit 98
'Dutch Disease' 173, 441

East Africa 69
East India Company (British) 49, 79–80
East India Company (Netherlands) 37, 429
Edwards, Michael 260
environmentally induced displacement 466–8
Estado da Índia 36, 38
Ethiopia 116, 126, 128, 129–30, 133, 159, 391
Euro-Mediterranean Partnership: see Barcelona
    Process
Eurocentrism 1–3, 239, 472
European Development Fund 408
European Common Foreign and Security Policy
    (CFSP) 406, 407, 408, 411, 414, 415, 417
European Common Security and Defence Policy
    (CSDP) 407–8, 409, 412, 413, 414, 415, 417
European Union (EU) 406–18
Ezulwini Consensus 324, 329

failed states 375–6, 383
faith-based organizations (FBOs) 76, 85–8
Fanon, Frantz 98, 99–100
Federation of Indian Chambers of Commerce and
    Industry (FICCI) 362
female–male ratio (FMR) 243
food security 390–92
forced migration 42, 424–5, 429, 431, 457–62,
    466–9
foreign direct investment (FDI) 443–5
Forum on China–Africa Cooperation (FOCAC)
    120, 121, 268, 283, 314–5, 323, 359
Foucault, Michel 112, 115
Frank, Andre Gunder 241
French Revolution 47
Fukuyama, Francis 203
Fukuzawa, Yukichi 114, 115, 122
fundamentalism 375
Furnivall, J.S. 243
Furuya, Komahei 117

G7/G8 354–6
G15 189
G20 355–6, 364–6
G77 145, 339–40
Gambia 212, 311
Gandhi, Indira 382
Gandhi, Mohandas K. (Mahatma) 81, 98, 100,
    221, 245
Gandhi, Rajiv 148
Garten, Jeffery E. 355
Garvey, Marcus 239
Geertz, Clifford 244
gender 273–86
Ghana 54–5, 56–7, 65, 128, 132, 133, 148, 339

Geiger, Susan 98
Gellner, Ernest 96
geopolitics 2, 4–5, 78, 118, 183, 201, 324, 359, 411,
    425, 435, 440–1, 446
geopolitical reconceptualization 16, 472–73
Global South 84, 87, 153–4, 157, 163, 188, 202,
    206, 267, 273, 275–7, 280, 294, 301, 318, 399,
    402, 440
globalization 4, 6–7, 11, 14, 61, 187–8, 219, 259,
    264, 317, 338, 357, 386, 426, 463, 472
Goa 36–7, 41
'Going Global' policy (China) 308, 317
Goldman Sachs 301
Gramsci, Antonio 98
Grand Canal (China) 396
Guha, Ranajit 98, 104
Guinea-Bissau 128, 322, 324, 325, 401
Gülen movement 256

Hankuk University of Foreign Studies 222, 224
Hindu reform movements 81
Hirschman, A.O. 242
Ho Chi Minh 98
Hobsbawm, Eric 96
Hu Jintao 312
human rights 294–6, 299–305
Human Rights Watch 299
Human Security Report Project 383
Hyderabad 41

Ijaw people 465
Iqbal, Muhammad 100
indentured/contact labor 3, 28, 51, 62, 429–31
Index of Philanthropic Freedom 260
India 53, 79–80, 148–50, 221–2, 262, 340, 359–61,
    464; see also BRICS countries
India–Africa Forum Summit (IAFS) 283, 323, 361
Indian Council for Africa 141
Indian rebellion (1857) (Indian Mutiny) 79, 430
Indian Ocean 2–3, 22, 33–42, 430, 473
Indian Ocean slave trade 27, 34, 39–40
Indian Technical and Economic Cooperation
    programme 148
Indo-China 50
Indonesia 56, 50, 53, 345
Industrial Revolution 2, 4, 11, 241, 428–9
internally displaced persons (IDPs) 425, 457, 463,
    467–8
International Institute for Asian Studies (IIAS) 227
International Islamic Relief Organisation (IIRO)
    250, 251
International Monetary Fund 56, 85, 354, 435
international relations theory 7, 233
Iran–Iraq war (1980–90) 143
Iraq 27, 337, 353, 375, 383
Isaacman, Allen 97
Islamic reform movements 80–1

Index

Islamic relief 249–56
'Islamic State' 460

Jackson, Randle 49
James, C.L.R. 239
Jammeh, Yahya 212
Japan 9, 40, 112–24, 159, 217–19, 265–6, 326, 340, 390
Japan Association for African Studies (JAAS) 217, 218, 219, 225, 229
Japan Bank for International Cooperation (JBIC) 120, 397, 398
Japan International Cooperation Agency (JICA) 119, 187, 323
Japan Monkey Center 217
jihadi transnational groups 383–4
Journal of Asian and African Studies 140

Kacchi Muslims 63
Kagame, Paul 135
Kanbur, Ravi 343
Katsumi, Hirano 120
Kedourie, Elie 96
Keegan, John 387
Kenya 23, 29, 62, 65, 67, 69, 70, 126, 132, 133, 147, 148, 159, 173, 189
Khoja Muslims 63–4, 65
knowledge 1–2, 4, 8–10, 14, 16, 23, 26, 53, 66, 68, 79, 120, 135, 141, 155, 208, 220, 223, 225, 237, 245, 253, 276, 280, 281, 283, 286, 339, 347, 361, 374, 376, 391, 403, 408, 450, 452, 472–73
Konkani Muslims 62
Korea 53; *see also* South Korea
Korea–Africa Forum (KAF) 126, 222, 268
Korean International Cooperation Agency (KOICA) 129, 133, 135, 323
Korean War 128–30, 157
Kragelund, Peter 335

Lagos Plan of Action (1980) 142
Lambie, Thomas 79
'lame leviathans' 399
League against Imperialism and Colonialism 143
League of Nations 94, 117, 118
Lederach, John Paul 376
Leopold II (Belgian king) 50–1
Lewis, W. Arthur 83, 239
Li Dazhao 238
Livingstone, David 79
Lomé Convention 410, 418
Louisiana sale 50
Lumumba, Patrice 98
Lusophone Africa 321–29

Maastricht Treaty 418
Macau 36, 41
Macau Forum 324

Macmillan, Harold 56, 157–8
Malaysia 52, 185–99, 263
Malcolm X 156
Malthusian assumption 234
Mandela, Nelson 98, 203, 205, 206–7
Mann, Gregory 264
Mao Zedong 53
Marx, Karl 297
Matsuoka, Yosuke 118
Mauritius 29, 193
Mazrui, Ali 164, 472
Mbeki, Thabo 203
Meiji Restoration 112, 122, 203, 265
Meman Muslims 63, 65
Menon, V. K. Krishna 103
Mentan, Tetah 294
Merchant of Venice 67
migration 424–35; *see also* refugees
military coups 56
Millennium Development Goals (MDGs) 273, 274, 283, 352, 356, 357, 439
Mobutu, Seko 170
Mogherini, Federica 419
Mozambique 126, 148, 322, 325, 326, 327, 339
Mudimbe, V.Y. 97
Muslim Brotherhood 84, 378
Mw Makumbe, John 262

Namibia 145, 389
Napoleon 50
Narmada dam project 464
Nasser, Gamal Abdel 101, 103
Nation of Islam 156
National Islamic Front (NIF) (Sudan) 378
nationalism 94–104
natural resources 439–52
Négritude 99
Nehru, Jawaharlal 100, 101, 103, 143, 148, 221
neo-colonialism 7, 15, 56–7, 446–7
Netherlands East Indies 431
New African Initiative (NAI) 340–2
New Asian–African Strategic Partnership (NAASP) 150, 160, 190, 335, 339, 343–8
New Development Bank (NDB) 298
New International Economic Order (NIEO) 145–6
New Partnership for African Development (NEPAD) 335, 342–3, 346, 411, 450–1
Niger 391, 397
Niger Delta Development Commission 465
Niger Expedition (1841) 78
Nigeria 88, 126, 132, 133, 149, 159, 173, 189, 464
Nkrumah, Kwame 54, 55, 56, 57, 98, 103, 239
Noguchi, Hideyo 218
Non-Alignment Movement (NAM) 5, 55, 56, 102, 103–4, 144–5

Index

non-governmental organisations (NGOs) 85, 88, 259–69
nongovernmentality 264
North Korea 130–1
Nuba people 379
Nyerere, Julius 56, 67, 87, 103, 145, 147, 188, 239–40, 246

O'Neill, Jim 300, 301
official development assistance (ODA) 127, 159, 267, 274, 336–7, 349, 475
Ogoni people 465
Okakura, Kakuzo 238
Okuro, Ong'wen 391–2
One China policy 202–12
Opium Wars: *see* Anglo-Chinese Wars
Organization of African States (OAS) 340
Organisation of African Unity (OAU) 55, 56, 57, 102, 140, 339
Organization of Arab Oil Exporting Countries 145
Organization of Petroleum Exporting States (OPEC) 146
Orientalism (Edward Said) 4, 8, 472
Ottomans 37

Padmore, George 239
Pakistan 53, 62, 65, 69, 83, 143, 149, 262, 383
Pan-African Conference (1900, London) 4, 52, 239
Pan-African Conference (1919, Paris) 117, 118, 239
Pan-African Conference (1945, Manchester) 54
Pan-Asianism 5, 234, 238–40
Pardo, Francisco Fontan 417
Parsons, Talcott 84
Peace of Westphalia 47, 48–9
Pedersen, Jørgen Dige 337
People's Republic of China (PRC) 53, 101, 103, 202
Petersberg tasks 412, 419
Petersen, Juul 252
Petronas 192, 193
Philip II, King of Spain 37
Pomeranz, Kenneth 241
population growth 235–7
Portugal 34–8, 40–1
'Publish What You Pay' movement 449
Punjabi Muslims 63–4

Quakers (Christian sect) 376
Quan, H.L.T. 154–5

Radcliffe-Brown, A.R. 243
Ranger, Terence 97
Red Crescent 251
refugees 434, 457–69

regional integration 228, 338, 342, 414–15, 433
Reid, Anthony 260
'religions of the book' 375
Renan, Ernest 95
Republic of Congo 173, 177
research 216–27
Robinson, Cedric J. 154
Rostow, W.W. 83–4
Roy, M.N. 100
Russel, J.W. 57
Russia 304, 354, 416; *see also* BRICS countries
Russo-Japanese war (1905) 4, 116
Rwanda 126, 135, 459

Sadat, Anwar el 139
Salamon, Lester 259
Salvadori, Cynthia 61
Sao Tome and Principe 170, 202, 212, 322, 324, 325
Satgar, Vishwas 298
Scalapino, Robert 143, 147
Schumacher, E.F. 245
Schuman Declaration 408, 419
Schweitzer, Albert 79
Scott, James 98
'Scramble for Africa' 79, 388
Senegal 126, 128
Senghor, Léopold 99, 103
Shafaeddin, S. M. 354
Shiva, Vandana 396
Sierra Leone 126
Sime Darby 193
slave trading 3, 427–9; *see also* antislavery movement, Atlantic slave trade, Indian Ocean slave trade, trans-Saharan slave trade
small-scale mining 450
Solomon, Steven 396
Somalia 85, 148, 251, 375, 383, 434
South Africa 23, 28, 29, 51, 65, 117, 119, 128, 147, 148, 149, 159, 173, 177, 191, 193, 195, 202–12, 339; *see also* Apartheid system, BRICS countries
South Asian Muslims 60–9
South Korea 126–36, 222–3, 266
South Sudan 312
South West African People's Organization (SWAPO) 145
South–South Commission 189
South–South cooperation (SSC) 336–40, 343, 345–6, 352, 358, 365, 440, 442, 475
South–South development cooperation (SSDC) 335
Spatial Development Programme (SDP) 450
special economic zones (SEZs) 326, 329
Sri Lanka 143, 380–3
St. Paul 375
Straits Exchange Foundation 210

482

Index

Strange, Susan 209
strategic partnership 13, 150, 160, 190, 198, 212, 315, 335
structural adjustment programmes (SAPs) 85, 133, 142
Subaltern Studies collective 98, 104
Sudan 85, 131, 161, 193, 251, 377–80, 385, 391
Sudan People's Liberation Army (SPLA) 379
Sukarno, Achmad 53, 56, 101, 103, 144
Sun Yat-sen 238–9, 246
Surati Muslims 63
Sustainable Development Goals (SDGs) 275, 285, 352, 353, 356–7, 364–6
Swaziland 170, 202
Sylvester-Williams, Henry 239
Syria 434, 457–8

Tagore, Rabindranath 238
Taiping Rebellion 50
Taiwan 170, 202–12, 325
Tamil Tigers (Liberation Tigers of Tamil Eelam) 381, 383
Tanganyika 65
Tanzania 67, 69, 70, 87, 98, 148, 262, 339
Tar, U.A. 262
Taylor, Ian 308
Telekom Malaysia 192, 193
Teny-Dhurgon, Machar 379
terrorism 316, 361, 362, 364, 375, 383, 407–8, 412, 414–15, 459, 473, 475
theory 5–7, 9, 56, 64, 82–5, 234, 243, 281, 286, 299, 426
Three Gorges Dam 396
Tito, Josip Broz 103
Tokyo International Conference on Africa Development (TICAD) 119–20, 121, 123, 159, 268, 323
total fertility rate (TFR) 234–5
Toynbee, Arnold 240
trans-Atlantic slave trade 164, 472
trans-regional partnership agreements 451
trans-Saharan slave trade 27
Treaty of Addis Ababa 116
Treaty of Nanking 50
Treaty of Tientsin 50
Treaty of Tordesillas 34, 386
Truman, Harry S 76, 82
Trump, Donald 317

Uganda 23, 61, 62, 65, 67, 68, 69, 126, 148, 268, 391
United Arab Republic 103
United Malays' National Organization (UMNO) 189
United Nations 47, 339
United Nations Development Programme (UNDP) 339
United Nations Population Division 234
Universal Declaration of Human Rights 296, 300

'vapour shift' 394
'victim diasporas' 24
Victoria (British Queen) 389
Vicwood Group 401
Vietnam 54
Vietnam War 54, 157
virtual water 393–4
Vivekananda, Swami 81

Wahhabism 84
'war on terror' 254
Washington Consensus 283, 302, 323, 329, 346, 354
water resources 388–90, 396–9
Wei Jianguo 393
Wells-Barnet, Ida B. 155
Wilhelm II (German Kaiser) 389
women 243; see also gender
World Bank 56, 85, 119, 142, 168, 285, 298, 336, 343, 391
World Islamic League 251
World Network of Friends 348
World Trade Organization (WTO) 210, 347

Xi Jinping 315

Yemen 64, 383
Yogyakarta Commemoration Group 6

Zaaj revolt (Iraq) 27
Zaire: see Democratic Republic of Congo
Zambia 126, 147, 149, 173, 177, 178
Zanzibar 65, 67, 68
Zha Daojiong 302
Zhou Enlai 101
Zimbabwe 97, 149, 189
Zulus 116